Microsoft®
Office 2007
Brief Concepts and Techniques

Gary B. Shelly
Thomas J. Cashman
Misty E. Vermaat

Contributing Authors
Steven G. Forsythe
Mary Z. Last
Philip J. Pratt
Jeffrey J. Quasney
Susan L. Sebok

THOMSON
COURSE TECHNOLOGY™

THOMSON COURSE TECHNOLOGY   25 THOMSON PLACE   BOSTON MA 02210

SHELLY
CASHMAN
SERIES®

Australia • Canada • Denmark • Japan • Mexico • New Zealand • Philippines • Puerto Rico • Singapore • South Africa • Spain • United Kingdom • United States

Microsoft Office 2007
Brief Concepts and Techniques

Gary B. Shelly

Thomas J. Cashman

Misty E. Vermaat

Executive Editor
Alexandra Arnold

Senior Product Managers
Reed Curry, Mali Jones

Product Manager
Heather Hawkins

Associate Product Manager
Klenda Martinez

Editorial Assistant
Jon Farnham

Senior Marketing Manager
Joy Stark-Vancs

Marketing Coordinator
Julie Schuster

Print Buyer
Julio Esperas

Director of Production
Patty Stephan

Lead Production Editor
Matthew Hutchinson

Production Editors
Cathie DiMassa,
Jill Klaffky, Phillipa Lehar

Developmental Editors
Jill Batistick, Amanda Brodkin,
Laurie Brown, Lyn Markowicz

Proofreaders
John Bosco,
Kim Kosmatka

Indexer
Rich Carlson

QA Manuscript Reviewers
John Freitas, Serge Palladino,
Chris Scriver, Danielle Shaw,
Marianne Snow, Teresa Storch

Art Director
Bruce Bond

Cover and Text Design
Joel Sadagursky

Cover Photo
Jon Chomitz

Compositor
GEX Publishing Services

Printer
Banta Menasha

Microsoft® Office 2007
Brief Concepts and Techniques

Contents

Microsoft Office **Word 2007**

Microsoft Office **Excel 2007**

CHAPTER ONE

Creating a Worksheet and an Embedded Chart

Microsoft Office Access 2007

Microsoft Office **PowerPoint 2007**

CHAPTER ONE
Creating and Editing a Presentation

Preface

The Shelly Cashman Series® offers the finest textbooks in computer education. We are proud of the fact that our series of Microsoft Office 4.3, Microsoft Office 95, Microsoft Office 97, Microsoft Office 2000, Microsoft Office XP, and Microsoft Office 2003 textbooks have been the most widely used books in education. With each new edition of our Office books, we have made significant improvements based on the software and comments made by instructors and students.

Microsoft Office 2007 contains more changes in the user interface and feature set than all other previous versions combined. Recognizing that the new features and functionality of Microsoft Office 2007 would impact the way that students are taught skills, the Shelly Cashman Series development team carefully reviewed our pedagogy and analyzed its effectiveness in teaching today's Office student. An extensive customer survey produced results confirming what the series is best known for: its step-by-step, screen-by-screen instructions, its project-oriented approach, and the quality of its content.

We learned, though, that students entering computer courses today are different than students taking these classes just a few years ago. Students today read less, but need to retain more. They need not only to be able to perform skills, but to retain those skills and know how to apply them to different settings. Today's students need to be continually engaged and challenged to retain what they're learning.

As a result, we've renewed our commitment to focusing on the user and how they learn best. This commitment is reflected in every change we've made to our Office 2007 books.

Objectives of This Textbook

Microsoft Office 2007: Brief Concepts and Techniques is intended for a course that includes a brief introduction to Office 2007. No experience with a computer is assumed, and no mathematics beyond the high school freshman level is required. The objectives of this book are:

- To teach the fundamentals of Microsoft Office Word 2007, Microsoft Office Excel 2007, Microsoft Office Access 2007, Microsoft Office PowerPoint 2007, and Microsoft Windows Vista

- To expose students to practical examples of the computer as a useful tool

- To acquaint students with the proper procedures to create documents, worksheets, databases, and presentations suitable for coursework, professional purposes, and personal use

- To help students discover the underlying functionality of Office 2007 so they can become more productive

- To develop an exercise-oriented approach that allows learning by doing

The Shelly Cashman Approach

Features of the Shelly Cashman Series Microsoft Office 2007 books include:

- **Project Orientation** Each chapter in the book presents a project with a practical problem and complete solution in an easy-to-understand approach.

- **Plan Ahead Boxes** The project orientation is enhanced by the inclusion of Plan Ahead boxes. These new features prepare students to create successful projects by encouraging them to think strategically about what they are trying to accomplish before they begin working.

- **Step-by-Step, Screen-by-Screen Instructions** Each of the tasks required to complete a project is clearly identified throughout the chapter. Now, the step-by-step instructions provide a context beyond point-and-click. Each step explains why students are performing a task, or the result of performing a certain action. Found on the screens accompanying each step, call-outs give students the information they need to know when they need to know it. Now, we've used color to distinguish the content in the call-outs. The Explanatory call-outs (in black) summarize what is happening on the screen and the Navigational call-outs (in red) show students where to click.

- **Q&A** Found within many of the step-by-step sequences, Q&As raise the kinds of questions students may ask when working through a step sequence and provide answers about what they are doing, why they are doing it, and how that task might be approached differently.

- **Experimental Steps** These new steps, within our step-by-step instructions, encourage students to explore, experiment, and take advantage of the features of the Office 2007 new user interface. These steps are not necessary to complete the projects, but are designed to increase the confidence with the software and build problem-solving skills.

- **Thoroughly Tested Projects** Unparalleled quality is ensured because every screen in the book is produced by the author only after performing a step, and then each project must pass Thomson Course Technology's Quality Assurance program.

- **Other Ways Boxes and Quick Reference Summary** The Other Ways boxes displayed at the end of most of the step-by-step sequences specify the other ways to do the task completed in the steps. Thus, the steps and the Other Ways box make a comprehensive reference unit. A Quick Reference Summary at the end of the book contains all of the tasks presented in the chapters, and all ways identified of accomplishing the tasks.

- **BTW** These marginal annotations provide background information, tips, and answers to common questions that complement the topics covered, adding depth and perspective to the learning process.

- **Integration of the World Wide Web** The World Wide Web is integrated into the Office 2007 learning experience by (1) BTW annotations that send students to Web sites for up-to-date information and alternative approaches to tasks; (2) a Microsoft Business Certification Program Web page so students can prepare for the certification examinations; (3) a Quick Reference Summary Web page that summarizes the ways to complete tasks (mouse, Ribbon, shortcut menu, and keyboard); and (4) the Learn It Online section at the end of each chapter, which has chapter reinforcement exercises, learning games, and other types of student activities.

- **End-of-Chapter Student Activities** Extensive student activities at the end of each chapter provide the student with plenty of opportunities to reinforce the materials learned in the chapter through hands-on assignments. Several new types of activities have been added that challenge the student in new ways to expand their knowledge, and to apply their new skills to a project with personal relevance.

What is a maximized window?

A maximized window fills the entire screen. When you maximize a window, the Maximize button changes to a Restore Down button.

Other Ways

1. Click Italic button on Mini toolbar
2. Right-click selected text, click Font on shortcut menu, click Font tab, click Italic in Font style list, click OK button
3. Click Font Dialog Box Launcher, click Font tab, click Italic in Font style list, click OK button
4. Press CTRL+I

Minimizing the Ribbon
If you want to minimize the Ribbon, right-click the Ribbon and then click Minimize the Ribbon on the shortcut menu, double-click the active tab, or press CTRL+F1. To restore a minimized Ribbon, right-click the Ribbon and then click Minimize the Ribbon on the shortcut menu, double-click any top-level tab, or press CTRL+F1. To use commands on a minimized Ribbon, click the top-level tab.

Organization of This Textbook

Microsoft Office 2007: Brief Concepts and Techniques consists of one chapter on Microsoft Windows Vista, two chapters each on Microsoft Office Word 2007, Microsoft Office Excel 2007, and Microsoft Office Access 2007, and Microsoft Office PowerPoint 2007, one PowerPoint Special Feature, seven appendices and a Quick Reference Summary.

End-of-Chapter Student Activities

A notable strength of the Shelly Cashman Series Microsoft Office 2007 books is the extensive student activities at the end of each chapter. Well-structured student activities can make the difference between students merely participating in a class and students retaining the information they learn. The activities in the Shelly Cashman Series Office books include the following.

CHAPTER SUMMARY A concluding paragraph, followed by a listing of the tasks completed within a chapter together with the pages on which the step-by-step, screen-by-screen explanations appear.

LEARN IT ONLINE Every chapter features a Learn It Online section that is comprised of six exercises. These exercises include True/False, Multiple Choice, Short Answer, Flash Cards, Practice Test, and Learning Games.

APPLY YOUR KNOWLEDGE This exercise usually requires students to open and manipulate a file from the Data Files that parallels the activities learned in the chapter. To obtain a copy of the Data Files for Students, follow the instructions on the inside back cover of this text.

EXTEND YOUR KNOWLEDGE This exercise allows students to extend and expand on the skills learned within the chapter.

MAKE IT RIGHT This exercise requires students to analyze a document, identify errors and issues, and correct those errors and issues using skills learned in the chapter.

IN THE LAB Three all new in-depth assignments per chapter require students to utilize the chapter concepts and techniques to solve problems on a computer.

CASES AND PLACES Five unique real-world case-study situations, including Make It Personal, an open-ended project that relates to student's personal lives, and one small-group activity.

Instructor Resources CD-ROM

The Shelly Cashman Series is dedicated to providing you with all of the tools you need to make your class a success. Information about all supplementary materials is available through your Thomson Course Technology representative or by calling one of the following telephone numbers: Colleges, Universities, and Continuing Ed departments, 1-800-648-7450; High Schools, 1-800-824-5179; and Career Colleges, Business, Government, Library and Resellers, 1-800-477-3692.

The Instructor Resources CD-ROM for this textbook include both teaching and testing aids. The contents of each item on the Instructor Resources CD-ROM (ISBN 1-4239-1226-8) are described on the following pages.

INSTRUCTOR'S MANUAL The Instructor's Manual consists of Microsoft Word files, which include chapter objectives, lecture notes, teaching tips, classroom activities, lab activities, quick quizzes, figures and boxed elements summarized in the chapters, and a glossary page. The new format of the Instructor's Manual will allow you to map through every chapter easily.

LECTURE SUCCESS SYSTEM The Lecture Success System consists of intermediate files that correspond to certain figures in the book, allowing you to step through the creation of a project in a chapter during a lecture without entering large amounts of data.

SYLLABUS Sample syllabi, which can be customized easily to a course, are included. The syllabi cover policies, class and lab assignments and exams, and procedural information.

FIGURE FILES Illustrations for every figure in the textbook are available in electronic form. Use this ancillary to present a slide show in lecture or to print transparencies for use in lecture with an overhead projector. If you have a personal computer and LCD device, this ancillary can be an effective tool for presenting lectures.

POWERPOINT PRESENTATIONS PowerPoint Presentations is a multimedia lecture presentation system that provides slides for each chapter. Presentations are based on chapter objectives. Use this presentation system to present well-organized lectures that are both interesting and knowledge based. PowerPoint Presentations provides consistent coverage at schools that use multiple lecturers.

SOLUTIONS TO EXERCISES Solutions are included for the end-of-chapter exercises, as well as the Chapter Reinforcement exercises. Rubrics and annotated solution files, as described below, are also included.

RUBRICS AND ANNOTATED SOLUTION FILES The grading rubrics provide a customizable framework for assigning point values to the laboratory exercises. Annotated solution files that correspond to the grading rubrics make it easy for you to compare students' results with the correct solutions whether you receive their homework as hard copy or via e-mail.

TEST BANK & TEST ENGINE In the ExamView test bank, you will find our standard question types (40 multiple-choice, 25 true/false, 20 completion) and new objective-based question types (5 modified multiple-choice, 5 modified true/false and 10 matching). Critical Thinking questions are also included (3 essays and 2 cases with 2 questions each) totaling the test bank to 112 questions for every chapter with page number references, and when appropriate, figure references. A version of the test bank you can print also is included. The test bank comes with a copy of the test engine, ExamView, the ultimate tool for your objective-based testing needs. ExamView is a state-of-the-art test builder that is easy to use. ExamView enables you to create paper-, LAN-, or Web-based tests from test banks designed specifically for your Thomson Course Technology textbook. Utilize the ultra-efficient QuickTest Wizard to create tests in less than five minutes by taking advantage of Thomson Course Technology's question banks, or customize your own exams from scratch.

LAB TESTS/TEST OUT The Lab Tests/Test Out exercises parallel the In the Lab assignments and are supplied for the purpose of testing students in the laboratory on the material covered in the chapter or testing students out of the course.

DATA FILES FOR STUDENTS All the files that are required by students to complete the exercises are included. You can distribute the files on the Instructor Resources CD-ROM to your students over a network, or you can have them follow the instructions on the inside back cover of this book to obtain a copy of the Data Files for Students.

ADDITIONAL ACTIVITIES FOR STUDENTS These additional activities consist of Chapter Reinforcement Exercises, which are true/false, multiple-choice, and short answer questions that help students gain confidence in the material learned.

Assessment & Training Solutions
SAM 2007

SAM 2007 helps bridge the gap between the classroom and the real world by allowing students to train and test on important computer skills in an active, hands-on environment.

SAM 2007's easy-to-use system includes powerful interactive exams, training or projects on critical applications such as Word, Excel, Access, PowerPoint, Outlook, Windows, the Internet, and much more. SAM simulates the application environment, allowing students to demonstrate their knowledge and think through the skills by performing real-world tasks.

Designed to be used with the Shelly Cashman series, SAM 2007 includes built-in page references so students can print helpful study guides that match the Shelly Cashman series textbooks used in class. Powerful administrative options allow instructors to schedule exams and assignments, secure tests, and run reports with almost limitless flexibility.

Student Edition Labs

Our Web-based interactive labs help students master hundreds of computer concepts, including input and output devices, file management and desktop applications, computer ethics, virus protection, and much more. Featuring up-to-the-minute content, eye-popping graphics, and rich animation, the highly interactive Student Edition Labs offer students an alternative way to learn through dynamic observation, step-by-step practice, and challenging review questions.

Online Content

Blackboard is the leading distance learning solution provider and class-management platform today. Thomson Course Technology has partnered with Blackboard to bring you premium online content. Instructors: Content for use with *Microsoft Office 2007: Brief Concepts and Techniques*, is available in a Blackboard Course Cartridge and may include topic reviews, case projects, review questions, test banks, practice tests, custom syllabi, and more.

Thomson Course Technology also has solutions for several other learning management systems. Please visit http://www.course.com today to see what's available for this title.

Workbook for Microsoft Office 2007: Introductory Concepts and Techniques

This highly popular supplement (ISBN 1-4188-4335-0) includes a variety of activities that help students recall, review, and master the concepts presented. The Workbook complements the end-of-chapter material with an outline; a self-test consisting of true/false, multiple-choice, short answer, and matching questions; and activities calculated to help students develop a deeper understanding of the information presented.

CourseCasts Learning on the Go. Always Available...Always Relevant.

Want to keep up with the latest technology trends relevant to you? Visit our site to find a library of podcasts, CourseCasts, featuring a "CourseCast of the Week," and download them to your portable media player at http://coursecasts.course.com.

Our fast-paced world is driven by technology. You know because you are an active participant — always on the go, always keeping up with technological trends, and always learning new ways to embrace technology to power your life.

Ken Baldauf, a faculty member of the Florida State University (FSU) Computer Science Department, is responsible for teaching technology classes to thousands of FSU students each year. He knows what you know; he knows what you want to learn. He is also an expert in the latest technology and will sort through and aggregate the most pertinent news and information so you can spend your time enjoying technology, rather than trying to figure it out.

Visit us at http://coursecasts.course.com to learn on the go!

CourseNotes

Course Technology's CourseNotes are six-panel quick reference cards that reinforce the most important and widely used features of a software application in a visual and user-friendly format. CourseNotes will serve as a great reference tool during and after the student completes the course. CourseNotes for Microsoft Office 2007, Word 2007, Excel 2007, Access 2007, PowerPoint 2007, Windows Vista, and more are available now!

course|notes™
quick reference guide

About Our New Cover Look

Learning styles of students have changed, but the Shelly Cashman Series' dedication to their success has remained steadfast for over 30 years. We are committed to continually updating our approach and content to reflect the way today's students learn and experience new technology. This focus on the user is reflected in our bold new cover design, which features photographs of real students using the Shelly Cashman Series in their courses. Each book features a different user, reflecting the many ages, experiences, and backgrounds of all of the students learning with our books. When you use the Shelly Cashman Series, you can be assured that you are learning computer skills using the most effective courseware available. We would like to thank the administration and faculty at the participating schools for their help in making our vision a reality. Most of all, we'd like to thank the wonderful students from all over the world who learn from our texts and now appear on our covers.

1 Introduction to Windows Vista

Objectives

You will have mastered the material in this chapter when you can:

- Start Windows Vista, log on to the computer, and identify the objects on the desktop

- Customize the Windows Sidebar with Gadgets

- Perform basic mouse operations

- Display the Start menu and start an application program

- Open, minimize, maximize, restore, move, size, scroll, and close a window

- Display drive and folder contents

- Create a folder in Folder Windows and WordPad

- Browse the Web using Windows Internet Explorer 7.0, a URL, and tabbed browsing

- Download folders from scsite.com

- Copy, move, rename, and delete files

- Search for files using a word or phrase in the file or by name

- Use Windows Help and Support

- Log off from the computer and turn it off

1 | Introduction to Windows Vista

What Is an Operating System?

An **operating system** is the set of computer instructions, called a computer program, that controls the allocation of computer hardware such as memory, disk devices, printers, and CD and DVD drives, and provides the capability for you to communicate with the computer. The most popular and widely used operating systems is **Microsoft Windows. Microsoft Windows Vista** is the newest version of Microsoft Windows. Windows Vista allows you to communicate with and control the computer.

Project Planning Guidelines

> Working with an operating system requires a basic knowledge of how to start the operating system, log on and log off the computer, and identify the objects on the Windows Vista desktop. As a starting point, you must be familiar with the Start menu and its commands, and be able to start an application. You should be able to personalize the operating system to allow you to work more efficiently. You will want to know how to manipulate windows as well as create a folder, display folder contents, recognize a disk drive, and download information from the Internet. You should be able to copy, move, rename, delete, and search for files. If you encounter a problem, Windows Help and Support is available to answer any questions you may have.

Overview

As you read through this chapter, you will learn how to use the Windows Vista operating system by performing these general tasks:

- Start the Windows Vista operating system.
- Log on to the computer.
- Perform basic mouse operations.
- Add and Remove a gadget to the Windows Sidebar.
- Open the Start menu and start an application program.
- Add and delete icons on the desktop.
- Open, minimize, maximize, restore, move, size, scroll, and close a window.
- Display drive and folder contents.
- Create folders and download folders from the Internet.
- Copy, move, rename, delete, and search for files.
- Use Help and Support.
- Log off and turn off the computer.

What Is a User Interface?

A **user interface** is the combination of hardware and software that you use to communicate with and control the computer. Through the user interface, you are able to make selections on the computer, request information from the computer, and respond to messages displayed by the computer.

Hardware and software together form the user interface. Among the hardware devices associated with a user interface are the monitor, keyboard, and mouse (Figure 1–1). The **monitor** displays messages and provides information. You respond by entering data in the form of a command or other response using an input device such as a **keyboard** or **mouse**.

Figure 1–1

The computer software associated with the user interface consists of the programs that engage you in dialogue. The computer software determines the messages you receive, the manner in which you should respond, and the actions that occur based on your responses.

The goal of an effective user interface is to be **user-friendly**, which means the software can be used easily by individuals with limited training. A **graphical user interface**, or **GUI** (pronounced gooey), is a user interface that displays graphics in addition to text when it communicates with the user.

To communicate with the operating system, you can use a mouse. A **mouse** is a pointing device used with Windows Vista that may be attached to the computer by a cable or may be wireless.

Many common tasks, such as logging on to the computer or logging off, are performed by pointing to an item and then clicking the item. **Point** means you move the mouse across a flat surface until the mouse pointer on the monitor rests on the item of choice. As you move the mouse across a flat surface, the optical sensor on the underside of the mouse senses the movement of mouse, and the mouse pointer moves across the computer desktop in the same direction. In Office 2007, you can point to buttons on the Ribbon in a window and observe a live preview of the effect of selecting that button.

Click means you press and release the primary mouse button, which in most cases is the left mouse button. In most cases, you must point to an item before you click it.

Windows Vista

The Windows Vista operating system simplifies the process of working with documents and applications by transferring data between documents, organizing the manner in which you interact with the computer, and using the computer to access information on the Internet or an intranet. Windows Vista is used to run **application programs**, which are programs that perform a specific function such as word processing.

In business, Windows Vista is commonly used on standalone computers, client computers, and portable computers. A standalone computer is not part of a computer network, and has access only to software that is installed on it, and hardware directly connected to it. A **client** is a computer connected to a server. A **server** is a computer that controls access to the hardware and software on a network and provides a centralized storage area for programs, data, and information. Portable computers, often referred to as laptop computers, can be used either as standalone computers or clients. Figure 1–2 illustrates a simple computer network consisting of a server, three client computers, and a laser printer connected to the server.

Figure 1–2

Windows Vista Operating System Editions

The Windows Vista operating systems is available in five editions: Windows Vista Home Basic, Windows Vista Home Premium, Windows Vista Business, Windows Vista Ultimate, and Windows Vista Enterprise. Windows Vista Ultimate (called **Windows Vista** for the rest of the chapter) is an operating system that performs every function necessary for you to communicate with and use the computer. The five editions of Windows Vista are described in Table 1–1.

Table 1–1 Windows Vista Editions

Edition	Description
Windows Vista Home Basic	This edition is easy to set up and maintain, provides security and parental controls, allows access to e-mail, simplifies searching for pictures and music, and allows the creation of simple documents.
Windows Vista Home Premium Edition	This edition is designed for individuals who have a home desktop or mobile PC. The built-in Windows Media Center allows you to watch and record television, play video games, listen to music, and burn and play CDs and DVDs.
Windows Vista Business Edition	This edition is the first operating system designed specifically for the needs of small and mid-sized businesses. Features include keeping PCs up-to-date and running smoothly, as well as powerful ways to find, organize, and share information on the road or in the office. Additional features include Windows Tablet PC capability, PC-to-PC synchronization, Domain Join, Group Policy support, and Encrypting File System.
Windows Vista Ultimate Edition	This edition, the most complete edition of the five, contains the most advanced capabilities, and is the choice of individuals who want the power, security, and mobility needed for work and the entertainment features desired for fun. The edition includes support for Windows Tablet and Touch Technology, Windows SideShow, Windows Mobility Center, Windows DreamScene, and Windows BitLocker Secure Online Key storage.
Windows Vista Enterprise	This edition was designed to help global organizations and enterprises with complex IT infrastructures to lower IT costs, reduce risk, and stay connected. This edition is only available to Volume License customers who have PCs covered by Microsoft Software Assurance. Windows BitLocker Drive Encryption is used to help prevent sensitive data and intellectual property from being lost or stolen.

Windows Vista Basic Interface and Windows Aero

Windows Vista offers two different GUIs, depending on your hardware configuration. Computers with up to 1 GB of RAM work with the Windows Vista Basic interface (Figure 1–3a). Computers with more than 1 GB of RAM can work also with the Windows Aero interface (Figure 1–3b), which provides an enhanced visual experience designed for Windows Vista, including additional navigation options, and animation. Windows Aero features a transparent glass design with subtle window animations and new window colors. The Windows Vista Business, Windows Vista Enterprise, Windows Vista Home Premium, and Windows Vista Ultimate editions have the ability to use Windows Aero. In this chapter, all figures were created on a computer using the Windows Vista Basic interface.

(a)

(b)

Figure 1–3

Starting Windows Vista

It is not an unusual occurrence for multiple people to use the same computer in a work, educational, recreational, or home setting. Windows Vista uses User Accounts to organize the resources that are made available to a person when they use the computer. A **user account** identifies to Windows Vista which resources a person can use when using the computer. Associated with a user account is a **user name**, which identifies the person to Windows Vista, and a **password**, a string of letters, numbers, and special characters, which is used to restrict access to a user account's resources to only those who know the password. In Windows Vista, you can choose a picture to associated with your user name as well.

In a work or school environment your user name and password may be set up for you automatically. Usually, you are given the option to reset the password to something that only you know. A good password is important for ensuring the security and privacy of your work. When you turn on the computer, an introductory black screen consisting of a progress bar and copyright message (© Microsoft Corporation) are displayed. After a short time, the Windows Vista logo and Welcome screen are displayed on the desktop (Figure 1–4).

Determine a user name and password.

Before logging on to the computer, you must have a unique user name and password.

1. Choose a user name that is unique and non-offensive. Your user name may be automatically set for you in a work or educational setting.

2. Choose a password that no one could guess. Do not use any part of your first or last name, your spouse's or child's name, telephone number, street address, license plate number, Social Security number, and so on.

3. Be sure your password is at least six characters long, mixed with letters and numbers.

4. Protect your password. Change your password frequently and do not disclose it to anyone or write it on a slip of paper kept near the computer. E-mail and telemarketing scams often ask you to disclose a password, so be wary, if you did not initiate the inquiry or telephone call.

Plan Ahead

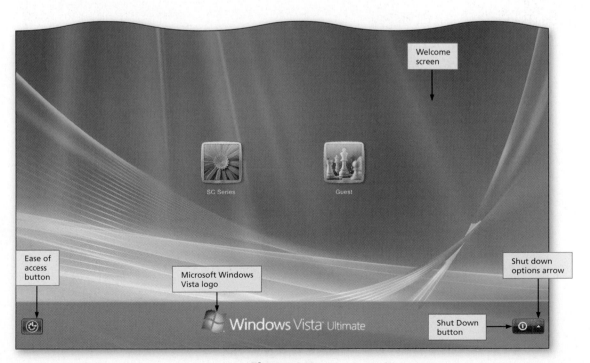

Figure 1–4

The **Welcome screen** shows the user names of every computer user on the computer. Clicking the user name or picture begins the process of logging on to the computer. The list of user names on your computer will be different.

At the bottom of the Welcome screen is the Ease of access button, Windows Vista logo, and a Shut down button. Clicking the **Ease of access button** displays the Ease of Access Center. The Ease of Access Center provides access to tools you can use to optimize your computer to accomodate the needs of the mobility, hearing and vision impaired. To the right of the Ease of access button is the Windows Vista logo. Located in the lower corner of the Welcome screen is the **Shut down button**. Clicking this button shuts down Windows Vista and the computer. To the right of the Shut down button is the **Shut down options arrow**, which provides access to a menu containing 3 commands, Restart, Sleep, and Shut Down.

The **Restart command** closes open programs, shuts down Windows Vista, and then restarts Windows Vista, and displays the Welcome screen. The **Sleep command** waits for Windows Vista to save your work and then turns off the fans and hard disk. To wake the computer from the Sleep state, press the Power button or lift the laptop cover, and log on to the computer. The **Shut Down command** shuts down and turns off the computer.

Logging On to the Computer

After starting Windows Vista, you must log on to the computer. **Logging on** to the computer opens your user account and makes the computer available for use.

If you are using a computer to step through the project in this chapter and you want your screen to match the figures in this book, you should change your screen's resolution to 1024 × 768. For information about how to change a computer's resolution, read Appendix E.

To Log On to the Computer

The following steps illustrate how to log on to the computer. In this chapter, the user name SC Series is used in the figures.

- Click your user name on the Welcome screen to display the password text box.

Q&A What is a text box?

A text box is a rectangular area in which you can enter text.

- Type your password in the password text box as shown in Figure 1–5.

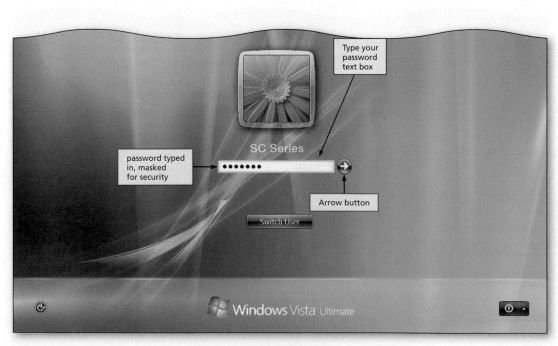

Figure 1–5

2

- Click the arrow button to log on to the computer to display the Welcome Center window and Windows Sidebar on the Windows Vista desktop (Figure 1–6).

Q&A

What is displayed on the desktop when I log on to the computer?

The Recycle Bin icon, Welcome Center, Windows Sidebar, and taskbar are displayed on the desktop.

Q&A

What if the Computer displays a different desktop design?

Windows Vista offers many standard desktop backgrounds, so any background is fine. The background design shown in Figure 1–6 is called img24.

Figure 1–6

The Windows Vista Desktop

The Windows Vista desktop is similar to a real physical desktop. It is the main work area when you are logged into Windows Vista. When you open a program, it appears on the desktop. Some items are on the desktop by default. For instance, the **Recycle Bin**, the location of files that have been deleted, sits on the desktop by default. You can customize your desktop so that programs and files you use often are out on your desktop and easily accessible.

Also on the Windows Vista desktop is the Windows Sidebar. The **Windows Sidebar** is a long, vertical strip on the right edge of the desktop that holds mini-programs called gadgets (Figure 1–6). A **gadget** is a mini-program that provides continuously updated information, such as current weather information, news updates, traffic information, and Internet radio streams. You can customize your Sidebar to hold gadgets that you choose.

Across the bottom of the Windows Vista desktop is the Windows Taskbar (Figure 1–6). The Windows Taskbar contains the Start button, which you use to access programs, files, folders, and settings on your computer. It also shows you which programs are currently running on your computer, by displaying a button per program.

In addition, the Windows Vista desktop may contain the Welcome Center Window. The **Welcome Center** is displayed when the computer is used for the first time and allows you to complete a set of tasks to optimize the computer. The tasks may include adding user accounts, transferring files and settings from another computer, and connecting to the Internet.

To Close the Welcome Center Window

The Welcome Center window is displayed when you launch Windows Vista for the first time, and subsequently unless you turn it off. If the Welcome Center window is displayed, you can close it prior to beginning any other operations using Windows Vista. This provides you with a clear desktop with which to work. The following step illustrates how to close the Welcome Center window.

- Click the Close button in the top right corner of the Welcome Center window to close the Welcome Center window (Figure 1–7).

Are there other ways to access the Welcome Center if it doesn't appear at startup?

Yes. The Welcome Center features are available in the Control Panel under System and Maintenance.

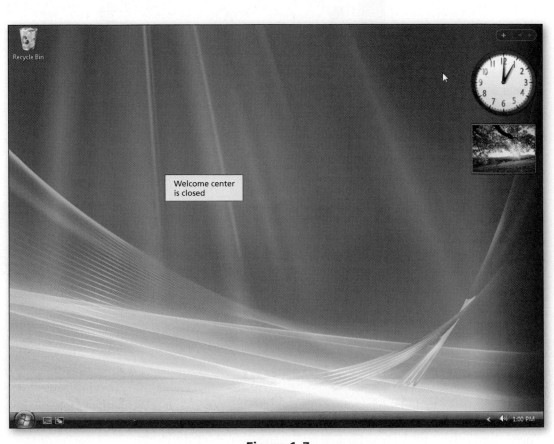

Figure 1–7

To Add a Gadget to the Windows Sidebar

When you start Windows Vista, some gadgets are attached to the Windows Sidebar. There are many additional gadgets that can be added according to personal preference. Gadgets can be found in the **Gadget Gallery**, which is a collection of gadgets. To use gadgets, they must be added to the Windows Sidebar. One method to add a gadget to the Windows Sidebar is to double-click the gadget in the Gadget Gallery. **Double-click** means you quickly press and release the left mouse button twice without moving the mouse. The steps on the following page illustrate how to open the Gadget Gallery and add a gadget to the Windows Sidebar.

①

- Click the Add Gadgets button to open the Gadget Gallery on the desktop. (Figure 1–8).

Q&A Where can I find additional gadgets?

You can find more gadgets on the www.microsoft.com website by searching for "sidebar gadgets".

Figure 1–8

②

- Double-click the Feed Headlines gadget in the Gadget Gallery to add the gadget to the top of the Windows Sidebar and display frequently updated headlines (Figure 1–9).

③

- Click the Close button to close the Gadget Gallery.

Q&A Can I customize the Windows Sidebar?

Yes. You can select which gadgets you want to add or remove, add multiple instances of a particular gadget, and detach one or more gadgets from the Sidebar and place them on the desktop

Figure 1–9

To Remove a Gadget from the Windows Sidebar

In addition to adding gadgets to the Windows Sidebar, you may want to customize the desktop by removing one or more gadgets from the sidebar. The following step illustrates how to remove a gadget from the Windows Sidebar.

- Point to the Feed Headlines gadget to make the Close button visible. (Figure 1–10).

- Click the Close button to remove the Feed Headlines gadget from the Windows Sidebar.

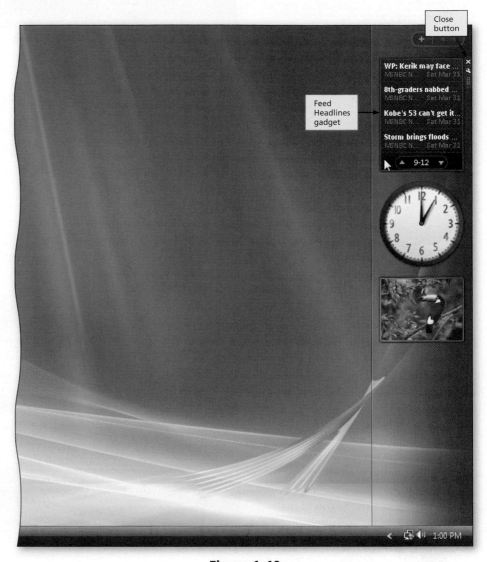

Figure 1–10

Other Ways
1. Right-click gadget, click Close Gadget

To Open the Start Menu

A **menu** is a list of related items, including folders, programs, and commands. Each **command** on a menu performs a specific action, such as searching for files or obtaining Help. The **Start menu** allows you to access programs and files on the computer and contains commands that allow you to connect to and browse the Internet, start an e-mail program, start application programs, store and search for documents, customize the computer, and obtain Help on thousands of topics. The Start menu contains the All Programs command, Search box, and right pane. The following steps open the Start menu, display the All Programs list, and then display the Accessories list.

1

- Click the Start button on the Windows Vista taskbar to open the Start menu (Figure 1–11).

Q&A

What are the various sections on the Start menu?

The left pane contains the pinned items list, frequently used programs list, All Programs command, and the Search box. The right pane contains the computer user name and illustration, list links, Power button, Lock this computer button, and Lock menu arrow.

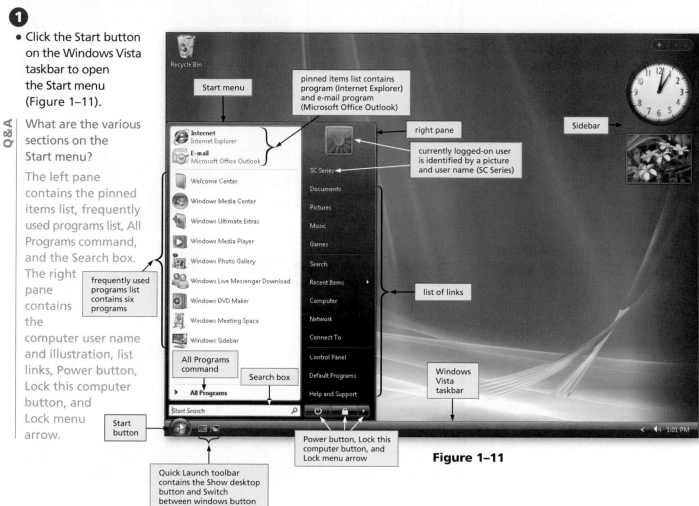

Figure 1–11

2

- Point to All Programs at the bottom of the left pane on the Start menu to display the All Programs list (Figure 1–12).

Q&A What happens when you point to All Programs on the Start menu?

The All Programs list is displayed and the word Back is displayed at the bottom of the All Programs list.

Figure 1–12

3

- Click Accessories to expand the list of programs and folders in the Accessories folder (Figure 1–13).

Q&A What are Accessories?

Accessories are application programs that accomplish a variety of tasks commonly required on a computer. For example, the Accessories programs include Calculator, Notepad, Paint, etc.

Figure 1–13

To Scroll Using Scroll Arrows, the Scroll Bar, and the Scroll Box

A **scroll bar** is a bar that displays when the contents of an area may not be completely visible. A vertical scroll bar contains an **up scroll arrow**, a **down scroll arrow**, and a **scroll box** that enables you to view areas that currently are not visible. In Figure 1–14, a vertical scroll bar displays along the right side of the All Programs list. Scrolling can be accomplished in three ways: (1) click the scroll arrows; (2) click the scroll bar; and (3) drag the scroll box. **Drag** means you point to an item, hold down the left mouse button, move the item to the desired location, and then release the left mouse button. The following steps scroll the items in the All Programs list.

1

- Click the down scroll arrow on the vertical scroll bar to display additional folders at the bottom of the All Programs list (Figure 1–14). You may need to click more than once to get to the bottom of the All Programs list.

Figure 1–14

- Click the scroll bar above the scroll box to move the scroll box to the top of the scroll bar and display the top of the All Programs list (Figure 1–15).

Figure 1–15

- Drag the scroll box down the scroll bar until the scroll box is about halfway down the scroll bar (Figure 1–16).

- Click an open area on the desktop to close the Start menu.

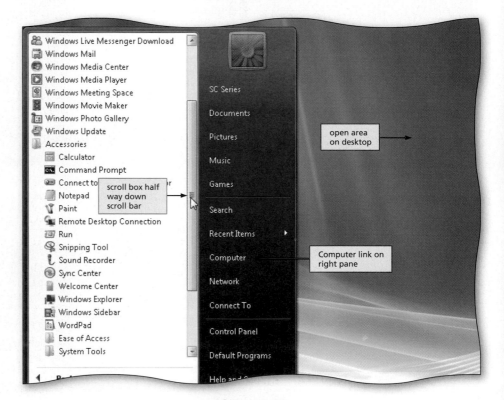

Figure 1–16

To Add an Icon to the Desktop

In addition to gadgets, you may want to add icons to the desktop. An **icon** is a picture that represents a file, folder, object, or program. For example, you may want to add the Computer icon to the desktop so you can view the contents of the computer folder without having to use the Start menu. The steps on the following page add the Computer icon to the desktop.

1

- Click the Start button to open the Start menu.

- Right-click Computer on the right pane to select the Computer link and display a shortcut menu (Figure 1–17).

Q&A What is a shortcut menu?

A shortcut menu appears when you right-click an object and includes commands specifically for use with the object clicked.

Figure 1–17

2

- Click Show on Desktop to close the shortcut menu and display the Computer icon on the desktop (Figure 1–18).

Q&A Why should I use a shortcut menu?

A shortcut menu speeds up your work and adds flexibility to your interaction with the computer by making often used items available in multiple locations.

3

- Click an open area on the desktop to close the Start menu.

Figure 1–18

To Open a Window Using a Desktop Icon

When an icon, like the Computer icon, is displayed on the desktop, you can use the icon to open the application or window it represents. One method for opening a window with a desktop icon is to double-click the icon. The following step opens the Computer window on the desktop by double-clicking the Computer icon on the desktop.

1

• Double-click the Computer icon on the desktop to open the Computer window (Figure 1–19).

Q&A

What does the Computer window allow me to do?

The Computer window allows you to view the contents of the computer.

Figure 1–19

Other Ways

1. Right-click desktop icon, click Open on shortcut menu
2. Press WINDOWS+E

Folder Windows

Folder windows are the key tools for finding, viewing, and managing information on the computer. Folder Windows have common design elements, illustrated in Figure 1–19. The three buttons to the left of the **Address bar** allow you to navigate the contents of the left pane and view recent pages. On the right of the title bar are the Minimize button, Maximize button, and Close button that can be used to specify the size of the window or close the window.

The two right arrows in the Address bar allow you to visit different locations on the computer and display a list of computer hardware. The **Previous Locations button** saves the locations you have visited and displays the locations using computer path names.

The **Refresh button** at the end of the Address bar refreshes the contents of the right pane of the Computer window. The **Search box** to the right of the Address bar contains the dimmed word, Search. You can type a term into the Search box for a list of files, folders, shortcuts, and such containing that term within the location you are searching.

The **Command Bar** contains five buttons used to accomplish various tasks on the computer related to organizing and managing the contents of the open window. The area below the Command Bar contains the Navigation pane and four column headers (Name, Type, Total Size, and Free Space) on the right. The **Navigation pane** on the left contains the Favorite Links section and the Folders list. The **Favorite Links list** contains your documents, pictures, music files, and more.

Four **column headers** displayed in the right pane allow you to sort and group the entries below the column header.

To Minimize and Redisplay a Window

Two buttons on the title bar, the Minimize button and the Maximize button, allow you to control the way a window is displayed on the desktop. The following steps minimize and then redisplay the Computer window.

❶

- Click the Minimize button on the title bar of the Computer window to minimize the Computer window (Figure 1–20).

Q&A What happens to the Computer window when I click the Minimize button?

The Computer window is still available, but it is no longer the active window. It collapses down to a non-recessed, light gray and black button on the task bar.

Figure 1–20

❷

- Click the Computer button on the taskbar to display the Computer window (Figure 1–21).

Q&A Why does the Computer button on the taskbar change?

The button changes to reflect the status of the Computer window. A recessed button indicates that the Computer window is active on the screen. A non-recessed button indicates that the Computer window is not active, but is open.

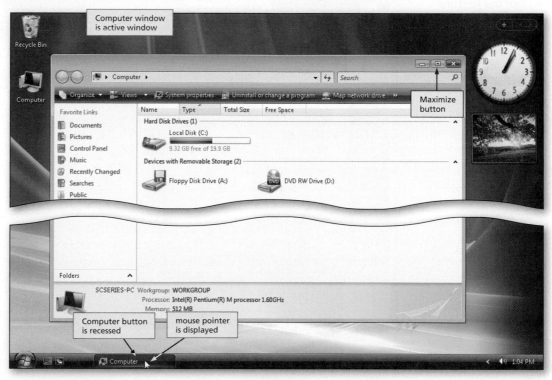

Figure 1–21

Other Ways
1. Right-click title bar, click Minimize, on taskbar click taskbar button   2. Press WINDOWS+M, press WINDOWS+SHIFT+M

To Maximize and Restore a Window

Sometimes information shown in a window is not completely visible. One method of displaying more contents in a window is to enlarge the window using the **Maximize button**, so the window fills the entire screen. If a window is filling the entire screen and you want to see part of the desktop, you can use the **Restore** button to return the window to its previous state. The following steps maximize and restore the Computer window.

- Click the Maximize button on the title bar of the Computer window to maximize the Computer window (Figure 1–22).

Q&A

When a window is maximized, can you also minimize it?

Yes. Click the Minimize button to minimize the window.

Figure 1–22

- Click the Restore Down button on the title bar of the Computer window to return the Computer window to its previous size (Figure 1–23).

Q&A

What happens to the Restore Down button when I click it?

The Maximize button replaces the Restore Down button on the title bar.

Other Ways

1. Right-click title bar, click Maximize, right-click title bar, click Restore
2. Double-click title bar, double-click title bar

Figure 1–23

To Close a Window

You can click the **Close button** on the title bar of a window to close the window and remove the taskbar button from the Windows taskbar. The following step closes the Computer window.

- Click the Close button on the title bar of the Computer window to close the Computer window (Figure 1–24).

Q&A

What happens to the Computer window when I click the Close button?

The Computer window closes and the Computer button no longer is displayed in the taskbar button area.

taskbar no longer displays Computer button

Figure 1–24

Other Ways
1. Right-click title bar, click Close   2. Press ALT+F4

To Open a Window Using the Start Menu

Previously, you opened the Computer window by double-clicking the Computer icon on the desktop. Another method of opening a window and viewing the contents of the window is to click a link on the Start menu. The **Pictures folder** is a convenient location to store your digital pictures, view and share your pictures, and edit pictures. The following steps open the Pictures window using the Pictures link on the Start menu.

- Open the Start menu (Figure 1–25).

Pictures link

Start menu

Start button

Figure 1–25

- Click Pictures on the Start menu to open the Pictures window (Figure 1–26).

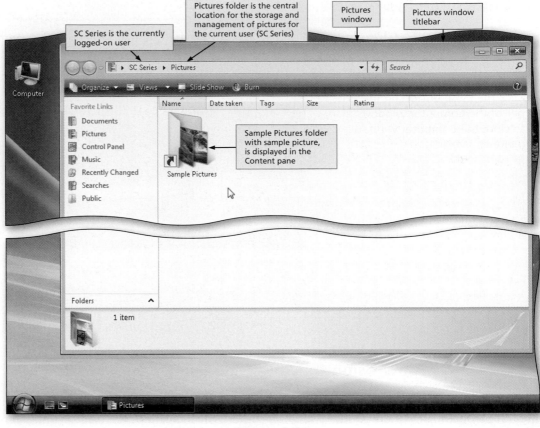

Figure 1–26

Other Ways

1. Click Start button, right-click Pictures, click Open

To Move a Window by Dragging

You can move any open window to another location on the desktop by pointing to the title bar of the window and then dragging the window. The following step drags the Pictures window to the top of the desktop.

- Drag the Pictures window title bar so the window moves to the top of the desktop as shown in Figure 1–27.

Figure 1–27

Other Ways

1. Right-click title bar, click Move, drag window

To Expand the Folders List

The Folders list in the Pictures window is collapsed and an up arrow appears to the right of the Folders name (see Figure 1–27 on the previous page). Clicking the up arrow or the Folders button expands the Folders list and reveals the contents of the Folders list. The following step expands the Folders list in the Pictures window.

1

- Click the Folders button to expand the Folders list in the Navigation pane of the Pictures window (Figure 1–28).

Q&A

What is shown in the Folders list?

The Folders list displays a hierarchical structure of files, folders, and drives on the computer.

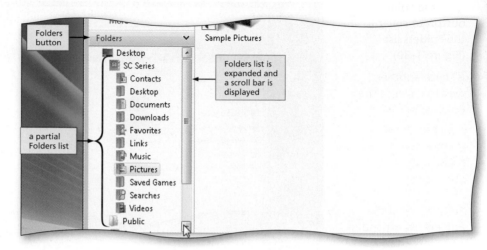

Figure 1–28

To Size a Window by Dragging

You can resize any open window to a more desirable size by pointing to one of the outside borders of the window and then dragging the window in or out. The following steps drag the bottom border of the Pictures window downward to enlarge the window until the contents of the Folders list is visible.

1

- Point to the bottom border of the Pictures window until the mouse pointer changes to a two-headed arrow.

- Drag the bottom border downward until the entire contents of the Folders list are visible and the scroll bar no longer appears (Figure 1–29).

Q&A

Can I drag anything else to enlarge or shrink the window?

You can drag the left, right, and top borders and any window corner.

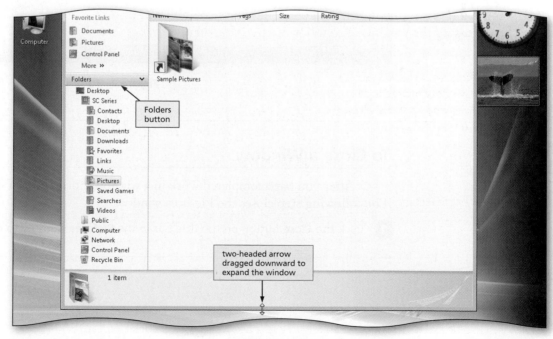

Figure 1–29

To Collapse the Folders List

When the Folders list is expanded, a down arrow is displayed. In the following step, you will collapse the list by clicking the Folders button.

- Click the Folders button to collapse the Folders list (Figure 1–30).

Q&A Is there another way to collapse the Folders list?

Yes. You can click the down arrow to collapse the Folders list.

Q&A Should I keep the Folders list expanded or collapsed?

If you need to use the contents within the Folders list, it is handy to keep the Folders list expanded. You can collapse the Folders list when the information is not needed.

Figure 1–30

To Close a Window

After you have completed work in a window, normally you will close the window. The following step closes the Pictures window.

1. Click the Close button on the title bar in the Pictures window to close the Pictures window.

To Delete a Desktop Icon by Right-Dragging

Sometimes, you will want to remove an icon from the desktop. One method of deleting an icon from the desktop is to right-drag the icon to the Recycle Bin icon on the desktop. **Right-drag** means you point to an item, hold down the right mouse button, move the item to the desired location, and then release the right mouse button. When you right-drag an object, a shortcut menu is displayed. The shortcut menu contains commands specifically for use with the object being dragged. The following steps delete the Computer icon by right-dragging the icon to the Recycle Bin icon. A **dialog box** is displayed whenever Windows Vista needs to supply information to you or wants you to enter information or select among several options. The Confirm Delete dialog box is used in the following steps.

- Point to the Computer icon on the desktop, hold down the right mouse button, drag the Computer icon over the Recycle Bin icon, and then release the right mouse button to display a shortcut menu (Figure 1–31).

Figure 1–31

- Click Move Here on the shortcut menu to close the shortcut menu and display the Confirm Delete dialog box (Figure 1–32).

 Why should I right-drag instead of simply dragging?

Although you can move icons by dragging with the primary (left) mouse button and by right-dragging with the secondary (right) mouse button, it is strongly suggested you right-drag because a shortcut menu appears and, in most cases, you can specify the exact operation you want to occur. When you drag using the left mouse button, a default operation takes place and that operation may not be the operation you intended to perform.

Figure 1–32

- Click the Yes button to delete the Computer icon and close the Confirm Delete dialog box.

Other Ways
1. Drag icon to Recycle Bin, click Yes button
2. Right-click icon, click Delete, click Yes button

Summary of Mouse and Windows Operations

You have seen how to use the mouse to point, click, right-click, double-click, drag, and right-drag in order to accomplish certain tasks on the desktop. The use of a mouse is an important skill when using Windows Vista. In addition, you have learned how to move around and use windows on the Windows Vista desktop.

The Keyboard and Keyboard Shortcuts

The **keyboard** is an input device on which you manually key in, or type, data. Figure 1–33 illustrates the rechargeable Wireless Entertainment Desktop 8000 keyboard designed for use with Microsoft Office and the Internet. Keyboards can be basic input devices, or in the case of the keyboard illustrated, can serve other purposes, such as providing USB ports for plugging in hardware, and specialized buttons such as the Windows Gadget button, which allow access to certain Windows Vista features at the touch of a button.

Figure 1–33

Many tasks you accomplish with a mouse can also be accomplished using a keyboard. To perform tasks using the keyboard, you must understand the notation used to identify which keys to press. This notation is used throughout Windows Vista to identify a **keyboard shortcut**.

Keyboard shortcuts consist of (1) pressing a single key (such as press the F1 key); or (2) pressing and holding down one key and pressing a second key, as shown by two key names separated by a plus sign (such as press CTRL+ESC). For example, to obtain help about Windows Vista, you can press the F1 key and to open the Start menu, hold down the CTRL key and then press the ESC key (press CRTL+ESC).

Starting an Application Program

One of the basic tasks you can perform using Windows Vista is starting an application program. A **program** is a set of computer instructions that carries out a task on the computer. An **application program** is a set of specific computer instructions that is designed to allow you to accomplish a particular task. For example, a **word processing program** is an application program that allows you to create written documents; a **presentation graphics program** is an application program that allows you to create graphic presentations for display on a computer; and a **Web browser program** is an application program that allows you to search for and display **Web pages**, documents designed to be viewed using a Web browser.

The **default Web browser program** (Internet Explorer) appears in the pinned items list on the Start menu shown in Figure 1–34. Because the default **Web browser** is selected during the installation of the Windows Vista operating system, the default Web browser on your computer may be different. In addition, you can easily select another Web browser as the default Web browser. Another frequently used Web browser program is **Mozilla Firefox**.

What Is Internet Explorer?

Internet Explorer is a **Web browsing program** that allows you to search for and view Web pages, save pages you find for use in the future, maintain a list of the pages you visit, send and receive e-mail messages, and edit Web pages. The Internet Explorer application program is included with the Windows Vista operating system software and Microsoft Office software, or you can download it from the Internet.

To Start an Application Using the Start Menu

A common activity performed on a computer is starting an application program to accomplish specific tasks. You can start an application program by using the Start menu. To illustrate the use of the Start menu to start an application program, the following steps start Internet Explorer using the Internet command on the Start menu.

- Open the Start menu (Figure 1–34).

Q&A

Is Internet Explorer included in the All Programs list?

Yes. All application programs stored on the computer are listed on the All Programs list. Internet Explorer also is on the pinned items list because it is used often, but you can start Internet Explorer from the All Programs list as well.

Figure 1–34

2

• Click the Internet icon in the pinned items list on the Start menu to start Windows Internet Explorer (Figure 1–35).

Q&A

What is displayed in the Windows Internet Explorer window?

A title bar, Address bar, Standard toolbar, Instant Search box, scroll bar, status bar, and display area where pages from the World Wide Web display.

Figure 1–35

Other Ways

1. Click Start button, point to All Programs, click Internet Explorer

BTW

Web Sites
A collection of related Web pages on a computer is called a **Web site**. The MSN.com Web page shown in Figure 1–35 is the first Web page you see when you access the MSN.com Web site and is, therefore, referred to as a **home page**, or **start page**.

Uniform Resource Locator (URL)

A **Uniform Resource Locator (URL)** is the address on the World Wide Web where a Web page is located. It often is composed of three parts (Figure 1–36 on page WIN 29). The first part is the **protocol**. A protocol is a set of rules. Most Web pages use the Hypertext Transfer Protocol. **Hypertext Transfer Protocol (HTTP)** describes the rules used to transmit Web pages electronically over the Internet. You enter the protocol in lowercase as http followed by a colon and two forward slashes (http://). If you do not begin a URL with a protocol, Internet Explorer will assume it is http, and automatically will append http:// to the front of the URL.

The second part of a URL is the domain name. The **domain name** is the Internet address of the computer on the Internet where the Web page is located. The domain name in the URL in Figure 1–36 on the next page is www.scsite.com.

The last part of the domain name (com in Figure 1–36 on the next page) indicates the type of organization that owns the Web site. Table 1–2 shows some types of organizations and their extensions. In addition to the 14 domain name extensions listed in the table, there are country specific extensions, such as .uk for the United Kingdom and .dk for Denmark.

Figure 1–36

Organization	Extension	Organization	Extension
Commercial	.com	aviation	.aero
Educational	.edu	businesses	.biz
Government	.gov	co-operatives	.coop
Military	.mil	general	.info
Major network support	.net	museums	.museum
Organizations not covered above	.org	individuals	.name
International	.int	professionals	.pro

Table 1–2 Organizations and their Domain Name Extensions

The optional third part of a URL is the file specification of the Web page. The **file specification** includes the file name and possibly a directory or folder name. This information is called the **path**. If no file specification of a Web page is specified in the URL, a default Web page is displayed.

Browsing the World Wide Web

One method to browse the World Wide Web is to find URLs that identify interesting Web sites in magazines or newspapers, on television, from friends, or even from just browsing the Web. URLs of well-known companies and organizations usually contain the company's name and institution's name. For example, ibm.com is the IBM Corporation URL, and umich.edu is the URL for the University of Michigan.

When you find a URL of a Web page you want to visit, enter the URL into the Address bar. The following steps show how to view a Web site provided by Thomson Course Technology and visit the Web page titled SC Site – Shelly Cashman Series Student Resources Web site, which contains student resources for use with Shelly Cashman Series textbooks. The URL for the SC Site – Shelly Cashman Series Student Resources Web site is:

www.scsite.com

You are not required to provide the leading http:// protocol when initially typing the URL in the Address bar. Internet Explorer will insert http:// and assume the www automatically, if you do not supply it.

To Browse the Web by Entering a URL

The SC Site — Shelly Cashman Series Student Resources Web site contains student resources for use with Shelly Cashman Series textbooks. The URL for this Web page is www.scsite.com.

When you find the URL of a Web page you want to visit, enter the URL into the Address bar. The following steps show how to display the Web page from the Shelly Cashman Series.

- Click the Address bar to select the URL in the Address bar (Figure 1–37).

Q&A What happens when I click the Address bar?

Internet Explorer selects the URL in the Address bar and the mouse pointer changes to an I-beam.

selected URL in Address bar   I-beam

Figure 1–37

- Type www.scsite.com in the Address bar to display the new URL in the Address bar (Figure 1–38).

Q&A Must I type www. in the URL?

No. If you type scsite.com, Internet Explorer automatically will add www.

new URL is displayed   Go to button

Figure 1–38

- Click the Go to button to display the SC Site –Shelly Cashman Series Student Resources Web site (Figure 1–39).

Q&A The Go to button changes after I click it. Why?

When you type the URL, the button changes to the Go to button. After the page is displayed, the button changes to the Refresh button. When you click the Refresh button, the Web page is downloaded again from the Web server, resulting in the most up-to-date version of the page being displayed.

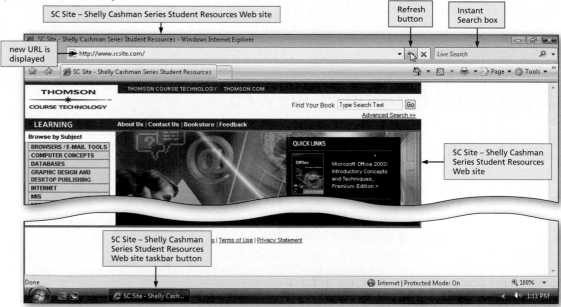

SC Site – Shelly Cashman Series Student Resources Web site   Refresh button   Instant Search box

new URL is displayed

SC Site – Shelly Cashman Series Student Resources Web site

SC Site – Shelly Cashman Series Student Resources Web site taskbar button

Figure 1–39

To Open a Link in a New Tab

You can view multiple Web pages in a single window using tabbed pages. A **tabbed page** consists of a tab in the Internet Explorer window and the associated Web page. When you start Internet Explorer only one tab is displayed, but you can open as many tabbed pages as you want. The following steps use the Instant Search box and the Course Technology – Shelly Cashman Series link to open a Web page on a new tabbed page.

 1

- Click the Instant Search box and type Shelly Cashman Series in the Instant Search box (Figure 1–40).

Q&A

What is an Instant Search box?

It is a text box in which you can type a term which then can be searched for by a Search engine. Internet Explorer provides an Instant Search box in the upper right corner of the window.

Figure 1–40

2

- Click the Search button to the right of the Instant Search box to display the results of the Web search (Figure 1–41).

Figure 1–41

3

- If necessary, scroll to view the Course Technology –Shelly Cashman Series link.

- Right-click the Course Technology –Shelly Cashman Series link to display a shortcut menu (Figure 1–42).

Q&A

What happens when I just click a link?

The Web page will open on the same tabbed page as the search results and will replace the search results page.

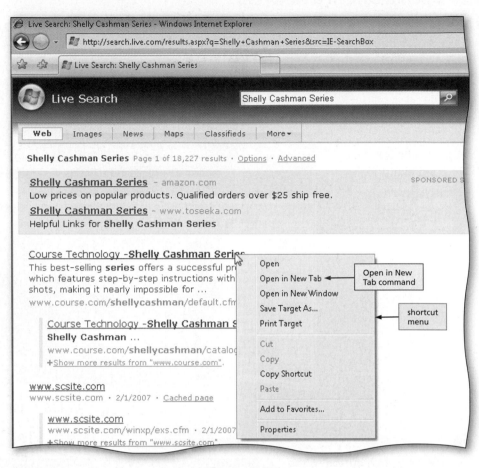

Figure 1–42

4

- Click the Open in New Tab command on the shortcut menu to close the shortcut menu and display the Course Technology –Shelly Cashman Series tab (Figure 1–43).

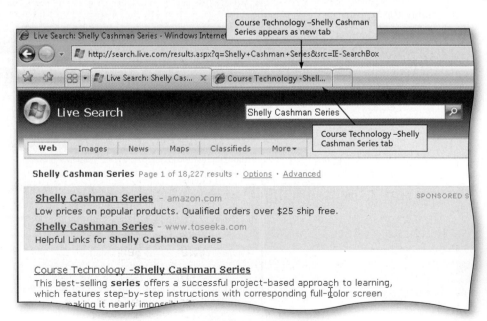

Figure 1–43

Other Ways

1. While holding down CTRL, click link

To Switch Between Tabs

You can display the contents of any tabbed page by clicking the tab, as shown in the following step which activates the Course Technology –Shelly Cashman Series tab.

1

• Click the Course Technology –Shelly Cashman Series tab to activate the tab and display The Shelly Cashman Series® Web page in the display area (Figure 1–44).

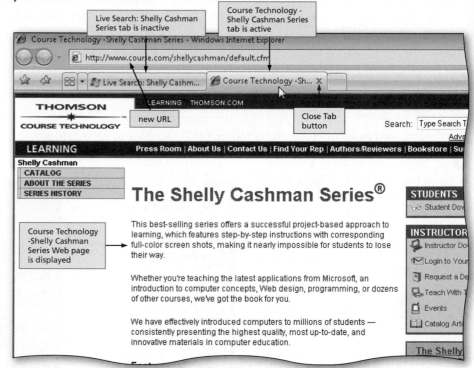

Figure 1–44

Other Ways	
1. Press CTRL+TAB, press CTRL+TAB	2. Press CTRL+2, press CTRL+1

To Close a Tab

You can keep as many tabbed pages open as necessary. If you no longer have a need for the tabbed page to be open, you can close the tab using the following steps.

• Click the Close Tab button in the Course Technology –Shelly Cashman Series tab to close the Course Technology –Shelly Cashman Series tab (Figure 1–45).

2

• Click the Close button on the title bar to close the Live Search: Shelly Cashman Series - Windows Internet Explorer window.

Figure 1–45

Working with Folders

The steps below allow you to view the contents of the computer, the hierarchy of drives and folders on the computer, and the files and folders in each folder. In this section, you will expand and collapse drives and folders, display drive and folder contents, create a new folder, copy a file between folders, and rename and then delete a file. These are common operations that you should understand how to perform.

To Work with Folders

First, you must open the Start menu, open the Computer window, and then maximize the window.

- Open the Start menu (Figure 1–46).

Figure 1–46

- Click Computer on the Start menu to display the Computer window (Figure 1–47).

Figure 1–47

3

- If necessary, double-click the Computer title bar to maximize the Computer window.

Figure 1–48

4

- If necessary, click the Folders button to display the Folders list (Figure 1–49).

Q&A

Is it possible to display my folders and drives in the right pane differently than what is shown in Figure 1–49?

You can display files and folders in the right pane in several different views. Currently, the drives and folders in the right pane are displayed in Tiles view.

Experiment

- Click a black arrow in the Folders list and observe the changes in the window. Then click the resulting white arrow to return the window to its previous state. Do the same for another black arrow and resulting white arrow.

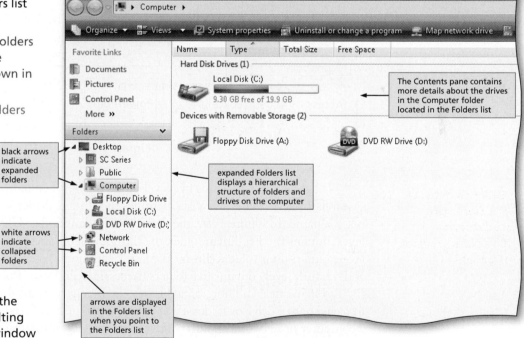

Figure 1–49

Other Ways

1. Click Start button, right-click Computer, click Explore on shortcut menu

2. Press WINDOWS+E

Using a Hierarchical Format to Organize Files and Folders

Besides navigating drives and folder, you also need to be able to create and organize the files and folders on the computer. A file may contain a spreadsheet assignment given by the computer teacher, a research paper assigned by the English teacher, an electronic quiz given by the Business teacher, or a study sheet designed by the Math teacher. You should organize and store these files in folders to avoid misplacing a file and to help you quickly find a file.

Assume you are a freshman taking four classes (Business, Computer, English, and Math). You want to design a series of folders for the four classes you are taking in the first semester of your freshman year. To accomplish this, you arrange the folders in a **hierarchical format**. The hierarchical structure of folders for the Freshman year is shown in Figure 1–50.

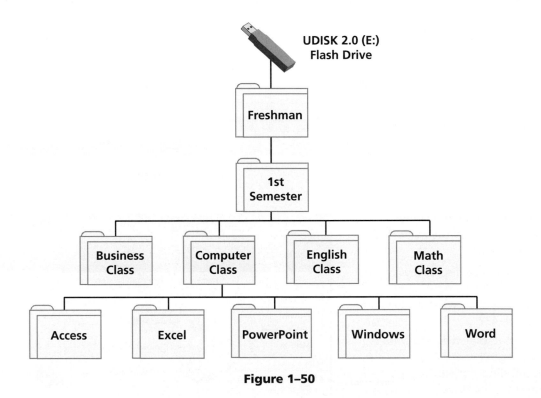

Figure 1–50

The hierarchy contains five levels. The first level contains the storage device, in this case a flash drive. Windows Vista identifies the storage device with a letter, and, in some cases, a name. In Figure 1–50, the flash drive is identified as UDISK 2.0 (E:). The second level contains the Freshman folder, the third level contains the 1st Semester folder, the fourth level contains four folders (Business Class, Computer Class, English Class, and Math Class), and the fifth level contains five folders (Access, Excel, PowerPoint, Windows, and Word).

The vertical and horizontal lines in the hierarchy chart form a pathway that allows you to navigate to a drive or folder. Each pathway is a means of navigation to a specific location on a computer or network. A **path** consists of a drive letter (preceded by a drive name when necessary) and colon, to identify the storage device, and one or more folder names. Each drive or folder in the hierarchy chart has a corresponding path. When you click a drive or folder icon in the Folders list, the corresponding path appears in the Address bar. Table 1–3 contains examples of paths and their corresponding drives and folders. These paths are referred to as **breadcrumb trails**, showing you where the current page or folder is in the hierarchy.

When the hierarchy in Figure 1–50 is created, the UDISK 2.0 (E:) drive is said "to contain" the Freshman folder, the Freshman folder is said "to contain" the 1st Semester folder, and so on. In addition, this hierarchy can easily be expanded to include folders from the Sophomore, Junior, and Senior years and any additional semesters.

Table 1–3 Paths and Corresponding Drives and Folders

Path	Drive and Folder
Computer ► UDISK 2.0 (E:)	Drive E (UDISK 2.0 (E:))
Computer ► UDISK 2.0 (E:) ► Freshman	Freshman folder on drive E
Computer ► UDISK 2.0 (E:) ► Freshman ► 1st Semester	1st Semester folder in Freshman folder on drive E
Computer ► UDISK 2.0 (E:) ► Freshman ► 1st Semester ► Computer Class ► Word	Word folder in Computer Class folder in 1st Semester folder in Freshman folder on drive E

Removable Media and Network Drives

Types of removable media such as USB flash drives are ideal for storing files and folders on a computer. A **USB flash drive**, sometimes called a **keychain drive**, is a flash memory storage device that plugs into a USB port on a computer. A **USB port**, short for universal serial bus port, can be found on most computers. USB flash drives, like the one shown in Figure 1–51, are convenient for mobile users because they are small and lightweight enough to be transported on a keychain or in a pocket.

USB ports

USB flash drive

Figure 1–51

Instead of a USB drive, you might use files stored on a network drive. A **network** is a collection of computers and devices connected together for the purpose of sharing information between computer users. In some cases, students might be required to store their files on a network drive found on the school's computer network. A **network drive** is a storage device that is connected to the server on the computer network. A **server** controls access to the hardware, software, and other resources on the network and provides a centralized storage area for programs, data, and information. If student files reside on the network drive on the school's network, files may be accessed from a school computer, or from a personal computer with permission from the school. Ask your teacher if the school requires you to use a network drive.

To Plug a USB Flash Drive into a USB Port

Although other removable media may be used for storage, the USB flash drive is one of the more popular drives. To store files and folders on the USB flash drive, you must plug the USB flash drive into a USB port on the computer. After you do, the flash drive window is displayed on the desktop. The removable media drive name on your computer may be different. The following step plugs a USB flash drive into a USB port.

- Plug the USB flash drive into a USB port on the computer to display the UDISK 2.0 (E:) window (Figure 1–52).

Q&A

What does UDISK 2.0 (E:) mean?

UDISK 2.0 is the name of a particular type of USB drive. (E:) is the drive letter assigned by Windows Vista to your removable drive. The name and drive letter of your USB drive might be different.

- Close the UDISK 2.0 (E:) window.

Figure 1–52

Naming a Folder

When you create a folder, such as the Freshman folder in Figure 1–50 on page 36, you must name the folder. A folder name should describe the folder and its contents. A folder name can contain up to 255 characters, including spaces. Any uppercase or lower-case character is valid when creating a folder name, except a backslash (\\), slash (/), colon (:), asterisk (*), question mark (?), quotation marks (''), less than symbol (<), greater than symbol (>), or vertical bar (|). Folder names cannot be CON, AUX, COM1, COM2, COM3, COM4, LPT1, LPT2, LPT3, PRN, or NUL. The same rules for naming folders also apply to naming files.

To Create a Folder on a Removable Drive

To create a folder on a removable drive, you must open the UDISK 2.0 (E:) drive and then create the folder in the right pane. The following steps create the Freshman folder on the UDISK 2.0 (E:) drive.

1

- Double-click the UDISK 2.0 (E:) icon in the Folders list to open it.

- Right-click an open area of the right pane to display a shortcut menu.

- Point to New on the shortcut menu to display the New submenu (Figure 1–53).

Figure 1–53

2

- Click Folder on the New submenu to display the new Folder icon.

- Type Freshman in the text box to name the folder.

- Press the ENTER key to create the Freshman folder on the UDISK 2.0 (E:) drive (Figure 1–54).

Q&A

What happens when I press the ENTER key?

The Freshman folder is displayed in the File list, which contains the folder name, date modified, and file folder type.

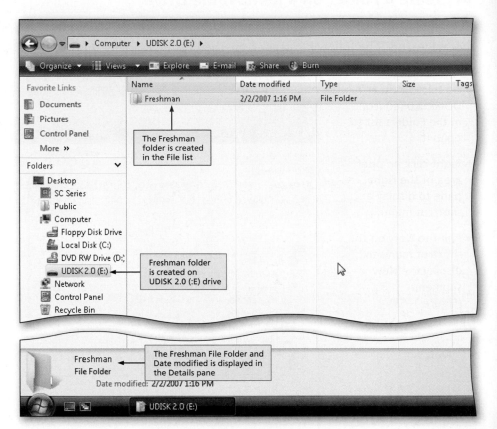

Figure 1–54

Downloading a Hierarchy of Folders into the Freshman Folder

After creating the Freshman folder on the UDISK 2.0 (E:) drive, the remaining folders in the hierarchical structure (see Figure 1–50), starting with the 1st Semester folder, should be downloaded to the Freshman folder. **Downloading** is the process of a computer receiving information, such as a set of files or folders from a Web site, from a server on the Internet. To make the task of creating the folders easier, the folders have been created and stored in a hierarchical structure on the SC Site - Shelly Cashman Series Student Resources Web site.

To Download a Hierarchy of Folders into the Freshman Folder

The following steps download the folders in the hierarchical structure into the Freshman folder.

1 Start Internet Explorer by clicking the Start button on the taskbar and then clicking Internet on the Start menu.

2 Click the Address box on the Address bar, type scsite.com in the Address box, and then click the Go button.

③ When the SC Site - Shelly Cashman Series Student Resources Web site is displayed, use the Browse by Subject navigation bar, click Office Suites, and then click Microsoft Office 2007.

④ In the center of the screen, locate your textbook and click the title (for example, Microsoft Office 2007: Introductory Concepts and Techniques, Windows Vista Edition).

⑤ Scroll down to display the Data Files for Students (Windows) area and then click the Windows Vista Chapter 1 Data Files link.

⑥ When the File Download – Security Warning dialog box is displayed, click the Run button.

⑦ When the Internet Explorer – Security Warning dialog box is displayed, click the Run button.

⑧ When the WinZip Self-Extractor dialog box is displayed, type the removable media drive letter of your removable media drive followed by a colon, backslash, and folder name (Freshman) (for example, E:\Freshman).

⑨ Click the Unzip button.

⑩ When Windows displays the WinZip Self-Extractor dialog box, click the OK button.

⑪ Click the Close button in the WinZip Self-Extractor dialog box.

⑫ Click the Close button in the SC Site – Shelly Cashman Series Student Resources Web site window (Figure 1–55).

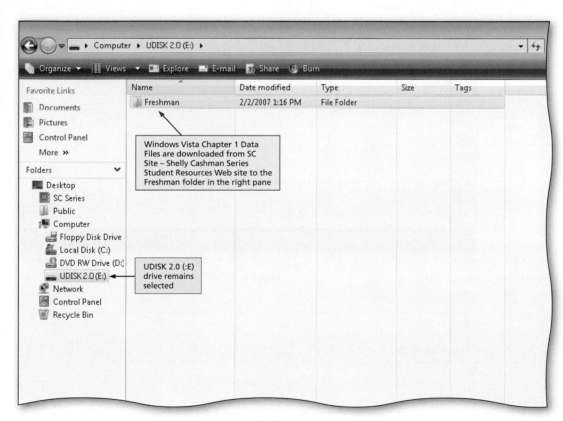

Figure 1–55

To Expand a Drive

Folder Windows display the hierarchy of items in the Folders list and the contents of drives and folders in the right pane. You might want to expand a drive to view its contents in the Folders list. The following step expands a drive.

- Point to any item in the Folders list to display arrows, and then click the white arrow to the left of the UDISK 2.0 (E:) icon in the Folders list to display the Freshman folder.

Q&A

Why are there black arrows and white arrows in the Folders list?

The black arrows represent folders and drives that contain other folders that have been expanded to show their contents. The white arrows represent folders and drives that contain other folders that have not been expanded.

- Click the white arrow next to the Freshman folder, and then click the white arrow next to the 1st Semester folder to display its contents (Figure 1–56).

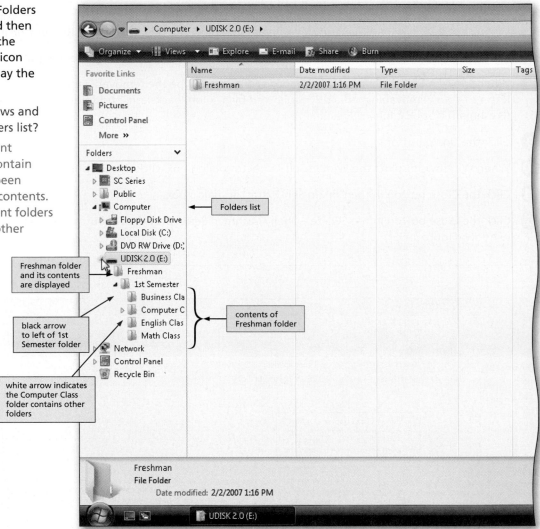

Figure 1–56

Other Ways

1. Double-click drive icon in Folders list
2. Select drive to expand using ARROW keys, press RIGHT ARROW on keyboard
3. Select drive to expand, press RIGHT ARROW

To Collapse a Folder

When a black arrow is displayed to the left of a folder icon in the Folders list, the folder is expanded and shows all the folders it contains. The following step collapses the 1st Semester folder.

1

• Click the black arrow to the left of the 1st Semester folder icon in the Folders list to collapse the 1st Semester folder (Figure 1–57).

Q&A Why is the 1st Semester folder indented below the Freshman folder in the Folders list?

The folder is indented below the Freshman icon to show that the folder is contained within the Freshman folder.

Figure 1–57

Other Ways

1. Double-click folder icon in Folders list
2. Select folder to collapse using ARROW keys, press LEFT ARROW on keyboard
3. Select folder to collapse, press LEFT ARROW

To Display the Contents of a Folder

Clicking a folder icon in the Folders list displays the contents of the drive or folder in the File list and displays the path in the Address bar. The following step displays the contents of the 1st Semester folder.

1

• Click the 1st Semester icon in the Folders list to display the contents of the 1st Semester folder in the File list (Figure 1–58).

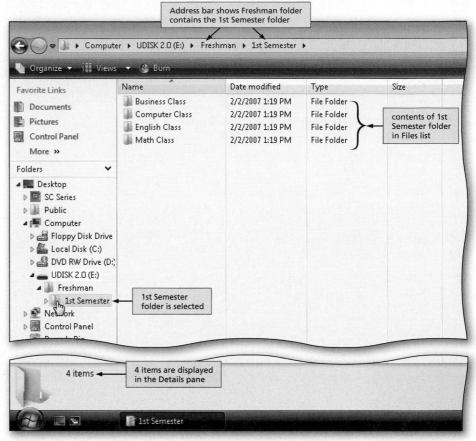

Figure 1–58

Other Ways

1. Right-click 1st Semester icon, click Explore on shortcut menu

Creating a Document and Folder Using WordPad

The Freshman folder was created in the UDISK 2.0 (E:) drive when you downloaded the files. You also can create a folder anytime you save a file in a Windows application. For example, you can use WordPad to create a document and then save the new document in a folder. **WordPad** is a word processing program included with Windows Vista that allows you to create a limited variety of personal and business documents.

As one of the programs in the Accessories list, one method to start the WordPad application is to display the Start menu, click All Programs, click Accessories, and click WordPad in the Accessories list.

An easier method to start WordPad is to use the Start Search box on the Start menu. The **Start Search** box allows you to find a specific application, file, e-mail, or Internet favorite by typing the first few letters in the Start Search box at the bottom of the Start menu.

To Start WordPad Using the Start Search Box

Assume you want to create a WordPad document that lists your homework for Friday, April 11. The first step is to start the WordPad application using the Start Search box. The following steps find and then start WordPad based on using the Start Search box at the bottom of the Start menu.

1

- Open the Start menu.

- Type w (the first letter in the WordPad name) in the Start Search box on the Start menu to display a list of programs, favorites, and history (Figure 1–59).

Q&A What is displayed on the Start menu when I type the letter w?

A list of programs, favorites, and history. The WordPad program does not appear yet. As you type the entire program name, fewer selections remain in the list until you find your selection or no items match your search term.

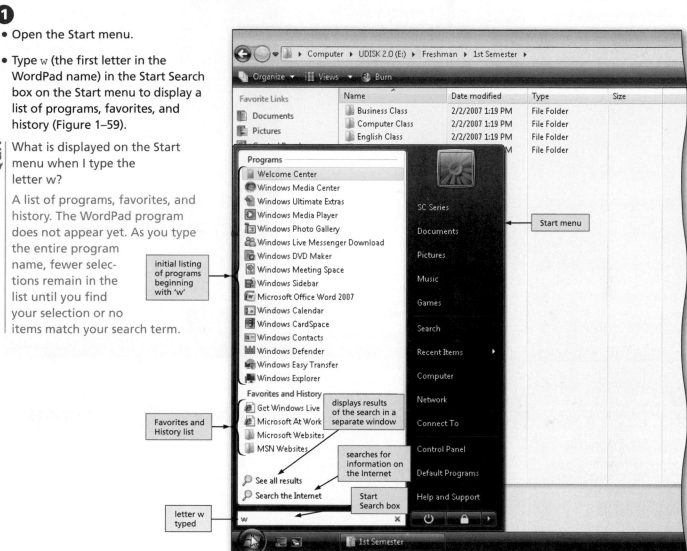

Figure 1–59

2

- Type the letter o (the second letter in the WordPad name) in the Start Search box on the Start menu to display a list of programs, favorites, history, and files (Figure 1–60).

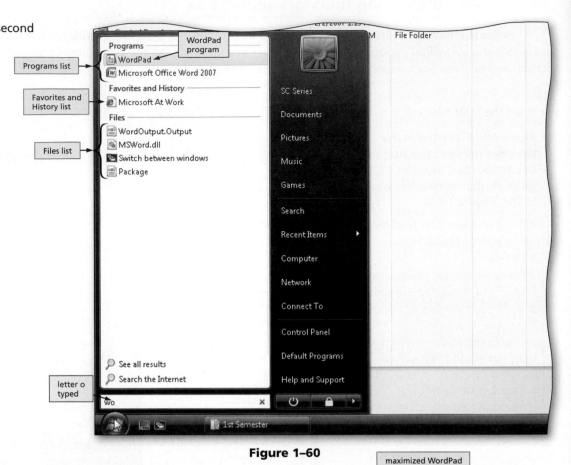

Figure 1–60

3

- Click WordPad in the Programs list to start the WordPad application and display a new blank document in the WordPad window (Figure 1–61).

- If the WordPad window is not maximized, click the Maximize button on the title bar to maximize the window.

Q&A Could I continue typing the remainder of the letters in the WordPad name?

Yes. To start the program you still need to click WordPad in the Programs list to start the WordPad application.

Figure 1–61

To Type Text

After starting WordPad, you can enter the text for a new document. To enter text in the document, you type on the keyboard. The following steps enter text in the new WordPad document.

- Type Friday, April 11 and then press the ENTER key twice.

- Type Finish – The Bike Delivers Data Base and then press the ENTER key.

- Type Read – Next Project and then press the ENTER key (Figure 1–62).

Q&A

What if I make an error while typing?

You can press the BACKSPACE key to delete the error and then retype the text correctly.

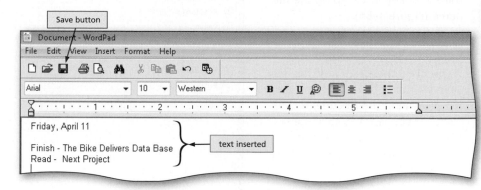

Figure 1–62

To Save a WordPad Document in a New Folder

After typing the text of a WordPad document, you can create a folder in which to save the document, and then save the document in the created folder. The following steps save the new document in a created folder named Homework, with a name of Friday, April 11. The Homework folder is created within the Computer Class folder (see the hierarchy in Figure 1–50 on page 36).

- Click the Save button on the Standard toolbar to display the Save As dialog box.

- If necessary, double-click the Save As dialog box title bar to maximize the Save As dialog box (Figure 1–63).

Q&A

Why is the Document file name selected in the File name text box?

It is selected in the File name text box as the default file name.
You can change the default file name by immediately typing the new name.

Figure 1–63

• Type `Friday, April 11` in the File name text box. Do not press the ENTER key after typing the file name (Figure 1–64).

Q&A

What happens if I press the ENTER key after typing the file name?

If you press the ENTER key, the Save As dialog box closes and the file is saved in the Documents folder. If you want to save the file in a folder other than the Documents folder, you must select the desired folder.

Q&A

What if the Navigation pane does not appear in the Save As dialog box?

Click the Browse Folders button.

Figure 1–64

• If necessary, click the Folders button to expand the Folders list.

• Click the white arrow next to the Computer icon in the Folders list to display a list of available disks and drives (Figure 1–65).

Q&A

What if I don't see the white arrows in the Folders list?

To display both the white and black arrows, point to any item in the Folders list.

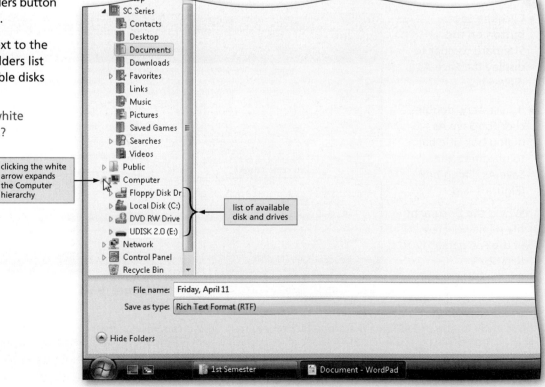

Figure 1–65

4

- Click UDISK 2.0 (E:) in the Folders list to display the contents of the UDISK 2.0 (E:) folder in the File list (Figure 1–66).

Is it OK if my list of drives and folders is different from the one in Figure 1–66?

Yes. Folders and drives can be unique for each computer.

Figure 1–66

5

- Double-click the Freshman folder in the File list of the Save As dialog box to display the 1st Semester folder in the File list (Figure 1–67).

Figure 1–67

- Double-click the 1st Semester folder in the File list of the Save As dialog box to display the contents of the 1st Semester folder (Figure 1–68)

Figure 1–68

- Double-click the Computer Class folder in the File list of the Save As dialog box to display the contents of the Computer Class folder (Figure 1–69).

Figure 1–69

8

- Click the New Folder button on the Save As dialog toolbar to create a new folder within the Computer Class folder.

- Type Homework as the name of the folder and then press the ENTER key (Figure 1–70).

Figure 1–70

9

- Click the Save button in the Save As dialog box to save the Friday, April 11 document to its new location in the Homework folder (Figure 1–71).

- Click the Close button in the Friday, April 11 - WordPad window to close the window.

Figure 1–71

To Verify the Contents of a Folder

After saving the Friday, April 11 document in the Homework folder, you can verify that the document was correctly saved in the Homework folder. The following step verifies the Homework folder contains the Friday, April 11 document.

- Click the white arrow next to the 1st Semester icon in the Folders list to display the folders within the 1st Semester folder.

- Click the white arrow next to the Computer Class icon in the Folders list to display the folders within the Computer Class folder.

- Click the Homework icon in the Folders list to select the Homework folder and display the contents of the Homework folder in the right pane (Figure 1–72).

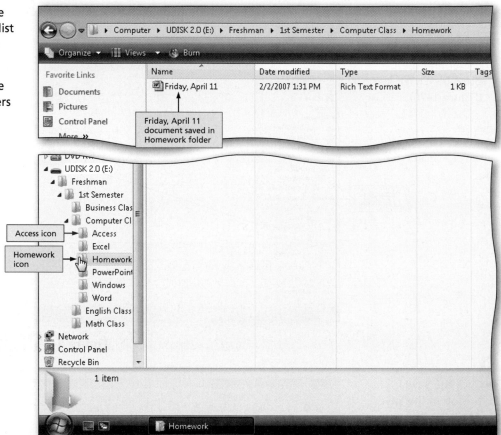

Figure 1–72

File Management

Being able to manage the files on the computer is one of the most important computer skills you can have. **File management** includes copying, moving, renaming, and deleting files and folders on the computer.

To Copy a File by Right-Dragging

When copying files, the drive and folder containing the files to be copied are called the **source drive** and **source folder**, respectively. The drive and folder to which the files are copied are called the **destination drive** and **destination folder**, respectively. The Access folder contains two Access database files (SciFi Scene and The Bike Delivers).

The following steps on the next page show one method of copying files - right-drag a file icon from the right pane to a folder or drive icon in the Folders list. The following steps on the next page copy the The Bike Delivers file from the Access folder (source folder) to the Homework (destination folder). The UDISK 2.0 (E:) drive is both the source drive and the destination drive.

1

• Click the Access folder in the Folders list to select the Access folder and display its contents in the right pane (Figure 1–73).

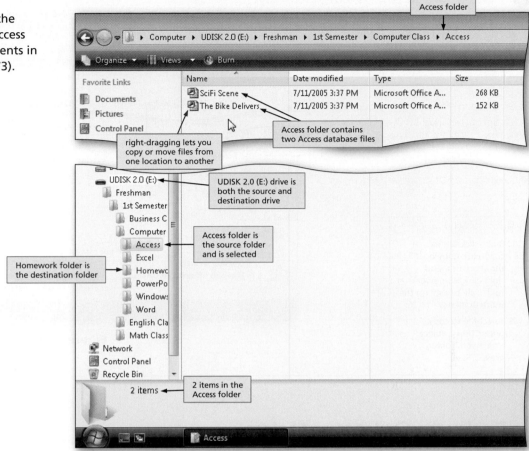

Figure 1–73

2

• Right-drag the The Bike Delivers icon from the right pane onto the Homework folder icon in the Folders list to open the shortcut menu (Figure 1–74).

Q&A

What should I do if I right-drag a file to the wrong folder?

Click Cancel on the shortcut menu, and then right-drag the file to the correct folder.

Figure 1–74

- Click Copy Here on the shortcut menu to copy The Bike Delivers file to the Homework folder.

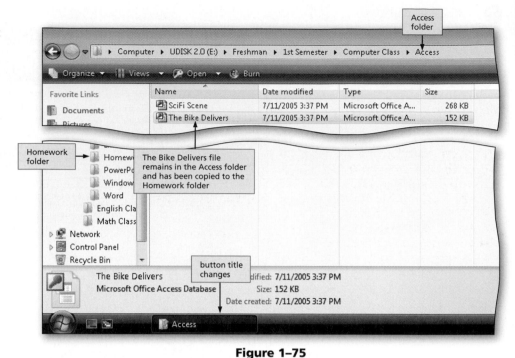

Figure 1–75

Other Ways

1. Right-click file to copy, click Copy on the shortcut menu, right-click Homework folder, click Paste on the shortcut menu
2. Select file to copy, press CTRL+C, select Homework folder, press CTRL+V

To Display the Contents of a Folder

After copying a file, you might want to examine the folder or drive where the file was copied to ensure it was copied properly. The following step displays the contents of the Homework folder.

- Click the Homework folder in the Folders list to display the contents of the Homework folder (Figure 1–76).

Q&A

Can I copy or move more than one file at a time?

Yes. To copy or move multiple files, select each file to be copied or moved by clicking the file icon while holding down the CTRL key. Then, right-drag the selected files to the destination folder using the same technique as right-dragging a single file.

Figure 1–76

To Rename a File

In some circumstances, you may want to rename a file or a folder. This could occur when you want to distinguish a file in one folder or drive from a copy, or if you decide you need a better name to identify a file. The Word folder in Figure 1–77 contains the three Word documents (Barn and Silo, Fall Harvest, and Lake at Sunset). In this case, you decide to change the Fall Harvest name to Great Fall Harvest. The following steps change the name of the Fall Harvest file in the Word folder to Great Fall Harvest.

1

- Click the Word folder in the left pane to display the three files it contains in the right pane.

- Right-click the Fall Harvest icon in the right pane to select the Fall Harvest icon and display a shortcut menu (Figure 1–77).

2

- Click Rename on the shortcut menu to select the file name for renaming.

- Type `Great Fall Harvest` and then press the ENTER key (Figure 1–78).

Q&A

Are there any risks to renaming files that are located on the hard disk?

If you inadvertently rename a file that is associated with certain programs, the programs may not be able to find the file and, therefore, may not execute properly. Always use caution when renaming files.

Figure 1–77

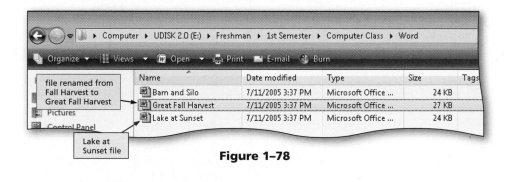

Figure 1–78

Other Ways

1. Right-click icon, press M, type name, press ENTER

2. Select icon, press F2, type name, press ENTER

3. Select icon, press ALT+F, press M, type name, press ENTER

To Delete a File by Right-Clicking

A final task you may want to perform is to delete a file. Exercise extreme caution when deleting a file or files. When you delete a file from a hard drive, the deleted file is stored in the Recycle Bin where you can recover it until you empty the Recycle Bin. If you delete a file from removable media, the file is gone permanently once you delete it. The following steps delete the Lake at Sunset file.

• Right-click the Lake at Sunset icon in the right pane to select the icon and open a shortcut menu (Figure 1–79).

Figure 1–79

• Click Delete on the shortcut menu to open the Delete File dialog box (Figure 1–80).

Figure 1–80

3

- Click the Yes button in the Delete File dialog box to remove the Lake at Sunset file (Figure 1–81).

Q&A Can I use this same technique to delete a folder?

Yes. Right-click the folder and then click Delete on the shortcut menu. When you delete a folder, all the files and folders contained in the folder you are deleting, together with any files and folders on lower hierarchical levels, are deleted as well.

Figure 1–81

Other Ways

1. Select icon, press ALT+F, press D, press Y

To Close Expanded Folders

Sometimes, after you have completed work with expanded folders, you will want to close the expanded folders while still leaving the Word window open. The following steps close the Computer Class folder, 1st Semester folder, Freshman folder, and UDISK 2.0 (E:) drive.

1

- Click the black arrow to the left of the Computer Class folder in the Folders list to collapse the Computer Class folder (Figure 1–82).

2

- Click the black arrow to the left of the 1st Semester folder to collapse the folder.

- Click the black arrow to the left of the Freshman folder to collapse the folder.

- Click the black arrow to the left of the UDISK 2.0 (E:) drive to collapse the drive.

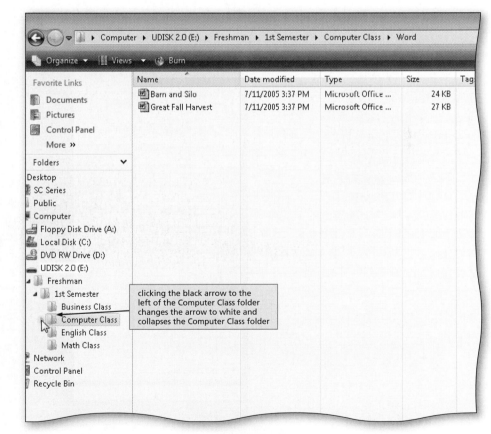

Figure 1–82

Other Ways

1. Click expanded folder icon, press LEFT ARROW

To Close the Computer Window

When you have finished working, you can close the Folders list and close the Computer window. The following steps close the Computer window.

1 Click the Close button on the Computer window title bar to close the Computer window.

2 Remove the USB flash drive from the USB port.

Using Help and Support

One of the more powerful Windows Vista features is Windows Help and Support. **Windows Help and Support** is available when using Windows Vista, or when using any application program running under Windows Vista. It contains answers to many questions you may ask with respect to the Windows Vista operating system.

To Start Windows Help and Support

Before you can access the Windows Help and Support services, you must start Help and Support. One method of starting Help and Support uses the Start menu. The following steps start Help and Support.

1

• Open the Start menu (Figure 1–83).

Figure 1–83

2

- Click Help and Support to display the Windows Help and Support window.

- If necessary, click the Maximize button on the Windows Help and Support title bar to maximize the Windows Help and Support window (Figure 1–84).

Q&A

What does Windows Help and Support contain?

Windows Help and Support contains a title bar, navigation toolbar, Find an answer area, Ask someone area, and Information from Microsoft area

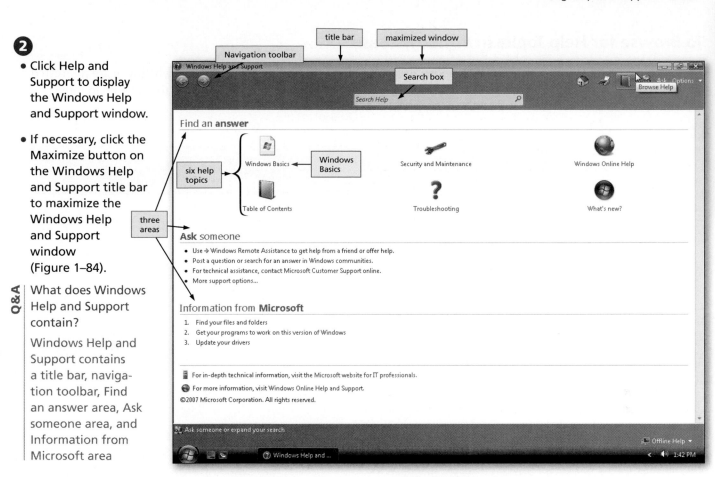

Figure 1–84

Table 1–4 shows the content areas in the Windows Help and Support Center.

Other Ways

1. Press CTRL+ESC, press RIGHT ARROW, press UP ARROW, Press ENTER
2. Press WINDOWS+F1

Table 1–4 Windows Help and Support Center Content Areas	
Area	**Function**
Find an answer	Area contains six Help topics: Windows Basics, Table of Contents, Security and Maintenance, Troubleshooting, Windows Online Help, and What's new? Clicking a category displays a list of subcategories and Help topics related to the category.
Ask someone	Area contains Windows Remote Assistance allowing you to get help from a friend or offer help, post a question or search for an answer in Windows communities, get technical assistance from Microsoft Customer Support online. Clicking the More support options link allows you to search the Knowledge Base, get in-depth technical information from Microsoft Website for IT professionals, and Windows Online Help and Support.
Information from Microsoft	Area contains links to Find your files and folders, Get your programs to work on this version of Windows, and Update your drives.

To Browse for Help Topics in Windows Basics

After starting Windows Help and Support, the next action is to find the Help topic in which you are interested. The following steps use the 'Find an answer' area in the Windows Help and Support Center to find a Help topic that describes how to use the Windows Help and Support Center.

- Click Windows Basics in the 'Find an answer' area to display the Windows Basics: all topics heading (Figure 1–85).

Figure 1–85

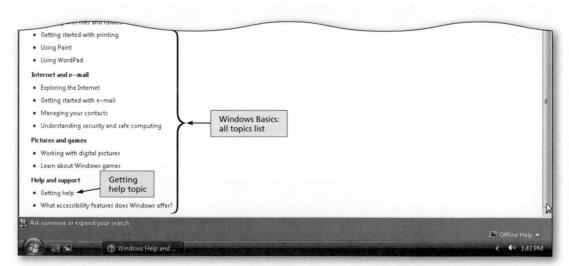

- Scroll down to view Getting help topic (Figure 1–86).

Figure 1–86

3

- Click the Getting help topic (Figure 1–87).

- Read the information in the Getting help topic.

Back button

Figure 1–87

4

- Click the Back button on the Navigation toolbar two times to return to the Find an answer area (Figure 1–88).

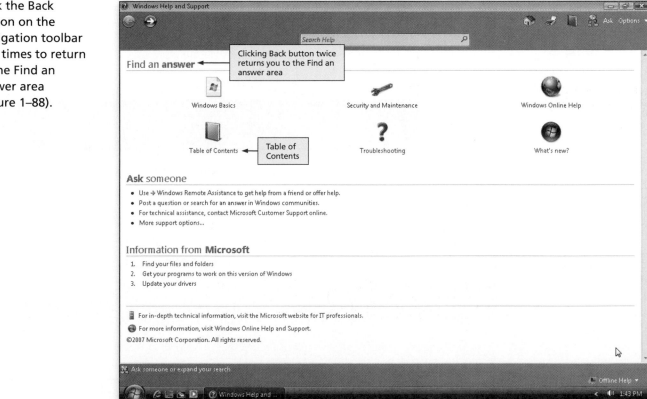

Figure 1–88

To Search for Help Topics Using the Table of Contents

A second method of finding answers to your questions about Windows Vista is to use the Table of Contents. The **Table of Contents** contains a list of entries, each of which references one or more Help topics. The following steps obtain help and information about what you need to set up a home network.

- Click the Table of Contents link in the Find an answer area to display the Table of Contents (Figure 1–89).

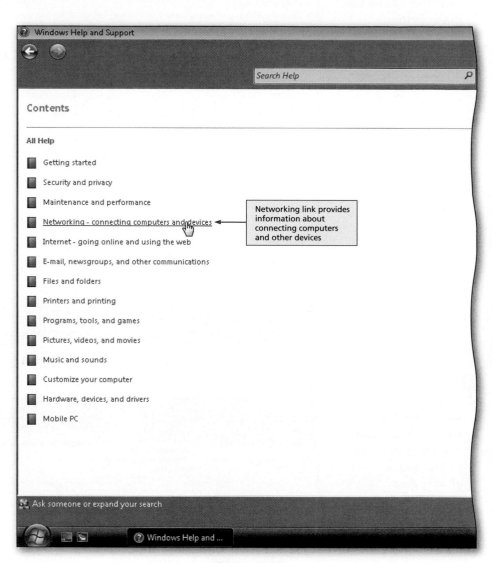

Figure 1–89

2

- Click the 'Networking – connecting computers and devices' link in the Contents area (Figure 1–90).

Q&A

What happens if the topic I am interested in is not included in the table of contents?

Type the term into the Search Help text box in the Windows Help and Support window, and then press ENTER to find information about your topic.

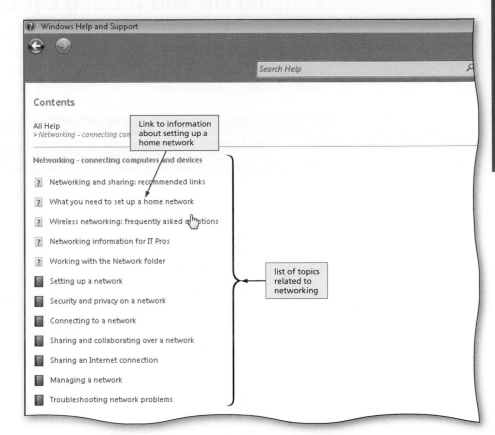

Figure 1–90

3

- Click the 'What you need to set up a home network' link (Figure 1–91).

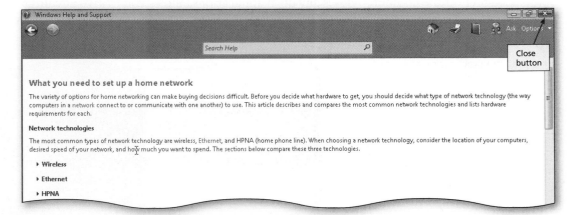

Figure 1–91

To Close Windows Help and Support

The following step shows how to close Windows Help and Support.

1 Click the Close button on the title bar of the Windows Help and Support window to close the Windows Help and Support window.

Logging Off and Turning Off the Computer

After completing your work with Windows Vista, you should close your user account by logging off the computer. In addition to logging off, there are several options available for ending your Windows Vista session. Table 1–5 illustrates the various options for ending your Windows Vista session.

Table 1–5 Options and Methods for Ending a Windows Vista Session	
Option	**Method**
Switch User	Click the Start button, point to the arrow next to the Lock button, and then click Switch User to keep your programs running in the background (but inaccessible until you log on again), which can allow another user to log on.
Log Off	Click the Start button, point to the arrow next to the Lock button, and then click Log Off to close all your programs but leave the computer running so that another user can log on.
Lock	Click the Start button, and then click the Lock button to deny anyone except those you have authorized access to log on to the computer.
Restart	Click the Start button, point to the arrow next to the Lock button, and then click Restart to shut down and then restart the computer.
Sleep	Click the Start button, click the Sleep button, wait for Windows to save your work, and then power down to a hibernating state.
Shut Down	Click the Start button, point to the arrow next to the Lock button, and then click Shut Down to close all your programs and turn off the computer.

To Log Off the Computer

Logging off the computer closes any open applications, allows you to save any unsaved documents, ends the Windows Vista session, and makes the computer available for other users. The following steps log off the computer.

• Open the Start menu (Figure 1–92).

Figure 1–92

2

- Point to the arrow to the right of the 'Lock this computer' button to display a menu. (Figure 1–93).

Figure 1–93

3

- Click the Log Off command, and then wait for Windows Vista to prompt you to save any unsaved and log off (Figure 1–94).

Q&A

Why should I log off the computer?

It is important to log off the computer so you do not lose your work. Some users of Windows Vista have turned off their computers without following the log off procedure only to find data they lost data thought they had stored on disk.

Figure 1–94

To Turn Off the Computer

After logging off, you also may want to shut down the computer using the Shut down button or the Shut down options arrow in the lower corner of the Welcome screen. Clicking the left button shuts down your computer, and clicking the right button displays a menu containing three commands (Restart, Sleep, and Shut Down) that can be used to restart the computer, put the computer into sleep mode, and shut down the computer). The following step turns off the computer. If you are not sure about turning off the computer, simply read the step.

• Click the Shut down button on the Welcome screen to shut down the computer.

Other Ways
1. Press ALT+F4, press the down arrow, select Shut Down, press OK

Chapter Summary

In this chapter you have learned about the Windows Vista graphical interface. You started Windows Vista, learned the components of the desktop and the six mouse operations. You opened, closed, moved, resized, minimized, maximized, and scrolled a window. You used Folder Windows to expand and collapse drives and folders, display drive and folder contents, create a folder, copy a file between folders, and rename and then delete a file. You used Internet Explorer to browse using a URL and tabs. You learned about the hierarchical format, removable media flash drives, and you used WordPad to type and save a document in a newly created folder. You searched for files using a word or phrase in the file or by name, you obtained help about using Windows Vista, and shut down Windows Vista.

1. Log On to the Computer (WIN 8)
2. Close the Welcome Center Window (WIN 10)
3. Add a Gadget to the Windows Sidebar (WIN 10)
4. Remove a Gadget from the Windows Sidebar (WIN 12)
5. Open the Start Menu (WIN 13)
6. Scroll Using Scroll Arrows, the Scroll Bar, and the Scroll Box (WIN 15)
7. Add an Icon to the Desktop (WIN 16)
8. Open a Window Using the Desktop Icon (WIN 18)
9. Minimize and Redisplay a Window (WIN 19)
10. Maximize and Restore a Window (WIN 20)
11. Close a Window (WIN 21, WIN 24)
12. Open a Window Using the Start Menu (WIN 21)
13. Move a Window by Dragging (WIN 22)
14. Expand the Folders List (WIN 23)
15. Size a Window by Dragging (WIN 23)
16. Collapse the Folders List (WIN 24)
17. Delete a Desktop Icon by Right-Dragging (WIN 25)
18. Start an Application Using the Start Menu (WIN 27)
19. Browse the Web by Entering a URL (WIN 30)
20. Open a Link in a New Tab (WIN 31)
21. Switch Between Tabs (WIN 33)
22. Close a Tab (WIN 33)
23. Work with Folders (WIN 34)
24. Plug a USB Flash Drive into a USB Port (WIN 38)
25. Create a Folder on a Removable Drive (WIN 39)
26. Download a Hierarchy of Folders (WIN 40)
27. Expand a Drive (WIN 42)
28. Collapse a Folder (WIN 43)
29. Display the Contents of a Folder (WIN 44)
30. Start WordPad Using the Start Search Box (WIN 45)
31. Type Text (WIN 47)
32. Save a WordPad Document in a New Folder (WIN 47)
33. Verify the Contents of a Folder (WIN 52)
34. Copy a File by Right-Dragging (WIN 52)
35. Display the Contents of a Folder (WIN 54)
36. Rename a File (WIN 55)
37. Delete a File by Right-Clicking (WIN 56)
38. Close Expanded Folders (WIN 57)
39. Start Windows Help and Support (WIN 58)

40. Browse for Help Topics in Windows Basics (WIN 60)
41. Search for Help Topics Using the Table of Contents (WIN 62)

42. Close Windows Help and Support (WIN 63)
43. Log Off from the Computer (WIN 64)
44. Turn Off the Computer (WIN 66)

If you have a SAM user profile, you may have access to hands-on instruction, practice, and assessment. Log in to your SAM account (http://sam2007.course.com) to launch any assigned training activities or exams that relate to the skills covered in this chapter.

Learn It Online

Test your knowledge of chapter content and key terms.

Instructions: To complete the Learn It Online exercises, start your browser, click the Address bar, and then enter the Web address scsite.com/winvista2007/learn. When the Windows Learn It Online page is displayed, click the link for the exercise you want to complete and then read the instructions.

Chapter Reinforcement TF, MC, and SA
A series of true/false, multiple choice, and short answer questions that test your knowledge of the chapter content.

Flash Cards
An interactive learning environment where you identify chapter key terms associated with displayed definitions.

Practice Test
A series of multiple choice questions that test your knowledge of chapter content and key terms.

Who Wants To Be a Computer Genius?
An interactive game that challenges your knowledge of chapter content in the style of a television quiz show.

Wheel of Terms
An interactive game that challenges your knowledge of chapter key terms in the style of the television show *Wheel of Fortune*.

Crossword Puzzle Challenge
A crossword puzzle that challenges your knowledge of key terms presented in the chapter.

In the Lab

Using the guidelines, concepts, and skills presented in this chapter, complete the following Labs.

Lab 1: Windows Vista Demos

Instructions: Use a computer to perform the following tasks.

Part 1:   Windows Vista Demos

1. If necessary, start Windows Vista and then log on to the computer.
2. Click the Start button and then click Help and Support on the Start menu.
3. If necessary, maximize the Windows Help and Support window.
4. Click What's new? in the 'Find an answer' area in the Windows Help and Support window.

Part 2:   What's New in Windows Vista?

1. In the Searching and organizing area, click the 'Demo: Working with files and folders' link, and then click the 'Watch the demo' link. As you watch the demo, answer the questions below.

   a. The Start menu provides access to several folders. What are the three folders mentioned?

   _____

   b. How do you create a new folder?

   _____

   c. If you use a folder frequently, where should you put the folder?

   _____

2. Click the Back button below the Windows Help and Support title to return to the What's new in Windows Vista heading.

Part 3:   What's New in Security?

1. In the Security area, click the green arrow to the left of the 'Click to open the Security Center' link. Answer the questions below.

   a. What are the four security essentials shown in the Windows Security Center.

   b. Close the Windows Security Center.

   c. In the Security area, click the 'Demo: Security basics' link and then click the Read the transcript' link.

   d. What's the quickest way to check your computer's security status and fix security problems.

   _____

   e. What does a firewall do?

   _____

   f. What does it mean when all the lights in the Security Center are green?

   _____

2. Click the Back button below the Windows Help and Support title to return to the 'What's new in Windows Vista Ultimate' page.

Part 4:   What's New in Parental Controls?

1. Scroll down to view the Parental Controls area.

   a. In the Parental Controls area, click the 'What can I control with Parental Controls?' link.

   b. What can I do with Parental Controls?

   _____

   _____

c. After setting up Parental Controls, how can a parent keep a record of a child's computer activity?

_____

2. Click the Back button below the Windows Help and Support title to view the topics in the Windows and Help Support window.

Part 5: What's New in the Pictures Area?

1. Scroll down the Windows Help and Support window to view the Pictures area.

a. In the Pictures area, click the 'Working with digital pictures' link.

b. What are the two main ways to import pictures?

_____

_____

2. Click the Back button below the Windows Help and Support title to view the topics in the Windows Help and Support window.

Part 6: What's New in the Mobile PC Features Area?

1. If necessary, scroll to view the Mobile PC features area, click the Using Windows Mobility Center link. Answer the following question.

a. How do you open the Mobility Center?

_____

_____

2. Click the Close button in the Windows Help and Support window.

In the Lab

Lab 2: Internet Explorer

Instructions: Use a computer to perform the following tasks.

1. Start Windows Vista and connect to the Internet.

2. Right-click the Start button on the taskbar, click Explore on the shortcut menu, and then maximize the Start Menu window.

3. If necessary, open the Folders list so the Start Menu and Programs icons are visible.

4. Click the Programs icon in the Start Menu folder.

5. Double-click the Internet Explorer shortcut icon in the Contents pane to start the Internet Explorer application. What is the URL of the Web page that appears in the Address bar in the Windows Internet Explorer window? _____

6. Click the URL in the Address bar in the Windows Internet Explorer window to select it. Type scsite.com and then press the ENTER key.

7. If necessary, scroll the Web page to display the Browse by Subject navigation bar containing the subject categories. Clicking a subject category displays the book titles in that category.

8. Click Operating Systems in the Browse by Subject navigation bar.

9. Click the Windows Vista link.

10. Right-click the first Windows Vista textbook cover image on the Web page, click Save Picture As on the shortcut menu, type Windows Vista Cover in the File name box, and then click the Save button in the Save Picture dialog box to save the image in the Pictures folder.

Continued >

In the Lab *continued*

11. Click the Close button in the Windows Internet Explorer window.

12. If necessary, scroll to the top of the Folders list to make the drive (C:) icon visible.

13. Click the black arrow to the left of the drive (C:) icon.

14. Click the Documents folder name in the Favorites Links list.

15. Click the Pictures folder name in the Folders list.

16. Right-click the Windows Vista Cover icon and then click Properties on the shortcut menu.

    a. What type of file is the Windows Vista Cover file? _____

    b. When was the file last modified? _____

    c. With what application does this file open? _____

17. Click the Cancel button in the Windows Vista Cover Properties dialog box.

18. If necessary, click the Close button in the Auto Play window.

19. Insert a USB flash drive into your computer.

19. Right-drag the Windows Vista Cover icon to the USB flash drive icon in the Folders list. Click Move Here on the shortcut menu. Click the USB flash drive icon in the Folders list.

    a. Is the Windows Vista Cover file stored on the USB flash drive? _____

20. Click the Close button in the USB flash drive window.

In the Lab

Lab 3: Getting Help

Instructions: Use a computer to perform the following tasks.

Part 1: Using Windows Basics to Get Help

1. If necessary, start Windows Vista and then log on to the computer.

2. Click the Start button and then click Help and Support on the Start menu.

3. If necessary, maximize the Windows Help and Support window.

4. Click Windows Basics icon in the 'Find an answer' area.

5. Click the 'Turning off your computer properly' link. Why are there two different looking Power buttons?

    _____

    _____

6. Click the Back button in the upper-left corner of the Windows Help and Support window.

Part 2: Using Desktop Fundamentals to Get Help

1. Look in the Desktop fundamentals area and identify the three parts of the desktop.

    _____

2. Click the 'Getting started with printing' link. List the three types of printers shown in the Getting started with printing area.

    _____

3. Click the Back button in the upper-left corner of the Windows Help and Support window.

4. If necessary, scroll to view the Getting help topic under the 'Help and support' heading. Click the Getting help link. List the eight ways to get help.

_____

_____

5. Click the Back button twice in the upper-left corner of the Windows Help and Support window.

Part 3:   Using Table of Contents to Get Help
1. Click the Table of Contents icon in the 'Find an answer' area.
2. Click the 'E-mail, newsgroups, and other communications' link. List six communication options.

_____

_____

3. Click Newsgroups in the Contents list.
4. Click the 'What are newsgroups?' in the Contents list.
5. Describe what a newsgroup is.

_____

_____

6. Click the Back button four times in the upper-left corner of the Windows Help and Support window.

Part 4:   Using Security and Maintenance to Get Help
1. Click the Security and Maintenance link in the 'Find an answer' area.
2. What does Windows Defender prevent?

_____

3. What's so important about Back up and Restore?

_____

_____

4. Click the Back button in the upper-left corner of the Windows Help and Support window.

Part 5:   Using Troubleshooting to Get Help
1. Click the Troubleshooting icon in the 'Find an answer' area.
2. Click the Connect to the Internet link under the 'Using the web' heading.
3. Click the 'What do I need to connect to the Internet?' link.
4. What do you use to connect to the Internet?

_____

5. Click the Back button three times in the upper-left corner of the Windows Help and Support.

Part 6:   Using Windows Online Help to Get Help
1. Click Windows the Online Help icon in the 'Find an answer' area to open Internet Explorer to the Windows Vista: Help and How-to window.
2. Click the 'Music and sounds' icon.
3. What can you do in the Music and sounds area in the Windows Help and How-to Web site?

_____

_____

4. Close the Windows Vista: Help Music window, and then close the Windows Help and Support window.

In the Lab

Lab 4: Downloading the Word 2007 Chapters 1–3 Data Files

Instructions: Use the SC Site—Shelly Cashman Series Student Resources Web site to download the Word 2007 Chapters 1–3 Data Files into the Word folder.

Part 1: *Plug the USB Flash Drive into the USB Port*

1. If necessary, launch Windows Vista and log on to the computer.
2. Plug the USB flash drive into the USB port on the computer. The UDISK 2.0 (E:) window should display on the desktop and should contain the Freshman folder.
3. If the Freshman folder does not display in the UDISK 2.0 (E:) window, follow the steps in Chapter One to create the hierarchy of folders shown in Figure 1–50 on page WIN 36.

Part 2: *Download the Word 2007 Chapters 1-3 Data Files into the Word Folder*

1. Start Internet Explorer by clicking the Start button on the taskbar and then clicking Internet on the Start menu.
2. Click the Address box on the Address bar, type `scsite.com` in the Address box, and then click the Go button.
3. When the SC Site — Shelly Cashman Series Student Resources Web site is displayed, use the Browse by Subject navigation bar, click Office Suites, and then click Microsoft Office 2007.
4. In the center of the screen, locate your textbook, and then click the title (for example, Microsoft Office 2007: Introductory Concepts and Techniques, Windows Vista Edition).
5. When the page for your textbook displays, click the Word Chapters 1–3 Data Files link (You may need to scroll down the page).
6. When the File Download – Security Warning dialog box is displayed, click the Run button.
7. When the Internet Explorer – Security Warning dialog box is displayed, click the Run button.
8. When the WinZip Self-Extractor dialog box displays, click the Browse button.
9. Click the plus sign to the left of the removable drive, click the plus sign to the left of the Freshman folder, click the plus sign to the left of the 1st Semester folder, click the plus sign to the left of the Computer Class folder, and then click the Word folder.
10. Click the OK button in the Browse for Folder dialog box.
11. Click the Unzip button in the WinZip Self-Extractor dialog box.
12. When a smaller WinZip Self-Extractor dialog box appears, click the OK button.
13. Click the Close button in the WinZip Self-Extractor dialog box.
14. Click the Close button in the SC Site — Shelly Cashman Series Student Resources Web site window.
15. Verify the Word 2007 Chapters 1–3 Data Files folder is contain in the Word folder.
16. Close the Word window. Unplug the USB flash drive from the USB port.

1 Creating and Editing a Word Document

Objectives

You will have mastered the material in this chapter when you can:

- Start and quit Word
- Describe the Word window
- Enter text in a document
- Check spelling as you type
- Save a document
- Format text, paragraphs, and document elements
- Undo and redo commands or actions

- Insert a picture and format it
- Print a document
- Change document properties
- Open a document
- Correct errors in a document
- Use Word's Help

1 | Creating and Editing a Word Document

What Is Microsoft Office Word 2007?

Microsoft Office Word 2007 is a full-featured word processing program that allows you to create professional-looking documents and revise them easily. A document is a printed or electronic medium people use to communicate with others. With Word, you can develop many types of documents, including flyers, letters, memos, resumes, reports, fax cover sheets, mailing labels, and newsletters. Word also provides tools that enable you to create Web pages. From within Word, you can place these Web pages directly on a Web server.

Word has many features designed to simplify the production of documents and make documents look visually appealing. Using Word, you easily can change the shape, size, and color of text. You can include borders, shading, tables, images, pictures, charts, and Web addresses in documents.

While you are typing, Word performs many tasks automatically. For example, Word detects and corrects spelling and grammar errors in several languages. Word's thesaurus allows you to add variety and precision to your writing. Word also can format text, such as headings, lists, fractions, borders, and Web addresses, as you type.

This latest version of Word has many new features to make you more productive. For example, Word has many predefined text and graphical elements designed to assist you with preparing documents. Word also includes new charting and diagramming tools; uses themes so that you can coordinate colors, fonts, and graphics; and has a tool that enables you to convert a document to a PDF format.

To illustrate the features of Word, this book presents a series of projects that use Word to create documents similar to those you will encounter in academic and business environments.

Project Planning Guidelines

The process of developing a document that communicates specific information requires careful analysis and planning. As a starting point, establish why the document is needed. Once the purpose is determined, analyze the intended readers of the document and their unique needs. Then, gather information about the topic and decide what to include in the document. Finally, determine the document design and style that will be most successful at delivering the message. Details of these guidelines are provided in Appendix A. In addition, each project in this book provides practical applications of these planning considerations.

Project — Document with a Picture

To advertise a sale, promote a business, publicize an event, or convey a message to the community, you may want to create a flyer and post it in a public location. Libraries, schools, churches, grocery stores, and other places often provide bulletin boards or windows for flyers. These flyers announce personal items for sale or rent (car, boat, apartment); garage or block sales; services being offered (animal care, housecleaning, lessons); membership, sponsorship, or donation requests (club, church, charity); and other messages. Flyers are an inexpensive means of reaching the community, yet many go unnoticed because they are designed poorly.

The project in this chapter follows general guidelines and uses Word to create the flyer shown in Figure 1–1. This colorful, eye-catching flyer advertises horseback riding lessons at Tri-Valley Stables. The picture of the horse and rider entices passersby to stop and look at the flyer. The headline on the flyer is large and colorful to draw attention into the text. The body copy below the headline briefly describes key points of the riding lessons, and the bulleted list below the picture concisely highlights important additional information. The signature line of the flyer calls attention to the stable name and telephone number. Finally, the graphical page border nicely frames and complements the contents of the flyer.

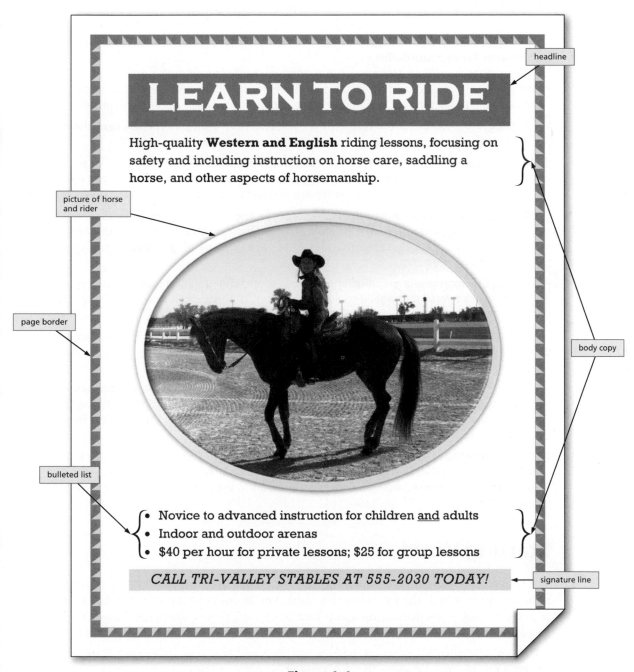

Figure 1–1

Overview

As you read this chapter, you will learn how to create the flyer shown in Figure 1–1 on the previous page by performing these general tasks:

- Enter text in the document.
- Save the document.
- Format the text in the document.
- Insert a picture in the document.
- Format the picture.
- Add a border to the page.
- Print the document.

Plan Ahead

General Project Guidelines

When creating a Word document, the actions you perform and decisions you make will affect the appearance and characteristics of the finished document. As you create a flyer, such as the project shown in Figure 1–1, you should follow these general guidelines:

1. **Choose the words for the text.** Follow the *less is more* principle. The less text, the more likely the flyer will be read. Use as few words as possible to make a point.

2. **Determine where to save the flyer.** You can store a document permanently, or **save** it, on a variety of storage media including a hard disk, USB flash drive, or CD. You also can indicate a specific location on the storage media for saving the document.

3. **Identify how to format various elements of the text.** The overall appearance of a document significantly affects its ability to communicate clearly. Examples of how you can modify the appearance, or **format**, of text include changing its shape, size, color, and position on the page.

4. **Find the appropriate graphical image.** An eye-catching graphical image should convey the flyer's overall message. It could show a product, service, result, or benefit, or visually convey a message that is not expressed easily with words.

5. **Establish where to position and how to format the graphical image.** The position and format of the graphical image should grab the attention of passersby and draw them into reading the flyer.

6. **Determine whether the flyer needs a page border, and if so, its style and format.** A graphical, color-coordinated page border can further draw attention to a flyer and nicely frame its contents. Be careful, however, that a page border does not make the flyer look too cluttered.

When necessary, more specific details concerning the above guidelines are presented at appropriate points in the chapter. The chapter also will identify the actions performed and decisions made regarding these guidelines during the creation of the flyer shown in Figure 1–1.

Starting Word

If you are using a computer to step through the project in this chapter and you want your screen to match the figures in this book, you should change your screen's resolution to 1024 × 768. For information about how to change a computer's resolution, read Appendix E.

Note: If you are using Windows XP, see Appendix F for alternate steps.

To Start Word

The following steps, which assume Windows Vista is running, start Word based on a typical installation. You may need to ask your instructor how to start Word for your computer.

- Click the Start button on the Windows Vista taskbar to display the Start menu.

- Click All Programs at the bottom of the left pane on the Start menu to display the All Programs list.

- Click Microsoft Office in the All Programs list to display the Microsoft Office list (Figure 1–2).

Figure 1–2

- Click Microsoft Office Word 2007 to start Word and display a new blank document in the Word window (Figure 1–3).

- If the Word window is not maximized, click the Maximize button next to the Close button on its title bar to maximize the window.

Q&A What is a maximized window?

A maximized window fills the entire screen. When you maximize a window, the Maximize button changes to a Restore Down button.

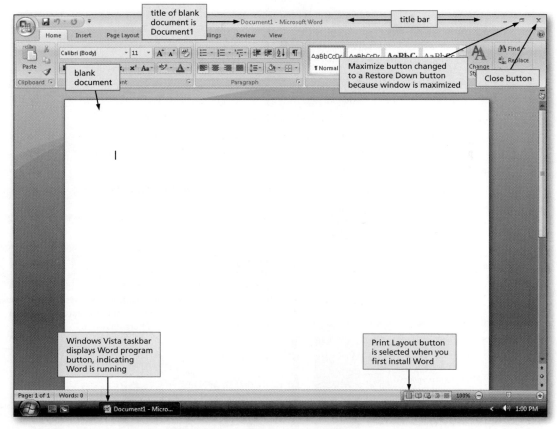

Figure 1–3

- If the Print Layout button is not selected, click it so that your screen layout matches Figure 1–3.

Other Ways
1. Double-click Word icon on desktop, if one is present   2. Click Microsoft Office Word 2007 on Start menu

The Word Window

The Word window consists of a variety of components to make your work more efficient and documents more professional. These include the document window, Ribbon, Mini toolbar and shortcut menus, Quick Access Toolbar, and Office Button. Some of these components are common to other Microsoft Office 2007 programs; others are unique to Word.

Document Window

You view a portion of a document on the screen through a **document window** (Figure 1–4). The default (preset) view is **Print Layout view**, which shows the document on a mock sheet of paper in the document window.

The Word document window in Figure 1–4 contains an insertion point, mouse pointer, scroll bar, and status bar. Other elements that may appear in the document window are discussed later in this and subsequent chapters.

Insertion Point   The **insertion point** is a blinking vertical bar that indicates where text, graphics, and other items will be inserted. As you type, the insertion point moves to the right, and when you reach the end of a line, it moves downward to the beginning of the next line.

Figure 1–4

Mouse Pointer   The **mouse pointer** becomes different shapes depending on the task you are performing in Word and the pointer's location on the screen. The mouse pointer in Figure 1–4 is the shape of an I-beam.

Scroll Bar   You use a **scroll bar** to display different portions of a document in the document window. At the right edge of the document window is a vertical scroll bar. If a document is too wide to fit in the document window, a horizontal scroll bar also appears at the bottom of the document window. On a scroll bar, the position of the **scroll box** reflects the location of the portion of the document that is displayed in the document window. A **scroll arrow** is located at each end of a scroll bar. To scroll through, or display different portions of the document in the document window, you can click a scroll arrow or drag the scroll box.

Status Bar   The **status bar**, located at the bottom of the document window above the Windows Vista taskbar, presents information about the document, the progress of current tasks, and the status of certain commands and keys; it also provides controls for viewing the document. As you type text or perform certain commands, various indicators and buttons may appear on the status bar.

The left edge of the status bar in Figure 1–4 shows the current page followed by the total number of pages in the document, the number of words in the document, and a button to check spelling and grammar. Toward the right edge are buttons and controls you can use to change the view of a document and adjust the size of the displayed document.

Ribbon

The **Ribbon**, located near the top of the Word window, is the control center in Word (Figure 1–5a). The Ribbon provides easy, central access to the tasks you perform while creating a document. The Ribbon consists of tabs, groups, and commands. Each **tab** surrounds a collection of groups, and each group contains related commands.

When you start Word, the Ribbon displays seven top-level tabs: Home, Insert, Page Layout, References, Mailings, Review, and View. The **Home tab**, called the primary tab, contains the more frequently used commands. To display a different tab on the Ribbon, click the top-level tab. That is, to display the Insert tab, click Insert on the Ribbon. To return to the Home tab, click Home on the Ribbon. The tab currently displayed is called the **active tab**.

To display more of the document in the document window, some users prefer to minimize the Ribbon, which hides the groups on the Ribbon and displays only the top-level tabs (Figure 1–5b). To use commands on a minimized Ribbon, click the top-level tab.

BTW

Minimizing the Ribbon
If you want to minimize the Ribbon, right-click the Ribbon and then click Minimize the Ribbon on the shortcut menu, double-click the active tab, or press CTRL+F1. To restore a minimized Ribbon, right-click the Ribbon and then click Minimize the Ribbon on the shortcut menu, double-click any top-level tab, or press CTRL+F1. To use commands on a minimized Ribbon, click the top-level tab.

Figure 1–5

Each time you start Word, the Ribbon appears the same way it did the last time you used Word. The chapters in this book, however, begin with the Ribbon appearing as it did at the initial installation of the software. If you are stepping through this chapter on a computer and you want your Ribbon to match the figures in this book, read Appendix E.

In addition to the top-level tabs, Word displays other tabs, called **contextual tabs**, when you perform certain tasks or work with objects such as pictures or tables. If you insert a picture in the document, for example, the Picture Tools tab and its related subordinate Format tab appear (Figure 1–6). When you are finished working with the picture, the Picture Tools and Format tabs disappear from the Ribbon. Word determines when contextual tabs should appear and disappear based on tasks you perform. Some contextual tabs, such as the Table Tools tab, have more than one related subordinate tab.

Figure 1–6

Commands on the Ribbon include buttons, boxes (text boxes, check boxes, etc.), and galleries (Figure 1–6). A **gallery** is a set of choices, often graphical, arranged in a grid or in a list. You can scroll through choices on an in-Ribbon gallery by clicking the gallery's scroll arrows. Or, you can click a gallery's More button to view more gallery options on the screen at a time. Some buttons and boxes have arrows that, when clicked, also display a gallery; others always cause a gallery to be displayed when clicked. Most galleries support **live preview**, which is a feature that allows you to point to a gallery choice and see its effect in the document — without actually selecting the choice (Figure 1–7).

Figure 1–7

Some commands on the Ribbon display an image to help you remember their function. When you point to a command on the Ribbon, all or part of the command glows in shades of yellow and orange, and an Enhanced ScreenTip appears on the screen. An **Enhanced ScreenTip** is an on-screen note that provides the name of the command, available keyboard shortcut(s), a description of the command, and sometimes instructions for how to obtain help about the command (Figure 1–8). Enhanced ScreenTips are more detailed than a typical ScreenTip, which usually only displays the name of the command.

Figure 1–8

The lower-right corner of some groups on the Ribbon has a small arrow, called a **Dialog Box Launcher**, that when clicked, displays a dialog box or a task pane with additional options for the group (Figure 1–9). When presented with a dialog box, you make selections and must close the dialog box before returning to the document. A **task pane**, by contrast, is a window that can remain open and visible while you work in the document.

Figure 1–9

Mini Toolbar and Shortcut Menus

The **Mini toolbar**, which appears automatically based on tasks you perform, contains commands related to changing the appearance of text in a document. All commands on the Mini toolbar also exist on the Ribbon. The purpose of the Mini toolbar is to minimize mouse movement. For example, if you want to use a command that currently is not displayed on the active tab, you can use the command on the Mini toolbar — instead of switching to a different tab to use the command.

When the Mini toolbar appears, it initially is transparent (Figure 1–10a). If you do not use the transparent Mini toolbar, it disappears from the screen. To use the Mini toolbar, move the mouse pointer into the toolbar, which causes the Mini toolbar to change from a transparent to bright appearance (Figure 1–10b).

Figure 1–10

A **shortcut menu**, which appears when you right-click an object, is a list of frequently used commands that relate to the right-clicked object. When you right-click a scroll bar, for example, a shortcut menu appears with commands related to the scroll bar. If you right-click an item in the document window, Word displays both the Mini toolbar and a shortcut menu (Figure 1–11).

Figure 1–11

Quick Access Toolbar

The **Quick Access Toolbar**, located by default above the Ribbon, provides easy access to frequently used commands (Figure 1–12a). The commands on the Quick Access Toolbar always are available, regardless of the task you are performing. Initially, the Quick Access Toolbar contains the Save, Undo, and Redo commands. If you click the Customize Quick Access Toolbar button, Word provides a list of commands you quickly can add to and remove from the Quick Access Toolbar (Figure 1–12b).

Figure 1–12

You also can add other commands to or delete commands from the Quick Access Toolbar so that it contains the commands you use most often. As you add commands to the Quick Access Toolbar, its commands may interfere with the document title on the title bar. For this reason, Word provides an option of displaying the Quick Access Toolbar below the Ribbon (Figure 1–13).

Figure 1–13

BTW

Quick Access Toolbar Commands
To add a Ribbon command to the Quick Access Toolbar, right-click the command on the Ribbon and then click Add to Quick Access Toolbar on the shortcut menu. To delete a command from the Quick Access Toolbar, right-click the command on the Quick Access Toolbar and then click Remove from Quick Access Toolbar on the shortcut menu. To display the Quick Access Toolbar below the Ribbon, right-click the Quick Access Toolbar and then click Show Quick Access Toolbar Below the Ribbon on the shortcut menu.

Each time you start Word, the Quick Access Toolbar appears the same way it did the last time you used Word. The chapters in this book, however, begin with the Quick Access Toolbar appearing as it did at the initial installation of the software. If you are stepping through this chapter on a computer and you want your Quick Access Toolbar to match the figures in this book, you should reset your Quick Access Toolbar. For more information about how to reset the Quick Access Toolbar, read Appendix E.

Office Button

While the Ribbon is a control center for creating documents, the **Office Button** is a central location for managing and sharing documents. When you click the Office Button, located in the upper-left corner of the window, Word displays the Office Button menu (Figure 1–14a). A **menu** contains a list of commands.

When you click the New, Open, Save As, and Print commands on the Office Button menu, Word displays a dialog box with additional options. The Save As, Print, Prepare, Send, and Publish commands have an arrow to their right. If you point to this arrow, Word displays a **submenu**, which is a list of additional commands associated with the selected command (Figure 1–14b). For the Prepare, Send, and Publish commands that do not display a dialog box when clicked, you can point either to the command or the arrow to display the submenu.

Figure 1–14

Key Tips

If you prefer using the keyboard instead of the mouse, you can press the ALT key on the keyboard to display a **Key Tip badge**, or keyboard code icon, for certain commands (Figure 1–15). To select a command using the keyboard, press its displayed code letter, or **Key Tip**. When you press a Key Tip, additional Key Tips related to the selected command may appear. For example, to select the New command on the Office Button menu, press the ALT key, then press the F key, and then press the N key.

To remove the Key Tip badges from the screen, press the ALT key or the ESC key until all Key Tip badges disappear, or click the mouse anywhere in the Word window.

Figure 1–15

Entering Text

The first step in creating a document is to enter its text by typing on the keyboard. By default, Word positions text you type at the left margin. In a later section of this chapter, you will learn how to format, or change the appearance of, the entered text.

Plan Ahead

Choose the words for the text.
The text in a flyer is organized into three areas: headline, body copy, and signature line.

- The headline is the first line of text on the flyer. It conveys the product or service being offered, such as a car for sale or personal lessons, or the benefit that will be gained, such as a convenience, better performance, greater security, higher earnings, or more comfort.

- The body text consists of all text between the headline and the signature line. This text highlights the key points of the message in as few words as possible. It should be easy to read and follow. While emphasizing the positive, the body text must be realistic, truthful, and believable.

- The signature line, which is the last line of text on the flyer, contains contact information or identifies a call to action.

To Type Text

To begin creating the flyer in this chapter, you type the headline in the document window. The following steps type this first line of text in the document.

- Type Learn to Ride as the headline (Figure 1–16).

Q&A What if I make an error while typing?

You can press the **BACKSPACE** key until you have deleted the text in error and then retype the text correctly.

Q&A Why did the Spelling and Grammar Check icon appear on the status bar?

When you begin typing text, the **Spelling and Grammar Check icon** appears on the status bar with an animated pencil writing on paper that indicates Word is checking for spelling and grammar errors. When you stop typing, the pencil changes to a blue check mark (no errors) or a red X (potential errors found). Word flags potential errors in the document with a red or green wavy underline. Later, this chapter shows how to fix flagged errors.

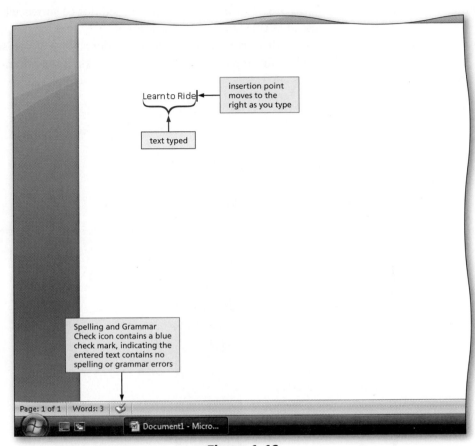

Figure 1–16

- Press the ENTER key to move the insertion point to the beginning of the next line (Figure 1–17).

Q&A Why did blank space appear between the headline and the insertion point?

Each time you press the ENTER key, Word creates a new paragraph and inserts blank space between the two paragraphs. Later in this chapter, you will learn how to adjust the spacing between paragraphs.

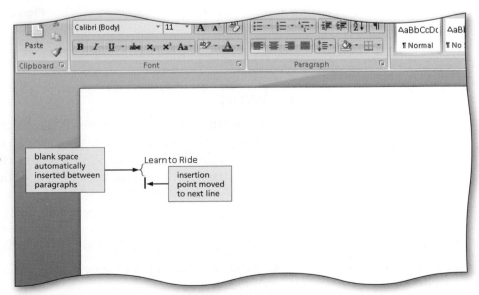

Figure 1–17

To Display Formatting Marks

To indicate where in a document you press the ENTER key or SPACEBAR, you may find it helpful to display formatting marks. A **formatting mark**, sometimes called a **nonprinting character**, is a character that Word displays on the screen but is not visible on a printed document. For example, the paragraph mark (¶) is a formatting mark that indicates where you pressed the ENTER key. A raised dot (·) shows where you pressed the SPACEBAR. Other formatting marks are discussed as they appear on the screen.

Depending on settings made during previous Word sessions, your Word screen already may display formatting marks (Figure 1–18). The following step displays formatting marks, if they do not show already on the screen.

1

- If necessary, click Home on the Ribbon to display the Home tab.

- If it is not selected already, click the Show/Hide ¶ button on the Home tab to display formatting marks on the screen (Figure 1–18).

Q&A What if I do not want formatting marks to show on the screen?

If you feel the formatting marks clutter the screen, you can hide them by clicking the Show/Hide ¶ button again. It is recommended that you display formatting marks so that you visually can identify when you press the ENTER key, SPACEBAR, and other keys associated with nonprinting characters; therefore, the document windows presented in this book show the formatting marks.

Figure 1–18

Other Ways

1. Press CTRL+SHIFT+*

Wordwrap

Wordwrap allows you to type words in a paragraph continually without pressing the ENTER key at the end of each line. When the insertion point reaches the right margin, Word automatically positions the insertion point at the beginning of the next line. As you type, if a word extends beyond the right margin, Word also automatically positions that word on the next line along with the insertion point.

Word creates a new paragraph each time you press the ENTER key. Thus, as you type text in the document window, do not press the ENTER key when the insertion point reaches the right margin. Instead, press the ENTER key only in these circumstances:

1. To insert blank lines in a document
2. To begin a new paragraph
3. To terminate a short line of text and advance to the next line
4. To respond to questions or prompts in Word dialog boxes, task panes, and other on-screen objects

To Wordwrap Text as You Type

The next step in creating the flyer is to type the body copy. The following step wordwraps the text in the body copy.

- **Type** High-quality Western and English riding lessons, focusing on safety and including instruction on horse care, saddling a horse, and other aspects of horsemanship.

Q&A

Why does my document wrap on different words?

Differences in wordwrap relate to the printer used by your computer. That is, the printer controls where wordwrap occurs for each line in your document. Thus, it is possible that the same document could wordwrap differently if printed on different printers.

- Press the ENTER key to position the insertion point on the next line in the document (Figure 1–19).

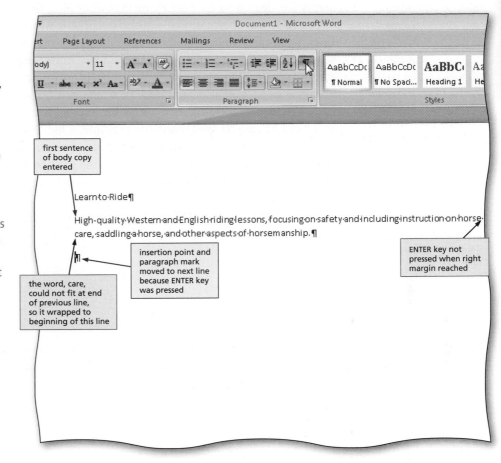

Figure 1–19

To Insert a Blank Line

In the flyer, the picture of the horse and rider should be positioned below the paragraph just entered. The picture will be inserted after all text is entered and formatted. Thus, you will leave a blank line in the document for the picture. To enter a blank line in a document, press the ENTER key without typing any text on the line. The following step inserts one blank line below the first paragraph of body copy.

- Press the ENTER key to insert a blank line in the document (Figure 1–20).

Figure 1–20

BTW

Automatic Spelling Correction
As you type, Word automatically corrects some misspelled words. For example, if you type recieve, Word automatically fixes the misspelling and displays the word, receive, when you press the SPACEBAR or type a punctuation mark. To see a complete list of automatically corrected words, click Office Button, click the Word Options button, click Proofing in the left pane of the Word Options dialog box, click the AutoCorrect Options button, and then scroll through the list of words near the bottom of the dialog box.

Spelling and Grammar Check

As you type text in a document, Word checks your typing for possible spelling and grammar errors. If all of the words you have typed are in Word's dictionary and your grammar is correct, as mentioned earlier, the Spelling and Grammar Check icon on the status bar displays a blue check mark. Otherwise, the icon shows a red X. In this case, Word flags the potential error in the document window with a red or green wavy underline. A red wavy underline means the flagged text is not in Word's dictionary (because it is a proper name or misspelled). A green wavy underline indicates the text may be incorrect grammatically. Although you can check the entire document for spelling and grammar errors at once, you also can check these flagged errors as they appear on the screen.

To display a list of corrections for flagged text, right-click the flagged text. When you right-click a flagged word, for example, a list of suggested spelling corrections appears on the screen. A flagged word, however, is not necessarily misspelled. For example, many names, abbreviations, and specialized terms are not in Word's main dictionary. In these cases, you tell Word to ignore the flagged word. As you type, Word also detects duplicate words while checking for spelling errors. For example, if your document contains the phrase, to the the store, Word places a red wavy underline below the second occurrence of the word, the.

To Check Spelling and Grammar as You Type

In the following steps, the word, instruction, has been misspelled intentionally as intrution to illustrate Word's check spelling as you type feature. If you are doing this project on a computer, your flyer may contain other misspelled words, depending on the accuracy of your typing.

- **Type** Novice to advanced intrution **and then press the SPACEBAR (Figure 1–21).**

Q&A

What if Word does not flag my spelling and grammar errors with wavy underlines?

To verify that the check spelling and grammar as you type features are enabled, click the Office Button and then click the Word Options button. When the Word Options dialog box is displayed, click Proofing, and then ensure the 'Check spelling as you type' and 'Mark grammar errors as you type' check boxes have check marks. Also ensure the 'Hide spelling errors in this document only' and 'Hide grammar errors in this document only' check boxes do not have check marks. Click the OK button.

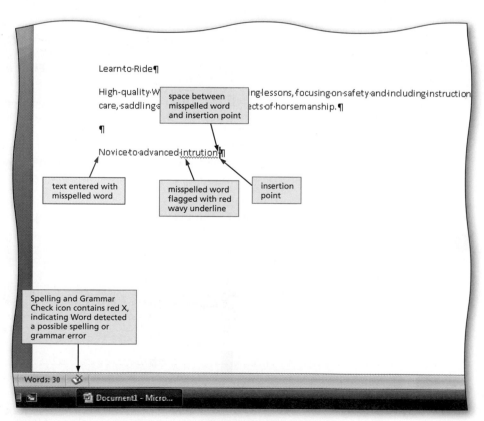

Figure 1–21

2

• Right-click the flagged word (intrution, in this case) to display a shortcut menu that includes a list of suggested spelling corrections for the flagged word (Figure 1–22).

Q&A

What if, when I right-click the misspelled word, my desired correction is not in the list on the shortcut menu?

You can click outside the shortcut menu to close the menu and then retype the correct word, or you can click Spelling on the shortcut menu to display the Spelling dialog box. Chapter 2 discusses the Spelling dialog box.

Q&A

What if a flagged word actually is, for example, a proper name and spelled correctly?

Right-click it and then click Ignore All on the shortcut menu to instruct Word not to flag future occurrences of the same word.

Figure 1–22

3

• Click instruction on the shortcut menu to replace the misspelled word in the document (intrution) with the word, instruction (Figure 1–23).

Figure 1–23

Other Ways

1. Click Spelling and Grammar Check icon on status bar, click correct word on shortcut menu

To Enter More Text

In the flyer, the text yet to be entered includes the remainder of the body copy, which will be formatted as a bulleted list, and the signature line. The following steps enter the remainder of text in the flyer.

1 Press the END key to move the insertion point to the end of the current line.

2 Type for children and adults and then press the ENTER key.

3 Type Indoor and outdoor arenas and then press the ENTER key.

4 Type $40 per hour for private lessons; $25 for group lessons and then press the ENTER key.

5 To complete the text in the flyer, type Call Tri-Valley Stables at 555-2030 today! (Figure 1–24).

BTW

Character Widths
Many word processing documents use variable character fonts, where some characters are wider than others; for example, the letter w takes up more space than the letter i.

Figure 1–24

Saving the Project

BTW

File Type
Depending on your Windows Vista settings, the file type .docx may be displayed immediately to the right of the file name after you save the file. The file type .docx is a Word 2007 document. Previous versions of Word had a file type of .doc.

While you are creating a document, the computer stores it in memory. When you save a document, the computer places it on a storage medium such as a USB flash drive, CD, or hard disk. A saved document is referred to as a **file**. A **file name** is the name assigned to a file when it is saved.

It is important to save a document frequently for the following reasons:

• The document in memory will be lost if the computer is turned off or you lose electrical power while Word is open.

• If you run out of time before completing your project, you may finish your document at a future time without starting over.

Determine where to save the document.

When saving a document, you must decide which storage medium to use.

Plan
Ahead

*   If you always work on the same computer and have no need to transport your projects to a different location, then your computer's hard disk will suffice as a storage location. It is a good idea, however, to save a backup copy of your projects on a separate medium in case the file becomes corrupted or the computer's hard disk fails.

*   If you plan to work on your projects in various locations or on multiple computers, then you should save your projects on a portable medium, such as a USB flash drive or CD. The projects in this book use a USB flash drive, which saves files quickly and reliably and can be reused. CDs are easily portable and serve as good backups for the final versions of projects because they generally can save files only one time.

To Save a Document

You have performed many tasks while creating this project and do not want to risk losing the work completed thus far. Accordingly, you should save the document. The following steps save a document on a USB flash drive using the file name, Horseback Riding Lessons Flyer.

Note: If you are using Windows XP, see Appendix F for alternate steps.

1

*   With a USB flash drive connected to one of the computer's USB ports, click the Save button on the Quick Access Toolbar to display the Save As dialog box (Figure 1–25).

*   If the Navigation pane is not displayed in the Save As dialog box, click the Browse Folders button to expand the dialog box.

*   If a Folders list is displayed below the Folders button, click the Folders button to remove the Folders list.

Q&A

Do I have to save to a USB flash drive?

No. You can save to any device or folder. A **folder** is a specific location on a storage medium. You can save to the default folder or a different folder. You also can create your own folders, which is explained later in this book.

Figure 1–25

2

- Type Horseback Riding Lessons Flyer in the File name text box to change the file name. Do not press the ENTER key after typing the file name (Figure 1–26).

Q&A What characters can I use in a file name?

A file name can have a maximum of 260 characters, including spaces. The only invalid characters are the backslash (\), slash (/), colon (:), asterisk (*), question mark (?), quotation mark ("), less than symbol (<), greater than symbol (>), and vertical bar (|).

Q&A What are file properties and tags?

File properties contain information about a file such as the file name, author name, date the file was modified, and tags. A tag is a file property that contains a word or phrase about a file. You can organize and locate files based on their file properties.

Figure 1–26

3

- If Computer is not displayed in the Favorite Links section, drag the top or bottom edge of the Save As dialog box until Computer is displayed.

- Click Computer in the Favorite Links section to display a list of available drives (Figure 1–27).

- If necessary, scroll until UDISK 2.0 (E:) appears in the list of available drives.

Q&A Why is my list of drives arranged and named differently?

The size of the Save As dialog box and your computer's configuration determine how the list is displayed and how the drives are named.

Q&A How do I save the file if I am not using a USB flash drive?

Use the same process, but select your desired save location in the Favorite Links section.

Figure 1–27

4

- Double-click UDISK 2.0 (E:) in the Computer list to select the USB flash drive, Drive E in this case, as the new save location (Figure 1–28).

Q&A

What if my USB flash drive has a different name or letter?

It is very likely that your USB flash drive will have a different name and drive letter and be connected to a different port. Verify the device in your Computer list is correct.

Figure 1–28

5

- Click the Save button in the Save As dialog box to save the document on the USB flash drive with the file name, Horseback Riding Lessons Flyer (Figure 1–29).

Q&A

How do I know that the project is saved?

While Word is saving your file, it briefly displays a message on the status bar indicating the amount of the file saved. In addition, your USB drive may have a light that flashes during the save process.

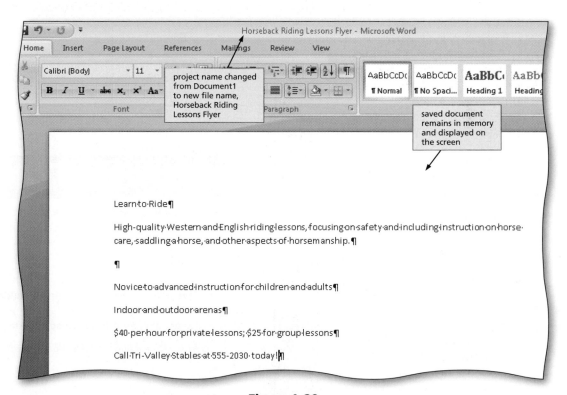

Figure 1–29

Other Ways	
1. Click Office Button, click Save, type file name, click Computer, select drive or folder, click Save button	2. Press CTRL+S or press SHIFT+F12, type file name, click Computer, select drive or folder, click Save button

Formatting Paragraphs and Characters in a Document

With the text for the flyer entered, the next step is to format its paragraphs and characters. Paragraphs encompass the text from the first character in a paragraph up to and including a paragraph mark (¶). **Paragraph formatting** is the process of changing the appearance of a paragraph. For example, you can center or indent a paragraph. Characters include letters, numbers, punctuation marks, and symbols. **Character formatting** is the process of changing the way characters appear on the screen and in print. You use character formatting to emphasize certain words and improve readability of a document. For example, you can italicize or underline characters. Often, you apply both paragraph and character formatting to the same text. For example, you may center a paragraph (paragraph formatting) and bold some of the characters in a paragraph (character formatting).

Although you can format paragraphs and characters before you type, many Word users enter text first and then format the existing text. Figure 1–30a shows the flyer in this chapter before formatting its paragraphs and characters. Figure 1–30b shows the flyer after formatting. As you can see from the two figures, a document that is formatted is easier to read and looks more professional. The following pages discuss how to format the flyer so that it looks like Figure 1–30b.

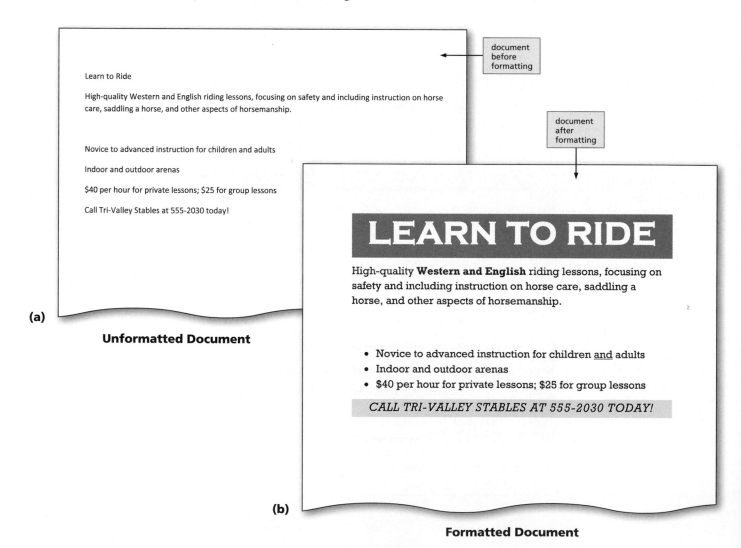

(a)

Unformatted Document

(b)

Formatted Document

Figure 1–30

Fonts, Font Sizes, Styles, and Themes

Characters that appear on the screen are a specific shape and size. The **font**, or typeface, defines the appearance and shape of the letters, numbers, and special characters. In Word, the default font usually is Calibri (Figure 1–31 on the next page). You can leave characters in the default font or change them to a different font. **Font size** specifies the size of the characters and is determined by a measurement system called points. A single **point** is about 1/72 of one inch in height. The default font size in Word typically is 11 (Figure 1–31). A character with a font size of 11 is about 11/72 or a little less than 1/6 of one inch in height. You can increase or decrease the font size of characters in a document.

When you create a document, Word formats the text using a particular style. A **style** is a named group of formatting characteristics, including font and font size. The default style in Word is called the **Normal style**, which most likely uses 11-point Calibri font. If you do not specify a style for text you type, Word applies the Normal style to the text. In addition to the Normal style, Word has many other built-in, or predefined, styles that you can use to format text. You also can create your own styles. Styles make it easy to apply many formats at once to text. After you apply a style to text, you easily can modify the text to include additional formats. You also can modify the style.

To assist you with coordinating colors and fonts and other formats, Word uses document themes. A document **theme** is a set of unified formats for fonts, colors, and graphics. The default theme fonts are Cambria for headings and Calibri for body text (Figure 1–31). Word includes a variety of document themes. By changing the document theme, you quickly give your document a new look. You also can define your own document themes.

Identify how to format various elements of the text.   **Plan Ahead**
By formatting the characters and paragraphs in a document, you can improve its overall appearance. In a flyer, consider the following formatting suggestions.

- **Increase the font size of characters.** Flyers usually are posted on a bulletin board or in a window. Thus, the font size should be as large as possible so that passersby easily can read the flyer. To give the headline more impact, its font size should be larger than the font size of the text in the body copy. If possible, make the font size of the signature line larger than the body copy but smaller than the headline.

- **Change the font of characters.** Use fonts that are easy to read. Try to use only two different fonts in a flyer, for example, one for the headline and the other for all other text. Too many fonts can make the flyer visually confusing.

- **Change paragraph alignment.** The default alignment for paragraphs in a document is **left-aligned**, that is, flush at the left margin of the document with uneven right edges. Consider changing the alignment of some of the paragraphs to add interest and variety to the flyer.

- **Highlight key paragraphs with bullets.** A **bullet** is a dot or other symbol positioned at the beginning of a paragraph. Use bullets to highlight important paragraphs in a flyer.

- **Emphasize important words.** To call attention to certain words or lines, you can underline them, italicize them, or bold them. Use these formats sparingly, however, because overuse will minimize their effect and make the flyer look too busy.

- **Use color.** Use colors that complement each other and convey the meaning of the flyer. Vary colors in terms of hue and brightness. Headline colors, for example, can be bold and bright. Signature lines should stand out more than body copy but less than headlines. Keep in mind that too many colors can detract from the flyer and make it difficult to read.

To Apply Styles

In the flyer, you want the headline and the signature line to be emphasized more than the other text. Word provides heading styles designed to emphasize this type of text. The first step in formatting the flyer is to apply the Heading 1 style to the headline and the Heading 2 style to the signature line. The default Heading 1 style is a 14-point Cambria bold font. The default Heading 2 style is a 13-point Cambria bold font. The default theme color scheme uses shades of blue for headings.

To apply a style to a paragraph, you first position the insertion point in the paragraph and then apply the style. The following steps apply heading styles to paragraphs.

- Press CTRL+HOME (that is, press and hold down the CTRL key, press the HOME key, and then release both keys) to position the insertion point at the top of the document (Figure 1–31).

Figure 1–31

- Point to Heading 1 in the Styles gallery to display a live preview in the document of the Heading 1 style (Figure 1–32).

Q&A

What happens if I move the mouse pointer?

If you move the mouse pointer away from the gallery, the text containing the insertion point returns to the Normal style.

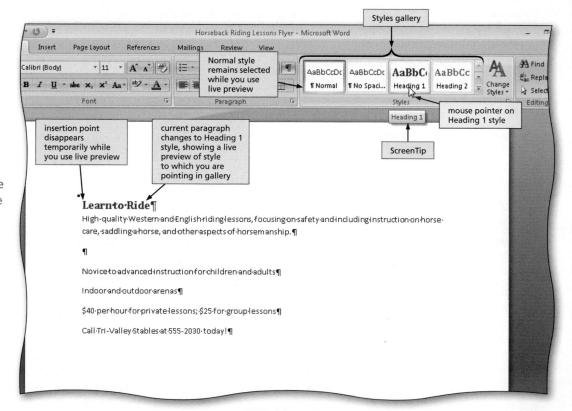

Figure 1–32

3

- Click Heading 1 in the Styles gallery to apply the Heading 1 style to the headline (Figure 1–33).

Q&A

Why did a square appear on the screen near the left edge of the headline?

The square is a nonprinting character, like the paragraph mark, that indicates text to its right has a special paragraph format applied to it.

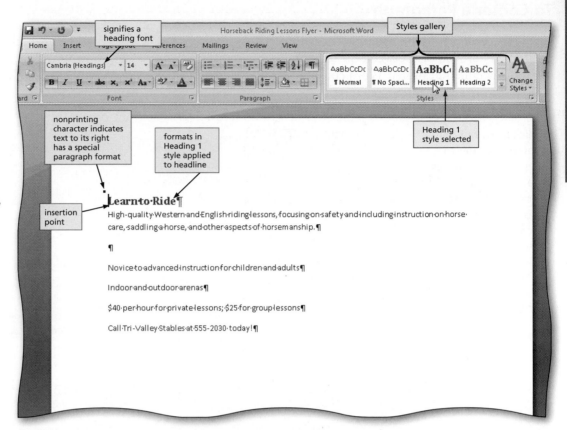

Figure 1–33

4

- Press CTRL+END (that is, press and hold down the CTRL key, press the END key, and then release both keys) to position the insertion point at the end of the document.

- Click Heading 2 in the Styles gallery to apply the Heading 2 style to the signature line (Figure 1–34).

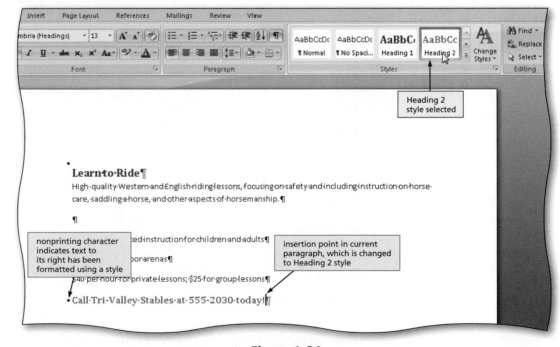

Figure 1–34

Other Ways
1. Click Styles Dialog Box Launcher, click desired style in Styles task pane   2. Press CTRL+SHIFT+S, click Style Name box arrow in Apply Styles task pane, click desired style in list

To Center a Paragraph

The headline in the flyer currently is left-aligned (Figure 1–35). You want the headline to be **centered**, that is, positioned horizontally between the left and right margins on the page. Thus, you will center the paragraph containing the headline. Recall that Word considers a single short line of text, such as the three-word headline, a paragraph. The following steps center a paragraph.

- Click somewhere in the paragraph to be centered (in this case, the headline) to position the insertion point in the paragraph to be formatted (Figure 1–35).

Figure 1–35

- Click the Center button on the Home tab to center the headline (Figure 1–36).

Q&A

What if I want to return the paragraph to left-aligned?

Click the Align Text Left button on the Home tab.

Figure 1–36

Other Ways

1. Right-click paragraph, click Center button on Mini toolbar
2. Right-click paragraph, click Paragraph on shortcut menu, click Indents and Spacing tab, click Alignment box arrow, click Centered, click OK button
3. Click Paragraph Dialog Box Launcher, click Indents and Spacing tab, click Alignment box arrow, click Centered, click OK button
4. Press CTRL+E

Formatting Single Versus Multiple Paragraphs and Characters

As shown in the previous pages, to format a single paragraph, simply move the insertion point in the paragraph and then format the paragraph. Likewise, to format a single word, position the insertion point in the word and then format the word.

To format *multiple* paragraphs or words, however, you first must select the paragraphs or words you want to format and then format the selection. If your screen normally displays dark letters on a light background, which is the default setting in Word, then selected text displays light letters on a dark background.

To Select a Line

The font size of characters in the Heading 1 style, 14 point, is too small for passersby to read in the headline of the flyer. To increase the font size of the characters in the headline, you must first select the line of text containing the headline. The following steps select a line.

- Move the mouse pointer to the left of the line to be selected (in this case, the headline) until the mouse pointer changes to a right-pointing block arrow (Figure 1–37).

Figure 1–37

- While the mouse pointer is a right-pointing block arrow, click the mouse to select the entire line to the right of the mouse pointer (Figure 1–38).

Figure 1–38

Other Ways	
1. Drag mouse through line	2. With insertion point at beginning of desired line, press SHIFT+DOWN ARROW

To Change the Font Size of Selected Text

The next step is to increase the font size of the characters in the selected headline. You would like the headline to be as large as possible and still fit on a single line, which in this case is 48 point. The following steps increase the font size of the headline from 14 to 48 point.

- With the text selected, click the Font Size box arrow on the Home tab to display the Font Size gallery (Figure 1–39).

Q&A Why are the font sizes in my Font Size gallery different from those in Figure 1–39?

Font sizes may vary depending on the current font and your printer driver.

Q&A What happened to the Mini toolbar?

The Mini toolbar disappears if you do not use it. These steps use the Font Size box arrow on the Home tab instead of the Font Size box arrow on the Mini toolbar. If a command exists both on the currently displayed tab and the Mini toolbar, this book uses the command on the tab. When the command is not on the currently displayed tab, the Mini toolbar is used.

Figure 1–39

- Point to 48 in the Font Size gallery to display a live preview of the headline at 48 point (Figure 1–40).

🔍 **Experiment**

- Point to various font sizes in the Font Size gallery and watch the font size of the headline change in the document window.

- Click 48 in the Font Size gallery to increase the font size of the selected text to 48.

Figure 1–40

Other Ways

1. Click Font Size box arrow on Mini toolbar, click desired font size in Font Size gallery
2. Right-click selected text, click Font on shortcut menu, click Font tab, select desired font size in Size list, click OK button
3. Click Font Dialog Box Launcher, click Font tab, select desired font size in Size list, click OK button
4. Press CTRL+SHIFT+P, click Font tab, select desired font size in Size list, click OK button

To Change the Font of Selected Text

As mentioned earlier, the default Heading 1 style uses the font called Cambria. Word, however, provides many other fonts to add variety to your documents. To draw more attention to the headline, you change its font so it differs from the font of other text in the flyer. The following steps change the font from Cambria to Copperplate Gothic Bold.

- With the text selected, click the Font box arrow on the Home tab to display the Font gallery (Figure 1–41).

Q&A

Will the fonts in my Font gallery be the same as those in Figure 1–41?

Your list of available fonts may differ, depending on the type of printer you are using.

Figure 1–41

- Scroll through the Font gallery, if necessary, and then point to Copperplate Gothic Bold (or a similar font) to display a live preview of the headline in Copperplate Gothic Bold font (Figure 1–42).

Experiment

- Point to various fonts in the Font gallery and watch the font of the headline change in the document window.

❸

- Click Copperplate Gothic Bold (or a similar font) to change the font of the selected text to Copperplate Gothic Bold.

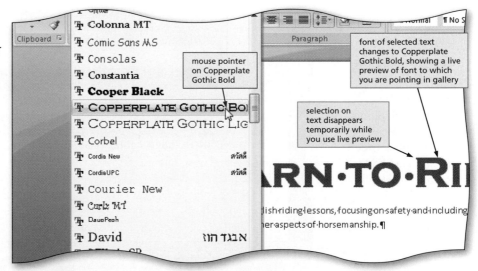

Figure 1–42

Other Ways

1. Click Font box arrow on Mini toolbar, click desired font in Font gallery

2. Right-click selected text, click Font on shortcut menu, click

   Font tab, select desired font in Font list, click OK button

3. Click Font Dialog Box Launcher, click Font tab, select desired font in Font list, click OK button

4. Press CTRL+SHIFT+F, click Font tab, select desired font in the Font list, click OK button

To Select Multiple Paragraphs

The next formatting step in creating the flyer is to increase the font size of the characters between the headline and the signature line so that they are easier to read from a distance. To change the font size of the characters in multiple lines, you first must select all the lines to be formatted. The following steps select multiple lines.

- Move the mouse pointer to the left of the first paragraph to be selected until the mouse pointer changes to a right-pointing block arrow (Figure 1–43).

Figure 1–43

- Drag downward to select all lines that will be formatted (Figure 1–44).

Q&A

How do I *drag* the mouse?

Dragging is the process of holding down the mouse button while moving the mouse and then releasing the mouse button.

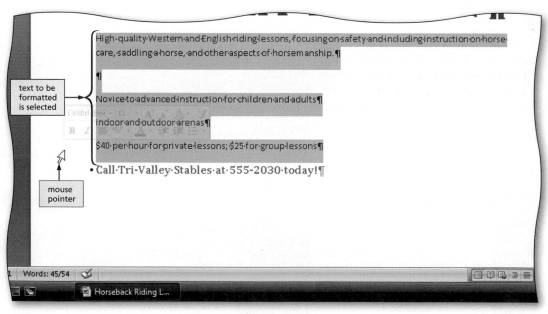

Figure 1–44

Other Ways

1. With insertion point at beginning of desired line, press SHIFT+DOWN ARROW repeatedly until all lines are selected

To Change the Font Size of Selected Text

The characters between the headline and the signature line in the flyer currently are 11 point. To make them easier to read from a distance, this flyer uses 16 point for these characters. The following steps change the font size of the selected text.

1 With the text selected, click the Font Size box arrow on the Home tab to display the Font Size gallery.

2 Click 16 in the Font Size gallery to increase the font size of the selected text to 16.

To Format a Line

In the flyer, the signature line is to be centered to match the paragraph alignment of the headline. Also, its text should have a font size larger than the rest of the body copy. The following steps center the line and increase its font size to 18.

1 Click somewhere in the paragraph to be centered (in this case, the signature line) to position the insertion point in the paragraph to be formatted.

2 Click the Center button on the Home tab to center the signature line.

3 Move the mouse pointer to the left of the line to be selected (in this case, the signature line) until the mouse pointer changes to a right-pointing block arrow and then click to select the line.

4 With the signature line selected, click the Font Size box arrow on the Home tab and then click 18 in the Font Size gallery to increase the font size of the selected text to 18 (Figure 1–45).

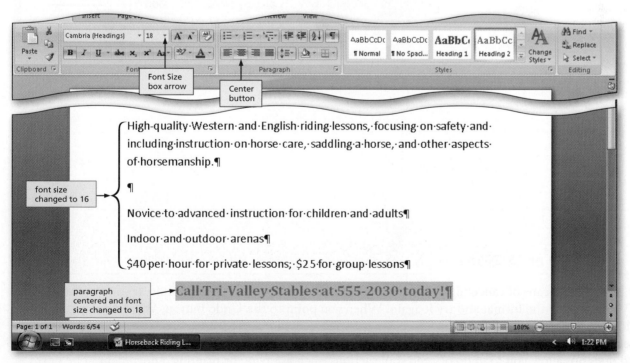

Figure 1–45

To Bullet a List of Paragraphs

The next step is to format the three important points above the signature line in the flyer as a bulleted list. A **bulleted list** is a series of paragraphs, each beginning with a bullet character. The three lines each end with a paragraph mark because you pressed the ENTER key at the end of each line. Thus, these three lines actually are three separate paragraphs.

To format a list of paragraphs with bullets, you first must select all the lines in the paragraphs. The following steps bullet a list of paragraphs.

1

- Move the mouse pointer to the left of the first paragraph to be selected until the mouse pointer changes to a right-pointing block arrow.

- Drag downward until all paragraphs (lines) that will be formatted with a bullet character are selected.

2

- Click the Bullets button on the Home tab to place a bullet character at the beginning of each selected paragraph (Figure 1–46).

Q&A

How do I remove bullets from a list or paragraph?

Select the list or paragraph and click the Bullets button again.

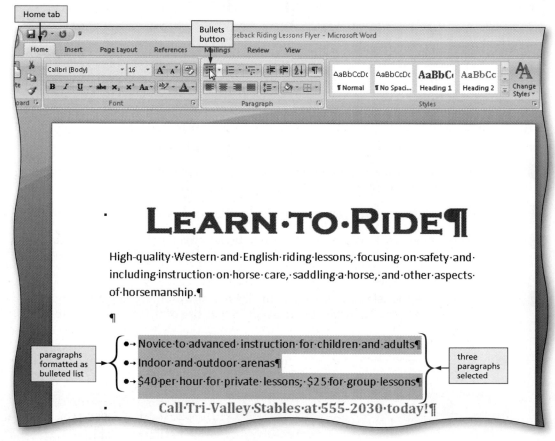

Figure 1–46

Other Ways
1. Right-click selected paragraphs, click Bullets button on Mini toolbar   2. Right-click selected paragraphs, point to Bullets on shortcut menu, click desired bullet style

To Undo and Redo an Action

Word provides a means of canceling your recent command(s) or action(s). For example, if you format text incorrectly, you can undo the format and try it again. When you point to the Undo button, Word displays the action you can undo as part of the ScreenTip.

If, after you undo an action, you decide you did not want to perform the undo, you can redo the undone action. Word does not allow you to undo or redo some actions, such as saving or printing a document. The next steps undo the bullet format just applied and then redo the bullet format.

1
- Click the Undo button on the Quick Access Toolbar to remove the bullets from the selected paragraphs (Figure 1–47).

2
- Click the Redo button on the Quick Access Toolbar to place a bullet character at the beginning of each selected paragraph again (shown in Figure 1–46).

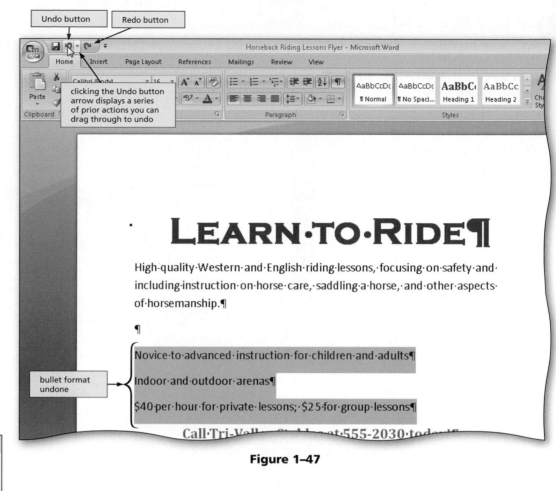

Figure 1–47

Other Ways
1. Press CTRL+Z; press CTRL+Y

To Select a Group of Words

To emphasize the types of riding lessons, Western and English, these words are bold in the flyer. To format a group of words, you first must select them. The following steps select a group of words.

1
- Position the mouse pointer immediately to the left of the first character of the text to be selected, in this case, the W in Western (Figure 1–48).

Q&A | Why did the shape of the mouse pointer change?

The mouse pointer's shape is an I-beam when positioned in unselected text in the document window.

Figure 1–48

- Drag the mouse pointer through the last character of the text to be selected, in this case, the h in English (Figure 1–49).

Q&A Why did the mouse pointer shape change again?

When the mouse pointer is positioned in selected text, its shape is a left-pointing block arrow.

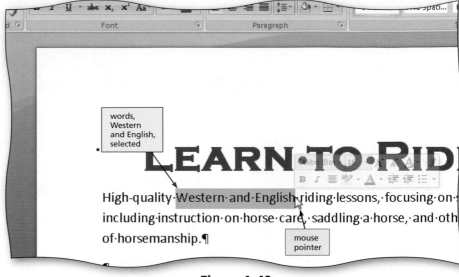

Figure 1–49

To Bold Text

Bold characters display somewhat thicker and darker than those that are not bold. The following step formats the selected words, Western and English, as bold.

- With the text selected, click the Bold button on the Home tab to format the selected text in bold (Figure 1–50).

Q&A How would I remove a bold format?

You would click the Bold button a second time, or you immediately could click the Undo button on the Quick Access Toolbar.

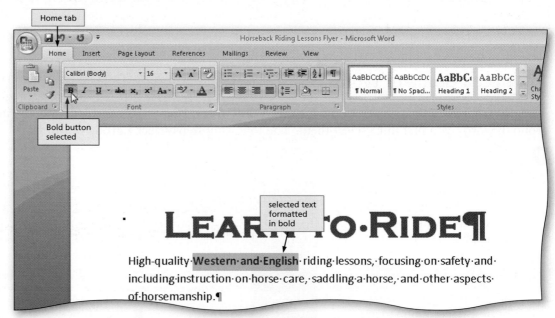

Figure 1–50

To Underline a Word

As with bold text, underlines are used to emphasize or draw attention to specific text. **Underlined** text prints with an underscore (_) below each character. In the flyer, the word, and, in the first bulleted paragraph is emphasized with an underline.

As with a single paragraph, if you want to format a single word, you do not need to select the word. Simply position the insertion point somewhere in the word and apply the desired format. The following step formats a word with an underline.

1

- Click somewhere in the word to be underlined (and, in this case).

- Click the Underline button on the Home tab to underline the word containing the insertion point (Figure 1–51).

Q&A

How would I remove an underline?

You would click the Underline button a second time, or you immediately could click the Undo button on the Quick Access Toolbar.

Q&A

Are other types of underlines available?

In addition to the basic solid underline shown in Figure 1–51, Word has many decorative underlines, such as double underlines, dotted underlines, and wavy underlines. You can access the decorative underlines and also change the color of an underline through the Underline gallery.

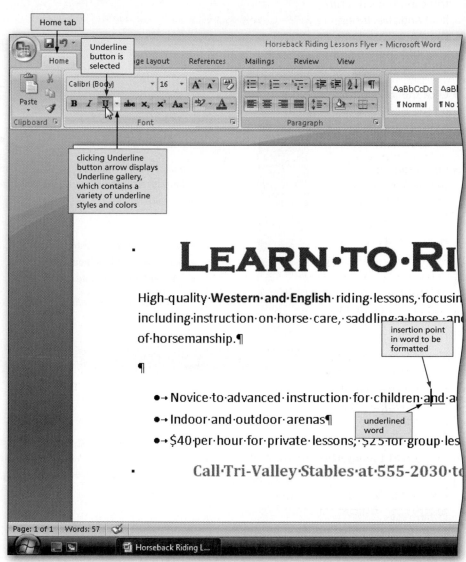

Figure 1–51

Other Ways

1. Right-click text, click Font on shortcut menu, click Font tab, click Underline style box arrow, click desired underline style, click OK button

2. Click Font Dialog Box Launcher, click Font tab, click Underline style box arrow, click desired underline style, click OK button

3. Press CTRL+U

To Italicize Text

To further emphasize the signature line, this line is italicized in the flyer. **Italicized** text has a slanted appearance. The following steps select the text and then italicize it.

- Point to the left of the line to be selected (in this case, the signature line) and click when the mouse pointer is a right-pointing block arrow.

- Click the Italic button on the Home tab to italicize the selected text.

- Click inside the selected text to remove the selection (Figure 1–52).

Q&A How would I remove an italic format?

You would click the Italic button a second time, or you immediately could click the Undo button on the Quick Access Toolbar.

Q&A How can I tell what formatting has been applied to text?

The selected buttons and boxes on the Home tab show formatting characteristics of the location of the insertion point. With the insertion point in the signature line, the Home tab shows these formats: 18-point Cambria bold italic font, centered paragraph, and Heading 2 style.

Figure 1–52

Other Ways

1. Click Italic button on Mini toolbar

2. Right-click selected text, click Font on shortcut menu, click Font tab, click Italic in Font style list, click OK button

3. Click Font Dialog Box Launcher, click Font tab, click Italic in Font style list, click OK button

4. Press CTRL+I

Document Formats

One advantage of using styles to format text is that you easily can change the formats of styles and themes in your document to give it a different or new look. Recall that a style is a named group of formatting characteristics and a theme is a set of unified formats for fonts, colors, and graphics. In Word, you can change the style set, theme colors, and theme fonts.

- The predefined styles in the Styles gallery, such as Heading 1 and Heading 2, each known as a **Quick Style**, are part of a style set. A **style set** consists of a group of frequently used styles formatted so they look pleasing when used together. When you change the style set, formats assigned to each Quick Style also change.

• Each **color scheme** in a theme identifies 12 complementary colors for text, background, accents, and links in a document. With more than 20 predefined color schemes, Word provides a simple way to select colors that work well together.

• Each theme has a **font set** that defines formats for two fonts: one for headings and another for body text. In Word, you can select from more than 20 predefined coordinated font sets to give the document's text a new look.

Use color.
When choosing color, associate the meaning of color to your message:

• Red expresses danger, power, or energy, and often is associated with sports or physical exertion.

• Brown represents simplicity, honesty, and dependability.

• Orange denotes success, victory, creativity, and enthusiasm.

• Yellow suggests sunshine, happiness, hope, liveliness, and intelligence.

• Green symbolizes growth, healthiness, harmony, blooming, and healing, and often is associated with safety or money.

• Blue indicates integrity, trust, importance, confidence, and stability.

• Purple represents wealth, power, comfort, extravagance, magic, mystery, and spirituality.

• White stands for purity, goodness, cleanliness, precision, and perfection.

• Black suggests authority, strength, elegance, power, and prestige.

• Gray conveys neutrality and thus often is found in backgrounds and other effects.

Plan Ahead

To Change the Style Set

To symbolize perfection and precision in the flyer, the characters in the headline are white. The style set, called Modern, formats Heading 1 characters in white. It also formats the Heading 1 and Heading 2 styles in all capital letters and places a background color around the paragraphs, which further emphasize the headline and signature line in the flyer. Thus, you will change the style set from Default to Modern. The following steps change a style set.

1

• Click the Change Styles button on the Home tab to display the Change Styles menu (Figure 1–53).

Figure 1–53

2

- Point to Style Set on the Change Styles menu to display the Style Set gallery.

- Point to Modern in the Style Set gallery to display a live preview of the formats associated with the Modern style set (Figure 1–54).

 Experiment

- Point to various style sets in the Style Set gallery and watch the formats of the styled text change in the document window.

3

- Click Modern in the Style Set gallery to change the document style set to Modern.

Q&A

What if I want to return to the original style set?

You would click the Change Styles button, click Style Set on the Change Styles menu, and then click Default in the Style Set gallery, or you could click the Undo button on the Quick Access Toolbar.

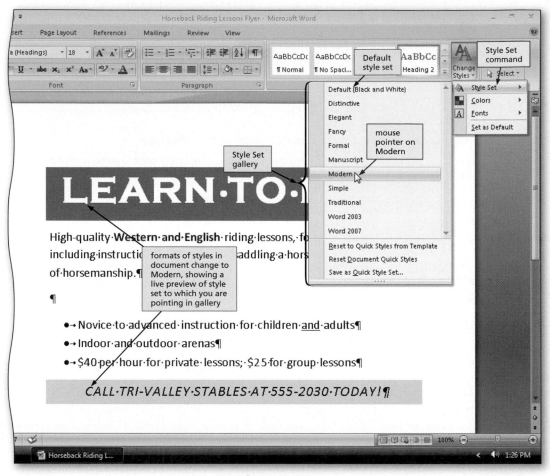

Figure 1–54

BTW

Style Formats
To see the formats assigned to a particular style in a document, click the Styles Dialog Box Launcher on the Home tab and then click the Style Inspector button in the Styles task pane. Position the insertion point in the style and then point to the Paragraph formatting or Text level formatting areas in the Style Inspector task pane to display an Enhanced ScreenTip describing formats assigned to the location of the insertion point. You also can click the Reveal Formatting button in the Style Inspector to display the Reveal Formatting task pane.

To Change Theme Colors

To suggest enthusiasm, success, and honesty, the background colors around the headline and signature line paragraphs in the flyer use shades of orange and brown. In Word, the color scheme called Aspect uses these colors. Thus, you will change the color scheme to Aspect. The following steps change theme colors.

1

- Click the Change Styles button on the Home tab to display the Change Styles menu.

- Point to Colors on the Change Styles menu to display the Colors gallery.

- Point to Aspect in the Colors gallery to display a live preview of the Aspect color scheme (Figure 1–55).

 Experiment

- Point to various color schemes in the Colors gallery and watch the paragraph background colors change in the document window.

2

- Click Aspect in the Colors gallery to change the document theme colors to Aspect.

Figure 1–55

Q&A What if I want to return to the original color scheme?

You would click the Change Styles button, click Colors on the Change Styles menu, and then click Office in the Colors gallery.

Other Ways

1. Click Theme Colors button arrow on Page Layout tab, select desired color scheme

To Change Theme Fonts

Earlier in this chapter, you changed the font of the headline to Copperplate Gothic Bold. In this flyer, all text below the headline should be the Rockwell font, instead of the Calibri font, because it better matches the western tone of the flyer. Thus, the next step is to change the current font set, which is called Office, to a font set called Foundry, which uses the Rockwell font for headings and body text.

If you previously changed a font using buttons on the Ribbon or Mini toolbar, Word will not alter those when you change the font set because changes to the font set are not applied to fonts changed individually. This means the font headline in the flyer will stay as Copperplate Gothic Bold when you change the font set. The following steps change the font set to Foundry.

- Click the Change Styles button on the Home tab.

- Point to Fonts on the Change Styles menu to display the Fonts gallery.

- Scroll through the Fonts gallery until Foundry is displayed and then point to Foundry to display a live preview of the Foundry font set (Figure 1–56).

 Experiment

- Point to various font sets in the Fonts gallery and watch the fonts below the headline change in the document window.

Figure 1–56

- Click Foundry in the Fonts gallery to change the document theme fonts to Foundry.

Q&A What if I want to return to the original font set?

You would click the Change Styles button, click Fonts on the Change Styles menu, and then click Office in the Fonts gallery.

Other Ways

1. Click Theme Fonts button arrow on Page Layout tab, select desired font set

Inserting and Formatting a Picture in a Word Document

With the text formatted in the flyer, the next step is to insert a picture in the flyer and format the picture. Flyers usually contain graphical images, such as a picture, to attract the attention of passersby.

Note: If you are using Windows XP, see Appendix F for alternate steps.

Plan
Ahead

Find the appropriate graphical image.
To use graphical images, also called graphics, in a Word document, the image must be stored digitally in a file. Files containing graphical images are available from a variety of sources:

- Word includes a collection of predefined graphical images that you can insert in a document.

- Microsoft has free digital images on the Web for use in a document. Other Web sites also have images available, some of which are free, while others require a fee.

- You can take a picture with a digital camera and **download** it, which is the process of copying the digital picture from the camera to your computer.

- With a scanner, you can convert a printed picture, drawing, or diagram to a digital file.

  If you receive a picture from a source other than yourself, do not use the file until you are certain it does not contain a virus. A **virus** is a computer program that can damage files and programs on your computer. Use an antivirus program to verify that any files you use are virus free.

Plan
Ahead

Establish where to position and how to format the graphical image.
The content, size, shape, position, and format of a graphic should capture the interest of passersby, enticing them to stop and read the flyer. Often, the graphic is the center of attraction and visually the largest element on a flyer. If you use colors in the graphical image, be sure they are part of the document's color scheme.

To Insert a Picture

The next step in creating the flyer is to insert the picture of the horse and rider so that it is centered on the blank line above the bulleted list. The picture, which was taken with a digital camera, is available on the Data Files for Students. See the inside back cover of this book for instructions on downloading the Data Files for Students, or contact your instructor for information about accessing the required files. The following steps insert a centered picture, which, in this example, is located on the same USB flash drive that contains the saved flyer.

1

- To position the insertion point where you want the picture to be located, press CTRL+HOME and then press the DOWN ARROW key four times.

- Click the Center button on the Home tab to center the paragraph that will contain the picture.

- Click Insert on the Ribbon to display the Insert tab (Figure 1–57).

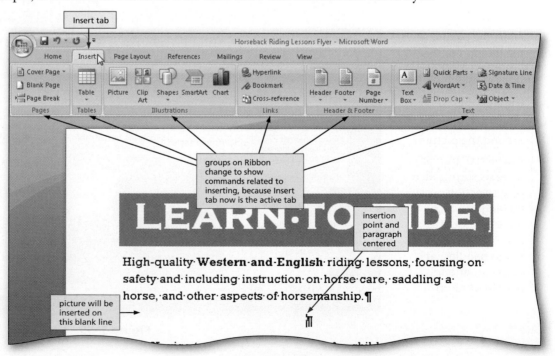

Figure 1–57

2

- With your USB flash drive connected to one of the computer's USB ports, click the Insert Picture from File button on the Insert tab to display the Insert Picture dialog box.

- If the Folders list is displayed below the Folders button, click the Folders button to remove the Folders list.

- If necessary, click Computer in the Favorite Links section and then scroll until UDISK 2.0 (E:) appears in the list of available drives.

- Double-click UDISK 2.0 (E:) to select the USB flash drive, Drive E in this case, as the device that contains the picture.

- Click Horse and Rider to select the file name (Figure 1–58).

Q&A What if the picture is not on a USB flash drive?

Use the same process, but select the device containing the picture in the Favorite Links section.

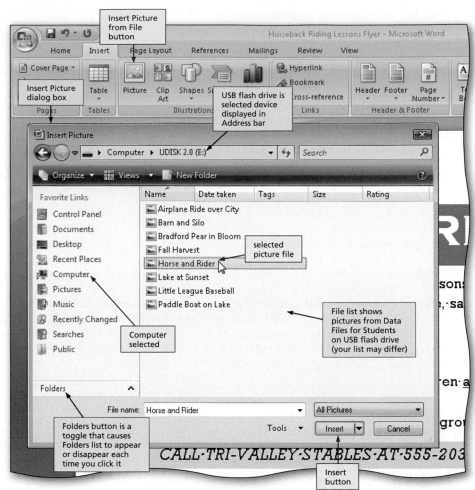

Figure 1–58

3

- Click the Insert button in the dialog box to insert the picture at the location of the insertion point in the document (Figure 1–59).

Q&A What are the symbols around the picture?

A selected graphic appears surrounded by a **selection rectangle**, which has small squares and circles, called **sizing handles**, at each corner and middle location.

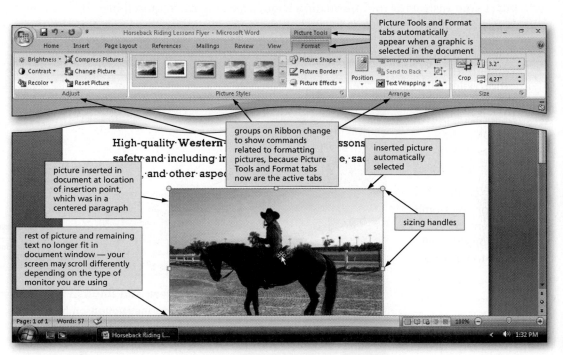

Figure 1–59

Scrolling

As mentioned at the beginning of this chapter, you view only a portion of a document on the screen through the document window. At some point when you type text or insert graphics, Word will **scroll** the top or bottom portion of the document off the screen. Although you cannot see the text and graphics once they scroll off the screen, they remain in the document.

As shown in Figure 1–59, when you insert the picture in the flyer, the text and graphics are too long to fit in the document window. Thus, to see the bottom of the flyer, you will need to scroll downward.

You may use either the mouse or the keyboard to scroll to a different location in a document. With the mouse, you can use the scroll arrows or the scroll box on the scroll bar to display a different portion of the document in the document window, and then click the mouse to move the insertion point to that location. Table 1–1 explains various techniques for using the scroll bar to scroll vertically with the mouse.

BTW

Minimize Wrist Injury
Computer users frequently switch between the keyboard and the mouse during a word processing session; such switching strains the wrist. To help prevent wrist injury, minimize switching. For instance, if your fingers already are on the keyboard, use keyboard keys to scroll. If your hand already is on the mouse, use the mouse to scroll.

Table 1–1 Using the Scroll Bar to Scroll with the Mouse	
SCROLL DIRECTION	**MOUSE ACTION**
Up	Drag the scroll box upward.
Down	Drag the scroll box downward.
Up one screen	Click anywhere above the scroll box on the vertical scroll bar.
Down one screen	Click anywhere below the scroll box on the vertical scroll bar.
Up one line	Click the scroll arrow at the top of the vertical scroll bar.
Down one line	Click the scroll arrow at the bottom of the vertical scroll bar.

When you use the keyboard to scroll, the insertion point automatically moves when you press the appropriate keys. Table 1–2 outlines various techniques to scroll through a document using the keyboard, some of which you have seen used in this chapter.

Table 1–2 Scrolling with the Keyboard	
SCROLL DIRECTION	**KEY(S) TO PRESS**
Left one character	LEFT ARROW
Right one character	RIGHT ARROW
Left one word	CTRL+LEFT ARROW
Right one word	CTRL+RIGHT ARROW
Up one line	UP ARROW
Down one line	DOWN ARROW
To end of line	END
To beginning of line	HOME
Up one paragraph	CTRL+UP ARROW
Down one paragraph	CTRL+DOWN ARROW
Up one screen	PAGE UP
Down one screen	PAGE DOWN
To top of document window	ALT+CTRL+PAGE UP
To bottom of document window	ALT+CTRL+PAGE DOWN
To beginning of document	CTRL+HOME
To end of document	CTRL+END

To Apply a Picture Style

Earlier in this chapter, you applied the heading styles to the headline and signature line in the flyer. Word also provides styles for pictures, allowing you easily to change the basic rectangle format to a more visually appealing style. Word provides a gallery of more than 25 picture styles, which include a variety of shapes, angles, borders, and reflections. The flyer in this chapter uses an oval picture style that has a border around its edges. The following steps apply a picture style to the picture in the flyer.

1

- Click the down scroll arrow on the vertical scroll bar as many times as necessary until the entire picture is displayed in the document window (Figure 1–60).

Q&A

What if the Picture Tools and Format tabs no longer are displayed on my Ribbon?

Double-click the picture to display the Picture Tools and Format tabs.

Figure 1–60

2

- Click the More button in the Picture Styles gallery, which shows more gallery options.

- Point to Metal Oval in the Picture Styles gallery to display a live preview of that style applied to the picture in the document (Figure 1–61).

 Experiment

- Point to various picture styles in the Picture Styles gallery and watch the format of the picture change in the document window.

3

- Click Metal Oval in the Picture Styles gallery to apply the selected style to the picture.

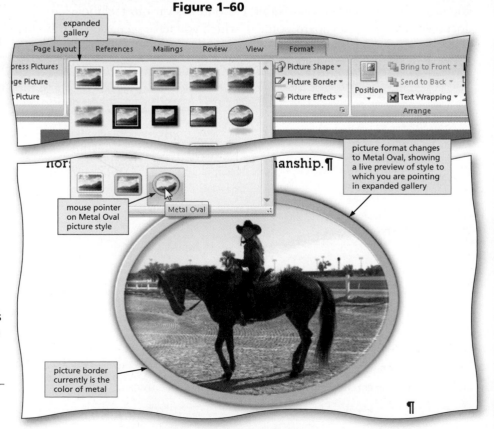

Figure 1–61

To Change a Picture Border Color

The flyer in this chapter has a tan border around the picture. Earlier in this chapter, you changed the color scheme to Aspect. To coordinate the border color with the other colors in the document, you will use a shade of tan in Aspect color scheme for the picture border. Any color galleries you display show colors defined in this current color scheme. The following steps change the picture border color.

1

- Click the Picture Border button arrow on the Format tab to display the Picture Border gallery.

Q&A What if the Picture Tools and Format tabs no longer are displayed on my Ribbon?

Double-click the picture to display the Picture Tools and Format tabs.

- Point to Tan, Background 2 (third theme color from left in the first row) in the Picture Border gallery to display a live preview of that border color on the picture (Figure 1–62).

Experiment

- Point to various colors in the Picture Border gallery and watch the border color on the picture change in the document window.

2

- Click Tan, Background 2 in the Picture Styles gallery to change the picture border color.

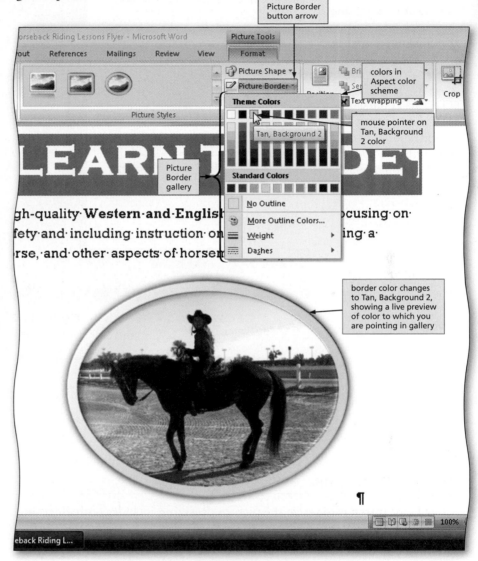

Figure 1–62

To Zoom the Document

The next step in formatting the picture is to resize it. Specifically, you will increase the size of the picture. You do not want it so large, however, that it causes the flyer text to flow to a second page. You can change the zoom so that you can see the entire document on the screen at once. Seeing the entire document at once helps you determine the appropriate size of the picture. The steps on the next page zoom the document.

1

 Experiment

- Repeatedly click the Zoom Out and Zoom In buttons on the status bar and watch the size of the document change in the document window.

2

- Click the Zoom Out or Zoom In button as many times as necessary until the Zoom level button displays 50% on its face (Figure 1–63).

Q&A If I change the zoom percentage, will the document print differently?

Changing the zoom has no effect on the printed document.

Figure 1–63

Other Ways		
1. Drag Zoom slider on status bar	2. Click Zoom level button on status bar, select desired zoom percent or type, click OK button	3. Click Zoom button on View tab, select desired zoom percent or type, click OK button

To Resize a Graphic

The next step is to resize the picture. **Resizing** includes both enlarging and reducing the size of a graphic. The picture in the flyer should be as large as possible, without causing any flyer text to flow to a second page.

With the entire document displaying in the document window, you will be able to see how the resized graphic will look on the entire page. The following steps resize a selected graphic.

1

- With the graphic still selected, point to the upper-right corner sizing handle on the picture so that the mouse pointer shape changes to a two-headed arrow (Figure 1–64).

Q&A What if my graphic (picture) is not selected?

To select a graphic, click it.

Figure 1–64

2

- Drag the sizing handle diagonally outward until the crosshair mouse pointer is positioned approximately as shown in Figure 1–65.

3

- Release the mouse button to resize the graphic.

What if the graphic is the wrong size?

Repeat Steps 1, 2, and 3.

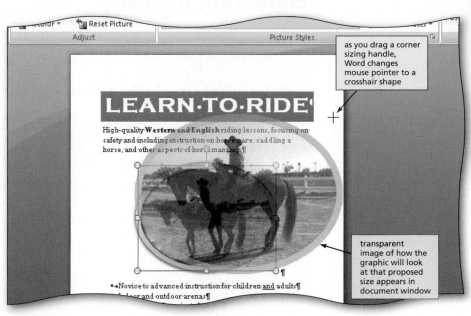

Figure 1–65

4

- Click outside the graphic to deselect it (Figure 1–66).

What happened to the Picture Tools and Format tabs?

When you click outside of a graphic or press a key to scroll through a document, Word deselects the graphic and removes the Picture Tools and Format tabs from the screen.

What if I want to return a graphic to its original size and start again?

With the graphic selected, click the Size Dialog Box Launcher on the Format tab to display the Size dialog box, click the Size tab, click the Reset button, and then click the Close button.

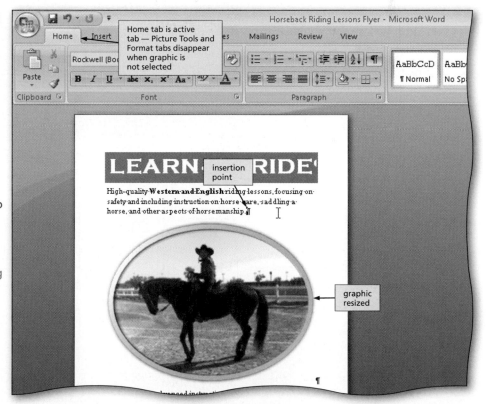

Figure 1–66

Other Ways
1. Enter graphic height and width in Shape Height and Shape Width text boxes in Size group on Format tab in Picture Tools tab   2. Click Size Dialog Box Launcher on Format tab in Picture Tools tab, click Size tab, enter desired height and width values in text boxes, click Close button

Enhancing the Page

With the text and graphics entered and formatted, the next step is to look at the page as a whole and determine if it looks finished in its current state. As you review the page, answer these questions:

- Does it need a page border to frame its contents, or would a page border make it look too busy?
- Is the spacing between paragraphs and graphics on the page adequate? Do any sections of text or graphics look as if they are positioned too closely to the items above or below them?

You determine that a graphical, color-coordinated border would enhance the flyer. You also notice that the flyer would look more proportionate if it had a little more space below the headline and above the graphic. The following pages make these enhancements to the flyer.

To Add a Page Border

In Word, you can add a border around the perimeter of an entire page. In this flyer, you add a graphical border that uses a shade of brown from the Aspect color scheme. The following steps add a graphical page border.

- Click Page Layout on the Ribbon to display the Page Layout tab.
- Click the Page Borders button on the Page Layout tab to display the Borders and Shading dialog box (Figure 1–67).

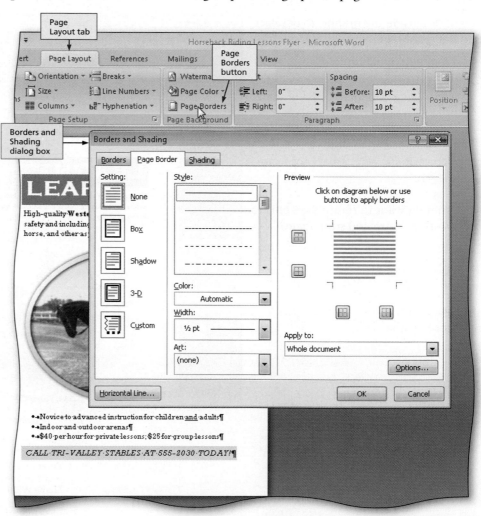

Figure 1–67

2

- Click the Art box arrow to display the Art gallery.

- Click the down scroll arrow in the Art gallery until the art border shown in Figure 1–68 appears.

Figure 1–68

3

- Click the art border shown in Figure 1–68 to display a preview of the selection in the Preview area of the dialog box.

- Click the Color box arrow to display a Color gallery (Figure 1–69).

Q&A Do I have to use an art border?

No. You can select a solid or decorative line in the Style list.

Q&A Can I add color to every border type?

You can color all of the line styles and many of the art borders.

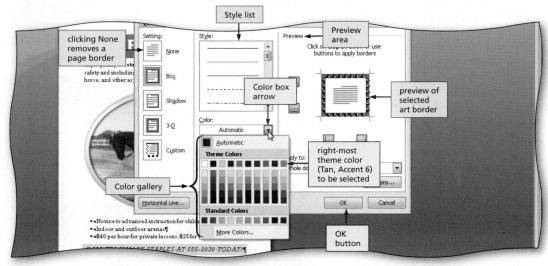

Figure 1–69

4

- Click the right-most theme color (Tan, Accent 6) in the Color gallery to display a preview of the selection in the Preview area.

- Click the OK button to add the border to the page (Figure 1–70).

Q&A What if I wanted to remove the border?

Click None in the Setting list in the Borders and Shading dialog box.

Figure 1–70

To Change Spacing Above and Below Paragraphs

The default spacing above a heading paragraph in Word is 10 points. In the flyer, you want to remove this spacing so the headline is closer to the page border. The default spacing below (after) a body text paragraph is 0 points. Below the first paragraph of body copy in the flyer, you want to increase this space. The following steps change the spacing above and below paragraphs.

1

- Position the insertion point in the paragraph to be adjusted, in this case, the headline.

- Click the Spacing Before box down arrow on the Page Layout tab as many times as necessary until 0 pt is displayed in the Spacing Before text box (Figure 1–71).

Q&A

Why is a blank space still between the border and the headline?

The space is a result of Word's preset left, right, top, and bottom margins and other settings.

2

- Position the insertion point in the paragraph below the headline.

- Click the Spacing After box up arrow on the Page Layout tab as many times as necessary until 24 pt is displayed in the Spacing After text box, shown in Figure 1–72. (If the text flows to two pages, resize the picture so that it is smaller.)

Figure 1–71

BTW

Centering Page Contents Vertically
You can center page contents vertically between the top and bottom margins. To do this, click the Page Setup Dialog Box Launcher on the Page Layout tab, click the Layout tab in the dialog box, click the Vertical alignment box arrow, click Center in the list, and then click the OK button.

To Zoom the Document

You are finished enhancing the page and no longer need to view the entire page in the document window. Thus, the following step changes the zoom back to 100 percent.

1 Click the Zoom In button as many times as necessary until the Zoom level button displays 100% on its face, shown in Figure 1–72.

Changing Document Properties and Saving Again

Word helps you organize and identify your files by using **document properties**, which are the details about a file. Document properties, also known as **metadata**, can include such information as the project author, title, or subject. **Keywords** are words or phrases that further describe the document. For example, a class name or document topic can describe the file's purpose or content.

Document properties are valuable for a variety of reasons:

- Users can save time locating a particular file because they can view a document's properties without opening the document.

- By creating consistent properties for files having similar content, users can better organize their documents.

- Some organizations require Word users to add document properties so that other employees can view details about these files.

Five different types of document properties exist, but the more common ones used in this book are standard and automatically updated properties. **Standard properties** are associated with all Microsoft Office documents and include author, title, and subject. **Automatically updated properties** include file system properties, such as the date you create or change a file, and statistics, such as the file size.

BTW

Printing Document Properties
To print document properties, click the Office Button to display the Office Button menu, point to Print on the Office Button menu to display the Print submenu, click Print on the Print submenu to display the Print dialog box, click the Print what box arrow, click Document properties to instruct Word to print the document properties instead of the document, and then click the OK button.

To Change Document Properties

The **Document Information Panel** contains areas where you can view and enter document properties. You can view and change information in this panel at any time while you are creating a document. Before saving the flyer again, you want to add your name and course information as document properties. The following steps use the Document Information Panel to change document properties.

1

- Click the Office Button to display the Office Button menu.

- Point to Prepare on the Office Button menu to display the Prepare submenu (Figure 1–72).

Q&A

What other types of actions besides changing properties can you take to prepare a document for distribution?

The Prepare submenu provides commands related to sharing a document with others, such as allowing or restricting people to view and modify your document, checking to see if your document will open in earlier versions of Word, and searching for hidden personal information.

Figure 1–72

● Click Properties on the Prepare submenu to display the Document Information Panel (Figure 1–73).

Q&A Why are some of the document properties in my Document Information Panel already filled in?

The person who installed Microsoft Office 2007 on your computer or network may have set or customized the properties.

Figure 1–73

● Click the Author text box, if necessary, and then type your name as the Author property. If a name already is displayed in the Author text box, delete it before typing your name.

● Click the Subject text box, if necessary delete any existing text, and then type your course and section as the Subject property.

● If an AutoComplete dialog box appears, click its Yes button.

● Click the Keywords text box, if necessary delete any existing text, and then type Tri-Valley Stables as the Keywords property (Figure 1–74).

Figure 1–74

Q&A What types of document properties does Word collect automatically?

Word records such details as how long you worked at creating your project, how many times you revised the document, and what fonts and themes are used.

● Click the Close the Document Information Panel button so that the Document Information Panel no longer is displayed.

To Save an Existing Document with the Same File Name

Saving frequently cannot be overemphasized. You have made several modifications to the document since you saved it earlier in the chapter. When you first saved the document, you clicked the Save button on the Quick Access Toolbar, the Save As dialog box appeared, and you entered the file name, Horseback Riding Lessons Flyer. If you want to use the same file name to save the changes made to the document, you again click the Save button on the Quick Access Toolbar. The following step saves the document again.

1

- Click the Save button on the Quick Access Toolbar to overwrite the previous Horseback Riding Lessons Flyer file on the USB flash drive (Figure 1–75).

Q&A

Why did the Save As dialog box not appear?

Word overwrites the document using the settings specified the first time you saved the document. To save the file with a different file name or on different media, display the Save As dialog box by clicking the Office Button and then clicking Save As on the Office Button menu. Then, fill in the Save As dialog box as described in Steps 2 through 5 on pages WD 20 and WD 21.

Figure 1–75

Other Ways

1. Press CTRL+S or press SHIFT+F12

Printing a Document

After you create a document, you often want to print it. A printed version of the document is called a **hard copy** or **printout**.

Printed copies of your document can be useful for the following reasons:

- Many people prefer proofreading a hard copy of the document rather than viewing it on the screen to check for errors and readability.

- Hard copies can serve as reference material if your storage medium is lost or becomes corrupted and you need to re-create the document.

It is a good practice to save a document before printing it, in the event you experience difficulties with the printer.

BTW

Conserving Ink and Toner
You can instruct Word to print draft quality documents to conserve ink or toner by clicking the Office Button, clicking the Word Options button, clicking Advanced in the left pane of the Word Options dialog box, scrolling to the Print area, placing a check mark in the 'Use draft quality' check box, and then clicking the OK button. To print the document with these settings, click the Office Button, point to Print, and then click Quick Print.

To Print a Document

With the completed document saved, you may want to print it. The following steps print the contents of the saved Horseback Riding Lessons Flyer project.

1
- Click the Office Button to display the Office Button menu.

- Point to Print on the Office Button menu to display the Print submenu (Figure 1–76).

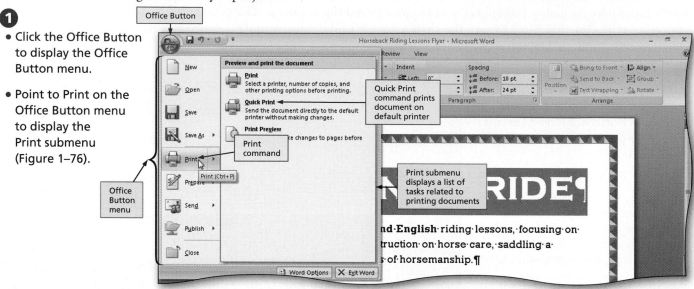

Figure 1–76

2
- Click Quick Print on the Print submenu to print the document.

- When the printer stops, retrieve the hard copy of the Horseback Riding Lessons Flyer (Figures 1–77).

Q&A How can I print multiple copies of my document other than issuing the Quick Print command twice?

Click the Office Button, point to Print on the Office Button menu, click Print on the Print submenu, increase the number in the Number of copies box, and then click the OK button.

Q&A Do I have to wait until my document is complete to print it?

No, you can follow these steps to print a document at any time while you are creating it.

BTW **Printed Borders**
If one or more of your borders do not print, click the Page Borders button on the Page Layout tab, click the Options button in the dialog box, click the Measure from box arrow and click Text, change the four text boxes to 15 pt, and then click the OK button in each dialog box. Try printing the document again. If the borders still do not print, adjust the text boxes in the dialog box to a number smaller than 15 point.

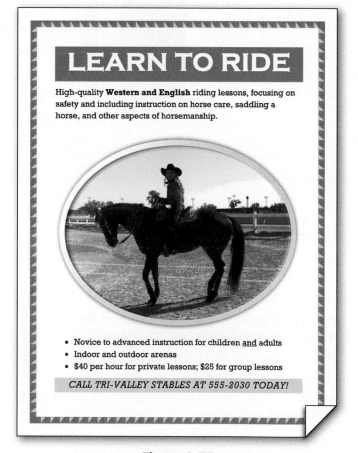

Figure 1–77

Other Ways

1. Press CTRL+P, press ENTER

Quitting Word

When you quit Word, if you have made changes to a document since the last time the file was saved, Word displays a dialog box asking if you want to save the changes you made to the file before it closes that window. The dialog box contains three buttons with these resulting actions: the Yes button saves the changes and then quits Word; the No button quits Word without saving changes; and the Cancel button closes the dialog box and redisplays the document without saving the changes.

If no changes have been made to an open document since the last time the file was saved, Word will close the window without displaying a dialog box.

To Quit Word with One Document Open

You saved the document prior to printing and did not make any changes to the project. The Horseback Riding Lessons Flyer project now is complete, and you are ready to quit Word. When one Word document is open, the following steps quit Word.

1
- Point to the Close button on the right side of the Word title bar (Figure 1–78).

2
- Click the Close button to quit Word.

Q&A What if I have more than one Word document open?

You would click the Close button for each open document. When you click the last open document's Close button, Word also quits. As an alternative, you could click the Office Button and then click the Exit Word button on the Office Button menu, which closes all open Word documents and then quits Word.

Figure 1–78

Other Ways

1. Double-click Office Button
2. With multiple documents open, click Office Button, click Exit Word on Office Button menu
3. Right-click Microsoft Word button on Windows Vista taskbar, click Close on shortcut menu
4. Press ALT+F4

Starting Word and Opening a Document

Once you have created and saved a document, you may need to retrieve it from your storage medium. For example, you might want to revise the document or reprint it. Opening a document requires that Word is running on your computer.

To Start Word

The following steps, which assume Windows Vista is running, start Word.

1 Click the Start button on the Windows Vista taskbar to display the Start menu.

2 Click All Programs at the bottom of the left pane on the Start menu to display the All Programs list and then click Microsoft Office in the All Programs list to display the Microsoft Office list.

3 Click Microsoft Office Word 2007 in the Microsoft Office list to start Word and display a new blank document in the Word window.

4 If the Word window is not maximized, click the Maximize button on its title bar to maximize the window.

Note: If you are using Windows XP, see Appendix F for alternate steps.

To Open a Document from Word

Earlier in this chapter you saved your project on a USB flash drive using the file name, Horseback Riding Lessons Flyer. The following steps open the Horseback Riding Lessons Flyer file from the USB flash drive.

1

- With your USB flash drive connected to one of the computer's USB ports, click the Office Button to display the Office Button menu (Figure 1–79).

Q&A

What files are shown in the Recent Documents list?

Word displays the most recently opened document file names in this list. If the name of the file you want to open appears in the Recent Documents list, you could click it to open the file.

Figure 1–79

2

- Click Open on the Office Button menu to display the Open dialog box.

- If the Folders list is displayed below the Folders button, click the Folders button to remove the Folders list.

- If necessary, click Computer in the Favorite Links section and then scroll until UDISK 2.0 (E:) appears in the list of available drives.

- Double-click UDISK 2.0 (E:) to select the USB flash drive, Drive E in this case, as the new open location.

- Click Horseback Riding Lessons Flyer to select the file name (Figure 1–80).

Q&A

How do I open the file if I am not using a USB flash drive?

Use the same process, but be certain to select your device in the Computer list.

Figure 1–80

3

• Click the Open button to open the selected file and display the Horseback Riding Lessons Flyer document in the Word window (Figure 1–81).

Q&A

Why is the Word icon and document name on the Windows Vista taskbar?

When you open a Word file, a Word program button is displayed on the taskbar. The button in Figure 1–81 contains an ellipsis because some of its contents do not fit in the allotted button space. If you point to a program button, its entire contents appear in a ScreenTip, which in this case would be the file name followed by the program name.

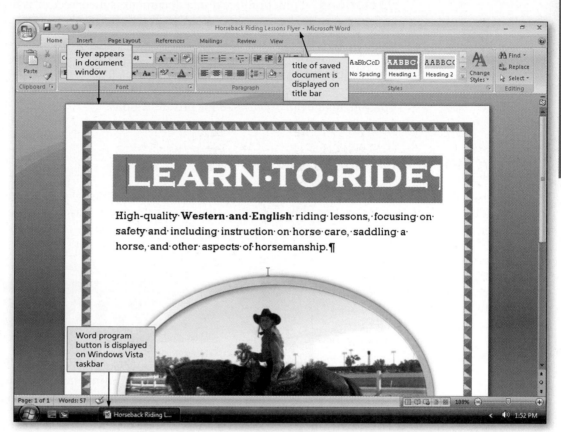

Figure 1–81

Other Ways

1. Click Office Button, click file name in Recent Documents list
2. Press CTRL+O, select file name, press ENTER

Correcting Errors

After creating a document, you often will find you must make changes to it. For example, the document may contain an error, or new circumstances may require you to add text to the document.

Types of Changes Made to Documents

The types of changes made to documents normally fall into one of the three following categories: additions, deletions, or modifications.

Additions Additional words, sentences, or paragraphs may be required in a document. Additions occur when you omit text from a document and want to insert it later. For example, additional types of riding lessons may be offered.

BTW

Print Preview
You can preview a document before printing it by clicking the Office Button, pointing to Print, and then clicking Print Preview. When finished previewing the document, click the Close Print Preview button.

Deletions   Sometimes, text in a document is incorrect or is no longer needed. For example, group lessons might not be offered. In this case, you would delete the words, $25 for group lessons, from the flyer.

Modifications   If an error is made in a document or changes take place that affect the document, you might have to revise a word(s) in the text. For example, the fee per hour may change from $40 to $50 for private lessons.

To Insert Text in an Existing Document

Word inserts text to the left of the insertion point. The text to the right of the insertion point moves to the right and downward to fit the new text. The following steps insert the word, various, to the left of the word, aspects, in the flyer.

- Scroll through the document and then click to the left of the location of text to be inserted (in this case, the a in aspects) to position the insertion point where text should be inserted (Figure 1–82).

Figure 1–82

- Type various and then press the SPACEBAR to insert the word, various, to the left of the insertion point (Figure 1–83).

Q&A

Why did the text move to the right as I typed?

In Word, the default typing mode is **insert mode**, which means as you type a character, Word moves all the characters to the right of the typed character one position to the right.

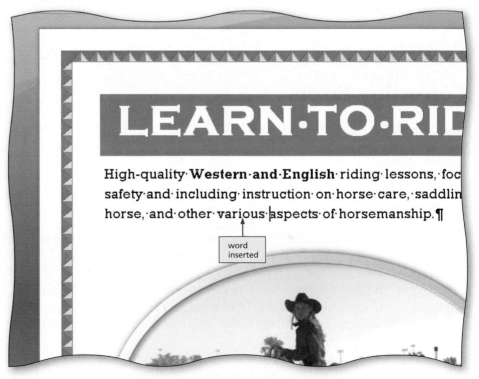

Figure 1–83

Deleting Text from an Existing Document

It is not unusual to type incorrect characters or words in a document. As discussed earlier in this chapter, you can click the Undo button on the Quick Access Toolbar to immediately undo a command or action — this includes typing. Word also provides other methods of correcting typing errors.

To delete an incorrect character in a document, simply click next to the incorrect character and then press the BACKSPACE key to erase to the left of the insertion point, or press the DELETE key to erase to the right of the insertion point.

To Select a Word and Delete It

To delete a word or phrase, you first must select the word or phrase. The following steps select the word, various, that was just added in the previous steps and then delete the selection.

- Position the mouse pointer somewhere in the word to be selected (in this case, various), as shown in Figure 1–84.

Figure 1–84

- Double-click the word to select it (Figure 1–85).

- With the text selected, press the DELETE key to delete the selected text (shown in Figure 1–82).

Figure 1–85

Closing the Entire Document

Sometimes, everything goes wrong. If this happens, you may want to close the document entirely and start over with a new document. You also may want to close a document when you are finished with it so you can begin your next document. If you wanted to close a document, you would use the steps on the next page.

To Close the Entire Document and Start Over

1. Click the Office Button and then click Close.

2. If Word displays a dialog box, click the No button to ignore the changes since the last time you saved the document.

3. Click the Office Button and then click New on the Office Button menu. When Word displays the New Document dialog box, click Blank document and then click the Create button.

Word Help

At any time while using Word, you can find answers to questions and display information about various topics through **Word Help**. Used properly, this form of assistance can increase your productivity and reduce your frustrations by minimizing the time you spend learning how to use Word.

This section introduces you to Word Help. Additional information about using Word Help is available in Appendix C.

To Search for Word Help

Using Word Help, you can search for information based on phrases such as save a document or format text, or key terms such as copy, save, or format. Word Help responds with a list of search results displayed as links to a variety of resources. The following steps, which use Word Help to search for information about selecting text, assume you are connected to the Internet.

- Click the Microsoft Office Word Help button near the upper-right corner of the Word window to open the Word Help window.

- Type select text in the 'Type words to search for' text box at the top of the Word Help window (Figure 1–86).

Figure 1–86

2

- Press the ENTER key to display the search results.

- Click the Maximize button on the Word Help window title bar to maximize the Help window (Figure 1–87).

Q&A

Where is the Word window with the Horseback Riding Lessons Flyer document?

Word is open in the background, but the Word Help window is overlaid on top of the Word window. When the Word Help window is closed, the document will reappear.

Figure 1–87

3

- Click the Select text link to display information about selecting text (Figure 1–88).

Q&A

What is the purpose of the buttons at the top of the Word Help window?

Use the buttons in the upper-left corner of the Word Help window to navigate through Help, change the display, show the Word Help table of contents, and print the contents of the window.

4

- Click the Close button on the Word Help window title bar to close the Word Help window and redisplay the Word window.

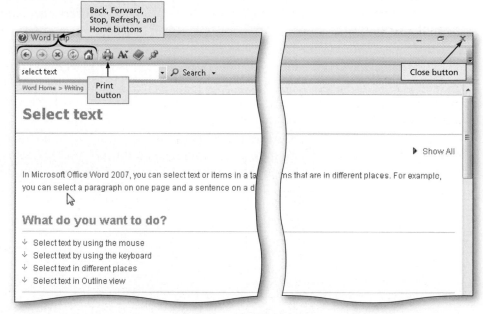

Figure 1–88

Other Ways
1. Press F1

BTW

Quick Reference
For a table that lists how to complete the tasks covered in this book using the mouse, Ribbon, shortcut menu, and keyboard, see the Quick Reference Summary at the back of this book, or visit the Word 2007 Quick Reference Web page (scsite.com/wd2007/qr).

To Quit Word

The following steps quit Word.

1 Click the Close button on the right side of the title bar to quit Word; or if you have multiple Word documents open, click the Office Button and then click the Exit Word button on the Office Button menu to close all open documents and quit Word.

2 If necessary, click the No button in the Microsoft Office Word dialog box so that any changes you have made are not saved.

Chapter Summary

In this chapter you have learned how to enter text in a document, format text, insert a picture, format a picture, add a page border, and print a document. The items listed below include all the new Word skills you have learned in this chapter.

1. Start Word (WD 5)
2. Type Text (WD 13)
3. Display Formatting Marks (WD 14)
4. Wordwrap Text as You Type (WD 15)
5. Insert a Blank Line (WD 15)
6. Check Spelling and Grammar as You Type (WD 16)
7. Save a Document (WD 19)
8. Apply Styles (WD 24)
9. Center a Paragraph (WD 26)
10. Select a Line (WD 27)
11. Change the Font Size of Selected Text (WD 28)
12. Change the Font of Selected Text (WD 29)
13. Select Multiple Paragraphs (WD 30)
14. Bullet a List of Paragraphs (WD 32)
15. Undo and Redo an Action (WD 32)
16. Select a Group of Words (WD 33)
17. Bold Text (WD 34)
18. Underline a Word (WD 35)
19. Italicize Text (WD 36)
20. Change the Style Set (WD 37)
21. Change Theme Colors (WD 39)
22. Change Theme Fonts (WD 39)
23. Insert a Picture (WD 41)
24. Apply a Picture Style (WD 44)
25. Change a Picture Border Color (WD 45)
26. Zoom the Document (WD 45)
27. Resize a Graphic (WD 46)
28. Add a Page Border (WD 48)
29. Change Spacing Above and Below Paragraphs (WD 50)
30. Change Document Properties (WD 51)
31. Save an Existing Document with the Same File Name (WD 53)
32. Print a Document (WD 54)
33. Quit Word with One Document Open (WD 55)
34. Open a Document from Word (WD 56)
35. Insert Text in an Existing Document (WD 58)
36. Select a Word and Delete It (WD 59)
37. Close the Entire Document and Start Over (WD 60)
38. Search for Word Help (WD 60)

If you have a SAM user profile, you may have access to hands-on instruction, practice, and assessment. Log in to your SAM account (http://sam2007.course.com) to launch any assigned training activities or exams that relate to the skills covered in this chapter.

BTW

Certification
The Microsoft Certified Application Specialist (MCAS) program provides an opportunity for you to obtain a valuable industry credential – proof that you have the Word 2007 skills required by employers. For more information, see Appendix G or visit the Word 2007 Certification Web page (scsite.com/wd2007/cert).

Learn It Online

Test your knowledge of chapter content and key terms.

Instructions: To complete the Learn It Online exercises, start your browser, click the Address bar, and then enter the Web address `scsite.com/wd2007/learn`. When the Word 2007 Learn It Online page is displayed, click the link for the exercise you want to complete and then read the instructions.

Chapter Reinforcement TF, MC, and SA
A series of true/false, multiple choice, and short answer questions that test your knowledge of the chapter content.

Flash Cards
An interactive learning environment where you identify chapter key terms associated with displayed definitions.

Practice Test
A series of multiple choice questions that test your knowledge of chapter content and key terms.

Who Wants To Be a Computer Genius?
An interactive game that challenges your knowledge of chapter content in the style of a television quiz show.

Wheel of Terms
An interactive game that challenges your knowledge of chapter key terms in the style of the television show *Wheel of Fortune*.

Crossword Puzzle Challenge
A crossword puzzle that challenges your knowledge of key terms presented in the chapter.

Apply Your Knowledge

Reinforce the skills and apply the concepts you learned in this chapter.

Modifying Text and Formatting a Document
Instructions: Start Word. Open the document, Apply 1-1 Autumn Fest Flyer Unformatted, from the Data Files for Students. See the inside back cover of this book for instructions on downloading the Data Files for Students, or contact your instructor for information about accessing the required files.

The document you open is an unformatted flyer. You are to modify text, format paragraphs and characters, and insert a picture in the flyer.

Perform the following tasks:
1. Delete the word, entire, in the sentence of body copy below the headline.
2. Insert the word, Creek, between the text, Honey Farm, in the sentence of body copy below the headline. The sentence should end: …Honey Creek Farm.
3. At the end of the signature line, change the period to an exclamation point. The sentence should end: …This Year's Fest!
4. Apply the Heading 1 style to the headline. Apply the Heading 2 style to the signature line.
5. Center the headline and the signature line.
6. Change the font and font size of the headline to 48-point Cooper Black, or a similar font.
7. Change the font size of body copy between the headline and the signature line to 22 point.
8. Change the font size of the signature line to 28 point.
9. Bullet the three lines (paragraphs) of text above the signature line.
10. Bold the text, October 4 and 5.

Continued >

Apply Your Knowledge *continued*

11. Underline the word, and, in the first bulleted paragraph.

12. Italicize the text in the signature line.

13. Change the theme colors to the Civic color scheme.

14. Change the theme fonts to the Opulent font set.

15. Change the zoom to 50 percent so the entire page is visible in the document window.

16. Change the spacing before the headline paragraph to 0 point. Change the spacing after the headline paragraph to 12 point.

17. Insert the picture of the combine centered on the blank line above the bulleted list. The picture is called Fall Harvest and is available on the Data Files for Students. Apply the Snip Diagonal Corner, White picture style to the inserted picture. Change the color of the picture border to Orange, Accent 6.

18. The entire flyer now should fit on a single page. If it flows to two pages, resize the picture or decrease spacing before and after paragraphs until the entire flyer text fits on a single page.

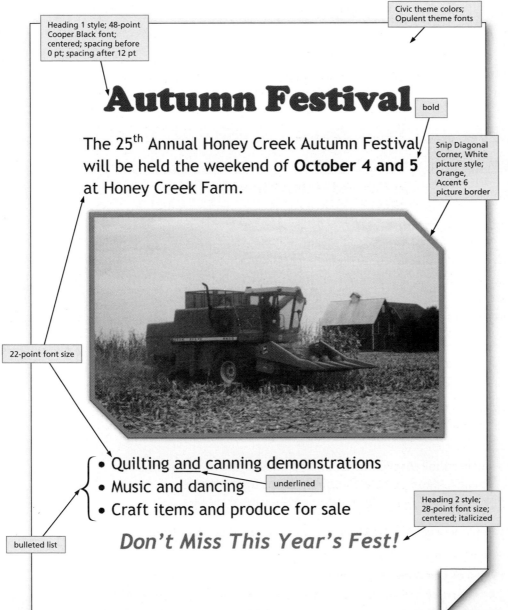

19. Enter the text, Honey Creek, as the keywords. Change the other document properties, as specified by your instructor.

20. Click the Office Button and then click Save As. Save the document using the file name, Apply 1-1 Autumn Fest Flyer Formatted.

21. Position the Quick Access Toolbar below the Ribbon. Save the document again by clicking the Save button. Reposition the Quick Access Toolbar above the Ribbon.

22. Submit the revised document, shown in Figure 1–89, in the format specified by your instructor.

Figure 1–89

Extend Your Knowledge

Extend the skills you learned in this chapter and experiment with new skills. You may need to use Help to complete the assignment.

Modifying Text and Graphics Formats

Instructions: Start Word. Open the document, Extend 1-1 Baseball Sign Ups Flyer, from the Data Files for Students. See the inside back cover of this book for instructions on downloading the Data Files for Students, or contact your instructor for information about accessing the required files.

You will enhance the look of the flyer shown in Figure 1–90.

Perform the following tasks:

1. Use Help to learn about the following formats: grow font, shrink font, change text color, decorative underline, and change bullet.

2. Select the headline and use the Grow Font button to increase its font size just enough so that the headline still fits on a single line. If it wraps to two lines, use the Shrink Font button.

3. Change the font color of all body copy between the headline and the signature line to a color other than Automatic, or Black.

4. Change the picture style of the picture so that it is not the Drop Shadow Rectangle picture style. Add a Glow picture effect to the picture of the baseball player.

5. Change the solid underline below the words, Indoor facility, to a decorative underline.

6. Change the color and width of the border.

7. Change the style of the bullets to a character other than the dot.

8. Change the document properties, including keywords, as specified by your instructor. Save the revised document with a new file name and then submit it in the format specified by your instructor.

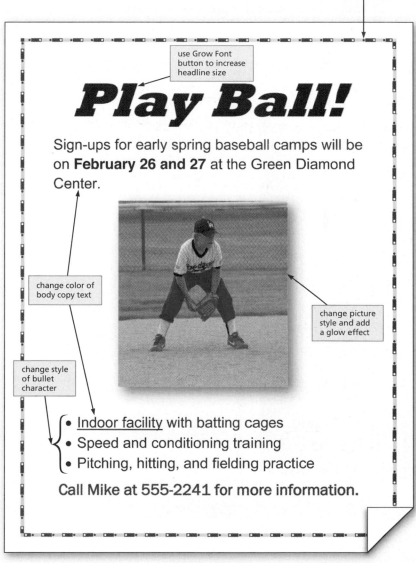

change color and width of border

use Grow Font button to increase headline size

change color of body copy text

change picture style and add a glow effect

change style of bullet character

Figure 1–90

Make It Right

Analyze a document and correct all errors and/or improve the design.

Correcting Spelling and Grammar Errors

Instructions: Start Word. Open the document, Make It Right 1-1 New York Tour Flyer, from the Data Files for Students. See the inside back cover of this book for instructions on downloading the Data Files for Students, or contact your instructor for information on accessing the required files.

The document is a flyer that contains spelling and grammar errors, as shown in Figure 1–91. You are to correct each spelling (red wavy underline) and grammar error (green wavy underline) by right-clicking the flagged text and then clicking the appropriate correction on the shortcut menu. If your screen does not display the wavy underlines, click the Office Button and then click the Word Options button. When the Word Options dialog box is displayed, click Proofing, be sure the 'Hide spelling errors in this document only' and 'Hide grammar errors in this document only' check boxes do not have check marks, and then click the OK button. If your screen still does not display the wavy underlines, redisplay the Word Options dialog box, click Proofing, and then click the Recheck Document button.

Change the document properties, including keywords, as specified by your instructor. Save the revised document with a new file name and then submit it in the format specified by your instructor.

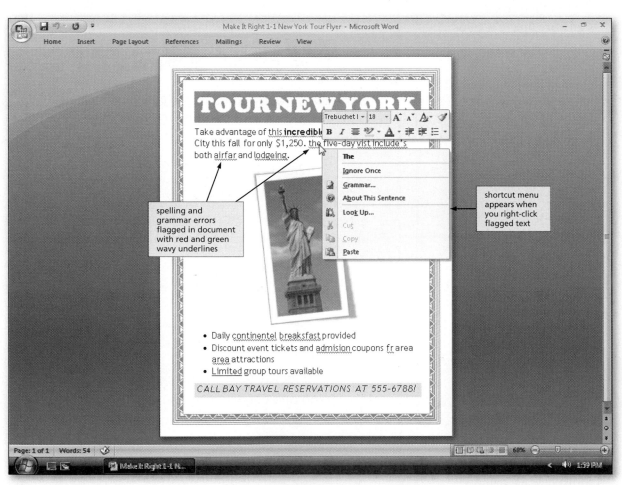

Figure 1–91

In the Lab

Design and/or create a document using the guidelines, concepts, and skills presented in this chapter. Labs are listed in order of increasing difficulty.

Lab 1: Creating a Flyer with a Picture

Problem: You work part-time at Scenic Air. Your boss has asked you to prepare a flyer that advertises aerial tours over the city of Campton. First, you prepare the unformatted flyer shown in Figure 1–92a, and then you format it so that it looks like Figure 1–92b on the next page. *Hint:* Remember, if you make a mistake while formatting the flyer, you can click the Undo button on the Quick Access Toolbar to undo your last action.

Instructions: Perform the following tasks:

1. Display formatting marks on the screen.
2. Type the flyer text, unformatted, as shown in Figure 1–92a. If Word flags any misspelled words as you type, check the spelling of these words and correct them.
3. Save the document on a USB flash drive using the file name, Lab 1-1 Airplane Rides Flyer.
4. Apply the Heading 1 style to the headline. Apply the Heading 2 style to the signature line.
5. Center the headline and the signature line.
6. Change the font and font size of the headline to 48-point Arial Rounded MT Bold, or a similar font.
7. Change the font size of body copy between the headline and the signature line to 22 point.
8. Change the font size of the signature line to 28 point.
9. Bullet the three lines (paragraphs) of text above the signature line.
10. Bold the text, change your view.
11. Italicize the word, aerial.

Airplane Rides

Gain an entirely new vision of Campton by taking an aerial tour. Visitor or local, business or pleasure, the trip will change your view of the city.

Pilots are licensed and experienced

15-, 30-, or 60-minute tours available during daylight hours

Individual and group rates

Call Scenic Air at 555-9883!

Figure 1–92a

Continued >

STUDENT ASSIGNMENTS

In the Lab continued

12. Underline the word, and, in the first bulleted paragraph.

13. Change the style set to Formal.

14. Change the theme fonts to the Metro font set.

15. Change the zoom to 50 percent so the entire page is visible in the document window.

16. Change the spacing before the headline to 0 point. Change the spacing after the first paragraph of body copy to 0 point. Change the spacing before the first bulleted paragraph to 12 point.

17. Insert the picture on the blank line above the bulleted list. The picture is called Airplane Ride over City and is available on the Data Files for Students. Apply the Relaxed Perspective, White picture style to the inserted picture.

18. The entire flyer should fit on a single page. If it flows to two pages, resize the picture or decrease spacing before and after paragraphs until the entire flyer text fits on a single page.

19. Change the document properties, including keywords, as specified by your instructor.

20. Save the flyer again with the same file name.

21. Submit the document, shown in Figure 1–92b, in the format specified by your instructor.

Figure 1–92b

In the Lab

Lab 2: Creating a Flyer with a Picture and a Border

Problem: Your boss at Danvers Nursery has asked you to prepare a flyer that promotes its expanded greenhouses and grounds. You prepare the flyer shown in Figure 1–93. *Hint:* Remember, if you make a mistake while formatting the flyer, you can click the Undo button on the Quick Access Toolbar to undo your last action.

Instructions: Perform the following tasks:

1. Display formatting marks on the screen.
2. Type the flyer text, unformatted. If Word flags any misspelled words as you type, check the spelling of these words and correct them.
3. Save the document on a USB flash drive using the file name, Lab 1-2 Nursery Expansion Flyer.

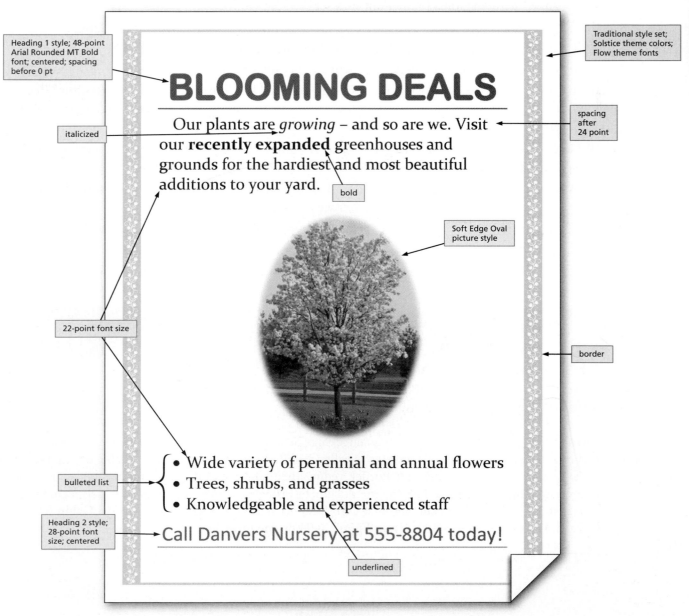

Figure 1–93

Continued >

In the Lab *continued*

4. Apply the Heading 1 style to the headline. Apply the Heading 2 style to the signature line.

5. Center the headline and the signature line.

6. Change the font and font size of the headline to 48-point Arial Rounded MT Bold, or a similar font.

7. Change the font size of body copy between the headline and the signature line to 22 point.

8. Change the font size of the signature line to 28 point.

9. Bullet the three lines (paragraphs) of text above the signature line.

10. Italicize the word, growing.

11. Bold the text, recently expanded.

12. Underline the word, and, in the third bulleted paragraph.

13. Change the style set to Traditional.

14. Change the theme colors to the Solstice color scheme.

15. Change the theme fonts to the Flow font set.

16. Change the zoom to 50 percent so the entire page is visible in the document window.

17. Change the spacing before the headline to 0 point. Change the spacing after the first paragraph of body copy to 24 point. Change the spacing before the first bulleted paragraph to 12 point.

18. Insert the picture on the blank line above the bulleted list. The picture is called Bradford Pear in Bloom and is available on the Data Files for Students. Apply the Soft Edge Oval picture style to the inserted picture.

19. The entire flyer should fit on a single page. If it flows to two pages, resize the picture or decrease spacing before and after paragraphs until the entire flyer text fits on a single page.

20. Add the graphic border, shown in Figure 1–93 on the previous page (about one-third down in the Art gallery). Change the color of the border to Tan, Background 2.

21. Change the document properties, including keywords, as specified by your instructor.

22. Save the flyer again with the same file name.

23. Submit the document, shown in Figure 1–93, in the format specified by your instructor.

In the Lab

Lab 3: Creating a Flyer with a Picture and Resized Border Art

Problem: Your neighbor has asked you to prepare a flyer that promotes her cabin rental business. You prepare the flyer shown in Figure 1–94.

Instructions: Enter the text in the flyer, checking spelling as you type, and then format it as shown in Figure 1–94. The picture to be inserted is called Paddle Boat on Lake and is available on the Data Files for Students. After adding the page border, reduce the point size of its width so that the border is not so predominant on the page. Change the document properties, including keywords, as specified by your instructor. Save the document on a USB flash drive using the file name, Lab 1-3 Cabin Rentals Flyer. Submit the document, shown in Figure 1–94, in the format specified by your instructor.

Figure 1–94

Cases and Places

Apply your creative thinking and problem solving skills to design and implement a solution.

● EASIER   ●● MORE DIFFICULT

● 1: Design and Create a Grand Reopening Flyer

Your friend owns the Craft Barn, a large, year-round craft fair. She recently has renovated and remodeled the facility and is planning a grand reopening. She has asked you to create a flyer advertising this fact. The flyer should contain the following headline: Craft Barn. The first paragraph of text below the headline should read: Pick up a jar of homemade jam or a handcrafted gift at the completely remodeled and renovated Craft Barn, located at 8701 County Road 300 West. Insert the photograph named, Barn and Silo, which is available on the Data Files for Students. The bullet items

Continued >

Cases and Places *continued*

under the photograph should read as follows: first bullet – Expanded and paved parking; second bullet – More than 150 booths; and third bullet – Open Monday through Saturday, 10:00 a.m. to 7:00 p.m. The last line should read: Call 555-5709 for more information! Use the concepts and techniques presented in this chapter to create and format this flyer. Be sure to check spelling and grammar.

• 2: Design and Create a Property Advertisement Flyer

As a part-time employee of Markum Realty, you have been assigned the task of preparing a flyer advertising lakefront property. The headline should read: Lakefront Lot. The first paragraph of text should read as follows: Build the house of your dreams or a weekend getaway on this beautiful lakeside property located on the north side of Lake Pleasant. Insert the photograph named, Lake at Sunset, which is available on the Data Files for Students. Below the photograph, insert the following bullet items: first bullet — City sewer and water available; second bullet – Lot size 110 × 300; third bullet – List price $65,000. The last line should read: Call Markum Realty at 555-0995 for a tour! Use the concepts and techniques presented in this chapter to create and format this flyer. Be sure to check spelling and grammar.

•• 3: Design and Create a Flyer for the Sale of a Business

After 25 years, your Uncle Mitch has decided to sell his ice cream shop and wants you to help him create a sales flyer. The shop is in a choice location at the corner of 135th and Main Street and has an established customer base. The building has an adjacent, paved parking lot, as well as an outdoor seating area. He wants to sell the store and all its contents, including the equipment, tables, booths, and chairs. The 1200-square-foot shop recently was appraised at $200,000, and your uncle is willing to sell for cash or on contract. Use the concepts and techniques presented in this chapter to create and format a sales flyer. Include a headline, descriptive body copy, a signature line, an appropriate photograph or clip art image, a bulleted list, a decorative underline, and if appropriate, a page border. Be sure to check spelling and grammar in the flyer.

•• 4: Design and Create a Flyer that Advertises You

Make It Personal

Everyone has at least one skill, talent, or special capability, which if shared with others, can lead to opportunity for growth, experience, and personal reward. Perhaps you play a musical instrument. If so, you could offer lessons. Maybe you are a skilled carpenter or other tradesman who could advertise your services. If you speak a second language, you could offer tutoring. Budding athletes might harbor a desire to pass on their knowledge by coaching a youth sports team. You may have a special knack for singing, sewing, knitting, photography, typing, housecleaning, or pet care. Carefully consider your own personal capabilities, skills, and talents and then use the concepts and techniques presented in this chapter to create a flyer advertising a service you can provide. Include a headline, descriptive body copy, a signature line, an appropriate photograph or clip art image, a bulleted list, a decorative underline, and if appropriate, a page border. Be sure to check spelling and grammar in the flyer.

•• 5: Redesign and Enhance a Poorly Designed Flyer

Working Together

Public locations, such as stores, schools, and libraries, have bulletin boards or windows for people to post flyers. Often, these bulletin boards or windows have so many flyers that some go unnoticed. Locate a posted flyer on a bulletin board or window that you think might be overlooked. Copy the text from the flyer and distribute it to each team member. Each member then independently should use this text, together with the techniques presented in this chapter, to create a flyer that would be more likely to catch the attention of passersby. Be sure to check spelling and grammar. As a group, critique each flyer and have team members redesign their flyer based on the group's recommendations. Hand in each team member's original and final flyers.

2 | Creating a Research Paper

Objectives

You will have mastered the material in this chapter when you can:

- Describe the MLA documentation style for research papers
- Change line and paragraph spacing in a document
- Use a header to number pages of a document
- Apply formatting using shortcut keys
- Modify paragraph indentation
- Create and modify styles

- Insert and edit citations and their sources
- Add a footnote to a document
- Insert a manual page break
- Create a bibliographical list of sources
- Move text
- Find and replace text
- Use the Research task pane to look up information

2 | Creating a Research Paper

Introduction

In both academic and business environments, you will be asked to write reports. Business reports range from proposals to cost justifications to five-year plans to research findings. Academic reports focus mostly on research findings. A **research paper** is a document you can use to communicate the results of research findings. To write a research paper, you learn about a particular topic from a variety of sources (research), organize your ideas from the research results, and then present relevant facts and/or opinions that support the topic. Your final research paper combines properly credited outside information along with personal insights. Thus, no two research papers — even if about the same topic — will or should be the same.

Project — Research Paper

When preparing a research paper, you should follow a standard documentation style that defines the rules for creating the paper and crediting sources. A variety of documentation styles exists, depending on the nature of the research paper. Each style requires the same basic information; the differences in styles relate to requirements for presenting the information. For example, one documentation style uses the term bibliography for the list of sources, whereas another uses references, and yet a third prefers the title works cited. Two popular documentation styles for research papers are the **Modern Language Association of America (MLA)** and **American Psychological Association (APA)** styles. This chapter uses the MLA documentation style because it is used in a wide range of disciplines.

The project in this chapter follows research paper guidelines and uses Word to create the short research paper shown in Figure 2–1. This paper, which discusses three types of wireless communications, follows the MLA documentation style. Each page contains a page number. The first two pages present the heading (name, course, and date information), paper title, an introduction with a thesis statement, details that support the thesis, and a conclusion. This section of the paper also includes references to research sources. The third page contains a detailed, alphabetical list of the sources used in the research paper.

Overview

As you read through this chapter, you will learn how to create the research paper shown in Figure 2–1 by performing these general tasks:

- Change the document settings.
- Type the research paper.
- Save the research paper.
- Create an alphabetical list of sources.
- Proof and revise the research paper.
- Print the research paper.

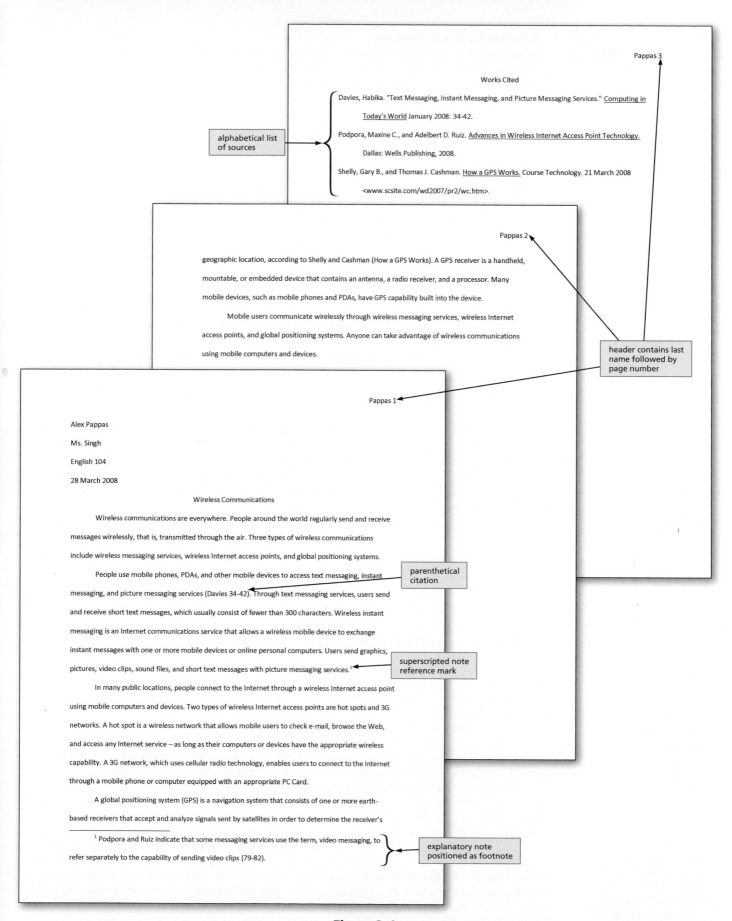

Figure 2–1

Plan
Ahead

General Project Guidelines

When creating a Word document, the actions you perform and decisions you make will affect the appearance and characteristics of the finished document. As you create a research paper, such as the project shown in Figure 2–1 on the previous page, you should follow these general guidelines:

1. **Select a topic.** Spend time brainstorming ideas for a topic. Choose one you find interesting. For shorter papers, narrow down the scope of the topic; for longer papers, broaden the scope. Identify a tentative thesis statement, which is a sentence describing the paper's subject matter.

2. **Research the topic and take notes.** Gather credible, relevant information about the topic that supports the thesis statement. Sources of research include books, magazines, newspapers, and the Internet. As you record facts and ideas, list details about the source: title, author, place of publication, publisher, date of publication, etc. When taking notes, be careful not to **plagiarize**. That is, do not use someone else's work and claim it to be your own. If you copy information directly, place it in quotation marks and identify its source.

3. **Organize your ideas.** Classify your notes into related concepts. Make an outline from the categories of notes. In the outline, identify all main ideas and supporting details.

4. **Write the first draft, referencing sources.** From the outline, compose the paper. Every research paper should include an introduction containing the thesis statement, supporting details, and a conclusion. Follow the guidelines identified in the required documentation style. Reference all sources of information.

5. **Create the list of sources.** Using the formats specified in the required documentation style, completely list all sources referenced in the body of the research paper in alphabetical order.

6. **Proofread and revise the paper.** If possible, proofread the paper with a fresh set of eyes, that is, at least one to two days after completing the first draft. Proofreading involves reading the paper with the intent of identifying errors (spelling, grammar, etc.) and looking for ways to improve the paper (wording, transitions, flow, etc.). Try reading the paper out loud, which helps to identify unclear or awkward wording. Ask someone else to proofread the paper and give you suggestions for improvements.

When necessary, more specific details concerning the above guidelines are presented at appropriate points in the chapter. The chapter also will identify the actions performed and decisions made regarding these guidelines during the creation of the research paper shown in Figure 2–1.

BTW

APA Documentation Style

In the APA style, a separate title page is required instead of placing name and course information on the paper's first page. Double-space all pages of the paper with 1.5" top, bottom, left, and right margins. Indent the first word of each paragraph .5" from the left margin. In the upper-right margin of each page, including the title page, place a running head that consists of the page number double-spaced below a brief summary of the paper title.

MLA Documentation Style

The research paper in this project follows the guidelines presented by the MLA. To follow the MLA style, double-space text on all pages of the paper using one-inch top, bottom, left, and right margins. Indent the first word of each paragraph one-half inch from the left margin. At the right margin of each page, place a page number one-half inch from the top margin. On each page, precede the page number by your last name.

The MLA style does not require a title page. Instead, place your name and course information in a block at the left margin beginning one inch from the top of the page. Center the title one double-space below your name and course information.

In the text of the paper, place author references in parentheses with the page number(s) of the referenced information. The MLA style uses in-text **parenthetical citations** instead of noting each source at the bottom of the page or at the end of the paper. In the MLA style, notes are used only for optional explanatory notes.

If used, explanatory notes elaborate on points discussed in the paper. Use a superscript (raised number) to signal that an explanatory note exists, and also to sequence the notes. Position explanatory notes either at the bottom of the page as footnotes or at the end of the paper as endnotes. Indent the first line of each explanatory note one-half inch from the left margin. Place one space following the superscripted number before beginning the note text. Double-space the note text. At the end of the note text, you may list bibliographic information for further reference.

The MLA style uses the term **works cited** to refer to the bibliographic list of sources at the end of the paper. The works cited page alphabetically lists sources that are referenced directly in the paper. Place the list of sources on a separate numbered page. Center the title, Works Cited, one inch from the top margin. Double-space all lines. Begin the first line of each source at the left margin, indenting subsequent lines of the same source one-half inch from the left margin. List each source by the author's last name, or, if the author's name is not available, by the title of the source. Underline or italicize the title of each source.

Changing Document Settings

The MLA documentation style defines some global formats that apply to the entire research paper. Some of these formats are the default in Word. For example, the default left, right, top, and bottom margin settings in Word are one inch, which meets the MLA style. You will modify, however, the paragraph and line spacing and header formats as required by the MLA style.

After starting Word, the following pages adjust line and paragraph spacing and define a header for the current document.

To Start Word

If you are using a computer to step through the project in this chapter and you want your screens to match the figures in this book, you should change your computer's resolution to 1024×768. For information about how to change a computer's resolution, read Appendix E.

The following steps, which assume Windows Vista is running, start Word based on a typical installation. You may need to ask your instructor how to start Word for your computer.

1 Click the Start button on the Windows Vista taskbar to display the Start menu and then click All Programs at the bottom of the left pane on the Start menu to display the All Programs list.

2 Click Microsoft Office in the All Programs list to display the Microsoft Office list and then click Microsoft Office Word 2007 to start Word and display a new blank document in the Word window.

3 If the Word window is not maximized, click the Maximize button next to the Close button on its title bar to maximize the window.

4 If the Print Layout button is not selected, click it so that your screen layout matches Figure 2–2 on the next page.

5 If your zoom percent is not 100, click the Zoom Out or Zoom In button as many times as necessary until the Zoom level button displays 100% on its face.

Note: If you are using Windows XP, see Appendix F for alternate steps.

To Display Formatting Marks

As discussed in Chapter 1, it is helpful to display formatting marks that indicate where in the document you pressed the ENTER key, SPACEBAR, and other keys. The following step displays formatting marks.

1 If necessary, click Home on the Ribbon to display the Home tab. If the Show/Hide ¶ button on the Home tab is not selected already, click it to display formatting marks on the screen.

BTW

Line Spacing
If the top of a set of characters or a graphical image is chopped off, then line spacing may be set to Exactly. To remedy the problem, change line spacing to 1.0, 1.15, 1.5, 2.0, 2.5, 3.0, or At least (in the Paragraph dialog box), all of which accommodate the largest font or image.

Adjusting Line and Paragraph Spacing

Line spacing is the amount of vertical space between lines of text in a paragraph. **Paragraph spacing** is the amount of space above and below a paragraph. By default, the Normal style places 10 points of blank space after each paragraph and inserts a vertical space equal to 1.15 lines between each line of text. It also automatically adjusts line height to accommodate various font sizes and graphics.

The MLA documentation style requires that you **double-space** the entire research paper. That is, the amount of vertical space between each line of text and above and below paragraphs should be equal to one blank line. The next sets of steps adjust line spacing and paragraph spacing according to the MLA documentation style.

To Double-Space Text

To double-space the lines in the research paper, change the line spacing to 2.0. The following steps change line spacing to double.

1
- Click the Line spacing button on the Home tab to display the Line spacing gallery (Figure 2–2).

Q&A
What do the numbers in the Line spacing gallery represent?

The default line spacing is 1.15 lines. The options 1.0, 2.0, and 3.0 set line spacing to single, double, and triple, respectively. Similarly, the 1.5 and 2.5 options set line spacing to 1.5 and 2.5 lines. All these options adjust line spacing automatically to accommodate the largest font or graphic on a line.

Figure 2–2

2
- Click 2.0 in the Line spacing gallery to change the line spacing to double at the location of the insertion point.

Q&A
Can I change the line spacing of existing text?

Yes. Select the text first and then change the line spacing as described in these steps.

Other Ways

1. Right-click paragraph, click Paragraph on shortcut menu, click Indents and Spacing tab, click Line spacing box arrow, click Double, click OK button
2. Click Paragraph Dialog Box Launcher, click Indents and Spacing tab, click Line spacing box arrow, click Double, click OK button
3. Press CTRL+2

To Remove Space after a Paragraph

The research paper should not have additional blank space after each paragraph. The following steps remove space after a paragraph.

- Click the Line spacing button on the Home tab to display the Line spacing gallery (Figure 2–3).

- Click Remove Space After Paragraph in the Line spacing gallery so that no blank space appears after a paragraph.

Q&A

Can I remove space after existing paragraphs?

Yes. Select the paragraphs first and then remove the space as described in these steps.

Figure 2–3

Other Ways

1. Click Spacing After box arrow on Page Layout tab until 0 pt is displayed

2. Right-click paragraph, click Paragraph on shortcut menu, click Indents and Spacing tab, click Spacing After box arrow until 0 pt is displayed, click OK button

3. Click Paragraph Dialog Box Launcher, click Indents and Spacing tab, click Spacing After box arrow until 0 pt is displayed, click OK button

Headers and Footers

A **header** is text and graphics that print at the top of each page in a document. Similarly, a **footer** is text and graphics that print at the bottom of every page. In Word, headers print in the top margin one-half inch from the top of every page, and footers print in the bottom margin one-half inch from the bottom of each page, which meets the MLA style. In addition to text and graphics, headers and footers can include document information such as the page number, current date, current time, and author's name.

In this research paper, you are to precede the page number with your last name placed one-half inch from the upper-right edge of each page. The procedures on the following pages enter your name and the page number in the header, as specified by the MLA style.

To Switch to the Header

To enter text in the header, you instruct Word to edit the header. The following steps switch from editing the document text to editing the header.

- Click Insert on the Ribbon to display the Insert tab.

- Click the Header button on the Insert tab to display the Header gallery (Figure 2–4).

Q&A

Can I use a built-in header for this research paper?

None of the built-in headers adhere to the MLA style. Thus, you enter your own header contents, instead of using a built-in header, for this research paper.

Figure 2–4

Experiment

- Click the down scroll arrow in the Header gallery to see the available built-in headers.

- Click Edit Header in the Header gallery to switch from the document text to the header, which allows you to edit the contents of the header (Figure 2–5).

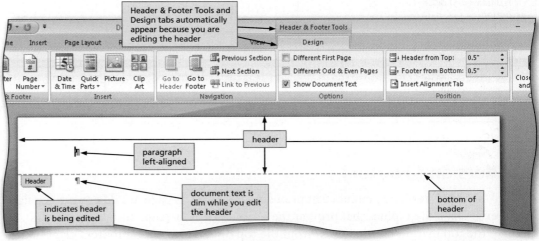

Figure 2–5

Q&A

How do I remove the Header & Footer Tools and Design tabs from the Ribbon?

When you are finished editing the header, you will close it, which removes the Header & Footer Tools tabs.

Other Ways

1. Double-click dimmed header

To Right-Align a Paragraph

The paragraph in the header currently is left-aligned (Figure 2–5). Your last name and the page number should print **right-aligned**, that is, at the right margin. The following step right-aligns a paragraph.

1

- Click Home on the Ribbon to display the Home tab.

- Click the Align Text Right button on the Home tab to right-align the paragraph in the header (Figure 2–6).

Q&A What if I wanted to return the paragraph to left-aligned?

Click the Align Text Right button again, or click the Align Text Left button.

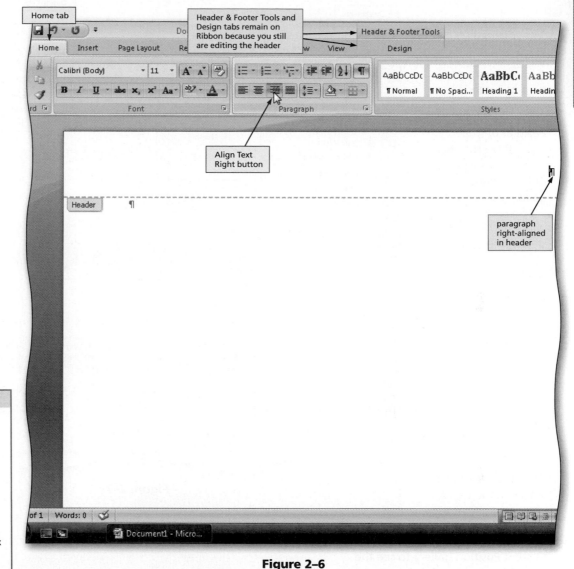

Figure 2–6

Other Ways

1. Right-click paragraph, click Paragraph on shortcut menu, click Indents and Spacing tab, click Alignment box arrow, click Right, click OK button

2. Click Paragraph Dialog Box Launcher, click Indents and Spacing tab, click Alignment box arrow, click Right, click OK button

3. Press CTRL+R

To Enter Text

The following steps enter your last name right-aligned in the header area.

1 Click Design on the Ribbon to display the Design tab.

2 Type Pappas and then press the SPACEBAR to enter the last name in the header.

BTW

Footers
If you wanted to create a footer, you would click the Footer button on the Insert tab and then select the desired built-in footer or click Edit Footer to create a customized footer.

To Insert a Page Number

The next task is to insert the current page number in the header. The following steps insert a page number at the location of the insertion point.

1

- Click the Insert Page Number button on the Design tab to display the Insert Page Number menu.

- Point to Current Position on the Insert Page Number menu to display the Current Position gallery (Figure 2–7).

Figure 2–7

2

 Experiment

- Click the down scroll arrow in the Current Position gallery to see the available page number formats.

3

- If necessary, scroll to the top of the Current Position gallery. Click Plain Number in the Current Position gallery to insert an unformatted page number at the location of the insertion point (Figure 2–8).

Figure 2–8

Other Ways
1. Click Insert Page Number button on Insert tab   2. Click Quick Parts button on Insert tab or on Design tab on Header & Footer Tools tab,   click Field on Quick Parts menu, select Page in Field names list, click OK button

To Close the Header

You are finished entering text in the header. Thus, the next task is to switch back to the document text. The following step closes the header.

- Click the Close Header and Footer button on the Design tab (shown in Figure 2–8) to close the header and switch back to the document text (Figure 2–9).

Q&A

How do I make changes to existing header text?

Switch to the header using the steps described on page WD 80, edit the header as you would edit text in the document window, and then switch back to the document text.

Figure 2–9

Other Ways

1. Double-click dimmed document text

Typing the Research Paper Text

The text of the research paper in this chapter encompasses the first two pages of the paper. You will type the text of the research paper and then modify it later in the chapter, so that it matches Figure 2–1 on page WD 75.

Plan Ahead

Write the first draft, referencing sources.
As you write the first draft of your research paper, be sure it includes the proper components, uses credible sources, and does not contain any plagiarism.

- **Include an introduction, body, and conclusion.** The first paragraph of the paper introduces the topic and captures the reader's attention. The body, which follows the introduction, consists of several paragraphs that support the topic. The conclusion summarizes the main points in the body and restates the topic.

- **Evaluate sources for authority, currency, and accuracy.** Be especially wary of information obtained from the Web. Any person, company, or organization can publish a Web page on the Internet. Ask yourself these questions about the source:

  - Authority: Does a reputable institution or group support the source? Is the information presented without bias? Are the author's credentials listed and verifiable?

  - Currency: Is the information up to date? Are dates of sources listed? What is the last date revised or updated?

  - Accuracy: Is the information free of errors? Is it verifiable? Are the sources clearly identified?

- **Acknowledge all sources of information; do not plagiarize.** Not only is plagiarism unethical, but it is considered an academic crime that can have severe punishments such as failing a course or being expelled from school.

  When you summarize, paraphrase (rewrite information in your own words), present facts, give statistics, quote exact words, or show a map, chart, or other graphical image, you

(continued)

Plan Ahead

(continued)

must acknowledge the source. Information that commonly is known or accessible to the audience constitutes common knowledge and does not need to be acknowledged. If, however, you question whether certain information is common knowledge, you should document it — just to be safe.

To Enter Name and Course Information

As discussed earlier in this chapter, the MLA style does not require a separate title page for research papers. Instead, place your name and course information in a block at the top of the page, below the header, at the left margin. The following steps enter the name and course information in the research paper.

Date Formats
The MLA style prefers the day-month-year (28 March 2008) or month-day-year (March 28, 2008) format. Whichever format you select, use it consistently throughout the paper.

1 Type `Alex Pappas` as the student name and then press the ENTER key.

2 Type `Ms. Singh` as the instructor name and then press the ENTER key.

3 Type `English 104` as the course name and then press the ENTER key.

4 Type `28 March 2008` as the paper due date and then press the ENTER key (Figure 2–10).

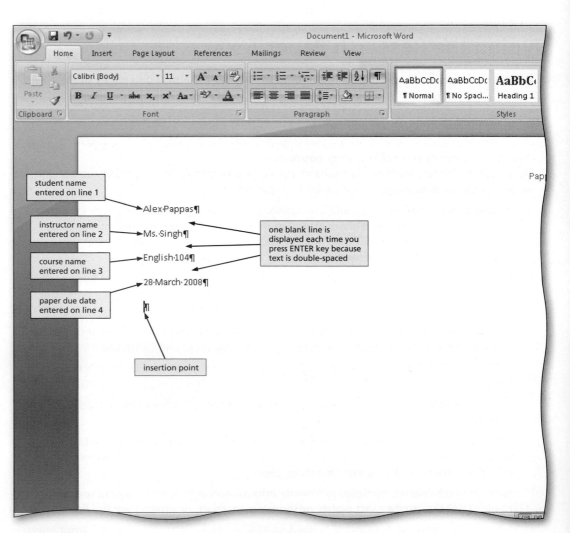

Figure 2–10

To Click and Type

The next step is to enter the title of the research paper centered between the page margins. In Chapter 1, you used the Center button on the Home tab to center text and graphics. As an alternative, you can use **Click and Type** to format and enter text, graphics, and other items. To use Click and Type, you double-click a blank area of the document window. Word automatically formats the item you enter according to the location where you just double-clicked. The following steps use Click and Type to center and then type the title of the research paper.

Experiment

- Move the mouse pointer around the document below the entered name and course information and observe the various icons that appear with the I-beam.

- Position the mouse pointer in the center of the document at the approximate location for the research paper title until a center icon appears below the I-beam (Figure 2–11).

Q&A

What are the other icons that appear in the Click and Type pointer?

A left-align icon appears to the right of the I-beam when the Click and Type pointer is in certain locations on the left side of the document window. A right-align icon appears to the left of the icon when the Click and Type pointer is in certain locations on the right side of the document window.

Figure 2–11

- Double-click to center the paragraph mark and insertion point between the left and right margins.

- Type `Wireless Communications` as the paper title and then press the ENTER key (Figure 2–12).

Figure 2–12

Shortcut Keys

Word has many shortcut keys for your convenience while typing. Table 2–1 lists the common shortcut keys for formatting characters. Table 2–2 lists common shortcut keys for formatting paragraphs.

Table 2–1 Shortcut Keys for Formatting Characters

Character Formatting Task	Shortcut Keys	Character Formatting Task	Shortcut Keys
All capital letters	CTRL+SHIFT+A	Italic	CTRL+I
Bold	CTRL+B	Remove character formatting (plain text)	CTRL+SPACEBAR
Case of letters	SHIFT+F3	Small uppercase letters	CTRL+SHIFT+K
Decrease font size	CTRL+SHIFT+<	Subscript	CTRL+EQUAL SIGN
Decrease font size 1 point	CTRL+[	Superscript	CTRL+SHIFT+PLUS SIGN
Double-underline	CTRL+SHIFT+D	Underline	CTRL+U
Increase font size	CTRL+SHIFT+>	Underline words, not spaces	CTRL+SHIFT+W
Increase font size 1 point	CTRL+]		

Table 2–2 Shortcut Keys for Formatting Paragraphs

Paragraph Formatting	Shortcut Keys	Paragraph Formatting	Shortcut Keys
1.5 line spacing	CTRL+5	Justify paragraph	CTRL+J
Add/remove one line above paragraph	CTRL+0 (ZERO)	Left-align paragraph	CTRL+L
Center paragraph	CTRL+E	Remove hanging indent	CTRL+SHIFT+T
Decrease paragraph indent	CTRL+SHIFT+M	Remove paragraph formatting	CTRL+Q
Double-space lines	CTRL+2	Right-align paragraph	CTRL+R
Hanging indent	CTRL+T	Single-space lines	CTRL+1
Increase paragraph indent	CTRL+M		

BTW

Shortcut Keys
To print a complete list of shortcut keys in Word, click the Microsoft Office Word Help button near the upper-right corner of the Word window, type `shortcut keys` in the 'Type words to search for' text box at the top of the Word Help window, press the ENTER key, click the Keyboard shortcuts for Microsoft Office Word link, click the Show All link in the upper-right corner of the Help window, click the Print button in the Help window, and then click the Print button in the Print dialog box.

To Format Text Using Shortcut Keys

The paragraphs below the paper title should be left-aligned, instead of centered. Thus, the next step is to left-align the paragraph below the paper title. When your fingers are already on the keyboard, you may prefer using **shortcut keys**, or keyboard key combinations, to format text as you type it. The following step left-aligns a paragraph using the shortcut keys CTRL+L. (Recall from Chapter 1 that a notation such as CTRL+L means to press the letter l on the keyboard while holding down the CTRL key.)

1 Press CTRL+L to left-align the current paragraph, that is, the paragraph containing the insertion point.

Q&A Why would I use a keyboard shortcut, instead of the Ribbon, to format text?

Switching between the mouse and the keyboard takes time. If your hands are already on the keyboard, use a keyboard shortcut. If your hand is on the mouse, use the Ribbon.

To Save a Document

You have performed many tasks while creating the research paper and do not want to risk losing the work completed thus far. Accordingly, you should save the document. For a detailed example of the procedure summarized below, refer to pages WD 19 through WD 21 in Chapter 1.

Note: If you are using Windows XP, see Appendix F for alternate steps.

1 With a USB flash drive connected to one of the computer's USB ports, click the Save button on the Quick Access Toolbar to display the Save As dialog box.

2 Type `Wireless Communications Paper` in the File name text box to change the file name.

3 If Computer is not displayed in the Favorite Links section, drag the top or bottom edge of the Save As dialog box until Computer is displayed. Click Computer in the Favorite Links section and then double-click your USB flash drive in the list of available drives.

4 Click the Save button in the Save As dialog box to save the document on the USB flash drive with the file name, Wireless Communications Paper.

To Display the Rulers

According to the MLA style, the first line of each paragraph in the research paper is to be indented one-half inch from the left margin. Although you can use a dialog box to indent paragraphs, Word provides a quicker way through the **horizontal ruler**. This ruler displays at the top edge of the document window just below the Ribbon. Word also provides a **vertical ruler** that displays along the left edge of the Word window. The following steps display the rulers.

Experiment

- Repeatedly click the View Ruler button on the vertical scroll bar to see the how this button is used to both show and hide the rulers.

- If the rulers are not displayed, click the View Ruler button on the vertical scroll bar because you want to use the ruler to indent paragraphs (Figure 2–13).

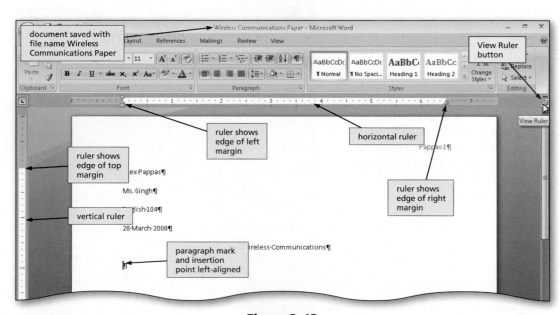

Figure 2–13

Q&A

Can I use the rulers for other tasks?

In addition to indenting paragraphs, you can use the rulers to set tab stops, change page margins, and adjust column widths.

Other Ways
1. Click View Ruler check box on View tab

To First-Line Indent Paragraphs

The first line of each paragraph in the research paper is to be indented one-half inch from the left margin. You can use the horizontal ruler, usually simply called the **ruler**, to indent just the first line of a paragraph, called **first-line indent**.

The left margin on the ruler contains two triangles above a square. The **First Line Indent marker** is the top triangle at the 0" mark on the ruler (Figure 2–14). The bottom triangle is discussed later in this chapter. The small square at the 0" mark is the Left Indent marker. The **Left Indent marker** allows you to change the entire left margin, whereas the First Line Indent marker indents only the first line of the paragraph. The following steps first-line indent paragraphs in the research paper.

- With the insertion point on the paragraph mark below the research paper title, point to the First Line Indent marker on the ruler (Figure 2–14).

Figure 2–14

- Drag the First Line Indent marker to the .5" mark on the ruler to display a vertical dotted line in the document window, which indicates the proposed location of the first line of the paragraph (Figure 2–15).

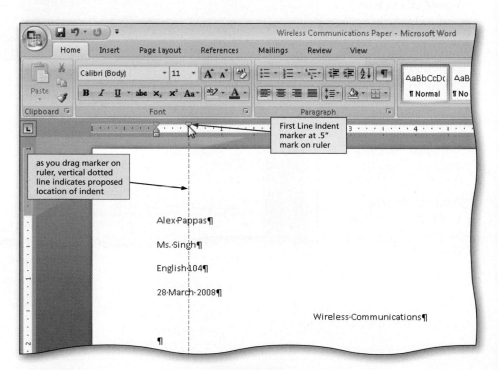

Figure 2–15

3

• Release the mouse button to place the First Line Indent marker at the .5" mark on the ruler, or one-half inch from the left margin (Figure 2–16).

Figure 2–16

4

• Type `Wireless communications are everywhere. People around the world regularly send and receive messages wirelessly, that is, transmitted through the air.` and notice that Word automatically indented the first line of the paragraph by one-half inch (Figure 2–17).

Will I have to set first-line indent for each paragraph in the paper?

No. Each time you press the ENTER key, paragraph formatting in the previous paragraph carries forward to the next paragraph. Thus, once you set the first-line indent, its format carries forward automatically to each subsequent paragraph you type.

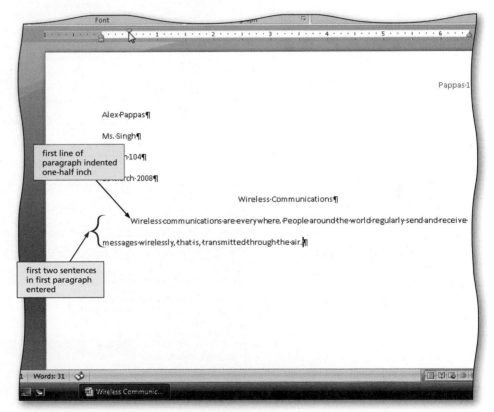

Figure 2–17

Other Ways

1. Right-click paragraph, click Paragraph on shortcut menu, click Indents and Spacing tab, click Special box arrow, click First line, click OK button

2. Click Paragraph Dialog Box Launcher, click Indents and Spacing tab, click Special box arrow, click First line, click OK button

3. Press TAB key at beginning of paragraph

To Create a Quick Style

Recall from Chapter 1 that a Quick Style is a predefined style that appears in the Styles gallery on the Ribbon. You use styles in the Styles gallery to apply defined formats to text. Later in this chapter, you will apply the formats of the research paper paragraph to the paragraphs in the footnote. To accomplish this task, you can create a Quick Style based on the formats in the current paragraph. That is, text is double-spaced with the first line of the paragraph indented and no space after the paragraph. The following steps first select the paragraph and then create a Quick Style based on the formats in the selected paragraph.

- Position the mouse pointer in the paragraph below the title and then triple-click; that is, press the mouse button three times in rapid succession, to select the paragraph.

- Right-click the selected paragraph to display a shortcut menu.

- Point to Styles on the shortcut menu to display the Styles submenu (Figure 2–18).

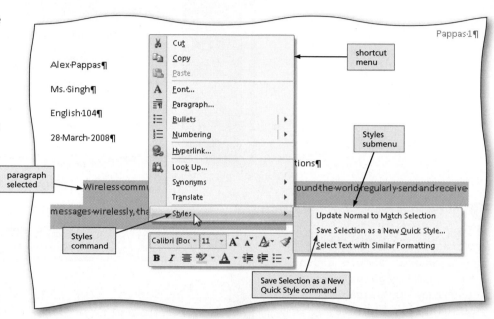

Figure 2–18

❷

- Click Save Selection as a New Quick Style on the Styles sub-menu to display the Create New Style from Formatting dialog box.

- Type Research Paper Paragraphs in the Name text box (Figure 2–19).

Figure 2–19

3

- Click the OK button to create the new Quick Style and add it to the Styles gallery (Figure 2–20).

Q&A

How can I see the formats assigned to a Quick Style?

Click the Styles Dialog Box Launcher. When the Styles task pane appears, position the mouse pointer on any style to display its formats in a ScreenTip. When finished, click the Close button in the task pane.

Research Paper Paragraphs Quick Style added to Styles gallery

Styles Dialog Box Launcher

Figure 2–20

Other Ways
1. Click More button in Styles gallery on Home tab, click Save Selection as a New   Quick Style, enter name of new Quick Style, click OK button

To AutoCorrect as You Type

As you type, you may make typing, spelling, capitalization, or grammar errors. For this reason, Word provides an **AutoCorrect** feature that automatically corrects these kinds of errors as you type them in the document. For example, if you type the text ahve, Word automatically changes it to the correct spelling, have, when you press the SPACEBAR or a punctuation mark key such as a period or comma.

Word has predefined many commonly misspelled words, which it automatically corrects for you. In the following steps, the word wireless is misspelled intentionally as wreless to illustrate the AutoCorrect as you type feature.

1

- Press CTRL+END to move the insertion point to the end of the document.

- Press the SPACEBAR.

- Type the beginning of the next sentence, misspelling the word, wireless, as follows: Three types of wireless communications include wireless messaging services, wreless (Figure 2–21).

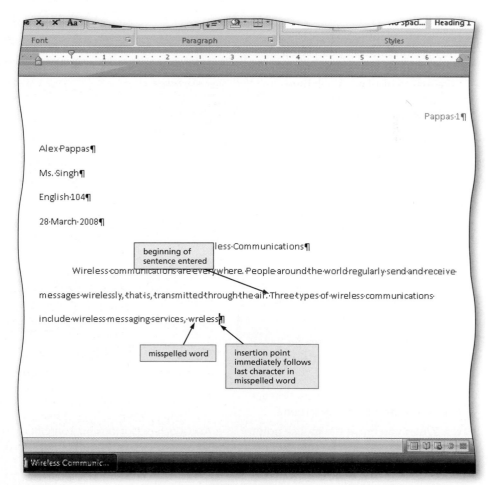

Pappas 1¶

Alex·Pappas¶

Ms.·Singh¶

English·104¶

28·March·2008¶

beginning of sentence entered

less·Communications¶

Wireless·communications·are·everywhere.·People·around·the·world·regularly·send·and·receive·

messages·wirelessly,·that·is,·transmitted·through·the·air.·Three·types·of·wireless·communications·

include·wireless·messaging·services,·wreless¶

misspelled word

insertion point immediately follows last character in misspelled word

Wireless·Communic...

Figure 2–21

2

- Press the SPACEBAR and watch Word automatically correct the misspelled word.

- Type the rest of the sentence (Figure 2–22): Internet access points, and global positioning systems.

Figure 2–22

To Use the AutoCorrect Options Button

When you position the mouse pointer on text that Word automatically corrected, a small blue box appears below the text. If you point to the small blue box, Word displays the AutoCorrect Options button. When you click the **AutoCorrect Options button**, Word displays a menu that allows you to undo a correction or change how Word handles future automatic corrections of this type. The following steps illustrate the AutoCorrect Options button and menu.

1

- Position the mouse pointer in the text automatically corrected by Word (in this case, the word wireless) to display a small blue box below the automatically corrected word (Figure 2–23).

Figure 2–23

2

- Point to the small blue box to display the AutoCorrect Options button.

- Click the AutoCorrect Options button to display the AutoCorrect Options menu (Figure 2–24).

- Press the ESCAPE key to remove the AutoCorrect Options menu from the screen.

Figure 2–24

Q&A

Do I need to remove the AutoCorrect Options button from the screen?

No. When you move the mouse pointer, the AutoCorrect Options button will disappear from the screen. If, for some reason, you wanted to remove the AutoCorrect Options button from the screen, you could press the ESCAPE key a second time.

To Create an AutoCorrect Entry

In addition to the predefined list of AutoCorrect spelling, capitalization, and grammar errors, you can create your own AutoCorrect entries to add to the list. For example, if you tend to type the word mobile as moble, you should create an AutoCorrect entry for it. The following steps create an AutoCorrect entry.

1
- Click the Office Button to display the Office Button menu (Figure 2–25).

Figure 2–25

2
- Click the Word Options button on the Office Button menu to display the Word Options dialog box.

- Click Proofing in the left pane to display proofing options in the right pane.

- Click the AutoCorrect Options button in the right pane to display the AutoCorrect dialog box.

- When Word displays the AutoCorrect dialog box, type moble in the Replace text box.

- Press the TAB key and then type mobile in the With text box (Figure 2–26).

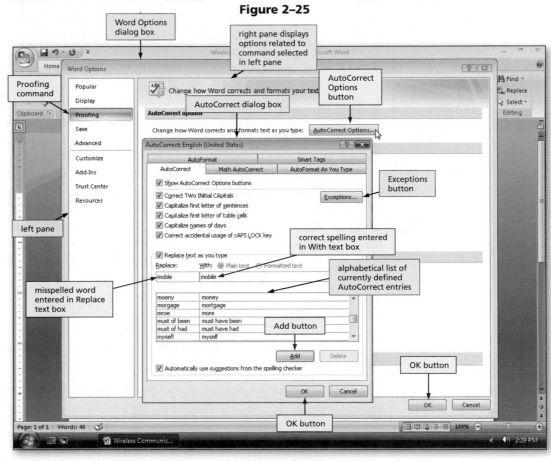

Figure 2–26

3
- Click the Add button in the AutoCorrect dialog box. (If your dialog box displays a Replace button instead, click it and then click the Yes button in the Microsoft Office Word dialog box.)

- Click the OK button to add the entry alphabetically to the list of words to correct automatically as you type.

- Click the OK button in the Word Options dialog box.

The AutoCorrect Dialog Box

In addition to creating AutoCorrect entries for words you commonly misspell or mistype, you can create entries for abbreviations, codes, and so on. For example, you could create an AutoCorrect entry for asap, indicating that Word should replace this text with the phrase, as soon as possible.

If, for some reason, you do not want Word to correct automatically as you type, you can turn off the Replace text as you type feature by clicking the Word Options button on the Office Button menu, clicking Proofing in the left pane of the Word Options dialog box, clicking the AutoCorrect Options button in the right pane of the Word Options dialog box (Figure 2–26 on the previous page), clicking the 'Replace text as you type' check box to remove the check mark, and then clicking the OK button in each open dialog box.

The AutoCorrect sheet in the AutoCorrect dialog box (Figure 2–26) contains other check boxes that correct capitalization errors if the check boxes are selected. If you type two capital letters in a row, such as TH, Word makes the second letter lowercase, Th. If you begin a sentence with a lowercase letter, Word capitalizes the first letter of the sentence. If you type the name of a day in lowercase, such as tuesday, Word capitalizes the first letter of the day, Tuesday. If you leave the CAPS LOCK key on and begin a new sentence, such as aFTER, Word corrects the typing, After, and turns off the CAPS LOCK key.

Sometimes you do not want Word to AutoCorrect a particular word or phrase. For example, you may use the code WD. in your documents. Because Word automatically capitalizes the first letter of a sentence, the character you enter following the period will be capitalized (in the previous sentence, it would capitalize the letter i in the word, in). To allow the code WD. to be entered into a document and still leave the AutoCorrect feature turned on, you should set an exception. To set an exception to an AutoCorrect rule, click the Word Options button on the Office Button menu, click Proofing in the left pane of the Word Options dialog box, click the AutoCorrect Options button in the right pane of the Word Options dialog box, click the Exceptions button (Figure 2–26), click the appropriate tab in the AutoCorrect Exceptions dialog box, type the exception entry in the text box, click the Add button, click the Close button in the AutoCorrect Exceptions dialog box, and then click the OK button in each of the remaining dialog boxes.

To Enter More Text

The next step is to continue typing text in the research paper up to the location of the citation.

1 Press the ENTER key, so that you can begin typing the text in the second paragraph.

2 Type `People use mobile phones, PDAs, and other mobile devices to access text messaging, instant messaging, and picture messaging services` and then press the SPACEBAR.

Citations

Both the MLA and APA guidelines suggest the use of in-text parenthetical citations (placed at the end of a sentence), instead of footnoting each source of material in a paper. These parenthetical acknowledgments guide the reader to the end of the paper for complete information about the source.

BTW

Automatic Corrections
If you do not want to keep a change automatically made by Word and you immediately notice the automatic correction, you can undo the change by clicking the Undo button on the Quick Access Toolbar or pressing CTRL+Z. You also can undo a correction through the AutoCorrect Options button, which was shown on page WD 92.

> **Reference all sources.**
> During your research, be sure to record essential publication information about each of your sources. Following is a sample list of types of required information.
>
> - Book: full name of author(s), complete title of book, edition (if available), volume (if available), publication city, publication year
> - Magazine: full name of author(s), complete title of article, magazine title, date of magazine, page numbers of article
> - Web site: full name of author(s), title of Web site, date viewed, Web address

Word provides tools to assist you with inserting citations in a paper and later generating a list of sources from the citations. With a documentation style selected, Word automatically formats the citations and list of sources. The process for adding citations in Word is as follows:

1. Modify the documentation style, if necessary.
2. Insert a citation placeholder.
3. Enter the source information for the citation.

You can combine Steps 2 and 3, where you insert the citation placeholder and enter the source information at once. Or, you can insert the citation placeholder as you write and then enter the source information for the citation at a later time. While entering the research paper in this chapter, you will use both methods.

To Change the Bibliography Style

The first step in inserting a citation is to be sure the citations and sources will be formatted using the correct documentation style, called the bibliography style in Word. The following steps change the specified documentation style.

- Click References on the Ribbon to display the References tab.

- Click the Bibliography Style box arrow on the References tab to display a gallery of predefined documentation styles (Figure 2–27).

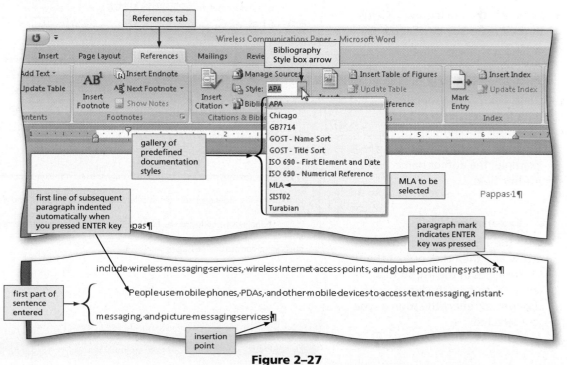

2

- Click MLA in the Bibliography Style gallery to change the documentation style to MLA.

Figure 2–27

To Insert a Citation and Create Its Source

With the documentation style selected, the next task is to insert a citation placeholder and enter the source information. You can accomplish these steps at once by instructing Word to add a new source. The following steps add a new source for a magazine (periodical) article.

- Click the Insert Citation button on the References tab to display the Insert Citation menu (Figure 2–28).

Figure 2–28

- Click Add New Source on the Insert Citation menu to display the Create Source dialog box (Figure 2–29).

Q&A

What are the Bibliography Fields in the Create Source dialog box?

A **field** is a placeholder for data whose contents can change. You enter data in some fields; Word supplies data for others. In this case, you enter the contents of the fields for a particular source, for example, the author name in the Author field.

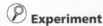 **Experiment**

- Click the Type of Source box arrow and then click one of the source types in the list, so that you can see how the list of fields changes to reflect the source type you selected.

Figure 2–29

- If necessary, click the Type of Source box arrow and then click Article in a Periodical, so that the list shows fields required for a magazine (periodical).

- Click the Author text box. Type Davies, Habika as the author.

- Click the Title text box. Type Text Messaging, Instant Messaging, and Picture Messaging as the article title.

- Press the TAB key and then type Computing in Today's World as the periodical title.

- Press the TAB key and then type 2008 as the year.

- Press the TAB key and then type January as the month.

- Press the TAB key twice and then type 34-42 as the pages (Figure 2–30).

Figure 2–30

- Click the OK button to close the dialog box, create the source, and insert the citation in the document at the location of the insertion point (Figure 2–31).

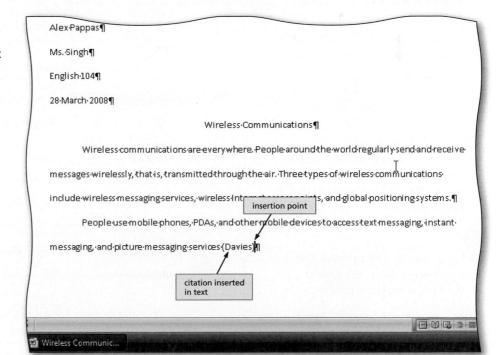

Figure 2–31

To Edit a Citation

In the MLA style, if a source has page numbers, you should include them in the citation. Thus, Word provides a means to enter the page numbers to be displayed in the citation. The following steps edit a citation, so that the page numbers appear in it.

- Click somewhere in the citation to be edited, in this case somewhere in (Davies), which selects the citation and displays the Citation Options box arrow.

- Click the Citation Options box arrow to display the Citation Options menu (Figure 2–32).

Q&A

What is the purpose of the tab to the left of the selected citation?

If, for some reason, you wanted to move a citation to a different location in the document, you would select it and then drag the citation tab to the desired location.

Figure 2–32

- Click Edit Citation on the Citation Options menu to display the Edit Citation dialog box.

- Type 34–42 in the Pages text box (Figure 2–33).

Figure 2–33

- Click the OK button to close the dialog box and add the page numbers to the citation in the document (Figure 2–34).

- Press the END key to move the insertion point to the end of the line, which also deselects the citation.

- Press the PERIOD key to end the sentence.

Figure 2–34

To Enter More Text

The next step is to continue typing text in the research paper up to the location of the footnote.

1 Press the SPACEBAR.

2 Type these three sentences (Figure 2–35): `Through text messaging services, users send and receive short text messages, which usually consist of fewer than 300 characters. Wireless instant messaging is an Internet communications service that allows a wireless mobile device to exchange instant messages with one or more mobile devices or online personal computers. Users send graphics, pictures, video clips, sound files, and short text messages with picture messaging services.`

BTW

Edit a Source
To edit a source, click somewhere in the citation, click the Citation Options box arrow, and then click Edit Source on the Citation Options menu to display the Edit Source dialog box (which resembles the Create Source dialog box). Make necessary changes and then click the OK button.

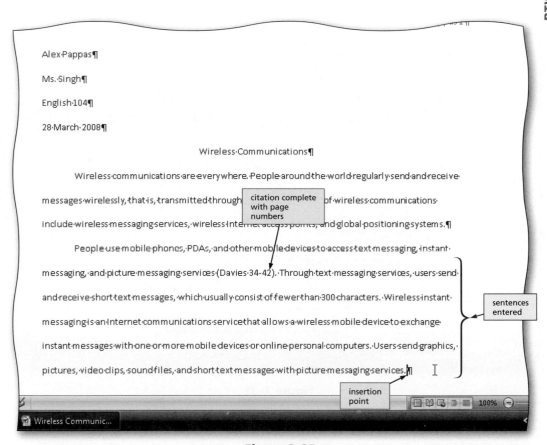

Figure 2–35

Footnotes

As discussed earlier in this chapter, explanatory notes are optional in the MLA documentation style. They are used primarily to elaborate on points discussed in the body of a research paper. The MLA style specifies that a superscript (raised number) be used for a **note reference mark** to signal that an explanatory note exists either at the bottom of the page as a **footnote** or at the end of the document as an **endnote**.

In Word, **note text** can be any length and format. Word automatically numbers notes sequentially by placing a note reference mark in the body of the document and also to the left of the note text. If you insert, rearrange, or remove notes, Word renumbers any subsequent note reference marks according to their new sequence in the document.

To Insert a Footnote Reference Mark

The following step inserts a footnote reference mark in the document at the location of the insertion point and also at the location where the footnote text will be typed.

• With the insertion point positioned as shown in Figure 2–35 on the previous page, click the Insert Footnote button on the References tab to display a note reference mark (a superscripted 1) in two places: (1) in the document window at the location of the insertion point and (2) at the bottom of the page where the footnote will be positioned, just below a separator line (Figure 2–36).

Q&A

What if I wanted explanatory notes to be positioned as endnotes instead of as footnotes?

You would click the Insert Endnote button on the References tab, which places the separator line and the endnote text at the end of the document, instead of the bottom of the page containing the reference.

Figure 2–36

Other Ways

1. Press CTRL+ALT+F

To Enter Footnote Text

The next step is to type the footnote text to the right of the note reference mark below the separator line.

1 Type the footnote text up to the citation: Podpora and Ruiz indicate that some messaging services use the term, video messaging, to refer separately to the capability of sending video clips and then press the SPACEBAR.

To Insert a Citation Placeholder

Earlier in this chapter, you inserted a citation and its source at once. Sometimes, you may not have the source information readily available and would prefer entering it at a later time.

In the footnote, you will insert a placeholder for the citation and enter the source information later. The following steps insert a citation placeholder.

1

- With the insertion point positioned as shown in Figure 2–37, click the Insert Citation button on the References tab to display the Insert Citation menu (Figure 2–37).

Figure 2–37

2

- Click Add New Placeholder on the Insert Citation menu to display the Placeholder Name dialog box.

- Type Podpora as the tag name for the source (Figure 2–38).

What is a tag name?

A tag name is an identifier that links a citation to a source. Word automatically creates a tag name when you enter a source. When you create a citation placeholder, enter a meaningful tag name, which will appear in the citation placeholder until you edit the source.

3

- Click the OK button to close the dialog box and insert the tag name in the citation placeholder.

- Press the PERIOD key to end the sentence.

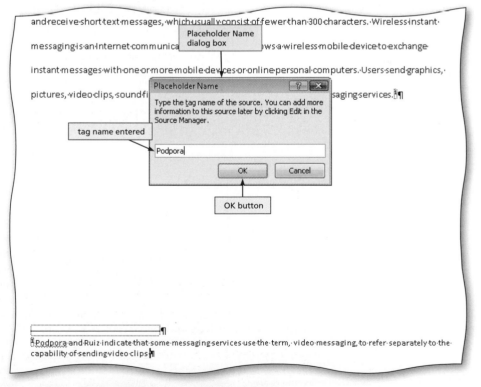

Figure 2–38

Footnote Text Style

When you insert a footnote, Word formats it using the Footnote Text style, which does not adhere to the MLA documentation style. For example, notice in Figure 2–38 on the previous page that the footnote text is single-spaced, left-aligned, and a smaller font size than the text in the research paper. According to the MLA style, notes should be formatted like all other paragraphs in the paper.

You could change the paragraph formatting of the footnote text to first-line indent and double-spacing and then change the font size from 10 to 11 point. If you use this technique, however, you will need to change the format of the footnote text for each footnote you enter into the document.

A more efficient technique is to modify the format of the Footnote Text style so that every footnote you enter in the document will use the formats defined in this style.

To Modify a Style Using a Shortcut Menu

The Footnote Text style should be based on the Research Paper Paragraphs style defined earlier in this chapter. Because the Footnote Text style specifically set paragraphs to single-spaced and the font size to 10 point, you will need to modify those formats to double-spaced paragraphs and 11-point font. The following steps modify the Footnote Text style.

- Right-click the note text in the footnote to display a shortcut menu related to footnotes (Figure 2–39).

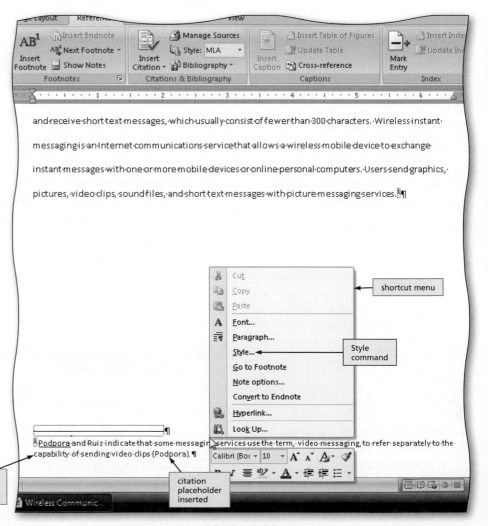

Figure 2–39

2

- Click Style on the shortcut menu to display the Style dialog box. If necessary, click Footnote Text in the Styles list.

- Click the Modify button in the Style dialog box to display the Modify Style dialog box.

- Click the 'Style based on' box arrow and then click Research Paper Paragraphs so that the Footnote Text style is based on the Research Paper Paragraphs style.

- Click the 'Style for following paragraph' box arrow and then scroll to and click Research Paper Paragraphs so that the additional footnote paragraphs are based on the Research Paper Paragraphs style.

Figure 2–40

- Click the Font Size box arrow and then click 11 in the Font Size list to change the font size to 11.

- Click the Double Space button to set the line spacing to double (Figure 2–40).

3

- Click the OK button in the Modify Style dialog box to close the dialog box.

- Click the Apply button in the Style dialog box to apply the style changes to the footnote text (Figure 2–41).

Q&A

Will all footnotes use this modified style?

Yes. Any future footnotes entered in the document will use an 11-point font with the paragraphs first-line indented and double-spaced.

Figure 2–41

Other Ways		
1. Click Styles Dialog Box Launcher, click Footnote Text in list, click Footnote Text box arrow, click Modify,	change settings, click OK button 2. Click Styles Dialog Box Launcher, click Manage Styles	button, scroll to Footnote Text and then select it, click Modify button, change settings, click OK button in each dialog box

To Edit a Source

When you typed the footnote text for this research paper, you inserted a citation placeholder for the source. You now have the source information and are ready to enter it. The following steps edit the source.

- Click somewhere in the citation placeholder to be edited, in this case (Podpora), to select the citation placeholder.

- Click the Citation Options box arrow to display the Citation Options menu (Figure 2–42).

Figure 2–42

- Click Edit Source on the Citation Options menu to display the Edit Source dialog box.

- If necessary, click the Type of Source box arrow and then click Book, so that the list shows fields required for a book.

- Click the Author text box. Type `Podpora, Maxine C., and Adelbert D. Ruiz` as the author.

- Click the Title text box. Type `Advances in Wireless Internet Access Point Technology` as the book title.

- Press the TAB key and then type `2008` as the year.

- Press the TAB key and then type `Dallas` as the city.

- Press the TAB key and then type `Wells Publishing` as the publisher (Figure 2–43).

- Click the OK button to close the dialog box and create the source.

Figure 2–43

Other Ways

1. Click Manage Sources button on References tab, click placeholder source in Current List, click Edit button

To Edit a Citation

In the MLA style, if you reference the author's name in the text, you should not list it again in the parenthetical citation. Instead, just list the page number in the citation. The following steps edit the citation, suppressing the author but displaying the page numbers.

1 If necessary, click somewhere in the citation to be edited, in this case (Podpora), to select the citation and display the Citation Options box arrow.

2 Click the Citation Options box arrow to display the Citation Options menu.

3 Click Edit Citation on the Citation Options menu to display the Edit Citation dialog box.

4 Type 79-82 in the Pages text box.

5 Click the Author check box to place a check mark in it (Figure 2–44).

6 Click the OK button to close the dialog box, remove the author name from the citation in the footnote, and add page numbers to the citation.

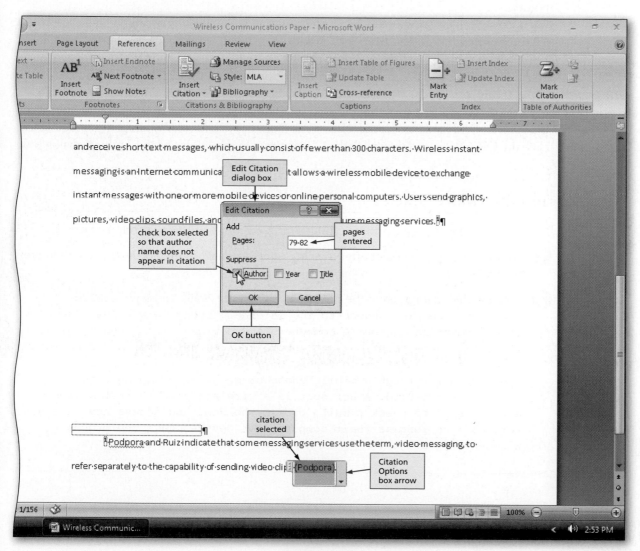

Figure 2–44

Working with Footnotes and Endnotes

You edit footnote text just as you edit any other text in the document. To delete or move a note reference mark, however, you must be in the document text (not in the footnote text).

To delete a note, select the note reference mark in the document text (not in the footnote text) by dragging through the note reference mark and then click the Cut button on the Home tab. Another way to delete a note is to click immediately to the right of the note reference mark in the document text and then press the BACKSPACE key twice, or click immediately to the left of the note reference mark in the document text and then press the DELETE key twice.

To move a note to a different location in a document, select the note reference mark in the document text (not in the footnote text), click the Cut button on the Home tab, click the location where you want to move the note, and then click the Paste button on the Home tab. When you move or delete notes, Word automatically renumbers any remaining notes in the correct sequence.

If you position the mouse pointer on the note reference mark, the note text displays above the note reference mark as a ScreenTip. To remove the ScreenTip, move the mouse pointer.

If, for some reason, you wanted to change the format of note reference marks in footnotes or endnotes (i.e., from 1, 2, 3, to A, B, C), you would click the Footnotes Dialog Box Launcher to display the Footnote and Endnote dialog box, click the Number format box arrow, click the desired number format in the list, and then click the OK button.

If, for some reason, you wanted to convert footnotes to endnotes, you would click the Footnotes Dialog Box Launcher to display the Footnote and Endnote dialog box, click the Convert button, make sure the 'Convert all footnotes to endnotes' option button is selected, click the OK button, and then click the Close button in the Footnote and Endnote dialog box.

To Enter More Text

The next step is to continue typing text in the body of the research paper.

1 Position the insertion point after the note reference mark in the document, and then press the ENTER key.

2 Type the third paragraph of the research paper (Figure 2–45): In many public locations, people connect to the Internet through a wireless Internet access point using mobile computers and devices. Two types of wireless Internet access points are hot spots and 3-G networks. A 3-G network, which uses cellular radio technology, enables users to connect to the Internet through a mobile phone or computer equipped with an appropriate PC Card. A hot spot is a wireless network that allows mobile users to check e-mail, browse the Web, and access any Internet service - as long as their computers or devices have the proper wireless capability.

BTW

Spacing after Punctuation
Because word processing documents use variable character fonts, it often is difficult to determine in a printed document how many times someone has pressed the SPACEBAR between sentences. The rule is to press the SPACEBAR only once after periods, colons, and other punctuation marks.

To Count Words

Often when you write papers, you are required to compose the papers with a minimum number of words. The minimum requirement for the research paper in this chapter is 325 words. You can look on the status bar and see the total number of words thus far in a document. For example, Figure 2–45 shows the research paper has 250 words, but you are not sure if that count includes the words in your footnote. The following steps display the Word Count dialog box, so that you can verify whether the footnote text is included in the count.

1

- Click the Word Count indicator on the status bar to display the Word Count dialog box.

- If necessary, place a check mark in the 'Include textboxes, footnotes and endnotes' check box (Figure 2-45).

Q&A Why do the statistics in my Word Count dialog box differ from Figure 2–45?

Depending on the accuracy of your typing, your statistics may differ.

2

- Click the Close button to close the dialog box.

Q&A Can I display statistics for just a section of the document?

Yes. Select the section and then click the Word Count indicator on the status bar to display statistics about the selected text.

Figure 2–45

Other Ways

1. Click Word Count button on Review tab
2. Press CTRL+SHIFT+G

Automatic Page Breaks

As you type documents that exceed one page, Word automatically inserts page breaks, called **automatic page breaks** or **soft page breaks**, when it determines the text has filled one page according to paper size, margin settings, line spacing, and other settings. If you add text, delete text, or modify text on a page, Word recomputes the location of automatic page breaks and adjusts them accordingly.

Word performs page recomputation between the keystrokes, that is, in between the pauses in your typing. Thus, Word refers to the automatic page break task as **background repagination**. The steps on the next page illustrate Word's automatic page break feature.

To Enter More Text and Insert a Citation Placeholder

The next task is to type the fourth paragraph in the body of the research paper.

1 With the insertion point positioned at the end of the third paragraph as shown in Figure 2–45 on the previous page, press the ENTER key. Type the fourth paragraph of the research paper (Figure 2–46): `A global positioning system (GPS) is a navigation system that consists of one or more earth-based receivers that accept and analyze signals sent by satellites in order to determine the receiver's geographic location, according to Shelly and Cashman` and then press the SPACEBAR.

2 Click the Insert Citation button on the References tab to display the Insert Citation menu. Click Add New Placeholder on the Insert Citation menu to display the Placeholder Name dialog box.

3 Type `Shelly` as the tag name for the source.

4 Click the OK button to close the dialog box and insert the tag name in the citation placeholder.

5 Press the PERIOD key to end the sentence. Press the SPACEBAR. Type `A GPS receiver is a handheld, mountable, or embedded device that contains an antenna, a radio receiver, and a processor. Many mobile devices, such as mobile phones and PDAs, have GPS capability built into the device.`

6 Press the ENTER key.

Figure 2–46

To Edit a Source

When you typed the fourth paragraph of the research paper, you inserted a citation placeholder, Shelly, for the source. You now have the source information, which is for a Web site, and are ready to enter it. The following steps edit the source for the Shelly citation placeholder.

1 Click somewhere in the citation placeholder to be edited, in this case (Shelly), to select the citation placeholder.

2 Click the Citation Options box arrow to display the Citation Options menu.

3 Click Edit Source on the Citation Options menu to display the Edit Source dialog box.

4 If necessary, click the Type of Source box arrow; scroll to and then click Web site, so that the list shows fields required for a Web site.

5 Place a check mark in the Show All Bibliography Fields check box to display more fields related to Web sites.

6 Click the Author text box. Type `Shelly, Gary B., and Thomas J. Cashman` as the author.

7 Click the Name of Web Page text box. Type `How a GPS Works` as the Web page title.

8 Click the Production Company text box. Type `Course Technology` as the production company.

9 Click the Year Accessed text box. Type `2008` as the year.

10 Press the TAB key and then type `March` as the month accessed.

Q&A

What if some of the text boxes disappear as I enter the Web site fields?

With the Show All Bibliography Fields check box selected, all Web site fields may not be able to be displayed in the dialog box at the same time. In this case, some may scroll up.

11 Press the TAB key and then type `21` as the day accessed.

12 Press the TAB key and then type `www.scsite.com/wd2007/ pr2/wc.htm` as the URL (Figure 2–47).

13 Click the OK button to close the dialog box and create the source.

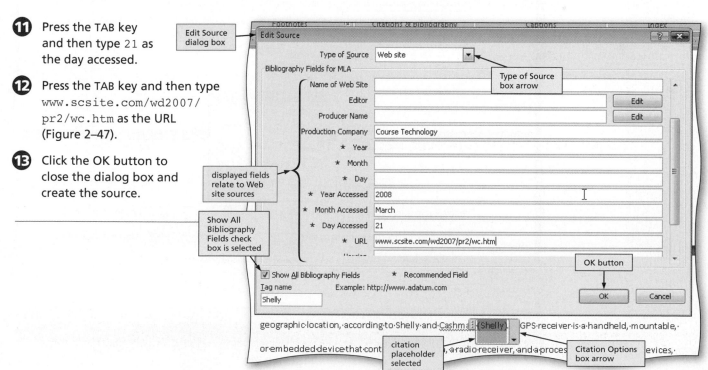

Figure 2–47

To Edit a Citation

As mentioned earlier, if you reference the author's name in the text, you should not list it again in the parenthetical citation. For Web site citations, when you suppress the author's name, the citation shows the Web site name because page numbers do not apply. The following steps edit the citation, suppressing the author and displaying the name of the Web site instead.

1 If necessary, click somewhere in the citation to be edited, in this case (Shelly), to select the citation and display the Citation Options box arrow.

2 Click the Citation Options box arrow and then click Edit Citation on the Citation Options menu to display the Edit Citation dialog box.

3 Click the Author check box to place a check mark in it (Figure 2–48).

4 Click the OK button to close the dialog box, remove the author name from the citation, and show the name of the Web site in the citation.

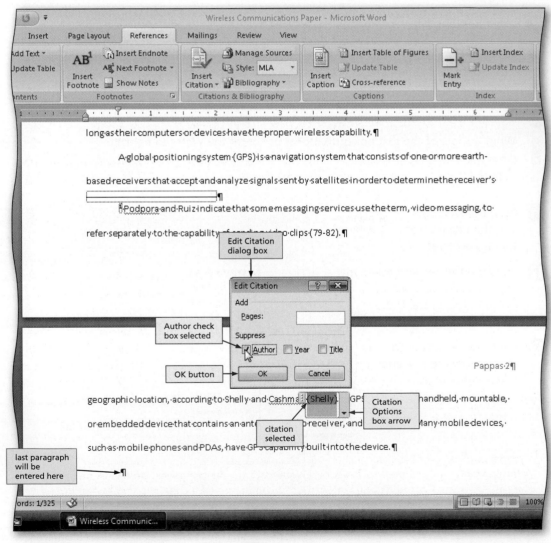

Figure 2–48

To Enter More Text

The next step is to type the last paragraph of text in the research paper.

1 Position the
insertion point
on the paragraph
mark below the
fourth paragraph in
the research paper
(Figure 2–48).

2 Type the last
paragraph of the
research paper
(Figure 2–49):
Mobile users
communicate
wirelessly
through
wireless

Pappas·2¶

geographic·location,·according·to·Shelly·and·Cashman·(How·a·GPS·Works).·A·GPS·receiver·is·a·handheld,·

mountable,·or·embedded·device·that·contains·an·anterna,·a·radio·receiver,·and·a·processor.·Many·

mobile·devices,·such·as·mobile·phones·and·P — — bility·built·into·the·device.¶

> *citation shows name of Web site*

Mobile·users·communicate·wirelessly·through·wireless·messaging·services,·wireless·Internet·

access·points,·and·global·positioning·systems.·Anyone·can·take·advantage·of·wireless·communications·

using·mobile·computers·and·devices.¶

> *last paragraph entered*

Words: 356

Figure 2–49

messaging services, wireless Internet access points, and global
positioning systems. Anyone can take advantage of wireless communications
using mobile computers and devices.

To Save an Existing Document with the Same File Name

You have made several edits to the research paper since you last saved it. Thus, you
should save it again. The following step saves the document again.

1 Click the Save button on the Quick Access Toolbar to overwrite the previous Wireless
Communications Paper file on the USB flash drive.

Creating an Alphabetical Works Cited Page

According to the MLA style, the **works cited page** is a list of sources that are referenced
directly in a research paper. You place the list on a separate numbered page with the title,
Works Cited, centered one inch from the top margin. The works are to be alphabetized
by the author's last name or, if the work has no author, by the work's title. The first line of
each entry begins at the left margin. Indent subsequent lines of the same entry one-half
inch from the left margin.

Create the list of sources.
A **bibliography** is an alphabetical list of sources referenced in a paper. Whereas the text of
the research paper contains brief references to the source (the citations), the bibliography
lists all publication information about the source. Documentation styles differ significantly
in their guidelines for preparing a bibliography. Each style identifies formats for various
sources including books, magazines, pamphlets, newspapers, Web sites, television programs,
paintings, maps, advertisements, letters, memos, and much more. You can find information
about various styles and their guidelines in printed style guides and on the Web.

**Plan
Ahead**

To Page Break Manually

The works cited are to be displayed on a separate numbered page. Thus, you must insert a manual page break following the body of the research paper so that the list of sources is displayed on a separate page. A **manual page break**, or **hard page break**, is one that you force into the document at a specific location.

Word never moves or adjusts manual page breaks; however, Word adjusts any automatic page breaks that follow a manual page break. Word inserts manual page breaks immediately above the location of the insertion point. The following step inserts a manual page break after the text of the research paper.

- With the insertion point at the end of the text of the research paper (Figure 2-49 on the previous page), press the ENTER key.

- Then, press CTRL+ENTER to insert a manual page break immediately above the insertion point and position the insertion point immediately below the manual page break (Figure 2–50).

- Scroll to position the top of the third page closer to the ruler.

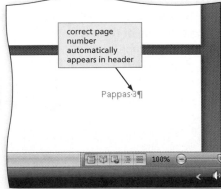

Figure 2–50

Other Ways

1. Click Page Break button on Insert tab

To Center the Title of the Works Cited Page

The works cited title is to be centered between the margins of the paper. If you simply issue the Center command, the title will not be centered properly. Instead, it will be one-half inch to the right of the center point because earlier you set first-line indent at one-half inch. Recall that Word is indenting the first line of every paragraph one-half inch.

To properly center the title of the works cited page, you must move the First Line Indent marker back to the left margin before centering the paragraph.

1 Drag the First Line Indent marker to the 0" mark on the ruler, which is at the left margin, to remove the first-line indent setting.

2 Press CTRL+E to center the paragraph mark.

3 Type Works Cited as the title.

4 Press the ENTER key.

5 Press CTRL+L to left-align the paragraph mark (Figure 2–51).

Figure 2–51

To Create the Bibliographical List

While typing the research paper, you created several citations and their sources. Word can format the list of sources and alphabetize them in a **bibliographical list**, saving you time looking up style guidelines. That is, Word will create a bibliographical list with each element of the source placed in its correct position with proper formatting and punctuation, according to the specified style. For example, in this research paper, the book source will list, in this order, the author name(s), book title, publisher city, publishing company name, and publication year with the book title underlined and the correct punctuation between each element according to the MLA style. The following steps create a MLA formatted bibliographical list from the sources previously entered.

- With the insertion point positioned as shown in Figure 2–52, click the Bibliography button on the References tab to display the Bibliography gallery (Figure 2–52).

Q&A

Will I select Works Cited from the Bibliography gallery?

No. The title it inserts is not formatted according to the MLA style. Thus, you will use the Insert Bibliography command instead.

Figure 2–52

- Click Insert Bibliography in the Bibliography gallery to insert a list of sources at the location of the insertion point.

- If necessary, scroll to display the entire list of sources in the document window (Figure 2–53).

Figure 2–53

To Modify a Style Using the Styles Task Pane

Although the format within each entry in the bibliographical list meets the MLA style, the paragraph formatting does not. Currently, entries are based on the Normal style, which does not have the correct line or paragraph spacing. Thus, you will modify the style so that it is based on the No Spacing style (no blank space before or after a paragraph) and change its line spacing to double. The following steps modify the Bibliography style.

- Click somewhere in the list of sources to position the insertion point in a paragraph formatted with the Bibliography style.

Q&A

Why did the list of sources turn gray?

The entire list of sources is a field that Word automatically updates each time you make a change to one of the sources. Word, by default, shades fields gray on the screen to help you identify them. The gray shading, however, will not appear in the printed document.

- Click Home on the Ribbon to display the Home tab.

- Click the Styles Dialog Box Launcher to display the Styles task pane.

- If necessary, scroll to Bibliography in the Styles task pane. Click Bibliography to select it, if necessary, and then click its box arrow to display the Bibliography menu (Figure 2–54).

Figure 2–54

2

- Click Modify on the Bibliography menu to display the Modify Style dialog box.

- Click the 'Style based on' box arrow and then click No Spacing to base the Bibliography style on the No Spacing style.

- Click the 'Style for following paragraph' box arrow and then click No Spacing to base additional bibliographical paragraphs on the No Spacing style.

- Click the Double Space button to set the line spacing to double.

- Place a check mark in the Automatically update check box so that any future changes you make to the bibliographical paragraphs will update the Bibliography style automatically (Figure 2–55).

Figure 2–55

3

- Click the OK button in the Modify Style dialog box to close the dialog box and apply the style changes to the paragraphs in the document.

- Click the Close button on the Styles task pane title bar to close the task pane (Figure 2–56).

Figure 2–56

Other Ways

1. Click Styles Dialog Box Launcher, click Manage Styles button, scroll to style and then select it, click Modify button, change settings, click OK button in each dialog box

To Create a Hanging Indent

Currently, the first line of each source entry begins at the left margin. Subsequent lines in the same paragraph are to be indented one-half inch from the left margin. In essence, the first line hangs to the left of the rest of the paragraph; thus, this type of paragraph formatting is called a **hanging indent**.

One method of creating a hanging indent is to use the horizontal ruler. The **Hanging Indent marker** is the bottom triangle at the 0" mark on the ruler (Figure 2–57). The following steps create a hanging indent using the horizontal ruler.

- With the insertion point in the paragraph to format, point to the Hanging Indent marker on the ruler (Figure 2–57).

Figure 2–57

- Drag the Hanging Indent marker to the .5" mark on the ruler to set the hanging indent to one-half inch from the left margin (Figure 2–58).

Q&A

Why were all three bibliographical paragraphs formatted with a hanging indent?

When you make a change to a paragraph based on the Bibliography style, the style is updated and all paragraphs based on that style also change because you selected the Automatically update check box in the Modify Style dialog box (shown in Figure 2–55 on the previous page).

Figure 2–58

Other Ways

1. Right-click paragraph, click Paragraph on shortcut menu, click Indents and Spacing tab, click Special box arrow, click Hanging, click OK button
2. Click Paragraph Dialog Box Launcher, click Indents and Spacing tab, click Special box arrow, click Hanging, click OK button
3. Press CTRL+T

To Modify a Source and Update the Bibliographical List

If you modify the contents of any source, the list of sources automatically updates because the list is a field. The following steps modify the title of the magazine article.

1

- Click References on the Ribbon to display the References tab.

- Click the Manage Sources button on the References tab to display the Source Manager dialog box.

- Click the source you wish to edit in the Current List.

- Click the Edit button to display the Edit Source dialog box.

- In the Title text box, add the word, Services, to the end of the title (Figure 2–59).

Figure 2–59

2

- Click the OK button to close the Edit Source dialog box.

- If a Microsoft Office Word dialog box appears, click its Yes button to update all occurrences of the source.

- Click the Close button in the Source Manager dialog box to update the list of sources in the document (Figure 2–60).

Q&A

What if the list of sources in the document does not update automatically?

Click in the list of sources and then press the F9 key, which is the shortcut key to update a field.

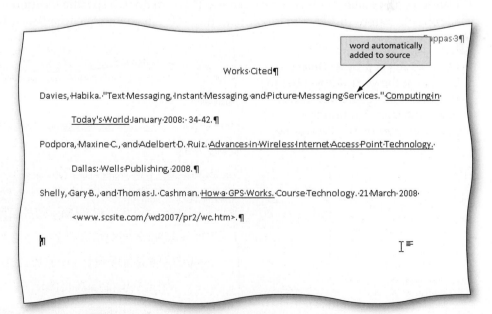

Figure 2–60

Proofing and Revising the Research Paper

As discussed in Chapter 1, once you complete a document, you might find it necessary to make changes to it. Before submitting a paper to be graded, you should proofread it. While **proofreading**, you look for grammatical errors and spelling errors. You want to be sure the transitions between sentences flow smoothly and the sentences themselves make sense.

<table>
<tr>
<td>

Plan Ahead

</td>
<td>

Proofread and revise the paper.
As you proofread the paper, look for ways to improve it. Check all grammar, spelling, and punctuation. Be sure the text is logical and transitions are smooth. Where necessary, add text, delete text, reword text, and move text to different locations. Ask yourself these questions:

- Does the title suggest the topic?
- Is the thesis clear?
- Is the purpose of the paper clear?
- Does the paper have an introduction, body, and conclusion?
- Does each paragraph in the body relate to the thesis?
- Is the conclusion effective?
- Are all sources acknowledged?

</td>
</tr>
</table>

To assist you with the proofreading effort, Word provides several tools. You can go to a specific location in a document, move text, find and replace text, insert a synonym, check spelling and grammar, and look up information. The following pages discuss these tools.

To Use the Select Browse Object Menu

Often, you would like to bring a certain page, footnote, or other object into view in the document window. To accomplish this, you could scroll through the document to find a desired page, footnote, or item. Instead of scrolling through the document, however, you can use Word to go to a specific location via the Select Browse Object menu. The following steps display the footnote in the research paper using the Select Browse Object menu.

- Click the Select Browse Object button on the vertical scroll bar to display the Select Browse Object menu and then position the mouse pointer on the Browse by Footnote icon (Figure 2–61).

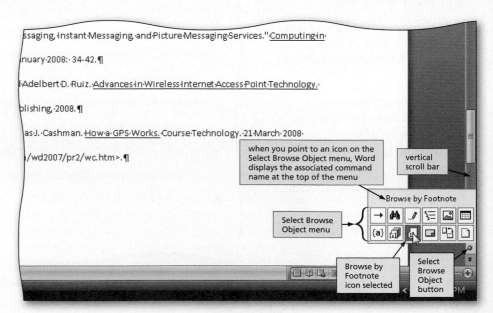

Figure 2–61

2

- Click the Browse by Footnote icon to set the browse object to footnotes.

- Position the mouse pointer on the Previous Footnote button on the vertical scroll bar (Figure 2–62).

Q&A

Did the function of the button change?

Yes. By default, it is the Previous Page button. Depending on the icon you click on the Select Browse Object menu, the function of the buttons above and below the Select Browse Object button on the vertical scroll bar changes.

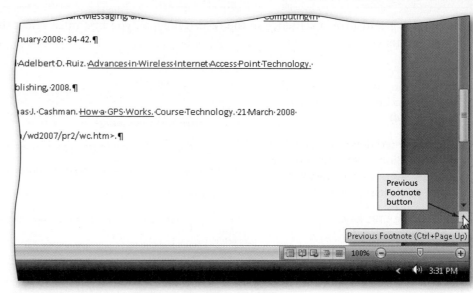

Figure 2–62

3

- Click the Previous Footnote button to display the footnote reference mark in the document window (Figure 2–63).

Other Ways

1. Click Page Number indicator on status bar, click desired object in Go to what list, type desired object number in Enter object number text box, click Go To button

2. Press ALT+CTRL+HOME

Figure 2–63

Moving Text

While proofreading the research paper, you realize that text in the third paragraph would flow better if the third sentence were moved to the end of the paragraph.

To move text, such as words, characters, sentences, or paragraphs, you first select the text to be moved and then use drag-and-drop editing or the cut-and-paste technique to move the selected text. With **drag-and-drop editing**, you drag the selected item to the new location and then insert, or *drop*, it there. **Cutting** involves removing the selected item from the document and then placing it on the Clipboard. The **Clipboard** is a temporary Windows storage area. **Pasting** is the process of copying an item from the Clipboard into the document at the location of the insertion point.

When moving text a long distance or between application programs, use the Clipboard task pane to cut and paste. When moving text a short distance, the drag-and-drop technique is more efficient. Thus, the steps on the following pages demonstrate drag-and-drop editing.

To Select a Sentence

To drag-and-drop a sentence in the research paper, you first must select the sentence. The following step selects a sentence.

- Position the mouse pointer in the sentence to be moved (shown in Figure 2–64).

- Press and hold down the CTRL key. While holding down the CTRL key, click the sentence to select the entire sentence.

- Release the CTRL key.

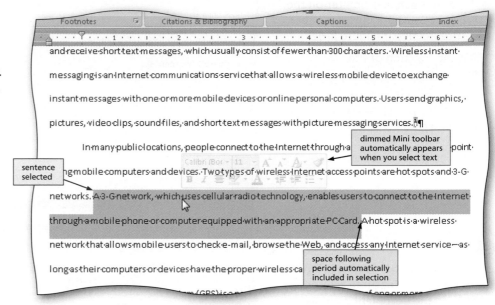

and receive short text messages, which usually consist of fewer than 300 characters. Wireless instant messaging is an Internet communications service that allows a wireless mobile device to exchange instant messages with one or more mobile devices or online personal computers. Users send graphics, pictures, video clips, sound files, and short text messages with picture messaging services.¶

In many public locations, people connect to the Internet through a ... point

dimmed Mini toolbar automatically appears when you select text

sentence selected

... ng mobile computers and devices. Two types of wireless Internet access points are hot spots and 3-G networks. A 3-G network, which uses cellular radio technology, enables users to connect to the Internet through a mobile phone or computer equipped with an appropriate PC Card. A hot spot is a wireless network that allows mobile users to check e-mail, browse the Web, and access any Internet service—as long as their computers or devices have the proper wireless ca

space following period automatically included in selection

Figure 2–64

Other Ways

1. Drag through the sentence
2. With insertion point at beginning of sentence, press CTRL+SHIFT+RIGHT ARROW until sentence is selected

Selecting Text

In the previous steps and throughout Chapters 1 and 2, you have selected text. Table 2–3 summarizes the techniques used to select various items with the mouse.

Selecting Nonadjacent Items

In Word, you can select nonadjacent items, that is, items not next to each other. This is helpful when you are formatting multiple items the same way. To select nonadjacent items (text or graphics), do the following: select the first item, such as a word or paragraph, as usual. Press and hold down the CTRL key. While holding down the CTRL key, select any additional items.

Table 2–3 Techniques for Selecting Items with the Mouse	
Item To Select	**Mouse Action**
Block of text	Click at beginning of selection, scroll to end of selection, position mouse pointer at end of selection, hold down SHIFT key and then click; or drag through the text
Character(s)	Drag through character(s)
Document	Move mouse to left of text until mouse pointer changes to a right-pointing block arrow and then triple-click
Graphic	Click the graphic
Line	Move mouse to left of line until mouse pointer changes to a right-pointing block arrow and then click
Lines	Move mouse to left of first line until mouse pointer changes to a right-pointing block arrow and then drag up or down
Paragraph	Triple-click paragraph; or move mouse to left of paragraph until mouse pointer changes to a right-pointing block arrow and then double-click
Paragraphs	Move mouse to left of paragraph until mouse pointer changes to a right-pointing block arrow, double-click, and then drag up or down
Sentence	Press and hold down CTRL key and then click sentence
Word	Double-click the word
Words	Drag through words

To Move Selected Text

With the sentence to be moved selected, you can use drag-and-drop editing to move it. You should be sure that drag-and-drop editing is enabled by clicking the Word Options button on the Office Button menu, clicking Advanced in the left pane of the Word Options dialog box, verifying the 'Allow text to be dragged and dropped' check box is selected, and then clicking the OK button.

The following steps move the selected sentence so that it becomes the last sentence in the paragraph.

- With the mouse pointer in the selected text, press and hold down the mouse button (Figure 2–65).

Figure 2–65

- Drag the mouse pointer to the location where the selected text is to be moved, as shown in Figure 2–66.

- Release the mouse button to move the selected text to the location of the mouse pointer.

- Click outside the selected text to remove the selection (Figure 2–67).

Q&A What if I accidentally drag text to the wrong location?

Click the Undo button on the Quick Access Toolbar and try again.

Q&A Can I use drag-and-drop editing to move any selected item?

Yes, you can select words, sentences, phrases, and graphics and then use drag-and-drop editing to move them.

Figure 2–66

Figure 2–67

Other Ways		
1. Click Cut button on Home tab, click where text is to be pasted, click Paste button on Home tab	2. Right-click selected text, click Cut on shortcut menu, right-click where text is to be pasted, click Paste on shortcut menu	3. Press CTRL+X, position insertion point where text is to be pasted, press CTRL+V

To Display the Paste Options Menu

When you drag-and-drop text, Word automatically displays a Paste Options button near the location of the drag-and-dropped text (Figure 2–67 on the previous page). If you click the **Paste Options button**, a menu appears that allows you to change the format of the item that was moved. The following steps display the Paste Options menu.

- Click the Paste Options button to display the Paste Options menu (Figure 2–68).

Q&A

What is the purpose of the commands on the Paste Options menu?

In general, the first command indicates the pasted text should look the same as it did in its original location. The second command formats the pasted text to match the rest of the text where it was pasted. The third command removes all formatting from the pasted text. The last command displays the Word Options dialog box.

- Press the ESCAPE key to remove the Paste Options menu from the window.

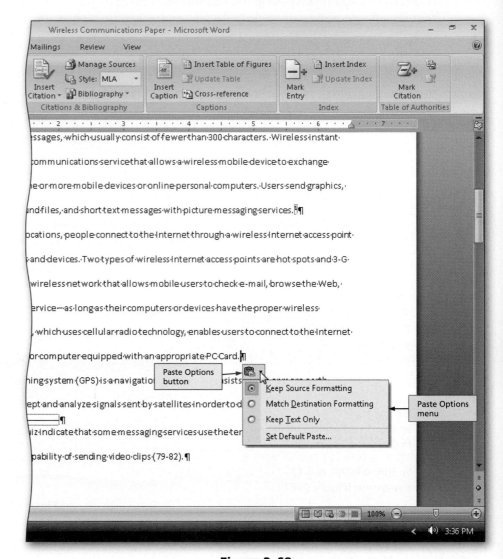

Figure 2–68

BTW

Dragging-and-Dropping
If you hold down the CTRL key while dragging a selected item, Word copies the item instead of moving it.

To Find and Replace Text

While proofreading the paper, you notice that you typed 3-G in the third paragraph (Figure 2–69). You prefer to use 3G, instead. Therefore, you need to change all occurrences of 3-G to 3G. To do this, you can use Word's find and replace feature, which automatically locates each occurrence of a word or phrase and then replaces it with specified text. The following steps use Find and Replace to replace all occurrences of 3-G with 3G.

- Click Home on the Ribbon to display the Home tab.

- Click the Replace button on the Home tab to display the Find and Replace dialog box.

- Type 3-G in the Find what text box.

- Press the TAB key. Type 3G in the Replace with text box (Figure 2–69).

Figure 2–69

- Click the Replace All button in the Find and Replace dialog box to instruct Word to replace all occurrences of the Find what text with the Replace with text (Figure 2–70).

- Click the OK button in the Microsoft Office Word dialog box.

- Click the Close button in the Find and Replace dialog box.

Other Ways

1. Click Select Browse Object button on vertical scroll bar, click Find icon, click Replace tab

2. Click Page Number indicator on status bar, click Replace tab in dialog box

3. Press CTRL+H

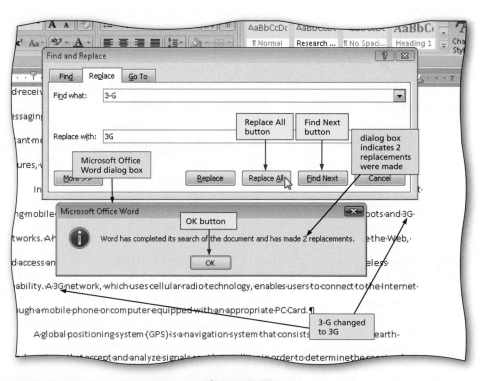

Figure 2–70

Find and Replace Dialog Box

The Replace All button in the Find and Replace dialog box replaces all occurrences of the Find what text with the Replace with text. In some cases, you may want to replace only certain occurrences of a word or phrase, not all of them. To instruct Word to confirm each change, click the Find Next button in the Find and Replace dialog box (Figure 2–70 on the previous page), instead of the Replace All button. When Word locates an occurrence of the text, it pauses and waits for you to click either the Replace button or the Find Next button. Clicking the Replace button changes the text; clicking the Find Next button instructs Word to disregard the replacement and look for the next occurrence of the Find what text.

If you accidentally replace the wrong text, you can undo a replacement by clicking the Undo button on the Standard toolbar. If you used the Replace All button, Word undoes all replacements. If you used the Replace button, Word undoes only the most recent replacement.

To Find Text

Sometimes, you may want only to find text, instead of finding and replacing text. To search for just a single occurrence of text, you would follow these steps.

1. Click the Find button on the Home tab; or click the Select Browse Object button on the vertical scroll bar and then click the Find icon on the Select Browse Object menu; or click the page indicator on the status bar and then click the Find tab; or press CTRL+F.

2. Type the text to locate in the Find what text box and then click the Find Next button. To edit the text, click the Cancel button in the Find and Replace dialog box; to find the next occurrence of the text, click the Find Next button.

To Find and Insert a Synonym

When writing, you may discover that you used the same word in multiple locations or that a word you used was not quite appropriate. In these instances, you will want to look up a **synonym**, or a word similar in meaning, to the duplicate or inappropriate word. A **thesaurus** is a book of synonyms. Word provides synonyms and a thesaurus for your convenience.

In this project, you would like a synonym for the word, proper, in the third paragraph of the research paper. The following steps show how to find a suitable synonym.

1

- Locate and then right-click the word for which you want to find a synonym (in this case, proper) to display a shortcut menu related to the word you right-clicked.

- Point to Synonyms on the shortcut menu to display a list of synonyms for the word you right-clicked (Figure 2–71).

Figure 2–71

2

- Click the synonym you want (appropriate) on the Synonyms submenu to replace the word, proper, in the document with the word, appropriate (Figure 2–72).

Q&A

What if the synonyms list on the shortcut menu does not display a suitable word?

You can display the thesaurus in the Research task pane by clicking Thesaurus on the Synonyms submenu. The Research task pane displays a complete thesaurus, in which you can look up synonyms for various meanings of a word. You also can look up an **antonym**, or word with an opposite meaning. The Research task pane is discussed later in this chapter.

Figure 2–72

Other Ways
1. Click Thesaurus on Review tab	2. Press SHIFT+F7

To Check Spelling and Grammar at Once

As discussed in Chapter 1, Word checks spelling and grammar as you type and places a wavy underline below possible spelling or grammar errors. Chapter 1 illustrated how to check these flagged words immediately. As an alternative, you can wait and check the entire document for spelling and grammar errors at once.

Note: In the following example the word, world, has been misspelled intentionally as wrld to illustrate the use of Word's check spelling and grammar at once feature. If you are completing this project on a personal computer, your research paper may contain different misspelled words, depending on the accuracy of your typing.

1

- Press CTRL+HOME because you want the spelling and grammar check to begin from the top of the document.

- Click Review on the Ribbon to display the Review tab.

- Click the Spelling & Grammar button on the Review tab to begin the spelling and grammar check at the location of the insertion point, which in this case, is at the beginning of the document (Figure 2–73).

Figure 2–73

- With the word, world, selected in the Suggestions list, click the Change button in the Spelling and Grammar dialog box to change the flagged word, wrld, to the selected suggestion, world, and then continue the spelling and grammar check until the next error is identified or the end of the document is reached (Figure 2–74).

❸

- Click the Ignore All button in the Spelling and Grammar dialog box to ignore this and future occurrences of the flagged proper noun and then continue the spelling and grammar check until the next error is identified or the end of the document is reached.

- When Word flags the proper noun, Podpora, click the Ignore All button.

- When the spelling and grammar check is finished and Word displays a dialog box, click its OK button.

Q&A

Can I check spelling of just a section of a document?

Yes, select the text before starting the spelling and grammar check.

Figure 2–74

Other Ways

1. Click Spelling and Grammar Check icon on status bar, click Spelling on shortcut menu
2. Right-click flagged word, click Spelling on shortcut menu
3. Press F7

BTW

Contextual Spelling Errors

You can instruct Word to check for misuse of homophones and other types of contextual spelling errors. (Homophones are two or more words that are pronounced the same but that have different spellings or meanings, such as one and won.) With this feature, Word flags a contextual spelling error with a blue wavy underline. For example, Word would place a blue wavy underline below the words, one and knight, in this sentence: The team one the game last knight. (The correct sentence would be written as follows: The team won the game last night.) To view Word's suggested replacements for the flagged words, you could right-click each of the flagged words or start the spelling and grammar check by clicking the Spelling & Grammar button on the Review tab. On many installations of Word, the contextual spelling check is not activated by default. To activate it, click the Office Button, click Word Options on the Office Button menu, click Proofing in the left pane, place a check mark in the 'Use contextual spelling' check box, and then click the OK button.

The Main and Custom Dictionaries

As shown in the previous steps, Word may flag a proper noun as an error because the proper noun is not in its main dictionary. To prevent Word from flagging proper nouns as errors, you can add the proper nouns to the custom dictionary. To add a correctly spelled word to the custom dictionary, click the Add to Dictionary button in the Spelling and Grammar dialog box (Figure 2–74) or right-click the flagged word and then click Add to Dictionary on the shortcut menu. Once you have added a word to the custom dictionary, Word no longer will flag it as an error.

To View or Modify Entries in a Custom Dictionary

To view or modify the list of words in a custom dictionary, you would follow these steps.

1. Click the Office Button and then click the Word Options button.
2. Click Proofing in the left pane of the Word Options dialog box.
3. Click the Custom Dictionaries button.
4. When Word displays the Custom Dictionaries dialog box, place a check mark next to the dictionary name to view or modify. Click the Edit Word List button. (In this dialog box, you can add or delete entries to and from the selected custom dictionary.)
5. When finished viewing and/or modifying the list, click the OK button in the dialog box.
6. Click the OK button in the Custom Dictionaries dialog box.
7. If the 'Suggest from main dictionary only' check box is selected in the Word Options dialog box, remove the check mark. Click the OK button in the Word Options dialog box.

To Set the Default Custom Dictionary

If you have multiple custom dictionaries, you can specify which one Word should use when checking spelling. To set the default custom dictionary, you would follow these steps.

1. Click the Office Button and then click the Word Options button.
2. Click Proofing in the left pane of the Word Options dialog box.
3. Click the Custom Dictionaries button.
4. When the Custom Dictionaries dialog box is displayed, place a check mark next to the desired dictionary name. Click the Change Default button.
5. Click the OK button in the Custom Dictionaries dialog box.
6. If the 'Suggest from main dictionary only' check box is selected in the Word Options dialog box, remove the check mark. Click the OK button in the Word Options dialog box.

To Use the Research Task Pane to Look Up Information

From within Word, you can search through various forms of reference information. Earlier, this chapter discussed the Research task pane with respect to looking up a synonym in a thesaurus. Other services available in the Research task pane include a dictionary and if you are connected to the Web, an encyclopedia, a search engine, and other Web sites that provide information such as stock quotes, news articles, and company profiles.

Assume you want to know more about the acronym, PDA. The following steps use the Research task pane to look up information about a word.

- Locate the word you want to look up.

- While holding down the ALT key, click the word you want to look up (in this case, PDAs) to open the Research task pane and display a dictionary entry for the ALT+CLICKED word. Release the ALT key (Figure 2–75).

- If the Research task pane does not display a dictionary entry for the ALT+CLICKED word, click the Search for box arrow and then click All Reference Books.

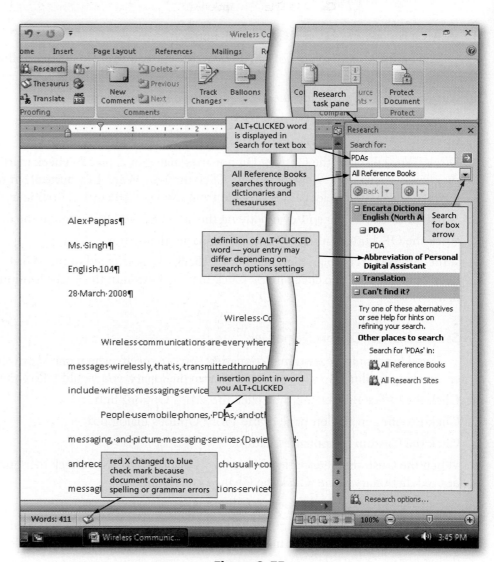

Figure 2–75

2

• Click the Search for box arrow and then click All Research Sites in the list to display Web sites with information about the ALT+CLICKED word (Figure 2–76).

Q&A

Can I copy information from the Research task pane into my document?

Yes, you can use the Copy and Paste commands. When using Word to insert material from the Research task pane or any other online reference, however, be very careful not to plagiarize.

3

• Click the Close button in the Research task pane.

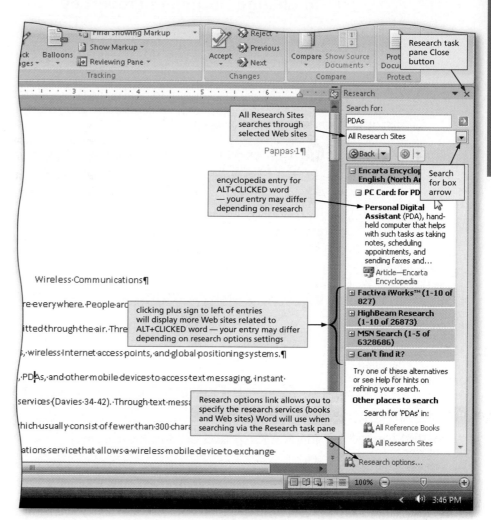

Figure 2–76

Other Ways

1. Click Research button on Review tab

2. Click Insert Citation button on References tab, click Search Libraries

Research Task Pane Options

When you install Word, it selects a series of services (reference books and Web sites) through which it searches when you use the Research task pane. You can view, modify, and update the list of services at any time.

Clicking the Research options link at the bottom of the Research task pane displays the Research Options dialog box, where you can view or modify the list of installed services. You can view information about any installed service by clicking the service in the list and then clicking the Properties button. To activate an installed service, click the check box to its left; likewise, to deactivate a service, remove the check mark. To add a particular Web site to the list, click the Add Services button, enter the Web address in the Address text box, and then click the Add button in the Add Services dialog box. To update or remove services, click the Update/Remove button, select the service in the list, click the Update (or Remove) button in the Update or Remove Services dialog box, and then click the Close button. You also can install parental controls through the Parental Control button in the Research Options dialog box, for example, if you want to restrict Web access from minor children who use Word.

To Change Document Properties

Before saving the research paper again, you want to add your name, course information, and some keywords as document properties. The following steps use the Document Information Panel to change document properties.

1 Click the Office Button to display the Office Button menu, point to Prepare on the Office Button menu, and then click Properties on the Prepare submenu to display the Document Information Panel.

2 Click the Author text box, if necessary, and then type your name as the Author property. If a name already is displayed in the Author text box, delete it before typing your name.

3 Click the Subject text box, if necessary delete any existing text, and then type your course and section as the Subject property.

4 Click the Keywords text box, if necessary delete any existing text, and then type instant messaging, Internet access points, global positioning systems as the Keywords property.

5 Click the Close the Document Information Panel button so that the Document Information Panel no longer is displayed.

To Save an Existing Document with the Same File Name

The document now is complete. You should save the research paper again. The following step saves the document again.

1 Click the Save button on the Quick Access Toolbar to overwrite the previous Wireless Communications Paper file on the USB flash drive.

To Print Document Properties and then the Document

With the document properties entered and the completed document saved, you may want to print the document properties along with the document. The following steps print the document properties, followed by the contents of the saved Wireless Communications Paper project.

1

• Click the Office Button to display the Office Button menu and then point to Print on the Office Button menu to display the Print submenu (Figure 2–77).

Figure 2–77

2

- Click Print on the Print submenu to display the Print dialog box.

- Click the Print what box arrow and then click Document properties to instruct Word to print the document properties instead of the document (Figure 2–78).

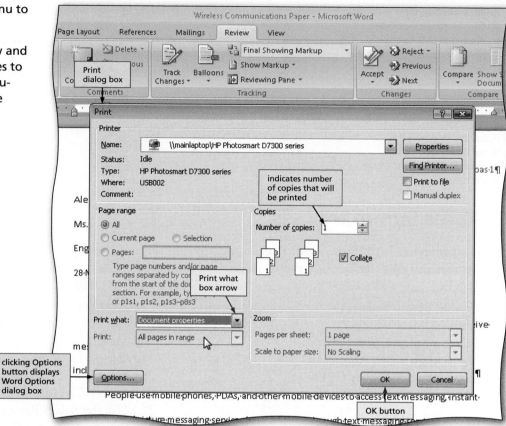

clicking Options button displays Word Options dialog box

People use mobile phones, PDAs, and other mobile devices to access text messaging, instant

Figure 2–78

3

- Click the OK button to print the document properties (Figure 2–79).

4

- Click the Office Button again to display the Office Button menu, point to Print on the Office Button menu, and then click Quick Print on the Print submenu to print the research paper (shown in Figure 2–1 on page WD 75).

printed document properties — your properties may differ, depending on settings

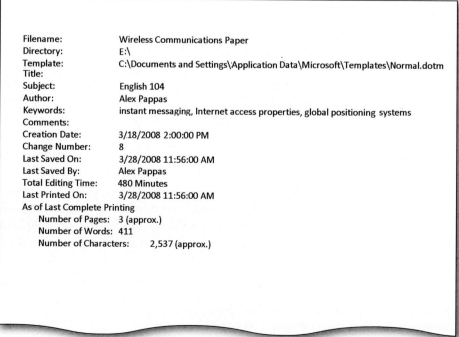

Filename:	Wireless Communications Paper
Directory:	E:\
Template:	C:\Documents and Settings\Application Data\Microsoft\Templates\Normal.dotm
Title:	
Subject:	English 104
Author:	Alex Pappas
Keywords:	instant messaging, Internet access properties, global positioning systems
Comments:	
Creation Date:	3/18/2008 2:00:00 PM
Change Number:	8
Last Saved On:	3/28/2008 11:56:00 AM
Last Saved By:	Alex Pappas
Total Editing Time:	480 Minutes
Last Printed On:	3/28/2008 11:56:00 AM

As of Last Complete Printing
    Number of Pages: 3 (approx.)
    Number of Words: 411
    Number of Characters: 2,537 (approx.)

Figure 2–79

BTW

Certification
The Microsoft Certified Application Specialist (MCAS) program provides an opportunity for you to obtain a valuable industry credential — proof that you have the Word 2007 skills required by employers. For more information, see Appendix G or visit the Word 2007 Certification Web page (scsite.com/wd2007/cert).

To Quit Word

This project is complete. The following steps quit Word.

1 Click the Close button on the right side of the title bar to quit Word; or if you have multiple Word documents open, click the Office Button and then click the Exit Word button on the Office Button menu to close all open documents and quit Word.

2 If necessary, click the Yes button in the Microsoft Office Word dialog box so that any changes you have made are saved.

Chapter Summary

In this chapter you have learned how to change document settings, use headers to number pages, create and modify styles, insert and edit citations and their sources, add footnotes, create a bibliographical list of sources, and use the Research task pane. The items listed below include all the new Word skills you have learned in this chapter.

1. Double-Space Text (WD 78)
2. Remove Space after a Paragraph (WD 79)
3. Switch to the Header (WD 80)
4. Right-Align a Paragraph (WD 81)
5. Insert a Page Number (WD 82)
6. Close the Header (WD 83)
7. Click and Type (WD 85)
8. Display the Rulers (WD 87)
9. First-Line Indent Paragraphs (WD 88)
10. Create a Quick Style (WD 90)
11. AutoCorrect as You Type (WD 91)
12. Use the AutoCorrect Options Button (WD 92)
13. Create an AutoCorrect Entry (WD 93)
14. Change the Bibliography Style (WD 95)
15. Insert a Citation and Create Its Source (WD 96)
16. Edit a Citation (WD 98)
17. Insert a Footnote Reference Mark (WD 100)
18. Insert a Citation Placeholder (WD 101)
19. Modify a Style Using a Shortcut Menu (WD 102)
20. Edit a Source (WD 104)
21. Count Words (WD 107)
22. Page Break Manually (WD 112)
23. Create the Bibliographical List (WD 113)
24. Modify a Style Using the Styles Task Pane (WD 114)
25. Create a Hanging Indent (WD 116)
26. Modify a Source and Update the Bibliographical List (WD 117)
27. Use the Select Browse Object Menu (WD 118)
28. Select a Sentence (WD 120)
29. Move Selected Text (WD 121)
30. Display the Paste Options Menu (WD 122)
31. Find and Replace Text (WD 123)
32. Find Text (WD 124)
33. Find and Insert a Synonym (WD 124)
34. Check Spelling and Grammar at Once (WD 125)
35. View or Modify Entries in a Custom Dictionary (WD 127)
36. Set the Default Custom Dictionary (WD 127)
37. Use the Research Task Pane to Look Up Information (WD 128)
38. Print Document Properties and then the Document (WD 130)

 If you have a SAM user profile, you may have access to hands-on instruction, practice, and assessment. Log in to your SAM account (http://sam2007.course.com) to launch any assigned training activities or exams that relate to the skills covered in this chapter.

BTW

Quick Reference
For a table that lists how to complete the tasks covered in this book using the mouse, Ribbon, shortcut menu, and keyboard, see the Quick Reference Summary at the back of this book, or visit the Word 2007 Quick Reference Web page (scsite.com/wd2007/qr).

Learn It Online

Test your knowledge of chapter content and key terms.

Instructions: To complete the Learn It Online exercises, start your browser, click the Address bar, and then enter the Web address scsite.com/wd2007/learn. When the Word 2007 Learn It Online page is displayed, click the link for the exercise you want to complete and then read the instructions.

Chapter Reinforcement TF, MC, and SA
A series of true/false, multiple choice, and short answer questions that test your knowledge of the chapter content.

Flash Cards
An interactive learning environment where you identify chapter key terms associated with displayed definitions.

Practice Test
A series of multiple choice questions that test your knowledge of chapter content and key terms.

Who Wants To Be a Computer Genius?
An interactive game that challenges your knowledge of chapter content in the style of a television quiz show.

Wheel of Terms
An interactive game that challenges your knowledge of chapter key terms in the style of the television show *Wheel of Fortune.*

Crossword Puzzle Challenge
A crossword puzzle that challenges your knowledge of key terms presented in the chapter.

Apply Your Knowledge

Reinforce the skills and apply the concepts you learned in this chapter.

Revising Text and Paragraphs in a Document
Instructions: Start Word. Open the document, Apply 2-1 Software Paragraphs Draft, from the Data Files for Students. See the inside back cover of this book for instructions on downloading the Data Files for Students, or contact your instructor for information about accessing the required files.

The document you open has a header and three paragraphs of text. You are to revise the document as follows: move a paragraph, move a word and change the format of the moved word, change paragraph indentation, change line spacing and paragraph spacing, replace all occurrences of a word with another word, and edit the header.

Perform the following tasks:
1. Select the last (third) paragraph. Use drag-and-drop editing to move this paragraph, so that it is the second paragraph in the document.
2. Select the underlined word, effectively, in the second sentence of the first paragraph. Use drag-and-drop editing to move the selected word, effectively, so that it follows the word, software, in the same sentence. Click the Paste Options button that displays to the right of the moved word, effectively. Remove the underline format from the moved sentence by clicking Keep Text Only on the shortcut menu.
3. Select the three paragraphs of text in the document.
4. Display the ruler, if necessary. With the paragraphs selected, use the ruler to indent the first line of the selected paragraphs one-half inch.
5. With the paragraphs still selected, change the line spacing of the selected paragraphs from single to double.

Continued >

Apply Your Knowledge *continued*

Figure 2–80

6. With the paragraphs still selected, use Line spacing box arrow to remove extra space below (after) the paragraphs. Click anywhere to remove the selection.

7. Use the Find and Replace dialog box to replace all occurrences of the word, Internet, with the word, Web. How many replacements were made? 4

8. Use the Find dialog box to locate the word, incorporated. Use Word's thesaurus to change the word, incorporated, to the word, integrated, in the first sentence of the second paragraph.

9. Switch to the header so that you can edit it. In the first line of the header, change the word, Draft, to the word, Modified, so that it reads: Software Paragraphs Modified. Change the first line of the header from the Normal style to the No Spacing style.

10. In the second line of the header, insert the page number (with no formatting) one space after the word, Page.

11. Change the alignment of both lines of text in the header from left-aligned to right-aligned. Switch back to the document text.

12. Change the document properties, as specified by your instructor.

13. Click the Office Button and then click Save As. Save the document using the file name, Apply 2-1 Software Paragraphs Modified.

14. Print the document properties and then print the revised document, shown in Figure 2–80.

15. Use the Research task pane to look up the definition of the word, online, in the first sentence of the second paragraph. Handwrite the COMPUTING definition of the word, online, on your printout.

16. Display the Research Options dialog box and on your printout, handwrite the currently active Reference Books, Research Sites, and Business and Financial Sites. If your instructor approves, activate one of the services.

Extend Your Knowledge

Extend the skills you learned in this chapter and experiment with new skills. You may need to use Help to complete the assignment.

Working with References and Proofing Tools

Instructions: Start Word. Open the document, Extend 2-1 Computing Options Paper Draft, from the Data Files for Students. See the inside back cover of this book for instructions on downloading the Data Files for Students, or contact your instructor for information on accessing the required files.

You will add another footnote to the paper, use the thesaurus, convert the document from MLA to APA style, convert the footnotes to endnotes, modify the Endnote Text style, change the format of the note reference marks, and translate the document to another language.

Perform the following tasks:

1. Insert a second footnote at an appropriate place in the research paper. Use the following footnote text: The Americans with Disabilities Act (ADA) requires any company with 15 or more employees to make reasonable attempts to accommodate the needs of physically challenged workers.

2. Use the Replace dialog box to find the word, imagine, in the document and then replace it with a word of your choice.

3. Save the document with a new file name and then print it. Select the entire document and then change the style of the citations and bibliography from MLA to APA. Save the APA version of the document with a new file name and then print it. Compare the two versions. Circle the differences between the two documents.

4. Convert the footnotes to endnotes.

5. Modify the Endnote Text style to 11-point Calibri font, double-spaced text with a first-line indent.

6. Change the format of the note reference marks to capital letters (A, B, etc.).

7. Save the revised document with endnotes with a new file name and then print it. On the printout with the endnotes, write the number of words, characters without spaces, characters with spaces, paragraphs, and lines in the document. Be sure to include endnote text in the statistics.

8. Translate the research paper into a language of your choice (Figure 2–81 on the next page) using the Translate button on the Review tab. Print the translated document.

Continued >

Extend Your Knowledge *continued*

Figure 2–81

Make It Right

Analyze a document and correct all errors and/or improve the design.

Inserting Missing Elements in an MLA Style Research Paper

Instructions: Start Word. Open the document, Make It Right 2-1 Certification Paper Draft, from the Data Files for Students. See the inside back cover of this book for instructions on downloading the Data Files for Students, or contact your instructor for information on accessing the required files.

The document is a research paper that is missing several elements. You are to insert these missing elements, all formatted according to the MLA documentation style: header with a page number, heading (name, course, and date information), paper title, footnote, and source information for the first citation and the citation in the footnote.

Perform the following tasks:

1. Insert a header with a page number, heading (use your own information: name, course information, and date), and an appropriate paper title, all formatted according to the MLA style.

2. Use the Select Browse Object button to go to page 2. How many bibliographical entries currently are on the Works Cited page? You will create additional source entries in Steps 3 and 4.

3. The Otoole placeholder (tag name) is missing its source information (Figure 2–82). Use the following source information to edit the source: magazine article titled "Career Builders and Boosts," written by Sarah W. O'Toole, magazine name is *IT World and Certifications*, publication date is March 2008, article is on pages 88-93. Edit the citation so that it displays the author name and the page numbers.

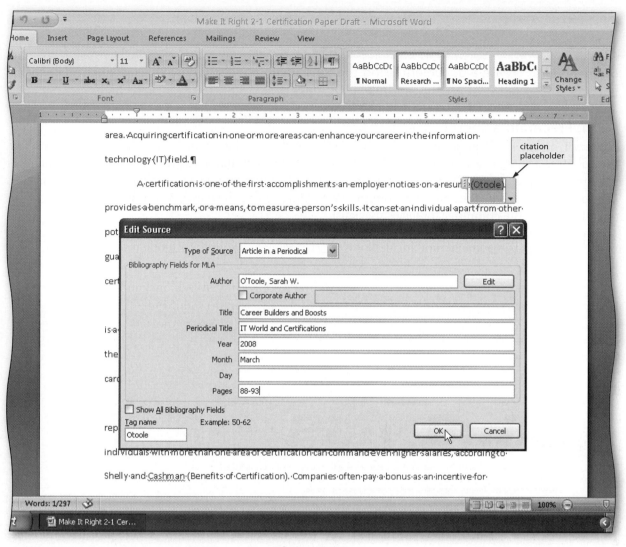

Figure 2–82

4. Insert the following footnote with the note reference at an appropriate place in the paper, formatted according to the MLA style: Debbins points out that, as an additional bonus, some certification training can be used for college credit. The citation for this footnote should be at the end of the footnote. The source information is as follows: book named *Preparing for the Future: IT Strategies*, authored by Floyd I. Debbins, published in 2008 at IT World Press in Chicago, pages 99-104. Edit the citation so that it displays only page numbers.

5. Use the Select Browse Object button to go to page 3. Be sure the bibliographical list on the Works Cited page contains all three entries. If necessary, use the F9 key to update the bibliographical list. Format the bibliographical paragraphs with a one-half inch hanging indent.

6. Modify the source of the book authored by Floyd I. Debbins, so that the publisher city is Boston instead of Chicago.

7. Use the Select Browse Object button to go to the footnote. Be sure the footnote is formatted properly.

8. Change the document properties, as specified by your instructor. Save the revised document with a new file name and then submit it in the format specified by your instructor.

In the Lab

Design and/or create a document using the guidelines, concepts, and skills presented in this chapter. Labs are listed in order of increasing difficulty.

Lab 1: Preparing a Short Research Paper

Problem: You are a college student currently enrolled in an introductory business class. Your assignment is to prepare a short research paper (300-350 words) about a computer-related job. The requirements are that the paper be presented according to the MLA documentation style and have three references. One of the three references must be from the Web. You prepare the paper shown in Figure 2–83, which discusses the computer forensics specialist.

Hankins 1

Mary Hankins

Mr. Habib

Business 102

14 March 2008

Computer Forensics Specialist

Computer forensics, also called digital forensics, network forensics, or cyberforensics, is a rapidly growing field that involves gathering and analyzing evidence from computers and networks. Because computers and the Internet are the fastest growing technology used for criminal activity, the need for computer forensics specialists will increase in years to come.

A computer forensics specialist examines computer media, programs, data, and log files on computers, servers, and networks. According to Shelly and Cashman (Computer Careers), many areas employ computer forensics specialists, including law enforcement, criminal prosecutors, military intelligence, insurance agencies, and information security departments in the private sector. A computer forensics specialist must have knowledge of the law, technical experience with many types of hardware and software products, superior communication skills, a willingness to learn and update skills, and a knack for problem solving.

When a problem occurs, it is the responsibility of the computer forensics specialist to carefully take several steps to identify and retrieve possible evidence that may exist on a suspect's computer. These steps include protecting the suspect's computer, discovering all files, recovering deleted files, revealing hidden files, accessing protected or encrypted files, analyzing all the data, and providing expert consultation and/or testimony as required (Reinman 52-58).

A computer forensics specialist must have knowledge of all aspects of the computer, from the operating system to computer architecture and hardware design. In the past, many computer forensics specialists were self-taught computer users. Today, extensive training, usually from several different

(a)

Figure 2–83

(b)

Hankins 2

sources, is required. A degree in Computer Science should be supplemented with graduate courses and university-level professional development certificates. Entry level salaries range from $45,000 to $75,000. With experience and certifications, salaries can exceed $125,000 (Turell 44-55).

With the growing use of computers in all areas of life, the number of computer crimes surely will continue to rise. As a result, the need for skilled specialists to battle these crimes will increase for many years to come.

(c)

Hankins 3

Works Cited

Reinman, David P. "Fighting Cybercriminals." Cybertech Monthly February 2008: 52-58.

Shelly, Gary B., and Thomas J. Cashman. "Computer Careers." Course Technology. 7 March 2008
        <www.scsite.com/wd2007/pr2/wc.htm>.

Turell, Marcia O., and Alex N. Gutierrez. Cybercrimes and Criminals. El Paso: Legal Works Publishing
        Company, 2008.

Figure 2–83 (continued)

Instructions: Perform the following tasks:

1. If necessary, display formatting marks on the screen.
2. Adjust line spacing to double.
3. Remove space below (after) paragraphs.
4. Create a header to number pages.
5. Type the name and course information at the left margin. Center and type the title.
6. Set first-line indent for paragraphs in the body of the research paper.
7. Create a Quick Style for the research paper paragraphs.
8. Type the research paper as shown in Figures 2–83a and 2–83b. Change the bibliography style to MLA. As you insert citations, enter their source information (shown in Figure 2–83c). Edit the citations so that they display according to Figures 2–83a and 2–83b.
9. At the end of the research paper text, press the ENTER key and then insert a manual page break so that the Works Cited page begins on a new page. Enter and format the works cited title (Figure 2–83c). Use Word to insert the bibliographical list (bibliography). Format the paragraphs in the list with a hanging indent.
10. Check the spelling and grammar of the paper at once.
11. Save the document on a USB flash drive using Lab 2-1 Computer Forensics Paper as the file name.
12. Print the research paper. Handwrite the number of words, paragraphs, and characters in the research paper above the title of your printed research paper.

In the Lab

Lab 2: Preparing a Research Report with a Footnote

Problem: You are a college student enrolled in an introductory English class. Your assignment is to prepare a short research paper in any area of interest to you. The requirements are that the paper be presented according to the MLA documentation style, contain at least one explanatory note positioned as a footnote, and have three references. One of the three references must be from the Internet. You prepare a paper about antivirus programs (Figure 2–84).

Yadav 1

Pahdi Yadav

Professor Milton

English 101

5 May 2008

Antivirus Programs

Today, people rely on computers to create, store, and manage critical information, many times via a home computer network. Information transmitted over networks has a higher degree of security risk than information kept in a user's home or company premises. Thus, it is crucial that they take measures to protect their computers and data from loss, damage, and misuse resulting from computer security risks. Antivirus programs are an effective way to protect a computer against viruses.

An antivirus program protects a computer against viruses by identifying and removing any computer viruses found in memory, on storage media, or on incoming files.[1] When you purchase a new computer, it often includes antivirus software. Antivirus programs work by scanning for programs that attempt to modify the boot program, the operating system, and other programs that normally are read from but not modified. In addition, many antivirus programs automatically scan files downloaded from the Web, e-mail attachments, opened files, and all types of removable media inserted in the computer (Karanos 201-205).

One technique that antivirus programs use to identify a virus is to look for virus signatures, or virus definitions, which are known specific patterns of virus code. According to Shelly and Cashman (Antivirus Programs), many vendors of antivirus programs allow registered users to update virus signature files automatically from the Web at no cost for a specified time. Updating the antivirus

_____

[1] Bulowski points out that most antivirus programs also protect against worms and Trojan horses (55-61).

(a)

Figure 2–84

Yadav 2

program's signature files regularly is important, because it will download any new virus definitions that

have been added since the last update.

      Methods that guarantee a computer or network is safe from computer viruses simply do not

exist. Installing, updating, and using an antivirus program, though, is an effective technique to safeguard

your computer from loss.

(b)

Figure 2–84 (continued)

Instructions: Perform the following tasks:

1. Adjust line spacing to double and remove space below (after) paragraphs. Create a header to number pages. Type the name and course information at the left margin. Center and type the title. Set first-line indent for paragraphs in the body of the research paper. Create a Quick Style for the research paper paragraphs.

2. Type the research paper as shown in Figures 2–84a and 2–84b. Add the footnote as shown in Figure 2–84a. Change the Footnote Text style to the format specified in the MLA style. Change the bibliography style to MLA. As you insert citations, use the following source information:

   a. Type of Source: Periodical
      Author: Bulowski, Dana
      Title: Protection and Precaution: Keeping Your Computer Healthy
      Periodical Title: Computing Today
      Year: 2008
      Month: February
      Pages 55-61
   b. Type of Source: Book
      Author: Karanos, Hector
      Title: Internet Security
      Year: 2008
      City: Indianapolis
      Publisher: Citywide Cyber Press
   c. Type of Source: Web site
      Author: Shelly, Gary B., and Thomas J. Cashman
      Name of Web page: Antivirus Programs
      Production Company: Course Technology
      Year Accessed: 2008
      Month Accessed: February
      Day Accessed: 7
      URL: www.scsite.com/wd2007/pr2/wc.htm

3. At the end of the research paper text, press the ENTER key once and insert a manual page break so that the Works Cited page begins on a new page. Enter and format the works cited title. Use Word to insert the bibliographical list. Format the paragraphs in the list with a hanging indent.

4. Check the spelling and grammar of the paper.

5. Save the document on a USB flash drive using Lab 2-2 Antivirus Programs Paper as the file name.

6. Print the research paper. Handwrite the number of words, including the footnotes, in the research paper above the title of your printed research paper.

In the Lab

Lab 3: Composing a Research Paper from Notes

Problem: You have drafted the notes shown in Figure 2–85. Your assignment is to prepare a short research paper from these notes.

Home networks:
- Home users connect multiple computers and devices together in a home network.
- Home networking saves money and provides conveniences.
- Approximately 39 million homes have more than one computer.
- Many vendors offer home networking packages that include all the necessary hardware and software to network a home using wired or wireless techniques.

Three types of wired home networks: Ethernet, powerline cable, and phoneline (source: "Wired vs. Wireless Networks," an article on pages 24-29 in March 2008 issue of Modern Networking by Mark A. Travis).
- Traditional Ethernet networks require that each computer have built-in network capabilities or contain a network card, which connects to a central network hub or similar device with a physical cable. This may involve running cable through walls, ceilings, and floors in the house.
- The hardware and software of an Ethernet network can be difficult to configure for the average home user (source: a book called <u>Home Networking</u> by Frank A. Deakins, published at Current Press in New York in 2008).
- A phoneline network is an easy-to-install and inexpensive network that uses existing telephone lines in the home.
- A home powerline cable network is a network that uses the same lines that bring electricity into the house. This network requires no additional wiring.

Two types of wireless home networks: HomeRF and Wi-Fi (source: a Web site titled "Wired and Wireless Networks" by Gary B. Shelly and Thomas J. Cashman of Course Technology, viewed on April 23, 2008. Web address is www.scsite.com/wd2007/pr2/wc.htm).
- Wireless networks have the disadvantage of interference, because walls, ceilings, and other electrical devices such as cordless telephones and microwave ovens can disrupt wireless communications.
- A HomeRF (radio frequency) network uses radio waves, instead of cables, to transmit data.
- A Wi-Fi network sends signals over a wider distance than the Home RF network, which can be up to 1,500 feet in some configurations.

Figure 2–85

Instructions: Perform the following tasks:

1. Review the notes in Figure 2–85 and then rearrange and reword them. Embellish the paper as you deem necessary. Present the paper according to the MLA documentation style. Create an AutoCorrect entry that automatically corrects the spelling of the misspelled word, wird, to the correct spelling, wired. Add a footnote that refers the reader to the Web for more information. Enter citations and their sources as shown. Create the works cited page (bibliography) from the listed sources.

2. Check the spelling and grammar of the paper. Save the document on a USB flash drive using Lab 2-3 Home Networks Paper as the file name.

3. Use the Research task pane to look up a definition of a word in the paper. Copy and insert the definition into the document as a footnote. Be sure to quote the definition and cite the source.

4. Print the research paper. Handwrite the number of words, including the footnotes, in the research paper above the title of the printed research paper.

Cases and Places

Apply your creative thinking and problem solving skills to design and implement a solution.

• EASIER   •• MORE DIFFICULT

• 1: Create a Research Paper about Word Using the MLA Documentation Style

Chapter 1 of this book discussed the components of the Word window (pages WD 6 through 11). Using the material presented on those pages, write a short research paper (350–400 words) that describes the purpose and functionality of one or more of these components: document window, Ribbon, Mini toolbar and shortcut menus, Quick Access Toolbar, and Office Button. Use your textbook and Word Help as sources. Include at least two citations and one explanatory note positioned as a footnote. Add an AutoCorrect entry to correct a word you commonly mistype. Use the concepts and techniques presented in this chapter to format the paper according to the MLA documentation style. Check spelling and grammar of the finished paper.

•• 2: Create the Research Paper Presented in this Chapter Using the APA Documentation Style

As discussed in this chapter, two popular documentation styles for research papers are the Modern Language Association of America (MLA) and American Psychological Association (APA) styles. In this chapter, you created a research paper that followed guidelines of the MLA documentation style. Using the school library, this textbook, other textbooks, the Internet, magazines, or other sources, research the guidelines of the APA documentation style. Then, prepare the Wireless Communications Paper from this chapter following the guidelines of the APA documentation style. Use Figure 2–1 on page WD 75 as a starting point for the text and source information. Check spelling and grammar of the finished paper.

•• 3: Create a Research Paper that Compares Documentation Styles

This chapter discussed the requirements of the MLA documentation style. The American Psychological Association (APA) and the Chicago Manual of Style (CMS) are two other documentation styles supported by Word. Using the school library, this textbook, other textbooks, the Internet, magazines, or other sources, research the guidelines of the APA and CMS documentation styles to learn more about the differences among the MLA, APA, and CMS documentation styles. Using what you learn, write a short research paper (450-500 words) that compares the requirements and formats of the three documentation styles. Include at least two references and one explanatory note positioned as a footnote. Use the documentation style specified by your instructor to format the paper. Check spelling and grammar of the finished paper.

•• 4: Create a Research Paper about the Month You Were Born

Make It Personal

Did you ever wonder what world events took place during the month you were born (besides your birth)? For example, what happened with respect to politics, world affairs, and the economy? What made headline news? Were there any scientific breakthroughs? What was on television and at the box office? Were any famous people born? Did anyone famous die? What songs topped the charts? What was happening in the world of sports? Research the newsworthy events that took place during the month and year you were born (i.e., July 1981) by looking through newspapers, magazines, searching the Web, and/or interviewing family and friends. Write a short research paper (450-500 words) that summarizes your findings. Include at least two references and one explanatory note. Use the documentation style specified by your instructor to format the paper. Check spelling and grammar of the finished paper.

Continued >

Cases and Places *continued*

•• 5: Create a Research Paper about Spring Break Vacation Destinations

Working Together

With spring break just two months away, you and your fellow classmates are thinking about various spring break vacation destinations. Many options are available. Should you vacation close to home or travel across the country? Stay at a hotel, rent a condominium, or camp outdoors? Travel by car, train, or airplane? Book through a travel agent or the Web? Each team member is to research the attractions, accommodations, required transportation, and total cost of one spring break destination by looking through newspapers, magazines, searching the Web, and/or visiting a travel agency. Each team member is to write a minimum of 200 words summarizing his or her findings. Each team member also is to write at least one explanatory note and supply his or her source information for the citation and bibliography. Then, the team should meet as a group to compose a research paper that includes all team members' write-ups. Start by copying and pasting the text into a single document and then write an introduction and conclusion as a group. Use the documentation style specified by your instructor to format the paper. Check spelling and grammar of the finished paper. Set the default dictionary. If Word flags any of your last names as an error, add the name(s) to the custom dictionary. Hand in printouts of each team member's original write-up, as well as the final research paper.

1 | Creating a Worksheet and an Embedded Chart

Objectives

You will have mastered the material in this chapter when you can:

- Start and quit Excel
- Describe the Excel worksheet
- Enter text and numbers
- Use the Sum button to sum a range of cells
- Copy the contents of a cell to a range of cells using the fill handle
- Save a workbook
- Format cells in a worksheet
- Create a 3-D Clustered Column chart

- Change document properties
- Save a workbook a second time using the same file name
- Print a worksheet
- Open a workbook
- Use the AutoCalculate area to determine statistics
- Correct errors on a worksheet
- Use Excel Help to answer questions

1 | Creating a Worksheet and an Embedded Chart

What Is Microsoft Office Excel 2007?

Microsoft Office Excel 2007 is a powerful spreadsheet program that allows users to organize data, complete calculations, make decisions, graph data, develop professional looking reports (Figure 1–1), publish organized data to the Web, and access real-time data from Web sites. The four major parts of Excel are:

- **Workbooks and Worksheets** Workbooks are a collection of worksheets. Worksheets allow users to enter, calculate, manipulate, and analyze data such as numbers and text. The terms worksheet and spreadsheet are interchangeable.
- **Charts** Excel can draw a variety of charts.
- **Tables** Tables organize and store data within worksheets. For example, once a user enters data into a worksheet, an Excel table can sort the data, search for specific data, and select data that satisfies defined criteria.
- **Web Support** Web support allows users to save Excel worksheets or parts of a worksheet in HTML format, so a user can view and manipulate the worksheet using a browser. Excel Web support also provides access to real-time data, such as stock quotes, using Web queries.

This latest version of Excel makes it much easier than in previous versions to perform common functions by introducing a new style of user interface. It also offers the capability of creating larger worksheets, improved formatting and printing, improved charting and table functionality, industry-standard XML support that simplifies the sharing of data within and outside an organization, improved business intelligence functionality, and the capability of performing complex tasks on a server.

In this chapter, you will create a worksheet that includes a chart. The data in the worksheet and chart includes sales data for several stores that a company owns and operates.

Project Planning Guidelines

The process of developing a worksheet that communicates specific information requires careful analysis and planning. As a starting point, establish why the worksheet is needed. Once the purpose is determined, analyze the intended users of the worksheet and their unique needs. Then, gather information about the topic and decide what to include in the worksheet. Finally, determine the worksheet design and style that will be most successful at delivering the message. Details of these guidelines are provided in Appendix A. In addition, each project developed in this book provides practical applications of these planning considerations.

Project — Worksheet with an Embedded Chart

The project in this chapter follows proper design guidelines and uses Excel to create the worksheet shown in Figure 1–1. The worksheet contains sales data for Walk and Rock Music stores. The Walk and Rock Music product line includes a variety of MP3 music players, called Rock-It MP3, including players that show pictures and video, as well as a complete line of headphones and other accessories. The company sells its products at kiosks in several malls throughout the United States. By concentrating its stores near colleges and universities and keeping the newest items in stock, the Walk and Rock Music stores quickly became trendy. As sales continued to grow in the past year, senior management requested an easy-to-read worksheet that shows product sales for the first quarter by region. In addition, they asked for a chart showing first quarter sales, because the president of the company likes to have a graphical representation of sales that allows him quickly to identify stronger and weaker product types by region.

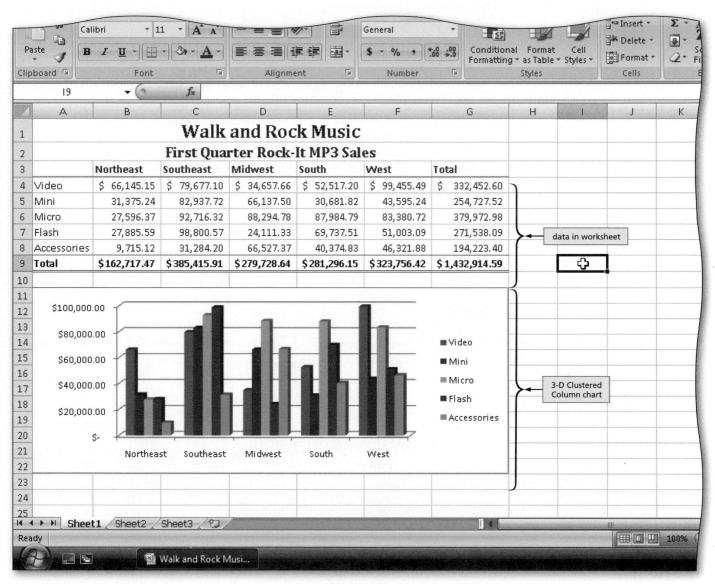

Figure 1–1

The first step in creating an effective worksheet is to make sure you understand what is required. The person or persons requesting the worksheet should supply their requirements in a requirements document. A **requirements document** includes a needs

BTW

Excel 2007 Features
With its what-if analysis tools, research capabilities, collaboration tools, streamlined user interface, smart tags, charting features, Web capabilities, hundreds of functions, and enhanced formatting capabilities, Excel 2007 is one of the easier and more powerful spreadsheet packages available.

statement, source of data, summary of calculations, and any other special requirements for the worksheet, such as charting and Web support. Figure 1–2 shows the requirements document for the new workbook to be created in this chapter.

requirements document ⟶

REQUEST FOR NEW WORKBOOK	
Date Submitted:	April 15, 2008
Submitted By:	Trisha Samuels
Worksheet Title:	Walk and Rock Music First Quarter Sales
Needs:	An easy-to-read worksheet that shows Walk and Rock Music's first quarter sales for each of our sales regions in which we operate (Northeast, Southeast, Midwest, South, West). The worksheet also should include total sales for each region, total sales for each product type, and total company sales for the first quarter.
Source of Data:	The data for the worksheet is available for the end of the first quarter from the chief financial officer (CFO) of Walk and Rock Music.
Calculations:	The following calculations must be made for the worksheet: (a) total first quarter sales for each of the five regions; (b) total first quarter sales for each of the five product types; and (c) total first quarter sales for the company.
Chart Requirements:	Below the data in the worksheet, construct a 3-D Clustered Column chart that compares the total sales for each region within each type of product.

Approvals

Approval Status:	X	Approved
		Rejected
Approved By:	Stan Maderbek	
Date:	April 22, 2008	
Assigned To:	J. Quasney, Spreadsheet Specialist	

Figure 1–2

BTW

Worksheet Development Cycle
Spreadsheet specialists do not sit down and start entering text, formulas, and data into a blank Excel worksheet as soon as they have a spreadsheet assignment. Instead, they follow an organized plan, or methodology, that breaks the development cycle into a series of tasks. The recommended methodology for creating worksheets includes: (1) analyze requirements (supplied in a requirements document); (2) design solution; (3) validate design; (4) implement design; (5) test solution; and (6) document solution.

Overview

As you read this chapter, you will learn how to create the worksheet shown in Figure 1–1 by performing these general tasks:

- Enter text in the worksheet
- Add totals to the worksheet
- Save the workbook that contains the worksheet
- Format the text in the worksheet
- Insert a chart in the worksheet
- Save the workbook a second time using the same file name
- Print the worksheet

Plan Ahead

General Project Guidelines
While creating an Excel worksheet, you need to make several decisions that will determine the appearance and characteristics of the finished worksheet. As you create the worksheet shown in Figure 1–1, you should follow these general guidelines:

1. **Select titles and subtitles for the worksheet.** Follow the *less is more* guideline. The less text in the titles and subtitles, the more impact the titles and subtitles will have. Use the fewest words possible to specify the information presented in the worksheet to the intended audience.

(continued)

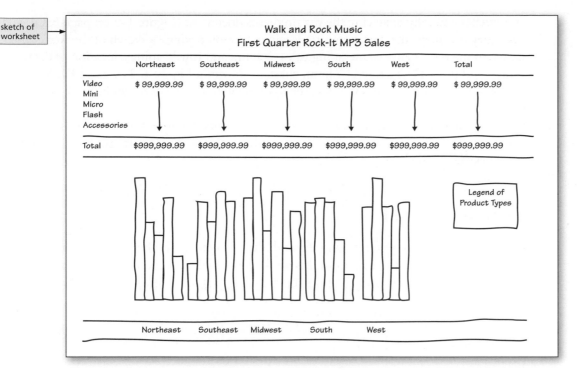

sketch of worksheet

Walk and Rock Music
First Quarter Rock-It MP3 Sales

	Northeast	Southeast	Midwest	South	West	Total
Video Mini Micro Flash Accessories	$ 99,999.99	$ 99,999.99	$ 99,999.99	$ 99,999.99	$ 99,999.99	$ 99,999.99
Total	$999,999.99	$999,999.99	$999,999.99	$999,999.99	$999,999.99	$999,999.99

Legend of Product Types

Northeast   Southeast   Midwest   South   West

Figure 1–3

(continued)

2. **Determine the contents for rows and columns.** Rows typically contain information that is analogous to items in a list, such as the products sold by a company. Columns typically contain descriptive information about items in rows or contain information that helps to group the data in the worksheet, such as company regions.

3. **Determine the calculations that are needed.** You can decide to total data in a variety of ways, such as across rows or in columns. You also can include a grand total.

4. **Determine where to save the workbook.** You can store a workbook permanently, or **save** it, on a variety of storage media including a hard disk, USB flash drive, or CD. You also can indicate a specific location on the storage media for saving the workbook.

5. **Identify how to format various elements of the worksheet.** The overall appearance of a worksheet significantly affects its ability to communicate clearly. Examples of how you can modify the appearance, or **format**, of text include changing its shape, size, color, and position on the worksheet.

6. **Decide on the type of chart needed.** Excel includes the capability of creating many different types of charts, such as bar charts and pie charts. Each chart type relays a different message about the data in the worksheet. Choose a chart type that relays the message that you want to convey.

7. **Establish where to position and how to format the chart.** The position and format of the chart should command the attention of the intended audience. If possible, position the chart so that it prints with the worksheet data on a single page.

When necessary, more specific details concerning the above guidelines are presented at appropriate points in the chapter. The chapter also will identify the actions performed and decisions made regarding these guidelines during the creation of the worksheet shown in Figure 1–1 on page EX 3.

Plan Ahead

After carefully reviewing the requirements document (Figure 1–2 on page EX 4) and necessary decisions, the next step is to design a solution or draw a sketch of the worksheet based on the requirements, including titles, column and row headings, location of data values, and the 3-D Clustered Column chart, as shown in Figure 1–3 on page EX 5. The dollar signs, 9s, and commas that you see in the sketch of the worksheet indicate formatted numeric values.

With a good understanding of the requirements document, an understanding of the necessary decisions, and a sketch of the worksheet, the next step is to use Excel to create the worksheet and chart.

Starting Excel

If you are using a computer to step through the project in this chapter and you want your screen to match the figures in this book, you should change your computer's resolution to 1024 × 768. For information about how to change a computer's resolution, read Appendix E.

To Start Excel

The following steps, which assume Windows Vista is running, start Excel based on a typical installation of Microsoft Office on your computer. You may need to ask your instructor how to start Excel for your computer.

Note: If you are using Windows XP, see Appendix F for alternate steps.

1

- Click the Start button on the Windows Vista taskbar to display the Start menu.

- Click All Programs at the bottom of left pane on the the Start menu to display the All Programs list.

- Click Microsoft Office in the All Programs list to display the Microsoft Office list (Figure 1–4).

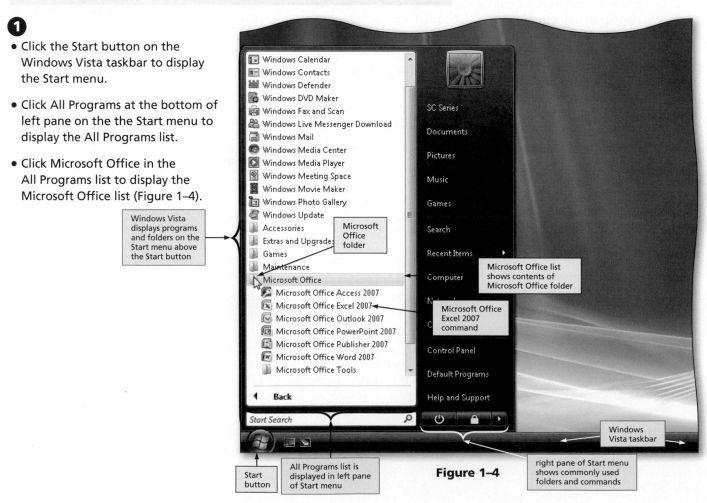

Figure 1–4

②

- Click Microsoft Office Excel 2007 to start Excel and display a new blank workbook titled Book1 in the Excel window (Figure 1–5).

- If the Excel window is not maximized, click the Maximize button next to the Close button on its title bar to maximize the window.

- If the worksheet window in Excel is not maximized, click the Maximize button next to the Close button on its title bar to maximize the worksheet window within Excel.

What is a maximized window?

A maximized window fills the entire screen. When you maximize a window, the Maximize button changes to a Restore Down button. When you restore a maximized window, the window returns to its previous size and the Restore Down button changes to a Maximize button.

Figure 1–5

Other Ways

1. Double-click Excel 2007 icon on desktop, if one is present
2. Click Microsoft Office Excel 2007 on Start menu

The Excel Workbook

The Excel window consists of a variety of components to make your work more efficient and worksheets more professional. These include the document window, Ribbon, Mini toolbar and shortcut menus, Quick Access Toolbar, and Office Button. Some of these components are common to other Microsoft Office 2007 programs; others are unique to Excel.

When Excel starts, it creates a new blank workbook, called Book1. The **workbook** (Figure 1–6) is like a notebook. Inside the workbook are sheets, each of which is called a **worksheet**. Excel opens a new workbook with three worksheets.

If necessary, you can add additional worksheets as long as your computer has enough memory to accommodate them. Each worksheet has a sheet name that appears on a **sheet tab** at the bottom of the workbook. For example, Sheet1 is the name of the active worksheet displayed in the Book1 workbook. If you click the sheet tab labeled Sheet2, Excel displays the Sheet2 worksheet. The project in this chapter uses only the Sheet1 worksheet.

The Worksheet

The worksheet is organized into a rectangular grid containing vertical columns and horizontal rows. A column letter above the grid, also called the **column heading**, identifies each column. A row number on the left side of the grid, also called the **row heading**, identifies

BTW

Excel Help
Help with Excel is no further away than the Help button on the right side of the Ribbon. Click the Help button, type help in the 'Type words to search for' box, and then press the ENTER key. Excel responds with a list of topics you can click to learn about obtaining Help on any Excel-related topic. To find out what is new in Excel 2007, type what is new in Excel in the 'Type words to search for' box.

each row. With the screen resolution set to 1024 × 768 and the Excel window maximized, Excel displays 15 columns (A through O) and 25 rows (1 through 25) of the worksheet on the screen, as shown in Figure 1–6.

Figure 1–6

The intersection of each column and row is a cell. A **cell** is the basic unit of a worksheet into which you enter data. Each worksheet in a workbook has 16,384 columns and 1,048,576 rows for a total of 17,179,869,180 cells. Only a small fraction of the active worksheet appears on the screen at one time.

A cell is referred to by its unique address, or **cell reference**, which is the coordinates of the intersection of a column and a row. To identify a cell, specify the column letter first, followed by the row number. For example, cell reference D11 refers to the cell located at the intersection of column D and row 11 (Figure 1–6).

One cell on the worksheet, designated the **active cell**, is the one into which you can enter data. The active cell in Figure 1–6 is A1. The active cell is identified in three ways. First, a heavy border surrounds the cell; second, the active cell reference shows immediately above column A in the Name box; and third, the column heading A and row heading 1 are highlighted so it is easy to see which cell is active (Figure 1–6).

The horizontal and vertical lines on the worksheet itself are called **gridlines**. Gridlines make it easier to see and identify each cell in the worksheet. If desired, you can turn the gridlines off so they do not show on the worksheet, but it is recommended that you leave them on for now.

The mouse pointer in Figure 1–6 has the shape of a block plus sign. The mouse pointer appears as a block plus sign whenever it is located in a cell on the worksheet. Another common shape of the mouse pointer is the block arrow. The mouse pointer turns into the block arrow whenever you move it outside the worksheet or when you drag cell contents between rows or columns. The other mouse pointer shapes are described when they appear on the screen.

Worksheet Window

You view the portion of the worksheet displayed on the screen through a **worksheet window** (Figure 1–6). The default (preset) view is **normal view**. Below and to the right of the worksheet window are **scroll bars**, **scroll arrows**, and **scroll boxes** that you can use to move the worksheet window around to view different parts of the active worksheet. To the right of the sheet tabs at the bottom of the screen is the tab split box. You can drag the **tab split box** to increase or decrease the view of the sheet tabs (Figure 1–6). When you decrease the view of the sheet tabs, you increase the length of the horizontal scroll bar, and vice versa.

Status Bar

The status bar is located immediately above the Windows Vista taskbar at the bottom of the screen (Figure 1–6). The **status bar** presents information about the worksheet, the function of the button the mouse pointer is pointing to, or the mode of Excel. **Mode indicators**, such as Enter and Ready, appear on the status bar and specify the current mode of Excel. When the mode is **Ready**, Excel is ready to accept the next command or data entry. When the mode indicator reads **Enter**, Excel is in the process of accepting data through the keyboard into the active cell.

Keyboard indicators, such as Scroll Lock, show which toggle keys are engaged. Keyboard indicators appear to the right of the mode indicator. Toward the right edge of the status bar are buttons and controls you can use to change the view of a document and adjust the size of the displayed document.

Ribbon

The **Ribbon**, located near the top of the Excel window, is the control center in Excel (Figure 1–7a). The Ribbon provides easy, central access to the tasks you perform while creating a worksheet. The Ribbon consists of tabs, groups, and commands. Each **tab** surrounds a collection of groups, and each **group** contains related commands.

BTW

The Worksheet Size and Window
Excel's 16,384 columns and 1,048,576 rows make for a huge worksheet that – if you could imagine – takes up the entire side of a building to display in its entirety. Your computer screen, by comparison, is a small window that allows you to view only a minute area of the worksheet at one time. While you cannot see the entire worksheet, you can move the window over the worksheet to view any part of it.

BTW

Increasing the Viewing Area
You can increase the size of the Excel window or viewing area to show more of the worksheet. Two ways exist to increase what you can see in the viewing area: (1) on the View tab on the Ribbon, click Full Screen; and (2) change to a higher resolution. See Appendix E for information about how to change to a higher resolution.

(a) The Excel Ribbon

(b) The Excel Ribbon Minimized

Figure 1–7

BTW

Minimizing the Ribbon
If you want to minimize the Ribbon, right-click the Ribbon and then click Minimize the Ribbon on the shortcut menu, double-click the active tab, or press CTRL+F1. To restore a minimized Ribbon, right-click the Ribbon and then click Minimize the Ribbon on the shortcut menu, double-click any top-level tab, or press CTRL+F1. To use commands on a minimized Ribbon, click the top-level tab.

When you start Excel, the Ribbon displays seven top-level tabs: Home, Insert, Page Layout, Formulas, Data, Review, and View. The **Home tab**, called the primary tab, contains groups with the more frequently used commands. To display a different tab on the Ribbon, click the top-level tab. That is, to display the Insert tab, click Insert on the Ribbon. To return to the Home tab, click Home on the Ribbon. The tab currently displayed is called the **active tab**.

To display more of the document in the document window, some users prefer to minimize the Ribbon, which hides the groups on the Ribbon and displays only the top-level tabs (Figure 1–7b). To use commands on a minimized Ribbon, click the top-level tab.

Each time you start Excel, the Ribbon appears the same way it did the last time you used Excel. The chapters in this book, however, begin with the Ribbon appearing as it did at the initial installation of the software. If you are stepping through this chapter on a computer and you want your Ribbon to match the figures in this book, read Appendix E.

In addition to the top-level tabs, Excel displays other tabs, called **contextual tabs**, when you perform certain tasks or work with objects such as charts or tables. If you insert a chart in the worksheet, for example, the Chart Tools tab and its related subordinate Design tab appear (Figure 1–8). When you are finished working with the chart, the Chart Tools and Design tabs disappear from the Ribbon. Excel determines when contextual tabs should appear and disappear, based on the tasks you perform.

Figure 1–8

Ribbon commands include buttons, boxes (text boxes, check boxes, etc.), and galleries (Figure 1–8). A **gallery** is a set of choices, often graphical, arranged in a grid or in a list. You can scroll through choices on an in-Ribbon gallery by clicking the gallery's scroll arrows. An **in-Ribbon** gallery shows common gallery choices on the Ribbon rather than in a dropdown list. Or, you can click a gallery's More button to view more gallery options on the screen at a time. Some buttons and boxes have arrows that, when clicked, also display a gallery; others always cause a gallery to be displayed when clicked. Most galleries support **live preview**, which is a feature that allows you to point to a gallery choice and see its effect in the worksheet without actually selecting the choice (Figure 1–9).

Some commands on the Ribbon display an image to help you remember their function. When you point to a command on the Ribbon, all or part of the command glows in shades of yellow and orange, and an Enhanced ScreenTip appears on the screen. An **Enhanced ScreenTip** is an on-screen note that provides the name of the command, available keyboard shortcut(s), a description of the command, and sometimes instructions for how to obtain Help about the command (Figure 1–10). Enhanced ScreenTips are more detailed than a typical **ScreenTip**, which usually displays only the name of the command.

The lower-right corner of some groups on the Ribbon has a small arrow, called a **Dialog Box Launcher**, that when clicked displays a dialog box or a task pane (Figure 1–11). A **dialog box** contains additional commands and options for the group. When presented with a dialog box, you make selections and must close the dialog box before returning to the worksheet. A **task pane**, by contrast, is a window that contains additional commands and can stay open and visible while you work on the worksheet.

Figure 1–9

Figure 1–10

Figure 1–11

Formula Bar

The formula bar appears below the Ribbon (Figure 1–12a). As you type, Excel displays the entry in the **formula bar**. You can make the formula bar larger by dragging the sizing handle (Figure 1–7) on the formula bar or clicking the expand button to the right of the formula bar. Excel also displays the active cell reference in the **Name box** on the left side of the formula bar.

Mini Toolbar and Shortcut Menus

The **Mini toolbar**, which appears automatically based on tasks you perform (such as selecting text), contains commands related to changing the appearance of text in a worksheet. All commands on the Mini toolbar also exist on the Ribbon. The purpose of the Mini toolbar is to minimize mouse movement. For example, if you want to format text using a command that currently is not displayed on the active tab, you can use the command on the Mini toolbar — instead of switching to a different tab to use the command.

When the Mini toolbar appears, it initially is transparent (Figure 1–12a). If you do not use the transparent Mini toolbar, it disappears from the screen. To use the Mini toolbar, move the mouse pointer into the toolbar, which causes the Mini toolbar to change from a transparent to bright appearance (Figure 1–12b).

(a) Transparent Mini Toolbar

(b) Bright Mini Toolbar

Figure 1–12

A **shortcut menu**, which appears when you right-click an object, is a list of frequently used commands that relate to the right-clicked object. If you right-click an item in the document window such as a cell, Excel displays both the Mini toolbar and a shortcut menu (Figure 1–13).

Figure 1–13

Quick Access Toolbar

The **Quick Access Toolbar**, located by default above the Ribbon, provides easy access to frequently used commands (Figure 1–14a). The commands on the Quick Access Toolbar always are available, regardless of the task you are performing. Initially, the Quick Access Toolbar contains the Save, Undo, and Redo buttons. If you click the Customize Quick Access Toolbar button, Excel provides a list of commands you quickly can add to and remove from the Quick Access Toolbar (Figure 1–14b).

You also can add other commands to or delete commands from the Quick Access Toolbar so that it contains the commands you use most often. As you add commands to the Quick Access Toolbar, its commands may interfere with the workbook title on the title bar. For this reason, Excel provides an option of displaying the Quick Access Toolbar below the Ribbon (Figure 1–14c).

BTW

Quick Access Toolbar Commands
To add a Ribbon command as a button to the Quick Access Toolbar, right-click the command on the Ribbon and then click Add to Quick Access Toolbar on the shortcut menu. To delete a button from the Quick Access Toolbar, right-click the button on the Quick Access Toolbar and then click Remove from Quick Access Toolbar on the shortcut menu. To display the Quick Access Toolbar below the Ribbon, right-click the Quick Access Toolbar and then click Show Quick Access Toolbar Below the Ribbon on the shortcut menu.

(a) Quick Access Toolbar above Ribbon

(c) Quick Access Toolbar below Ribbon

(b) Customize Quick Access Toolbar Menu

Figure 1–14

Each time you start Excel, the Quick Access Toolbar appears the same way it did the last time you used Excel. The chapters in this book, however, begin with the Quick Access Toolbar appearing as it did at the initial installation of the software. If you are stepping through this chapter on a computer and you want your Quick Access Toolbar to match the figures in this book, you should reset your Quick Access Toolbar. For more information about how to reset the Quick Access Toolbar, read Appendix E.

Office Button

While the Ribbon is a control center for creating worksheets, the **Office Button** is a central location for managing and sharing workbooks. When you click the Office Button, located in the upper-left corner of the window, Excel displays the Office Button menu (Figure 1–15). A **menu** contains a list of commands.

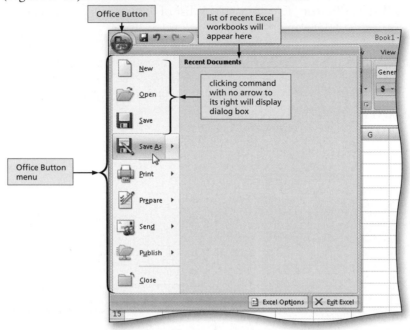

Figure 1–15

When you click the New, Open, Save As, and Print commands on the Office Button menu, Excel displays a dialog box with additional options. The Save As, Print, Prepare, Send, and Publish commands have an arrow to their right. If you point to a button that includes an arrow, Excel displays a **submenu**, which is a list of additional commands associated with the selected command (Figure 1–16). For the Prepare, Send, and Publish commands that do not display a dialog box when clicked, you can point either to the command or the arrow to display the submenu.

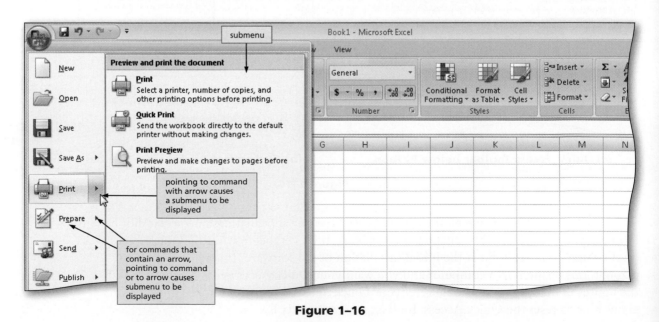

Figure 1–16

Key Tips

If you prefer using the keyboard, instead of the mouse, you can press the ALT key on the keyboard to display a **Key Tip badge**, or keyboard code icon, for certain commands (Figure 1–17). To select a command using the keyboard, press its displayed code letter, or **Key Tip**. When you press a Key Tip, additional Key Tips related to the selected command appear. For example, to select the New command on the Office Button menu, press the ALT key, then press the F key, then press the N key.

Figure 1–17

To remove the Key Tip badges from the screen, press the ALT key or the ESC key on the keyboard until all Key Tip badges disappear or click the mouse anywhere in the Excel window.

Selecting a Cell

To enter data into a cell, you first must select it. The easiest way **to select a cell** (make it active) is to use the mouse to move the block plus sign mouse pointer to the cell and then click.

An alternative method is to use the arrow keys that are located just to the right of the typewriter keys on the keyboard. An arrow key selects the cell adjacent to the active cell in the direction of the arrow on the key.

You know a cell is selected, or active, when a heavy border surrounds the cell and the active cell reference appears in the Name box on the left side of the formula bar. Excel also changes the active cell's column heading and row heading to a gold color.

Entering Text

In Excel, any set of characters containing a letter, hyphen (as in a telephone number), or space is considered text. **Text** is used to place titles, such as worksheet titles, column titles, and row titles, on the worksheet.

Plan Ahead	**Select titles and subtitles for the worksheet.**
	As previously stated, worksheet titles and subtitles should be as brief and meaningful as possible. As shown in Figure 1–18, the worksheet title, Walk and Rock Music, identifies the company for whom the worksheet is being created in Chapter 1. The worksheet subtitle, First Quarter Rock-It MP3 Sales, identifies the type of report.

Plan Ahead	**Determine the contents of rows and columns.**
	As previously mentioned, rows typically contain information that is similar to items in a list. For the Walk and Rock Music sales data, the list of product types meets this criterion. It is more likely that in the future, the company will add more product types as opposed to more regions. Each product type, therefore, should be placed in its own row. The row titles in column A (Video, Mini, Micro, Flash, Accessories, and Total) identify the numbers in each row.
	Columns typically contain descriptive information about items in rows or contain information that helps to group the data in the worksheet. In the case of the Walk and Rock Music sales data, the regions classify the sales of each product type. The regions, therefore, are placed in columns. The column titles in row 3 (Northeast, Southeast, Midwest, South, West, and Total) identify the numbers in each column.

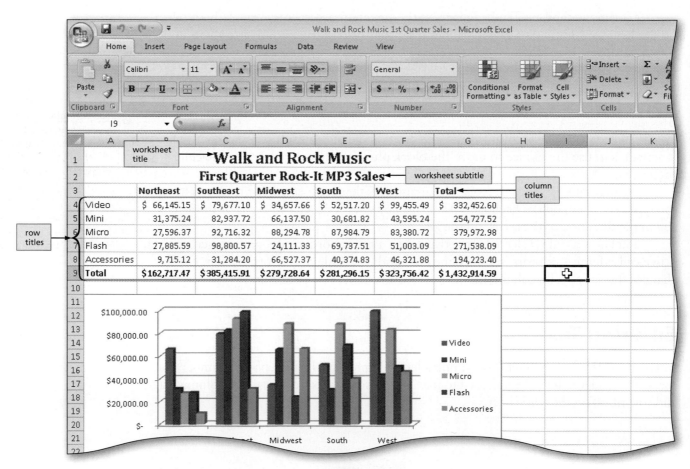

Figure 1–18

To Enter the Worksheet Titles

The following steps show how to enter the worksheet titles in cells A1 and A2. Later in this chapter, the worksheet titles will be formatted so they appear as shown in Figure 1–18.

1

• Click cell A1 to make cell A1 the active cell (Figure 1–19).

Figure 1–19

2

• Type Walk and Rock Music in cell A1, and then point to the Enter box in the formula bar.

Q&A

Why did the appearance of the formula bar change?

Excel displays the title in the formula bar and in cell A1. When you begin typing a cell entry, Excel displays two additional boxes in the formula bar: the Cancel box and the Enter box. Clicking the **Enter box** completes an entry. Clicking the **Cancel box** cancels an entry.

Q&A

What is the vertical line in cell A1?

In Figure 1–20, the text in cell A1 is followed by the insertion point. The **insertion point** is a blinking vertical line that indicates where the next typed character will appear.

Figure 1–20

③

- Click the Enter box to complete the entry and enter the worksheet title in cell A1 (Figure 1–21).

Figure 1–21

④

- Click cell A2 to select it.

- Type First Quarter Rock-It MP3 Sales as the cell entry.

- Click the Enter box to complete the entry and enter the worksheet subtitle in cell A2 (Figure 1–22).

Figure 1–22

Other Ways

1. To complete entry, click any cell other than active cell

2. To complete entry, press ENTER key

3. To complete entry, press HOME, PAGE UP, PAGE DOWN, or END key

4. To complete entry, press UP, DOWN, LEFT, or RIGHT key.

Entering Text in a Cell

When you complete a text entry into a cell, a series of events occurs. First, Excel positions the text left-aligned in the cell. **Left-aligned** means the cell entry is positioned at the far left in the cell. Therefore, the W in the worksheet title, Walk and Rock Music, begins in the leftmost position of cell A1.

Second, when the text is longer than the width of a column, Excel displays the overflow characters in adjacent cells to the right as long as these adjacent cells contain no data. In Figure 1–22, the width of cell A1 is approximately nine characters. The text consists of 19 characters. Therefore, Excel displays the overflow characters from cell A1 in cells B1 and C1, because cells B1 and C1 are empty. If cell B1 contained data, Excel would hide the overflow characters, so that only the first nine characters in cell A1 would appear on the worksheet. Excel stores the overflow characters in cell A1 and displays them in the formula bar whenever cell A1 is the active cell.

Third, when you complete an entry by clicking the Enter box, the cell in which the text is entered remains the active cell.

Correcting a Mistake while Typing

If you type the wrong letter and notice the error before clicking the Enter box or pressing the ENTER key, use the BACKSPACE key to delete all the characters back to and including the incorrect letter. To cancel the entire entry before entering it into the cell, click the Cancel box in the formula bar or press the ESC key. If you see an error in a cell after entering the text, select the cell and retype the entry. Later in this chapter, additional error-correction techniques are discussed.

AutoCorrect

The **AutoCorrect feature** of Excel works behind the scenes, correcting common mistakes when you complete a text entry in a cell. AutoCorrect makes three types of corrections for you:

1. Corrects two initial capital letters by changing the second letter to lowercase.

2. Capitalizes the first letter in the names of days.

3. Replaces commonly misspelled words with their correct spelling. For example, it will change the misspelled word *recieve* to *receive* when you complete the entry. AutoCorrect will correct the spelling of hundreds of commonly misspelled words automatically.

BTW

The ENTER Key
When you first install Excel, the ENTER key not only completes the entry, but it also moves the selection to an adjacent cell. You can instruct Excel not to move the selection after pressing the ENTER key by clicking the Excel Options button on the Office Button menu, clicking the Advanced option, removing the checkmark from the 'After pressing Enter, move selection' check box, and then clicking the OK button.

To Enter Column Titles

To enter the column titles in row 3, select the appropriate cell and then enter the text. The following steps enter the column titles in row 3.

1

• Click cell B3 to make cell B3 the active cell (Figure 1–23).

Figure 1–23

2

- Type Northeast in cell B3 (Figure 1–24).

Figure 1–24

3

- Press the RIGHT ARROW key to enter the column title, Northeast, in cell B3 and make cell C3 the active cell (Figure 1–25).

Q&A

Why is the RIGHT ARROW key used to complete the entry in the cell?

If the next entry is in an adjacent cell, use the arrow keys to complete the entry in a cell. When you press an arrow key to complete an entry, the adjacent cell in the direction of the arrow (up, down, left, or right) becomes the active cell. If the next entry is in a nonadjacent cell, complete an entry by clicking the next cell in which you plan to enter data. You also can click the Enter box or press the ENTER key and then click the appropriate cell for the next entry.

Figure 1–25

4

- Repeat Steps 2 and 3 to enter the remaining column titles in row 3; that is, enter `Southeast` in cell C3, `Midwest` in cell D3, `South` in cell E3, `West` in cell F3, and `Total` in cell G3 (complete the last entry in cell G3 by clicking the Enter box in the formula bar) (Figure 1–26).

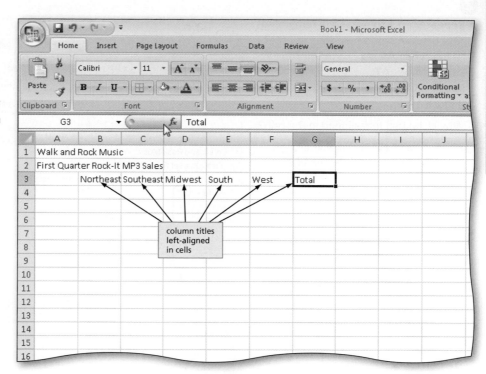

Figure 1–26

To Enter Row Titles

The next step in developing the worksheet for this project is to enter the row titles in column A. This process is similar to entering the column titles. The following steps enter the row titles in the worksheet.

- Click cell A4 to select it.

- Type `Video` and then press the DOWN ARROW key to enter the row title and make cell A5 the active cell (Figure 1–27).

Figure 1–27

2

• Repeat Step 1 to enter the remaining row titles in column A; that is, enter `Mini` in cell A5, `Micro` in cell A6, `Flash` in cell A7, `Accessories` in cell A8, and `Total` in cell A9 (Figure 1–28).

Q&A

Why is the text left-aligned in the cells?

When you enter text, Excel automatically left-aligns the text in the cell. Excel treats any combination of numbers, spaces, and nonnumeric characters as text. For example, the following entries are text:

401AX21, 921-231, 619 321, 883XTY

You can change the text alignment in a cell by realigning it. Several alignment techniques are discussed later in the chapter.

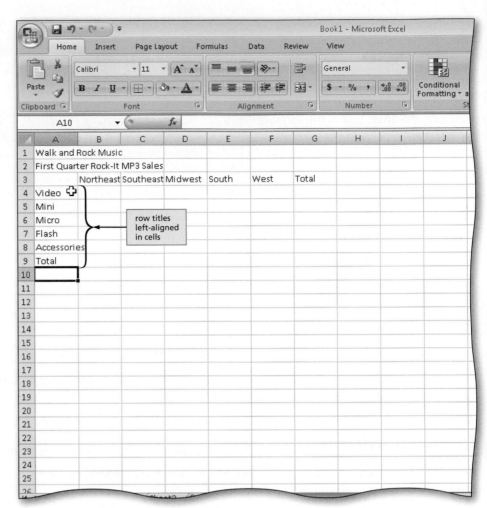

Figure 1–28

BTW

Numeric Limitations
In Excel, a number can be between approximately -1×10^{308} and 1×10^{308}, that is, between a negative 1 followed by 308 zeros and a positive 1 followed by 308 zeros. To enter a number such as 6,000,000,000,000,000, you can type 6,000,000,000,000,000, or you can type 6E15, which stands for 6×10^{15}.

Entering Numbers

In Excel, you can enter numbers into cells to represent amounts. A **number** can contain only the following characters:

0 1 2 3 4 5 6 7 8 9 + - ( ) , / . $ % E e

If a cell entry contains any other keyboard character (including spaces), Excel interprets the entry as text and treats it accordingly. The use of the special characters is explained when they are used in this book.

To Enter Numbers

The Walk and Rock Music First Quarter Rock-It MP3 Sales numbers used in Chapter 1 are summarized in Table 1–1. These numbers, which represent sales revenue for each of the product types and regions, must be entered in rows 4, 5, 6, 7, and 8.

Table 1–1 Walk and Rock Music First Quarter Rock-It MP3 Sales					
	Northeast	**Southeast**	**Midwest**	**South**	**West**
Video	66145.15	79677.10	34657.66	52517.20	99455.49
Mini	31375.24	82937.72	66137.50	30681.82	43595.24
Micro	27596.37	92716.32	88294.78	87984.79	83380.72
Flash	27885.59	98800.57	24111.33	69737.51	51003.09
Accessories	9715.12	31284.20	66527.37	40374.83	46321.88

The following steps enter the numbers in Table 1–1 one row at a time.

1

- Click cell B4.

- Type 66145.15 and then press the RIGHT ARROW key to enter the data in cell B4 and make cell C4 the active cell (Figure 1–29).

Do I need to enter dollar signs, commas, or trailing zeros for the quarterly sales numbers?

You are not required to type dollar signs, commas, or trailing zeros. When you enter a dollar value that has cents, however, you must add the decimal point and the numbers representing the cents. Later in this chapter, the numbers will be formatted to use dollar signs, commas, and trailing zeros to improve the appearance and readability of the numbers.

Figure 1–29

2

- Enter 79677.1 in cell C4, 34657.66 in cell D4, 52517.2 in cell E4, and 99455.49 in cell F4 (Figure 1–30).

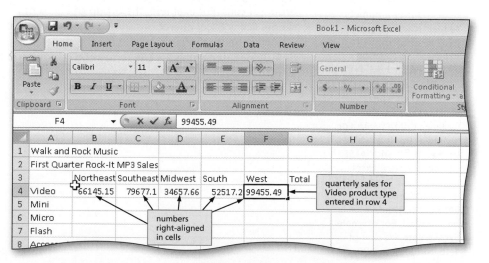

Figure 1–30

3

- Click cell B5.

- Enter the remaining first quarter sales numbers provided in Table 1–1 for each of the four remaining offerings in rows 5, 6, 7, and 8 to display the quarterly sales in the worksheet (Figure 1–31).

row title partially displayed because adjacent cell on right contains data

data entered into worksheet

Figure 1–31

Calculating a Sum

The next step in creating the worksheet is to perform any necessary calculations, such as calculating the column and row totals.

Plan Ahead

Determine calculations that are needed.
As stated in the requirements document in Figure 1–2 on page EX 4, totals are required for each region, each product type, and the company. The first calculation is to determine the quarterly sales for the stores in the Northeast region in column B. To calculate this value in cell B9, Excel must add, or sum, the numbers in cells B4, B5, B6, B7, and B8. Excel's **SUM function**, which adds all of the numbers in a range of cells, provides a convenient means to accomplish this task.

A **range** is a series of two or more adjacent cells in a column or row or a rectangular group of cells. For example, the group of adjacent cells B4, B5, B6, B7, and B8 is called a range. Many Excel operations, such as summing numbers, take place on a range of cells.

After the total quarterly sales for the stores in the Northeast region in column B is determined, the totals for the remaining regions and totals for each product type will be determined.

To Sum a Column of Numbers

The following steps sum the numbers in column B.

1

• Click cell B9 to make it the active cell and then point to the Sum button on the Ribbon (Figure 1–32).

Figure 1–32

2

• Click the Sum button on the Ribbon to display =SUM(B4: B8) in the formula bar and in the active cell B9 (Figure 1–33).

Q&A

How does Excel know which cells to sum?

When you enter the SUM function using the Sum button, Excel automatically selects what it considers to be your choice of the range to sum. When proposing the range to sum, Excel first looks for a range of cells with numbers above the active cell and then to the left. If Excel proposes the wrong range, you can correct it by dragging through the correct range before pressing the ENTER key. You also can enter the correct range by typing the beginning cell reference, a colon (:), and the ending cell reference.

Figure 1–33

3

- Click the Enter box in the formula bar to enter the sum of the first quarter sales for the five product types for the Northeast region in cell B9 (Figure 1-34).

Q&A

What is the purpose of the Sum button arrow?

If you click the Sum button arrow on the right side of the Sum button (Figure 1–34), Excel displays a list of often-used functions from which you can choose. The list includes functions that allow you to determine the average, the number of items in the selected range, the minimum value, or the maximum value of a range of numbers.

Figure 1–34

Using the Fill Handle to Copy a Cell to Adjacent Cells

Excel also must calculate the totals for the Southeast in cell C9, the Midwest in cell D9, the South in cell E9, and for the West in cell F9. Table 1–2 illustrates the similarities between the entry in cell B9 and the entries required to sum the totals in cells C9, D9, E9, and F9.

Table 1–2 Sum Function Entries in Row 9		
Cell	**Sum Function Entries**	**Remark**
B9	=SUM(B4:B8)	Sums cells B4, B5, B6, B7, and B8
C9	=SUM(C4:C8)	Sums cells C4, C5, C6, C7, and C8
D9	=SUM(D4:D8)	Sums cells D4, D5, D6, D7, and D8
E9	=SUM(E4:E8)	Sums cells E4, E5, E6, E7, and E8
F9	=SUM(F4:F8)	Sums cells F4, F5, F6, F7, and F8

To place the SUM functions in cells C9, D9, E9, and F9, you could follow the same steps shown previously in Figures 1–32 through 1–34. A second, more efficient method is to copy the SUM function from cell B9 to the range C9:F9. The cell being copied is called the **source area** or **copy area**. The range of cells receiving the copy is called the **destination area** or **paste area**.

Although the SUM function entries in Table 1–2 are similar, they are not exact copies. The range in each SUM function entry uses cell references that are one column to the right of the previous column. When you copy cell references, Excel automatically adjusts them for each new position, resulting in the SUM function entries illustrated in Table 1–2. Each adjusted cell reference is called a **relative reference**.

To Copy a Cell to Adjacent Cells in a Row

The easiest way to copy the SUM formula from cell B9 to cells C9, D9, E9, and F9 is to use the fill handle. The **fill handle** is the small black square located in the lower-right corner of the heavy border around the active cell. The following steps use the fill handle to copy cell B9 to the adjacent cells C9:F9.

- With cell B9 active, point to the fill handle (Figure 1–35).

Figure 1–35

- Drag the fill handle to select the destination area, range C9:F9, to display a shaded border around the destination area, range C9:F9, and the source area, cell B9 (Figure 1–36). Do not release the mouse button.

Figure 1–36

3

• Release the mouse button to copy the SUM function in cell B9 to the range C9:F9 (Figure 1–37) and calculate the sums in cells C9, D9, E9, and F9.

Q&A

What is the purpose of the Auto Fill Options button?

When you copy one range to another, Excel displays an Auto Fill Options button (Figure 1–37). The Auto Fill Options button allows you to choose whether you want to copy the values from the source area to the destination area with formatting, without formatting, or copy only the format. To view the available fill options, click the Auto Fill Options button. The Auto Fill Options button disappears when you begin another activity.

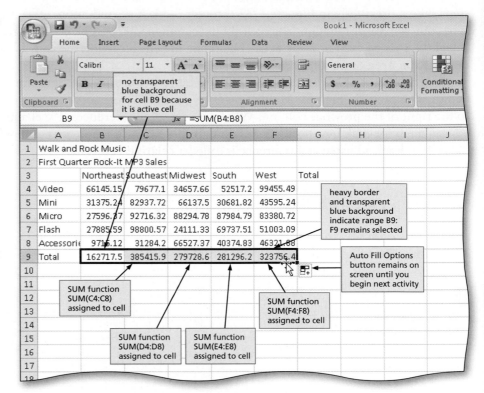

Figure 1–37

Other Ways

1. Select source area, click Copy button on Ribbon, select destination area, click Paste button on Ribbon

2. Right-click source area, click Copy on shortcut menu, right-click destination area, click Paste on shortcut menu

3. Select source area and then point to border of range; while holding down CTRL key, drag source area to destination area

To Determine Multiple Totals at the Same Time

The next step in building the worksheet is to determine the quarterly sales for each product type and total quarterly sales for the company in column G. To calculate these totals, you can use the SUM function much as it was used to total the quarterly sales by region in row 9. In this example, however, Excel will determine totals for all of the rows at the same time. The following steps illustrate this process.

1

• Click cell G4 to make it the active cell (Figure 1–38).

Figure 1–38

- With the mouse pointer in cell G4 and in the shape of a block plus sign, drag the mouse pointer down to cell G9 to highlight the range G4:G9 with a transparent view (Figure 1–39).

Figure 1–39

- Click the Sum button on the Ribbon to calculate and display the sums of the corresponding rows of sales in cells G4, G5, G6, G7, G8, and G9 (Figure 1–40).

- Select cell A10 to deselect the range G4:G9.

Q&A

Why does Excel create totals for each row?

If each cell in a selected range is next to a row of numbers, Excel assigns the SUM function to each cell when you click the Sum button.

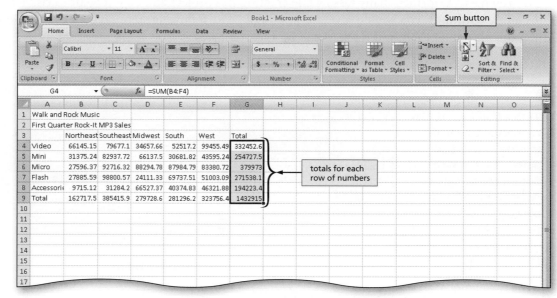

Figure 1–40

Saving the Project

While you are building a worksheet in a workbook, the computer stores it in memory. When you save a workbook, the computer places it on a storage medium such as a USB flash drive, CD, or hard disk. A saved workbook is referred to as a **file**. A **file name** is the name assigned to a file when it is saved. It is important to save the workbook frequently for the following reasons:

- The worksheet in memory will be lost if the computer is turned off or you lose electrical power while Excel is open.
- If you run out of time before completing your workbook, you may finish your worksheet at a future time without starting over.

BTW

Saving
Excel allows you to save a workbook in more than 30 different file formats. Choose the file format by clicking the 'Save as type' box arrow at the bottom of the Save As dialog box (Figure 1–41 on the next page). Excel Workbook is the default file format.

<table>
<tr><td>**Plan**
Ahead</td><td>**Determine where to save the workbook.**
When saving a workbook, you must decide which storage medium to use.

• If you always work on the same computer and have no need to transport your projects to a different location, then your computer's hard drive will suffice as a storage location. It is a good idea, however, to save a backup copy of your projects on a separate medium in case the file becomes corrupted or the computer's hard drive fails.

• If you plan to work on your workbooks in various locations or on multiple computers, then you should save your workbooks on a portable medium, such as a USB flash drive or CD. The workbooks used in this book are saved to a USB flash drive, which saves files quickly and reliably and can be reused. CDs are easily portable and serve as good backups for the final versions of workbooks because they generally can save files only one time.</td></tr>
</table>

To Save a Workbook

You have performed many tasks while creating this project and do not want to risk losing the work completed thus far. Accordingly, you should save the workbook. The following steps save a workbook on a USB flash drive using the file name, Walk and Rock Music 1st Quarter Sales.

Note: If you are using Windows XP, see Appendix F for alternate steps.

1
• With a USB flash drive connected to one of the computer's USB ports, click the Save button on the Quick Access Toolbar to display the Save As dialog box (Figure 1–41).

• If the Navigation pane is not displayed in the Save As dialog box, click the Browse Folders button to expand the dialog box.

• If a Folders list is displayed below the Folders button, click the Folders button to remove the Folders list.

Q&A
Do I have to save to a USB flash drive?

No. You can save to any device or folder. A **folder** is a specific location on a storage medium. You can save to the default folder or a different folder. You also can create your own folders, which is explained later in this book.

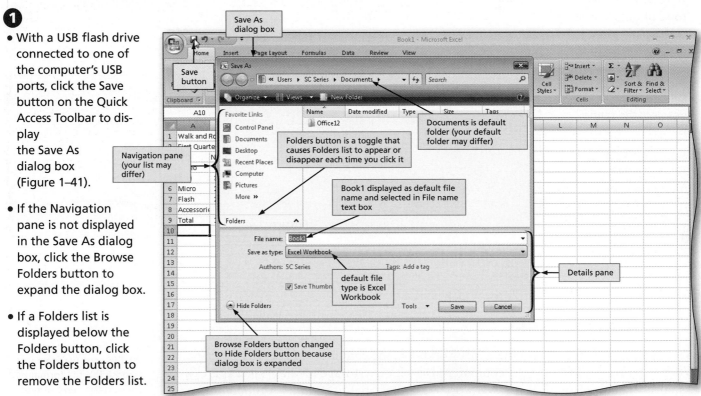

Figure 1–41

2

- Type `Walk and Rock Music 1st Quarter Sales` in the File name text box to change the file name. Do not press the ENTER key after typing the file name (Figure 1–42).

Q&A

What characters can I use in a file name?

A file name can have a maximum of 255 characters, including spaces. The only invalid characters are the backslash (\), slash (/), colon (:), asterisk (*), question mark (?), quotation mark ("), less than symbol (<), greater than symbol (>), and vertical bar (|).

Figure 1–42

3

- If Computer is not displayed in the Favorite Links section, drag the top or bottom edge of the Save As dialog box until Computer is displayed.

- Click Computer in the Favorite Links section to display a list of available drives (Figure 1–43).

- If necessary, scroll until UDISK 2.0 (E :) appears in the list of available drives.

Q&A

Why is my list of files, folders, and drives arranged and named differently from those shown in the figure?

Your computer's configuration determines how the list of files and folders is displayed and how drives are named. You can change the save location by clicking links on the **Favorite Links section**.

Figure 1–43

Q&A

How do I save the file if I am not using a USB flash drive?

Use the same process, but be certain to select your device in the list of available drives.

4

- Double-click UDISK 2.0 (E:) in the Save in list to select the USB flash drive, Drive E in this case, as the new save location (Figure 1–44).

What if my USB flash drive has a different name or letter?

It is very likely that your USB flash drive will have a different name and drive letter and be connected to a different port.

Figure 1–44

5

- Click the Save button in the Save As dialog box to save the workbook on the USB flash drive with the file name, Walk and Rock Music 1st Quarter Sales (Figure 1–45).

How do I know that Excel saved the workbook?

While Excel is saving your file, it briefly displays a message on the status bar indicating the amount of the file saved. In addition, your USB drive may have a light that flashes during the save process.

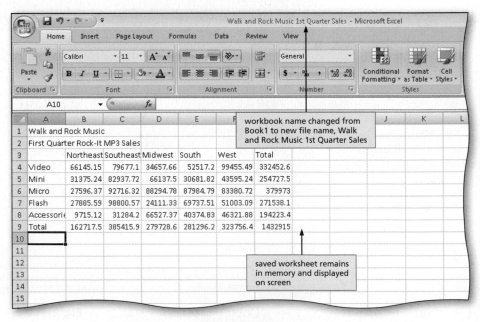

Figure 1–45

Other Ways

1. Click Office Button, click Save, type file name, select drive or folder, click Save button

2. Press CTRL+S or press SHIFT+F12, type file name, select drive or folder, click Save button

Formatting the Worksheet

The text, numeric entries, and functions for the worksheet now are complete. The next step is to format the worksheet. You **format** a worksheet to emphasize certain entries and make the worksheet easier to read and understand.

Figure 1–46a shows the worksheet before formatting. Figure 1–46b shows the worksheet after formatting. As you can see from the two figures, a worksheet that is formatted not only is easier to read but also looks more professional.

(a) Before Formatting

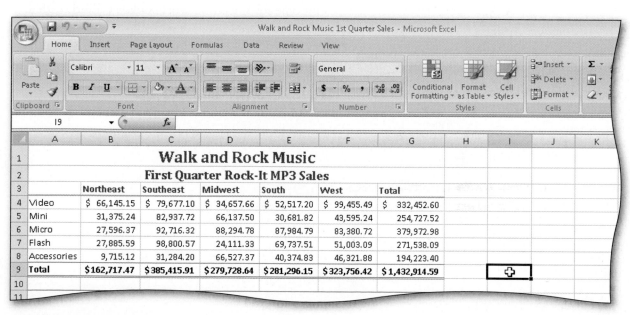

(b) After Formatting

Figure 1–46

<table>
<tr>
<td>

**Plan
Ahead**

</td>
<td>

Identify how to format various elements of the worksheet.
To change the unformatted worksheet in Figure 1–46a to the formatted worksheet in Figure 1–46b, the following tasks must be completed:

1. Change the font type, change the font style to bold, increase the font size, and change the font color of the worksheet titles in cells A1 and A2. These changes make the worksheet title prominently display to the user and inform the user of the purpose of the worksheet.

2. Center the worksheet titles in cells A1 and A2 across columns A through G.

3. Format the body of the worksheet. The body of the worksheet, range A3:G9, includes the column titles, row titles, and numbers. Formatting the body of the worksheet changes the numbers to use a dollars-and-cents format, with dollar signs in the first row (row 4) and the total row (row 9); adds underlining that emphasizes portions of the worksheet; and modifies the column widths to make the text and numbers readable.

</td>
</tr>
</table>

The remainder of this section explains the process required to format the worksheet. Although the format procedures are explained in the order described above, you should be aware that you could make these format changes in any order. Modifying the column widths, however, usually is done last.

Font Type, Style, Size, and Color

The characters that Excel displays on the screen are a specific font type, style, size, and color. The **font type**, or font face, defines the appearance and shape of the letters, numbers, and special characters. Examples of font types include Calibri, Cambria, Times New Roman, Arial, and Courier. **Font style** indicates how the characters are emphasized. Common font styles include regular, bold, underline, or italic. The **font size** specifies the size of the characters on the screen. Font size is gauged by a measurement system called points. A single point is about 1/72 of one inch in height. Thus, a character with a **point size** of 10 is about 10/72 of one inch in height. The **font color** defines the color of the characters. Excel can display characters in a wide variety of colors, including black, red, orange, and blue.

When Excel begins, the preset font type for the entire workbook is Calibri, with a font size, font style, and font color of 11-point regular black. Excel allows you to change the font characteristics in a single cell, a range of cells, the entire worksheet, or the entire workbook.

To Change a Cell Style

Excel includes the capability of changing several characteristics of a cell, such as font type, font size, and font color, all at once by assigning a predefined cell style to a cell. The following steps assign the Title cell style to the worksheet title in cell A1.

1

- Click cell A1 to make cell A1 the active cell.

- Click the Cell Styles button on the Ribbon to display the Cell Styles gallery (Figure 1–47).

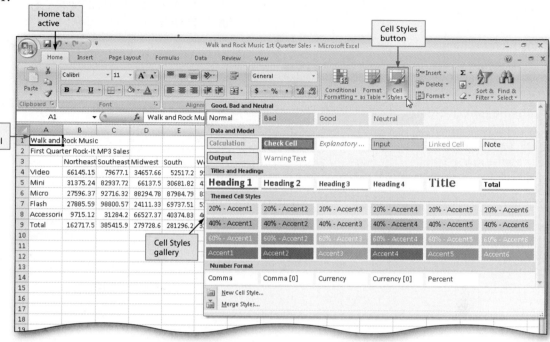

Figure 1–47

2

- Point to the Title cell style in the Titles and Headings area of the Cell Styles gallery to see a live preview of the cell style in cell A1 (Figure 1–48).

 Experiment

- Point to several other cell styles in the Cell Styles gallery to see a live preview of other cell styles in cell A1.

Q&A

Why does the font type, font size, and font color change in cell A1 when I point to it?

The change in cell A1 is a result of live preview. Live preview is a feature of Excel 2007 that allows you to preview cell styles as you point to them in the Cell Styles gallery.

Figure 1–48

3

- Click the Title cell style to apply the cell style to cell A1 (Figure 1–49).

Q&A

Why do several items in the Font group on the Ribbon change?

The changes to the Font box, Bold button, and Font Size box indicate the font changes applied to the active cell, cell A1, as a result of applying the Title cell style.

Figure 1–49

To Change the Font Type

Different font types often are used in a worksheet to make it more appealing to the reader. The following steps show how to change the worksheet subtitle's font type from Calibri to Cambria.

1

- Click cell A2 to make cell A2 the active cell.

- Click the Font box arrow on the Ribbon to display the Font gallery (Figure 1–50).

Q&A

Which fonts are displayed in the Font gallery?

Because many applications supply additional font types beyond what comes with the Windows Vista operating system, the number of font types available on your computer will depend on the applications installed. This book uses only font types that come with the Windows Vista operating system and Microsoft Office.

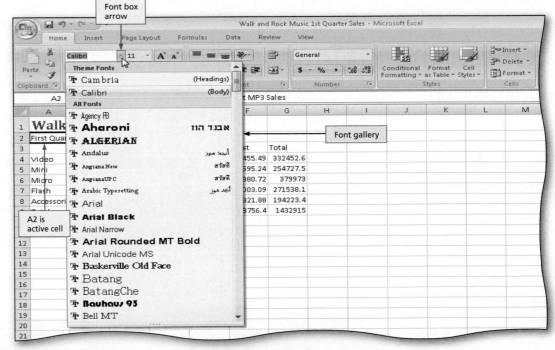

Figure 1–50

2

- Point to Cambria in the Theme Fonts area of the Font gallery to see a live preview of the Cambria font in cell A2 (Figure 1–51).

🔍 **Experiment**

- Point to several other fonts in the Font gallery to see a live preview of other fonts in cell A2.

What is the Theme Fonts area?

Excel applies the same default theme to any new workbook that you start. A **theme** is a collection of cell styles and other styles that have common characteristics, such as a color scheme and font type. The default theme for an Excel workbook is the Office theme. The Theme Fonts area of the Font gallery includes the fonts included in the default Office theme. Cambria is recommended for headings and Calibri is recommended for cells in the body of the worksheet (Figure 1–51).

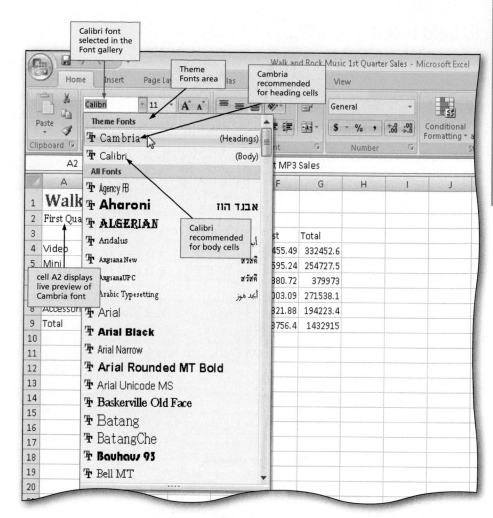

Figure 1–51

3

- Click Cambria in the Theme Fonts area to change the font type of the worksheet subtitle in cell A2 from Calibri to Cambria (Figure 1–52).

Figure 1–52

Other Ways

1. Select font type from Font list on Mini toolbar

2. Right-click cell, click Format Cells on shortcut menu, click Font tab, click desired font type, click OK button

To Bold a Cell

You **bold** an entry in a cell to emphasize it or make it stand out from the rest of the worksheet. The following step shows how to bold the worksheet subtitle in cell A2.

1

- With cell A2 active, click the Bold button on the Ribbon to change the font style of the worksheet subtitle to bold (Figure 1–53).

Q&A What if a cell already includes a bold style?

If you point to the Bold button and the active cell already is bold, then Excel displays the button with a transparent orange background.

Q&A How do I remove the bold style from a cell?

Clicking the Bold button a second time removes the bold font style.

Figure 1–53

Other Ways
1. Click Bold button on Mini toolbar	click Font tab, click Bold, click OK button
2. Right-click cell, click Format Cells on shortcut menu,	3. Press CTRL+B

To Increase the Font Size of a Cell Entry

Increasing the font size is the next step in formatting the worksheet subtitle. You increase the font size of a cell so the entry stands out and is easier to read. The following steps increase the font size of the worksheet subtitle in cell A2.

1

- With cell A2 selected, click the Font Size box arrow on the Ribbon to display the Font Size list.

- Point to 14 in the Font Size list to see a live preview of cell A2 with a font size of 14 (Figure 1–54).

 Experiment

- Point to several other font sizes in the Font Size list to see a live preview of other font sizes in cell A2.

Figure 1–54

2

• Click 14 in the Font Size list to change the font in cell A2 from 11 point to 14 point (Figure 1–55).

Q&A

Can I assign a font size that is not in the Font Size list?

Yes. An alternative to clicking a font size in the Font Size list is to click the Font Size box, type the font size, and then press the ENTER key. This procedure allows you to assign a font size not available in the Font Size list to a selected cell entry.

Figure 1–55

Other Ways

1. Click Increase Font Size button or Decrease Font Size button on Ribbon
2. Select font size from Font Size list on Mini toolbar
3. Right-click cell, click Format Cells on shortcut menu, click Font tab, select font size in Size box, click OK button

To Change the Font Color of a Cell Entry

The next step is to change the color of the font in cell A2 from black to dark blue. The following steps change the font color of a cell entry.

1

• With cell A2 selected, click the Font Color button arrow on the Ribbon to display the Font Color palette.

• Point to Dark Blue, Text 2 (dark blue color in column 4, row 1) in the Theme Colors area of the Font Color palette to see a live preview of the font color in cell A2 (Figure 1–56).

Experiment

• Point to several other colors in the Font Color palette to see a live preview of other font colors in cell A2.

Q&A

Which colors does Excel make available on the Font Color palette?

Figure 1–56

You can choose from more than 60 different font colors on the Font Color palette (Figure 1–56). Your Font Color palette may have more or fewer colors, depending on color settings of your operating system. The Theme Colors area includes colors that are included in the current workbook's theme.

- Click Dark Blue, Text 2 (column 4, row 1) on the Font Color palette to change the font of the worksheet subtitle in cell A2 from black to dark blue (Figure 1–57).

Q&A

Why does the Font Color button change after I select the new font color?

When you choose a color on the Font Color palette, Excel changes the Font Color button on the Formatting toolbar to the chosen color. Thus, to change the font color of the cell entry in another cell to the same color, you need only to select the cell and then click the Font Color button.

Figure 1–57

Other Ways

1. Select font color from Font Color list on Mini toolbar
2. Right-click cell, click Format Cells on shortcut menu, click Font tab, select color on Font Color palette, click OK button

To Center Cell Entries across Columns by Merging Cells

The final step in formatting the worksheet title and subtitle is to center them across columns A through G. Centering a title across the columns used in the body of the worksheet improves the worksheet's appearance. To do this, the seven cells in the range A1:G1 are combined, or merged, into a single cell that is the width of the columns in the body of the worksheet. The seven cells in the range A2:G2 also are merged in a similar manner. **Merging cells** involves creating a single cell by combining two or more selected cells. The following steps center the worksheet title and subtitle across columns by merging cells.

- Select cell A1 and then drag to cell G1 to highlight the range A1:G1 (Figure 1–58).

Q&A

What if a cell in the range B1:G1 contained data?

For the Merge & Center button to work properly, all the cells except the leftmost cell in the selected range must be empty.

Figure 1–58

2

• Click the Merge & Center button on the Ribbon to merge cells A1 through G1 and center the contents of cell A1 across columns A through G (Figure 1–59).

Q&A

What happened to cells B1 through G1?

After the merge, cells B1 through G1 no longer exist. Cell A1 now extends across columns A through G.

Figure 1–59

3

• Repeat Steps 1 and 2 to merge and center the worksheet subtitle across cells A2 through G2 (Figure 1–60).

Q&A

Are cells B1 through G1 and B2 through G2 lost forever?

No. The opposite of merging cells is **splitting a merged cell**. After you have merged multiple cells to create one merged cell, you can unmerge, or split, the merged cell to display the original cells on the worksheet. You split a merged cell by selecting it and clicking the Merge & Center button. For example, if you click the Merge & Center button a second time in Step 2, it will split the merged cell A1 to cells A1, B1, C1, D1, E1, F1, and G1.

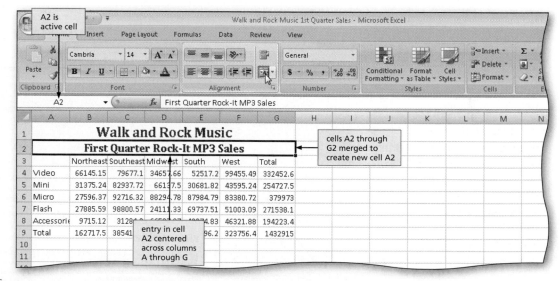

Figure 1–60

Other Ways

1. Right-click selection, click Merge & Center button on Mini toolbar

2. Right-click selection, click Format Cells on shortcut menu, click Alignment tab, select Center Across Selection in Horizontal list, click OK button

To Format Column Titles and the Total Row

The next step to format the worksheet is to format the column titles in row 3 and the total row, row 9. Column titles and the total row should be formatted so anyone who views the worksheet can quickly distinguish the column titles and total row from the data in the body of the worksheet. The following steps format the column titles and total row using cell styles in the default worksheet theme.

- Click cell A3 and then drag the mouse pointer to cell G3 to select the range A3:G3.

- Point to the Cell Styles button on the Ribbon (Figure 1–61).

Q&A

Why is cell A3 selected in the range for the column headings?

The style to be applied to the column headings includes an underline that will help to distinguish the column headings from the rest of the worksheet. Including cell A3 in the range ensures that the cell will include the underline, which is visually appealing and further helps to separate the data in the worksheet.

Figure 1–61

- Click the Cell Styles button to display the Cell Styles gallery.

- Point to the Heading 3 cell style in the Titles and Headings area of the Cell Styles gallery to see a live preview of the cell style in the range A3:G3 (Figure 1–62).

Experiment

- Point to other cell styles in the Titles and Headings area of the Cell Styles gallery to see a live preview of other cell styles in the range A3:G3.

Figure 1–62

③

- Click the Heading 3 cell style to apply the cell style to the range A3:G3.

- Click cell A9 and then drag the mouse pointer to cell G9 to select the range A9:G9.

- Point to the Cell Styles button on the Ribbon (Figure 1–63).

Q&A

Why should I choose Heading 3 instead of another heading cell style?

Excel includes many types of headings, such as Heading 1 and Heading 2, because worksheets often include many levels of headings above columns. In the case of the worksheet created for this project, the Heading 3 title includes formatting that makes the column titles' font size smaller than the title and subtitle and makes the column titles stand out from the data in the body of the worksheet.

Figure 1–63

④

- Click the Cell Styles button on the Ribbon to display the Cell Styles gallery and then click the Total cell style in the Titles and Headings area to apply the Total cell style to the cells in the range A9:G9.

- Click cell A11 to select the cell (Figure 1–64).

Figure 1–64

To Format Numbers in the Worksheet

As previously noted, the numbers in the worksheet should be formatted to use a dollar-and-cents format, with dollar signs in the first row (row 4) and the total row (row 9). Excel allows you to format numbers in a variety of ways, and these methods are discussed in other chapters in this book. The following steps use buttons on the Ribbon to format the numbers in the worksheet.

1

- Select cell B4 and drag the mouse pointer to cell G4 to select the range B4:G4.

- Point to the Accounting Number Format button on the Ribbon to display the Enhanced ScreenTip (Figure 1–65).

Figure 1–65

2

- Click the Accounting Number Format button on the Ribbon to apply the Accounting Number format to the cells in the range B4:G4.

- Select the range B5:G8 (Figure 1–66).

Q&A

What effect does the Accounting Number format have on the selected cells?

The Accounting Number format causes the cells to display with two decimal places so that decimal places in cells below the selected cells align vertically. Cell widths are automatically adjusted to accommodate the new formatting.

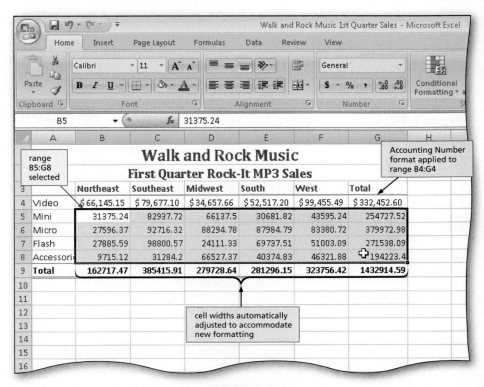

Figure 1–66

3

- Click the Comma Style button on the Ribbon to apply the Comma Style to the range B5:G8.

- Select the range B9:G9 (Figure 1–67).

Q&A

What effect does the Comma Style format have on the selected cells?

The Comma Style format causes the cells to display with two decimal places and commas as thousands separators.

Figure 1–67

4

- Click the Accounting Number Format button on the Ribbon to apply the Accounting Number format to the cells in the range B9:G9.

- Select cell A11 (Figure 1-68).

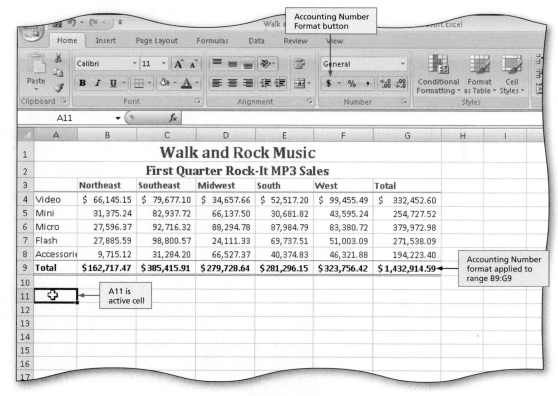

Figure 1–68

Other Ways	
1. Click Accounting Number Format or Comma button on Mini toolbar	2. Right-click selection, click Format Cells on the shortcut menu, click Number tab, select Accounting in Category list or select Number and click Use 1000 Separator, click OK button

To Adjust the Column Width

The last step in formatting the worksheet is to adjust the width of column A so that the word Accessories in cell A8 is shown in its entirety in the cell. Excel includes several methods for adjusting cell widths and row heights, and these methods are discussed later in this book. The following steps adjust the width of column A so that the contents of cell A8 are displayed in the cell.

1

• Point to the boundary on the right side of the column A heading above row 1 to change the mouse pointer to a split double arrow (Figure 1–69).

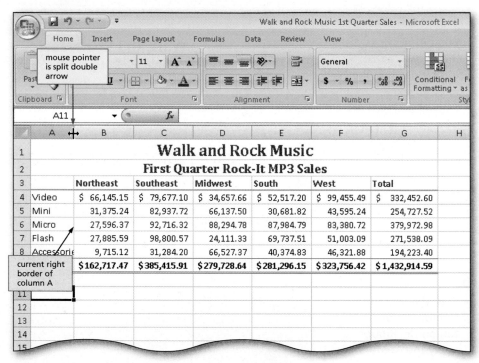

Figure 1–69

2

• Double-click on the boundary to adjust the width of column A to the width of the largest item in the column (Figure 1–70).

Q&A

What if none of the items in column A extended through the entire width of the column?

If all of the items in column A were shorter in length than the width of the column when you double-click the right side of the column A heading, then Excel still would adjust the column width to the largest item in the column. That is, Excel would reduce the width of the column to the largest item.

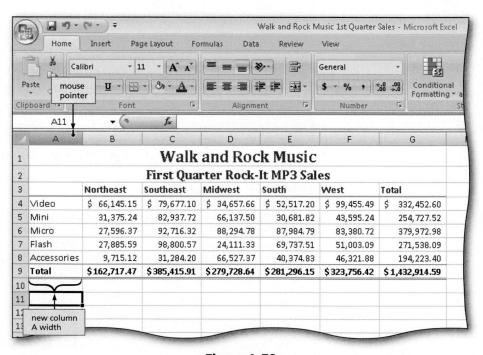

Figure 1–70

Using the Name Box to Select a Cell

The next step is to chart the quarterly sales for the five product types sold by the company. To create the chart, you must select the cell in the upper-left corner of the range to chart (cell A3). Rather than clicking cell A3 to select it, the next section describes how to use the Name box to select the cell.

To Use the Name Box to Select a Cell

As previously noted, the Name box is located on the left side of the formula bar. To select any cell, click the Name box and enter the cell reference of the cell you want to select. The following steps select cell A3.

1

- Click the Name box in the formula bar and then type a3 as the cell to select (Figure 1–71).

Q&A

Why is cell A11 still selected?

Even though cell A11 is the active cell, Excel displays the typed cell reference a3 in the Name box until you press the ENTER key.

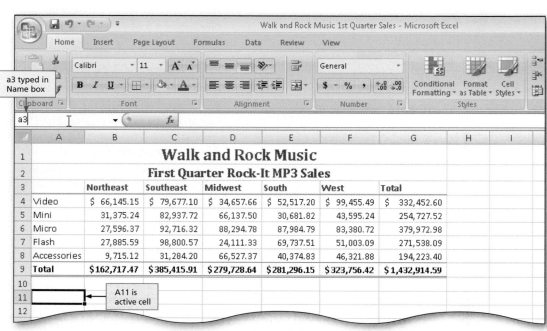

Figure 1–71

2

- Press the ENTER key to change the active cell from A11 to cell A3 (Figure 1–72).

Figure 1–72

Other Ways to Select Cells

As you will see in later chapters, in addition to using the Name box to select any cell in a worksheet, you also can use it to assign names to a cell or range of cells. Excel supports several additional ways to select a cell, as summarized in Table 1–3.

BTW

Find & Select
You can find and select cells based on their content. Click the Find & Select button on the Home tab on the Ribbon. Then, click the Go To Special command. Choose your desired option in the Select area of the Go To Special dialog box and then click the OK button.

Table 1–3 Selecting Cells in Excel

Key, Box, or Command	Function
ALT+PAGE DOWN	Selects the cell one worksheet window to the right and moves the worksheet window accordingly.
ALT+PAGE UP	Selects the cell one worksheet window to the left and moves the worksheet window accordingly.
ARROW	Selects the adjacent cell in the direction of the arrow on the key.
CTRL+ARROW	Selects the border cell of the worksheet in combination with the arrow keys and moves the worksheet window accordingly. For example, to select the rightmost cell in the row that contains the active cell, press CTRL+RIGHT ARROW. You also can press the END key, release it, and then press the appropriate arrow key to accomplish the same task.
CTRL+HOME	Selects cell A1 or the cell one column and one row below and to the right of frozen titles and moves the worksheet window accordingly.
Find command on Find and Select menu or SHIFT+F5	Finds and selects a cell that contains specific contents that you enter in the Find dialog box. If necessary, Excel moves the worksheet window to display the cell. You also can press CTRL+F to display the Find dialog box.
Go To command on Find and Select menu or F5	Selects the cell that corresponds to the cell reference you enter in the Go To dialog box and moves the worksheet window accordingly. You also can press CTRL+G to display the Go To dialog box.
HOME	Selects the cell at the beginning of the row that contains the active cell and moves the worksheet window accordingly.
Name box	Selects the cell in the workbook that corresponds to the cell reference you enter in the Name box.
PAGE DOWN	Selects the cell down one worksheet window from the active cell and moves the worksheet window accordingly.
PAGE UP	Selects the cell up one worksheet window from the active cell and moves the worksheet window accordingly.

Plan Ahead

Decide on the type of chart needed.
Excel includes 11 chart types from which you can choose including column, line, pie, bar, area, X Y (scatter), stock, surface, doughnut, bubble, and radar. The type of chart you choose depends on the type of data that you have, how much data you have, and the message you want to convey.

A column chart is a good way to compare values side-by-side. A Clustered Column chart can go even further in comparing values across categories. In the case of the Walk and Rock Music quarterly sales data, comparisons of product types within each region can be made side-by-side with a Clustered Column chart.

Establish where to position and how to format the chart.

- When possible, try to position charts so that both the data and chart appear on the screen on the worksheet together and so that the data and chart can be printed in the most readable manner possible. By placing the chart below the data on the Walk and Rock Music 1st Quarter Sales worksheet, both of these goals are accomplished.

- When choosing/selecting colors for a chart, consider the color scheme of the rest of the worksheet. The chart should not present colors that are in stark contrast to the rest of the worksheet. If the chart will be printed in color, minimize the amount of dark colors on the chart so that the embedded chart both prints quickly and preserves ink.

Adding a 3-D Clustered Column Chart to the Worksheet

As outlined in the requirements document in Figure 1–2 on page EX 4, the worksheet should include a 3-D Clustered Column chart to graphically represent quarterly sales for each product type that the company sells. The 3-D Clustered Column chart shown in Figure 1–73 is called an **embedded chart** because it is drawn on the same worksheet as the data.

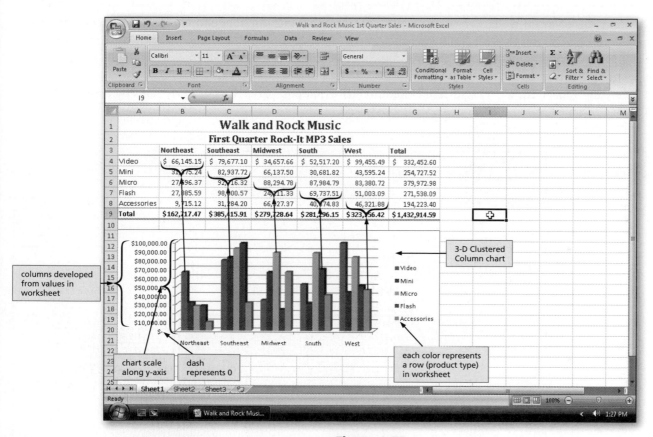

Figure 1–73

The chart uses different colored columns to represent sales for different product types. Each region uses the same color scheme for identifying product types, which allows for easy identification and comparison. For the Northeast sales region, for example, the dark blue column representing Video products shows quarterly sales of $66,145.15; for the Southeast sales region, the maroon column representing Mini products shows quarterly sales of $82,937.72; for the Midwest sales region, the pale green column representing Micro products shows quarterly sales of $88,294.78; for the South sales region, the violet column representing Flash products shows quarterly sales of $69,737.51; and for the West sales region, the light blue column representing Accessories shows quarterly sales of $46,321.88. Because the same color scheme is used in each region to represent the five product types, you easily can compare sales of product types among the sales regions. The totals from the worksheet are not represented, because the totals are not in the range specified for charting.

BTW

Cell Values and Charting

When you change a cell value on which a chart is dependent, Excel redraws the chart instantaneously, unless automatic recalculation is disabled. If automatic recalculation is disabled, then you must press the F9 key to redraw the chart. To enable or disable automatic recalculation, click the Calculations Options button on the Formulas tab on the Ribbon.

Excel derives the chart scale based on the values in the worksheet and then displays the scale along the vertical axis (also called the **y-axis** or **value axis**) of the chart. For example, no value in the range B4:F8 is less than 0 or greater than $100,000.00, so the scale ranges from 0 to $100,000.00. Excel also determines the $10,000.00 increments of the scale automatically. For the numbers along the y-axis, Excel uses a format that includes representing the 0 value with a dash (Figure 1–73 on the previous page).

To Add a 3-D Clustered Column Chart to the Worksheet

The commands to insert a chart are located on the Insert tab. With the range to chart selected, you click the Column button on the Ribbon to initiate drawing the chart. The area on the worksheet where the chart appears is called the chart location. As shown in Figure 1–73, the chart location in this worksheet is the range A11:G22, immediately below the worksheet data.

The following steps draw a 3-D Clustered Column chart that compares the quarterly sales by product type for the five sales regions.

- Click cell A3 and then drag the mouse pointer to the cell F8 to select the range A3:F8 (Figure 1–74).

Figure 1–74

2

- Click the Insert tab to make the Insert tab the active tab (Figure 1–75).

Q&A

What tasks can I perform with the Insert tab?

The Insert tab includes commands that allow you to insert various objects, such as shapes, tables, illustrations, and charts, into a work-sheet. These objects will be discussed as they are used throughout this book.

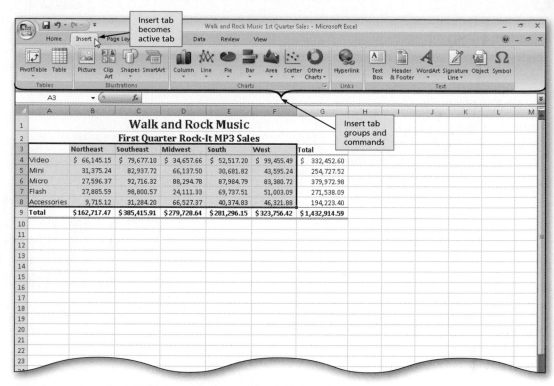

Figure 1–75

3

- Click the Column button on the Ribbon to display the Column gallery.

- Point to the 3-D Clustered Column chart type in the 3-D Column area of the Column gallery (Figure 1–76).

Figure 1–76

4

- Click the 3-D Clustered Column chart type in the 3-D Column area of the Column gallery to add a 3-D Clustered Column chart to the middle of the worksheet in a selection rectangle.

- Click the top-right edge of the selection rectangle but do not release the mouse to grab the chart and change the mouse pointer to a crosshair with four arrowheads (Figure 1–77).

Why is a new tab displayed on the Ribbon?

When you select objects such as shapes or charts, Excel displays contextual tabs that include special commands that are used to work with the type of object selected. Because a chart is selected, Excel displays the Chart Tools contextual tab. The three tabs below the Chart Tools contextual tab, Design, Layout, and Format, are tabs that include commands to work with charts.

Figure 1–77

5

- Continue holding down the left mouse button while dragging the chart down and to the left to position the upper-left corner of the dotted line rectangle over the upper-left corner of cell A11. Release the mouse button to complete the move of the chart.

- Click the middle sizing handle on the right edge of the chart and do not release the mouse button (Figure 1–78).

How does Excel know how to create the chart?

Excel automatically selects the entries in the topmost row of the chart range (row 3) as the titles for the horizontal axis (also called the **x-axis** or **category axis**) and draws a column for each of the 25 cells in the range containing numbers.

Figure 1–78

6

- While continuing to hold down the mouse button, press the ALT key and drag the right edge of the chart to the right edge of column G and then release the mouse button to resize the chart.

- Point to the middle sizing handle on the bottom edge of the selection rectangle and do not release the mouse button (Figure 1–79).

 Q&A

Why should I hold the ALT key down while I resize a chart?

Holding down the ALT key while you drag a chart **snaps** (aligns) the edge of the chart area to the worksheet gridlines. If you do not hold down the ALT key, then you can place an edge of a chart in the middle of a column or row.

Figure 1–79

7

- While continuing to hold down the mouse button, press the ALT key and drag the bottom edge of the chart up to the bottom edge of row 22 and then release the mouse button to resize the chart.

- Click the More button in the Chart Styles gallery to expand the gallery and point to Style 2 in the gallery (column 2, row 1) (Figure 1–80).

chart resized so that bottom edge of chart aligns with bottom edge of row 22

Figure 1–80

8

- Click Style 2 in the Chart Styles gallery to apply the chart style Style 2 to the chart.

🔎 **Experiment**

- Select other chart styles in the Chart Styles gallery to apply other chart styles to the chart, but select Style 2 as your final choice.

- Click cell I9 to deselect the chart and complete the worksheet (Figure 1–81).

Q&A

What is the purpose of the items on the right side of the chart?

The items to the right of the column chart in Figure 1–81 are the **legend**, which identifies the colors assigned to each bar in the chart. Excel automatically selects the entries in the leftmost column of the chart range (column A) as titles within the legend.

Figure 1–81

Changing Document Properties and Saving Again

BTW

Document Properties
Excel allows you to assign additional document properties by clicking the Document Properties button arrow in the Document Information Panel and then clicking Advanced Properties. You can assign custom properties, such as Department, Purpose, and Editor. Or, you can create your own document properties.

Excel helps you organize and identify your files by using **document properties**, which are the details about a file. Document properties, also known as **metadata**, can include such information as the project author, title, or subject. **Keywords** are words or phrases that further describe the document. For example, a class name or worksheet topic can describe the file's purpose or content. Document properties are valuable for a variety of reasons:

- Users can save time locating a particular file because they can view a document's properties without opening the workbook.

- By creating consistent properties for files having similar content, users can better organize their workbooks.

- Some organizations require Excel users to add document properties so that other employees can view details about these files.

Five different types of document properties exist, but the more common ones used in this book are standard and automatically updated properties. **Standard properties** are associated with all Microsoft Office documents and include author, title, and subject. **Automatically updated properties** include file system properties, such as the date you create or change a file, and statistics, such as the file size.

To Change Document Properties

The **Document Information Panel** contains areas where you can view and enter document properties. You can view and change information in this panel at any time while you are creating your workbook. Before saving the workbook again, you want to add your name and class name as document properties. The following steps use the Document Information Panel to change document properties.

1

- Click the Office Button to display the Office Button menu.

- Point to Prepare on the Office Button menu to display the Prepare submenu (Figure 1–82).

Q&A

What other types of actions besides changing properties can you take to prepare a document for distribution?

The Prepare submenu provides commands related to sharing a document with others, such as allowing or restricting people to view and modify your document, checking to see if your worksheet will work in earlier versions of Excel, and searching for hidden personal information.

Figure 1–82

2

- Click Properties on the Prepare submenu to display the Document Information Panel (Figure 1–83).

Q&A

Why are some of the document properties in my Document Information Panel already filled in?

The person who installed Microsoft Office 2007 on your computer or network may have set or customized the properties.

Figure 1–83

3

- Click the Author text box and then type your name as the Author property. If a name already is displayed in the Author text box, delete it before typing your name.

- Click the Subject text box, if necessary delete any existing text, and then type your course and section as the Subject property.

- Click the Keywords text box, if necessary delete any existing text, and then type First Quarter Rock-It MP3 Sales (Figure 1-84).

Q&A

What types of document properties does Excel collect automatically?

Excel records such details as how long you worked at creating your project, how many times you revised the document, and what fonts and themes are used.

Figure 1–84

4

- Click the Close the Document Information Panel button so that the Document Information Panel no longer is displayed.

To Save an Existing Workbook with the Same File Name

Saving frequently cannot be overemphasized. Several modifications have been made to the workbook since it was saved earlier in the chapter. Earlier in this chapter, the Save button on the Quick Access Toolbar caused the Save As dialog box to appear, and the file name, Walk and Rock Music 1st Quarter Sales, was entered. Clicking the Save button on the Quick Access Toolbar causes Excel to save the changes made to the workbook since the last time it was saved. The following step saves the workbook again.

1
- With your USB flash drive connected to one of the computer's USB ports, click the Save button on the Quick Access Toolbar to overwrite the previous Walk and Rock Music 1st Quarter Sales file on the USB flash drive (Figure 1–85).

Q&A

Why did the Save As dialog box not appear?

Excel overwrites the document using the settings specified the first time the document was saved. To save the file with a different file name or on different media, display the Save As dialog box by clicking the Office Button and then clicking Save As on the Office Button menu. Then, fill in the Save As dialog box as described in Steps 2 through 5 on pages EX 31 and EX 32.

Figure 1–85

Other Ways

1. Press CTRL+S or press SHIFT+F12, press ENTER

Printing a Worksheet

After you create a worksheet, you often want to print it. A printed version of the worksheet is called a **hard copy** or **printout**. Printed copies of your worksheet can be useful for the following reasons:

- Many people prefer proofreading a hard copy of the worksheet rather than viewing the worksheet on the screen to check for errors and readability.
- Someone without computer access can view the worksheet's content.
- Copies can be distributed as handouts to people during a meeting or presentation.
- Hard copies can serve as reference material if your storage medium is lost or becomes corrupted and you need to recreate the worksheet.

It is a good practice to save a workbook before printing it, in the event you experience difficulties with the printer.

BTW

Conserving Ink and Toner
You can print a presentation in black and white to conserve ink or toner by clicking the Office Button, pointing to Print on the Office Button menu, and then clicking Print Preview on the Print submenu. Click the Page Setup button on the Print Preview tab, click the Sheet tab, and then click the Black and White check box in the Print area. Click the OK button to close the Page Setup dialog box. Click the Office Button, point to Print, and then click Quick Print.

To Print a Worksheet

With the completed worksheet saved, you may want to print it. The following steps print the worksheet in the saved Walk and Rock Music 1st Quarter Sales workbook.

1

- Click the Office Button to display the Office Button menu.

- Point to Print on the Office Button menu to display the Print submenu (Figure 1–86).

Figure 1–86

2

- Click Quick Print on the Print submenu to print the document (Figure 1–87).

Q&A

Can I print my document in black and white to conserve ink or toner?

Yes. Click the Office Button and then click the Excel Options button on the Office Button menu. When the Excel Options dialog box is displayed, click Advanced, scroll to the Print area, place a check mark in the Use draft quality check box if it is displayed, and then click the OK button. Click the Office Button, point to Print, and then click Quick Print.

Walk and Rock Music
First Quarter Rock-It MP3 Sales

	Northeast	Southeast	Midwest	South	West	Total
Video	$ 66,145.15	$ 79,677.10	$ 34,657.66	$ 52,517.20	$ 99,455.49	$ 332,452.60
Mini	31,375.24	82,937.72	66,137.50	30,681.82	43,595.24	254,727.52
Micro	27,596.37	92,716.32	88,294.78	87,984.79	83,380.72	379,972.98
Flash	27,885.59	98,800.57	24,111.33	69,737.51	51,003.09	271,538.09
Accessories	9,715.12	31,284.20	66,527.37	40,374.83	46,321.88	194,223.40
Total	**$ 162,717.47**	**$ 385,415.91**	**$ 279,728.64**	**$ 281,296.15**	**$ 323,756.42**	**$ 1,432,914.59**

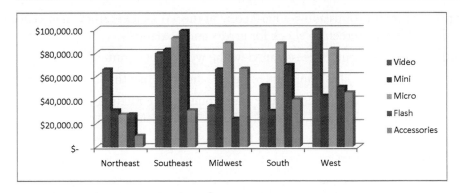

Figure 1–87

Other Ways

1. Press CTRL+P, press ENTER

Quitting Excel

When you quit Excel, if you have made changes to a workbook since the last time the file was saved, Excel displays a dialog box asking if you want to save the changes you made to the file before it closes that window. The dialog box contains three buttons with these resulting actions:

- Yes button — Saves the changes and then quits Excel
- No button — Quits Excel without saving changes
- Cancel button — Closes the dialog box and redisplays the worksheet without saving the changes

If no changes have been made to an open workbook since the last time the file was saved, Excel will close the window without displaying a dialog box.

To Quit Excel with One Workbook Open

The Walk and Rock 1st Quarter Sales worksheet is complete. The following steps quit Excel if only one workbook is open.

1

- Point to the Close button on the right side of the Excel title bar (Figure 1–88).

2

- Click the Close button to quit Excel.

Q&A

What if I have more than one Excel workbook open?

You would click the Close button on the Excel title bar for each open workbook. When you click the Close button with the last workbook open, Excel also quits. As an alternative, you could click the Office Button and then click the Exit Excel button on the Office Button menu, which closes all open workbooks and then quits Excel.

Figure 1–88

Other Ways

1. Double-click Office Button
2. With multiple workbooks open, click Office Button, click Exit Excel on Office Button menu
3. Right-click Microsoft Excel button on Windows Vista taskbar, click Close on shortcut menu
4. Press ALT+F4

BTW

Print Preview
You can preview the printout on your screen using the Print Preview command on the Print submenu (Figure 1–86 on page EX 58), make adjustments to the worksheet, and then print it only when it appears exactly as you want. Each time you preview rather than print, you save both ink and paper.

Starting Excel and Opening a Workbook

Once you have created and saved a workbook, you may need to retrieve it from your storage medium. For example, you might want to revise a worksheet or reprint it. Opening a workbook requires that Excel is running on your computer.

To Start Excel

The following steps, which assume Windows Vista is running, start Excel.

Note: If you are using Windows XP, please see Appendix F for alternate steps.

1 Click the Start button on the Windows Vista taskbar to display the Start menu.

2 Click All Programs at the bottom of the left pane on the Start menu to display the All Programs list and then click Microsoft Office in the All Programs list to display the Microsoft Office list.

3 Click Microsoft Office Excel 2007 in the Microsoft Office list to start Excel and display a new blank worksheet in the Excel window.

4 If the Excel window is not maximized, click the Maximize button on its title bar to maximize the window.

To Open a Workbook from Excel

Earlier in this chapter, the workbook was saved on a USB flash drive using the file name, Walk and Rock Music 1st Quarter Sales. The following steps open the Walk and Rock Music 1st Quarter Sales file from the USB flash drive.

1

- With your USB flash drive connected to one of the computer's USB ports, click the Office Button to display the Office Button menu (Figure 1–89).

Q&A

What files are shown in the Recent Documents list?

Excel displays the most recently opened document file names in this list. If the name of the file you want to open appears in the Recent Documents list, you could double-click it to open the file.

Figure 1–89

2

- Click Open on the Office Button menu to display the Open dialog box.

- If the Folders list is displayed below the Folders button, click the Folders button to remove the Folders list.

- If necessary, click Computer in the Favorite Links section and then scroll until UDISK 2.0 (E:) appears in the list of available drives.

- Double-click UDISK 2.0 (E:) to select the USB flash drive, Drive E in this case, as the new open location.

- Click Walk and Rock Music 1st Quarter Sales to select the file name (Figure 1–90).

Q&A How do I open the file if I am not using a USB flash drive?

Use the same process, but be certain to select your device in the Computer list.

3

- Click the Open button to open the selected file and display the worksheet in the Excel window (Figure 1–91).

Q&A Why do I see the Microsoft Excel icon and name on the Windows Vista taskbar?

When you open an Excel file, the application name (Microsoft Excel) is displayed on a selected button on the Windows Vista taskbar. If you point to this button, the file name also appears in a ScreenTip.

Figure 1–90

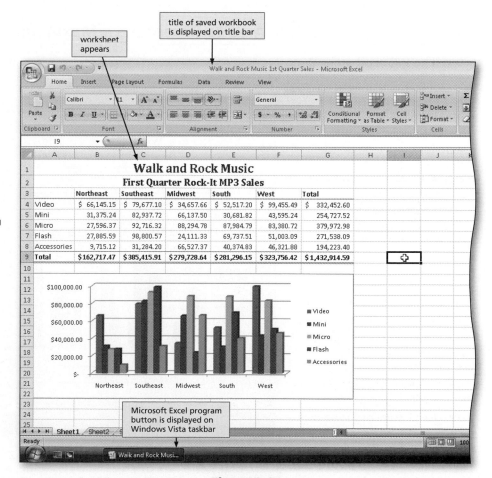

Figure 1–91

Other Ways

1. Click Office Button, double-click file name in Recent Documents list

2. Press CTRL+O, select file name, press ENTER

BTW

AutoCalculate
Use the AutoCalculate area on the status bar to check your work as you enter data in a worksheet. If you enter large amounts of data, you select a range of data and then check the AutoCalculate area to provide insight into statistics about the data you entered. Often, you will have an intuitive feel for whether the numbers are accurate or if you may have made a mistake while entering the data.

AutoCalculate

You easily can obtain a total, an average, or other information about the numbers in a range by using the **AutoCalculate area** on the status bar. First, select the range of cells containing the numbers you want to check. Next, right-click the AutoCalculate area to display the Status Bar Configuration shortcut menu (Figure 1–92). The check mark to the left of the active functions (Average, Count, and Sum) indicates that the sum, count, and average of the selected range are displayed in the AutoCalculate area on the status bar. The functions of the AutoCalculate commands on the Status Bar Configuration shortcut menu are described in Table 1–4.

Table 1–4 AutoCalculate Shortcut Menu Commands	
Command	**Function**
Average	AutoCalculate area displays the average of the numbers in the selected range
Count	AutoCalculate area displays the number of nonblank cells in the selected range
Numerical Count	AutoCalculate area displays the number of cells containing numbers in the selected range
Minimum	AutoCalculate area displays the lowest value in the selected range
Maximum	AutoCalculate area displays the highest value in the selected range
Sum	AutoCalculate area displays the sum of the numbers in the selected range

To Use the AutoCalculate Area to Determine a Maximum

The following steps show how to display the largest quarterly sales for any region for the Micro product type.

1

• Select the range B6:F6 and then right-click the AutoCalculate area on the status bar to display the Status Bar Configuration shortcut menu (Figure 1–92).

Q&A

What is displayed on the Status Bar Configuration shortcut menu?

This shortcut menu includes several commands that allow you to control the items displayed on the Customize Status Bar shortcut menu. The AutoCalculate area of the shortcut menu includes six commands as well as the result of the associated calculation on the right side of the menu.

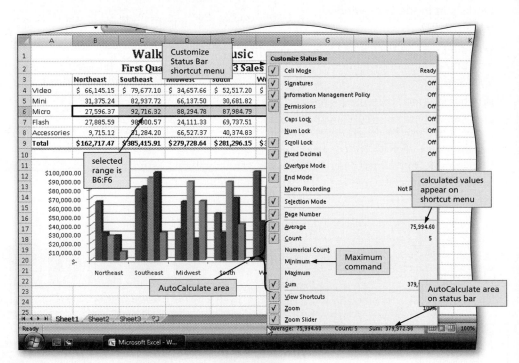

Figure 1–92

2

- Click Maximum on the shortcut menu to display the Maximum value in the range B6:F6 in the AutoCalculate area of the status bar.

- Click anywhere on the worksheet to cause the shortcut menu to disappear (Figure 1–93).

3

- Right-click the AutoCalculate area and then click Maximum on the shortcut menu to cause the Maximum value to no longer appear in the AutoCalculate area.

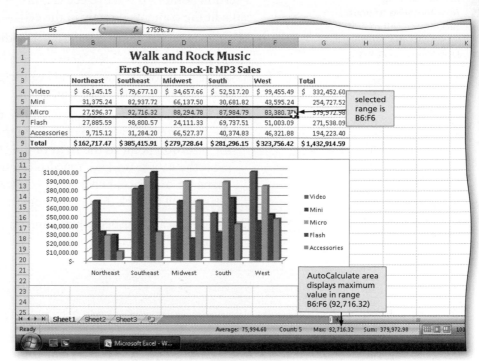

Figure 1–93

Correcting Errors

You can correct errors on a worksheet using one of several methods. The method you choose will depend on the extent of the error and whether you notice it while typing the data or after you have entered the incorrect data into the cell.

Correcting Errors while You Are Typing Data into a Cell

If you notice an error while you are typing data into a cell, press the BACKSPACE key to erase the incorrect characters and then type the correct characters. If the error is a major one, click the Cancel box in the formula bar or press the ESC key to erase the entire entry and then reenter the data from the beginning.

Correcting Errors after Entering Data into a Cell

If you find an error in the worksheet after entering the data, you can correct the error in one of two ways:

1. If the entry is short, select the cell, retype the entry correctly, and then click the Enter box or press the ENTER key. The new entry will replace the old entry.

2. If the entry in the cell is long and the errors are minor, using Edit mode may be a better choice than retyping the cell entry. Use the Edit mode as described below.

   a. Double-click the cell containing the error to switch Excel to Edit mode. In **Edit mode**, Excel displays the active cell entry in the formula bar and a flashing

BTW

In-Cell Editing
An alternative to double-clicking the cell to edit it is to select the cell and then press the F2 key.

insertion point in the active cell (Figure 1–94). With Excel in Edit mode, you can edit the contents directly in the cell — a procedure called **in-cell editing**.

b. Make changes using in-cell editing, as indicated below.

(1) To insert new characters between two characters, place the insertion point between the two characters and begin typing. Excel inserts the new characters at the location of the insertion point.

(2) To delete a character in the cell, move the insertion point to the left of the character you want to delete and then press the DELETE key or place the insertion point to the right of the character you want to delete and then press the BACKSPACE key. You also can use the mouse to drag through the character or adjacent characters you want to delete and then press the DELETE key or click the Cut button on the Home tab on the Ribbon.

(3) When you are finished editing an entry, click the Enter box or press the ENTER key.

Figure 1–94

When Excel enters the Edit mode, the keyboard usually is in Insert mode. In **Insert mode**, as you type a character, Excel inserts the character and moves all characters to the right of the typed character one position to the right. You can change to Overtype mode by pressing the INSERT key. In **Overtype mode**, Excel overtypes, or replaces, the character to the right of the insertion point. The INSERT key toggles the keyboard between Insert mode and Overtype mode.

While in Edit mode, you may have reason to move the insertion point to various points in the cell, select portions of the data in the cell, or switch from inserting characters to overtyping characters. Table 1–5 summarizes the more common tasks used during in-cell editing.

BTW

Editing the Contents of a Cell
Rather than using in-cell editing, you can select the cell and then click the formula bar to edit the contents.

	Task	Mouse	Keyboard
	Table 1–5 Summary of In-Cell Editing Tasks		
1	Move the insertion point to the beginning of data in a cell.	Point to the left of the first character and click.	Press HOME
2	Move the insertion point to the end of data in a cell.	Point to the right of the last character and click.	Press END
3	Move the insertion point anywhere in a cell.	Point to the appropriate position and click the character.	Press RIGHT ARROW or LEFT ARROW
4	Highlight one or more adjacent characters.	Drag the mouse pointer through adjacent characters.	Press SHIFT+RIGHT ARROW or SHIFT+LEFT ARROW
5	Select all data in a cell.	Double-click the cell with the insertion point in the cell if there are no spaces in the data in the cell.	
6	Delete selected characters.	Click the Cut button on the Home tab on the Ribbon.	Press DELETE
7	Delete characters to the left of the insertion point.		Press BACKSPACE
8	Delete characters to the right of the insertion point.		Press DELETE
9	Toggle between Insert and Overtype modes.		Press INSERT

Undoing the Last Cell Entry

Excel provides the Undo command on the Quick Access Toolbar (Figure 1–95), which allows you to erase recent cell entries. Thus, if you enter incorrect data in a cell and notice it immediately, click the Undo button and Excel changes the cell entry to what it was prior to the incorrect data entry.

Figure 1–95

Excel remembers the last 100 actions you have completed. Thus, you can undo up to 100 previous actions by clicking the Undo button arrow to display the Undo list and then clicking the action to be undone (Figure 1–95). You can drag through several actions in the Undo list to undo all of them at once. If no actions are available for Excel to undo, then the Undo button is dimmed and inoperative.

The Redo button, next to the Undo button on the Quick Access Toolbar, allows you to repeat previous actions.

BTW

Quick Reference
For a table that lists how to complete the tasks covered in this book using the mouse, Ribbon, shortcut menu, and keyboard, see the Quick Reference Summary at the back of this book, or visit the Excel 2007 Quick Reference Web page (scsite.com/ex2007/qr).

Clearing a Cell or Range of Cells

If you enter data into the wrong cell or range of cells, you can erase, or clear, the data using one of the first four methods listed below. The fifth method clears the formatting from the selected cells.

To Clear Cell Entries Using the Fill Handle

1. Select the cell or range of cells and then point to the fill handle so the mouse pointer changes to a crosshair.
2. Drag the fill handle back into the selected cell or range until a shadow covers the cell or cells you want to erase. Release the mouse button.

To Clear Cell Entries Using the Shortcut Menu

1. Select the cell or range of cells to be cleared.
2. Right-click the selection.
3. Click Clear Contents on the shortcut menu.

To Clear Cell Entries Using the delete Key

1. Select the cell or range of cells to be cleared.
2. Press the delete key.

To Clear Cell Entries and Formatting Using the Clear Button

1. Select the cell or range of cells to be cleared.
2. Click the Clear button on the Home tab (Figure 1–95 on the previous page).
3. Click Clear Contents on the menu.

To Clear Formatting Using the Cell Styles Button

1. Select the cell or range of cells from which you want to remove the formatting.
2. Click the Cell Styles button on the Home tab and point to Normal.
3. Click Normal in the Live Preview Gallery.

The Clear button on the Home tab is the only command that clears both the cell entry and the cell formatting. As you are clearing cell entries, always remember that you should *never press the* spacebar *to clear a cell*. Pressing the spacebar enters a blank character. A blank character is text and is different from an empty cell, even though the cell may appear empty.

BTW

Certification
The Microsoft Certified Application Specialist (MCAS) program provides an opportunity for you to obtain a valuable industry credential – proof that you have the Excel 2007 skills required by employers. For more information, see Appendix G or visit the Excel 2007 Certification Web page (scsite.com/ex2007/cert).

Clearing the Entire Worksheet

If required worksheet edits are extremely extensive, you may want to clear the entire worksheet and start over. To clear the worksheet or delete an embedded chart, use the following steps.

To Clear the Entire Worksheet

1. Click the Select All button on the worksheet (Figure 1–95).
2. Click the Clear button on the Home tab to delete both the entries and formats.

BTW

Getting Back to Normal
If you accidentally assign unwanted formats to a range of cells, you can use the Normal cell style selection in the Cell Styles gallery. Click Cell Styles on the Home tab on the Ribbon and then click Normal. Doing so changes the format to Normal style. To view the characteristics of the Normal style, right-click the style in the Cell Styles gallery and then click Modify, or press ALT+APOSTROPHE (').

The Select All button selects the entire worksheet. Instead of clicking the Select All button, you also can press CTRL+A. To clear an unsaved workbook, click the workbook's Close Window button or click the Close command on the Office Button menu. Click the No button if the Microsoft Excel dialog box asks if you want to save changes. To start a new, blank workbook, click the New command on the Office Button menu.

To delete an embedded chart, complete the following steps.

To Delete an Embedded Chart

1. Click the chart to select it.
2. Press the DELETE key.

Excel Help

At any time while using Excel, you can find answers to questions and display information about various topics through **Excel Help**. This section introduces you to Excel Help.

To Search for Excel Help

Using Excel Help, you can search for information based on phrases such as save a workbook or format a chart, or key terms such as copy, save, or format. Excel Help responds with a list of search results displayed as links to a variety of resources. The following steps, which use Excel Help to search for information about formatting a chart, assume you are connected to the Internet.

1

- Click the Microsoft Office Excel Help button near the upper-right corner of the Excel window to open the Excel Help window.

- Type format a chart in the Type words to search for text box at the top of the Excel Help window (Figure 1–96).

Figure 1–96

2

- Press the ENTER key to display the search results.

- Click the Maximize button on the Excel Help window title bar to maximize the Help window (Figure 1–97).

Q&A

Where is the Excel window with the Walk and Rock Music 1st Quarter Sales worksheet?

Excel is open in the background, but the Excel Help window is overlaid on top of the Microsoft Excel window. When the Excel Help window is closed, the worksheet will reappear.

Figure 1–97

3

- Click the Format chart elements link to display information regarding formatting chart elements (Figure 1–98).

Q&A

What is the purpose of the buttons at the top of the Excel Help window?

Use the buttons in the upper-left corner of the Excel Help window to navigate through the Help system, change the display, show the Excel Help table of contents, and print the contents of the window.

Figure 1–98

4

- Click the Close button on the Excel Help window title bar to close the Excel Help window and make Excel active.

Other Ways
1. Press F1

To Quit Excel

The following steps quit Excel.

1 Click the Close button on the right side of the title bar to quit Excel; or if you have multiple Excel workbooks open, click the Office Button and then click the Exit Excel button on the Office Button menu to close all open workbooks and quit Excel.

2 If necessary, click the No button in the Microsoft Office Excel dialog box so that any changes you have made are not saved.

 Quitting Excel
Do not forget to remove your USB flash drive from the USB port after quitting Excel, especially if you are working in a laboratory environment. Nothing can be more frustrating than leaving all of your hard work behind on a USB flash drive for the next user.

Chapter Summary

In this chapter you have learned about the Excel window, how to enter text and numbers to create a worksheet, how to select a range, how to use the Sum button, save a workbook, format cells, insert a chart, print a worksheet, quit Excel, and use Excel Help. The items listed below include all the new Excel skills you have learned in this chapter.

1. Start Excel (EX 6)
2. Enter the Worksheet Titles (EX 17)
3. Enter Column Titles (EX 19)
4. Enter Row Titles (EX 21)
5. Enter Numbers (EX 23)
6. Sum a Column of Numbers (EX 25)
7. Copy a Cell to Adjacent Cells in a Row (EX 27)
8. Determine Multiple Totals at the Same Time (EX 28)
9. Save a Workbook (EX 30)
10. Change a Cell Style (EX 35)
11. Change the Font Type (EX 36)
12. Bold a Cell (EX 38)
13. Increase the Font Size of a Cell Entry (EX 38)
14. Change the Font Color of a Cell Entry (EX 39)
15. Center Cell Entries across Columns by Merging Cells (EX 40)
16. Format Column Titles and the Total Row (EX 42)
17. Format Numbers in the Worksheet (EX 44)
18. Adjust the Column Width (EX 46)
19. Use the Name Box to Select a Cell (EX 47)
20. Add a 3-D Clustered Column Chart to the Worksheet (EX 50)
21. Change Document Properties (EX 55)
22. Save an Existing Workbook with the Same File Name (EX 58)
23. Print a Worksheet (EX 58)
24. Quit Excel with One Workbook Open (EX 59)
25. Open a Workbook from Excel (EX 60)
26. Use the AutoCalculate Area to Determine a Maximum (EX 62)
27. Clear Cell Entries Using the Fill Handle (EX 66)
28. Clear Cell Entries Using the Shortcut Menu (EX 66)
29. Clear Cell Entries Using the DELETE Key (EX 66)
30. Clear Cell Entries and Formatting Using the Clear Button (EX 66)
31. Clear Formatting Using the Cell Styles Button (EX 66)
32. Clear the Entire Worksheet (EX 66)
33. Delete an Embedded Chart (EX 67)
34. Search for Excel Help (EX 67)

 If you have a SAM user profile, you may have access to hands-on instruction, practice, and assessment. Log in to your SAM account (http://sam2007.course.com) to launch any assigned training activities or exams that relate to the skills covered in this chapter.

Learn It Online

Test your knowledge of chapter content and key terms.

Instructions: To complete the Learn It Online exercises, start your browser, click the Address bar, and then enter the Web address scsite.com/ex2007/learn. When the Excel 2007 Learn It Online page is displayed, click the link for the exercise you want to complete and then read the instructions.

Chapter Reinforcement TF, MC, and SA
A series of true/false, multiple choice, and short answer questions that test your knowledge of the chapter content.

Flash Cards
An interactive learning environment where you identify chapter key terms associated with displayed definitions.

Practice Test
A series of multiple choice questions that test your knowledge of chapter content and key terms.

Who Wants To Be a Computer Genius?
An interactive game that challenges your knowledge of chapter content in the style of a television quiz show.

Wheel of Terms
An interactive game that challenges your knowledge of chapter key terms in the style of the television show *Wheel of Fortune*.

Crossword Puzzle Challenge
A crossword puzzle that challenges your knowledge of key terms presented in the chapter.

Apply Your Knowledge

Reinforce the skills and apply the concepts you learned in this chapter.

Changing the Values in a Worksheet
Instructions: Start Excel. Open the workbook Apply 1-1 Bicycle Shop 3rd Quarter Sales (Figure 1–99a). See the inside back cover of this book for instructions for downloading the Data Files for Students, or see your instructor for information on accessing the files required in this book.

1. Make the changes to the worksheet described in Table 1–6 so that the worksheet appears as shown in Figure 1–99b. As you edit the values in the cells containing numeric data, watch the totals in row 8, the totals in column G, and the chart change.

2. Change the worksheet title in cell A1 to the Title cell style and then merge and center it across columns A through G. Use commands in the Font group on the Home tab on the Ribbon to change the worksheet subtitle in cell A2 to 16-point Corbel red, bold font and then center it across columns A through G. Use the Accent 1 theme color (column 5, row 1 on the Font palette) for the red font color.

3. Update the document properties with your name, course number, and name for the workbook. Save the workbook using the file name, Apply 1-1 Spoke-Up Bicycle Shop 3rd Quarter Sales. Submit the assignment as requested by your instructor.

Table 1–6 New Worksheet Data	
Cell	**Change Cell Contents To**
A1	Spoke-Up Bicycle Shop
B4	11869.2
E4	9157.83
D6	5217.92
F6	6239.46
B7	3437.64

(a) Before

(b) After

Figure 1–99

Extend Your Knowledge

Extend the skills you learned in this chapter and experiment with new skills. You may need to use Help to complete the assignment.

Formatting Cells and Inserting Multiple Charts

Instructions: Start Excel. Open the workbook Extend 1-1 Pack-n-Away Shipping. See the inside back cover of this book for instructions for downloading the Data Files for Students, or see your instructor for information on accessing the files required in this book. Perform the following tasks to format cells in the worksheet and to add two charts to the worksheet.

1. Use the commands in the Font group on the Home tab on the Ribbon to change the font of the title in cell A1 to 24-point Arial, red; bold and subtitle of the worksheet to 16-point Arial Narrow, blue, bold.

2. Select the range A3:E8, click the Insert tab on the Ribbon, and then click the Dialog Box Launcher in the Charts group on the Ribbon to open the Insert Chart dialog box (Figure 1–100).

Figure 1–100

3. Insert a Stacked Line chart by clicking the Stacked Line chart in the gallery and then clicking the OK button. Move the chart either below or to the right of the data in the worksheet. Click the Design tab and apply a chart style to the chart.

4. With the same range selected, follow Step 3 above to insert a 3-D Area chart in the worksheet. You may need to use the scroll box on the right side of the Insert Chart dialog box to view the Area charts in the gallery. Move the chart either below or to the right of the data so that each chart does not overlap the Stacked Line chart. Choose a different chart style for this chart than the one you selected for the Stacked Line chart.

5. Resize each chart so that each snaps to the worksheet gridlines. Make certain that both charts are visible with the worksheet data without the need to scroll the worksheet.

6. Update the document properties with your name, course number, and name for the workbook.

7. Save the workbook using the file name, Extend 1-1 Pack-n-Away Shipping Charts. Submit the assignment as requested by your instructor.

Make It Right

Analyze a workbook and correct all errors and/or improve the design.

Correcting Formatting and Values in a Worksheet

Instructions: Start Excel. Open the workbook Make It Right 1-1 Book Sales. See the inside back cover of this book for instructions for downloading the Data Files for Students, or see your instructor for information on accessing the files required for this book. Correct the following formatting problems and data errors (Figure 1–101) in the worksheet, while keeping in mind the guidelines presented in this chapter.

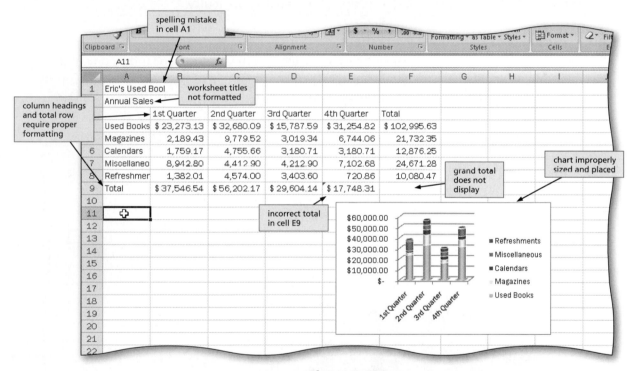

Figure 1–101

1. Merge and center the worksheet title and subtitle appropriately.

2. Format the worksheet title with a cell style appropriate for a worksheet title.

3. Format the subtitle using commands in the Font group on the Ribbon.

4. Correct the spelling mistake in cell A1 by changing Bool to Books.

5. Apply proper formatting to the column headers and total row.

Continued >

Make It Right *continued*

6. Adjust column sizes so that all data in each column is visible.

7. Use the SUM function to create the grand total for annual sales.

8. The SUM function in cell E9 does not sum all of the numbers in the column. Correct this error by editing the range for the SUM function in the cell.

9. Resize and move the chart so that it is below the worksheet data and does not extend past the right edge of the worksheet data. Be certain to snap the chart to the worksheet gridlines by holding down the ALT key as you resize the chart.

10. Update the document properties with your name, course number, and name for the workbook. Save the workbook using the file name, Make It Right 1-1 Eric's Used Books Annual Sales. Submit the assignment as requested by your instructor.

In the Lab

Design and/or create a workbook using the guidelines, concepts, and skills presented in this chapter. Labs 1, 2, and 3 are listed in order of increasing difficulty.

Lab 1: Annual Cost of Goods Worksheet

Problem: You work part-time as a spreadsheet specialist for Kona's Expresso Coffee, one of the up-and-coming coffee franchises in the United States. Your manager has asked you to develop an annual cost of goods analysis worksheet similar to the one shown in Figure 1–102.

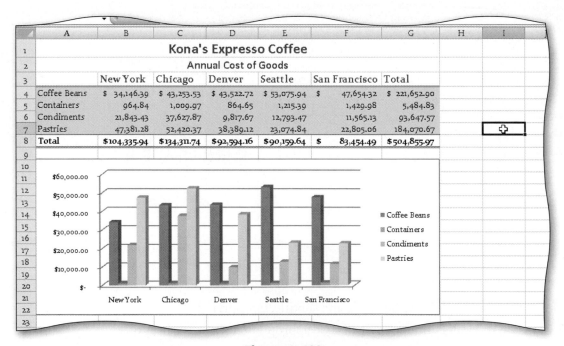

Figure 1–102

Instructions: Perform the following tasks.

1. Start Excel. Enter the worksheet title, Kona's Expresso Coffee, in cell A1 and the worksheet subtitle, Annual Cost of Goods, in cell A2. Beginning in row 3, enter the store locations, costs of goods, and supplies categories shown in Table 1–7.

Table 1–7 Kona's Expresso Coffee Annual Cost of Goods					
	New York	**Chicago**	**Denver**	**Seattle**	**San Franscisco**
Coffee Beans	34146.39	43253.53	43522.72	53075.94	47654.32
Containers	964.84	1009.97	864.65	1215.39	1429.98
Condiments	21843.43	37627.87	9817.67	12793.47	11565.13
Pastries	47381.28	52420.37	38389.12	23074.84	22805.06

2. Use the SUM function to determine the totals for each store location, type of supply, and company grand total.

3. Use Cell Styles in the Styles group on the Home tab on the Ribbon to format the worksheet title with the Title cell style. Center the title across columns A through G. Do not be concerned if the edges of the worksheet title are not displayed.

4. Use buttons in the Font group on the Home tab on the Ribbon to format the worksheet subtitle to 14-point Calibri dark blue, bold font, and center it across columns A through G.

5. Use Cell Styles in the Styles group on the Home tab on the Ribbon to format the range A3:G3 with the Heading 2 cell style, the range A4:G7 with the 20% - Accent1 cell style, and the range A8:G8 with the Total cell style. Use the buttons in the Number group on the Home tab on the Ribbon to apply the Accounting Number format to the range B4:G4 and the range B8:G8. Use the buttons in the Number group on the Home tab on the Ribbon to apply the Comma Style to the range B5:G7. Adjust any column widths to the widest text entry in each column.

6. Select the range A3:F7 and then insert a 3-D Clustered Column chart. Apply the Style 8 chart style to the chart. Move and resize the chart so that it appears in the range A10:G22. If the labels along the horizontal axis (x-axis) do not appear as shown in Figure 1-102, then drag the right side of the chart so that it is displayed in the range A10:H22.

7. Update the document properties with your name, course number, and name for the workbook.

8. Save the workbook using the file name Lab 1-1 Konas Expresso Coffee Annual Cost of Goods.

9. Print the worksheet.

10. Make the following two corrections to the sales amounts: $9,648.12 for Seattle Condiments (cell E6), $12,844.79 for Chicago Pastries (cell C7). After you enter the corrections, the company totals in cell G8 should equal $462,135.04.

11. Print the revised worksheet. Close the workbook without saving the changes. Submit the assignment as requested by your instructor.

In the Lab

Lab 2: Annual Sales Analysis Worksheet

Problem: As the chief accountant for Scissors Office Supply, Inc., you have been asked by the sales manager to create a worksheet to analyze the annual sales for the company by location and customer type category (Figure 1–103). The office locations and corresponding sales by customer type for the year are shown in Table 1–8.

Continued >

In the Lab *continued*

Instructions: Perform the following tasks.

1. Create the worksheet shown in Figure 1–103 using the data in Table 1–8.

2. Use the SUM function to determine totals sales for the four offices, the totals for each customer type, and the company total. Add column and row headings for the totals row and totals column, as appropriate.

Table 1–8 Scissors Office Supply Annual Sales

	Boston	Miami	St. Louis	Santa Fe
Consumer	206348.81	113861.40	69854.13	242286.82
Small Business	235573.28	133511.24	199158.35	228365.51
Large Business	237317.55	234036.08	126519.10	111773.38
Government	178798.04	144548.80	135470.86	132599.75
Nonprofit	15180.63	28837.75	63924.48	21361.42

3. Format the worksheet title with the Title cell style and center it across columns A through F. Use the Font group on the Ribbon to format the worksheet subtitle to 16-point Cambria green, and bold font. Center the title across columns A through F.

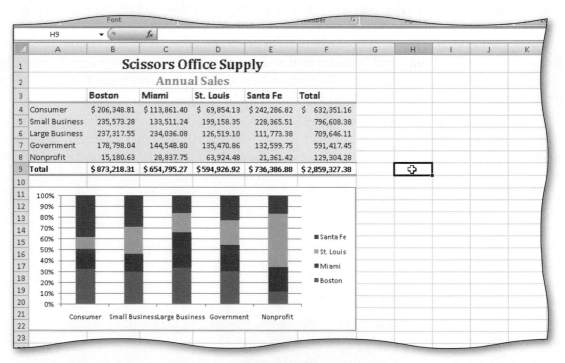

Figure 1–103

4. Format the range A3:F3 with the Heading 2 cell style, the range A4:F8 with the 20% - Accent3 cell style, and the range B9:F9 with the Total cell style. Use the Number group on the Ribbon to format cells B4:F4 and B9:F9 with the Accounting Number Format and cells B5:F8 with the Comma Style numeric format.

5. Chart the range A3:E8. Insert a 100% Stacked Column chart for the range A3:E8, as shown in Figure 1–103, by using the Column button on the Insert tab on the Ribbon. Use the chart location A11:F22.

6. Update the document properties with your name, course number, and name for the workbook.

7. Save the workbook using the file name, Lab 1-2 Scissors Office Supply Annual Sales. Print the worksheet.

8. Two corrections to the figures were sent in from the accounting department. The correct sales are $98,342.16 for Miami's annual Small Business sales (cell C5) and $48,933.75 for St. Louis's annual Nonprofit sales (cell D8). After you enter the two corrections, the company total in cell F9 should equal $2,809,167.57. Print the revised worksheet.

9. Use the Undo button to change the worksheet back to the original numbers in Table 1–8. Use the Redo button to change the worksheet back to the revised state.

10. Close Excel without saving the latest changes. Start Excel and open the workbook saved in Step 7. Double-click cell E6 and use in-cell editing to change the Santa Fe annual Large Business sales (cell E6) to $154,108.49. Write the company total in cell F9 at the top of the first printout. Click the Undo button.

11. Click cell A1 and then click the Merge & Center button to split cell A1 into cells A1, B1, C1, D1, E1, and F1. To merge the cells into one again, select the range A1:F1 and then click the Merge & Center button on the Home tab on the Ribbon.

12. Close the workbook without saving the changes. Submit the assignment as requested by your instructor.

In the Lab

Lab 3: College Cost and Financial Support Worksheet

Problem: Attending college is an expensive proposition and your resources are limited. To plan for your four-year college career, you have decided to organize your anticipated resources and costs in a worksheet. The data required to prepare your worksheet is shown in Table 1–9.

Table 1–9 College Cost and Resources				
Cost	**Freshman**	**Sophomore**	**Junior**	**Senior**
Books	450.00	477.00	505.62	535.95
Room & Board	7500.00	7950.00	8427.00	8932.62
Tuition	8200.00	8692.00	9213.52	9766.33
Entertainment	1325.00	1404.50	1488.77	1578.10
Miscellaneous	950.00	1007.00	1067.42	1131.47
Clothes	725.00	768.50	814.61	863.49
Financial Support	**Freshman**	**Sophomore**	**Junior**	**Senior**
Job	3400.00	3604.00	3820.24	4049.45
Savings	4350.00	4611.00	4887.66	5180.92
Parents	4700.00	4982.00	5280.92	5597.78
Financial Aid	5500.00	5830.00	6179.80	6550.59
Other	1200.00	1272.00	1348.32	1429.22

Continued >

In the Lab *continued*

Instructions Part 1: Using the numbers in Table 1–9, create the worksheet shown in columns A through F in Figure 1–104. Format the worksheet title as Calibri 24-point bold red. Merge and center the worksheet title in cell A1 across columns A through F. Format the worksheet subtitles in cells A2 and A11 as Calibri 16-point bold green. Format the ranges A3:F3 and A12:F12 with the Heading 2 cell style, the ranges A4:F9 and A13:F17 with the 20% - Accent cell style, and the ranges A10:F10 and A18:F18 with the Total cell style.

Update the document properties, including the addition of at least one keyword to the properties, and save the workbook using the file name, Lab 1-3 Part 1 College Cost and Financial Support. Print the worksheet. Submit the assignment as requested by your instructor.

Figure 1–104

After reviewing the numbers, you realize you need to increase manually each of the Junior-year expenses in column D by $600. Change the Junior-year expenses to reflect this change. Manually change the financial aid for the Junior year by the amount required to cover the increase in costs. The totals in cells F10 and F18 should equal $87,373.90. Print the worksheet. Close the workbook without saving changes.

Instructions Part 2: Open the workbook Lab 1-3 Part 1 College Cost and Financial Support and then save the workbook using the file name, Lab 1-3 Part 2 College Cost and Financial Support. Insert an Exploded pie in 3-D chart in the range G3:K10 to show the contribution of each category of cost for the Freshman year. Chart the range A4:B9 and apply the Style 8 chart style to the chart. Add the Pie chart title as shown in cell G2 in Figure 1–104. Insert an Exploded pie in 3-D chart in the range G12:K18 to show the contribution of each category of financial support for the Freshman year. Chart the range A13:B17 and apply the Style 8 chart style to the chart. Add the Pie chart title shown in cell G11 in Figure 1–104. Update the identification area with the exercise part number and save the workbook. Print the worksheet. Submit the assignment as requested by your instructor.

Instructions Part 3: Open the workbook Lab 1-3 Part 2 College Cost and Financial Support. Do not save the workbook in this part. A close inspection of Table 1–9 shows that both cost and financial support figures increase 6% each year. Use Excel Help to learn how to enter the data for the last three years using a formula and the Copy and Paste buttons on the Home tab on the Ribbon. For example, the formula to enter in cell C4 is =B4*1.06. Enter formulas to replace all the numbers in the range C4:E9 and C13:E17. If necessary, reformat the tables, as described in Part 1. The worksheet should appear as shown in Figure 1–104, except that some of the totals will be off by 0.01 due to rounding errors. Save the worksheet using the file name, Lab 1-3 Part 3 College Cost and Financial Support. Print the worksheet. Press CTRL+ACCENT MARK (`) to display the formulas. Print the formulas version. Submit the assignment as requested by your instructor. Close the workbook without saving changes.

Cases and Places

Apply your creative thinking and problem solving skills to design and implement a solution.

● EASIER   ●● MORE DIFFICULT

● 1: Design and Create a Workbook to Analyze Yearly Sales

You are working as a summer intern for Hit-the-Road Mobile Services. Your manager has asked you to prepare a worksheet to help her analyze historical yearly sales by type of product (Table 1–10). Use the concepts and techniques presented in this chapter to create the worksheet and an embedded 3-D Clustered Column chart.

Table 1–10 Hit-the-Road Mobile Services Sales				
	2005	**2006**	**2007**	**2008**
Standard Mobile Phones	87598	99087	129791	188785
Camera Phones	71035	75909	96886	100512
Music Phones	65942	24923	34590	15696
Wireless PDAs	67604	58793	44483	35095
Satellite Radios	15161	27293	34763	43367
Headsets	9549	6264	2600	4048
Other Accessories	47963	108059	100025	62367

● 2: Design and Create a Worksheet and Chart to Analyze a Budget

To estimate the funds needed by your school's Environmental Club to make it through the upcoming year, you decide to create a budget for the club itemizing the expected quarterly expenses. The anticipated expenses are listed in Table 1–11. Use the concepts and techniques presented in this chapter to create the worksheet and an embedded 3-D Column chart using an appropriate chart style that compares the quarterly cost of each expense. Use the AutoCalculate area to determine the average amount spent per quarter on each expense. Manually insert the averages with appropriate titles in an empty area on the worksheet.

Table 1–11 Quarterly Environmental Club Budget				
	Jan – Mar	**April – June**	**July – Sept**	**Oct – Dec**
Meeting Room Rent	300	300	150	450
Copies and Supplies	390	725	325	640
Travel	450	755	275	850
Refreshments	105	85	215	155
Speaker Fees	200	200	0	500
Miscellaneous	125	110	75	215

Continued >

Cases and Places *continued*

•• 3: Create a 3-D Pie Chart to Analyze Quarterly Revenue

In-the-Villa DVD Rental is a DVD movie rental store. The owner of the store is trying to decide if it is feasible to hire more employees during certain times of the year. You have been asked to develop a worksheet totaling all the revenue received last year by quarter. The revenue per quarter is: Quarter 1, $52,699.23; Quarter 2, $111,244.32; Quarter 3, $70,905.03; and Quarter 4, $87,560.10. Create a 3-D Pie chart to illustrate quarterly revenue contribution by quarter. Use the AutoCalculate area to find the average, maximum, and minimum quarterly revenue and manually enter them and their corresponding identifiers in an empty area of the worksheet.

•• 4: Design and Create a Workbook to Analyze Your Field of Interest

Make It Personal

Based on your college major, area of interest, or career, use an Internet search engine or other research material to determine the total number of people employed in your chosen field of interest in the country over the past five years. For each year, break the yearly number down into two or more categories. For example, the number for each year can be broken into management and nonmanagement employees. Create an Excel worksheet that includes this data. Place the data in appropriate rows and columns for each year and category. Create totals for each row, totals for each column, and a grand total. Format the worksheet title, column headings, and data using the concepts presented in this chapter. Create a properly formatted Clustered Cone chart for the data and place it below the data in the worksheet. Make certain that years are on the X axis and number of employees is on the Y axis.

•• 5: Design and Create a Workbook to Analyze Your School

Working Together

Visit the registrar's office at your school and obtain data, such as age, gender, and full-time versus part-time status, for the students majoring in at least six different academic departments this semester. Have each member of your team divide the data into different categories. For example, separate the data by:

1. Age, divided into four different age groups

2. Gender, divided into male and female

3. Status, divided into full-time and part-time

After coordinating the data as a group, have each member independently use the concepts and techniques presented in this chapter to create a worksheet and appropriate chart to show the total students by characteristics by academic department. As a group, critique each worksheet and have each member modify his or her worksheet based on the group recommendations.

2 Formulas, Functions, Formatting, and Web Queries

Objectives

You will have mastered the material in this chapter when you can:

- Enter formulas using the keyboard and Point mode
- Apply the AVERAGE, MAX, and MIN functions
- Verify a formula using Range Finder
- Apply a theme to a workbook
- Add conditional formatting to cells
- Change column width and row height
- Check the spelling of a worksheet

- Set margins, headers and footers in Page Layout View
- Preview and print versions of a worksheet
- Use a Web query to get real-time data from a Web site
- Rename sheets in a workbook
- E-mail the active workbook from within Excel

2 | Formulas, Functions, Formatting, and Web Queries

Introduction

In Chapter 1, you learned how to enter data, sum values, format the worksheet to make it easier to read, and draw a chart. You also learned about using Help and saving, printing, and opening a workbook. This chapter continues to highlight these topics and presents some new ones.

The new topics covered in this chapter include using formulas and functions to create a worksheet. A **function** is a prewritten formula that is built into Excel. Other new topics include smart tags and option buttons, verifying formulas, applying a theme to a worksheet, adding borders, formatting numbers and text, using conditional formatting, changing the widths of columns and heights of rows, spell checking, e-mailing from within an application, renaming worksheets, using alternative types of worksheet displays and printouts, and adding page headers and footers to a worksheet. One alternative worksheet display and printout shows the formulas in the worksheet, instead of the values. When you display the formulas in the worksheet, you see exactly what text, data, formulas, and functions you have entered into it. Finally, this chapter covers Web queries to obtain real-time data from a Web site.

Project — Worksheet with Formulas, Functions, and Web Queries

The project in the chapter follows proper design guidelines and uses Excel to create the two worksheets shown in Figure 2–1. The Silver Dollars Stock Club was started and is owned by a national academic fraternity, which pools contributions from a number of local chapters. Each local chapter contributes $150 per month; the money is then invested in the stock market for the benefit of the organization and as a tool to help members learn about investing. At the end of each month, the club's treasurer summarizes the club's financial status in a portfolio summary. This summary includes information such as the stocks owned by the club, the cost of the stocks to the club, and the gain or loss that the club has seen over time on the stock. As the complexity of the task of creating the summary increases, the treasurer wants to use Excel to create the monthly portfolio summary. The treasurer also sees an opportunity to use Excel's built-in capability to access real-time stock quotes over the Internet.

Recall that the first step in creating an effective worksheet is to make sure you understand what is required. The people who will use the worksheet usually provide requirements. The requirements document for the Silver Dollars Stock Club Portfolio Summary worksheet includes the following: needs, source of data, summary of calculations, Web requirements, and other facts about its development (Figure 2–2 on page EX 84). The real-time stock quotes (shown in Figure 2–1b) will be accessed via a Web query. The stock quotes will be returned to the active workbook on a separate worksheet. Microsoft determines the content and format of the Real-Time Stock Quotes worksheet.

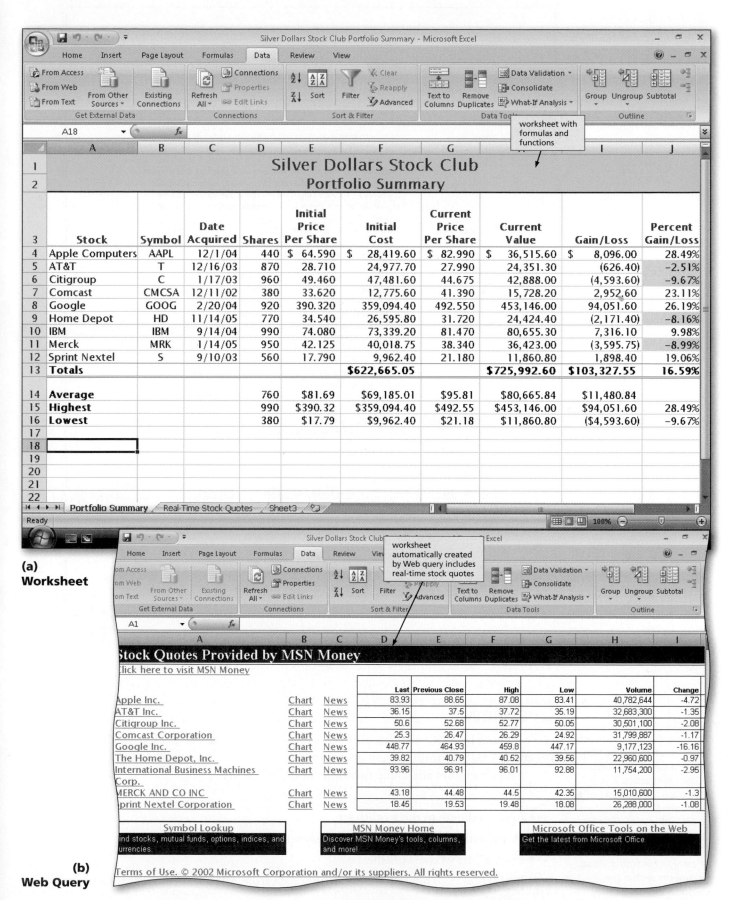

Figure 2–1

REQUEST FOR NEW WORKSHEET

Date Submitted:	April 8, 2008
Submitted By:	Juan Castillo
Worksheet Title:	Silver Dollars Stock Club Portfolio Summary
Needs:	An easy-to-read worksheet that summarizes the club's investments (Figure 2-3). For each stock, the worksheet is to include the stock name, stock symbol, date acquired, shares, initial price per share, initial cost, current price per share, current value, gain/loss, and percent gain/loss. Also include totals and the average, highest value, and lowest value for each column of numbers. Use the import data capabilities of Excel to access real-time stock quotes using Web queries.
Source of Data:	The data supplied by Juan includes the stock names, symbols, dates acquired, number of shares, initial price per share, and current price per share. This data is shown in Table 2-1 on page EX 89.
Calculations:	The following calculations must be made for each of the stocks: 1. Initial Cost = Shares × Initial Price Per Share 2. Current Value = Shares × Current Price Per Share 3. Gain/Loss = Current Value − Initial Cost 4. Percent Gain/Loss = Gain/Loss / Initial Cost 5. Compute the totals for initial cost, current value, and gain/loss. 6. Use the AVERAGE function to determine the average for the number of shares, initial price per share, initial cost per share, current price per share, current value, and gain/loss. 7. Use the MAX and MIN functions to determine the highest and lowest values for the number of shares, initial price per share, initial cost per share, current price per share, current value, gain/loss, and percent gain/loss.
Web Requirements:	Use the Web query feature of Excel to get real-time stock quotes for the stocks owned by the Silver Dollars Stock Club.

Approvals

Approval Status:	X	Approved
		Rejected
Approved By:	Members of the Silver Dollars Stock Club	
Date:	April 15, 2008	
Assigned To:	J. Quasney, Spreadsheet Specialist	

Figure 2–2

Aesthetics versus Function

In designing a worksheet, functional considerations should come first, before visual aesthetics. The function, or purpose, of a worksheet is to provide a user with direct ways to accomplish tasks. Avoid the temptation to use flashy or confusing visual elements within the worksheet, unless they will help the user more easily complete a task.

Overview

As you read this chapter, you will learn how to create the worksheet shown in Figure 2–1 by performing these general tasks:

- Enter formulas and apply functions in the worksheet
- Add conditional formatting to the worksheet
- Apply a theme to the worksheet
- Work with the worksheet in Page Layout View
- Print a part of the worksheet
- Perform a Web query to get real-time data from a Web site and create a new worksheet
- E-mail the worksheet

Plan
Ahead

General Project Decisions
While creating an Excel worksheet, you need to make several decisions that will determine the appearance and characteristics of the finished worksheet. As you create the worksheet required to meet the requirements shown in Figure 2–2, you should follow these general guidelines:

1. **Plan the layout of the worksheet.** As discussed in Chapter 1 and shown in Figure 2–3, rows typically contain items analogous to items in a list. In the case of the stock club's data, the individual stocks serve this purpose and each stock should be placed in a row. As the club adds more stocks, the number of rows in the worksheet will increase. Information about each stock and associated calculations should appear in columns.

2. **Determine the necessary formulas and functions needed.** Values such as initial cost and current value are calculated from known values. The formulas for these calculations should be known in advance of creating the worksheet. Values such as the average, highest, and lowest values can be calculated using Excel functions as opposed to relying on complex formulas.

3. **Identify how to format various elements of the worksheet.** As discussed in Chapter 1 and shown in Figure 2–3, the appearance of the worksheet affects its ability to communicate clearly. Numeric data should be formatted in generally accepted formats, such as using commas as thousands separators and parentheses for negative values.

4. **Establish rules for conditional formatting.** Conditional formatting allows you to format a cell based on the contents of the cell. Decide under which circumstances you would like a cell to stand out from similar cells and determine in what way the cell will stand out. In the case of the Percent Gain/Loss column on the worksheet, placing a different background color in cells that show losses is an appropriate format for the column.

5. **Specify how the printed worksheet should appear.** When it is possible that a person will want to print a worksheet, care should be taken in the development of the worksheet to ensure that the contents can be printed in a readable manner. Excel prints worksheets in landscape or portrait orientation and margins can be adjusted to fit more or less data on each page. Headers and footers add an additional level of customization to the printed page.

(continued)

Figure 2–3

Plan Ahead

(continued)

6. **Gather information regarding the needed Web query.** You must also know what information the Web query requires in order for it to generate results that you can use in Excel.

7. **Choose names for the worksheets.** When a workbook includes multiple worksheets, each worksheet should be named. A good worksheet name is succinct, unique to the workbook, and meaningful to any user of the workbook.

In addition, using a sketch of the worksheet can help you visualize its design. The sketch for Silver Dollars Stock Club Portfolio Summary worksheet (Figure 2–3 on the previous page) includes a title, a subtitle, column and row headings, and the location of data values. It also uses specific characters to define the desired formatting for the worksheet as follows:

1. The row of Xs below the leftmost column defines the cell entries as text, such as stock names and stock symbols.

2. The rows of Zs and 9s with slashes, dollar signs, decimal points, commas, and percent signs in the remaining columns define the cell entries as numbers. The Zs indicate that the selected format should instruct Excel to suppress leading 0s. The 9s indicate that the selected format should instruct Excel to display any digits, including 0s.

3. The decimal point means that a decimal point should appear in the cell entry and indicates the number of decimal places to use.

4. The commas indicate that the selected format should instruct Excel to display a comma separator only if the number has enough digits to the left of the decimal point.

5. The slashes in the third column identify the cell entry as a date.

6. The dollar signs that are not adjacent to the Zs in the first row below the column headings and in the total row signify a fixed dollar sign. The dollar signs that are adjacent to the Zs below the total row signify a floating dollar sign, or one that appears next to the first significant digit.

7. The percent sign (%) in the far right column indicates a percent sign should appear after the number.

When necessary, more specific details concerning the above guidelines are presented at appropriate points in the chapter. The chapter also will identify the actions you perform and decisions made regarding these guidelines during the creation of the worksheet shown in Figure 2–3 on page EX 85.

With a good understanding of the requirements document, an understanding of the necessary decisions, and a sketch of the worksheet, the next step is to use Excel to create the worksheet.

To Start Excel

If you are using a computer to step through the project in this chapter and you want your screen to match the figures in this book, you should change your computer's resolution to 1024×768. For information about how to change a computer's resolution, read Appendix E.

The following steps, which assume Windows Vista is running, start Excel based on a typical installation of Microsoft Office on your computer. You may need to ask your instructor how to start Excel for your computer.

Note: If you are using Windows XP, see Appendix F for alternate steps.

1 Click the Start button on the Windows Vista taskbar to display the Start menu.

2 Point to All Programs at the bottom of the left pane on the Start menu to display the All Programs list.

3 Click Microsoft Office in the All Programs list to display the Microsoft Office list.

4 Click Microsoft Office Excel to start Excel and display a blank worksheet in the Excel window.

5 If the Excel window is not maximized, click the Maximize button next to the Close button on its title bar to maximize the window.

6 If the worksheet window in Excel is not maximized, click the Maximize button next to the Close button on its title bar to maximize the worksheet window within Excel.

BTW

Starting Excel
You can use a command-line switch to start Excel and control how it starts. First, click the Start button on the Windows Vista taskbar, and then click the Start Search box. Next, enter the complete path to Excel's application file including the switch (for example, C:\Program Files\Microsoft Office\ Office12\Excel.exe/e). The switch /e starts Excel without opening a new workbook; /i starts Excel with a maximized window; /p "folder" sets the active path to folder and ignores the default folder; /r "filename" opens filename in read-only mode; and /s starts Excel in safe mode.

Entering the Titles and Numbers into the Worksheet

The first step in creating the worksheet is to enter the titles and numbers into the worksheet.

To Enter the Worksheet Title and Subtitle

The following steps enter the worksheet title and subtitle into cells A1 and A2.

1 If necessary, select cell A1. Type `Silver Dollars Stock Club` in the cell and then press the DOWN ARROW key to enter the worksheet title in cell A1.

2 Type `Portfolio Summary` in cell A2 and then press the DOWN ARROW key to enter the worksheet subtitle in cell A2 (Figure 2–4 on page EX 89).

To Enter the Column Titles

The column titles in row 3 begin in cell A3 and extend through cell J3. The column titles in Figure 2–3 include multiple lines of text. To start a new line in a cell, press ALT+ENTER after each line, except for the last line, which is completed by clicking the Enter box, pressing the ENTER key, or pressing one of the arrow keys. When you see ALT+ENTER in a step, press the ENTER key while holding down the ALT key and then release both keys.

The stock names and the row titles Totals, Average, Highest, and Lowest in the leftmost column begin in cell A4 and continue down to cell A16. This data is entered into rows 4 through 12 of the worksheet. The remainder of this section explains the steps required to enter the column titles, stock data, and row titles as shown in Figure 2–4 on page EX 89 and then save the workbook.

1 With cell A3 selected, type `Stock` and then press the RIGHT ARROW key.

2 Type `Symbol` in cell B3 and then press the RIGHT ARROW key.

BTW

Wrapping Text

If you have a long text entry, such as a paragraph, you can instruct Excel to wrap the text in a cell, rather than pressing ALT+ENTER to end a line. To wrap text, right-click in the cell, click Format Cells on the shortcut menu, click the Alignment tab, click Wrap text, and then click OK. Excel will increase the height of the cell automatically so the additional lines will fit. If you want to control where each line ends in the cell, rather than letting Excel wrap based on the cell width, however, then you must end each line with ALT+ENTER.

③ In cell C3, type Date and then press ALT+ENTER. Type Acquired and then press the RIGHT ARROW key.

④ In cell D3, type Shares and then press the RIGHT ARROW key.

⑤ In cell E3, type Initial and then press ALT+ENTER. Type Price and then press ALT+ENTER. Type Per Share and then press the RIGHT ARROW key.

⑥ Type Initial in cell F3 and then press ALT+ENTER. Type Cost and then press the RIGHT ARROW key.

⑦ In cell G3, type Current and then press ALT+ENTER. Type Price and then press ALT+ENTER. Type Per Share and then press the RIGHT ARROW key.

⑧ Type Current in cell H3 and then press ALT+ENTER. Type Value and then press the RIGHT ARROW key.

⑨ In cell I3, type Gain/Loss and then press the RIGHT ARROW key.

⑩ In cell J3, type Percent and then press ALT+ENTER. Type Gain/Loss.

To Enter the Portfolio Summary Data

BTW

Two-Digit Years

When you enter a two-digit year value, Excel changes a two-digit year less than 30 to 20xx and a two-digit year of 30 and greater to 19xx. Use four-digit years to ensure that Excel interprets year values the way you intend, if necessary.

The portfolio summary data in Table 2–1 includes a purchase date for each stock. Excel considers a date to be a number and, therefore, it displays the date right-aligned in the cell. The following steps enter the portfolio summary data shown in Table 2–1.

① Select cell A4, type Apple Computers, and then press the RIGHT ARROW key.

② Type AAPL in cell B4 and then press the RIGHT ARROW key.

③ Type 12/1/04 in cell C4 and then press the RIGHT ARROW key.

④ Type 440 in cell D4 and then press the RIGHT ARROW key.

⑤ Type 64.59 in cell E4 and then click cell G4.

⑥ Type 82.99 in cell G4 and then click cell A5.

⑦ Enter the portfolio summary data in Table 2–1 for the eight remaining stocks in rows 5 through 12 (Figure 2–4).

To Enter the Row Titles

BTW

Formatting a Worksheet

With early worksheet programs, users often skipped rows to improve the appearance of the worksheet. With Excel it is not necessary to skip rows because you can increase row heights to add white space between information.

① Select cell A13. Type Totals and then press the DOWN ARROW key. Type Average in cell A14 and then press the DOWN ARROW key.

② Type Highest in cell A15 and then press the DOWN ARROW key. Type Lowest in cell A16 and then press the ENTER key. Select cell F4 (Figure 2–4).

Table 2–1 Silver Dollars Stock Club Portfolio Summary Data					
Stock	**Symbol**	**Date Acquired**	**Shares**	**Initial Price Per Share**	**Current Price Per Share**
Apple Computers	AAPL	12/1/04	440	64.59	82.99
AT&T	T	12/16/03	870	28.71	27.99
Citigroup	C	1/17/03	960	49.46	44.675
Comcast	CMCSA	12/11/02	380	33.62	41.39
Google	GOOG	2/20/04	920	390.32	492.55
Home Depot	HD	11/14/05	770	34.54	31.72
IBM	IBM	9/14/04	990	74.08	81.47
Merck	MRK	1/14/05	950	42.125	38.34
Sprint Nextel	S	9/10/03	560	17.79	21.18

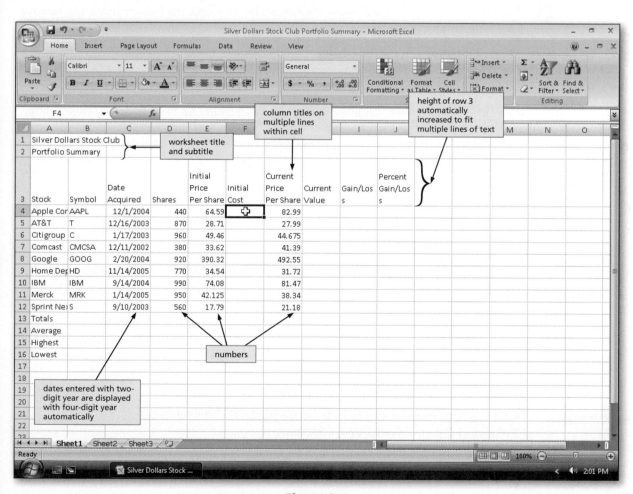

Figure 2–4

To Change Workbook Properties and Save the Workbook

With the data entered into the worksheet, the following steps save the workbook using the file name, Silver Dollars Stock Club Portfolio Summary. As you are building a workbook, it is a good idea to save it often so that you do not lose your work if the computer is turned off or if you lose electrical power. The first time you save a workbook, you should change the workbook properties.

1 Click the Office Button, click Prepare on the Office Button menu, and then click Properties.

2 Update the document properties with your name and any other information required.

3 Click the Close button on the Document Properties pane.

Note: If you are using Windows XP, see Appendix F for alternate steps.

4 With a USB flash drive connected to one of the computer's USB ports, click the Save button on the Quick Access Toolbar.

5 When Excel displays the Save As dialog box, type `Silver Dollars Stock Club Portfolio Summary` in the File name text box.

6 If the Folders list is displayed below the Folders button, click the Folders button to remove the Folders list.

7 If Computer is not displayed in the Favorite Links section, drag the top or bottom edge of the Save As dialog box until Computer is displayed.

8 Click Computer in the Favorite Links section. If necessary, scroll until UDISK 2.0 (E:) appears in the list of available drives. Double-click UDISK 2.0 (E:) (your USB flash drive may have a different name and letter). Click the Save button in the Save As dialog box to save the workbook on the USB flash drive using the file name, Silver Dollars Stock Club Portfolio Summary.

Entering Formulas

One of the reasons Excel is such a valuable tool is that you can assign a **formula** to a cell and Excel will calculate the result. Consider, for example, what would happen if you had to multiply 440×64.59 and then manually enter the product, 28,419.60, in cell F4. Every time the values in cells D4 or E4 changed, you would have to recalculate the product and enter the new value in cell F4. By contrast, if you enter a formula in cell F4 to multiply the values in cells D4 and E4, Excel recalculates the product whenever new values are entered into those cells and displays the result in cell F4.

Plan Ahead

Determine the necessary formulas and functions needed.
The formulas needed in the worksheet are noted in the requirements document as follows:

1. Initial Cost (column F) = Shares × Initial Price Per Share

2. Current Value (column H) = Shares × Current Price Per Share

3. Gain/Loss (column I) = Current Value – Initial Cost

4. Percent Gain/Loss (column J) = Gain/Loss / Initial Cost

The necessary functions to determine the average, highest, and lowest numbers are discussed shortly.

To Enter a Formula Using the Keyboard

The initial cost for each stock, which appears in column F, is equal to the number of shares in column D times the initial price per share in column E. Thus, the initial cost for Apple Computers in cell F4 is obtained by multiplying 440 (cell D4) by 64.59 (cell E4) or =D4*E4. The following steps enter the initial cost formula in cell F4 using the keyboard.

1

- With cell F4 selected, type =d4*e4 in the cell to display the formula in the formula bar and in cell F4 and to display colored borders around the cells referenced in the formula (Figure 2–5).

Q&A

What is happening on the worksheet as I enter the formula?

The **equal sign** (=) preceding d4*e4 is an important part of the formula. It alerts Excel that you are entering a formula or function and not text. Because the most common error when entering a formula is to reference the wrong cell in a formula mistakenly, Excel colors the borders of the cells referenced in the formula. The coloring helps in the reviewing process to ensure the cell references are correct. The **asterisk** (*) following d4 is the arithmetic operator that directs Excel to perform the multiplication operation.

Figure 2–5

2

- Press the RIGHT ARROW key twice to complete the arithmetic operation indicated by the formula, display the result, 28419.6, and to select cell H4 (Figure 2–6).

Figure 2–6

Arithmetic Operations

Table 2–2 describes multiplication and other valid Excel arithmetic operators.

Table 2–2 Summary of Arithmetic Operators			
Arithmetic Operator	**Meaning**	**Example of Usage**	**Meaning**
–	Negation	–34	Negative 34
%	Percentage	=72%	Multiplies 72 by 0.01
^	Exponentiation	=4 ^ 6	Raises 4 to the sixth power
*	Multiplication	=22.6 * F4	Multiplies the contents of cell F4 by 22.6
/	Division	=C3 / C6	Divides the contents of cell C3 by the contents of cell C6
+	Addition	=7 + 3	Adds 7 and 3
–	Subtraction	=F12 – 22	Subtracts 22 from the contents of cell F12

BTW

Troubling Formulas
If Excel does not accept a formula, remove the equal sign from the left side and complete the entry as text. Later, after you have entered additional data or determined the error, reinsert the equal sign to change the text back to a formula and edit the formula as needed.

You can enter the cell references in formulas in uppercase or lowercase, and you can add spaces before and after arithmetic operators to make the formulas easier to read. The formula, =d4*e4, is the same as the formulas, =d4 * e4, =D4 * e4, or =D4 * E4.

Order of Operations

When more than one arithmetic operator is involved in a formula, Excel follows the same basic order of operations that you use in algebra. Moving from left to right in a formula, the **order of operations** is as follows: first negation (–), then all percentages (%), then all exponentiations (^), then all multiplications (*) and divisions (/), and finally, all additions (+) and subtractions (–).

You can use parentheses to override the order of operations. For example, if Excel follows the order of operations, 5 * 9 + 8 equals 53. If you use parentheses, however, to change the formula to 5 * (9 + 8), the result is 85, because the parentheses instruct Excel to add 9 and 8 before multiplying by 5. Table 2–3 illustrates several examples of valid Excel formulas and explains the order of operations.

Table 2–3 Examples of Excel Formulas	
Formula	**Meaning**
=K12	Assigns the value in cell K12 to the active cell.
=10 + 4^2	Assigns the sum of 10 + 16 (or 26) to the active cell.
=3 * C20 or =C20 * 3 or =(3 * C20)	Assigns three times the contents of cell C20 to the active cell.
=50% * 12	Assigns the product of 0.50 times 12 (or 6) to the active cell.
– (H3 * Q30)	Assigns the negative value of the product of the values contained in cells H3 and Q30 to the active cell.
=12 * (N8 – O8)	Assigns the product of 12 times the difference between the values contained in cells N8 and O8 to the active cell.
=M9 / Z8 – C3 * Q19 + A3 ^ B3	Completes the following operations, from left to right: exponentiation (A3 ^ B3), then division (M9 / Z8), then multiplication (C3 * Q19), then subtraction (M9 / Z8) – (C3 * Q19), and finally addition (M9 / Z8 – C3 * Q19) + (A3 ^ B3). If cells A3 = 2, B3 = 4, C3 = 6, M9 = 3, Q19 = 4, and Z8 = 3, then Excel assigns the active cell the value 18; that is, 3 / 3 – 6 * 4 + 2 ^ 4 = -7.

To Enter Formulas Using Point Mode

The sketch of the worksheet in Figure 2–3 on page EX 85 calls for the current value, gain/loss, and percent gain/loss of each stock to appear in columns H, I, and J respectively. All three of these values are calculated using formulas in row 4:

> Current Value (cell H4) = Shares × Current Price Per Share or =D4*G4
> Gain/Loss (cell I4) = Current Value – Initial Cost or H4-F4
> Percent Gain/Loss (cell J4) = Gain/Loss / Initial Cost or I4/F4

An alternative to entering the formulas in cells H4, I4, and J4 using the keyboard is to enter the formulas using the mouse and Point mode. **Point mode** allows you to select cells for use in a formula by using the mouse. The following steps enter formulas using Point mode.

1

- With cell H4 selected, type = (equal sign) to begin the formula and then click cell D4 to add a reference to cell D4 to the formula (Figure 2–7).

Figure 2–7

2

- Type * (asterisk) and then click cell G4 to add a multiplication operator and reference to cell G4 to the formula (Figure 2–8).

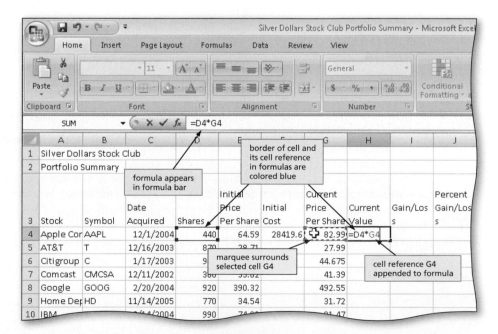

Figure 2–8

❸

- Click the Enter box and then click cell I4 to select cell I4.

- Type = (equal sign) and then click cell H4 to add a reference to cell H4 to the formula.

- Type − (minus sign) and then click cell F4 to add a subtraction operator and reference to cell F4 to the formula (Figure 2–9).

Q&A

When should I use Point mode to enter formulas?

Using Point mode to enter formulas often is faster and more accurate than using the keyboard to type the entire formula when the cell you want to select does not require you to scroll. In many instances, as in these steps, you may want to use both the keyboard and mouse when entering a formula in a cell. You can use the keyboard to begin the formula, for example, and then use the mouse to select a range of cells.

Figure 2–9

❹

- Click the Enter box to enter the formula in cell I4.

- Select cell J4. Type = (equal sign) and then click cell I4 to add a reference to cell I4 to the formula.

- Type / (forward slash) and then click cell F4 to add a reference to cell F4 to the formula.

- Click the Enter box to enter the formula in cell J4 (Figure 2–10).

Q&A

Why do only six decimal places show in cell J4?

The actual value assigned by Excel to cell J4 from the division operation in Step 4 is 0.284873819. While not all the decimal places appear in Figure 2–10, Excel maintains all of them for computational purposes. Thus, if referencing cell J4 in a formula, the value used for computational purposes is 0.284873819, not 0.284874. Excel displays the value in cell J4 as 0.284874 because the cell formatting is set to display only six digits after the decimal point. If you change the cell formatting of column J to display nine digits after the decimal point, then Excel displays the true value 0.284873819.

Figure 2–10

To Copy Formulas Using the Fill Handle

The four formulas for Apple Computers in cells F4, H4, I4, and J4 now are complete. You could enter the same four formulas one at a time for the eight remaining stocks. A much easier method of entering the formulas, however, is to select the formulas in row 4 and then use the fill handle to copy them through row 12. Recall from Chapter 1 that the fill handle is a small rectangle in the lower-right corner of the active cell or active range. The following steps copy the formulas using the fill handle.

- Select cell F4 and then point to the fill handle.

- Drag the fill handle down through cell F12 and continue to hold the mouse button to select the destination range (Figure 2–11).

Figure 2–11

- Release the mouse button to copy the formula in cell F4 to the cells in the range F5:F12.

- Select the range H4:J4 and then point to the fill handle (Figure 2–12).

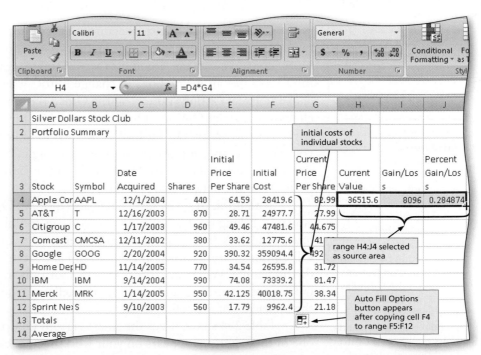

Figure 2–12

3

- Drag the fill handle down through the range H5:J12 to copy the three formulas =D4*G4 in cell H4, =H4-F4 in cell I4, and =I4/F4 in cell J4 to the range H5:J12 (Figure 2–13).

Q&A How does Excel adjust the cell references in the formulas in the destination area?

Recall that when you copy a formula, Excel adjusts the cell references so the new formulas contain references corresponding to the new location and performs calculations using the appropriate values. Thus, if you copy downward, Excel adjusts the row portion of cell references. If you copy across, then Excel adjusts the column portion of cell references. These cell references are called **relative cell references**.

Figure 2–13

Other Ways

1. Select source area, click Copy button on Ribbon, select destination area, click Paste button on Ribbon

2. Select source area, right-click copy area, click Copy on shortcut menu, select destination area, right-click paste area, click Paste on shortcut menu

Automatic Recalculation
Every time you enter a value into a cell in the worksheet, Excel automatically recalculates all formulas. You can change to manual recalculation by clicking the Calculation Options button on the Formulas tab on the Ribbon and then clicking Manual. In manual calculation mode, press the F9 key to instruct Excel to recalculate all formulas.

Smart Tags and Option Buttons

Excel can identify certain actions to take on specific data in workbooks using **smart tags**. Data labeled with smart tags includes dates, financial symbols, people's names, and more. To use smart tags, you must turn on smart tags using the AutoCorrect Options in the Excel Options dialog box. To change AutoCorrect options, click the Office Button, click the Excel Options button on the Office Button menu, point to Proofing, and then click AutoCorrect Options. Once smart tags are turned on, Excel places a small purple triangle, called a **smart tag indicator**, in a cell to indicate that a smart tag is available. When you move the insertion point over the smart tag indicator, the Smart Tag Actions button appears. Clicking the Smart Tag Actions button arrow produces a list of actions you can perform on the data in that specific cell.

In addition to smart tags, Excel also displays Options buttons in a workbook while you are working on it to indicate that you can complete an operation using automatic features such as AutoCorrect, Auto Fill, error checking, and others. For example, the Auto Fill Options button shown in Figure 2–13 appears after a fill operation, such as dragging the fill handle. When an error occurs in a formula in a cell, Excel displays the Trace Error button next to the cell and identifies the cell with the error by placing a green triangle in the upper left of the cell.

Table 2–4 summarizes the smart tag and Options buttons available in Excel. When one of these buttons appears on your worksheet, click the button arrow to produce the list of options for modifying the operation or to obtain additional information.

Table 2–4 Smart Tag and Options Buttons in Excel

Button	Name	Menu Function
	Auto Fill Options	Gives options for how to fill cells following a fill operation, such as dragging the fill handle.
	AutoCorrect Options	Undoes an automatic correction, stops future automatic corrections of this type, or causes Excel to display the AutoCorrect Options dialog box.
	Insert Options	Lists formatting options following an insertion of cells, rows, or columns.
	Paste Options	Specifies how moved or pasted items should appear (for example, with original formatting, without formatting, or with different formatting).
	Smart Tag Actions	Lists information options for a cell containing data recognized by Excel, such as a stock symbol.
	Trace Error	Lists error checking options following the assignment of an invalid formula to a cell.

To Determine Totals Using the Sum Button

The next step is to determine the totals in row 13 for the initial cost in column F, current value in column H, and gain/loss in column I. To determine the total initial cost in column F, the values in the range F4 through F12 must be summed. To do so, enter the function =sum(f4:f12) in cell F13 or select cell F13 and then click the Sum button on the Ribbon and then press the ENTER key. Recall that a function is a prewritten formula that is built into Excel. Similar SUM functions or the Sum button can be used in cells H13 and I13 to determine total current value and total gain/loss, respectively.

1 Select cell F13. Click the Sum button on the Ribbon and then click the Enter button.

2 Select the range H13:I13. Click the Sum button on the Ribbon to display the totals in row 13 as shown in Figure 2–14.

BTW

Selecting a Range
You can select a range using the keyboard. Press the F8 key and then use the arrow keys to select the desired range. After you are finished, make sure to press the F8 key to turn off the selection or you will continue to select ranges.

Figure 2–14

To Determine the Total Percent Gain/Loss

With the totals in row 13 determined, the next step is to copy the percent gain/loss formula in cell J12 to cell J13 as performed in the following steps.

1 Select cell J12 and then point to the fill handle.

2 Drag the fill handle down through cell J13 to copy the formula in cell J12 to cell J13 (Figure 2–15).

Q&A Why was the formula I13/F13 not copied to cell J13 earlier?

The formula, I13/F13, was not copied to cell J13 when cell J4 was copied to the range J5:J12 because both cells involved in the computation (I13 and F13) were blank, or zero, at the time. A **blank cell** in Excel has a numerical value of zero, which would have resulted in an error message in cell J13. Once the totals were determined, both cells I13 and F13 (especially F13, because it is the divisor) had nonzero numerical values.

	Stock	Symbol	Date Acquired	Shares	Initial Price Per Share	Initial Cost	Current Price Per Share	Current Value	Gain/Loss	Percent Gain/Loss
3	Stock	Symbol	Acquired	Shares	Per Share	Cost	Per Share	Value	s	s
4	Apple Cor	AAPL	12/1/2004	440	64.59	28419.6	82.99	36515.6	8096	0.284874
5	AT&T	T	12/16/2003	870	28.71	24977.7	27.99	24351.3	-626.4	-0.02508
6	Citigroup	C	1/17/2003	960	49.46	47481.6	44.675	42888	-4593.6	-0.09674
7	Comcast	CMCSA	12/11/2002	380	33.62	12775.6	41.39	15728.2	2952.6	0.231112
8	Google	GOOG	2/20/2004	920	390.32	359094.4	492.55	453146	94051.6	0.261913
9	Home De	HD	11/14/2005	770	34.54	26595.8	31.72	24424.4	-2171.4	-0.08164
10	IBM	IBM	9/14/2004	990	74.08	73339.2	81.47	80655.3	7316.1	0.099757
11	Merck	MRK	1/14/2005	950	42.125	40018.75	38.34	36423	-3595.75	-0.08985
12	Sprint Ne	S	9/10/2003	560	17.79	9962.4	21.18	11860.8	1898.4	0.190556
13	Totals					622665.1		725992.6	103327.6	0.165944
14	Average									
15	Highest									
16	Lowe									

formula is =I12/F12

formula is =I13/F13

Auto Fill Options button appears after copying cell J12 to cell J13

Figure 2–15

Entering Functions
You can drag the Function Arguments dialog box (Figure 2–20 on page EX 101) out of the way in order to select a range. You also can click the Collapse Dialog button to the right of the Number 1 box to hide the Function Arguments dialog box. After selecting the range, click the Collapse Dialog button a second time.

Statistical Functions
Excel usually considers a blank cell to be equal to 0. The statistical functions, however, ignore blank cells. Excel thus calculates the average of 3 cells with values of 7, blank, and 5 to be 6 or (7 + 5) / 2 and not 4 or (7 + 0 + 5) / 3.

Using the AVERAGE, MAX, and MIN Functions

The next step in creating the Silver Dollars Stock Club Portfolio Summary worksheet is to compute the average, highest value, and lowest value for the number of shares listed in the range D4:D12 using the AVERAGE, MAX, and MIN functions in the range D14:D16. Once the values are determined for column D, the entries can be copied across to the other columns.

Excel includes prewritten formulas called functions to help you compute these statistics. A **function** takes a value or values, performs an operation, and returns a result to the cell. The values that you use with a function are called **arguments**. All functions begin with an equal sign and include the arguments in parentheses after the function name. For example, in the function =AVERAGE(D4:D12), the function name is AVERAGE, and the argument is the range D4:D12.

With Excel, you can enter functions using one of five methods: (1) the keyboard or mouse; (2) the Insert Function box in the formula bar; (3) the Sum menu; (4) the AutoSum command on the Formulas tab on the Ribbon; and (5) the Name box area in the formula bar (Figure 2–16). The method you choose will depend on your typing skills and whether you can recall the function name and required arguments.

In the following pages, each of the first three methods will be used. The keyboard and mouse method will be used to determine the average number of shares (cell D14). The Insert Function button in the formula bar method will be used to determine the highest number of shares (cell D15). The Sum menu method will be used to determine the lowest number of shares (cell D16).

To Determine the Average of a Range of Numbers Using the Keyboard and Mouse

The **AVERAGE function** sums the numbers in the specified range and then divides the sum by the number of nonzero cells in the range. The following steps use the AVERAGE function to determine the average of the numbers in the range D4:D12.

- Select cell D14.

- Type =av in the cell to display the Formula AutoComplete list.

- Point to the AVERAGE function name (Figure 2–16).

Q&A

What is happening as I type?

As you type the equal sign followed by the characters in the name of a function, Excel displays the Formula AutoComplete list. This list contains those functions that alphabetically match the letters you have typed. Because you typed =av, Excel displays all the functions that begin with the letters av.

Figure 2–16

②

- Double-click AVERAGE in the Formula AutoComplete list to select the AVERAGE function.

- Select the range D4:D12 to insert the range as the argument to the AVERAGE function (Figure 2–17).

Q&A

As I drag, why does the function in cell D14 change?

When you click cell D4, Excel appends cell D4 to the left parenthesis in the formula bar and surrounds cell D4 with a marquee. When you begin dragging, Excel appends to the argument a colon (:) and the cell reference of the cell where the mouse pointer is located.

③

- Click the Enter box to compute the average of the nine numbers in the range D4:D12 and display the result in cell D14 (Figure 2–18).

Q&A

Can I use the arrow keys to complete the entry instead?

No. When you use Point mode you cannot use the arrow keys to complete the entry. While in Point mode, the arrow keys change the selected cell reference in the range you are selecting.

Q&A

What is the purpose of the parentheses in the function?

The AVERAGE function requires that the argument (in this case, the range D4:D12) be included within parentheses following the function name. Excel automatically appends the right parenthesis to complete the AVERAGE function when you click the Enter box or press the ENTER key.

Figure 2–17

SUM ▾ × ✓ ƒ𝑥 =AVERAGE(D4:D12

AVERAGE function with range to average shows in active cell and formula bar

	A	B	C	D	E	F	G	H	I	J
1	Silver Dollars Stock Club									
2	Portfolio Summary									
3	Stock	Symbol	Date Acquired	Shares	Initial Price Per Share	Initial Cost	Current Price Per Share	Current Value	Gain/Loss	Percent Gain/Loss
4	Apple Cor	AAPL	12/1/2004	440	64.59	28419.6	82.99	36515.6	8096	0.28487
5			/16/2003	870	28.71	24977.7	27.99	24351.3	-626.4	-0.0250
6			/17/2003	960	49.46	47481.6	44.675	42888	-4593.6	-0.0967
7	Comcast	CMCSA	12/11/2002	380	33.62	12775.6	41.39	15728.2	2952.6	0.231112
8	Google	GOOG	2/20/2004	920	390.32	359094.4	492.55	453146	94051.6	0.261913
9	Home Dep	HD	11/14/2005	770	34.54	26595.8	31.72	24424.4	-2171.4	-0.08164
10	IBM	IBM	9/14/2004	990	74.08	73339.2	81.47	80655.3	7316.1	0.099757
11	Merck	MRK	1/14/2005	950	42.125	40018.75	38.34	36423	-3595.75	-0.08985
12	Sprint Nex	S	9/10/2003	560	17.79	9962.4	21.18	11860.8	1898.4	0.190556
13	Total					622665.1		725992.6	103327.6	0.165944
14	Aver			=AVERAGE(D4:D12						
15	Highest									
16	Lowest									
17										

Enter box

marquee surrounds selected range D4:D12

AVERAGE function ScreenTip

AVERAGE(**number1**, [number2], ...)

Figure 2–18

Function box changes back to Name box

when cell D14 is active cell, formula bar displays AVERAGE function

right parenthesis automatically appended when Enter box clicked or ENTER key pressed

D14 ▾ ƒ𝑥 =AVERAGE(D4:D12)

	A	B	C	D	E	F	G	H	I	J
1	Silver Dollars Stock Club									
2	Portfolio Summary									
3	Stock	Symbol	Date Acquired	Shares	Initial Price Per Share	Initial Cost	Current Price Per Share	Current Value	Gain/Loss	Percent Gain/Loss
4	Apple Cor	AAPL	12/1/2004	440	64.59	28419.6	82.99	36515.6	8096	0.28487
5	AT&T	T	12/16/2003	870	28.71	24977.7	27.99	24351.3	-626.4	-0.0250
6	Citigroup	C	1/17/2003	960	49.46	47481.6	44.675	42888	-4593.6	-0.0967
7	Comcast	CMCSA	12/11/2002	380	33.62	12775.6	41.39	15728.2	2952.6	0.231112
8	Google	GOOG	2/20/2004	920	390.32	359094.4	492.55	453146	94051.6	0.261913
9	Home Dep	HD	11/14/2005	770	34.54	26595.8	31.72	24424.4	-2171.4	-0.08164
10	IBM	IBM	9/14/2004	990	74.08	73339.2	81.47	80655.3	7316.1	0.099757
11	Merck	MRK	1/14/2005	950	42.125	40018.75	38.34	36423	-3595.75	-0.08985
12	Sprint Nex	S	9/10/2003	560	17.79	9962.4	21.18	11860.8	1898.4	0.190556
13	Totals							725992.6	103327.6	0.165944
14	Average			760						
15	Hi									

average shares per stock

Other Ways

1. Click Insert Function box in formula bar, click AVERAGE function

2. Click Sum button arrow on Ribbon, click Average function

3. Click Formulas tab on Ribbon, click AutoSum button arrow, click Average function

To Determine the Highest Number in a Range of Numbers Using the Insert Function Box

The next step is to select cell D15 and determine the highest (maximum) number in the range D4:D12. Excel has a function called the **MAX function** that displays the highest value in a range. Although you could enter the MAX function using the keyboard and Point mode as described in the previous steps, an alternative method to entering the function is to use the Insert Function box in the formula bar, as performed in the following steps.

- Select cell D15.

- Click the Insert Function box in the formula bar to display the Insert Function dialog box.

- When Excel displays the Insert Function dialog box, click MAX in the 'Select a function' list (Figure 2–19).

Figure 2–19

- Click the OK button.

- When Excel displays the Function Arguments dialog box, type d4:d12 in the Number1 box (Figure 2–20).

Q&A

Why did numbers appear in the Function Arguments dialog box?

As shown in Figure 2–20, Excel displays the value the MAX function will return to cell D15 in the Function Arguments dialog box. It also lists the first few numbers in the selected range, next to the Number1 box.

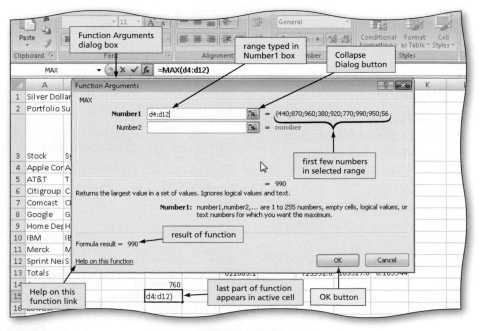

Figure 2–20

③

- Click the OK button to display the highest value in the range D4:D12 in cell D15 (Figure 2–21).

Q&A

Why should I not just enter the highest value that I see in the range D4:D12 in cell D15?

In this example, rather than entering the MAX function, you easily could scan the range D4:D12, determine that the highest number of shares is 990, and manually enter the number 990 as a constant in cell D15. Excel would display the number the same as in Figure 2–21. Because it contains a constant, however, Excel will continue to display 990 in cell D15, even if the values in the range D4:D12 change. If you use the MAX function, Excel will recalculate the highest value in the range D4:D9 each time a new value is entered into the worksheet.

	D15		fx	=MAX(D4:D12)					
	A	B	C	D	E	F	G	H	I	J
1	Silver Dollars Stock Club									
2	Portfolio Summary									
3	Stock	Symbol	Date Acquired	Shares	Initial Price Per Share	Initial Cost	Current Price Per Share	Current Value	Gain/Loss	Percent Gain/Loss
4	Apple Cor	AAPL	12/1/2004	440	64.59	28419.6	82.99	36515.6	8096	0.28487
5	AT&T	T	12/16/2003	870	28.71	24977.7	27.99	24351.3	-626.4	-0.0250
6	Citigroup	C	1/17/2003	960	49.46	47481.6	44.675	42888	-4593.6	-0.0967
7	Comcast	CMCSA	12/11/2002	380	33.62	12775.6	41.39	15728.2	2952.6	0.231112
8	Google	GOOG	2/20/2004	920	390.32	359094.4	492.55	453146	94051.6	0.261913
9	Home Dep	HD	11/14/2005	770	34.54	26595.8	31.72	24424.4	-2171.4	-0.08164
10	IBM	IBM	9/14/2004	990	74.08	73339.2	81.47	80655.3	7316.1	0.099757
11	Merck	MRK	1/14/2005	950	42.125	40018.75	38.34	36423	-3595.75	-0.08985
12	Sprint Ne>	S	9/10/2003	560	17.79	9962.4	21.18	11860.8	1898.4	0.190556
13	Totals					622665.1		725992.6	103327.6	0.165944
14	Average			760						
15	Highest			990						
16	Lowest									
17										

MAX function determines highest value in range D4:D12

highest value in range D4:D12

Figure 2–21

Other Ways

1. Click Sum button arrow on Ribbon, click Max function
2. Click Formulas tab on Ribbon, click AutoSum button arrow, click Max function
3. Type =MAX in cell

To Determine the Lowest Number in a Range of Numbers Using the Sum Menu

The next step is to enter the **MIN function** in cell D16 to determine the lowest (minimum) number in the range D4:D12. Although you can enter the MIN function using either of the methods used to enter the AVERAGE and MAX functions, the following steps perform an alternative using the Sum button on the Ribbon.

①

- Select cell D16.

- Click the Sum button arrow on the Ribbon to display the Sum button menu (Figure 2–22).

Q&A

Why should I use the Sum button menu?

Using the Sum button menu allows you to enter one of five often-used functions easily into a cell, without having to memorize its name or the required arguments.

Sum button arrow

Sum button menu

Min function

Σ Sum
Average
Count Numbers
Max
Min
More Functions...

D16 is active cell

Figure 2–22

2

- Click Min to display the function =MIN(D14:D15) in the formula bar and in cell D16 (Figure 2–23).

Q&A

Why does Excel select the range D14:D15?

The range D14:D15 automatically selected by Excel is not correct. Excel attempts to guess which cells you want to include in the function by looking for adjacent ranges to the selected cell that contain numeric data.

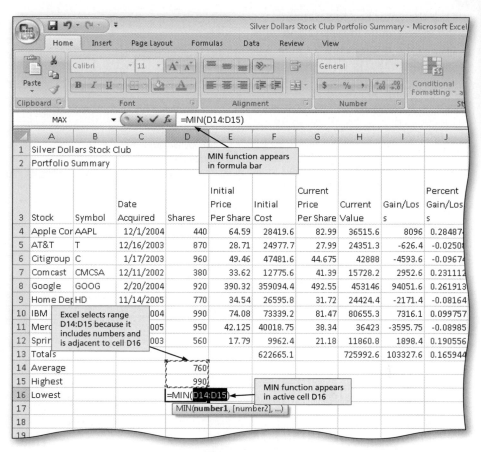

Figure 2–23

3

- Click cell D4 and then drag through cell D12 to display the function in the formula bar and in cell D14 with the new range (Figure 2–24).

Figure 2–24

4

- Click the Enter box to determine the lowest value in D4:D12 and display the result in the formula bar and in cell D14 (Figure 2–25).

Q&A

How can I use other functions?

Excel has more than 400 additional functions that perform just about every type of calculation you can imagine. These functions are categorized in the Insert Function dialog box shown in Figure 2–19 on page EX 101. To view the categories, click the 'Or select a category' box arrow. To obtain a description of a selected function, select its name in the Insert Function dialog box. Excel displays the description of the function below the Select a function list in the dialog box.

Figure 2–25

Other Ways

1. Click Insert Function box in formula bar, click MIN function
2. Click Formulas tab on Ribbon, click AutoSum button arrow, click Min function
3. Type =MIN in cell

To Copy a Range of Cells across Columns to an Adjacent Range Using the Fill Handle

The next step is to copy the AVERAGE, MAX, and MIN functions in the range D14:D16 to the adjacent range E14:J16. The following steps use the fill handle to copy the functions.

1

- Select the range D14:D16.

- Drag the fill handle in the lower-right corner of the selected range through cell J16 and continue to hold down the mouse button (Figure 2–26).

Figure 2–26

2

- Release the mouse button to copy the three functions to the range E14:J16 (Figure 2–27).

Q&A

How can I be sure that the function arguments are proper for the cells in range E14:J16?

Remember that Excel adjusts the cell references in the copied functions so each function refers to the range of numbers above it in the same column. Review the numbers in rows 14 through 16 in Figure 2–27. You should see that the functions in each column return the appropriate values, based on the numbers in rows 4 through 12 of that column.

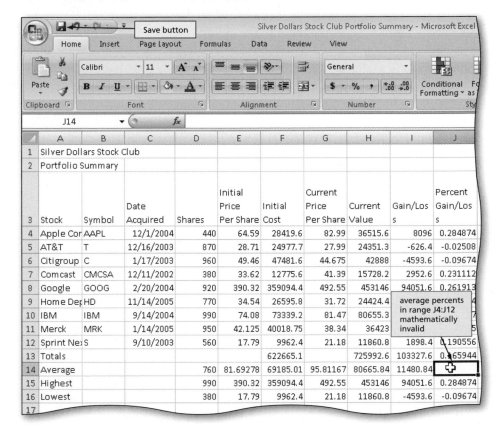

Figure 2–27

3

- Select cell J14 and press the DELETE key to delete the average of the percent gain/loss (Figure 2–28).

Q&A

Why is the formula in cell J14 deleted?

The average of the percent gain/loss in cell J14 is deleted because an average of percentages of this type is mathematically invalid.

Other Ways

1. Select source area and point to border of range, while holding down CTRL key, drag source area to destination area

2. Select source area, on Ribbon click Copy button, select destination area, on Ribbon click Paste button

3. Right-click source area, click Copy on shortcut menu, right-click destination area, click Paste on shortcut menu

4. Select source area, press CTRL+C, select destination area, press CTRL+V

Figure 2–28

To Save a Workbook Using the Same File Name

Earlier in this project, an intermediate version of the workbook was saved using the file name, Silver Dollars Stock Club Portfolio Summary. The following step saves the workbook a second time using the same file name.

1 Click the Save button on the Quick Access Toolbar to save the workbook on the USB flash drive using the file name, Silver Dollars Stock Club Portfolio Summary.

Q&A

Why did Excel not display the Save As dialog box?

When you save a workbook a second time using the same file name, Excel will not display the Save As dialog box as it does the first time you save the workbook. Excel automatically stores the latest version of the workbook using the same file name, Silver Dollars Stock Club Portfolio Summary. You also can click Save on the Office Button menu or press SHIFT+F12 or CTRL+S to save a workbook again.

Verifying Formulas Using Range Finder

One of the more common mistakes made with Excel is to include a wrong cell reference in a formula. An easy way to verify that a formula references the cells you want it to reference is to use Excel's Range Finder. Use the **Range Finder** to check which cells are referenced in the formula assigned to the active cell. Range Finder allows you to make immediate changes to the cells referenced in a formula.

To use Range Finder to verify that a formula contains the intended cell references, double-click the cell with the formula you want to check. Excel responds by highlighting the cells referenced in the formula so you can check that the cell references are correct.

To Verify a Formula Using Range Finder

The following steps use Range Finder to check the formula in cell J4.

1

- Double-click cell J4 to activate Range Finder (Figure 2–29).

2

- Press the ESC key to quit Range Finder and then select cell A18.

Figure 2–29

Formatting the Worksheet

Although the worksheet contains the appropriate data, formulas, and functions, the text and numbers need to be formatted to improve their appearance and readability.

In Chapter 1, cell styles were used to format much of the worksheet. This section describes how to change the unformatted worksheet in Figure 2–30a to the formatted worksheet in Figure 2–30b using a theme and other commands on the Ribbon. A **theme** is a predefined set of colors, fonts, chart styles, cell styles, and fill effects that can be applied to an entire workbook. Every new workbook that you create is assigned a default theme named Office. The colors and fonts that are used in the worksheet shown in Figure 2–30b are those that are associated with the Concourse theme.

(a) **Unformatted Worksheet**

(b) **Formatted Worksheet**

Figure 2–30

Identify how to format various elements of the worksheet.

The following outlines the formatting suggested in the sketch of the worksheet in Figure 2–3 on page EX 85:

1. Workbook theme - Concourse

2. Worksheet title and subtitle

   a. Alignment — center across columns A through J

   b. Cell style —Title

   c. Font size — title 18; subtitle 16

   d. Background color (range A1:J2) — Turquoise Accent 1, Lighter 60%

   e. Border — thick box border around range A1:J2

3. Column titles

   a. Cell style — Heading 3

   b. Alignment — center

4. Data

   a. Alignment — center data in column B

   b. Dates in column C — mm/dd/yy format

   c. Numbers in top row (range E4:I4) — Accounting style

   d. Numbers below top row (range E5:I12) — Comma style and decimal places

5. Total line

   a. Cell style — Total

   b. Numbers — Accounting style

6. Average, Highest, and Lowest rows

   a. Font style of row titles in range A14:A16 — bold

   b. Numbers — Currency style with floating dollar sign in the range E14:I16

7. Percentages in column J

   a. Numbers — Percentage style with two decimal places; if a cell in range J4:J12 is less than zero, then cell appears with background color of light red

8. Column widths

   a. Column A — 14.11 characters

   b. Columns B and C — best fit

   c. Column D — 6.00 characters

   d. Column E, G, and J — 9.00 characters

   e. Columns F, H, and I — 12.67 characters

9. Row heights

   a. Row 3 — 60.00 points

   b. Row 14 — 26.25 points

   c. Remaining rows — default

To Change the Workbook Theme

The Concourse theme includes fonts and colors that provide the worksheet a professional and subtly colored appearance. The following steps change the workbook theme to the Concourse theme.

1

- Click the Page Layout tab on the Ribbon.

- Click the Themes button on the Ribbon to display the Theme gallery (Figure 2–31).

Experiment

- Point to several themes in the Theme gallery to see a live preview of the themes.

Q&A

Why should I change the theme of a workbook?

A company or department may standardize on a specific theme so that all of their documents have a similar appearance. Similarly, an individual may want to have a theme that sets their work apart from others. Other Office applications, such as Word and PowerPoint, include the same themes included with Excel, meaning that all of your Microsoft Office documents can share a common theme.

Figure 2–31

2

- Click Concourse in the Theme gallery to change the workbook theme to Concourse (Figure 2–32).

Q&A

Why did the cells in the worksheet change?

The cells in the worksheet originally were formatted with the default font for the default Office theme. The default font for the Concourse theme is different than that of the default font for the Office theme and therefore changed on the worksheet when you changed the theme. If you had modified the font for any of the cells, those cells would not receive the default font for the Concourse theme.

Figure 2–32

To Format the Worksheet Titles

The following steps merge and center the worksheet titles, apply the Title cells style to the worksheet titles, and decrease the font of the worksheet subtitle.

1 Click the Home tab on the Ribbon.

2 Select the range A1:J1 and then click the Merge & Center button on the Ribbon.

3 Select the range A2:J2 and then click the Merge & Center button on the Ribbon.

4 Select the range A1:A2, click the Cell Styles button on the Ribbon, and then click the Title cell style in the Cell Styles gallery.

5 Select cell A2 and then click the Decrease Font Size button on the Ribbon (Figure 2–33).

Q&A What is the effect of clicking the Decrease Font Size button?

When you click the Decrease Font Size button Excel assigns the next lowest font size in the Font Size gallery to the selected range. The Increase Font Size button works in a similar manner, but causes Excel to assign the next highest font size in the Font Size gallery to the selected range.

Figure 2–33

To Change the Background Color and Apply a Box Border to the Worksheet Title and Subtitle

The final formats assigned to the worksheet title and subtitle are the turquoise background color and thick box border (Figure 2–30b on page EX 107). The following steps complete the formatting of the worksheet titles.

- Select the range A1:A2 and then click the Fill Color button arrow on the Ribbon to display the Fill Color palette (Figure 2–34).

Figure 2–34

2
- Click Turquoise Accent 1, lighter 60% (column 5, row 3) on the Fill Color palette to change the background color of cells A1 and A2 from white to turquoise (Figure 2–35).

Figure 2–35

3
- Click the Borders button arrow on the Ribbon to display the Borders gallery (Figure 2–36).

Figure 2–36

- Click the Thick Box Border command on the Borders gallery to display a thick box border around the range A1:A2.

- Click cell A18 to deselect the range A1:A2 (Figure 2–37).

Other Ways

1. On Ribbon click Format Cells Dialog Box Launcher, click appropriate tab, click desired format, click OK button

2. Right-click range, click Format Cells on shortcut menu, click appropriate tab, click desired format, click OK button

3. Press CTRL+1, click appropriate tab, click desired format, click OK button

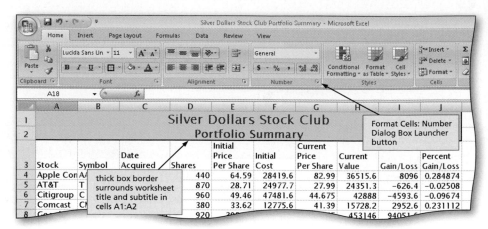

Figure 2–37

To Apply a Cell Style to the Column Headings and Format the Total Rows

As shown in Figure 2–30b on page EX 107, the column titles (row 3) have the Heading 3 cell style and the total row (row 13) has the Total cell style. The summary information headings in the range A14:A16 should be bold. The following steps assign these styles to row 3 and row 13 and the range A14:A16.

1 Select the range A3:J3.

2 Apply the Heading 3 cell style to the range A3:J3.

3 Apply the Total cell style to the range A13:J13.

4 Select the range A14:A16 and then click the Bold button on the Ribbon (Figure 2–38).

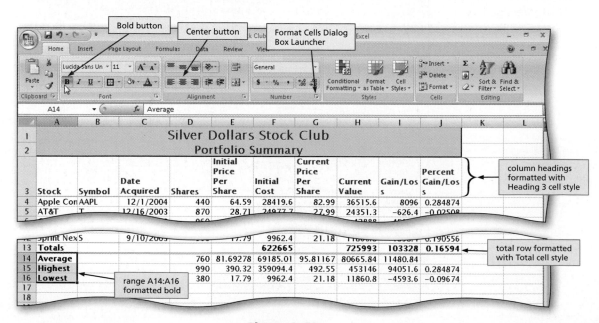

Figure 2–38

To Center Data in Cells and Format Dates

With the column titles and total rows formatted, the next step is to center the stock symbols in column B and format the dates in column C. If a cell entry is short, such as the stock symbols in column B, centering the entries within their respective columns improves the appearance of the worksheet. The following steps center the data in the range B4:B12 and format the dates in the range C4:C12.

1

- Select the range B4:B12 and then click the Center button on the Ribbon to center the data in the range B4:B12.

2

- Select the range C4:C12.

- Click the Format Cells: Number Dialog Box Launcher on the Ribbon to display the Format Cells dialog box.

- When Excel displays the Format Cells dialog box, if necessary click the Number tab, click Date in the Category list, and then click 3/14/01 in the Type list to choose the format for the range C4:C12 (Figure 2–39).

Figure 2–39

3

- Click the OK button to format the dates in column C using the date format style, mm/dd/yy.

- Select cell E4 to deselect the range C4:C13 (Figure 2–40).

Q&A

Can I format an entire column at once?

Yes. Rather than selecting the range B4:B12 in Step 1, you could have clicked the column B heading immediately above cell B1, and then clicked the Center button on the Ribbon. In this case, all cells in column B down to the last cell in the worksheet would have been formatted to use center alignment. This same procedure could have been used to format the dates in column C.

	A	B	C	D	E	F	G	H
1					Silver Dollars Stock Club			
2					Portfolio Summary			
3	Stock	Symbol	Date Acquired	Shares	Initial Price Per Share	Initial Cost	Current Price Per Share	Currer Value
4	Apple Con	AAPL	12/1/04	440	64.59	28419.6	82.99	3651
5	AT&T	T	12/16/03	870	28.71	24977.7	27.99	2435
6	Citigroup	C	1/17/03	960	49.46	47481.6	44.675	428
7	Comcast	CMCSA	12/11/02	380	33.62	12775.6	41.39	15728
8	Google	GOOG	2/20/04	920	390.32	359094.4	492.55	4531
9	Home Dep	HD	11/14/05	770	34.54	26595.8	31.72	24424
10	IBM	IBM	9/14/04	990	74.08	73339.2	81.47	80655
11	Merck	MRK	1/14/05			018.75	38.34	3642
12	Sprint Nex	S	9/10/03			9962.4	21.18	11860
13	Totals					22665		7259
14	Average					185.01	95.81167	80665.
15	Highest				990	390.32	359094.4	492.55	4531
16	Lowest				380	17.79	9962.4	21.18	1186

Excel displays dates in range C4:C12 using date style format, mm/dd/yy

Figure 2–40

BTW

Rotating and Shrinking Entries in Cells
In addition to aligning entries horizontally and vertically, you also can rotate and shrink entries to fit in a cell. To rotate or shrink entries to fit in a cell, click Format Cells on the shortcut menu, click the Alignment tab in the Format Cells dialog box, and then select the type of control you want.

Formatting Numbers Using the Ribbon

As shown in Figure 2–30b on page EX 107, the worksheet is formatted to resemble an accounting report. For example, in columns E through I, the numbers in the first row (row 4), the totals row (row 13), and the rows below the totals (rows 14 through 16) have dollar signs, while the remaining numbers (rows 5 through 12) in columns E through I do not.

To append a dollar sign to a number, you should use the Accounting number format. Excel displays numbers using the **Accounting number format** with a dollar sign to the left of the number, inserts a comma every three positions to the left of the decimal point, and displays numbers to the nearest cent (hundredths place). Clicking the Accounting Number Format button on the Ribbon assigns the desired Accounting number format. When you use the Accounting Number Format button to assign the Accounting number format, Excel displays a **fixed dollar sign** to the far left in the cell, often with spaces between it and the first digit. To assign a **floating dollar sign** that appears immediately to the left of the first digit with no spaces, use the Currency style in the Format Cells dialog box.

The Comma style format is used to instruct Excel to display numbers with commas and no dollar signs. The **Comma style format**, which can be assigned to a range of cells by clicking the Comma Style button on the Ribbon, inserts a comma every three positions to the left of the decimal point and causes numbers to be displayed to the nearest hundredths.

To Apply an Accounting Style Format and Comma Style Format Using the Ribbon

The following steps show how to assign formats using the Accounting Number Format button and the Comma Style button on the Ribbon.

1

- Select the range E4:I4.

- While holding down the CTRL key, select the ranges F13:I13.

- Click the Accounting Number Format button on the Ribbon (Figure 2–41) to apply the Accounting style format with fixed dollar signs to the nonadjacent ranges E4:I4 and F13:I13 (Figure 2–41).

Q&A What is the effect of applying the Accounting style format?

The Accounting Number Format button assigns a fixed dollar sign to the numbers in the ranges E4:I4 and F13:I13. In each cell in these ranges, Excel displays the dollar sign to the far left with spaces between it and the first digit in the cell.

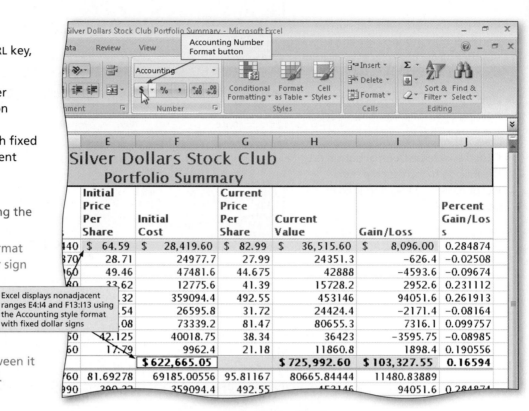

Figure 2–41

2

- Select the range E5:I12.

- Click the Comma Style button on the Ribbon to assign the Comma style format to the range E5:I12 (Figure 2–42).

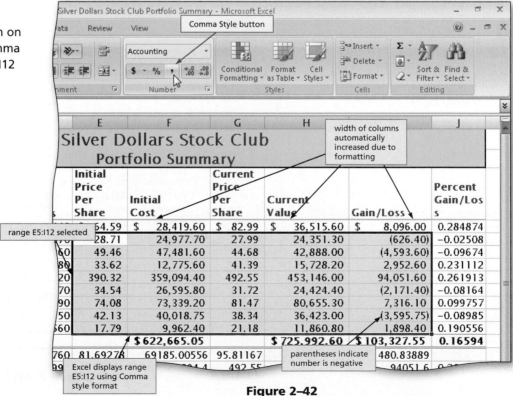

Figure 2–42

3

- Click cell E4.

- While holding down the CTRL key, select cell G4.

- Click the Increase Decimal button on the Ribbon to increase the number of decimal places displayed in cell E4 and G4.

- Select the range E5:E12. While holding down the CTRL key, select the range G5:G12.

- Click the Increase Decimal button on the Ribbon to increase the number of decimal places displayed in selected ranges (Figure 2–43).

Q&A | What is the effect of clicking the Increase Decimal button?

The Increase Decimal button instructs Excel to display additional decimal places in a cell. Each time you click the Increase Decimal button, Excel adds a decimal place to the selected cell.

Figure 2–43

To Apply a Currency Style Format with a Floating Dollar Sign Using the Format Cells Dialog Box

The following steps use the Format Cells dialog box to apply the Currency style format with a floating dollar sign to the numbers in the ranges E14:I16.

1

- Select the range E14:I16 and then point to the Format Cells: Number Dialog Box Launcher on the Ribbon (Figure 2–44).

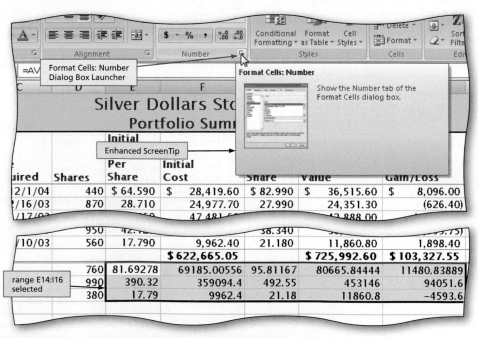

Figure 2–44

2

- Click the Format Cells: Number Dialog Box Launcher.

- If necessary, click the Number tab in the Format Cells dialog box.

- Click Currency in the Category list and then click the third style ($1,234.10) in the Negative numbers list (Figure 2–45).

Q&A How do I select the proper format?

You can choose from 12 categories of formats. Once you select a category, you can select the number of decimal places, whether or not a dollar sign should be displayed, and how negative numbers should appear. Selecting the appropriate negative numbers format is important, because doing so adds a space to the right of the number in order to align the numbers in the worksheet on the decimal points. Some of the available negative number formats do not align the numbers in the worksheet on the decimal points.

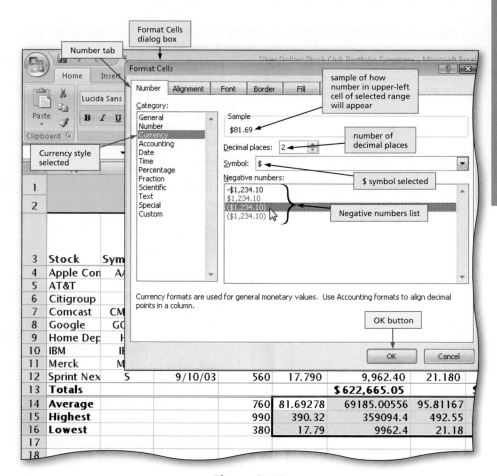

Figure 2–45

3

- Click the OK button to assign the Currency style format with a floating dollar sign to the range E14:I16 (Figure 2–46).

Q&A Should I click the Accounting Number Style button on the Ribbon or use the Format Cells dialog box?

Recall that a floating dollar sign always appears immediately to the left of the first digit, and the fixed dollar sign always appears on the left side of the cell. Cell E4, for example, has a fixed dollar sign, while cell E14 has a floating dollar sign. The Currency style was assigned to cell E14 using the Format Cells dialog box and the result is a floating dollar sign.

40	$ 64.390		32.990	$ 36,9		0.284874
70	28.710	24,977.70	27.990	24,351.30	(626.40)	–0.02508
60	49.460	47,481.60	44.675	42,888.00	(4,593.60)	–0.09674
80	33.620	12,775.60	41.390	15,728.20	2,952.60	0.231112
920	390.320	359,094.40	492.550	453,146.00	94,051.60	0.261913
77		6,595.80	31.720	24,424.40	(2,171.40)	–0.08164
9		3,339.20	81.470	80,655.20	7,316.10	0.099757
5		0,018.75	38.340		(3,595.75)	–0.08985
60	17.790	9,962.40	21.180		1,898.40	0.190556
		$ 622,665.05		$ 725,992.60	$ 103,327.55	0.16594
50	$81.69	$69,185.01	$95.81	$80,665.84	$11,480.84	
90	$390.32	$359,094.40	$492.55	$453,146.00	$94,051.60	0.284874
80	$17.79	$9,962.40	$21.18	$11,860.80	($4,593.60)	–0.09674

Excel displays range E14:I16 using Currency style format with floating dollar signs

parentheses surround negative numbers

Figure 2–46

Other Ways

1. Press CTRL+1, click Number tab, click Currency in Category list, select format, click OK button

2. Press CTRL+SHIFT+ DOLLAR SIGN ($)

To Apply a Percent Style Format and Use the Increase Decimal Button

The next step is to format the percent gain/loss in column J. Currently, Excel displays the numbers in column J as a decimal fraction (for example, 0.284874 in cell J4). The following steps format the range J4:J16 to the Percent style format with two decimal places.

- Select the range J4:J16.

- Click the Percent Style button on the Ribbon to display the numbers in column J as a rounded whole percent.

Q&A

What is the result of clicking the Percent Style button?

The Percent Style button instructs Excel to display a value as a percentage, determined by multiplying the cell entry by 100, rounding the result to the nearest percent, and adding a percent sign. For example, when cell J4 is formatted using the Percent Style and Increase Decimal buttons, Excel displays the actual value 0.284874 as 28.49%.

- Click the Increase Decimal button on the Ribbon two times to display the numbers in column J with the Percent style format and two decimal places (Figure 2–47).

Figure 2–47

Other Ways

1. Right-click range, click Format Cells on shortcut menu, click Number tab, click Percentage in Category list, select format, click OK button

2. Press CTRL+1, click Number tab, click Percentage in Category list, select format, click OK button

3. Press CTRL+SHIFT+ PERCENT SIGN (%)

Conditional Formatting

The next step is to emphasize the negative percentages in column J by formatting them to appear with a tinted background. The Conditional Formatting button on the Ribbon will be used to complete this task.

Excel lets you apply formatting that appears only when the value in a cell meets conditions that you specify. This type of formatting is called **conditional formatting**. You can apply conditional formatting to a cell, a range of cells, the entire worksheet, or the entire workbook. Usually, you apply conditional formatting to a range of cells that contains values you want to highlight, if conditions warrant. For example, you can instruct Excel to change the color of the background of a cell if the value in the cell meets a condition, such as being less than 0 as shown in Figure 2–48.

A **condition**, which is made up of two values and a relational operator, is true or false for each cell in the range. If the condition is true, then Excel applies the formatting. If the condition is false, then Excel suppresses the formatting. What makes conditional formatting so powerful is that the cell's appearance can change as you enter new values in the worksheet.

To Apply Conditional Formatting

The following steps assign conditional formatting to the range J4:J12, so that any cell value less than zero will cause Excel to display the number in the cell with a light red background.

- Select the range J4:J12.

- Click the Conditional Formatting button on the Ribbon to display the Conditional Formatting gallery (Figure 2–48).

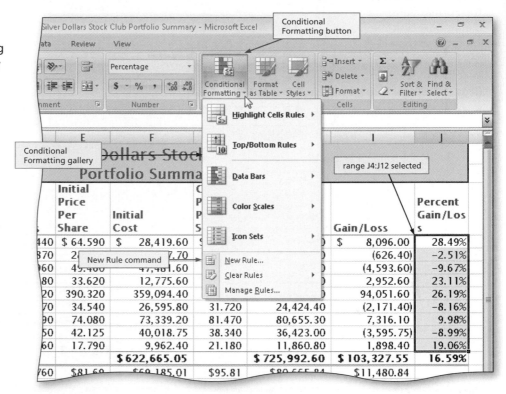

Figure 2–48

- Click New Rule in the Conditional Formatting gallery to display the New Formatting Rule dialog box.

- Click 'Format only cells that contain' in the Select a Rule Type area.

- In the Edit the Rule Description area, click the box arrow in the relational operator box (second text box) and then select less than.

- Type 0 (zero) in the rightmost box in the Edit the Rule Description area (Figure 2–49).

Figure 2–49

- Click the Format button.

- When Excel displays the Format Cells dialog box, click the Fill tab and then click the light red color in column 6, row 2 (Figure 2–50).

Figure 2–50

- Click the OK button to close the Format Cells dialog box and display the New Formatting Rule dialog box with the desired color displayed in the Preview box (Figure 2–51).

Figure 2–51

5

- Click the OK button to assign the conditional format to the range J4:J12.

- Click cell A18 to deselect the range J4:J12 (Figure 2–52).

	C	D	E	F	G	H	I	J

Silver Dollars Stock Club

Portfol...

Excel displays negative numbers in range J4:J12 with a light red background

		Initial Price Per Share	Initial Cost	Per Share	Current Value	Gain/Loss	Percent Gain/Loss
uired	Shares						s
2/1/04	440	$ 64.590	$ 28,419.60	$ 82.990	$ 36,515.60	$ 8,096.00	28.49%
2/16/03	870	28.710	24,977.70	27.990	24,351.30	(626.40)	-2.51%
/17/03	960	49.460	47,481.60	44.675	42,888.00	(4,593.60)	-9.67%
/11/02	380	33.620	12,775.60	41.390	15,728.20	2,952.60	23.11%
/20/04	920	390.320	359,094.40	492.550	453,146.00	94,051.60	26.19%
/14/05	770	34.540	26,595.80	31.720	24,424.40	(2,171.40)	-8.16%
/14/04	990	74.080	73,339.20	81.470	80,655.30	7,316.10	9.98%
/14/05	950	42.125	40,018.75	38.340	36,423.00	(3,595.75)	-8.99%
/10/03	560	17.790	9,962.40	21.180	11,860.80	1,898.40	19.06%
			$ 622,665.05		$ 725,992.60	$ 103,327.55	16.59%
	760	$81.69	$69,185.01	$95.81	$80,665.84	$11,480.84	
	990	$390.32	$359,094.40	$492.55	$453,146.00	$94,051.60	28.49%
	380	$17.79	$9,962.40	$21.18	$11,860.80	($4,593.60)	-9.67%

Figure 2–52

Conditional Formatting Operators

As shown in Figure 2–49 on page EX 119, the second text box in the New Formatting Rule dialog box allows you to select a relational operator, such as less than, to use in the condition. The eight different relational operators from which you can choose for conditional formatting in the New Formatting Rule dialog box are summarized in Table 2–5.

Table 2–5 Summary of Conditional Formatting Relational Operators	
Relational Operator	**Description**
Between	Cell value is between two numbers
Not between	Cell value is not between two numbers
Equal to	Cell value is equal to a number
Not equal to	Cell value is not equal to a number
Greater than	Cell value is greater than a number
Less than	Cell value is less than a number
Greater than or equal to	Cell value is greater than or equal to a number
Less than or equal to	Cell value is less than or equal to a number

BTW

Conditional Formatting
You can assign any format to a cell, a range of cells, a worksheet, or an entire workbook conditionally. If the value of the cell changes and no longer meets the specified condition, Excel suppresses the conditional formatting.

BTW

Hidden Columns
Trying to unhide a range of columns using the mouse can be frustrating. An alternative is to use the keyboard: select the columns to the right and left of the hidden columns and then press CTRL+SHIFT+) (RIGHT PARENTHESIS). To use the keyboard to hide a range of columns, press CTRL+0 (ZERO).

Changing the Widths of Columns and Heights of Rows

When Excel starts and displays a blank worksheet on the screen, all of the columns have a default width of 8.43 characters, or 64 pixels. A character is defined as a letter, number, symbol, or punctuation mark in 11-point Calibri font, the default font used by Excel. An average of 8.43 characters in 11-point Calibri font will fit in a cell.

Another measure of the height and width of cells is pixels, which is short for picture element. A **pixel** is a dot on the screen that contains a color. The size of the dot is based on your screen's resolution. At a common resolution of 1024 × 768, 1024 pixels appear across the screen and 768 pixels appear down the screen for a total of 786,432 pixels. It is these 786,432 pixels that form the font and other items you see on the screen.

The default row height in a blank worksheet is 15 points (or 20 pixels). Recall from Chapter 1 that a point is equal to 1/72 of an inch. Thus, 15 points is equal to about 1/5 of an inch. You can change the width of the columns or height of the rows at any time to make the worksheet easier to read or to ensure that Excel displays an entry properly in a cell.

To Change the Widths of Columns

When changing the column width, you can set the width manually or you can instruct Excel to size the column to best fit. **Best fit** means that the width of the column will be increased or decreased so the widest entry will fit in the column. Sometimes, you may prefer more or less white space in a column than best fit provides. Excel thus allows you to change column widths manually.

When the format you assign to a cell causes the entry to exceed the width of a column, Excel automatically changes the column width to best fit. If you do not assign a format to a cell or cells in a column, the column width will remain 8.43 characters. To set a column width to best fit, double-click the right boundary of the column heading above row 1.

The following steps change the column widths: column A to 14.11 characters; columns B and C to best fit; column D to 6.00 characters; columns E, G, and J to 9.00 characters; and columns F, H, and I to 12.67 characters.

- Point to the boundary on the right side of the column A heading above row 1.

- When the mouse pointer changes to a split double arrow, drag until the ScreenTip indicates Width: 14.11 (134 pixels). Do not release the mouse button (Figure 2–53).

Q&A

What happens if I change the column width to zero (0)?

If you decrease the column width to 0, the column is hidden. **Hiding cells** is a technique you can use to hide data that might not be relevant to a particular report or sensitive data that you do not want others to see. To instruct Excel to display a hidden column, position the mouse pointer to the right of the column heading boundary where the hidden column is located and then drag to the right.

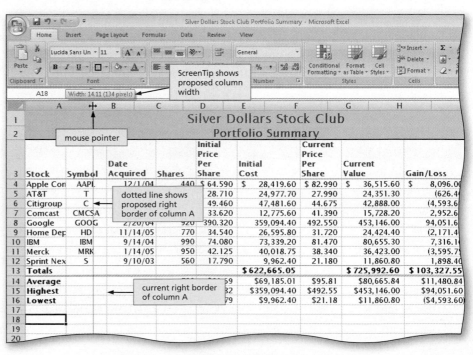

Figure 2–53

2

- Release the mouse button.

- Drag through column headings B and C above row 1.

- Point to the boundary on the right side of column heading C to cause the mouse pointer to become a split double arrow (Figure 2–54).

Q&A

What if I want to make a large change to the column width?

If you want to increase or decrease column width significantly, you can right-click a column heading and then use the Column Width command on the shortcut menu to change the column's width. To use this command, however, you must select one or more entire columns.

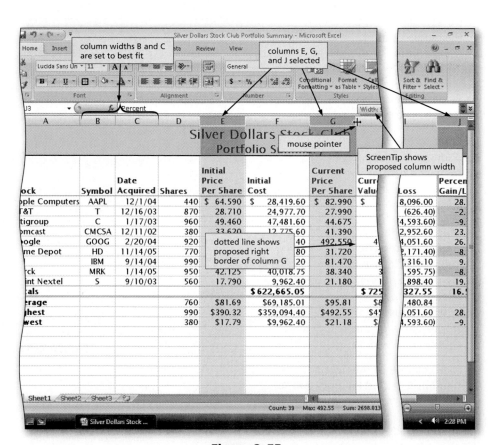

Figure 2–54

3

- Double-click the right boundary of column heading C to change the width of columns B and C to best fit.

- Click the column E heading above row 1.

- While holding down the CTRL key, click the column G heading and then the column J heading above row 1 so that columns E, G, and J are selected.

- If necessary, scroll the worksheet to the right so that the right border of column J is visible. Point to the boundary on the right side of the column J heading above row 1.

- Drag until the ScreenTip indicates Width: 9.00 (88 pixels). Do not release the mouse button (Figure 2–55).

Figure 2–55

- Release the mouse button.

- Click the column F heading above row 1 to select column F.

- While holding down the CTRL key, click the column H heading and then the column I heading above row 1, to select columns F, H, and I.

- Point to the boundary on the right side of the column I heading above row 1.

- Drag to the left until the ScreenTip indicates Width: 12.67 (121 pixels). Do not release the mouse button (Figure 2–56).

Figure 2–56

- Release the mouse button.

- Point to the boundary on the right side of the column D heading above row 1.

- Drag to the left until the ScreenTip indicates Width: 6.00 (61 pixels) and then release the mouse button to display the worksheet with the new column widths.

- Click cell A18 to deselect columns F, H, and I (Figure 2–57).

Figure 2–57

Other Ways

1. Right-click column heading or drag through multiple column headings and right-click, click Column Width on shortcut menu, enter desired

   column width, click OK button

2. Right-click column heading or drag through multiple column headings and right-

   click, click Format button on Ribbon, click Column Width in Format gallery, enter desired column width, click OK button

To Change the Heights of Rows

When you increase the font size of a cell entry, such as the title in cell A1, Excel automatically increases the row height to best fit so it can display the characters properly. Recall that Excel did this earlier when multiple lines were entered in a cell in row 3, and when the cell style of the worksheet title and subtitle was changed.

You also can increase or decrease the height of a row manually to improve the appearance of the worksheet. The following steps show how to improve the appearance of the worksheet by increasing the height of row 3 to 60.00 points, and increasing the height of row 14 to 26.25 points.

1

- Point to the boundary below row heading 3.

- Drag down until the ScreenTip indicates Height: 60.00 (80 pixels). Do not release the mouse button (Figure 2–58).

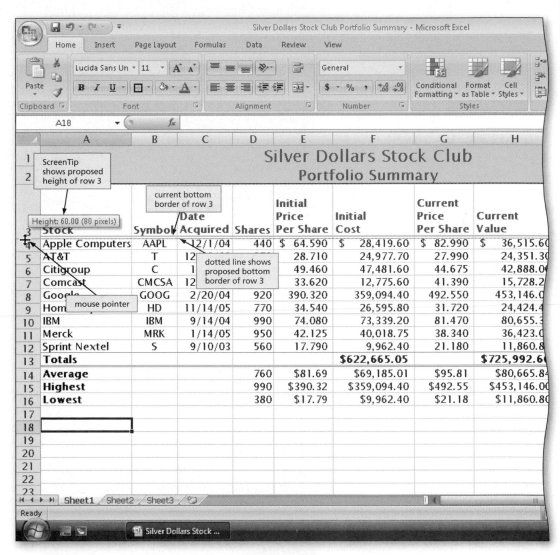

Figure 2–58

2

- Release the mouse button.

- Point to the boundary below row heading 14.

- Drag down until the ScreenTip indicates Height: 26.25 (35 pixels). Do not release the mouse button (Figure 2–59).

row 3 height is 60.00 points

ScreenTip shows proposed height of row 14

dotted line shows proposed bottom border of row 14

Height: 26.25 (35 pixels)

mouse pointer

current bottom border of row 14

Silver Dollars Stock Club
Portfolio Summary

	A	B	C	D	E	F	G
3	Stock	Symbol	Date Acquired	Shares	Initial Price Per Share	Initial Cost	Current Price Per Share
4	Apple Computers	AAPL	12/1/04	440	$ 64.590	$ 28,419.60	$ 82.990
5	AT&T	T	12/16/03	870	28.710	24,977.70	27.990
6	Citigroup	C	1/17/03	960	49.460	47,481.60	44.675
7	Comcast	CMCSA	12/11/02	380	33.620	12,775.60	41.390
8	Google	GOOG	2/20/04	920	390.320	359,094.40	492.550
9	Home Depot	HD	11/14/05	770	34.540	26,595.80	31.720
10	IBM	IBM	9/14/04	990	74.080	73,339.20	81.470
11	Merck			950		018.75	38.340
12	Sprint Nextel		03	560		962.40	21.180
13						$622,665.05	
	Average			760	$81.69	$69,185.01	$95.81
14	Highest			990	$390.32	$359,094.40	$492.55
15	Lowest				$17.79	$9,962.40	$21.18
16							
17							
18							

Figure 2–59

3

- Release the mouse button to change the row height of row 14 to 26.25.

- Select cells A3:J3 and then click the Center button on the Ribbon to center the column headings.

- Select cell A18 (Figure 2–60).

Q&A

Can I hide a row?

Yes. As with column widths, when you decrease the row height to 0, the row is hidden. To instruct Excel to display a hidden row, position the mouse pointer just below the row heading boundary where the row is hidden and then drag down. To set a row height to best fit, double-click the bottom boundary of the row heading.

formatting of worksheet complete

Silver Dollars Stock Club
Portfolio Summary

	A	B	C	D	E	F	G
3	Stock	Symbol	Date Acquired	Shares	Initial Price Per Share	Initial Cost	Current Price Per Share
4	Apple Computers	AAPL	12/1/04	440	$ 64.590	$ 28,419.60	$ 82.990
5	AT&T	T	12/16/03	870	28.710	24,977.70	27.990
6	Citigroup	C	1/17/03	960	49.460	47,481.60	44.675
7	Comcast	CMCSA	12/11/02	380	33.620	12,775.60	41.390
8	Google	GOOG	2/20/04	920	390.320	359,094.40	492.550
9	Home Depot	HD	11/14/05	770	34.540	26,595.80	31.720
10	IBM	IBM	9/14/04	990	74.080	73,339.20	81.470
11	Merck	MRK	1/14/05			40,018.75	38.340
12	Sprint Nextel	S	9/10/03			9,962.40	21.180
13	Totals					$622,665.05	
14	Average			760	$81.69	$69,185.01	$95.81
15	Highest			990	$390.32	$359,094.40	$492.55
16	Lowest			380	$17.79	$9,962.40	$21.18
17							
18							

row 14 height is 26.25 points

added white space in row 14 improves appearance of worksheet

Figure 2–60

Other Ways

1. Right-click row heading or drag through multiple row headings and right-click, click Row Height on shortcut menu, enter desired row height, click OK button

Checking Spelling

Excel has a **spell checker** you can use to check the worksheet for spelling errors. The spell checker looks for spelling errors by comparing words on the worksheet against words contained in its standard dictionary. If you often use specialized terms that are not in the standard dictionary, you may want to add them to a custom dictionary using the Spelling dialog box.

When the spell checker finds a word that is not in either dictionary, it displays the word in the Spelling dialog box. You then can correct it if it is misspelled.

BTW

Hidden Rows
You can use the keyboard to unhide a range of rows by selecting the rows immediately above and below the hidden rows and then pressing CTRL+SHIFT+((LEFT PARENTHESIS). To use the keyboard to hide a range of rows, press CTRL+9.

To Check Spelling on the Worksheet

To illustrate how Excel responds to a misspelled word, the word, Stock, in cell A3 is misspelled purposely as the word, Stcok, as shown in Figure 2–61.

1

- Click cell A3 and then type Stcok to misspell the word Stock.

- Click cell A1.

- Click the Review tab on the Ribbon.

- Click the Spelling button on the Ribbon to run the spell checker and display the misspelled word, Stcok, in the Spelling dialog box (Figure 2–61).

Q&A

What happens when the spell checker finds a misspelled word?

When the spell checker identifies that a cell contains a word not in its standard or custom dictionary, it selects that cell as the active cell and displays the Spelling dialog box. The Spelling dialog box (Figure 2–61) lists the word not found in the dictionary and a list of suggested corrections.

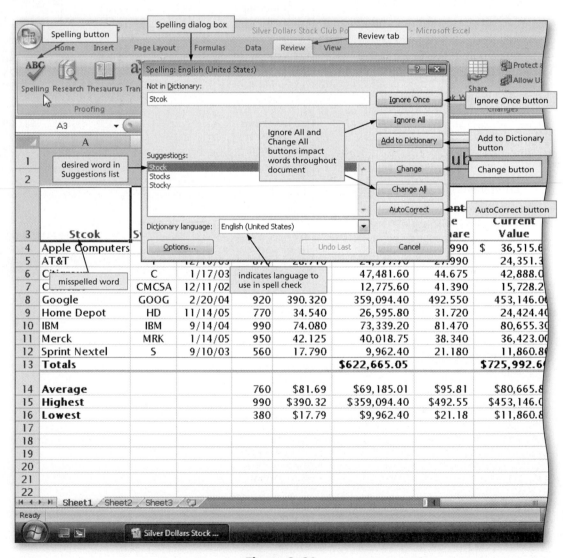

Figure 2–61

2

- With the word Stock highlighted in the Suggestions list, click the Change button to change the misspelled word, Stcok, to the correct word, Stock (Figure 2–62).

- If the Microsoft Office Excel dialog box is displayed, click the OK button.

3

- Select cell A18.

- Click the Home tab on the Ribbon.

- Click the Save button on the Quick Access Toolbar to save the workbook.

Q&A

What other actions can I take in the Spelling dialog box?

If one of the words in the Suggestions list is correct, click it and then click the Change button. If none of the suggestions is correct, type the correct word in the Not in Dictionary text box and then click the Change button. To change the word throughout the worksheet, click the Change All button instead of the Change button. To skip correcting the word, click the Ignore Once button. To have Excel ignore the word for the remainder of the worksheet, click the Ignore All button.

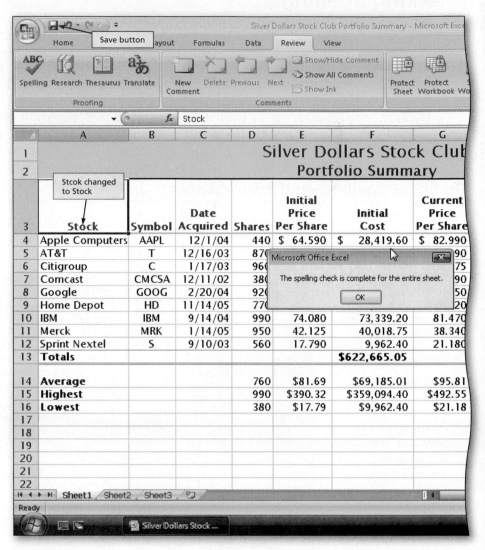

Figure 2–62

Other Ways

1. Press F7

Additional Spell Checker Considerations

Consider these additional guidelines when using the spell checker:

- To check the spelling of the text in a single cell, double-click the cell to make the formula bar active and then click the Spelling button on the Review tab on the Ribbon.

- If you select a single cell so that the formula bar is not active and then start the spell checker, Excel checks the remainder of the worksheet, including notes and embedded charts.

- If you select a cell other than cell A1 before you start the spell checker, Excel will display a dialog box when the spell checker reaches the end of the worksheet, asking if you want to continue checking at the beginning.

- If you select a range of cells before starting the spell checker, Excel checks the spelling of the words only in the selected range.

- To check the spelling of all the sheets in a workbook, click Select All Sheets on the sheet tab shortcut menu and then start the spell checker. To instruct Excel to display the sheet tab shortcut menu, right-click any sheet tab.

- To add words to the dictionary such as your last name, click the Add to Dictionary button in the Spelling dialog box (Figure 2–61 on page EX 127) when Excel identifies the word as not in the dictionary.

- Click the AutoCorrect button (Figure 2–61) to add the misspelled word and the correct version of the word to the AutoCorrect list. For example, suppose you misspell the word, do, as the word, dox. When the spell checker displays the Spelling dialog box with the correct word, do, in the Change to box, click the AutoCorrect button. Then, anytime in the future that you type the word, dox, Excel automatically will change it to the word, do.

Preparing to Print the Worksheet

Excel allows for a great deal of customization in how a worksheet appears when printed. For example, the margins on the page can be adjusted. A header or footer can be added to each printed page as well. Excel also has the capability to work on the worksheet in Page Layout View. **Page Layout View** allows you to create or modify a worksheet while viewing how it will look in printed format. The default view that you have worked in up until this point in the book is called **Normal View**.

Specify how the printed worksheet should appear.
Before printing a worksheet, you should consider how the worksheet will appear when printed. In order to fit as much information on the printed page as possible, the margins of the worksheet should be set to a reasonably small width and height. The current Portfolio Summary worksheet will print on one page. If, however, the club added more data to the worksheet, then it may extend to multiple pages. It is, therefore, a good idea to add a page header to the worksheet that prints in the top margin of each page.

In Chapter 1, the worksheet was printed in **portrait orientation**, which means the printout is printed across the width of the page. **Landscape orientation** means the printout is printed across the length of the page. Landscape orientation is a good choice for the Silver Dollars Stock Club Portfolio Summary because the printed worksheet's width is greater than its length.

Plan Ahead

BTW

Spell Checking
While Excel's spell checker is a valuable tool, it is not infallible. You should proofread your workbook carefully by pointing to each word and saying it aloud as you point to it. Be mindful of misused words such as its and it's, through and though, and to and too. Nothing undermines a good impression more than a professional looking report with misspelled words.

BTW

Error Checking
Always take the time to check the formulas of a worksheet before submitting it to your supervisor. You can check formulas by clicking the Error Checking button on the Formulas tab on the Ribbon. You also should test the formulas by employing data that tests the limits of formulas. Experienced spreadsheet specialists spend as much time testing a workbook as they do creating it, before placing it into production.

BTW

Certification
The Microsoft Certified Application Specialist (MCAS) program provides an opportunity for you to obtain a valuable industry credential – proof that you have the Excel 2007 skills required by employers. For more information, see Appendix G or visit the Excel 2007 Certification Web page (scsite.com/ex2007/cert).

To Change the Worksheet's Margins, Header, and Orientation in Page Layout View

The following steps change to Page Layout View, narrow the margins of the worksheet, change the header of the worksheet, and set the orientation of the worksheet to landscape.

1

- Click the Page Layout View button on the status bar to view the worksheet in Page Layout View (Figure 2–63).

What are some key features of Page Layout View?

Page Layout View shows the worksheet divided into pages. A blue background separates each page. The white areas surrounding each page indicate the print margins. The top of each page includes a Header area, and the bottom of each page includes a Footer area. Page Layout View also includes a ruler at the top of the page that assists you in placing objects on the page, such as charts and pictures.

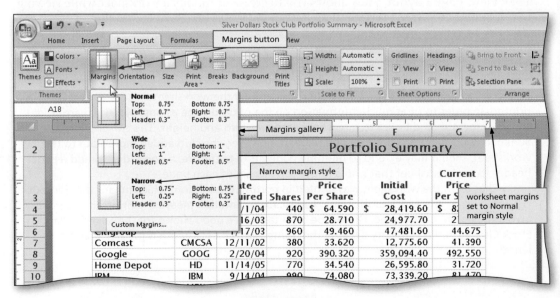

Figure 2–63

2

- Click the Page Layout tab on the Ribbon.

- Click the Margins button on the Ribbon to display the Margins gallery (Figure 2–64).

Figure 2–64

3

- Click Narrow in the Margins gallery to change the worksheet margins to the Narrow margin style.

- Drag the scroll bar on the right side of the worksheet to the top so that row 1 of the worksheet is displayed.

- Click above the worksheet title in cell A1 in the Header area.

- Type `Treasurer: Juan Castillo` and then press the ENTER key. Type `castillo_ juan37@hotmail. com` to complete the worksheet header (Figure 2–65).

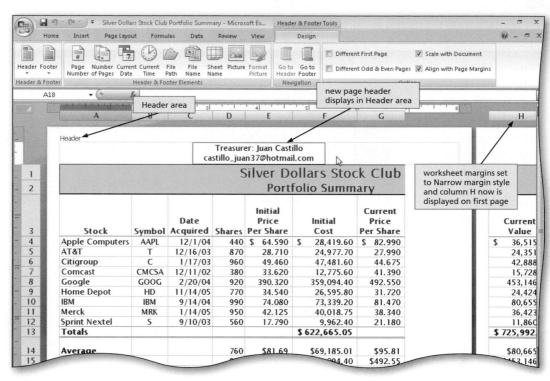

Figure 2–65

4

- Select cell B16 to deselect the header. Click the Orientation button on the Ribbon to display the Orientation gallery.

- Point to Landscape but do not click the mouse button (Figure 2–66).

Figure 2–66

- Click Landscape in the Orientation gallery to change the worksheet's orientation to landscape (Figure 2–67).

Q&A

Do I need to change the orientation every time I want to print the worksheet?

No. Once you change the orientation and save the workbook, Excel will save the orientation setting for that workbook until you change it. When you open a new workbook, Excel sets the orientation to portrait.

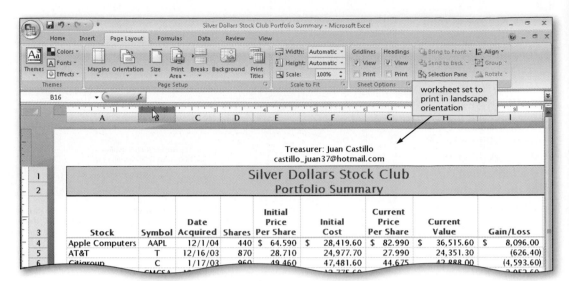

Figure 2–67

Other Ways

1. Click Page Layout tab on Ribbon, click Page Setup Dialog Box Launcher, click Page tab, click Portrait or Landscape, click OK button

Previewing and Printing the Worksheet

In Chapter 1, the worksheet was printed without first previewing it on the screen. By **previewing the worksheet**, however, you see exactly how it will look without generating a printout. Previewing a worksheet using the Print Preview command can save time, paper, and the frustration of waiting for a printout only to discover it is not what you want.

To Preview and Print a Worksheet

The following steps preview and then print the worksheet.

- Click the Office Button and then point to Print on the Office Button menu to display the Print submenu (Figure 2–68).

Figure 2–68

2

- Click Print Preview on the Print submenu to display a preview of the worksheet in landscape orientation (Figure 2–69).

Q&A

What is the purpose of the buttons in the Print Preview area?

The Print button displays the Print dialog box and allows you to print the worksheet. The Page Setup button displays the Page Setup dialog box. The Zoom button allows you to zoom in and out of the page displayed in the Preview window. You also can click the previewed page in the Preview window when the mouse pointer shape is a magnifying glass to carry out the function of the Zoom button.

Figure 2–69

3

- Click the Print button to display the Print dialog box (Figure 2–70).

Q&A

How can I use the Print dialog box?

When you click the Print command on the Print submenu of the Office Button menu or a Print button in a dialog box or Preview window, Excel displays the Print dialog box shown in Figure 2–70. Excel does not display the Print dialog box when you use the Print button on the Quick Access Toolbar, as was the case in Chapter 1. The Print dialog box allows you to select a printer, instruct Excel what to print, and indicate how many copies of the printout you want.

Figure 2–70

- Click the OK button to print the worksheet (Figure 2–71).

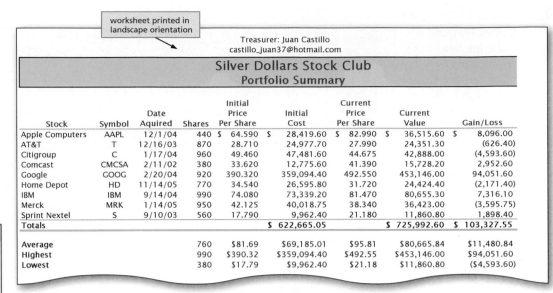

worksheet printed in landscape orientation

Treasurer: Juan Castillo
castillo_juan37@hotmail.com

Silver Dollars Stock Club
Portfolio Summary

Stock	Symbol	Date Aquired	Shares	Initial Price Per Share		Initial Cost		Current Price Per Share		Current Value		Gain/Loss	
Apple Computers	AAPL	12/1/04	440	$	64.590	$	28,419.60	$	82.990	$	36,515.60	$	8,096.00
AT&T	T	12/16/03	870		28.710		24,977.70		27.990		24,351.30		(626.40)
Citigroup	C	1/17/04	960		49.460		47,481.60		44.675		42,888.00		(4,593.60)
Comcast	CMCSA	2/11/02	380		33.620		12,775.60		41.390		15,728.20		2,952.60
Google	GOOG	2/20/04	920		390.320		359,094.40		492.550		453,146.00		94,051.60
Home Depot	HD	11/14/05	770		34.540		26,595.80		31.720		24,424.40		(2,171.40)
IBM	IBM	9/14/04	990		74.080		73,339.20		81.470		80,655.30		7,316.10
Merck	MRK	1/14/05	950		42.125		40,018.75		38.340		36,423.00		(3,595.75)
Sprint Nextel	S	9/10/03	560		17.790		9,962.40		21.180		11,860.80		1,898.40
Totals						$	622,665.05			$	725,992.60	$	103,327.55
Average			760		$81.69		$69,185.01		$95.81		$80,665.84		$11,480.84
Highest			990		$390.32		$359,094.40		$492.55		$453,146.00		$94,051.60
Lowest			380		$17.79		$9,962.40		$21.18		$11,860.80		($4,593.60)

Figure 2–71

Other Ways

1. Click Page Layout tab on Ribbon, click Page Setup Dialog Box Launcher, click appropriate tab, change desired options, click Print, click OK button

To Print a Section of the Worksheet

You might not always want to print the entire worksheet. You can print portions of the worksheet by selecting the range of cells to print and then clicking the Selection option button in the Print what area in the Print dialog box. The following steps print the range A3:F16.

- Select the range A3:F16.

- Click the Office Button and then click Print on the Office Button menu to display the Print dialog box.

- Click Selection in the Print what area to instruct Excel to print only the selected range (Figure 2–72).

Figure 2–72

2

- Click the OK button to print the selected range of the worksheet on the printer (Figure 2–73).

- Click the Normal View button on the status bar.

- Click cell A18 to deselect the range A3:F13.

Q&A

What are the options in the Print what area?

The Print what area of the Print dialog box includes four option buttons (Figure 2–72). As shown in the previous steps, the Selection option button instructs Excel to print the selected range. The Active sheet(s) option button instructs Excel to print the active worksheet (the worksheet currently on the screen) or the selected worksheets. Finally, the Entire workbook option button instructs Excel to print all of the worksheets in the workbook.

| | | | | Initial | |
| | | Date | | Price | Initial |
Stock	Symbol	Acquired	Shares	Per Share	Cost
Apple Computers	AAPL	12/1/04	440	$ 64.590	$ 28,419.60
AT&T	T	12/16/03	870	28.710	24,977.70
Citigroup	C	1/17/04	960	49.460	47,481.60
Comcast	CMCSA	2/11/02	380	33.620	12,775.60
Google	GOOG	2/20/04	920	390.320	359,094.40
Home Depot	HD	11/14/05	770	34.540	26,595.80
IBM	IBM	9/14/04	990	74.080	73,339.20
Merck	MRK	1/14/05	950	42.125	40,018.75
Sprint Nextel	S	9/10/03	560	17.790	9,962.40
Totals					$ 622,665.05
Average			760	$81.69	$69,185.01
Highest			990	$390.32	$359,094.40
Lowest			380	$17.79	$9,962.40

header prints → Treasurer: Juan Castillo
castillo_juan37@hotmail.com ← selected range prints

Figure 2–73

Other Ways

1. Select range, click Page Layout tab on Ribbon, click Print Area button, click Set Print Area, click Quick Print button on Quick Access Toolbar, click Print Area button, click Clear Print Area button

Displaying and Printing the Formulas Version of the Worksheet

Thus far, you have been working with the **values version** of the worksheet, which shows the results of the formulas you have entered, rather than the actual formulas. Excel also can display and print the **formulas version** of the worksheet, which shows the actual formulas you have entered, rather than the resulting values. You can toggle between the values version and formulas version by holding down the CTRL key while pressing the ACCENT MARK (`) key, which is located to the left of the number 1 key on the keyboard.

The formulas version is useful for debugging a worksheet. **Debugging** is the process of finding and correcting errors in the worksheet. Viewing and printing the formulas version instead of the values version makes it easier to see any mistakes in the formulas.

When you change from the values version to the formulas version, Excel increases the width of the columns so the formulas and text do not overflow into adjacent cells on the right. The formulas version of the worksheet thus usually is significantly wider than the values version. To fit the wide printout on one page, you can use landscape orientation, which has already been selected for the workbook, and the Fit to option in the Page sheet in the Page Setup dialog box.

BTW

Values versus Formulas
When completing class assignments, do not enter numbers in cells that require formulas. Most instructors require their students to hand in both the values version and formulas version of the worksheet. The formulas version verifies that you entered formulas, rather than numbers, in formula-based cells.

To Display the Formulas in the Worksheet and Fit the Printout on One Page

The following steps change the view of the worksheet from the values version to the formulas version of the worksheet and then print the formulas version on one page.

1

- Press CTRL+ACCENT MARK (`).

- When Excel displays the formulas version of the worksheet, click the right horizontal scroll arrow until column J appears to display the worksheet with formulas (Figure 2–74).

2

- If necessary, click the Page Layout tab on the Ribbon and then click the Page Setup Dialog Box Launcher to display the Page Setup dialog box.

- If necessary, click Landscape to select it and then click Fit to in the Scaling area.

	G	H	I	J	K
1	b				
2		numbers displayed using General format		formulas displayed as entered	
3	Current Price Per Share	Current Value	Gain/Loss	Percent Gain/Loss	
4	82.99	=D4*G4	=H4–F4	=I4/F4	
5	27.99	=D5*G5	=H5–F5	=I5/F5	
6	44.675	=D6*G6	=H6–F6	=I6/F6	
7	41.39	=D7*G7	=H7–F7	=I7/F7	
8	492.55	=D8*G8	=H8–F8	=I8/F8	
9	31.72	=D9*G9	=H9–F9	=I9/F9	
10	81.47	=D10*G10	=H10–F10	=I10/F10	
11	38.34	=D11*G11	=H11–F11	=I11/F11	
12	21.18	=D12*G12	=H12–F12	=I12/F12	
13		=SUM(H4:H12)	=SUM(I4:I12)	=I13/F13	
14	=AVERAGE(G4:G12)	=AVERAGE(H4:H12)	=AVERAGE(I4:I12)		
15	=MAX(G4:G12)	=MAX(H4:H12)	=MAX(I4:I12)	=MAX(J4:J12)	
16	=MIN(G4:G12)	=MIN(H4:H12)	=MIN(I4:I12)	=MIN(J4:J12)	
17					

Figure 2–74

3

- Click the Print button in the Page Setup dialog box to print the formulas in the worksheet on one page in landscape orientation (Figure 2–75).

- When Excel displays the Print dialog box, click the OK button.

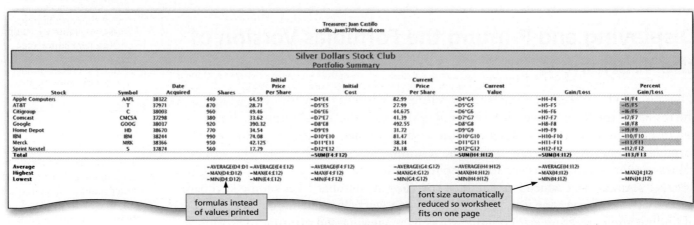

Figure 2–75

4

- After viewing and printing the formulas version, press CTRL+ACCENT MARK (`) to instruct Excel to display the values version.

- Click the left horizontal scroll arrow until column A appears.

Other Ways

1. Click Show Formulas button on Formulas tab on Ribbon

To Change the Print Scaling Option Back to 100%

Depending on your printer, you may have to change the Print Scaling option back to 100% after using the Fit to option. The following steps reset the Print Scaling option so future worksheets print at 100%, instead of being resized to print on one page.

1 If necessary, click the Page Layout tab on the Ribbon and then click the Page Setup Dialog Box Launcher to display the Page Setup dialog box.

2 Click Adjust to in the Scaling area.

3 If necessary, type 100 in the Adjust to box.

4 Click the OK button to set the print scaling to normal.

5 Click the Home tab on the Ribbon.

Q&A

What is the purpose of the Adjust to box in the Page Setup dialog box?

The Adjust to box allows you to specify the percentage of reduction or enlargement in the printout of a worksheet. The default percentage is 100%. When you click the Fit to option, this percentage automatically changes to the percentage required to fit the printout on one page.

Importing External Data from a Web Source Using a Web Query

One of the major features of Excel is its capability of importing external data from Web sites. To import external data from a Web site, you must have access to the Internet. You then can import data stored on a Web site using a **Web query**. When you run a Web query, Excel imports the external data in the form of a worksheet. As described in Table 2–6, three Web queries are available when you first install Excel. All three Web queries relate to investment and stock market activities.

BTW

Web Queries
Most Excel specialists that build Web queries use the worksheet returned from the Web query as an engine to supply data to another worksheet in the workbook. With 3-D cell references, you can create a worksheet similar to the Silver Dollars Stock Club worksheet to feed the Web query stock symbols and get refreshed stock prices in return.

Table 2–6 Excel Web Queries

Query	External Data Returned
MSN MoneyCentral Investor Currency Rates	Currency rates
MSN MoneyCentral Investor Major Indices	Major indices
MSN MoneyCentral Investor Stock Quotes	Up to 20 stocks of your choice

Plan Ahead

Gather information regarding the needed Web query.
As shown in Table 2–6, the MSN Money Central Investor Stock Quotes feature that is included with Excel allows you to retrieve information on up to 20 stocks of your choice. The Web query requires that you supply the stock symbols. The stock symbols are located in column B of the Portfolio Summary worksheet.

To Import Data from a Web Source Using a Web Query

Although you can have a Web query return data to a blank workbook, the following steps have the data for the nine stock symbols in column B of the Portfolio Summary worksheet returned to a blank worksheet in the Silver Dollars Stock Club Portfolio Summary workbook. The data returned by the stock-related Web queries is real time in the sense that it is no more than 20 minutes old during the business day.

- With the Silver Dollars Stock Club Portfolio Summary workbook open, click the Sheet2 tab at the bottom of the window.

- With cell A1 active, click the Data tab on the Ribbon, and then click the Existing Connections button to display the Existing Connections dialog box (Figure 2–76).

Figure 2–76

2

- Double-click MSN MoneyCentral Investor Stock Quotes to display the Import Data dialog box (Figure 2–77).

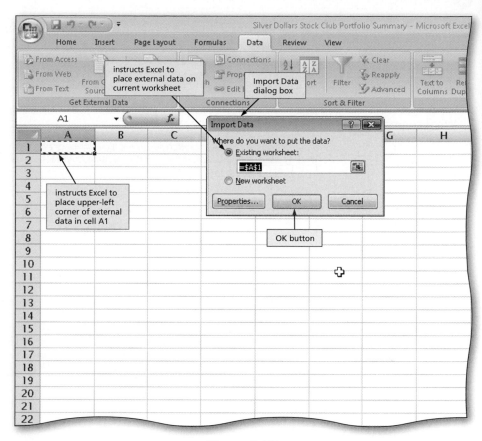

Figure 2–77

3

- Click the OK button.

- When Excel displays the Enter Parameter Value dialog box, type the nine stock symbols `aapl t c cmcsa goog hd ibm mrk s` in the text box.

- Click the 'Use this value/reference for future refreshes' check box to select it (Figure 2–78).

Q&A

What is the purpose of clicking the check box?

Once Excel displays the worksheet, you can refresh the data as often as you want. To refresh the data for all the stocks, click the Refresh All button on the Data tab on the Ribbon. Because the 'Use this value/reference for future refreshes' check box was selected, Excel will continue to use the same stock symbols each time it refreshes.

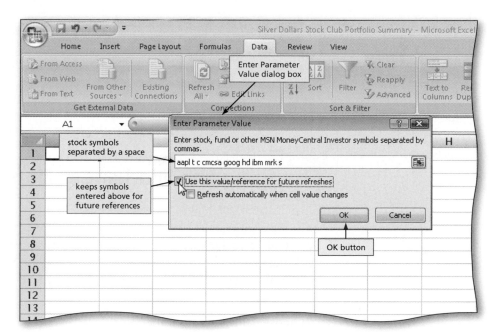

Figure 2–78

4

- Click the OK button to retrieve the stock quotes and display a new worksheet with the desired data (Figure 2–79).

Q&A

What composes the new worksheet?

As shown in Figure 2–79, Excel displays the data returned from the Web query in an organized, formatted worksheet, which has a worksheet title, column titles, and a row of data for each stock symbol entered. Other than the first column, which contains the stock name and stock symbol, you have no control over the remaining columns of data returned. The latest price of each stock appears in column D.

Figure 2–79

Other Ways

1. Press ALT+A, X, select data source

Changing the Worksheet Names

The sheet tabs at the bottom of the window allow you to view any worksheet in the workbook. You click the sheet tab of the worksheet you want to view in the Excel window. By default, Excel presets the names of the worksheets to Sheet1, Sheet2, and so on. The worksheet names become increasingly important as you move towards more sophisticated workbooks, especially workbooks in which you reference cells between worksheets.

Plan Ahead

Choose names for the worksheets.
Use simple, meaningful names for each worksheet. Name the first worksheet that includes the portfolio summary Portfolio Summary. The second worksheet that includes the stock quotes should be named Real-Time Stock Quotes to reflect its contents.

To Change the Worksheet Names

The following steps show how to rename worksheets by double-clicking the sheet tabs.

1

- Double-click the sheet tab labeled Sheet2 in the lower-left corner of the window.

- Type `Real-Time Stock Quotes` as the worksheet name and then press the ENTER key to display the new worksheet name on the sheet tab (Figure 2–80).

Q&A

What is the maximum length for a worksheet tab?

Worksheet names can be up to 31 characters (including spaces) in length. Longer worksheet names, however, mean that fewer sheet tabs will show. To view more sheet tabs, you can drag the tab split box (Figure 2–81) to the right. This will reduce the size of the scroll bar at the bottom of the screen. Double-click the tab split box to reset it to its normal position.

	AT&T Inc.		Chart	News	
6	Citigroup Inc.		Chart	News	50.6	52.68
7	Comcast Corporation		Chart	News	25.3	26.47
8	Google Inc.		Chart	News	448.77	464.93
9	The Home Depot, Inc.		Chart	News	39.82	40.79
	International Business Machines		Chart	News	93.96	96.91
10	Corp.					
11	MERCK AND CO INC		Chart	News	43.18	44.48
12	Sprint Nextel Corporation		Chart	News	18.45	19.53

Symbol Lookup
Find stocks, mutual funds, options, indices, and currencies.

MSN Money Home
Discover MSN Money's tools, columns, and more!

17 Terms of Use. © 2002 Microsoft Corporation and/or its suppliers. All rights reserved.

Sheet2 name changed to Real-Time Stock Quotes

20 Data providers
21 Canadian investment fund pricing (c) 2007 CANNEX Financial Exchanges Limited.
22 Analyst Recommendations data provided by Zacks Investment Research.
23 Fund data provided by Morningstar, Inc. © 2007. All rights reserved.
24 Copyright © 2007 Reuters. Click for Restrictions.

Sheet1 **Real-Time Stock Quotes** Sheet3

Ready

Silver Dollars Stock ...

Figure 2–80

2

- Double-click the sheet tab labeled Sheet1 in the lower-left corner of the window.

- Type `Portfolio Summary` as the worksheet name and then press the ENTER key to change the name of the worksheet from Sheet 1 to Portfolio Summary (Figure 2–81).

Q&A

How can I quickly move between worksheet tabs?

You can use the tab scrolling buttons to the left of the sheet tabs (Figure 2–81) to move between worksheets. The leftmost and rightmost scroll buttons move to the first or last worksheet in the workbook. The two middle scroll buttons move one worksheet to the left or right.

	Apple Computers				$ 64.590		
5	AT&T	T	12/16/03	870	28.710	24,977.70	27.990
6	Citigroup	C	1/17/03	960	49.460	47,481.60	44.675
7	Comcast	CMCSA	12/11/02	380	33.620	12,775.60	41.390
8	Google	GOOG	2/20/04	920	390.320	359,094.40	492.550
9	Home Depot	HD	11/14/05	770	34.540	26,595.80	31.720
10	IBM	IBM	9/14/04	990	74.080	73,339.20	81.470
11	Merck	MRK	1/14/05	950	42.125	40,018.75	38.340
12	Sprint Nextel	S	9/10/03	560	17.790	9,962.40	21.180
13	**Totals**					**$622,665.05**	
14	**Average**			760	$81.69	$69,185.01	$95.81
15	**Highest**			990	$390.32	$359,094.40	$492.55
16	**Lowest**			380	$17.79	$9,962.40	$21.18

tab scrolling buttons

Sheet1 name changed to Portfolio Summary

tab split box

Portfolio Summary Real-Time Stock Quotes Sheet3

Ready

Silver Dollars Stock ...

Figure 2–81

3

- Click the Home tab on the Ribbon.

BTW

Obtaining an E-Mail Account
Several Web sites that allow you to sign up for free e-mail are available. Some choices are MSN Hotmail, Yahoo! Mail, and Google Gmail.

E-Mailing a Workbook from within Excel

The most popular service on the Internet is electronic mail, or **e-mail**, which is the electronic transmission of messages and files to and from other computers using the Internet. Using e-mail, you can converse with friends across the room or on another continent. One of the features of e-mail is the capability to attach Office files, such as Word documents or Excel workbooks, to an e-mail message and send it to a coworker. In the past, if you wanted to e-mail a workbook, you saved the workbook, closed the file, started your e-mail program, and then attached the workbook to the e-mail message before sending it. With Excel, you have the capability of e-mailing a worksheet or workbook directly from within Excel. For these steps to work properly, you must have an e-mail address and one of the following as your e-mail program: Microsoft Outlook, Microsoft Outlook Express, Microsoft Exchange Client, or another 32-bit e-mail program compatible with Messaging Application Programming Interface.

To E-Mail a Workbook from within Excel

The following steps show how to e-mail the Silver Dollars Stock Club Portfolio Summary workbook from within Excel to Juan Castillo at the e-mail address castillo_juan37@hotmail.com.

- With the Silver Dollars Stock Club Portfolio Summary workbook open, click the Office Button and then click Send to display the Send submenu (Figure 2–82).

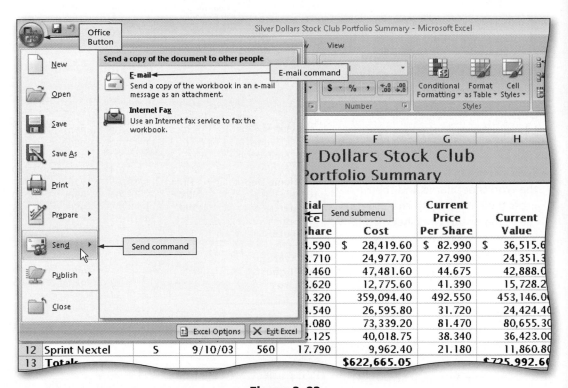

Figure 2–82

2

- Click E-mail on the Send submenu.

- When the e-mail Message window appears, type castillo_ juan37@hotmail. com in the To text box.

- Type the message shown in the message area in Figure 2–83.

3

- Click the Send button to send the e-mail with the attached workbook to castillo_juan37@ hotmail.com.

Q&A

How can the recipient use the attached workbook?

Because the workbook was sent as an attachment, Juan Castillo can double-click the attachment in the e-mail to open it in Excel, or he can save it on disk and then open it later.

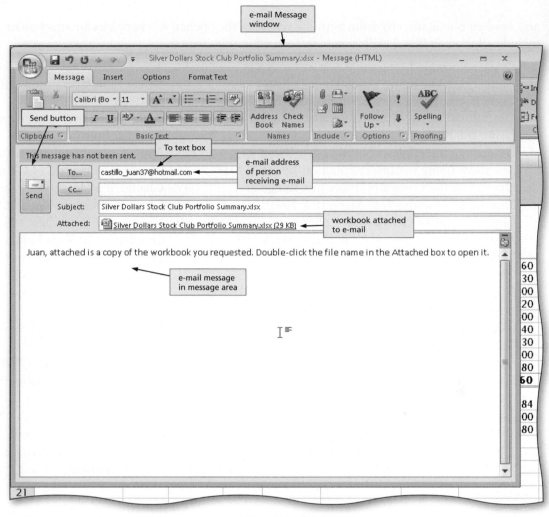

Figure 2–83

To Save the Workbook and Quit Excel

With the workbook complete and e-mailed, the following steps save the workbook and quit Excel.

1 Click the Save button on the Quick Access Toolbar.

2 Click the Close button on the upper-right corner of the title bar.

BTW

Quick Reference
For a table that lists how to complete the tasks covered in this book using the mouse, Ribbon, shortcut menu, and keyboard, see the Quick Reference Summary at the back of this book, or visit the Excel 2007 Quick Reference Web page (scsite.com/ex2007/qr).

Chapter Summary

In creating the Silver Dollars Stock Club Portfolio Summary workbook, you learned how to enter formulas, calculate an average, find the highest and lowest numbers in a range, verify formulas using Range Finder, draw borders, align text, format numbers, change column widths and row heights, and add conditional formatting to a range of numbers. In addition, you learned to spell check a worksheet, preview a worksheet, print a section of a worksheet, display and print the formulas version of the worksheet using the Fit to option, complete a Web query, rename sheet tabs, and send an e-mail directly from within Excel with the opened workbook as an attachment. The items listed below include all the new Excel skills you have learned in this chapter.

1. Enter a Formula Using the Keyboard (EX 91)
2. Enter Formulas Using Point Mode (EX 93)
3. Copy Formulas Using the Fill Handle (EX 95)
4. Determine the Average of a Range of Numbers Using the Keyboard and Mouse (EX 99)
5. Determine the Highest Number in a Range of Numbers Using the Insert Function Box (EX 101)
6. Determine the Lowest Number in a Range of Numbers Using the Sum Menu (EX 102)
7. Copy a Range of Cells across Columns to an Adjacent Range Using the Fill Handle (EX 104)
8. Verify a Formula Using Range Finder (EX 106)
9. Change the Workbook Theme (EX 109)
10. Change the Background Color and Apply a Box Border to the Worksheet Title and Subtitle (EX 110)
11. Center Data in Cells and Format Dates (EX 113)
12. Apply an Accounting Number Format and Comma Style Format Using the Ribbon (EX 115)
13. Apply a Currency Style Format with a Floating Dollar Sign Using the Format Cells Dialog Box (EX 116)
14. Apply a Percent Style Format and Use the Increase Decimal Button (EX 118)
15. Apply Conditional Formatting (EX 119)
16. Change the Widths of Columns (EX 122)
17. Change the Heights of Rows (EX 125)
18. Check Spelling on the Worksheet (EX 127)
19. Change the Worksheet's Margins, Header, and Orientation in Page Layout View (EX 130)
20. Preview and Print a Worksheet (EX 132)
21. Print a Section of the Worksheet (EX 134)
22. Display the Formulas in the Worksheet and Fit the Printout on One Page (EX 136)
23. Import Data from a Web Source Using a Web Query (EX 138)
24. Change the Worksheet Names (EX 141)
25. E-Mail a Workbook from within Excel (EX 142)

If you have a SAM user profile, you may have access to hands-on instruction, practice, and assessment. Log in to your SAM account (http://sam2007.course.com) to launch any assigned training activities or exams that relate to the skills covered in this chapter.

Learn It Online

Learn It Online is a series of online student exercises that test your knowledge of chapter content and key terms.

Instructions: To complete the Learn It Online exercises, start your browser, click the Address bar, and then enter the Web address `scsite.com/ex2007/learn`. When the Excel 2007 Learn It Online page is displayed, click the link for the exercise you want to complete and then read the instructions.

Chapter Reinforcement TF, MC, and SA
A series of true/false, multiple choice, and short answer questions that test your knowledge of the chapter content.

Flash Cards
An interactive learning environment where you identify chapter key terms associated with displayed definitions.

Practice Test
A series of multiple choice questions that test your knowledge of chapter content and key terms.

Who Wants To Be a Computer Genius?
An interactive game that challenges your knowledge of chapter content in the style of a television quiz show.

Wheel of Terms
An interactive game that challenges your knowledge of chapter key terms in the style of the television show *Wheel of Fortune*.

Crossword Puzzle Challenge
A crossword puzzle that challenges your knowledge of key terms presented in the chapter.

Apply Your Knowledge

Reinforce the skills and apply the concepts you learned in this chapter.

Profit Analysis Worksheet

Instructions Part 1: Start Excel. Open the workbook Apply 2-1 Car-B-Clean Profit Analysis. See the inside back cover of this book for instructions for downloading the Data Files for Students or see your instructor for information on accessing the files required in this book. The purpose of this exercise is to open a partially completed workbook, enter formulas and functions, copy the formulas and functions, and then format the worksheet titles and numbers. As shown in Figure 2–84, the completed worksheet analyzes profits by product.

	A	B	C	D	E	F	G	H
					Car–B–Clean Accessories			
					Profit Analysis			
3	Item	Unit Cost	Unit Profit	Units Sold	Total Sales	Total Profit	% Total Profit	
4	Brush	$ 5.84	$ 3.15	36,751	$ 330,391.49	$ 115,765.65	35.039%	
5	Bucket	7.14	2.75	57,758	571,226.62	158,834.50	27.806%	
6	Drying Cloth	3.52	1.17	42,555	199,582.95	49,789.35	24.947%	
7	Duster	2.55	1.04	78,816	282,949.44	81,968.64	28.969%	
8	Polish	7.19	7.80	57,758	865,792.42	450,512.40	52.035%	
9	Soap	8.52	4.09	50,646	638,646.06	207,142.14	32.435%	
10	Sponge	2.05	1.84	23,154	90,069.06	42,603.36	47.301%	
11	Wax	10.15	7.44	53,099	934,011.41	395,056.56	42.297%	
12	Vacuum	43.91	33.09	17,780	1,369,060.00	588,340.20	42.974%	
13	Totals			418,317	$5,281,729.45	$2,090,012.80	39.571%	
14	Lowest	$2.05	$1.04	17,780	$90,069.06	$42,603.36	24.947%	
15	Highest	$43.91	$33.09	78,816	$1,369,060.00	$588,340.20	52.035%	
16	Average	$10.10	$6.93	46,480	$586,858.83	$232,223.64		

Figure 2–84

Perform the following tasks.

1. Use the following formulas in cells E4, F4, and G4:

   Total Sales (cell E4) = Units Sold * (Unit Cost + Unit Profit) or =D4 * (B4 + C4)

   Total Profit (cell F4) = Units Sold * Unit Profit or = D4 * C4

   % Total Profit (cell G4) = Total Profit / Total Sales or = F4 / E4

   Use the fill handle to copy the three formulas in the range E4:G4 to the range E5:G12.

2. Determine totals for the units sold, total sales, and total profit in row 13. Copy cell G12 to G13 to assign the formula in cell G12 to G13 in the total line.

Continued >

STUDENT ASSIGNMENTS

3. In the range B14:B16, determine the lowest value, highest value, and average value, respectively, for the values in the range B4:B12. Use the fill handle to copy the three functions to the range C14:G16. Delete the average from cell G16, because an average of percentages of this type is mathematically invalid.

4. Format the worksheet as follows:

   a. change the workbook theme to Concourse by using the Themes button on the Page Layout tab on the Ribbon

   b. cell A1 — change to font size 24 with a green (column 6 of standard colors) background and white font color by using the buttons in the Font group on the Home tab on the Ribbon

   c. cell A2 — change to a green (column 6 of standard colors) background and white font color

   d. cells B4:C4, E4:F4, and E13:F13 — Accounting style format with two decimal places and fixed dollar signs (use the Accounting Style button on the Home tab on the Ribbon)

   e. cells B5:C12 and E5:F12 — Comma style format with two decimal places (use the Comma Style button on the Home tab on the Ribbon)

   f. cells D4:D16 — Comma style format with no decimal places

   g. cells G4:G15 — Percent style format with three decimal places

   h. cells B14:C16 and E14:F16 — Currency style format with floating dollar signs (use the Format Cells: Number Dialog Box Launcher on the Home tab on the Ribbon)

5. Switch to Page Layout View and enter your name, course, laboratory assignment number (Apply 2-1), date, and any other information requested by your instructor in the Header area. Preview and print the worksheet in landscape orientation. Change the document properties, as specified by your instructor. Save the workbook using the file name, Apply 2-1 Car-B-Clean Profit Analysis Complete in the format specified by your instructor.

6. Use Range Finder to verify the formula in cell F4.

7. Print the range A3:E16. Press CTRL+ACCENT MARK (`) to change the display from the values version of the worksheet to the formulas version. Print the formulas version in landscape orientation on one page (Figure 2–85) by using the Fit to option in the Page sheet in the Page Setup dialog box. Press CTRL+ACCENT MARK (`) to change the display of the worksheet back to the values version. Do not save the workbook. If requested, submit the three printouts to your instructor.

Instructions Part 2:

1. Do not save the workbook in this part. In column C, use the keyboard to add manually $1.00 to the profit of each product with a unit profit less than $7.00 and $3.00 to the profits of all other products. You should end up with $2,765,603.80 in cell F13.

2. Print the worksheet. Do not save the workbook. If requested, submit the revised workbook in the format specified by your instructor.

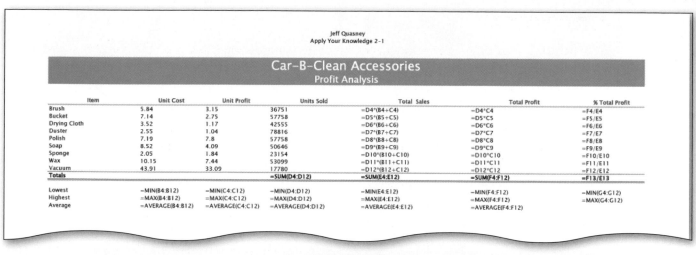

Figure 2–85

Extend Your Knowledge

Extend the skills you learned in this chapter and experiment with new skills. You may need to use Help to complete the assignment.

Applying Conditional Formatting to Cells

Instructions: Start Excel. Open the workbook Extend 2-1 Biology 201 Midterm Scores. See the inside back cover of this book for instructions for downloading the Data Files for Students, or see your instructor for information on accessing the files required in this book. Perform the following tasks to apply new conditional formatting to the worksheet.

1. Select the range C4:C18. Click the Conditional Formatting button on the Home tab on the Ribbon and then select New Rule in the Conditional Formatting gallery. Select 'Format only top or bottom ranked values' in the Select a Rule Type area (Figure 2–86). Enter a value between 20 and 35 of your choosing in the text box in the Edit the Rule Description area and click the '% of the selected range' check box to select it. Click the Format button and choose a format to assign to this conditional format. Click the OK button in each dialog box to close the dialog boxes and view the worksheet.

2. With range C4:C18 selected, apply a conditional format to the range that highlights scores that are below average.

3. With range D4:D18 selected, apply a conditional format to the range that highlights any grade that is a D or an F.

4. With range B4:B18 selected, apply a conditional format to the range that uses a red color to highlight any duplicate student names.

5. Change the document properties, as specified by your instructor. Change the worksheet header with your name, course number, and other information requested by your instructor. Save the workbook using the file name, Extend 2-1 Biology 201 Midterm Scores Complete, and submit the revised workbook as specified by your instructor.

Figure 2–86

Make It Right

Analyze a workbook and correct all errors and/or improve the design.

Correcting Functions and Formulas in a Worksheet

Instructions: Start Excel. Open the workbook Make It Right 2-1 El Centro Diner Payroll Report. See the inside back cover of this book for instructions for downloading the Data Files for Students, or see your instructor for information on accessing the files required for this book. Correct the following formatting, function, and formula problems (Figure 2–87) in the worksheet.

	Employee	Dependents	Rate per Hou	Hours Worked	Gross Pay	Federal Tax	State Tax	Net Pay	% Taxes
	El Centro Diner								
	Payrol Report								
4	Vincent Flores	1	$9.90	20.00	$198.00	$34.97	$7.92	$162.03	21.660%
5	Wonda Jefferson	2	11.20	40.00	448.00	80.33	17.92	365.67	21.931%
6	Anthony Sanchez	2	15.90	21.25	337.88	58.31	13.52	277.57	21.257%
7	Alexa Martin	3	11.30	23.50	265.55	39.21	10.62	223.34	18.765%
8	Maria Reyes	1	10.30	21.25	218.88	39.14	8.76	178.73	21.883%
9	Lori Romanoff	2	10.75	40.00	430.00	76.73	17.20	351.27	21.845%
10	Carmen Alvarez	1	12.60	21.50	270.90	49.55	10.84	220.35	22.289%
11	Peter Lane	4	14.50	37.50	543.75	90.21	21.75	449.54	20.591%
12	Claudi Moreno	1	16.00	33.00	528.00	100.97	21.12	426.03	23.122%
13	Wayne Vargas	3	8.00	29.25	234.00	32.90	9.36	198.10	18.059%
14	**Totals**			287.25	$3,474.95	$ 602.31	$ 139.00	$2,852.64	21.333%
15	Average	1.8888889	$12.49	28.67	$360.11	$60.23	$13.90	$294.95	21.140%
16	Highest	4	$16.00	40.00	$543.75	$100.97	$21.75	$449.54	23.122%
17	Lowest	1	$8.00	20.00	$198.00	$32.90	$7.92	$162.03	18.059%

Figure 2–87

1. Adjust the width of column B to 11.25 pixels so that the word in the column header does not wrap.
2. Spell check the worksheet and correct any spelling mistakes that are found, but ignore any spelling mistakes found with the worksheet title and the employee names.
3. The averages in several columns do not include the employee in row 13. Adjust the functions in these cells so that all employees are included in the calculation.
4. The net pay calculation should be:

    Net Pay = Gross Pay – (Federal Taxes + State Taxes)

    Adjust the formulas in the range H4:H13 so that the correct formula is used.
5. The value for the highest value in column C was entered as a number rather than as a function. Replace the value with the appropriate function.
6. The currency values in row 4 should be formatted with the Accounting Number Format button on the Home tab on the Ribbon. They are currently formatted with the Currency format.
7. Delete the function in the cell containing the average of % Taxes because it is mathematically invalid.

8. Change the document properties, as specified by your instructor. Change the worksheet header with your name, course number, and other information requested by your instructor. Save the workbook using the file name, Make It Right 2-1 El Centro Diner Payroll Report Corrected. Submit the revised workbook as specified by your instructor.

In the Lab

Create a workbook using the guidelines, concepts, and skills presented in this chapter. Labs are listed in order of increasing difficulty.

Lab 1: Sales Analysis Worksheet

Problem: You have been asked to build a sales analysis worksheet for Facade Importers that determines the sales quota and percentage of quota met for the sales representatives in Table 2–8. The desired worksheet is shown in Figure 2–88.

Table 2–8 Facade Importers Sales Data

Sales Representative	Sales Amount	Sales Return	Sales Quota
Polizzi, Bernard	591518	12638	765130
Li, Grace	895050	12015	776381
Volpe, Pamela	716502	18141	733309
Khan, Anwer	709672	22326	566940
Hudson, Emma	802525	11138	712222
Huerta, Teresa	885156	18721	778060

	A	B	C	D	E	F
	Facade Importers Sales Analysis					
	Sales Representative	Sales Amount	Sales Return	Net Sales	Sales Quota	Above Quota
	Polizzi, Bernard	$591,518.00	$12,638.00	$578,880.00	$765,130.00	($186,250.00)
	Li, Grace	895,050.00	12,015.00	883,035.00	776,381.00	106,654.00
	Volpe, Pamela	716,502.00	18,141.00	698,361.00	733,309.00	(34,948.00)
	Khan, Anwer	709,672.00	22,326.00	687,346.00	566,940.00	120,406.00
	Hudson, Emma	802,525.00	11,138.00	791,387.00	712,222.00	79,165.00
	Huerta, Terese	885,156.00	18,721.00	866,435.00	778,060.00	88,375.00
	Total	$4,600,423.00	$94,979.00	$4,505,444.00	$4,332,042.00	$173,402.00
	Average	$766,737.17	$15,829.83	$750,907.33	$722,007.00	$28,900.33
	Highest	$895,050.00	$22,326.00	$883,035.00	$778,060.00	$120,406.00
	Lowest	$591,518.00	$11,138.00	$578,880.00	$566,940.00	($186,250.00)
	% of Quota Sold ====>	104.00%				

Figure 2–88

Continued >

In the Lab *continued*

Instructions Part 1: Perform the following tasks to build the worksheet shown in Figure 2–88.

1. Apply the Aspect theme to the worksheet by using the Themes button on the Page Layout tab on the Ribbon.

2. Increase the width of column A to 19.00 points and the width of columns B through F to 13.50 points.

3. Enter the worksheet title `Facade Importers` in cell A1 and the worksheet subtitle `Sales Analysis` in cell A2. Enter the column titles in row 3 as shown in Figure 2–88. In row 3, use ALT+ENTER to start a new line in a cell.

4. Enter the sales data described in Table 2–8 in columns A, B, C, and E in rows 4 through 9. Enter the row titles in the range A10:A14 as shown in Figure 2–88 on the previous page.

5. Obtain the net sales in column D by subtracting the sales returns in column C from the sales amount in column B. Enter the formula in cell D4 and copy it to the range D5:D9.

6. Obtain the above quota amounts in column F by subtracting the sales quota in column E from the net sales in column D. Enter the formula in cell F4 and copy it to the range F5:F9.

7. Obtain the totals in row 10 by adding the column values for each salesperson. In the range B11:B13, use the AVERAGE, MAX, and MIN functions to determine the average, highest value, and lowest value in the range B4:B9. Copy the range B11:B13 to the range C11:F13.

8. Determine the percent of quota sold in cell B14 by dividing the total net sales amount in cell D10 by the total sales quota amount in cell E10. Center this value in the cell.

9. If necessary, click the Home tab on the Ribbon. One at a time, merge and center the worksheet title and subtitle across columns A through F. Select cells A1 and A2 and change the background color to red (column 2 in the Standard Colors area on the Fill Color palette). Apply the Title cell style to cells A1 and B1 by clicking the Cell Styles button on the Home tab on the Ribbon and clicking the Title cell style in the Titles and Headings area in the Cell Styles gallery. Change the worksheet title in cell A1 to 28-point white (column 1, row 1 on the Font Color gallery). Change the worksheet subtitle to the same color. Assign a thick box border from the Borders gallery to the range A1:A2.

10. Center the titles in row 3, columns A through F. Apply the Heading 3 cell style to the range A3:F3. Use the Italic button on the Home tab on the Ribbon to italicize the column titles in row 3 and the row titles in the range A10:A14.

11. Apply the Total cell style to the range A10:F10. Assign a thick box to cell B14. Change the background and font colors for cell B14 to the same colors applied to the worksheet title in Step 9.

12. Change the row heights of row 3 to 33.00 points and rows 11 and 14 to 30.00 points.

13. Select cell B14 and then click the Percent Style button on the Home tab on the Ribbon. Click the Increase Decimal button on the Ribbon twice to display the percent in cell B14 to hundredths.

14. Use the CTRL key to select the ranges B4:F4 and B10:F13. That is, select the range B4:F4 and then while holding down the CTRL key, select the range B10:F13. Use the Format Cells: Number Dialog Box Launcher button on the Home tab on the Ribbon to display the Format Cells dialog box to assign the selected ranges a Floating Dollar Sign style format with two decimal places and parentheses to represent negative numbers. Select the range B5:F9 and click the Comma Style button on the Home tab on the Ribbon.

15. Rename the sheet tab as Sales Analysis. Change the document properties, as specified by your instructor. Change the worksheet header with your name, course number, and other information requested by your instructor.

16. Save the workbook using the file name Lab 2-1 Part 1 Facade Importers Sales Analysis. Print the entire worksheet in landscape orientation. Print only the range A3:B10.

17. Display the formulas version by pressing CTRL+ACCENT MARK (`). Print the formulas version using the Fit to option button in the Scaling area on the Page tab in the Page Setup dialog box. After printing the worksheet, reset the Scaling option by selecting the Adjust to option button on the Page tab in the Page Setup dialog box and changing the percent value to 100%. Change the display from the formulas version to the values version by pressing CTRL+ACCENT MARK (`). Do not save the workbook.

18. Submit the assignment as specified by your instructor.

Instructions Part 2:   Open the workbook created in Part 1 and save the workbook as Lab 2-1 Part 2 Facade Importers Sales Analysis. Manually decrement each of the six values in the net sales column by $10,000.00 until the percent of quota sold in cell B14 is below, yet as close as possible to, 100%. All six values in column E must be incremented the same number of times. The percent of quota sold in B14 should equal 99.85%. Update the worksheet header and save the workbook. Print the worksheet. Submit the assignment as specified by your instructor.

Instructions Part 3:   Open the workbook created in Part 2 and then save the workbook as Lab 2-1 Part 3 Facade Importers Sales Analysis. With the percent of quota sold in cell B14 equal to 99.85% from Part 2, manually decrement each of the six values in the sales return column by $1,000.00 until the percent of quota sold in cell B14 is above, yet as close as possible to, 100%. Decrement all six values in column C the same number of times. Your worksheet is correct when the percent of quota sold in cell B14 is equal to 100.12%. Update the worksheet header and save the workbook. Print the worksheet. Submit the assignment as specified by your instructor.

In the Lab

Lab 2: Balance Due Worksheet

Problem: You are a spreadsheet intern for Jackson's Bright Ideas, a popular Denver-based light fixture store with outlets in major cities across the western United States. You have been asked to use Excel to generate a report (Figure 2–89) that summarizes the monthly balance due. A graphic breakdown of the data also is desired. The customer data in Table 2–9 is available for test purposes.

Table 2–9 Jackson's Bright Ideas Monthly Balance Due Data				
Customer	**Beginning Balance**	**Credits**	**Payments**	**Purchases**
Costa, Dan	160.68	18.70	99.33	68.28
Hernandez, Abraham	138.11	48.47	75.81	46.72
Mc Cartan, John	820.15	32.11	31.23	29.19
Paoli, Pam	167.35	59.32	52.91	33.90
Ramirez, Alberto	568.34	55.17	18.53	36.34
Vaughn, Noah	449.92	25.90	82.05	99.77
Xiong, James	390.73	48.12	19.35	92.13

Continued >

In the Lab *continued*

Instructions Part 1: Create a worksheet similar to the one shown in Figure 2–89. Include the five columns of customer data in Table 2–9 in the report, plus two additional columns to compute a service charge and a new balance for each customer. Assume no negative unpaid monthly balances.

	A	B	C	D	E	F	G	H
	Customer	**Beginning Balance**	**Credits**	**Payments**	**Purchases**	**Service Charge**	**New Balance**	
1	Jackson's Bright Ideas							
2	Monthly Balance Due Report							
4	Costa, Dan	$160.68	$18.70	$99.33	$68.28	$1.17	$112.10	
5	Hernandez, Abraham	138.11	48.47	75.81	46.72	0.38	60.93	
6	Mc Cartan, John	820.15	32.11	31.23	29.19	20.81	806.81	
7	Paoli, Pam	167.35	59.32	52.91	33.90	1.52	90.54	
8	Ramirez, Alberto	568.34	55.17	18.53	36.34	13.60	544.58	
9	Vaughn, Noah	449.92	25.90	82.05	99.77	9.40	451.14	
10	Xiong, James	390.73	48.12	19.35	92.13	8.89	424.28	
11	**Totals**	$2,695.28	$287.79	$379.21	$406.33	$55.78	$2,490.39	
12	**Highest**	$820.15	$59.32	$99.33	$99.77	$20.81	$806.81	
13	**Lowest**	$138.11	$18.70	$18.53	$29.19	$0.38	$60.93	
14	**Average**	$385.04	$41.11	$54.17	$58.05	$7.97	$355.77	

Figure 2–89

Perform the following tasks:

1. Enter and format the worksheet title `Jackson's Bright Ideas` and worksheet subtitle `Monthly Balance Due Report` in cells A1 and A2. Change the theme of the worksheet to the Technic theme. Apply the Title cell style to cells A1 and A2. Change the font size in cell A1 to 28 points. One at a time, merge and center the worksheet title and subtitle across columns A through G. Change the background color of cells A1 and A2 to yellow (column 4 in the Standard Colors area in the Font Color palette). Draw a thick box border around the range A1:A2.

2. Change the width of column A to 20.00 characters. Change the widths of columns B through G to 12.00. Change the heights of row 3 to 36.00 and row 12 to 30.00 points.

3. Enter the column titles in row 3 and row titles in the range A11:A14 as shown in Figure 2–89. Center the column titles in the range A3:G3. Apply the Heading 3 cell style to the range A3:G3. Bold the titles in the range A11:A14. Apply the Total cell style to the range A11:G11. Change the font size of the cells in the range A3:G14 to 12 points.

4. Enter the data in Table 2–9 in the range A4:E10.

5. Use the following formulas to determine the service charge in column F and the new balance in column G for the first customer. Copy the two formulas down through the remaining customers.

   a. Service Charge (cell F4) = 2.75% * (Beginning Balance – Payments – Credits)
      or = 0.0275 * (B4 – D4 – C4)

   b. New Balance (G4) = Beginning Balance + Purchases – Credits – Payments + Service Charge
      or =B4 + E4 – C4 – D4 + F4

6. Determine the totals in row 11.

7. Determine the maximum, minimum, and average values in cells B12:B14 for the range B4:B10 and then copy the range B12:B14 to C12:G14.

8. Use the Format Cells command on the shortcut menu to format the numbers as follows: (a) assign the Currency style with a floating dollar sign to the cells containing numeric data in the ranges B4:G4 and B11:G14; and (b) assign the Comma style (currency with no dollar sign) to the range B5:G10.

9. Use conditional formatting to change the formatting to white font on a red background in any cell in the range C4:C10 that contains a value greater than 50.

10. Change the worksheet name from Sheet1 to Balance Due. Change the document properties, as specified by your instructor. Change the worksheet header with your name, course number, and other information requested by your instructor.

11. Spell check the worksheet. Preview and then print the worksheet in landscape orientation. Save the workbook using the file name, Lab 2-2 Part 1 Jackson's Bright Ideas Monthly Balance Due Report.

12. Print the range A3:D14. Print the formulas version on one page. Close the workbook without saving the changes. Submit the assignment as specified by your instructor.

Instructions Part 2: This part requires that a 3-D Bar chart with a cylindrical shape be inserted on a new worksheet in the workbook. If necessary, use Excel Help to obtain information on inserting a chart on a separate sheet in the workbook.

1. With the Lab 2-2 Part 1 Jackson's Bright Ideas Monthly Balance Due Report workbook open, save the workbook using the file name, Lab 2-2 Part 2 Jackson's Bright Ideas Monthly Balance Due Report. Draw the 3-D Bar chart with cylindrical shape showing each customer's total new balance as shown in Figure 2–90.

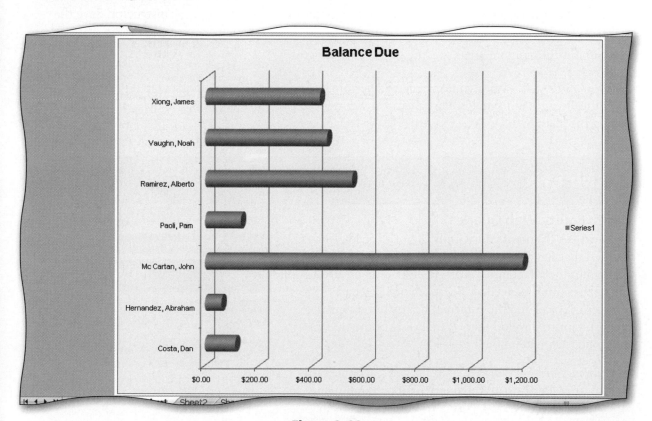

Figure 2–90

2. Use the CTRL key and mouse to select the nonadjacent chart ranges A4:A10 and G4:G10. That is, select the range A4:A10 and then while holding down the CTRL key, select the range G4:G10. The customer names in the range A4:A10 will identify the cylindrical bars, while the data series in the range G4:G10 will determine the length of the bars.

Continued >

In the Lab *continued*

3. Click the Insert tab on the Ribbon. Click the Bar button in the Charts group on the Ribbon and then select Clustered Horizontal Cylinder in the Cylinder area. When the chart is displayed on the worksheet, click the Move Chart button on the Ribbon. When the Move Chart dialog box appears, click New sheet and then type Bar Chart for the sheet name. Click the OK button.

4. When the chart is displayed on the new worksheet, click the chart area, which is a blank area near the edge of the chart, and then click the Format contextual tab. Click the Shape Fill button on the Ribbon and then select Gold, Accent 2, Lighter 80% in the gallery (column 6, row 2). Click the Layout contextual tab. Click the Chart Title button on the Ribbon and then select Above Chart in the Chart Title gallery. If necessary, use the scroll bar on the right side of the worksheet to scroll to the top of the chart. Click the edge of the chart title to select it and then type Balance Due as the chart title.

5. Drag the Balance Due tab at the bottom of the worksheet to the left of the Bar Chart tab to reorder the sheets in the workbook. Preview and print the chart.

6. Click the Balance Due sheet tab. Change the following purchases: customer John Mc Cartan to $406.58, and customer Pam Paoli to $74.99. The company also decided to change the service charge from 2.75% to 3.25% for all customers. After copying the adjusted formula in cell F4 to the range F5:F10, click the Auto Fill Options button and then click Fill without Formatting to maintain the original formatting in the range F5:F10. The total new balance in cell G11 should equal $2,919.01.

7. Select both sheets by holding down the SHIFT key and then clicking the Bar Chart tab. Preview and print the selected sheets. Submit the assignment as requested by your instructor. Save the workbook.

8. Submit the assignment as specified by your instructor.

Instructions Part 3: With your instructor's permission, e-mail the workbook created in this exercise with the changes indicated in Part 2 as an attachment to your instructor. Close the workbook without saving the changes.

In the Lab

Lab 3: Equity Web Queries

Problem: A friend of your family, Benson Yackley, has learned that Excel can connect to the Web, download real-time stock data into a worksheet, and then refresh the data as often as needed. Because you have had courses in Excel and the Internet, he has hired you as a consultant to develop a stock analysis workbook. His portfolio is shown in Table 2–10.

Instructions Part 1: Start Excel. If necessary, connect to the Internet. Perform a Web query to obtain multiple stock quotes (Figure 2–91), using the stock symbols in the second column of Table 2–10. Place the results of the Web query in a new worksheet. Rename the worksheet Real-Time Stock Quotes. Change the document properties, as specified by your instructor. Add a header with your name, course number, and other information requested by your instructor. Save the workbook using the file name, Lab 2-3 Part 1 Benson Yackley Equities Online. Preview and then print the worksheet in landscape orientation using the Fit to option.

Table 2–10 Benson Yackley's Stock Portfolio	
Company	**Stock Symbol**
Exxon Mobil	XOM
Dell	DELL
Hewlett-Packard	HPQ
Intel	INTC
MetLife	MET
PepsiCo	PEP

Click the following links and print the Web page that appears in the browser window: Click here to visit MSN Money; Dell Inc.; Chart (to the right of MetLife, Inc.); and News (to the right of PepsiCo, Inc.). Submit the assignment as specified by your instructor.

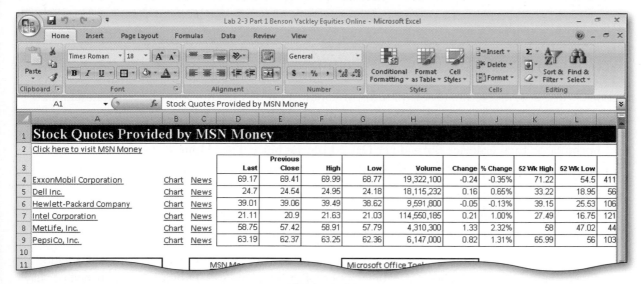

Figure 2–91

Instructions Part 2: While connected to the Internet and with the Lab 2-3 Benson Yackley Equities Online workbook open, create a worksheet listing the major indices and their current values on Sheet2 of the workbook (Figure 2–92). After clicking the Sheet2 tab, create the worksheet by double-clicking MSN MoneyCentral Investor Major Indices in the Existing Connections dialog box. The dialog box is displayed when you click the Existing Connections button on the Data tab on the Ribbon. Rename the worksheet Major Indices. Preview and then print the Major Indices worksheet in landscape orientation using the Fit to option. Save the workbook using the same file name as in Part 1. Submit the assignment as specified by your instructor.

Stock Quotes Provided by MSN Money

Click here to visit MSN Money

			Last	Previous Close	High	Low	Volume	Change	% Change	52 Wk High	52 Wk Low
DOW JONES INDUSTRIAL AVERAGE INDEX	Chart	News	11992.68	11950.02	12049.03	11947.62	276,354,912	42.66	0.36%	11997.25	10193.45
DOW JONES COMPOSITE INDEX	Chart	News	4030.49	4028.71	4068.22	4013.22	344,654,987	1.78	0.04%	4053.4	3346.66
DOW JONES TRANSPORTATION AVERAGE INDEX	Chart	News	4605.27	4648.65	4718.13	4574.62	44,944,975	-43.38	-0.93%	5013.67	3550.55
DOW JONES UTILITIES INDEX	Chart	News	442.81	439.33	443.03	439.35	23,355,100	3.48	0.79%	443.49	378.95
$DAX (Invalid symbol)	???	???	???	???	???	???	???	???	???	???	???
$FTSE (Invalid symbol)	???	???	???	???	???	???	???	???	???	???	???
Hang Seng	Chart	News	18048.09	18014.84	18048.09	17881.78	0	33.25	0.18%	0	0
AMEX INTERACTIVE WEEK INTERNET INDEX	Chart	News	186.5	187.51	188.97	186.09	0	-1.01	-0.54%	192.64	156.16
NASDAQ COMPOSITE INDEX	Chart	News	2337.15	2344.95	2362.09	2330.49	2,091,566,611	-7.8	-0.33%	2375.54	2012.78
$NI225 (Invalid symbol)	???	???	???	???	???	???	???	???	???	???	???
$CAC (Invalid symbol)	???	???	???	???	???	???	???	???	???	???	???
PHLX SEMICONDUCTOR SECTOR INDEX	Chart	News	450.79	463.74	462.46	449.51	0	-12.95	-2.79%	559.6	384.28
PH...	Chart	News				761.46				784.62	618...

Figure 2–92

Cases and Places

Apply your creative thinking and problem solving skills to design and implement a solution.

• EASIER • • MORE DIFFICULT

• 1: Design and Create a Weight-Loss Plan Worksheet

As a summer intern working for Choose to Lose, a local weight-loss clinic, you have been asked to create a worksheet that estimates the monthly weight lost for an individual based on recommended average daily activities. You have been given the numbers of calories burned per hour and the average number of hours for each activity (Table 2–11). Use the following formulas:

Formula A: Total Calories Burned per Day = Calories burned per Hour $\times$ Average Hours Daily

Formula B: Total Pounds Lost per Month (30 days) = 30 $\times$ Total Calories Burned per Day / 3500

Formula C: Average function

Formula D: Max function

Formula E: Min function

Use the concepts and techniques presented in this project to create and format the worksheet. Include an embedded 3-D Pie chart that shows the contribution of each activity to the total calories burned per day. Use Microsoft Excel Help to create a professional looking 3-D Pie chart with title and data labels.

Table 2–11 Activities with Corresponding Calories Burned per Hour and Worksheet Layout				
Activity	**Calories Burned per Hour**	**Average Hours Daily**	**Total Calories Burned per Day**	**Total Pounds Lost per Month (30 Days)**
Aerobics class	450	0.50	Formula A	Formula B
Brisk walking	350	0.50		
House work	150	1.00		
Office work/sitting	120	6.00		
Sleeping	70	9.00		
Standing	105	2.00		
Swimming	290	0.50		
Tennis	315	0.25		
Walking	240	4.25		
Totals	—		—	—
Average	Formula C			
Highest	Formula D			
Lowest	Formula E			

• 2: Create a Profit Potential Worksheet

You work part-time for Doze-Now, a retailer of sleep-related products. Your manager wants to know the profit potential of their inventory based on the categories of inventory in Table 2–12. Table 2–12 contains the format of the desired report. The required formulas are shown in Table 2–13. Use the concepts and techniques developed in this project to create and format the worksheet. Submit a printout of the values version and formulas version of the worksheet. The company just received a shipment of 175 additional comforters and 273 items of sleepwear. Update the appropriate cells in the Units on Hand column.

Table 2–12 Doze-Now Profit Potential Data and Worksheet Layout

Item	Units on Hand	Average Unit Cost	Total Cost	Average Unit Price	Total Value	Potential Profit
Comforters	216	46.52	Formula A	Formula B	Formula C	Formula D
Night lights	4,283	6.89				
Pillows	691	47.64				
Sleep sound machines	103	45.06				
Sleepwear	489	16.77				
Total	—		—	—	—	—
Average	Formula E					
Lowest	Formula F					
Highest	Formula G					

Table 2–13 Doze-Now Profit Potential Formulas

Formula A = Units on Hand * Average Unit Cost

Formula B = Average Unit Cost * (1 / (1 − .58))

Formula C = Units on Hand * Average Unit Price

Formula D = Total Value − Total Cost

Formula E = AVERAGE function

Formula F = MIN function

Formula G = MAX function

Continued >

Cases and Places *continued*

•• 3: Create a Fund-Raising Analysis Worksheet

You are the chairperson of the fund-raising committee for a local charity. You want to compare various fund-raising ideas to determine which will give you the best profit. The data obtained from six businesses about their products and the format of the desired report are shown in Table 2–14. The required formulas are shown in Table 2–15. Use the concepts and techniques presented in this project to create and format the worksheet.

Table 2–14 Fund-Raising Data and Worksheet Layout

Product	Company	Cost per Unit	Margin	Selling Price	Profit per 2000 Sales	Profit per 5000 Sales
Candles	Woodland Farms	$4.75	40%	Formula A	Formula B	Formula C
Candy	Polkandy	3.00	70%			
Coffee	Garcia Coffee	6.50	45%			
Cookie dough	Oh, Dough!	2.90	65%			
Flower bulbs	Early Bloom	2.40	50%			
T-shirts	Zed's Sports	5.75	42%			
Minimum		Formula D				
Maximum		Formula E				

Table 2–15 Band Fund-Raising Formulas

Formula A = Cost per Unit / (1 – Margin)

Formula B = 2000 * (Selling Price – Cost per Unit)

Formula C = 5000 *110% * (Selling Price – Cost per Unit)

Formula D = MIN function

Formula E = MAX function

•• 4: Design and Create a Projected Budget

Make It Personal

For the next six-month period, forecast your income for each month, your base expenditures for each month, and your special expenditures for each month. Base expenditures include expenses that occur each month, such as food and loan payments. Special expenditures include expenses that are out of the ordinary, such as the purchase of gifts, automobile insurance, and medical expenses. With this data, develop a worksheet calculating the amount of remaining money at the end of each month. You can determine this amount by subtracting both expenses from the anticipated income.

Include a total, average value, highest value, and lowest value for income, base expenditures, special expenditures, and remaining money. Use the concepts and techniques presented in this project to create and format the worksheet.

Create a 3-D Pie chart on a separate sheet illustrating the portion each month's special expenditures deducts from the total remaining money after all six months have passed. Use Microsoft Excel Help to create a professional looking 3-D Pie chart with title and data labels.

•• 5: Design and Create a Stock Analysis Worksheet

Working Together

Have each member of your team select six stocks — two bank stocks, two communications stocks, and two Internet stocks. Each member should submit the stock names, stock symbols, and an approximate six-month-old price. Create a worksheet that lists the stock names, symbols, price, and number of shares for each stock (use 350 shares as the number of shares for all stocks). Format the worksheet so that it has a professional appearance and is as informative as possible.

Have the group do research on the use of 3-D references, which is a reference to a range that spans two or more worksheets in a workbook (use Microsoft Excel Help). Use what the group learns to create a Web query on the Sheet2 worksheet by referencing the stock symbols on the Sheet1 worksheet. On the Sheet1 worksheet, change the cells that list current price per share numbers on the Sheet1 worksheet so that they use 3-D cell references that refer to the worksheet created by the Web query on the Sheet2 worksheet. Present your workbook and findings to the class.

1 | Creating and Using a Database

Objectives

You will have mastered the material in this chapter when you can:

- Describe databases and database management systems
- Design a database to satisfy a collection of requirements
- Start Access
- Describe the features of the Access window
- Create a database
- Create a table and add records

- Close a table
- Close a database and quit Access
- Open a database
- Print the contents of a table
- Create and print custom reports
- Create and use a split form
- Use the Access Help system

1 | Creating and Using a Database

What Is Microsoft Office Access 2007?

Microsoft Office Access 2007, usually referred to as simply Access, is a database management system. A database management system, such as Access, is a software tool that allows you to use a computer to create a database; add, change, and delete data in the database; sort the data in the database; retrieve data in the database; and create forms and reports using the data in the database. The term **database** describes a collection of data organized in a manner that allows access, retrieval, and use of that data. Some of the key features in Access are:

- **Data entry and update** Access provides easy mechanisms for adding, changing, and deleting data, including the capability of making mass changes in a single operation.

- **Queries (questions)** Access makes it possible to ask complex questions concerning the data in the database and then receive instant answers.

- **Forms** Access allows the user to produce attractive and useful forms for viewing and updating data.

- **Reports** Access includes report creation tools that make it easy to produce sophisticated reports for presenting data.

- **Web support** Access allows you to save objects, reports, and tables in HTML format so they can be viewed using a browser. You also can import and export documents in XML format as well as share data with others using SharePoint Services.

This latest version of Access has many new features to help you be more productive. Like the other Office applications, it features a new, improved interface utilizing the Ribbon. The new Navigation Pane makes navigating among the various objects in a database easier and more intuitive than in the past. The new version includes several professionally designed templates that you can use to quickly create a database. Sorting and filtering has been enhanced in this version. The new Layout view allows you to make changes to the design of forms and reports at the same time you are browsing the data. Datasheet view also has been enhanced to make creating tables more intuitive. Split form, a new form object, combines both a datasheet and a form as a single unit. Memo fields now support rich text, and there is a new Attachment data type. Using the Attachment data type, a field can contain an attached file, such as a document, image, or spreadsheet.

Project Planning Guidelines

The process of developing a database that communicates specific information requires careful analysis and planning. As a starting point, establish why the database is needed. Once the purpose is determined, analyze the intended users of the database and their unique needs. Then, gather information about the topic and decide what to include in the database. Finally, determine the database design and style that will be most successful at delivering the message. Details of these guidelines are provided in Appendix A. In addition, each project in this book provides practical applications of these planning considerations.

Project — Database Creation

JSP Recruiters is a recruiting firm that specializes in job placement for health care professionals. Because the recruiters at JSP have previous experience in the health care industry, the firm is able to provide quality candidates for employment in hospitals, clinics, medical laboratories, doctors' offices, and other health care facilities.

JSP Recruiters works with clients in need of health care professionals. It assigns each client to a specific recruiter. The recruiter works with the client to determine the necessary qualifications for each job candidate. The recruiter then contacts and does a preliminary review of the qualifications for each candidate before setting up a job interview between the client and the candidate. If the candidate is hired, the client pays a percentage of the new employee's annual salary to the recruiting firm, which then distributes a percentage of that client fee to the recruiter.

To ensure that operations run smoothly, JSP Recruiters organizes data on its clients and recruiters in a database, managed by Access. In this way, JSP keeps its data current and accurate while the firm's management can analyze the data for trends and produce a variety of useful reports.

In Access, a database consists of a collection of tables, each of which contains information on a specific subject. Figure 1–1 shows the database for JSP Recruiters. It consists of two tables. The Client table (Figure 1–1a) contains information about the clients to whom JSP provides services. The Recruiter table (Figure 1–1b) contains information about the recruiters to whom these clients are assigned.

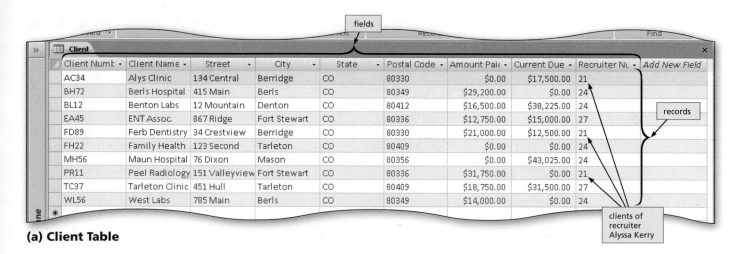

(a) Client Table

(b) Recruiter Table

Figure 1–1

The rows in the tables are called **records**. A record contains information about a given person, product, or event. A row in the Client table, for example, contains information about a specific client.

The columns in the tables are called fields. A **field** contains a specific piece of information within a record. In the Client table, for example, the fourth field, City, contains the city where the client is located.

The first field in the Client table is the Client Number. JSP Recruiters assigns a number to each client. As is common to the way in which many organizations format client numbers, JSP Recruiters calls it a *number*, although it actually contains letters. The JSP client numbers consist of two uppercase letters followed by a two-digit number.

These numbers are unique; that is, no two clients are assigned the same number. Such a field can be used as a **unique identifier**. This simply means that a given client number will appear only in a single record in the table. Only one record exists, for example, in which the client number is BH72. A unique identifier also is called a **primary key**. Thus, the Client Number field is the primary key for the Client table.

The next seven fields in the Client table are Client Name, Street, City, State, Postal Code, Amount Paid, and Current Due. Note that the default width of the columns cuts off the names of some of the columns. The Amount Paid column contains the amount that the client has paid JSP Recruiters year to date (YTD) prior to the current period. The Current Due column contains the amount due to JSP for the current period. For example, client BL12 is Benton Labs. The address is 12 Mountain in Denton, Colorado. The postal code is 80412. The client has paid $16,500 for recruiting services so far this year. The amount due for the current period is $38,225.

JSP assigns each client a single recruiter. The last column in the Client table, Recruiter Number, gives the number of the client's recruiter.

The first field in the Recruiter table, Recruiter Number, is the number JSP Recruiters assigns to the recruiter. These numbers are unique, so Recruiter Number is the primary key of the Recruiter table.

The other fields in the Recruiter table are Last Name, First Name, Street, City, State, Postal Code, Rate, and Commission. The Rate field contains the percentage of the client fee that the recruiter earns, and the Commission field contains the total amount that JSP has paid the recruiter so far this year. For example, Recruiter 27 is Jaime Fernandez. His address is 265 Maxwell in Charleston, Colorado. The Postal Code is 80380. His commission rate is .09 (9%), and his commission is $9,450.

The recruiter number appears in both the Client table and the Recruiter table. It relates clients and recruiters. For example, in the Client table, you see that the recruiter number for client BL12 is 24. To find the name of this recruiter, look for the row in the Recruiter table that contains 24 in the Recruiter Number column. After you have found it, you know the client is assigned to Camden Reeves. To find all the clients assigned to Camden Reeves, you must look through the Client table for all the clients that contain 24 in the Recruiter Number column. His clients are BH72 (Berls Hospital), BL12 (Benton Labs), FH22 (Family Health), MH56 (Maun Hospital), and WL56 (West Labs).

The last recruiter in the Recruiter table, Jan Lee, has not been assigned any clients yet; therefore, her recruiter number, 34, does not appear on any row in the Client table.

Overview

As you read this chapter, you will learn how to create the database shown in Figure 1–1 on the previous page by performing these general tasks:

• Design the database.

• Create a new blank database.

- Create a table and add the records.
- Preview and print the contents of a table.
- Create a second table and add the records.
- Create four reports.
- Create a form.

Plan
Ahead

Database design guidelines.

Database design refers to the arrangement of data into tables and fields. In the example in this chapter the design is specified, but in many cases, you will have to determine the design based on what you want the system to accomplish.

When designing a database, the actions you take and the decisions you make will determine the tables and fields that will be included in the database. As you create a database, such as the project shown in Figure 1–1 on page AC 3, you should follow these general guidelines:

1. **Identify the tables.** Examine the requirements for the database in order to identify the main objects that are involved. There will be a table for each object you identified.

   In one database, for example, the main objects might be departments and employees. Thus, there would be two tables: one for departments and the other for employees. In another database, the main objects might be clients and recruiters. In this case, there would also be two tables: one for clients and the other for recruiters. In still another database, the main objects might be books, publishers, and authors. Here there would be three tables: one for books, a second for publishers, and a third for authors.

2. **Determine the primary keys.** Recall that the primary key is the unique identifier for records in the table. For each table, determine the unique identifier, if there is one. For a Department table, for example, the unique identifier might be the Department Code. For a Book table, the unique identifier might be the ISBN number.

3. **Determine the additional fields.** The primary key will be a field or combination of fields in a table. There typically will be many additional fields, each of which contains a type of data. Examine the project requirements to determine these additional fields. For example, in an Employee table, the additional fields might include such fields as Employee Name, Street Address, City, State, Postal Code, Date Hired, Salary, and so on.

4. **Determine relationships among the tables.** Examine the list of tables you have created to see which tables are related. When you determine two tables are related, include matching fields in the two tables. For example, in a database containing employees and departments, there is a relationship between the two tables because one department can have many employees assigned to it. Department Code could be the matching field in the two tables.

5. **Determine data types for the fields.** For each field, determine the type of data the field can contain. One field, for example, might contain only numbers. Another field might contain currency amounts, while a third field might contain only dates. Some fields contain text data, meaning any combination of letters, numbers and special characters (!, ;, ', &, and so on). For example, in an Employee table, the Date Hired field would contain dates, the Salary field would contain currency amounts, and the Hours Worked field would contain numbers. The other fields in the Employee table would contain text data, such as Employee Name and Department Code.

6. **Identify and remove any unwanted redundancy. Redundancy** is the storing of a piece of data in more than one place. Redundancy usually, but not always, causes problems, such as wasted space, difficulties with update, and possible data inconsistency. Examine each table you have created to see if it contains redundancy and, if so, determine whether the redundancy causes these problems. If it does, remove the redundancy by splitting the table into two tables. For example, you may have a single table of employees. In addition to typical employee data (name, address, earnings, and so on), the table might contain Department Number and Department Name. If so, the Department Name could repeat multiple times.

(continued)

**Plan
Ahead**

(continued)

Every employee whose department number is 12, for example, would have the same department name. It would be better to split the table into two tables, one for Employees and one for Department. In the Department table, the Department Name is stored only once.

7. **Determine a location for the database. The database you have designed will be stored in a single file. You need to determine a location in which to store the file.**

When necessary, more specific details concerning the above guidelines are presented at appropriate points in the chapter. The chapter also will identify the actions performed and decisions made regarding these guidelines during the creation of the database shown in Figure 1–1 on page AC 3.

BTW

Database Design
For more information on database design methods and for techniques for identifying and eliminating redundancy, visit the Access 2007 Database Design Web page (scsite.com/ac2007/dbdesign).

Designing a Database

This section illustrates the database design process by showing how you would design the database for JSP Recruiters from a set of requirements. In this section, you will use a commonly accepted shorthand to represent the tables and fields that make up the database as well as the primary keys for the tables. For each table, you give the name of the table followed by a set of parentheses. Within the parentheses is a list of the fields in the table separated by columns. You underline the primary key. For example,

Product (<u>Product Code</u>, Description, On Hand, Price)

represents a table called Product. The Product table contains four fields: Product Code, Description, On Hand, and Price. The Product Code field is the primary key.

Database Requirements

JSP Recruiters needs to maintain information on both clients and recruiters. It currently keeps this data in the two Word tables and two Excel workbooks shown in Figure 1–2. They use Word tables for address information and Excel workbooks for financial information.

Client Number	Client Name	Street	City	State	Postal Code
AC34	Alys Clinic	134 Central	Berridge	CO	80330
BH72	Berls Hospital	415 Main	Berls	CO	80349
BL12	Benton Labs	12 Mountain	Denton	CO	80412
EA45	ENT Assoc.	867 Ridge	Fort Stewart	CO	80336
FD89	Ferb Dentistry	34 Crestview	Berridge	CO	80330
FH22	Family Health	123 Second	Tarleton	CO	80409
MH56	Maun Hospital	76 Dixon	Mason	CO	80356
PR11	Peel Radiology	151 Valleyview	Fort Stewart	CO	80336
TC37	Tarleton Clinic	451 Hull	Tarleton	CO	80409
WL56	West Labs	785 Main	Berls	CO	80349

**(a)
Client Address
Information
(Word Table)**

Figure 1–2

(b) Client Financial Information (Excel Workbook)

	A	B	C	D
1	Client Number	Client Name	Amount Paid	Current Due
2	AC34	Alys Clinic	$0.00	$17,500.00
3	BH72	Berls Hospital	$29,200.00	$0.00
4	BL12	Benton Labs	$16,500.00	$38,225.00
5	EA45	ENT Assoc.	$12,750.00	$15,000.00
6	FD89	Ferb Dentistry	$21,000.00	$12,500.00
7	FH22	Family Health	$0.00	$0.00
8	MH56	Maun Hospital	$0.00	$43,025.00
9	PR11	Peel Radiology	$31,750.00	$0.00
10	TC37	Tarleton Clinic	$18,750.00	$31,500.00
11	WL56	West Labs	$14,000.00	$0.00

(c) Recruiter Address Information (Word Table)

Recruiter Number	Last Name	First Name	Street	City	State	Postal Code
21	Kerry	Alyssa	261 Pointer	Tourin	CO	80416
24	Reeves	Camden	3135 Brill	Denton	CO	80412
27	Fernandez	Jaime	265 Maxwell	Charleston	CO	80380
34	Lee	Jan	1827 Oak	Denton	CO	80413

(d) Recruiter Financial Information (Excel Workbook)

	A	B	C	D	E
1	Recruiter Number	Last Name	First Name	Rate	Commission
2	21	Kerry	Alyssa	0.10	$17,600.00
3	24	Reeves	Camden	0.10	$19,900.00
4	27	Fernandez	Jaime	0.09	$9,450.00
5	34	Lee	Jan	0.08	$0.00

Figure 1–2 (continued)

For clients, JSP needs to maintain address data. It currently keeps this address data in a Word table (Figure 1–2a). It also maintains financial data for each client. This includes the amount paid and the current due from the client. It keeps these amounts along with the client name and number in the Excel workbook shown in Figure 1–2b.

JSP keeps recruiter address data in a Word table as shown in Figure 1–2c. Just as with clients, it keeps financial data for recruiters, including their rate and commission, in a separate Excel workbook, as shown in Figure 1–2d.

Finally, it keeps track of which clients are assigned to which recruiters. Currently, for example, clients AC34 (Alys Clinic), FD89 (Ferb Dentistry), and PR11 (Peel Radiology) are assigned to recruiter 21 (Alyssa Kerry). Clients BH72 (Berls Hospital), BL12 (Benton Labs), FH22 (Family Health), MH56 (Maun Hospital), and WL56 (West Labs) are assigned to recruiter 24 (Camden Reeves). Clients EA45 (ENT Assoc.) and TC37 (Tarleton Clinic) are assigned to recruiter 27 (Jaime Fernandez). JSP has an additional recruiter, Jan Lee, whose number has been assigned as 34, but who has not yet been assigned any clients.

Naming Tables and Fields

In designing your database, you must name the tables and fields. Thus, before beginning the design process, you must understand the rules for table and field names, which are:

1. Names can be up to 64 characters in length.
2. Names can contain letters, digits, and spaces, as well as most of the punctuation symbols.
3. Names cannot contain periods (.), exclamation points (!), accent graves (`), or square brackets ([ ]).
4. The same name cannot be used for two different fields in the same table.

The approach to naming tables and fields used in this text is to begin the names with an uppercase letter and to use lowercase for the other letters. In multiple-word names, each word begins with an uppercase letter, and there is a space between words (for example, Client Number). You should know that there are other approaches. Some people omit the space (ClientNumber). Still others use an underscore in place of the space (Client_Number). Finally, some use an underscore in place of a space, but use the same case for all letters (CLIENT_NUMBER or client_number).

Identifying the Tables

Now that you know the rules for naming tables and fields, you are ready to begin the design process. The first step is to identify the main objects involved in the requirements. For the JSP Recruiters database, the main objects are clients and recruiters. This leads to two tables, which you must name. Reasonable names for these two tables are:

Client

Recruiter

Determining the Primary Keys

The next step is to identify the fields that will be the primary keys. Client numbers uniquely identify clients, and recruiter numbers uniquely identify recruiters. Thus, the primary key for the Client table is the client number, and the primary key for the Recruiter table is the recruiter number. Reasonable names for these fields would be Client Number and Recruiter Number, respectively. Adding these primary keys to the tables gives:

Client (<u>Client Number</u>)

Recruiter (<u>Recruiter Number</u>)

Determining Additional Fields

After identifying the primary keys, you need to determine and name the additional fields. In addition to the client number, the Client Address Information shown in Figure 1–2a on page AC 6 contains the client name, street, city, state, and postal code. These would be fields in the Client table. The Client Financial Information shown in Figure 1–2b also contains the client number and client name, which are already included in the Client table. The financial information also contains the amount paid and the current due. Adding the amount paid and current due fields to those already identified in the Client table and assigning reasonable names gives:

Client (<u>Client Number</u>, Client Name, Street, City, State, Postal Code, Amount Paid, Current Due)

Similarly, examining the Recruiter Address Information in Figure 1–2c on page AC 7 adds the last name, first name, street, city, state, and postal code fields to the Recruiter table. In addition to the recruiter number, last name, and first name, the Recruiter Financial Information in Figure 1–2d would add the rate and commission. Adding these fields to the Recruiter table and assigning reasonable names gives:

Recruiter (<u>Recruiter Number</u>, Last Name, First Name, Street, City, State, Postal Code, Rate, Commission)

Determining and Implementing Relationships Between the Tables

Plan
Ahead

Determine relationships among the tables.
The most common type of relationship you will encounter between tables is the **one-to-many relationship**. This means that each row in the first table may be associated with *many* rows in the second table, but each row in the second table is associated with only *one* row in the first. The first table is called the "one" table and the second is called the "many" table. For example, there may be a relationship between departments and employees, in which each department can have many employees, but each employee is assigned to only one department. In this relationship, there would be two tables, Department and Employee. The Department table would be the "one" table in the relationship. The Employee table would be the "many" table.

To determine relationships among tables, you can follow these general guidelines:

1. Identify the "one" table.

2. Identify the "many" table.

3. Include the primary key from the "one" table as a field in the "many" table.

According to the requirements, each client has one recruiter, but each recruiter can have many clients. Thus, the Recruiter table is the "one" table, and the Client table is the "many" table. To implement this one-to-many relationship between recruiters and clients, add the Recruiter Number field (the primary key of the Recruiter table) to the Client table. This produces:

Client (<u>Client Number</u>, Client Name, Street, City, State, Postal Code, Amount Paid, Current Due, Recruiter Number)

Recruiter (<u>Recruiter Number</u>, Last Name, First Name, Street, City, State, Postal Code, Rate, Commission)

Determining Data Types for the Fields

Each field has a **data type**. This indicates the type of data that can be stored in the field. Three of the most commonly used data types are:

1. **Text** — The field can contain any characters. A maximum number of 255 characters is allowed in a field whose data type is Text.

2. **Number** — The field can contain only numbers. The numbers either can be positive or negative. Fields are assigned this type so they can be used in arithmetic operations. Fields that contain numbers but will not be used for arithmetic operations usually are assigned a data type of Text.

3. **Currency** — The field can contain only monetary data. The values will appear with currency symbols, such as dollar signs, commas, and decimal points, and with

BTW

Currency Symbols
To show the symbol for the Euro (€) instead of the dollar sign, change the Format property for the field whose data type is currency. To change the default symbols for currency, change the settings in the operating system using the Control Panel.

two digits following the decimal point. Like numeric fields, you can use currency fields in arithmetic operations. Access assigns a size to currency fields automatically.

Table 1–1 shows the other data types that are available.

Table 1–1 Additional Data Types	
Data Type	**Description**
Memo	Field can store a variable amount of text or combinations of text and numbers where the total number of characters may exceed 255.
Date/Time	Field can store dates and times.
AutoNumber	Field can store a unique sequential number that Access assigns to a record. Access will increment the number by 1 as each new record is added.
Yes/No	Field can store only one of two values. The choices are Yes/No, True/False, or On/Off.
OLE Object	Field can store an OLE object, which is an object linked to or embedded in the table.
Hyperlink	Field can store text that can be used as a hyperlink address.
Attachment	Field can contain an attached file. Images, spreadsheets, documents, charts, and so on can be attached to this field in a record in the database. You can view and edit the attached file.

In the Client table, because the Client Number, Client Name, Street, City, and State can all contain letters, their data types should be Text. The data type for Postal Code is Text instead of Number, because postal codes are not used in arithmetic operations. You do not add postal codes or find an average postal code, for example. The Amount Paid and Current Due fields both contain monetary data, so their data types should be Currency.

Similarly, in the Recruiter table, the data type for the Recruiter Number, Last Name, First Name, Street, City, State, and Postal Code fields all should be Text. The Commission field contains monetary amounts, so its data type should be Currency. The Rate field contains a number that is not a currency amount, so its data type should be Number.

Identifying and Removing Redundancy

Redundancy means storing the same fact in more than one place. It usually results from placing too many fields in a table — fields that really belong in separate tables — and often causes serious problems. If you had not realized there were two objects, clients and recruiters, for example, you might have placed all the data in a single Client table. Figure 1–3 shows a portion of this table with some sample data. Notice that the data for a given Recruiter (number, name, address, and so on) occurs on more than one record. The data for Camden Reeves is repeated in the figure.

Client Table

clients of recruiter 24

name of recruiter 24 appears more than once

Client Number	Client Name	Street	...	Recruiter Number	Last Name	First Name	...
AC34	Alys Clinic	134 Central	...	21	Kerry	Alyssa	...
BH72	Berls Hospital	415 Main	...	24	Reeves	Camden	...
BL12	Benton Labs	12 Mountain	...	24	Reeves	Camden	...
...	...	...	...	...	...	...	...

Figure 1–3

Storing this data on multiple records is an example of redundancy, which causes several problems, including:

1. Wasted storage space. The name of Recruiter 24 (Camden Reeves), for example, should be stored only once. Storing this fact several times is wasteful.

2. More difficult database updates. If, for example, Camden Reeves's name is spelled wrong and needs to be changed in the database, his name would need to be changed in several different places.

3. A possibility of inconsistent data. There is nothing to prohibit the recruiter's last name from being Reeves on client BH72's record and Reed on client BL12's record. The data would be inconsistent. In both cases, the recruiter number is 24, but the last names are different.

The solution to the problem is to place the redundant data in a separate table, one in which the data no longer will be redundant. If, for example, you place the data for recruiters in a separate table (Figure 1–4), the data for each recruiter will appear only once.

Client Table

Client Number	Client Name	Street	...	Recruiter Number
AC34	Alys Clinic	134 Central	...	21
BH72	Berls Hospital	415 Main	...	24
BL12	Benton Labs	12 Mountain	...	24
...	...	...	...	...

clients of recruiter 24

Recruiter Table

Recruiter Number	Last Name	First Name	...
21	Kerry	Alyssa	...
24	Reeves	Camden	...
...	...	...	...

name of recruiter 24 appears only once

Figure 1–4

Notice that you need to have the recruiter number in both tables. Without it, there would be no way to tell which recruiter is associated with which client. The remaining recruiter data, however, was removed from the Client table and placed in the Recruiter table. This new arrangement corrects the problems of redundancy in the following ways:

1. Because the data for each recruiter is stored only once, space is not wasted.

2. Changing the name of a recruiter is easy. You have only to change one row in the Recruiter table.

3. Because the data for a recruiter is stored only once, inconsistent data cannot occur. Designing to omit redundancy will help you to produce good and valid database designs.

You should always examine your design to see if it contains redundancy. If it does, you should decide whether you need to remove the redundancy by creating a separate table.

Postal Codes
Some organizations with many customers spread throughout the country will, in fact, have a separate table of postal codes, cities, and states. If you call such an organization to place an order, they typically will ask you for your postal code (or ZIP code), rather than asking for your city, state, and postal code. They then will indicate the city and state that correspond to that postal code and ask you if that is correct.

If you examine your design, you'll see that there is one area of redundancy (see the data in Figure 1–1 on page AC 3). Cities and states are both repeated. Every client whose postal code is 80330, for example, has Berridge as the city and CO as the state. To remove this redundancy, you would create a table whose primary key is Postal Code and that contains City and State as additional fields. City and State would be removed from the Client table. Having City, State, and Postal Code in a table is very common, however, and usually you would not take such action. There is no other redundancy in your tables.

Starting Access

If you are using a computer to step through the project in this chapter, and you want your screen to match the figures in this book, you should change your screen's resolution to 1024 × 768. For information about how to change a computer's resolution, read Appendix E.

Note: If you are using Windows XP, see Appendix F for alternate steps.

To Start Access

The following steps, which assume Windows Vista is running, start Access based on a typical installation. You may need to ask your instructor how to start Access for your computer.

1

- Click the Start button on the Windows Vista taskbar to display the Start menu.

- Click All Programs at the bottom of the left pane on the Start menu to display the All Programs list.

- Click Microsoft Office in the All Programs list to display the Microsoft Office list (Figure 1–5).

Figure 1–5

2

- Click Microsoft Office Access 2007 to start Access and display the Getting Started with Microsoft Office Access screen (Figure 1–6).

- If the Access window is not maximized, click the Maximize button next to the Close button on its title bar to maximize the window.

Q&A

What is a maximized window?

A maximized window fills the entire screen. When you maximize a window, the Maximize button changes to a Restore Down button.

Figure 1–6

Creating a Database

In Access, all the tables, reports, forms, and queries that you create are stored in a single file called a database. Thus, before creating any of these objects, you first must create the database that will hold them. You can use either the Blank Database option or a template to create a new database. If you already know the tables and fields you want in your database, you would use the Blank Database option. If not, you can use a template. Templates can guide you by suggesting some commonly used databases. If you choose to create a database using a template, you would use the following steps.

TO CREATE A DATABASE USING A TEMPLATE

1. If the template you wish to use is not already visible on the Getting Started with Microsoft Office Access page, double-click the links in the Template Categories pane to display the desired template.

2. Click the template you wish to use.

3. Enter a file name (or accept the suggested file name) and select a location for the database.

4. Click the Create button to create the database or the Download button to download the database and create the database, if necessary.

When you create a database, the computer places it on a storage medium, such as a USB flash drive, CD, or hard disk. A saved database is referred to as a **file**. A **file name** is the name assigned to a file when it is saved.

Other Ways

1. Double-click Access icon on desktop, if one is present

2. Click Microsoft Office Access 2007 on Start menu

BTW

Naming Files
File names can be a maximum of 260 characters including the file extension. The file extension for Access 2007 is .accdb. You can use either uppercase or lowercase letters in file names.

Plan Ahead	**Determine where to create the database.** When creating a database, you must decide which storage medium to use. If you always work on the same computer and have no need to transport your database to a different location, then your computer's hard drive will suffice as a storage location. It is a good idea, however, to save a backup copy of your database on a separate medium in case the file becomes corrupted, or the computer's hard drive fails. If you plan to work on your database in various locations or on multiple computers, then you can consider saving your projects on a portable medium, such as a USB flash drive or CD. The projects in this book are stored on a USB flash drive, which saves files quickly and reliably and can be reused. CDs are easily portable and serve as good backups for the final versions of projects because they generally can save files only one time.

To Create a Database

Because you already know the tables and fields you want in the JSP Recruiters database, you would use the Blank Database option rather than using a template. The following steps create a database, using the file name JSP Recruiters, on a USB flash drive.

Note: If you are using Windows XP, see Appendix F for alternate steps.

- With a USB flash drive connected to one of the computer's USB ports, click Blank Database to create a new blank database (Figure 1–7).

Figure 1–7

2

- Repeatedly press the DELETE key to delete the default name of Database1.

- Type `JSP Recruiters` in the File Name text box to replace the default file name of Database1 (your screen may show Database1.accdb). Do not press the ENTER key after typing the file name (Figure 1–8).

Q&A What characters can I use in a file name?

A file name can have a maximum of 260 characters, including spaces. The only invalid characters are the back-slash (\), slash (/), colon (:), asterisk (*), question mark (?), quotation mark ("), less than symbol (<), greater than symbol (>), and vertical bar (|).

3

- Click the 'Browse for a location to put your database' button to display the File New Database dialog box.

- If the Navigation Pane is not displayed in the Save As dialog box, click the Browse Folders button to expand the dialog box.

- If a Folders list is displayed below the Folders button, click the Folders button to remove the Folders list (Figure 1-9).

Q&A Do I have to save to a USB flash drive?

No. You can save to any device or folder. A **folder** is a specific location on a storage medium. You can save to the default folder or a different folder. You also can create your own folders, which is explained later in this book.

Figure 1–8

Figure 1–9

- If Computer is not displayed in the Favorite Links section, drag the top or bottom edge of the Save As dialog box until Computer is displayed.

- Click Computer in the Favorite Links section to display a list of available drives (Figure 1–10).

- If necessary, scroll until UDISK 2.0 (E:) appears in the list of available drives.

Q&A Why is my list of drives arranged and named differently?

The size of the Save As dialog box and your computer's configuration determine how the list is displayed and how the drives are named.

Figure 1–10

Q&A How do I save the file if I am not using a USB flash drive?

Use the same process, but select your desired save location in the Favorite Links section.

- Double-click UDISK 2.0 (E:) in the Computer list to select the USB flash drive, Drive E in this case, as the new save location (Figure 1–11).

Q&A What if my USB flash drive has a different name or letter?

It is very likely that your USB flash drive will have a different name and drive letter and be connected to a different port. Verify that the device in your Computer list is correct.

Figure 1–11

- Click the OK button to select the USB flash drive as the location for the database and to return to the Getting Started with Microsoft Office Access screen (Figure 1–12).

Figure 1–12

7
- Click the Create button to create the database on the USB flash drive with the file name, JSP Recruiters (Figure 1–13).

Q&A

How do I know that the JSP Recruiters database is created?

The name of the database appears in the title bar.

Figure 1–13

8
- If a Field List appears, click its Close button to remove the Field List from the screen (Figure 1–14).

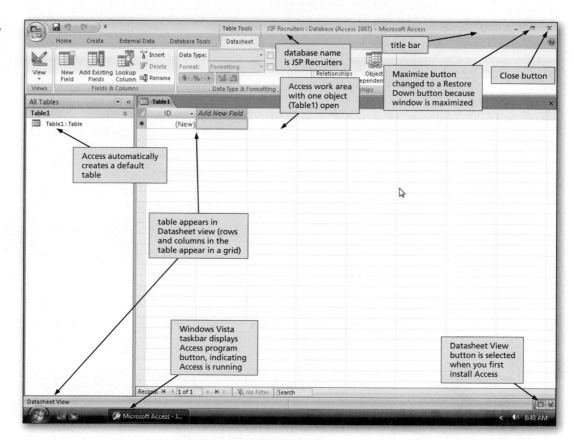

Figure 1–14

The Access Window

The Access window consists of a variety of components to make your work more efficient and documents more professional. These include the Navigation Pane, Access work area, Ribbon, Mini toolbar and shortcut menus, Quick Access Toolbar, and Office Button. Some of these components are common to other Microsoft Office 2007 programs; others are unique to Access.

Other Ways

1. Click Office Button, click Save, type file name, click Computer, select drive or folder, click Save button

2. Press CTRL+S or press SHIFT+F12, type file name, click Computer, select drive or folder, click Save button

Navigation Pane and Access Work Area

You work on objects such as tables, forms, and reports in the **Access work area**. In the work area in Figure 1–14 on the previous page, a single table, Table1, is open in the work area. Figure 1–15 shows a work area with multiple objects open. **Object tabs** for the open objects appear at the top of the work area. You can select one of the open objects by clicking its tab. In the figure, the Client Form is the selected object. To the left of the work area is the Navigation Pane. The Navigation Pane contains a list of all the objects in the database. You use this pane to open an object. You also can customize the way objects are displayed in the Navigation Pane.

Figure 1–15

The Access work area in Figure 1–15 contains an insertion point, mouse pointer, scroll bar, and status bar. Other elements that may appear in the work area are discussed later in this and subsequent chapters.

Insertion Point   The **insertion point** is a blinking vertical bar that indicates where text, graphics, and other items will be inserted. As you type, the insertion point moves to the right.

Mouse Pointer   The **mouse pointer** becomes different shapes depending on the task you are performing in Access and the pointer's location on the screen. The mouse pointer in Figure 1–15 is the shape of an I-beam.

Scroll Bar   You use a **scroll bar** to display different portions of a database object in the Access window. At the right edge of the window is a **vertical scroll bar**. If an object is too wide to fit in the Access window, a **horizontal scroll bar** also appears at the bottom of the window. On a scroll bar, the position of the **scroll box** reflects the location of the portion of the database object that is displayed in the Access window. A **scroll arrow** is located at each end of a scroll bar. To scroll through, or display different portions of the object in the Access window, you can click a scroll arrow or drag the scroll box.

Status Bar   The **status bar**, located at the bottom of the Access window above the Windows Vista taskbar, presents information about the database object, the progress of current tasks, and the status of certain commands and keys; it also provides controls for viewing the object. As you type text or perform certain commands, various indicators may appear on the status bar.

The left edge of the status bar in Figure 1–15 shows that the form object is open in Form view. Toward the right edge are View buttons, which you can use to change the view that is currently displayed.

Ribbon

The **Ribbon**, located near the top of the Access window, is the control center in Access (Figure 1–16a). The Ribbon provides easy, central access to the tasks you perform while creating a database object. The Ribbon consists of tabs, groups, and commands. Each **tab** surrounds a collection of groups, and each group contains related commands.

When you start Access, the Ribbon displays four top-level tabs: Home, Create, External Data, and Database Tools. The **Home tab**, called the primary tab, contains the more frequently used commands. To display a different tab on the Ribbon, click the top-level tab. That is, to display the Create tab, click Create on the Ribbon. To return to the Home tab, click Home on the Ribbon. The tab currently displayed is called the **active tab**.

To allow more space in the Access work area, some users prefer to minimize the Ribbon, which hides the groups on the Ribbon and displays only the top-level tabs (Figure 1–16b). To use commands on a minimized Ribbon, click the top-level tab.

Each time you start Access, the Ribbon appears the same way it did the last time you used Access. The chapters in this book, however, begin with the Ribbon appearing as it did at the initial installation of the software. If you are stepping through this chapter on a computer and you want your Ribbon to match the figures in this book, read Appendix E.

BTW

Minimizing the Ribbon
If you want to minimize the Ribbon, right-click the Ribbon and then click Minimize the Ribbon on the shortcut menu, double-click the active tab, or press CTRL+F1. To restore a minimized Ribbon, right-click the Ribbon and then click Minimize the Ribbon on the shortcut menu, double-click any top-level tab, or press CTRL+F1. To use commands on a minimized Ribbon, click the top-level tab.

(a) Ribbon at Initial Installation (Default Ribbon)

(b) Minimized Ribbon

Figure 1–16

In addition to the top-level tabs, Access displays other tabs, called **contextual tabs**, when you perform certain tasks or work with objects such as datasheets. If you are working with a table in Datasheet view, for example, the Table Tools tab and its related subordinate Datasheet tab appear (Figure 1–17). When you are finished working with the table, the Table Tools and Datasheet tabs disappear from the Ribbon. Access determines when contextual tabs should appear and disappear based on tasks you perform. Some contextual tabs have more than one related subordinate tab.

Figure 1–17

Figure 1–18

Commands on the Ribbon include buttons, boxes (text boxes, check boxes, etc.), and galleries (Figure 1–18). A **gallery** is a set of choices, often graphical, arranged in a grid or in a list. You can scroll through choices on an in-Ribbon gallery by clicking the gallery's scroll arrows. Or, you can click a gallery's More button to view more gallery options on the screen at a time. Some buttons and boxes have arrows that, when clicked, also display a gallery; others always cause a gallery to be displayed when clicked. Many galleries support **live preview**, which is a feature that allows you to point to a gallery choice and see its effect in the database object — without actually selecting the choice.

Some commands on the Ribbon display an image to help you remember their function. When you point to a command on the Ribbon, all or part of the command glows in shades of yellow and orange, and an Enhanced ScreenTip appears on the screen. An **Enhanced ScreenTip** is an on-screen note that provides the name of the command, available keyboard shortcut(s), a description of the command, and sometimes instructions for how to obtain help about the command (Figure 1–19). Enhanced ScreenTips are more detailed than a typical ScreenTip, which usually only displays the name of the command.

The lower-right corner of some groups on the Ribbon has a small arrow, called a **Dialog Box Launcher**, which, when clicked, displays a dialog box or a task pane with additional options for the group (Figure 1–20). When presented with a dialog box, you make selections and must close the dialog box before returning to the database object. A **task pane**, by contrast, is a window that can remain open and visible while you work in the database object.

Figure 1–19

Figure 1–20

Mini Toolbar and Shortcut Menus

The **Mini toolbar**, which appears automatically based on tasks you perform, contains commands related to changing the appearance of text in a database object. All commands on the Mini toolbar also exist on the Ribbon. The purpose of the Mini toolbar is to minimize mouse movement. For example, if you want to use a command that currently is not displayed on the active tab, you can use the command on the Mini toolbar — instead of switching to a different tab to use the command.

When the Mini toolbar appears, it initially is transparent (Figure 1–21a). If you do not use the transparent Mini toolbar, it disappears from the screen. To use the Mini toolbar, move the mouse pointer into the toolbar, which causes the Mini toolbar to change from a transparent to bright appearance (Figure 1–21b).

A **shortcut menu**, which appears when you right-click an object, is a list of frequently used commands that relate to the right-clicked object. When you right-click a table, for example, a shortcut menu appears with commands related to the table (Figure 1–21c).

(a) Transparent Mini Toolbar

(b) Bright Mini Toolbar

(c) Shortcut Menu

Figure 1–21

Quick Access Toolbar

The **Quick Access Toolbar**, located by default above the Ribbon, provides easy access to frequently used commands (Figure 1–22a). The commands on the Quick Access Toolbar always are available, regardless of the task you are performing. Initially, the Quick Access Toolbar contains the Save, Undo, and Redo commands. If you click the Customize Quick Access Toolbar button, Access provides a list of commands you quickly can add to and remove from the Quick Access Toolbar (Figure 1–22b).

You also can add other commands to or delete commands from the Quick Access Toolbar so that it contains the commands you use most often. As you add commands to the Quick Access Toolbar, its commands may interfere with the title of the database object on the title bar. For this reason, Access provides an option of displaying the Quick Access Toolbar below the Ribbon (Figure 1–22c).

Figure 1–22

Each time you start Access, the Quick Access Toolbar appears the same way it did the last time you used Access. The chapters in this book, however, begin with the Quick Access Toolbar appearing as it did at the initial installation of the software. If you are stepping through this chapter on a computer, and you want your Quick Access Toolbar to match the figures in this book, you should reset your Quick Access Toolbar. For more information about how to reset the Quick Access Toolbar, read Appendix E.

Office Button

While the Ribbon is a control center for creating database objects, the **Office Button** is a central location for managing and sharing database objects. When you click the Office Button, located in the upper-left corner of the window, Access displays the Office Button menu (Figure 1–23). A **menu** contains a list of commands.

When you click the New, Open, and Print commands on the Office Button menu, Access displays a dialog box with additional options. The Save As, Print, Manage, and Publish commands have an arrow to their right. If you point to this arrow, Access displays a **submenu**, which is a list of additional commands associated with the selected command (Figure 1–24). For the Save As, Print, Manage, and Publish commands that do not display a dialog box when clicked, you can point either to the command or the arrow to display the submenu.

Figure 1–23

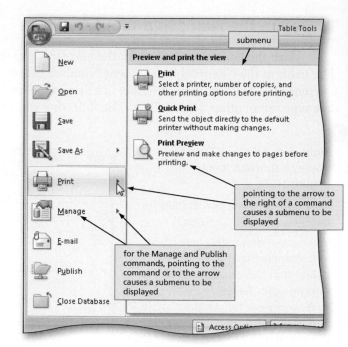

Figure 1–24

Key Tips

If you prefer using the keyboard instead of the mouse, you can press the ALT key on the keyboard to display a **Key Tip badge**, or keyboard code icon, for certain commands (Figure 1–25). To select a command using the keyboard, press its displayed code letter, or **Key Tip**. When you press a Key Tip, additional Key Tips related to the selected command may appear. For example, to select the New command on the Office Button menu, press the ALT key, then press the F key, then press the N key.

To remove the Key Tip badges from the screen, press the ALT key or the ESC key until all Key Tip badges disappear, or click the mouse anywhere in the Access window.

Figure 1–25

Creating a Table

When you first create your database, Access automatically creates a table for you. You can immediately begin defining the fields. If, for whatever reason, you do not have this table or inadvertently delete it, you can create the table by clicking Create on the Ribbon and then clicking the Table button on the Create tab. In either case, you are ready to define the fields.

To Define the Fields in a Table

With the table already created, the next step is to define the fields in the table and to assign them data types. The fields in the Client table are Client Number, Client Name, Street, City, State, Postal Code, Amount Paid, Current Due, and Recruiter Number. The data type for the Amount Paid and Current Due fields is Currency. The data type for all other fields is Text. The following steps define the fields in the table.

- Right-click Add New Field to display a shortcut menu (Figure 1–26).

Q&A Why don't I delete the ID field first, before adding other fields?

You cannot delete the primary key in Datasheet view; you only can delete it in Design view. After adding the other fields, you will move to Design view, delete the ID field, and then make the Client Number the primary key.

Q&A Why does my shortcut menu look different?

You right-clicked within the column instead of right-clicking the column heading.

Figure 1–26

- Click Rename Column on the shortcut menu to display an insertion point.

- Type Client Number to assign a name to the new field.

- Press the DOWN ARROW key to complete the addition of the field (Figure 1–27).

Q&A Why doesn't the whole name appear?

The default column size is not large enough for Client Number to appear in its entirety. Later in this book, you will learn how to resize columns so that the entire name can appear.

Figure 1–27

3

- Right-click Add New Field to display a shortcut menu, click Rename Column on the shortcut menu to display an insertion point, type `Client Name` to assign a name to the new field, and then press the DOWN ARROW key to complete the addition of the field.

Did I have to press the DOWN ARROW key? Couldn't I have just moved to the next field or pressed the ENTER key?

You could have pressed the TAB key or the ENTER key to move to the column heading for the next field. Pressing the DOWN ARROW key, however, completes the entry of the Client Number field and allows you to ensure that the column is assigned the correct data type.

- Using the same technique add the fields in the Client table up through and including the Amount Paid field.

- Click the Data Type box arrow to display the Data Type box menu (Figure 1–28).

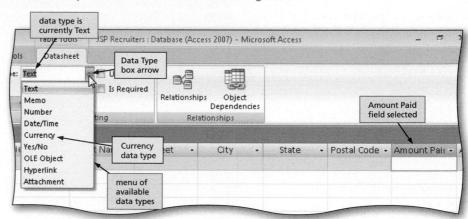

Figure 1–28

4

- Click Currency to select Currency as the data type for the Amount Paid field (Figure 1–29).

Why does Currency appear twice?

The second Currency is the format, which indicates how the data will be displayed. For the Currency data type, Access automatically sets the format to Currency, which is usually what you would want. You could change it to something else, if desired, by clicking the arrow and selecting the desired format.

Figure 1–29

5

- Click the right scroll arrow to shift the fields to the left and display the Add New Field column (Figure 1–30).

Figure 1–30

6

- Make the remaining entries from the Client table structure shown in Figure 1–31 to complete the structure. Be sure to select Currency as the data type for the Current Due field.

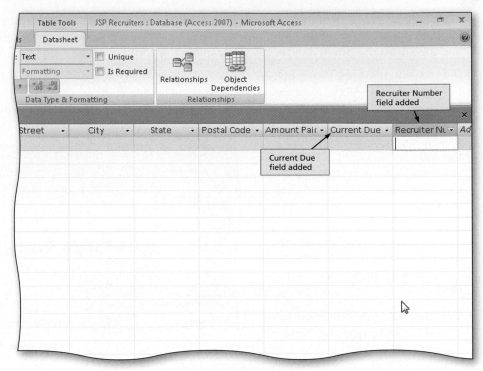

Figure 1–31

BTW

Creating a Table: Table Templates
Access includes table templates that assist you in creating some commonly used tables and fields. To use a template, click Create on the Ribbon and then click the Table Templates button on the Create tab. Click the desired template, make any adjustments you wish to the table that Access creates, and then save the table.

Making Changes to the Structure

When creating a table, check the entries carefully to ensure they are correct. If you discover a mistake while still typing the entry, you can correct the error by repeatedly pressing the BACKSPACE key until the incorrect characters are removed. Then, type the correct characters. If you do not discover a mistake until later, you can use the following techniques to make the necessary changes to the structure:

- To undo your most recent change, click the Undo button on the Quick Access Toolbar. If there is nothing that Access can undo, this button will be dim, and clicking it will have no effect.

- To delete a field, right-click the column heading for the field (the position containing the field name), and then click Delete Column on the shortcut menu.

- To change the name of a field, right-click the column heading for the field, click Rename Column on the shortcut menu, and then type the desired field name.

- To insert a field as the last field, right-click the Add New Field column heading, click Rename Column on the shortcut menu, type the desired field name, click the down arrow, and then ensure the correct data type is already selected.

- To insert a field between existing fields, right-click the column heading for the field that will follow the new field, and then click Insert Column on the shortcut menu. You then proceed just as you do when you insert a field as the last field.

As an alternative to these steps, you may want to start over. To do so, click the Close button for the window containing the table, and then click the No button in the Microsoft Office Access dialog box. Click Create on the Ribbon and then click the Table button to create a table. You then can repeat the process you used earlier to define the fields in the table.

To Save a Table

The Client table structure now is complete. The final step is to save and close the table within the database. At this time, you should give the table a name.

The following steps save the table, giving it the name, Client.

1

- Click the Save button on the Quick Access Toolbar to save the structure of the table (Figure 1–32).

Q&A

I have an extra row between the row containing the field names and the row that begins with the asterisk. What happened? Is this a problem? If so, how do I fix it?

You inadvertently added a record to the table by pressing some key after you pressed the DOWN ARROW key. Even pressing the Spacebar would add a record. You now have a record you do not want and it will cause problems when you attempt to assign a different primary key. To fix it, you need to delete the record, which you will do in Step 3.

Figure 1–32

2

- Type Client to change the name to be assigned to the table (Figure 1–33).

Figure 1–33

3

- Click the OK button to save the structure with the name, Client (Figure 1–34).

- If you have an additional record between the field names and the asterisk, click the record selector (the box at the beginning of the record), press the DELETE key, and then click the Yes button when Access asks you if you want to delete the record.

Figure 1–34

Other Ways
1. Click Office Button, click Save on the Office Button menu
2. Right-click tab for table, click Save on shortcut menu
3. Press CTRL+S

To Change the Primary Key

To change the primary key, you must first delete the ID field that Access created automatically. You then can designate the Client Number field as the primary key. To delete the ID field, the table must appear in Design view rather than Datasheet view. You also can designate the Client Number field as the primary key within Design view. As you define or modify the fields, the **row selector**, the small box or bar that, when you click it, selects the entire row, indicates the field you currently are describing. The following steps move to Design view and then change the primary key.

- Click the Design View button on the status bar to move to Design view.

- Confirm that your data types match those shown in the figure. Make any necessary corrections to the data types (Figure 1-35).

Q&A

Did I have to save the table before moving to Design view?

Yes. If you had not saved it yourself, Access would have asked you to save it.

Figure 1–35

- Click the row selector for the ID field to select the field.

- Press the DELETE key to delete the field (Figure 1–36).

Q&A

What if I click the row selector for the wrong field before pressing the DELETE key?

Click the No button in the Microsoft Office Access dialog box. If you inadvertently clicked the Yes button, you have deleted the wrong field. You can fix this by clicking the Close button for the Client table, and then clicking the No button when asked if you want to save your changes.

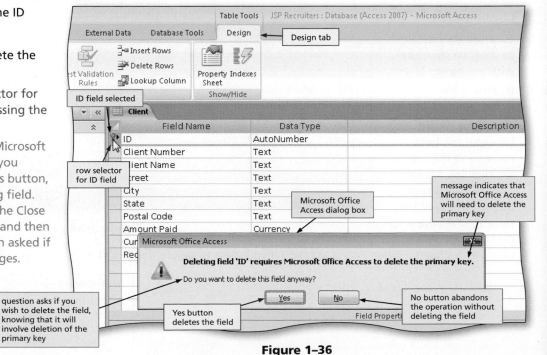

Figure 1–36

❸

- Click the Yes button to complete the deletion of the field.

- With the Client Number field selected, click the Primary Key button to designate the Client Number field as the primary key.

- Click the Save button to save the changes (Figure 1–37).

Q&A

When I attempted to save the table I got an error message that indicates index or primary key cannot contain a null value. What did I do wrong and how do I fix it?

You inadvertently added a record to the table by pressing some key after you pressed the DOWN ARROW key. To fix it, click the OK button (you will need to do it twice) and then click the Primary Key button to remove the primary key. Click the Save button to save the table and then click the View button near the upper-left corner of the screen to return to datasheet view. Click the little box immediately to the left of the record you added and press the DELETE key. Click the Yes button when Access asks if it is OK to delete the record. Click the View button again and continue with these steps.

Figure 1–37

❹

- Close the Client table by clicking the Close 'Client' button (Figure 1–38).

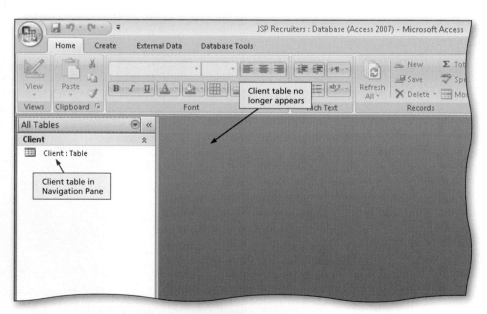

Figure 1–38

To Add Records to a Table

Creating a table by building the structure and saving the table is the first step in a two-step process. The second step is to add records to the table. To add records to a table, the table must be open. When making changes to tables, you work in Datasheet view. In **Datasheet view**, the table is represented as a collection of rows and columns called a **datasheet**.

You often add records in phases. You may, for example, not have enough time to add all the records in one session. The following steps open the Client table in Datasheet view and then add the first two records in the Client table (Figure 1–39).

Client Numb ▾	Client Name ▾	Street ▾	City ▾	State ▾	Postal Code ▾	Amount Paic ▾	Current Due ▾	Recruiter Nu ▾
AC34	Alys Clinic	134 Central	Berridge	CO	80330	$0.00	$17,500.00	21
BH72	Berls Hospital	415 Main	Berls	CO	80349	$29,200.00	$0.00	24

Figure 1–39

● Right-click the Client table in the Navigation Pane to display the shortcut menu (Figure 1–40).

Figure 1–40

2

- Click Open on the shortcut menu to open the Client table in Datasheet view.

What if I want to return to Design view?

There are two ways to get to Design view. You could click Design View on the shortcut menu. Alternatively, you could click Open on the shortcut menu to open the table in Datasheet view and then click the Design View button on the Access status bar.

- Click the Shutter Bar Open/Close Button to hide the Navigation Pane (Figure 1–41).

Figure 1–41

3

- Click in the Client Number field and type AC34 to enter the first client number. Be sure you type the letters in uppercase so they are entered in the database correctly (Figure 1–42).

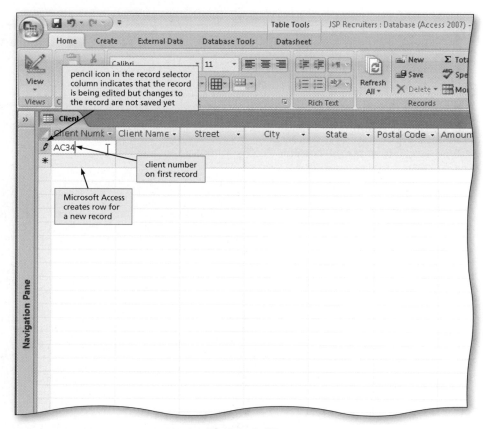

Figure 1–42

4

- Press the TAB key to complete the entry for the Client Number field.

- Enter the client name, street, city, state, and postal code by typing the following entries, pressing the TAB key after each one: Alys Clinic as the client name, 134 Central as the street, Berridge as the city, CO as the state, and 80330 as the postal code.

- Type 0 to enter the amount paid (Figure 1–43).

 Q&A Do I need to type a dollar sign?

You do not need to type dollar signs or commas. In addition, because the digits to the right of the decimal point are both zeros, you do not need to type either the decimal point or the zeros.

Figure 1–43

5

- Press the TAB key to complete the entry for the Amount Paid field.

- Type 17500 to enter the current due amount and then press the TAB key to move to the next field.

- Type 21 as the Recruiter number to complete data entry for the record (Figure 1–44).

Figure 1–44

6

- Press the TAB key to complete the entry of the first record (Figure 1–45).

How and when do I save the record?

As soon as you have entered or modified a record and moved to another record, the original record is saved. This is different from other applications. The rows entered in an Excel worksheet, for example, are not saved until the entire worksheet is saved.

Figure 1–45

7

- Use the techniques shown in Steps 3 through 6 to enter the data for the second record in the Client table (Figure 1–46).

Figure 1–46

Undo and Redo
You also can undo multiple actions. To see a list of recent actions that you can undo, click the down arrow next to the Undo button on the Quick Access Toolbar. To redo the most recent action, click the Redo button on the Quick Access Toolbar. You also can redo multiple actions by clicking the down arrow next to the button.

Cut, Copy, and Paste
Just as in other Office applications, you can use buttons in the Clipboard group on the Home tab to cut, copy, and paste data. To cut data, select the data to be cut and click the Cut button. To copy data, select the data and click the Copy button. To paste data, select the desired location and click the Paste button.

AutoCorrect Options
Using the Office AutoCorrect feature, you can create entries that will replace abbreviations with spelled-out names and phrases automatically. For example, you can create the abbreviated entry *dbms* for *database management system*. Whenever you type dbms followed by a space or punctuation mark, Access automatically replaces dbms with database management system. To specify AutoCorrect rules and exceptions to the rules, click Access Options on the Office Button menu and then click Proofing in the Access Options dialog box.

Making Changes to the Data

Check your entries carefully to ensure they are correct. If you make a mistake and discover it before you press the TAB key, correct it by pressing the BACKSPACE key until the incorrect characters are removed and then typing the correct characters. If you do not discover a mistake until later, you can use the following techniques to make the necessary corrections to the data:

- To undo your most recent change, click the Undo button on the Quick Access Toolbar. If there is nothing that Access can undo, this button will be dim, and clicking it will have no effect.

- To add a record, click the New (blank) record button, shown in Figure 1–46 on the previous page, and then add the record. Do not worry about it being in the correct position in the table. Access will reposition the record based on the primary key, in this case, the Client Number.

- To delete a record, click the Record selector, shown in Figure 1–46, for the record to be deleted. Then press the DELETE key to delete the record, and click the Yes button when Access asks you to verify that you do indeed wish to delete the record.

- To change the contents of one or more fields in a record, the record must be on the screen. If it is not, use any appropriate technique, such as the UP ARROW and DOWN ARROW keys or the vertical scroll bar, to move to it. If the field you want to correct is not visible on the screen, use the horizontal scroll bar along the bottom of the screen to shift all the fields until the one you want appears. If the value in the field is currently highlighted, you can simply type the new value. If you would rather edit the existing value, you must have an insertion point in the field. You can place the insertion point by clicking in the field or by pressing F2. Once you have produced an insertion point, you can use the arrow keys, the DELETE key, and the BACKSPACE key in making the correction. You also can use the INSERT key to switch between Insert and Overtype mode. When you have made the change, press the TAB key to move to the next field.

If you cannot determine how to correct the data, you may find that you are "stuck" on the record. Access neither allows you to move to any other record until you have made the correction, nor allows you to close the table. If you encounter this situation, simply press the ESC key. Pressing the ESC key will remove from the screen the record you are trying to add. You then can move to any other record, close the table, or take any other action you desire.

AutoCorrect

Not visible in the Access window, the **AutoCorrect** feature of Access works behind the scenes, correcting common mistakes when you complete a text entry in a cell. AutoCorrect makes three types of corrections for you:

1. Corrects two initial capital letters by changing the second letter to lowercase.

2. Capitalizes the first letter in the names of days.

3. Replaces commonly misspelled words with their correct spelling. For example, it changes the misspelled word *recieve* to *receive* when you complete the entry. AutoCorrect will correct the spelling automatically of more than 400 commonly misspelled words.

To Close a Table

It is a good idea to close a table as soon as you have finished working with it. It keeps the screen from getting cluttered and prevents you from making accidental changes to the data in the table. The following steps close the Client table.

- Click the Close 'Client' button, shown in Figure 1–46 on page AC 33, to close the table (Figure 1–47).

Figure 1–47

Other Ways

1. Right-click tab for table, click Close on shortcut menu

Quitting Access

If you save the object on which you are currently working and then quit Access, all Access windows close. If you have made changes to an object since the last time the object was saved, Access displays a dialog box asking if you want to save the changes you made before it closes that window. The dialog box contains three buttons with these resulting actions:

- Yes button — Saves the changes and then quits Access
- No button — Quits Access without saving changes
- Cancel button — Closes the dialog box and redisplays the database without saving the changes

If no changes have been made to any object since the last time the object was saved, Access will close all windows without displaying any dialog boxes.

To Quit Access

You saved your changes to the table and did not make any additional changes. You are ready to quit Access. The following step quits Access.

1 Click the Close button on the right side of the Access title bar, shown in Figure 1–47 on the previous page, to quit Access.

Starting Access and Opening a Database

Once you have created and later closed a database, you will need to open it in the future in order to use it. Opening a database requires that Access is running on your computer.

Note: If you are using Windows XP, see Appendix F for alternate steps.

To Start Access

The following steps, which assume Windows Vista is running, start Access.

1 Click the Start button on the Windows Vista taskbar to display the Start menu.

2 Click All Programs at the bottom of the left pane on the Start menu to display the All Programs list and then click Microsoft Office in the All Programs list to display the Microsoft Office list.

3 Click Microsoft Office Access 2007 on the Microsoft Office submenu to start Access and display the Getting Started with Microsoft Office Access window (Figure 1–48).

4 If the Access window is not maximized, click the Maximize button on its title bar to maximize the window.

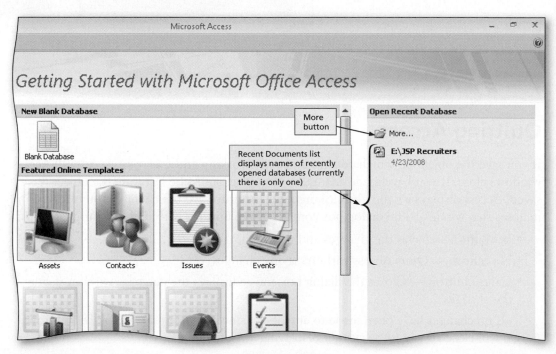

Figure 1–48

To Open a Database from Access

Note: If you are using Windows XP, see Appendix F for alternate steps.

Earlier in this chapter you created your database on a USB flash drive using the file name, JSP Recruiters. There are two ways to open the file containing your database. If the file you created appears in the Recent Documents list, you could click it to open the file. If not, you can use the More button to open the file. The following steps use the More button to open the JSP Recruiters database from the USB flash drive.

1

- With your USB flash drive connected to one of the computer's USB ports, click the More button, shown in Figure 1–48, to display the Open dialog box.

- If the Folders list is displayed below the Folders button, click the Folders button to remove the Folders list.

- If necessary, click Computer in the Favorite Links section.

- Double-click UDISK 2.0 (E:) to select the USB flash drive, Drive E in this case, as the new open location.

- Click JSP Recruiters to select the file name (Figure 1–49).

 Q&A How do I open the file if I am not using a USB flash drive?

Use the same process, but be certain to select your device in the Look in list. You might need to open multiple folders.

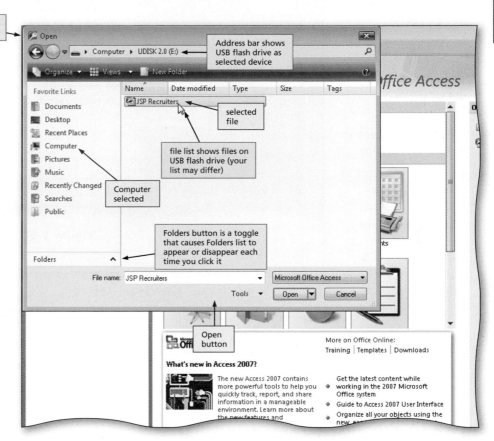

Figure 1–49

2

- Click the Open button to open the database (Figure 1–50).

Q&A Why do I see the Access icon and name on the Windows Vista taskbar?

When you open an Access database, an Access program button is displayed on the taskbar. If the contents of a button cannot fit in the allotted button space, an ellipsis appears. If you point to a program button, its entire contents appear in a ScreenTip, which in this case would be the program name followed by the file name.

Figure 1–50

- If a Security Warning appears, as shown in Figure 1–50 on the previous page, click the Options button to display the Microsoft Office Security Options dialog box (Figure 1–51).

- Click the 'Enable this content' option button.

- Click the OK button to enable the content.

Q&A When would I want to disable the content?

You would want to disable the content if you suspected that your database might contain harmful content or damaging macros. Because you are the one who created the database and no one else has used it, you should have no such suspicions.

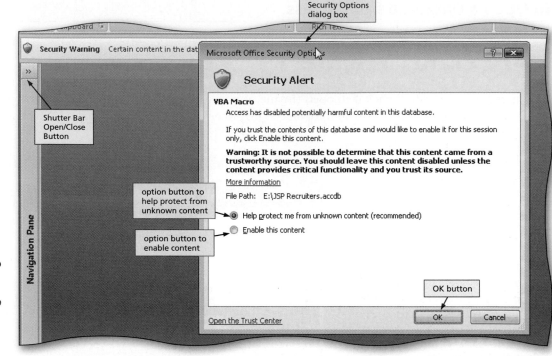

Figure 1–51

Other Ways

1. Click Office Button, double-click file name in Recent Documents list

2. Press CTRL+O, select file name, press ENTER

To Add Additional Records to a Table

You can add records to a table that already contains data using a process almost identical to that used to add records to an empty table. The only difference is that you place the insertion point after the last data record before you enter the additional data. To do so, use the **Navigation buttons**, which are buttons used to move within a table, found near the lower-left corner of the screen when a table is open. The purpose of each of the Navigation buttons is described in Table 1–2.

Table 1–2 Navigation Buttons in Datasheet View	
Button	**Purpose**
First record	Moves to the first record in the table
Previous record	Moves to the previous record
Next record	Moves to the next record
Last record	Moves to the last record in the table
New (blank) record	Moves to the end of the table to a position for entering a new record

The following steps add the remaining records (Figure 1–52) to the Client table.

Client Numb ▾	Client Name ▾	Street ▾	City ▾	State ▾	Postal Code ▾	Amount Paic ▾	Current Due ▾	Recruiter Nu ▾
BL12	Benton Labs	12 Mountain	Denton	CO	80412	$16,500.00	$38,225.00	24
EA45	ENT Assoc.	867 Ridge	Fort Stewart	CO	80336	$12,750.00	$15,000.00	27
FD89	Ferb Dentistry	34 Crestview	Berridge	CO	80330	$21,000.00	$12,500.00	21
FH22	Family Health	123 Second	Tarleton	CO	80409	$0.00	$0.00	24
MH56	Maun Hospital	76 Dixon	Mason	CO	80356	$0.00	$43,025.00	24
PR11	Peel Radiology	151 Valleyview	Fort Stewart	CO	80336	$31,750.00	$0.00	21
TC37	Tarleton Clinic	451 Hull	Tarleton	CO	80409	$18,750.00	$31,500.00	27
WL56	West Labs	785 Main	Berls	CO	80349	$14,000.00	$0.00	24

Figure 1–52

1

- If the Navigation Pane is hidden, click the Shutter Bar Open/Close Button, shown in Figure 1–51, to show the Navigation Pane (Figure 1–53).

Figure 1–53

2

- Right-click the Client table in the Navigation Pane to display a shortcut menu.

- Click Open on the shortcut menu to open the Client table in Datasheet view.

- Hide the Navigation Pane by clicking the Shutter Bar Open/Close button (Figure 1–54).

Figure 1–54

- Click the New (blank) record button to move to a position to enter a new record (Figure 1–55).

Q&A

Why click the New (blank) record button? Could you just click the Client Number on the first open record and then add the record?

You could click the Client Number on the first open record, provided that record appears on the screen. With only two records in the table, this is not a problem. Once a table contains more records than will fit on the screen, it is easier to click the New (blank) record button.

Figure 1–55

- Add the records shown in Figure 1–52 on the previous page, using the same techniques you used to add the first two records (Figure 1–56).

- Click the Close 'Client' button to close the table.

Figure 1–56

Other Ways

1. Click New button in Records group on Ribbon
2. Press CTRL+PLUS SIGN (+)

Previewing and Printing the Contents of a Table

When working with a database, you often will need to print a copy of the table contents. Figure 1–57 shows a printed copy of the contents of the Client table. (Yours may look slightly different, depending on your printer.) Because the Client table is wider substantially than the screen, it also will be wider than the normal printed page in portrait orientation. **Portrait orientation** means the printout is across the width of the page.

Client Number	Client Name	Street	City	State	Postal Code	Amount Paid	Current Due	Recruiter Numb
AC34	Alys Clinic	134 Central	Berridge	CO	80330	$0.00	$17,500.00	21
BH72	Berls Hospital	415 Main	Berls	CO	80349	$29,200.00	$0.00	24
BL12	Benton Labs	12 Mountain	Denton	CO	80412	$16,500.00	$38,225.00	24
EA45	ENT Assoc.	867 Ridge	Fort Stewart	CO	80336	$12,750.00	$15,000.00	27
FD89	Ferb Dentistry	34 Crestview	Berridge	CO	80330	$21,000.00	$12,500.00	21
FH22	Family Health	123 Second	Tarleton	CO	80409	$0.00	$0.00	24
MH56	Maun Hospital	76 Dixon	Mason	CO	80356	$0.00	$43,025.00	24
PR11	Peel Radiology	151 Valleyview	Fort Stewart	CO	80336	$31,750.00	$0.00	21
TC37	Tarleton Clinic	451 Hull	Tarleton	CO	80409	$18,750.00	$31,500.00	27
WL56	West Labs	785 Main	Berls	CO	80349	$14,000.00	$0.00	24

Client   4/23/2008

Figure 1–57

Landscape orientation means the printout is across the length (height) of the page. Thus, to print the wide database table, use landscape orientation. If you are printing the contents of a table that fit on the screen, you will not need landscape orientation. A convenient way to change to landscape orientation is to preview what the printed copy will look like by using Print Preview. This allows you to determine whether landscape orientation is necessary and, if it is, to change the orientation easily to landscape. In addition, you also can use Print Preview to determine whether any adjustments are necessary to the page margins.

To Preview and Print the Contents of a Table

The following steps use Print Preview to preview and then print the Client table.

1

- If the Navigation Pane is hidden, show the Navigation Pane by clicking the Shutter Bar Open/Close Button.

- Be sure the Client table is selected (Figure 1–58).

Q&A | Why do I have to be sure the Client table is selected? It is the only object in the database.

Figure 1–58

There is no issue when the database contains only one object. Ensuring that the correct object is selected is a good habit to form, however, to make sure that the object you print is the one you want.

2

- Click the Office Button to display the Office Button menu.

- Point to the Print command arrow to display the Print submenu (Figure 1–59).

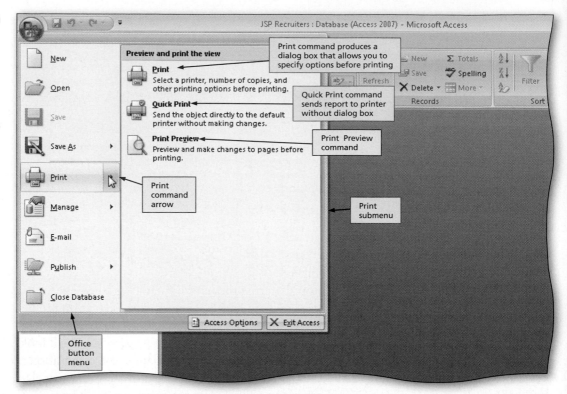

Figure 1–59

3

- Click Print Preview on the Print submenu to display a preview of the report (Figure 1–60).

Q&A

I can't read the report. Can I magnify a portion of the report?

Yes. Point the mouse pointer, whose shape will change to a magnifying glass, at the portion of the report that you wish to magnify, and then click. You can return the view of the report to the one shown in the figure by clicking a second time.

Figure 1–60

4

- Click the mouse pointer in the position shown in Figure 1–60 to magnify the upper-right section of the report (Figure 1–61).

My report was already magnified in a different area. How can I see the area shown in the figure?

There are two ways. You can use the scroll bars to move to the desired portion of the report. You also can click the mouse pointer anywhere in the report to produce a screen like the one in Figure 1–60, and then click in the location shown in the figure.

Figure 1–61

5

- Click the Landscape button to change to landscape orientation (Figure 1–62).

6

- Click the Print button on the Print Preview tab to print the report.

- When the printer stops, retrieve the hard copy of the Client table.

- Click the Close 'Client' button to close the Print Preview window.

How can I print multiple copies of my document other than clicking the Print button multiple times?

Click the Office Button, point to the arrow next to Print on the Office Button menu, click Print on the Print submenu, increase the number in the Number of Copies: box, and then click the OK button.

How can I print a range of pages rather than printing the whole report?

Click the Office Button, point to the arrow next to Print on the Office Button menu, click Print on the Print submenu, click the Pages option button in the Print Range box, enter the desired page range, and then click the OK button.

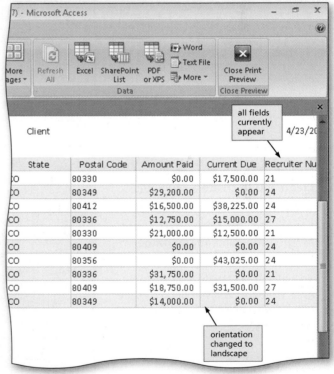

Figure 1–62

Other Ways

1. Press CTRL+P, press ENTER

Creating Additional Tables

The JSP Recruiters database contains two tables, the Client table and the Recruiter table. You need to create the Recruiter table and add records to it. Because you already used the default table that Access created when you created the database, you will need to first create the table. You can then add fields as you did with the Client table.

To Create an Additional Table

The fields to be added are Recruiter Number, Last Name, First Name, Street, City, State, Postal Code, Rate, and Commission. The data type for the Rate field is Number, and the data type for the Commission field is Currency. The data type for all other fields is Text. The following steps create the Recruiter table.

- Click Create on the Ribbon to display the Create tab (Figure 1–63).

Figure 1–63

- Click the Table button on the Create tab to create a new table (Figure 1–64).

Q&A

Could I save the table now so I can assign it the name I want, rather than Table1?

You certainly can. Be aware, however, that you will still need to save it again once you have added all your fields.

Figure 1–64

3

- Right-click Add New Field to display a shortcut menu.

- Click Rename Column on the short-cut menu to display an insertion point.

- Type Recruiter Number to assign a name to the new field.

- Press the DOWN ARROW key to com-plete the addition of the field.

- Using the same technique, add the Last Name, First Name, Street, City, State, Postal Code, and Rate fields.

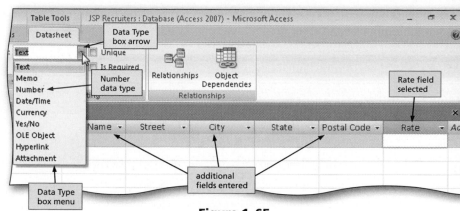

Figure 1–65

- Click the Data Type box arrow to display the Data Type box menu (Figure 1–65).

4

- Click Number on the Data Type box menu to select the Number data type and assign the Number data type to the Rate field.

- Add the Commission field and assign it the Currency data type.

- Click the Save button to display the Save As dialog box (Figure 1–66).

Figure 1–66

- Type Recruiter to assign a name to the table.

- Click the OK button (Figure 1–67).

Figure 1–67

To Modify the Primary Key and Field Properties

Fields whose data type is Number often require you to change the field size. Table 1–3 shows the possible field sizes for Number fields.

Table 1–3 Field Sizes for Number Fields	
Field Size	**Description**
Byte	Integer value in the range of 0 to 255.
Integer	Integer value in the range of -32,768 to 32,767.
Long Integer	Integer value in the range of -2,147,483,648 to 2,147,483,647.
Single	Numeric values with decimal places to seven significant digits — requires four bytes of storage.
Double	Numeric values with decimal places to more accuracy than Single — requires eight bytes of storage.
Replication ID	Special identifier required for replication.
Decimal	Numeric values with decimal places to more accuracy than Single — requires 12 bytes of storage.

Because the values in the Rate field have decimal places, only Single, Double, or Decimal would be possible choices. The difference between these choices concerns the amount of accuracy. Double is more accurate than Single, for example, but requires more storage space. Because the rates are only two decimal places, Single is a perfectly acceptable choice.

In addition to changing the field size, you should also change the format to Fixed (a fixed number of decimal places) and the number of decimal places to 2.

The following steps move to Design view, delete the ID field, and make the Recruiter Number field the primary key. They then change the field size of the Rate field to Single, the format to Fixed, and the number of decimal places to 2.

1

- Click the Design View button on the status bar to move to Design view (Figure 1–68).

Figure 1–68

2

- Click the row selector for the ID field to select the field.

- Press the DELETE key to delete the field.

- Click the Yes button to complete the deletion of the field.

- With the Recruiter Number field selected, click the Primary Key button to designate the Recruiter Number field as the primary key.

- Click the row selector for the Rate field to select the field (Figure 1–69).

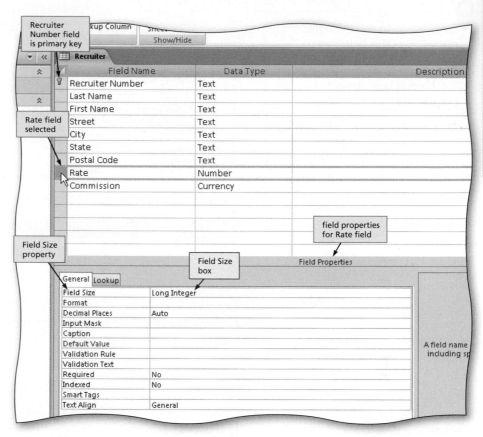

Figure 1–69

3

- Click the Field Size box to display the Field Size box arrow.

- Click the Field Size box arrow to display the Field Size box menu (Figure 1–70).

 Q&A

What would happen if I left the field size set to Integer?

If the field size is Integer, no decimal places can be stored. Thus a value of .10 would be stored as 0. If you enter your rates and the values all appear as 0, chances are you did not change the field size.

Figure 1–70

4

- Click Single to select single precision as the field size.

- Click the Format box to display the Format box arrow (Figure 1–71).

- Click the Format box arrow to open the Format box menu.

Figure 1–71

5

- Click Fixed to select fixed as the format.

- Click the Decimal Places box to display the Decimal Places box arrow.

- Click the Decimal Places box arrow to enter the number of decimal places.

- Click 2 to select 2 as the number of decimal places.

- Click the Save button to save your changes (Figure 1–72).

Q&A

What is the purpose of the error checking button?

You changed the number of decimal places. The error checking button gives you a quick way of making the same change everywhere Rate appears. So far, you have not added any data, nor have you created any forms or reports that use the Rate field, so no such changes are necessary.

Figure 1–72

6

- Close the Recruiter table by clicking the Close 'Recruiter' button (Figure 1–73).

Figure 1–73

To Add Records to an Additional Table

The following steps add the records shown in Figure 1–74 to the Recruiter table.

Recruiter Nu ▾	Last Name ▾	First Name ▾	Street ▾	City ▾	State ▾	Postal Code ▾	Rate ▾	Commission ▾
21	Kerry	Alyssa	261 Pointer	Tourin	CO	80416	0.10	$17,600.00
24	Reeves	Camden	3135 Brill	Denton	CO	80412	0.10	$19,900.00
27	Fernandez	Jaime	265 Maxwell	Charleston	CO	80380	0.09	$9,450.00
34	Lee	Jan	1827 Oak	Denton	CO	80413	0.08	$0.00

Figure 1–74

- Open the Recruiter table in Datasheet view by right-clicking the Recruiter table in the Navigation Pane and then clicking Open on the shortcut menu.

- Enter the Recruiter data from Figure 1–74 (Figure 1–75).

Experiment

- Click in the Rate field on any of the records. Be sure the Datasheet tab is selected. Click the Format box arrow and then click each of the formats in the Format box menu to see the effect on the values in the Rate field. When finished, click Fixed in the Format box menu.

Figure 1–75

- Click the Close 'Recruiter' button to close the table and remove the datasheet from the screen.

Creating a Report

JSP Recruiters needs the following reports. You will create the four reports shown in Figure 1–76 in this section.

Figure 1–76

To Create a Report

You will first create the report shown in Figure 1–76a. The records in the report are sorted (ordered) by Client Number. To ensure that the records appear in this order, you will specify that the records are to be sorted on the Client Number field. The following steps create the report in Figure 1–76a.

❶

- Be sure the Client table is selected in the Navigation Pane.

- Click Create on the Ribbon to display the Create tab.

- Click the Report Wizard button to display the Report Wizard dialog box (Figure 1–77).

Q&A What would have happened if the Recruiter table were selected instead of the Client table?

The list of available fields would have contained fields from the Recruiter table rather than the Client table.

Q&A If the list contained Recruiter table fields, how could I make it contain Client table fields?

Click the arrow in the Tables/Queries box and then click the Client table in the list that appears.

Figure 1–77

❷

- Click the Add Field button to add the Client Number field.

- Click the Add Field button to add the Client Name field.

- Click the Amount Paid field, and then click the Add Field button to add the Amount Paid field.

- Click the Add Field button to add the Current Due field.

- Click the Add Field button to add the Recruiter Number field (Figure 1–78).

Figure 1–78

3

• Click the Next button to display the next Report Wizard screen (Figure 1–79).

Q&A

What is grouping?

Grouping means creating separate collections of records sharing some common characteristic. For example, you might want to group clients in the same Postal code or that have the same recruiter.

Q&A

What if I realize that I have selected the wrong fields?

You can click the Back button to return to the previous screen and then correct the list of fields. You also could click the Cancel button and start over.

Figure 1–79

4

• Because you will not specify any grouping, click the Next button in the Report Wizard dialog box to display the next Report Wizard screen.

• Click the box arrow in the text box labeled 1 to display a list of available fields for sorting (Figure 1–80).

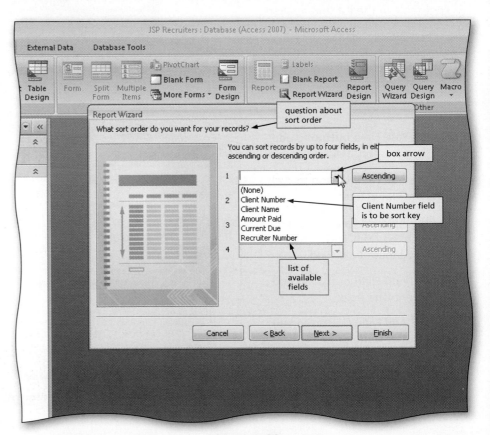

Figure 1–80

5

- Click the Client Number field to select the field as the sort key (Figure 1–81).

What if I want Descending order?

Click the Ascending button next to the sort key to change Ascending order to Descending. If you decide you want Ascending after all, click the button a second time.

Figure 1–81

6

- Click the Next button to display the next Report Wizard screen (Figure 1–82).

 Experiment

- Click different layouts and orientations and observe the effect on the sample report. When you have finished experimenting, click the Tabular option button for the layout and the Portrait option button for the orientation.

Figure 1–82

- Make sure that Tabular is selected as the Layout. (If it is not, click the Tabular option button to select Tabular layout.)

- Make sure Portrait is selected as the Orientation. (If it is not, click the Portrait option button to select Portrait orientation.)

- Click the Next button to display the next Report Wizard screen (Figure 1–83).

Experiment

- Click different styles and observe the effect on the sample report. When you have finished experimenting, click the Module style.

Figure 1–83

- Be sure the Module style is selected. (If it is not, click Module to select the Module style.)

- Click the Next button to display the next Report Wizard screen (Figure 1–84).

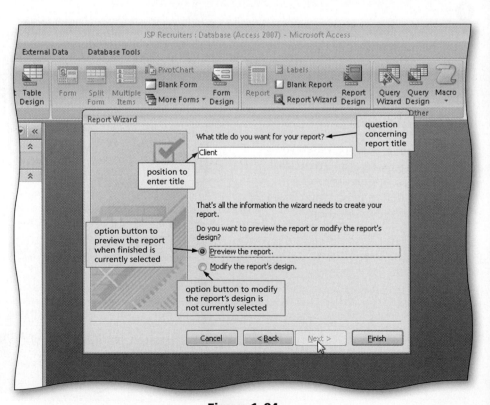

Figure 1–84

Creating a Report   **AC** 55

9

- Erase the current title, and then type Client Financial Report as the new title (Figure 1–85).

Q&A How do I erase the title?

You can highlight the existing title and then press the DELETE key. You can click at the end of the title and repeatedly press the BACKSPACE key. You can click at the beginning of the title and repeatedly press the DELETE key.

Q&A Could I just click after the word, Client, press the Spacebar, and then type Financial Report?

Yes. In general, you can edit the current title to produce the new title using the method with which you are most comfortable.

Figure 1–85

- Click the Finish button to produce the report (Figure 1–86).

10

- Click the Close 'Client Financial Report' button to remove the report from the screen.

Q&A Why didn't I have to save the report?

The Report Wizard saves the report automatically.

Figure 1–86

BTW

Quick Reference
For a table that lists how to complete the tasks covered in this book using the mouse, Ribbon, shortcut menu, and keyboard, see the Quick Reference Summary at the back of this book, or visit the Access 2007 Quick Reference Web page (scsite.com/ac2007/qr).

To Print a Report

Once you have created a report, you can print it at any time. The printed layout will reflect the layout you created. The data in the report will always reflect current data. The following step prints the Client Financial Report.

- With the Client Financial Report selected in the Navigation Pane, click the Office Button.

- Point to the arrow next to Print on the Office Button menu and then click Quick Print on the Print submenu to print the report.

To Create Additional Reports

The following steps produce the reports shown in Figure 1–76b, Figure 1–76c, and Figure 1–76d on page AC 50.

1 If necessary, click Create on the Ribbon to display the Create tab, and then click the Report Wizard button to display the Report Wizard dialog box.

2 Add the Client Number, Client Name, Street, City, State, and Postal Code fields by clicking each field and then clicking the Add Field button.

3 Click the Next button to move to the screen asking about grouping, and then click the Next button a second time to move to the screen asking about sort order.

4 Click the box arrow in the text box labeled 1, click the Client Number field to select the field as the sort key, and then click the Next button.

5 Make sure that Tabular is selected as the Layout and that Portrait is selected as the Orientation, and then click the Next button.

6 Make sure the Module style is selected, and then click the Next button.

7 Enter `Client Address Report` as the title and click the Finish button to produce the report.

8 Click the Close 'Client Address Report' button to close the Print Preview window.

9 Click the Recruiter table in the Navigation Pane, and then use the techniques shown in Steps 1 through 8 to produce the Recruiter Financial Report. The report is to contain the Recruiter Number, Last Name, First Name, Rate, and Commission fields. It is to be sorted by Recruiter Number. It is to have tabular layout, portrait orientation, and the Module Style. The title is to be Recruiter Financial Report.

10 With the Recruiter table selected in the Navigation Pane, use the techniques shown in Steps 1 through 8 to produce the Recruiter Address Report. The report is to contain the Recruiter Number, Last Name, First Name, Street, City, State, and Postal Code fields. It is to be sorted by Recruiter Number. It is to have tabular layout, landscape orientation, and the Module Style. The title is to be Recruiter Address Report.

11 Click the Close 'Recruiter Address Report' button to close the Print Preview window.

Using a Form to View Data

In Datasheet view, you can view many records at once. If there are many fields, however, only some of the fields in each record might be visible at a time. In **Form view**, where data is displayed in a form on the screen, you usually can see all the fields, but only for one record. To get the advantages from both, many database management systems allow you to easily switch between Datasheet view and Form view while maintaining position within the database. In Access 2007, you can view both a datasheet and a form simultaneously using a split form.

To Create a Split Form

A **split form** combines both a datasheet and a form, thus giving the advantages of both views. The following steps create a split form.

1
- Select the Client table in the Navigation Pane.

- If necessary, click Create on the Ribbon to display the Create tab (Figure 1–87).

Figure 1–87

2
- Click the Split Form button to create a split form. If a Field List appears, click its Close button to remove the Field List from the screen (Figure 1–88).

Q&A

Is the form automatically saved the way the report was created when I used the Report Wizard?

No. You must take specific action if you wish to save the form.

Figure 1–88

- Click the Save button to display the Save As dialog box (Figure 1–89).

Figure 1–89

- Type `Client Form` as the form name, and then click the OK button to save the form.

- If the form appears in Layout view, click the Form View button on the Access status bar to display the form in Form view (Figure 1–90).

Q&A

How can I recognize Layout view?

There are three ways. The left end of the Status bar will contain the words Layout View. There will be shading around the outside of the selected field in the form. The Layout View button will be selected in the right end of the Status bar.

Figure 1–90

To Use a Split Form

After you have saved a form, you can use it at any time by right-clicking the form in the Navigation Pane and then clicking Open in the shortcut menu. If you plan to use the form to enter data, you must ensure you are viewing the form in Form view.

1
- Click the Next Record button four times to move to record 5 (Figure 1–91).

Q&A I inadvertently closed the form at the end of the previous steps. What should I do?

Right-click the form in the Navigation Pane and then click Open on the shortcut menu.

Q&A Do I have to take any special action for the form to be positioned on the same record as the datasheet?

No. The advantage to the split form is that changing the position on either the datasheet or the form automatically changes the position on the other.

Figure 1–91

2
- Click the Postal Code field on the second record in the data-sheet to select the second record in both the datasheet and the form (Figure 1–92).

Experiment
- Click several fields in various records in the datasheet and observe the effect on the form.

3
- Click the Close 'Client Form' button to remove the form from the screen.

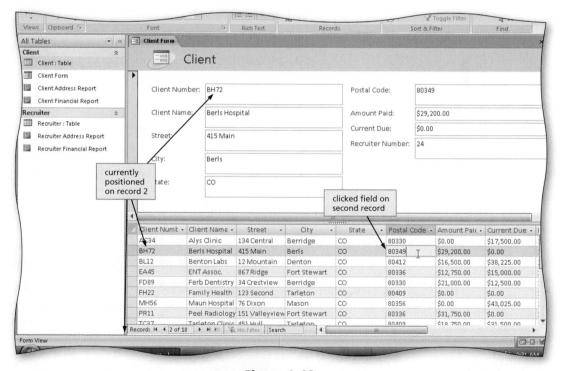

Figure 1–92

Changing Database Properties

Access helps you organize and identify your databases by using **database properties,** which are the details about a file. Database properties, also known as **metadata,** can include such information as the project author, title, or subject. **Keywords** are words or phrases that further describe the database. For example, a class name or database topic can describe the file's purpose or content.

Five different types of document properties exist, but the more common ones used in this book are standard and automatically updated properties. **Standard properties** are associated with all Microsoft Office documents and include author, title, and subject. **Automatically updated properties** include file system properties, such as the date you create or change a file, and statistics, such as the file size.

To Change Database Properties

The Database Properties dialog box contains areas where you can view and enter document properties. You can view and change information in this dialog box at any time while you are working on your database. It is a good idea to add your name and class name as database properties. The following steps use the Properties dialog box to change database properties.

1

- Click the Office Button to display the Office Button menu.

- Point to Manage on the Office Button menu to display the Manage submenu (Figure 1–93).

Q&A What other types of actions besides changing properties can you take to prepare a database for distribution?

The Manage submenu provides commands to compact and repair a database as well as to back up a database.

Figure 1–93

2

- Click Database Properties on the Manage submenu to display the JSP Recruiters.accdb Properties dialog box (Figure 1–94).

Q&A Why are some of the document properties in my Properties dialog box already filled in?

The person who installed Microsoft Office 2007 on your computer or network may have set or customized the properties.

Figure 1–94

③

- If necessary, click the Summary tab.

- Click the Author text box and then type your name as the Author property. If a name already is displayed in the Author text box, delete it before typing your name.

- Click the Subject text box, if necessary delete any existing text, and then type your course and section as the Subject property.

- Click the Keywords text box, if necessary delete any existing text, and then type Healthcare, Recruiter as the Keywords property (Figure 1–95).

Q&A

What types of properties does Access collect automatically?

Access records such details as when the database was created, when it was last modified, total editing time, and the various objects contained in the database.

Figure 1–95

④

- Click the OK button to save your changes and remove the JSP Recruiters.accdb Properties dialog box from the screen.

Access Help

At any time while using Access, you can find answers to questions and display information about various topics through **Access Help**. Used properly, this form of assistance can increase your productivity and reduce your frustrations by minimizing the time you spend learning how to use Access.

This section introduces you to Access Help. Additional information about using Access Help is available in Appendix C.

To Search for Access Help

Using Access Help, you can search for information based on phrases, such as create a form or change a data type, or key terms, such as copy, save, or format. Access Help responds with a list of search results displayed as links to a variety of resources. The following steps, which use Access Help to search for information about creating a form, assume you are connected to the Internet.

- Click the Microsoft Office Access Help button near the upper-right corner of the Access window to open the Access Help window.

- Type create a form in the 'Type words to search for' text box at the top of the Access Help window (Figure 1–96).

Figure 1–96

- Press the ENTER key to display the search results.

- Click the Maximize button on the Access Help window title bar to maximize the Help window unless it is already maximized (Figure 1–97).

Q&A

Where is the Access window with the JSP Recruiters database?

Access is open in the background, but the Access Help window sits on top of the Microsoft Access window. When the Access Help window is closed, the database will reappear.

Figure 1–97

3

- Click the 'Create a split form' link to display information regarding creating a split form (Figure 1–98).

Q&A

What is the purpose of the buttons at the top of the Access Help window?

Use the buttons in the upper-left corner of the Access Help window to navigate through the Help system, change the display, show the Access Help table of contents, and print the contents of the window.

4

- Click the Close button on the Access Help window title bar to close the Access Help window and make the database active.

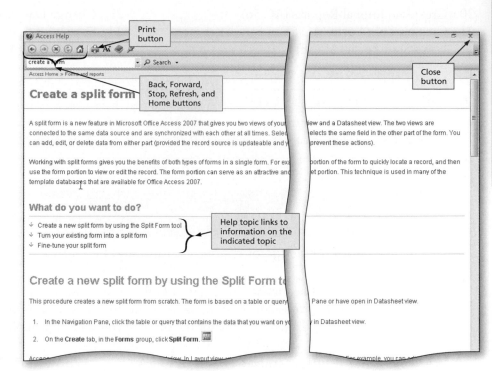

Figure 1–98

Other Ways
1. Press F1

To Quit Access

You saved all your changes and are ready to quit Access. The following step quits Access.

1 Click the Close button on the right side of the Access title bar to quit Access.

Chapter Summary

In this chapter you have learned to design a database, create an Access database, create tables and add records to them, print the contents of tables, create reports, and create forms. The items listed below include all the new Access skills you have learned in this chapter.

1. Start Access (AC 12)
2. Create a Database Using a Template (AC 13)
3. Create a Database (AC 14)
4. Define the Fields in a Table (AC 24)
5. Create a Table Using a Template (AC 26)
6. Save a Table (AC 27)
7. Change the Primary Key (AC 28)
8. Add Records to a Table (AC 30)
9. Close a Table (AC 35)
10. Quit Access (AC 36)
11. Start Access (AC 36)
12. Open a Database from Access (AC 37)
13. Add Additional Records to a Table (AC 38)
14. Preview and Print the Contents of a Table (AC 41)
15. Create an Additional Table (AC 44)
16. Modify the Primary Key and Field Properties (AC 46)
17. Add Records to an Additional Table (AC 49)
18. Create a Report (AC 51)
19. Print a Report (AC 56)

If you have a SAM user profile, you may have access to hands-on instruction, practice, and assessment. Log in to your SAM account (http://sam2007.course.com) to launch any assigned training activities or exams that relate to the skills covered in this chapter.

Learn It Online

Test your knowledge of chapter content and key terms.

Instructions: To complete the Learn It Online exercises, start your browser, click the Address bar, and then enter the Web address scsite.com/ac2007/learn. When the Access 2007 Learn It Online page is displayed, click the link for the exercise you want to complete and then read the instructions.

Chapter Reinforcement TF, MC, and SA
A series of true/false, multiple choice, and short answer questions that test your knowledge of the chapter content.

Flash Cards
An interactive learning environment where you identify chapter key terms associated with displayed definitions.

Practice Test
A series of multiple choice questions that test your knowledge of chapter content and key terms.

Who Wants To Be a Computer Genius?
An interactive game that challenges your knowledge of chapter content in the style of a television quiz show.

Wheel of Terms
An interactive game that challenges your knowledge of chapter key terms in the style of the television show *Wheel of Fortune*.

Crossword Puzzle Challenge
A crossword puzzle that challenges your knowledge of key terms presented in the chapter.

Apply Your Knowledge

Reinforce the skills and apply the concepts you learned in this chapter.

Changing Data, Creating a Form, and Creating a Report

Instructions: Start Access. Open the The Bike Delivers database. See the inside back cover of this book for instructions for downloading the Data Files for Students, or see your instructor for information on accessing the files required in this book.

The Bike Delivers uses motorbikes to provide courier services for local businesses. The Bike Delivers has a database that keeps track of its couriers and customers. The database has two tables. The Customer table (Figure 1–99a) contains data on the customers who use the services of The Bike Delivers. The Courier table (Figure 1–99b) contains data on the individuals employed by The Bike Delivers.

(a) Customer Table

(b) Courier Table

Figure 1–99

Perform the following tasks:

1. Open the Customer table and change the Courier Number for customer KL55 to 113.

2. Close the Customer table.

3. Create a split form for the Courier table. Use the name Courier for the form.

4. Open the form you created and change the street address for Michelle Hyde to 65 Park.

5. Close the Courier form.

6. Create the report shown in Figure 1–100 for the Customer table. The report uses the Module style.

7. Change the database properties, as specified by your instructor. Submit the revised database in the format specified by your instructor.

Figure 1–100

Extend Your Knowledge

Extend the skills you learned in this chapter and experiment with new skills. You may need to use Help to complete the assignment.

Changing Formats and Creating Grouped and Sorted Reports

Instructions: Start Access. Open the Camden Scott College database. See the inside back cover of this book for instructions for downloading the Data Files for Students, or see your instructor for information on accessing the files required in this book.

Continued >

Extend Your Knowledge *continued*

Camden Scott College is a small liberal arts college. The Human Resources Director has created an Access database in which to store information about candidates applying for faculty positions. You will make some changes to the Candidate table so that it looks like that shown in Figure 1–101 and create a report that both groups records and sorts them in ascending order.

Figure 1–101

Perform the following tasks:

1. Open the Candidate table in Datasheet view and change the column heading for the ID field to Candidate ID.

2. Save the change and open the table in Design view.

3. Select a format for the App Date field that will produce the look shown in Figure 1–101.

4. Change the data type for the Documentation field so that it will match that shown in Figure 1–101.

5. Save the changes.

6. Open the table in Datasheet view. The Human Resources department has received an application from Edward Klinger. Edward applied for the same position as Sarah Klinger on the same date as Sarah. Edward's phone number is 610-555-1111. He did submit all his documentation with his application. Add this record.

7. Add the Quick Print button to the Quick Access Toolbar.

8. Create a report for the Candidate table that lists the Department Code, App Date, Last Name, and First Name. Group the report by Department Code. Sort the report by App Date, Last Name, and then First Name. Choose your own report style and use Candidate by Department as the title of the report.

9. Remove the Quick Print button from the Quick Access Toolbar.

10. Change the database properties, as specified by your instructor. Submit the revised database in the format specified by your instructor.

Make It Right

Analyze a database and correct all errors and/or improve the design.

Correcting Errors in the Table Structure

Instructions: Start Access. Open the SciFi Scene database. See the inside back cover of this book for instructions for downloading the Data Files for Students, or see your instructor for information on accessing the files required in this book.

SciFi Scene is a database containing information on science fiction books. The Book table shown in Figure 1–102 contains a number of errors in the table structure. You are to correct these errors before any additional records can be added to the table. Book Code, not ID, is the primary key for the Book table. The column heading Titel is misspelled. The On Hand field represents the number of books on hand. The field will be used in arithmetic operations. Only whole numbers should be stored in the field. The Price field represents the price of the book. The current data type does not reflect this information.

Change the database properties, as specified by your instructor. Submit the revised database in the format specified by your instructor.

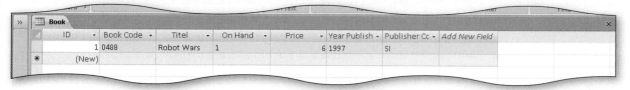

Figure 1–102

In the Lab

Design, create, modify, and/or use a database using the guidelines, concepts, and skills presented in this chapter. Labs are listed in order of increasing difficulty.

Lab 1: Creating the JMS TechWizards Database

Problem: JMS TechWizards is a local company that provides technical services to several small businesses in the area. The company currently keeps its records in two Excel workbooks. One Excel workbook (Figure 1–103a) contains information on the clients that JMS TechWizards serves. The other Excel workbook (Figure 1–103b) contains information on the technicians that JMS employs. JMS would like to store this data in a database and has asked for your help.

	A	B	C	D	E	F	G	H	I	J	K	L	M
1	Client Number	Client Name	Street	City	State	Postal Code	Telephone Number	Billed	Paid	Technician Number			
2	AM53	Ashton-Mills	216 Rivard	Anderson	TX	78077	512-555-4070	$315.50	$255.00	22			
3	AR76	The Artshop	722 Fisher	Liberty Corner	TX	78080	254-555-0200	$535.00	$565.00	23			
4	BE29	Bert's Supply	5752 Maumee	Liberty Corner	TX	78080	254-555-2024	$229.50	$0.00	23			
5	DE76	D & E Grocery	464 Linnell	Anderson	TX	78077	512-555-6050	$485.70	$400.00	29			
6	GR56	Grant Cleaners	737 Allard	Kingston	TX	78084	512-555-1231	$215.00	$225.00	22			
7	GU21	Grand Union	247 Fuller	Kingston	TX	78084	512-555-5431	$228.00	$0.00	23			
8	JE77	Jones Electric	57 Giddings	Anderson	TX	78077	512-555-6895	$0.00	$0.00	23			
9	ME17	Merry Café	665 Whittier	Kingston	TX	78084	512-555-9780	$312.50	$323.50	22			
10	SA56	Sawyer Ind.	31 Lafayette	Anderson	TX	78077	512-555-4567	$372.25	$350.00	29			
11	ST21	Steed's	752 Cadieux	Liberty Corner	TX	78080	254-555-9080	$0.00	$0.00	23			
12													
13													

(a) Client Data (Excel Workbook)

	A	B	C	D	E	F	G	H	I	J
1	Technician Number	Last Name	First Name	Street	City	State	Postal Code	Hourly Rate	YTD Earnings	
2	22	Levin	Joe	26 Cotton	Anderson	TX	78077	$25.00	$8,245.00	
3	23	Rogers	Brad	79 Marsden	Liberty Corner	TX	78080	$30.00	$9,143.30	
4	29	Rodriguez	Maria	263 Topper	Kingston	TX	78084	$35.00	$9,745.50	
5	32	Torres	Lee	34 Red Poppy	Liberty Corner	TX	78080	$23.00	$0.00	
6										
7										
8										

(b) Technician Data (Excel Workbook)

Figure 1–103

Continued >

In the Lab *continued*

Instructions: Perform the following tasks:

1. Create a new database in which to store all the objects related to the technical services data. Call the database JMS TechWizards.

2. Create a table in which to store the data related to clients. Use the name Client for the table. The fields for the Client table are: Client Number, Client Name, Street, City, State, Postal Code, Telephone Number, Billed, Paid, and Technician Number. Client Number is the primary key. The Billed and Paid fields are currency data type.

3. Create a table in which to store the data related to technicians. Use the name Technician for the table. The fields for the Technician table are: Technician Number, Last Name, First Name, Street, City, State, Postal Code, Hourly Rate, and YTD Earnings. The primary key for the Technician table is Technician Number. Hourly rate and YTD Earnings are currency data type.

4. Add the data from the Client workbook in Figure 1–103a to the Client table.

5. Add the data from the Technician workbook in Figure 1–103b to the Technician table.

6. Create and save the reports shown in Figure 1–104a for the Client table and Figure 1–104b for the Technician table.

7. Change the database properties, as specified by your instructor. Submit the revised database in the format specified by your instructor.

(a) Billing Summary Report

(b) Salary Report

Figure 1–104

In the Lab

Lab 2: Creating the Hockey Fan Zone Database

Problem: Your town has a minor league hockey team. The team store sells a variety of items with the team logo. The store purchases the items from suppliers that deal in specialty items for sports teams. Currently, the information about the items and suppliers is stored in the Excel workbook shown in Figure 1–105. You work part-time at the store, and your boss has asked you to create a database that will store the item and supplier information. You have already determined that you need two tables: an Item table and a Supplier table in which to store the information.

Instructions: Perform the following tasks:

1. Design a new database in which to store all the objects related to the items for sale. Call the database Hockey Fan Zone.

2. Use the information shown in Figure 1–105 to determine the primary keys and determine additional fields. Then, determine the relationships among tables and the data types.

3. Create the Item table using the information shown in Figure 1–105.

4. Create the Supplier table using the information shown in Figure 1–105.

5. Add the appropriate data to the Item table.

6. Add the appropriate data to the Supplier table.

7. Create a split form for the Item table. Use the name Item for the form.

8. Create the report shown in Figure 1–106 for the Item table.

9. Change the database properties, as specified by your instructor. Submit the database in the format specified by your instructor.

	A	B	C	D	E	F	G	H
1	Item Number	Description	On Hand	Cost	Selling Price	Supplier Code	Supplier Name	Telephone Number
2	3663	Ball Cap	30	$11.15	$18.95	LG	Logo Goods	517-555-3853
3	3683	Bumper Sticker	50	$0.95	$1.50	MN	Mary's Novelties	317-555-4747
4	4563	Earrings	10	$4.50	$7.00	LG	Logo Goods	517-555-3853
5	4593	Foam Finger	25	$2.95	$5.00	LG	Logo Goods	517-555-3853
6	5923	Jersey	12	$21.45	$24.75	AC	Ace Clothes	616-555-9228
7	6189	Koozies	35	$2.00	$4.00	MN	Mary's Novelties	317-555-4747
8	6343	Note Cube	7	$5.75	$8.00	MN	Mary's Novelties	317-555-4747
9	7810	Tee Shirt	32	$9.50	$14.95	AC	Ace Clothes	616-555-9228
10	7930	Visor	9	$11.95	$17.00	LG	Logo Goods	517-555-3853
11								

Figure 1–105

Inventory Status Report

Item Number	Description	On Hand	Cost
3663	Ball Cap	30	$11.15
3683	Bumper Sticker	50	$0.95
4563	Earrings	10	$4.50
4593	Foam Finger	25	$2.95
5923	Jersey	12	$21.45
6189	Koozies	35	$2.00
6343	Note Cube	7	$5.75
7810	Tee Shirt	32	$9.50
7930	Visor	9	$11.95

Figure 1–106

In the Lab

Lab 3: Creating the Ada Beauty Supply Database

Problem: A distribution company supplies local beauty salons with items needed in the beauty industry. The distributor employs sales representatives who receive a base salary as well as a commission on sales. Currently, the distributor keeps data on customers and sales reps in two Word documents and two Excel workbooks.

Instructions: Using the data shown in Figure 1–107 on the next page, design the Ada Beauty Supply database. Use the database design guidelines in this chapter to help you in the design process.

Continued >

In the Lab *continued*

Customer Number	Customer Name	Street	Telephone
AM23	Amy's Salon	223 Johnson	555-2150
BB34	Bob the Barber	1939 Jackson	555-1939
BL15	Blondie's	3294 Devon	555-7510
CM09	Cut Mane	3140 Halsted	555-0604
CS12	Curl n Style	1632 Clark	555-0804
EG07	Elegante	1805 Boardway	555-1404
JS34	Just Cuts	2200 Lawrence	555-0313
LB20	Le Beauty	13 Devon	555-5161
NC25	Nancy's Place	1027 Wells	555-4210
RD03	Rose's Day Spa	787 Monroe	555-7657
TT21	Tan and Tone	1939 Congress	555-6554

(a) Customer Address Information (Word table)

	A	B	C	D	E
1	Customer Number	Customer Name	Balance	Amount Paid	Sales Rep Nun
2	AM23	Amy's Salon	$195.00	$1,695.00	44
3	BB34	Bob the Barber	$150.00	$0.00	51
4	BL15	Blondie's	$555.00	$1,350.00	49
5	CM09	Cut Mane	$295.00	$1,080.00	51
6	CS12	Curl n Style	$145.00	$710.00	49
7	EG07	Elegante	$0.00	$1,700.00	44
8	JS34	Just Cuts	$360.00	$700.00	49
9	LB20	Le Beauty	$200.00	$1,250.00	51
10	NC25	Nancy's Place	$240.00	$550.00	44
11	RD03	Rose's Day Spa	$0.00	$975.00	51
12	TT21	Tan and Tone	$160.00	$725.00	44
13					
14					
15					
16					

(c) Customer Financial Information (Excel Workbook)

Sales Rep Number	Last Name	First Name	Street	City	State	Postal Code
44	Jones	Pat	43 Third	Lawncrest	WA	98084
49	Gupta	Pinn	678 Hillcrest	Manton	WA	98085
51	Ortiz	Gabe	982 Victoria	Lawncrest	WA	98084
55	Sinson	Terry	45 Elm	Manton	WA	98084

(b) Sales Rep Address Information (Word table)

	A	B	C	D	E	F
1	Sales Rep Number	Last Name	First Name	Salary	Comm Rate	Commission
2	44	Jones	Pat	$ 23,000.00	0.05	$613.50
3	49	Gupta	Pinn	$ 24,000.00	0.06	$616.60
4	51	Ortiz	Gabe	$ 22,500.00	0.05	$492.75
5	55	Sinson	Terry	$ 20,000.00	0.05	$0.00
6						

(d) Sales Rep Financial Information (Excel Workbook)

Figure 1–107

When you have completed the database design, create the database, create the tables, and add the data to the appropriate tables. Be sure to determine the correct data types.

Finally, prepare the Customer Status Report shown in Figure 1–108a and the Sales Rep Salary Report shown in Figure 1–108b. Change the database properties, as specified by your instructor. Submit the database in the format specified by your instructor.

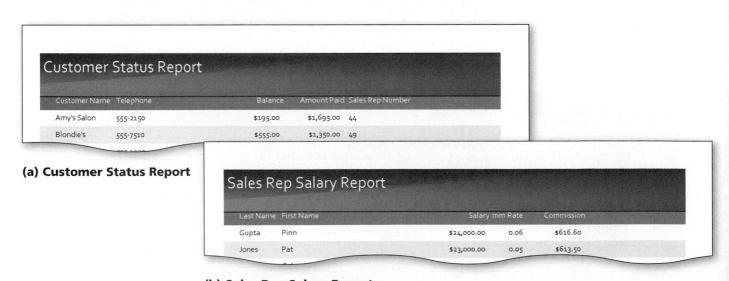

(a) Customer Status Report

(b) Sales Rep Salary Report

Figure 1–108

Cases and Places

Apply your creative thinking and problem solving skills to design and implement a solution.

• Easier   •• More Difficult

• 1: Design and Create an E-Commerce Database

Students often have very little money to furnish dorm rooms and apartments. You and two of your friends have decided to use the skills you learned in your e-commerce class to create a Web site specifically for college students to buy and sell used household furnishings.

Design and create a database to store the data that you need to manage this new business. Then create the necessary tables and enter the data from the Case 1-1 Second-Hand Goods document. See the inside back cover of this book for instructions for downloading the Data Files for Students, or see your instructor for information on accessing the files required in this book. Submit your assignment in the format specified by your instructor.

• 2: Design and Create a Rental Database

You are a part-time employee of BeachCondo Rentals. BeachCondo Rentals provides a rental service for condo owners who want to rent their units. The company rents units by the week. Currently, the company keeps information about its rentals in an Excel workbook.

Design and create a database to store the rental data. Then create the necessary tables and enter the data from the Case 1-2 BeachCondo Rentals workbook. See the inside back cover of this book for instructions for downloading the Data Files for Students, or see your instructor for information on accessing the files required in this book. Create an Available Rentals Report that lists the unit number, weekly rate, and owner number. Submit your assignment in the format specified by your instructor.

•• 3: Design and Create a Restaurant Database

Your school is sponsoring a conference that will draw participants from a wide geographical area. The conference director has asked for your help in preparing a database of restaurants that might be of interest to the participants. At a minimum, she needs to know the following: the type of restaurant (vegetarian, fast-food, fine dining, and so on), street address, telephone number, and opening and closing times and days. Because most of the participants will stay on campus, she also would like to know the approximate distance from campus. Additionally, she would like to know about any unique or special features the restaurants may have.

Design and create a database to meet the conference director's needs. Create the necessary tables, determine the necessary fields, enter some sample data, and prepare a sample report to show the director. Submit your assignment in the format specified by your instructor.

•• 4: Design and Create a Database to Help You Find a Job

Make It Personal

Conducting a job search requires careful preparation. In addition to preparing a resume and cover letter, you will need to research the companies for which you are interested in working and contact these companies to let them know of your interest and qualifications.

Microsoft Access includes a Contacts table template that can create a table that will help you keep track of your job contacts. Create a database to keep track of the companies that are of interest to you. Submit your assignment in the format specified by your instructor.

Continued >

STUDENT ASSIGNMENTS

Cases and Places *continued*

•• 5: Design a Database that Tracks Student Data

Working Together

Keeping track of students is an enormous task for school administrators. Microsoft Access can help school administrators manage student data. The Database Wizard includes a Students template that can create a database that will maintain many different types of data on students, such as allergies, medications, and emergency contact information.

Have each member of your team explore the features of the Database Wizard and determine individually which tables and fields should be included in a Students database. As a group, review your choices and decide on one common design. Prepare a short paper for your instructor that explains why your team chose the particular database design.

After agreeing on the database design, assign one member to create the database using the Database Wizard. Every other team member should contribute data and add the data to the database. Submit your assignment in the format specified by your instructor.

2 | Querying a Database

Objectives

You will have mastered the material in this chapter when you can:

- Create queries using the Simple Query Wizard
- Print query results
- Create queries using Design view
- Include fields in the design grid
- Use text and numeric data in criteria
- Create and use parameter queries
- Save a query and use the saved query

- Use compound criteria in queries
- Sort data in queries
- Join tables in queries
- Create a report from a query
- Perform calculations in queries
- Calculate statistics in queries
- Create crosstab queries
- Customize the Navigation Pane

2 | Querying a Database

Introduction

A database management system such as Access offers many useful features, among them the capability of answering questions, the answers to which are found in the database. When you pose a question to Access, or any other database management system, the question is called a query. A **query** is simply a question presented in a way that Access can process.

Thus, to find the answer to a question, you first create a corresponding query using the techniques illustrated in this chapter. After you have created the query, you instruct Access to display the query results; that is, to perform the steps necessary to obtain the answer. Access then displays the answer in Datasheet view.

Project — Querying a Database

Organizations and individuals achieve several benefits from storing data in a database and using Access to manage the database. One of the most important benefits is the capability of easily finding the answers to questions such as those shown in Figure 2-1 and the following, which concern the data in the JSP Recruiters database:

1. What are the number, name, the amount paid, and the current due of client FD89?
2. Which clients' names begin with Be?
3. Which clients are located in Berridge?
4. Which clients have a current due of $0.00?
5. Which clients have an amount paid that is more than $20,000.00?
6. Which clients of recruiter 21 have an amount paid that is more than $20,000.00?
7. In what cities are all the clients located?
8. What is the total amount (amount paid + current due) for each client?
9. What is the client number and name of each client, and what is the number and name of the recruiter to whom each client is assigned?

In addition to these questions, JSP Recruiters needs to find information about clients located in a specific city, but they want to enter a different city each time they ask the question. A parameter query would enable this. The agency also has a special way it wants to summarize data. A crosstab query will present the data in the desired form.

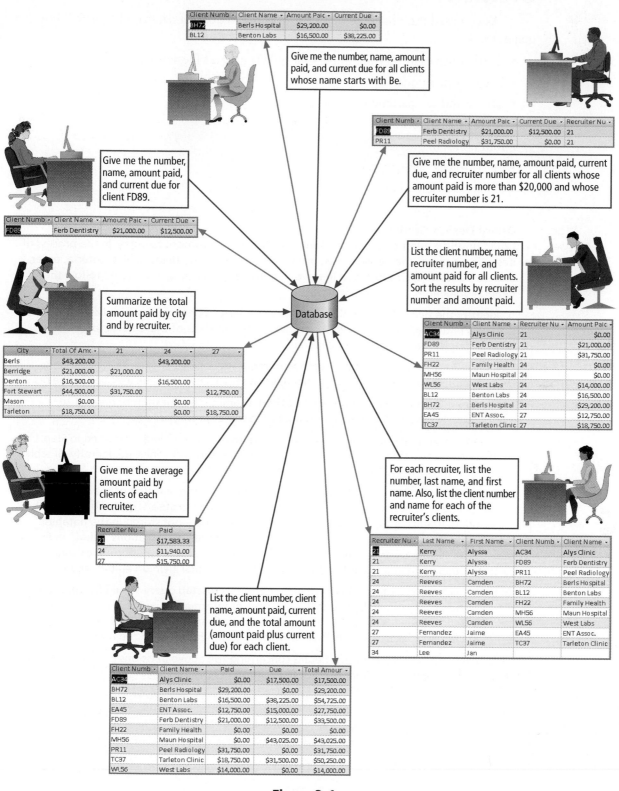

Figure 2–1

Overview

As you read this chapter, you will learn how to query a database by performing these general tasks:

- Create queries using the Simple Query Wizard and Design view
- Use criteria in queries
- Create and use parameter queries
- Sort data in queries
- Join tables in queries
- Perform calculations in queries
- Create crosstab queries

Plan Ahead

Query Design Guidelines

When posing a question to Access, you must design an appropriate query. In the process of designing a query, the decisions you make will determine the fields, tables, criteria, order, and special calculations included in the query. To design a query, you should follow these general guidelines:

1. **Identify the fields.** Examine the question or request to determine which fields from the tables in the database are involved. Examine the contents of these fields to make sure you understand how the data is stored.

2. **Identify restrictions.** Unless the question or request calls for all records, determine the restrictions, that is, the conditions records must satisfy in order to be included in the results.

3. **Determine whether special order is required.** Examine the question or request to determine whether the results must appear in some specific order.

4. **Determine whether more than one table is required.** If all the fields identified in Step 1 are in the same table, no special action is required. If this is not the case, identify all tables represented by those fields.

5. **Determine whether calculations are required.** Examine the question or request to determine whether, in addition to the fields determined in Step 1, calculations must be included. Results of mathematical operations typically are not stored in the database because they can be calculated easily when necessary. Such calculations include individual record calculations (for example, adding the values in two fields) or group calculations (for example, finding the total of the values in a particular field on all the records).

6. **If data is to be summarized, determine whether a crosstab query would be appropriate.** If data is to be grouped by two different types of information, you can use a crosstab query. You will need to identify the two types of information. One of the types will form the row headings and the other will form the column headings in the query results.

When necessary, more specific details concerning the above decisions and/or actions are presented at appropriate points in the chapter.

Starting Access

If you are using a computer to step through the project in this chapter and you want your screen to match the figures in this book, you should change your screen's resolution to 1024 × 768. For information about how to change a computer's resolution, read Appendix E.

To Start Access

The following steps, which assume Windows Vista is running, start Access.

Note: If you are using Windows XP, see Appendix F for alternate steps.

1 Click the Start button on the Windows Vista taskbar to display the Start menu.

2 Click All Programs at the bottom of the left Pane on the Start menu to display the All Programs list and then click Microsoft Office in the All Programs list to display the Microsoft Office list.

3 Click Microsoft Office Access 2007 on the Microsoft Office list to start Access and display the Getting Started with Microsoft Office Access window.

4 If the Access window is not maximized, click the Maximize button on its title bar to maximize the window.

To Open a Database

In Chapter 1, you created your database on a USB flash drive using the file name, JSP Recruiters. There are two ways to open the file containing your database. If the file you created appears in the Recent Documents list, you can click it to open the file. If not, you can use the More button to open the file. The following steps use the More button to open the JSP Recruiters database from the USB flash drive.

Note: If you are using Windows XP, see Appendix F for alternate steps.

1 With your USB flash drive connected to one of the computer's USB ports, click the More button to display the Open dialog box.

2 If the Folders list is displayed below the Folders button, click the Folders button to remove the Folders list.

3 If necessary, click Computer in the Favorite Links section and then double-click UDISK 2.0 (E:) to select the USB flash drive, Drive E in this case, as the new open location. (Your drive letter might be different.)

4 Click JSP Recruiters to select the file name.

5 Click the Open button to open the database.

6 If a Security Warning appears, click the Options button to display the Microsoft Office Security Options dialog box.

7 With the option button to enable this content selected, click the OK button to enable the content.

Creating Queries

Queries are simply questions, the answers to which are in the database. Access contains a powerful query feature. Through the use of this feature, you can find the answers to a wide variety of complex questions.

To Use the Simple Query Wizard to Create a Query

Once you have examined the question you wish to ask to determine the fields involved in the question, you can begin creating the query. If there are no restrictions involved in the query, nor any special order or calculations, you can use the Simple Query wizard. The following steps use the Simple Query wizard to create a query to display the number, name, and recruiter number of all clients.

1

- If the Navigation Pane is hidden, click the Shutter Bar Open/Close Button to show the Navigation Pane.

- Be sure the Client table is selected.

- Click Create on the Ribbon to display the Create tab.

- Click the Query Wizard button on the Create tab to display the New Query dialog box (Figure 2–2).

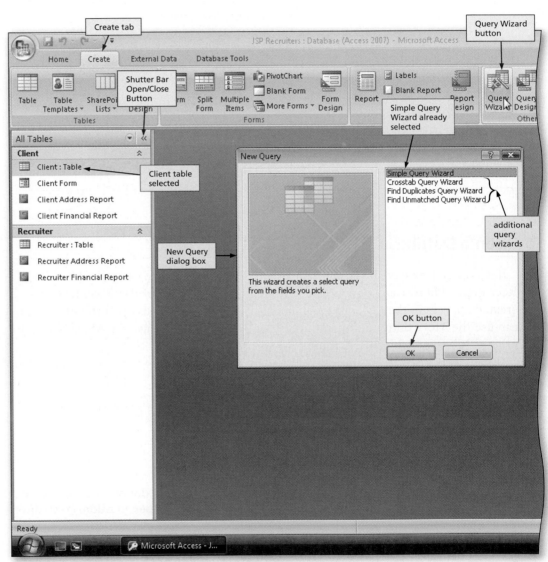

Figure 2–2

2

- Be sure Simple Query Wizard is selected, and then click the OK button to display the Simple Query Wizard dialog box (Figure 2–3).

Q&A

This looks like the screen I saw in the Report Wizard. Do I select fields in the same way?

Yes. In fact, you will see a similar screen in other wizards and you always select the fields just as you did in the Report Wizard.

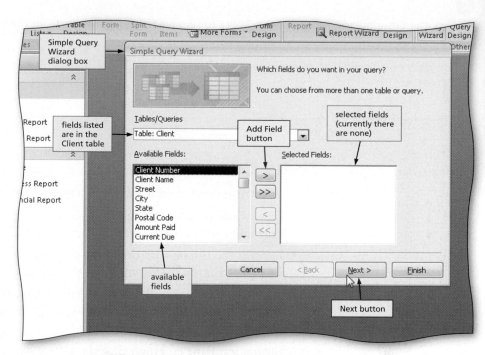

Figure 2–3

3

- Click the Add Field button to add the Client Number field.

- Click the Add Field button a second time to add the Client Name field.

- Click the Recruiter Number field, and then click the Add Field button to add the Recruiter Number field.

- Click the Next button.

- Be sure the title of the query is Client Query.

- Click the Finish button to create the query (Figure 2–4).

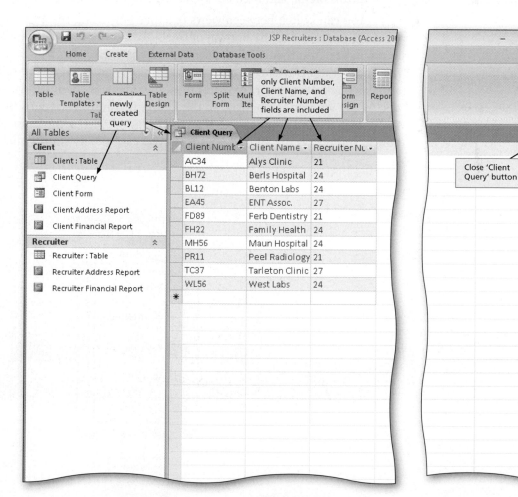

Figure 2–4

4

• Click the Close button for the Client Query to remove the query results from the screen.

If I want to use this query in the future, do I need to save the query?

Normally you would. The one exception is a query created by the wizard. The wizard automatically saves the query it creates.

Using Queries

After you have created and saved a query, you can use it in a variety of ways:

• To view the results of the query, open it by right-clicking the query in the Navigation Pane and clicking Open on the shortcut menu.

• To print the results with the query open, click the Office Button, point to Print on the Office Button menu, and then click Quick Print on the Print submenu.

• If you want to change the design of the query, right-click the query and then click Design View on the shortcut menu to open the query in Design view.

• To print the query without first opening it, be sure the query is selected in the Navigation Pane and then click the Office Button, point to Print on the Office Button menu, and then click Quick Print on the Print submenu.

You can switch between views of a query by using the View button (Figure 2–5). Clicking the arrow at the bottom of the button produces the View button menu as shown in the figure. You then click the desired view in the menu. The two views you will use in this chapter are Datasheet view (see the results) and Design view (change the design). You also can click the top part of the button, in which case, you will switch to the view identified by the icon on the button. In the figure, the button contains the icon for Design view, so clicking the button would change to Design view. For the most part, the icon on the button represents the view you want, so you can usually simply click the button.

Figure 2–5

To Use a Criterion in a Query

After you have determined the fields to be included in a query, you will determine whether there are any restrictions on the records that are to be included. For example, you might only want to include those clients whose recruiter number is 24. In such a case, you need to enter the 24 as a **criterion**, which is a condition that the records to be included must satisfy. To do so, you will open the query in Design view, enter the criterion below the appropriate field, and then view the results of the query. The following steps enter a criterion to include only the clients of recruiter 24 and then view the query results.

1

• Right-click Client Query to produce a shortcut menu (Figure 2–6).

Figure 2–6

2

• Click Design View on the shortcut menu to open the query in Design view (Figure 2–7). (Your field names may be enclosed in brackets.)

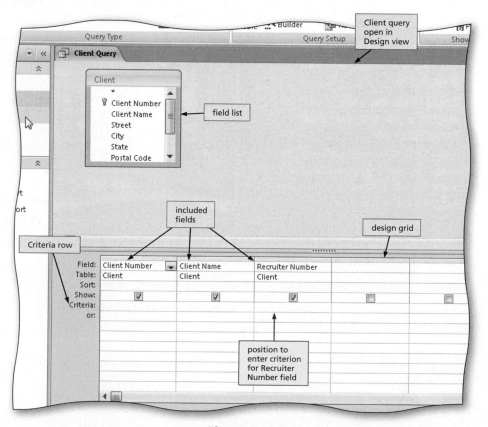

Figure 2–7

3

- Click the Criteria row in the Recruiter Number column of the grid, and then type 24 as the criterion (Figure 2–8).

Q&A

The Recruiter Number field is a text field. Do I need to enclose the value for a text field in quotation marks?

You could, but it is not necessary, because Access inserts the quotation marks for you automatically.

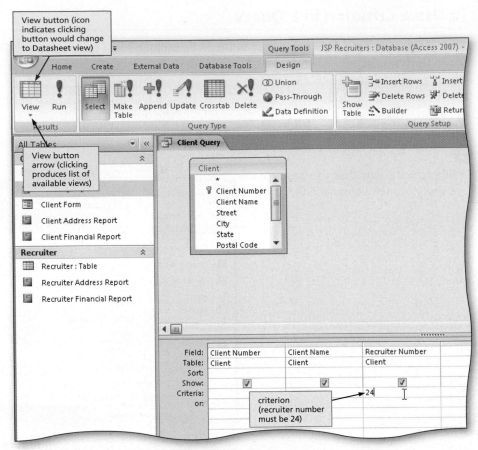

Figure 2–8

4

- Click the View button to display the results in Datasheet view (Figure 2–9).

Q&A

Could I click the View button arrow and then click Datasheet view?

Yes. If the icon representing the view you want appears on the View button, however, it is easier just to click the button.

Figure 2–9

5

- Close the Client Query window by clicking the Close 'Client Query' button.

- When asked if you want to save your changes, click the No button.

Q&A

If I saved the query, what would happen the next time I ran the query?

You would see only clients of recruiter 24.

Other Ways

1. Click Run button on Ribbon

2. Click Datasheet View button on status bar

To Print the Results of a Query

To print the results of a query, use the same techniques you learned in Chapter 1 on pages AC 41 and AC 42 to print the data in the table. The following steps print the current query results.

1 With the Client Query selected in the Navigation Pane, click the Office Button.

2 Point to Print on the Office Button menu.

3 Click Quick Print on the Print submenu.

To Create a Query in Design View

Most of the time you will use Design view to create queries. Once you have created a new query in Design view, you can specify fields, criteria, sorting, calculations, and so on. The following steps create a new query in Design view.

1

- Hide the Navigation Pane.

- Click Create on the Ribbon to display the Create tab.

- Click the Query Design button to create a new query (Figure 2–10).

Q&A

Is it necessary to hide the Navigation Pane?

No. It gives you more room for the query, however, so it is usually a good practice to hide it.

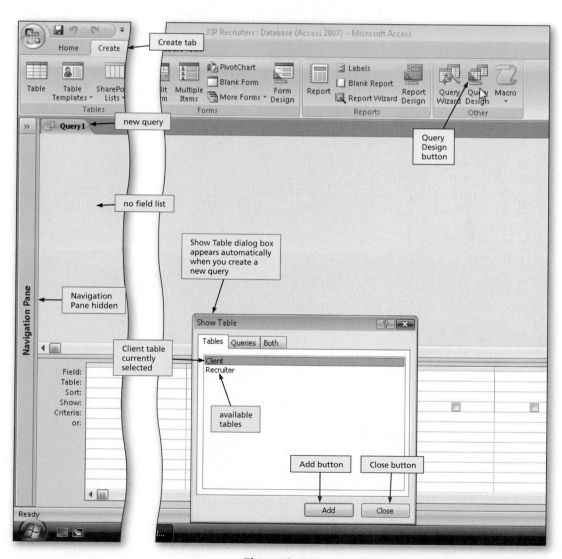

Figure 2–10

2

- With the Client table selected, click the Add button in the Show Table dialog box to add the Client table to the query.

- Click the Close button in the Show Table dialog box to remove the dialog box from the screen.

Q&A

What if I inadvertently add the wrong table?

Right-click the table that you added in error and click Remove Table on the shortcut menu. You also can just close the query, indicate that you don't want to save it, and then start over.

- Drag the lower edge of the field box down far enough so all fields in the Client table appear (Figure 2–11).

Q&A

How do I drag the lower edge?

Point to the lower edge, press and hold the left mouse button, move the mouse pointer to the new position for the lower edge, and then release the left mouse button. While the mouse pointer points to the lower edge of the field list, its shape changes to a double-headed arrow.

Q&A

Is it essential that I resize the field box?

No. You can always scroll through the list of fields using the scroll bar. If you can resize the field box so all fields appear, it is usually more convenient.

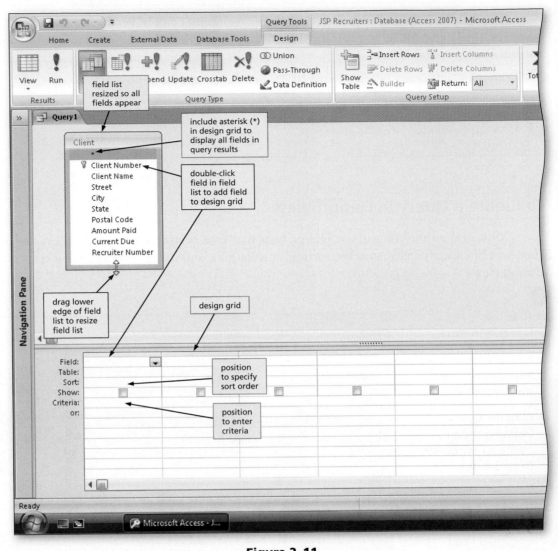

Figure 2–11

To Add Fields to the Design Grid

Once you have a new query displayed in Design view, you are ready to create the query by making entries in the design grid in the lower Pane of the window. You add the fields you want included in the Field row in the grid. Only the fields that appear in the design grid will be included in the results of the query. The following step includes the client number, client name, amount paid, and current due for all clients by adding only those fields in the design grid.

1

- Double-click the Client Number field in the field list to add the Client Number field to the query.

Q&A What if I add the wrong field?

Click just above the field name in the design grid to select the column and then press the DELETE key to remove the field.

- Double-click the Client Name field in the field list to add the Client Name field to the query.

- Add the Amount Paid field to the query by double-clicking the Amount Paid field in the field list.

- Add the Current Due field to the query (Figure 2–12).

Q&A What if I want to include all fields? Do I have to add each field individually?

No. Instead of adding individual fields, you can double-click the asterisk (*) to add the asterisk to the design grid.

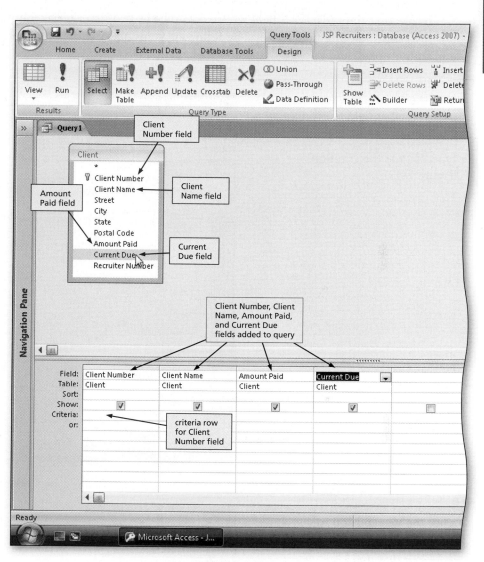

Figure 2–12

Entering Criteria

When you use queries, usually you are looking for those records that satisfy some criterion. In the simple query you created earlier, for example, you entered a criterion to restrict the records that were included to those on which the recruiter number was 24. In another query, you might want the name, amount paid, and current due amounts of the client whose number is FD89, for example, or of those clients whose names start with the letters, Be. You enter criteria in the Criteria row in the design grid below the field name to which the criterion applies. For example, to indicate that the client number must be FD89, you first must add the Client Number field to the design grid. You then would type FD89 in the Criteria row below the Client Number field.

To Use Text Data in a Criterion

To use **text data** (data in a field whose data type is Text) in criteria, simply type the text in the Criteria row below the corresponding field name. The following steps query the Client table and display the client number, client name, amount paid, and current due amount of client FD89.

1

- Click the Criteria row for the Client Number field to produce an insertion point.

- Type FD89 as the criterion (Figure 2–13).

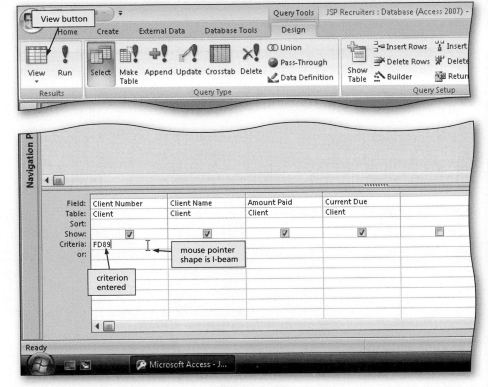

Figure 2–13

2

- Click the View button to display the query results (Figure 2–14).

 I noticed that there is a View button on both the Home tab and the Design tab. Do they both have the same effect?

Yes. Use whichever one you find most convenient.

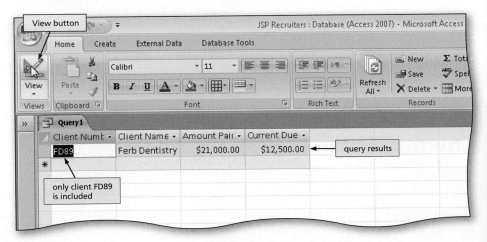

Figure 2–14

To Use a Wildcard

Microsoft Access supports wildcards. **Wildcards** are symbols that represent any character or combination of characters. One common wildcard, the **asterisk** (*), represents any collection of characters. Thus Be* represents the letters, Be, followed by any collection of characters. Another wildcard symbol is the **question mark** (?), which represents any individual character. Thus T?m represents the letter, T, followed by any single character followed by the letter, m, such as Tim or Tom.

The following steps use a wildcard to find the number, name, and address of those clients whose names begin with Be. Because you do not know how many characters will follow the Be, the asterisk is appropriate.

1

• Click the View button to return to Design view.

• If necessary, click the Criteria row below the Client Number field to produce an insertion point.

• Use the DELETE or BACKSPACE key as necessary to delete the current entry.

• Click the Criteria row below the Client Name field to produce an insertion point.

• Type Be* as the criterion (Figure 2–15).

Figure 2–15

2

• View the query results by clicking the View button (Figure 2–16).

 Experiment

• Vary the case of the letters in the criteria and view the results to determine whether case makes a difference when entering a wildcard.

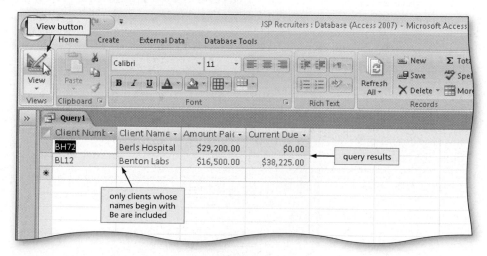

Figure 2–16

To Use Criteria for a Field Not Included in the Results

In some cases, you may have criteria for a particular field that should not appear in the results of the query. For example, you may want to see the client number, client name, address, and amount paid for all clients located in Berridge. The criteria involve the City field, which is not one of the fields to be included in the results.

To enter a criterion for the City field, it must be included in the design grid. Normally, this also would mean it would appear in the results. To prevent this from happening, remove the check mark from its Show check box in the Show row of the grid. The following steps display the client number, client name, amount paid, and current due for clients located in Berridge.

- Click the View button to return to Design view.

- Erase the criterion in the Client Name field.

- Include the City field in the query.

- Type Berridge as the criterion for the City field (Figure 2–17).

Figure 2–17

- Click the Show check box for the City field to remove the check mark (Figure 2–18).

Q&A

Could I have removed the check mark before entering the criterion?

Yes. The order in which you performed the two operations does not matter.

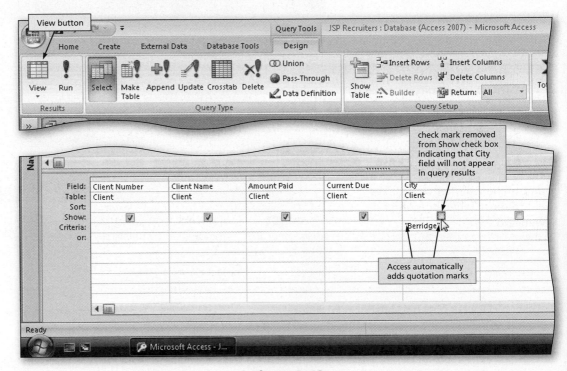

Figure 2–18

3

• View the query results (Figure 2–19).

🔍 **Experiment**

• Click the View button to return to Design view, enter a different city name, and view the results. Repeat this process with a variety of city names, including at least one city name that is not in the database.

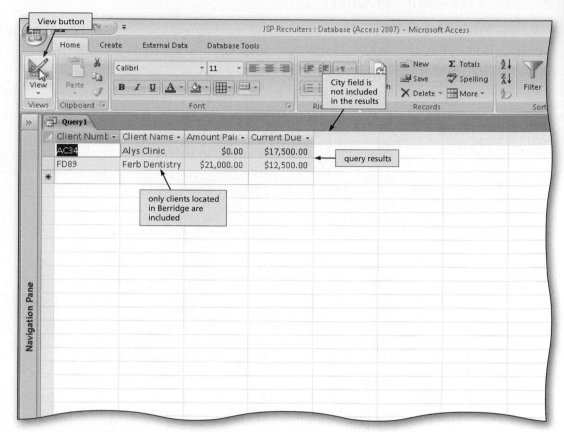

Figure 2–19

Creating a Parameter Query

If you wanted to find clients located in Fort Stewart rather than Berridge, you would either have to create a new query or modify the existing query by replacing Berridge with Fort Stewart as the criterion. Rather than giving a specific criterion when you first create the query, on occasion, you may want to be able to enter part of the criterion when you view the query results and then have the appropriate results appear. For example, to include all the clients located in Berridge, you could enter Berridge as a criterion in the City field. From that point on, every time you ran the query, only the clients in Berridge would appear.

A better way is to allow the user to enter the city at the time the user wants to view the results. Thus a user could view the query results, enter Berridge as the city and then see all the clients in Berridge. Later, the user could use the same query, but enter Fort Stewart as the city, and then see all the clients in Fort Stewart.

To enable this flexibility, you create a **parameter query**, which is a query that prompts for input whenever it is used. You enter a parameter, rather than a specific value, as the criterion. You create a parameter by enclosing a value in a criterion in square brackets. It is important that the value in the brackets does not match the name of any field. If you enter a field name in square brackets, Access assumes you want that particular field and does not prompt the user for input. For example, you could place [Enter City] as the criterion in the City field.

BTW

Removing a Table from a Query
If you add the wrong table to a query or have an extra table in the query, you can remove it by right-clicking the field list for the table and then clicking Remove Table on the shortcut menu.

To Create a Parameter Query

The following steps create a parameter query that prompts the user to enter a city, and then displays the client number, client name, amount paid, and current due for all clients located in that city.

1

- Return to Design view.

- Erase the current criterion in the City column, and then type [Enter City] as the new criterion (Figure 2–20).

Q&A

What is the purpose of the square brackets?

The square brackets indicate that the text entered is not text that the value in the column must match. Without the brackets, for example, Access would search for records on which the city is Enter City.

Q&A

What if I typed a field name in the square brackets?

Access would simply use the value in that field. In order to create a parameter query, it is essential that the text typed in the square brackets not be a field name.

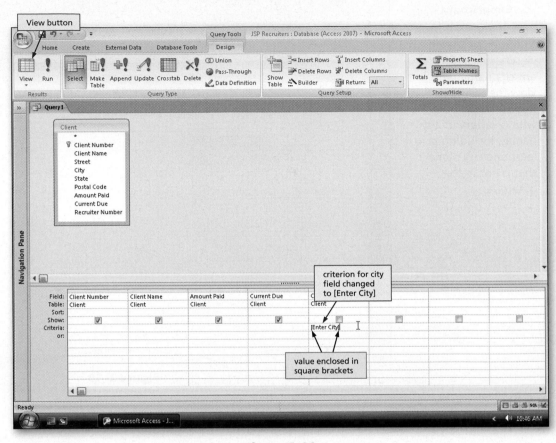

Figure 2–20

2

- Click the View button to display the Enter Parameter Value dialog box (Figure 2–21).

Figure 2–21

3

- Type `Fort Stewart` as the parameter value in the Enter City text box and then click the OK button (Figure 2–22).

Experiment

- Try other characters between the square brackets. In each case, view the results. When finished, change the characters between the square brackets back to Enter City.

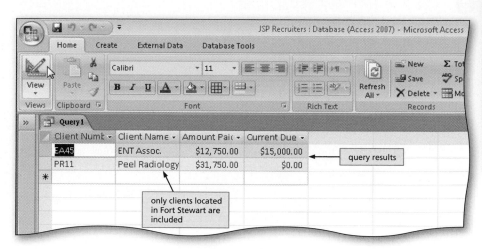

Figure 2–22

Each time you use this query, you will be asked to enter a city. Only clients in the city you enter will be included in the results.

To Save a Query

In many cases, you will want to repeatedly use the queries you construct. By saving the query, you eliminate the need to repeat all your entries. The following steps save the query you just have created and assign it the name Client-City Query.

1

- Click the Save button on the Quick Access Toolbar to open the Save As dialog box.

Q&A Can I also save from Design view?

Yes. You can save the query when you view it in Design view just as you can save the query when you view the query results in Datasheet view.

- Type `Client-City Query` in the Query Name text box (Figure 2–23).

Figure 2–23

- Click the OK button to save the query (Figure 2–24).

- Click the Close 'Client-City Query' button to close the query and remove it from the screen.

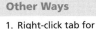

Other Ways

1. Right-click tab for query, click Save on shortcut menu
2. Press CTRL+S

Figure 2–24

To Use a Saved Query

Once you have saved a query, you can use and manipulate it at any time in the future by opening it. When you right-click the query in the Navigation Pane, Access displays a shortcut menu containing commands that allow you to open and change the design of the query. You also can print the results by clicking the Office Button, pointing to Print on the Office button menu, and then clicking Quick Print on the Print submenu.

The query always uses the data that is currently in the table. Thus, if changes have been made to the data since the last time you ran the query, the results of the query may be different. The following steps use the query named Client-City Query.

- Show the Navigation Pane.

- Right-click the Client-City Query to produce a shortcut menu.

- Click Open on the shortcut menu to open the query and display the Enter Parameter Value dialog box (Figure 2–25).

Q&A

What would have happened if there were no parameters?

You would immediately see the results without needing to furnish any additional information.

Figure 2–25

- Type `Fort Stewart` in the Enter City text box, and then click the OK button to display the results using Fort Stewart as the city as shown in Figure 2–24.

- Click the Close 'Client-City Query' button, shown in Figure 2–24, to close the query.

To Use a Number in a Criterion

To enter a number in a criterion, type the number without any dollar signs or commas. The following steps display all clients whose current due amount is $0.00.

1

- Hide the Navigation Pane.

- Click Create on the Ribbon to display the Create tab.

- Click the Query Design button to create a new query.

- With the Client table selected, click the Add button in the Show Table dialog box to add the Client table to the query.

- Click the Close button in the Show Table dialog box to remove the dialog box from the screen.

- Drag the lower edge of the field box down far enough so all fields in the Client table are displayed.

- Include the Client Number, Client Name, Amount Paid, and Current Due fields in the query.

- Type 0 as the criterion for the Current Due field (Figure 2–26).

Q&A Do I need to enter a dollar sign and decimal point?

No. Access will interpret 0 as $0.00, because the data type for the Current Due field is currency.

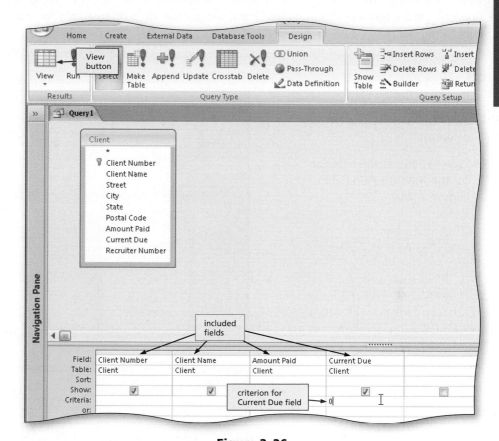

Figure 2–26

2

- View the query results (Figure 2–27).

Q&A Why did Access display the results as $0.00 when I only entered 0?

Access uses the format for the field to determine how to display the result. In this case the format indicated that Access should include the dollar sign and decimal point.

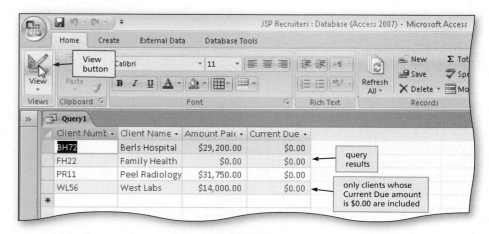

Figure 2–27

To Use a Comparison Operator in a Criterion

Unless you specify otherwise, Access assumes that the criteria you enter involve equality (exact matches). In the last query, for example, you were requesting those clients whose current due amount is equal to 0 (zero). If you want something other than an exact match, you must enter the appropriate **comparison operator**. The comparison operators are > (greater than), < (less than), >= (greater than or equal to), <= (less than or equal to), and NOT (not equal to).

The following steps use the > operator to find all clients whose amount paid is more than $20,000.00.

- Return to Design view.

- Erase the 0 in the Current Due column.

- Type >20000 as the criterion for the Amount Paid field (Figure 2–28).

Figure 2–28

- View the query results (Figure 2–29).

 Experiment

- Return to Design view. Try a different criterion involving a comparison operator in the Amount Paid field and view the results. When finished, return to Design view, enter the original criterion (>20000) in the Amount Paid field, and view the results.

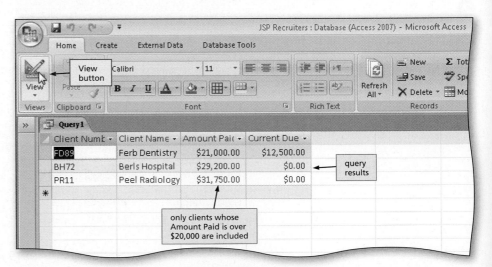

Figure 2–29

Using Compound Criteria

Often you will have more than one criterion that the data for which you are searching must satisfy. This type of criterion is called a **compound criterion**. Two types of compound criteria exist.

In an **AND criterion**, each individual criterion must be true in order for the compound criterion to be true. For example, an AND criterion would allow you to find those clients that have an amount paid greater than $20,000.00 and whose recruiter is recruiter 21.

Conversely, an **OR criterion** is true provided either individual criterion is true. An OR criterion would allow you to find those clients that have an amount paid greater than $20,000.00 or whose recruiter is recruiter 21. In this case, any client whose amount paid is greater than $20,000.00 would be included in the answer, regardless of whether the client's recruiter is recruiter 21. Likewise, any client whose recruiter is recruiter 21 would be included, regardless of whether the client had an amount paid greater than $20,000.00.

To Use a Compound Criterion Involving AND

To combine criteria with AND, place the criteria on the same line. The following steps use an AND criterion to find those clients whose amount paid is greater than $20,000.00 and whose recruiter is recruiter 21.

1

- Return to Design view.

- Include the Recruiter Number field in the query.

- Type 21 as the criterion for the Recruiter Number field (Figure 2–30).

Figure 2–30

- View the query results (Figure 2–31).

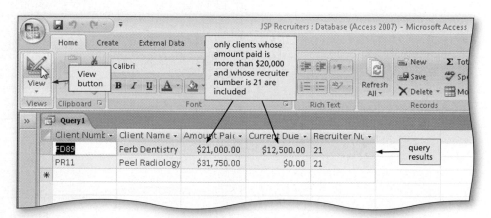

Figure 2–31

To Use a Compound Criterion Involving OR

To combine criteria with OR, the criteria must go on separate lines in the Criteria area of the grid. The following steps use an OR criterion to find those clients whose amount paid is greater than $20,000.00 or whose recruiter is recruiter 21 (or both).

- Return to Design view.

- If necessary, click the Criteria entry for the Recruiter Number field and then use the BACKSPACE key or the DELETE key to erase the entry ("21").

- Click the or: row (the row below the Criteria row) for the Recruiter Number field and then type 21 as the entry (Figure 2–32).

Figure 2–32

- View the query results (Figure 2–33).

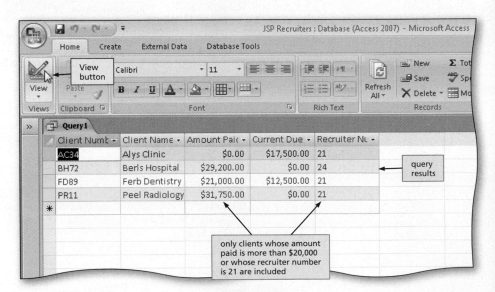

Figure 2–33

Sorting

In some queries, the order in which the records appear really does not matter. All you need to be concerned about are the records that appear in the results. It does not matter which one is first or which one is last.

In other queries, however, the order can be very important. You may want to see the cities in which clients are located and would like them arranged alphabetically. Perhaps you want to see the clients listed by recruiter number. Further, within all the clients of any given recruiter, you might want them to be listed by amount paid from largest amount to smallest.

To order the records in the answer to a query in a particular way, you **sort** the records. The field or fields on which the records are sorted is called the **sort key**. If you are sorting on more than one field (such as sorting by amount paid within recruiter number), the more important field (Recruiter Number) is called the **major key** (also called the **primary sort key**) and the less important field (Amount Paid) is called the **minor key** (also called the **secondary sort key**).

To sort in Microsoft Access, specify the sort order in the Sort row of the design grid below the field that is the sort key. If you specify more than one sort key, the sort key on the left will be the major sort key and the one on the right will be the minor key.

The following are guidelines related to sorting in queries.

BTW

OR Criteria in a Single Field
If you want to combine two criteria with OR in a single field, you can place the criteria on separate lines, or you can place the criteria on the same line with the word OR in between them. For example, to include those records in which the city is Berls or Mason, you could type Berls OR Mason in the Criteria row. You also can use the IN operator, which consists of the word IN followed by the criteria in parentheses. For example, you would type IN (Berls, Mason).

Plan Ahead

Determine whether special order is required.

1. **Determine whether sorting is required.** Examine the query or request to see if it contains words such as "order" or "sort" that would imply that the order of the query results is important. If so, you need to sort the query.

2. **Determine the sort key(s).** If sorting is required, identify the field or fields on which the results are to be sorted. Look for words such as "ordered by" or "sort the results by," both of which would indicate that the specified field is a sort key.

3. **If using two sort keys, determine major and minor key.** If you are using two sort keys, determine which one is more important. That will be the major key. Look for words such as "sort by amount paid within recruiter number," which imply that the overall order is by recruiter number. Thus, the Recruiter Number field would be the major sort key and the Amount Paid field would be the minor sort key.

4. **Determine sort order.** Words such as "increasing," "ascending," or "low-to-high" imply Ascending order. Words such as "decreasing," "descending," or "high-to-low" imply Descending order. Sorting in alphabetical order implies Ascending order. If there are no words to imply a particular order, you would typically use Ascending.

5. **Determine restrictions.** Examine the query or request to see if there are any special restrictions. One common restriction is to exclude duplicates. Another common restriction is to list only a certain number of records, for example to list only the first five records.

To Clear the Design Grid

If the fields you want to include in the next query are different from those in the previous query, it is usually simpler to start with a clear grid, that is, one with no fields already in the design grid. You always can clear the entries in the design grid by closing the query and then starting over. A simpler approach to clearing the entries is to select all the entries and then press the DELETE key. The following steps return to Design view and clear the design grid.

- Return to Design view.

- Click just above the Client Number column heading in the grid to select the column.

Q&A

I clicked above the column heading, but the column is not selected. What should I do?

You didn't point to the correct location. Be sure the mouse pointer turns to a down-pointing arrow and then click again.

- Hold the SHIFT key down and click just above the Recruiter Number column heading to select all the columns (Figure 2–34).

Figure 2–34

- Press the DELETE key to clear the design grid.

To Sort Data in a Query

If you have determined in the design process that a query is to be sorted, you must identify the sort key, that is, the field on which the results are to be sorted. In creating the query, you will need to specify the sort key to Access. The following steps sort the cities in the Client table by indicating that the City field is to be sorted. The steps specify Ascending sort order.

- Include the City field in the design grid.

- Click the Sort row below the City field, and then click the Sort row arrow to display a menu of possible sort orders (Figure 2–35).

Figure 2–35

2

• Click Ascending to select Ascending sort order (Figure 2–36).

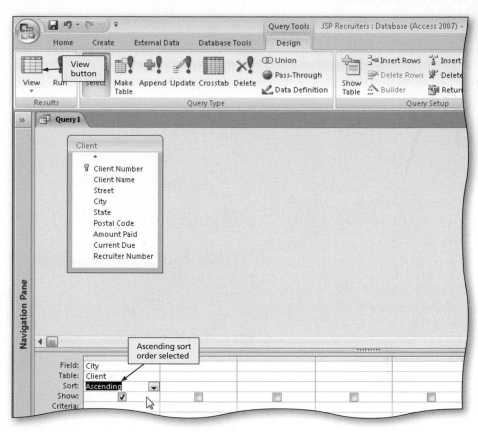

Figure 2–36

3

• View the query results (Figure 2–37).

🔎 **Experiment**

• Return to Design view and change the sort order to Descending. View the results. Return to Design view and change the sort order back to Ascending. View the results.

Why do some cities appear more than once?

More than one client is located in those cities.

Figure 2–37

To Omit Duplicates

When you sort data, duplicates normally are included. In Figure 2–37 on the previous page, for example, Berridge appeared twice, as did Fort Stewart and Tarleton. These duplicates do not add any value, so you can eliminate them from the results. To eliminate duplicates, display the query's property sheet. A **property sheet** is a window containing the various properties of the object. To omit duplicates, you will use the property sheet to change the Unique Values property from No to Yes.

The following steps produce a sorted list of the cities in the Client table in which each city is listed only once.

- Return to Design view.

- Click the second field in the design grid (the empty field following City).

- If necessary, click Design on the Ribbon to display the Design tab.

- Click the Property Sheet button on the Design tab to display the property sheet (Figure 2–38).

Q&A

My property sheet looks different. What should I do?

If your sheet looks different, you clicked the wrong place and will have to close the property sheet and repeat this step.

Figure 2–38

- Click the Unique Values property box, and then click the arrow that appears to produce a menu of available choices for Unique Values (Figure 2–39).

Figure 2–39

- Click Yes and then close the Query Properties sheet by clicking its Close button.

- View the query results (Figure 2–40).

Other Ways

1. Right-click second field in design grid, click Properties on shortcut menu

Figure 2–40

To Sort on Multiple Keys

The following steps sort on multiple keys. Specifically, the data is to be sorted by amount paid (low to high) within recruiter number, which means that the Recruiter Number field is the major key and the Amount Paid field is the minor key.

- Return to Design view.

- Clear the design grid.

- Include the Client Number, Client Name, Recruiter Number, and Amount Paid fields in the query in this order.

- Select Ascending as the sort order for both the Recruiter Number field and the Amount Paid field (Figure 2–41).

Figure 2–41

• View the query results (Figure 2–42).

Figure 2–42

Experiment

• Return to Design view and try other sort combinations for the Recruiter Number and Amount Paid fields, such as Ascending for Recruiter Number and Descending for Amount Paid. In each case, view the results to see the effect of the changes. When finished, select Ascending as the sort order for both fields.

Q&A

What if the Amount Paid field is to the left of the Recruiter Number?

It is important to remember that the major sort key must appear to the left of the minor sort key in the design grid. If you attempted to sort by amount paid within recruiter number, but placed the Amount Paid field to the left of the Recruiter Number field, your results would be incorrect.

To Create a Top-Values Query

Rather than show all the results of a query, you may want to show only a specified number of records or a percentage of records. Creating a **top-values query** allows you to quantify the results. When you sort records, you can limit results to those records having the highest (descending sort) or lowest (ascending sort) values. To do so, first create a query that sorts the data in the desired order. Next, use the Return box on the Design tab to change the number of records to be included from All to the desired number or percentage. The following steps show the first five records that were included in the results of the previous query.

• Return to Design view.

• If necessary, click Design on the Ribbon to display the Design tab.

• Click the Return box arrow on the Design tab to display the Return box menu (Figure 2–43).

Figure 2–43

2

- Click 5 in the Return box menu to specify that the query results should contain the first five rows.

Q&A
Could I have typed the 5? What about other numbers that do not appear in the list?

Yes, you could have typed the 5. For numbers not appearing in the list, you must type the number.

- View the query results (Figure 2–44).

3

- Close the query by clicking the Close 'Query1' button.

- When asked if you want to save your changes, click the No button.

Q&A
Do I need to close the query before creating my next query?

Not necessarily. When you use a top-values query, however, it is important to change the value in the Return box back to All. If you do not change the Return value back to All, the previous value will remain in effect. Consequently, you may very well not get all the records you should in the next query. A good practice whenever you use a top-values query is to close the query as soon as you are done. That way, you will begin your next query from scratch, which guarantees that the value is set back to All.

Figure 2–44

Joining Tables

In designing a query, you need to determine whether more than one table is required. If the question being asked involves data from both the Client and Recruiter tables, for example, both tables are required for the query. Such a query may require listing the number and name of each client along with the number and name of the client's recruiter. The client's name is in the Client table, whereas the recruiter's name is in the Recruiter table. Thus, this query cannot be completed using a single table; both the Client and Recruiter tables are required. You need to **join** the tables; that is, to find records in the two tables that have identical values in matching fields (Figure 2–45). In this example, you need to find records in the Client table and the Recruiter table that have the same value in the Recruiter Number fields.

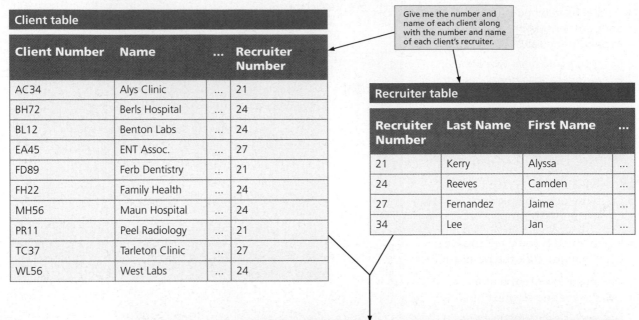

Join Types
The type of join that finds records from both tables that have identical values in matching fields is called an inner join. An inner join is the default join in Access. Outer joins are used to show all the records in one table as well as the common records; that is, the records that share the same value in the join field. In a left outer join, all rows from the table on the left are included. In a right outer join, all rows from the table on the right are included.

Figure 2–45

The following are guidelines related to joining tables.

Plan Ahead

Determine whether more than one table is required.

1. **Determine whether more than one table is required.** Examine the query or request to see if all the fields involved in the request are in one table. If the fields are in two (or more) tables, you need to join the tables.

2. **Determine the matching fields.** If joining is required, identify the matching fields in the two tables that have identical values. Look for the same column name in the two tables or for column names that are similar.

(continued)

(continued)

3. **Determine whether sorting is required.** Queries that join tables often are used as the basis for a report. If this is the case, it may be necessary to sort the results. For example, the Recruiter-Client Report is based on a query that joins the Recruiter and Client tables. The query is sorted by recruiter number and client number.

4. **Determine restrictions.** Examine the query or request to see if there are any special restrictions. For example, the query may only want clients whose current due amount is $0.00.

5. **Determine join properties.** Examine the query or request to see if you only want records from both tables that have identical values in matching fields. If you want to see records in one of the tables that do not have identical values, then you need to change the join properties. When two tables have fields with the same name, you also need to determine which table contains the field to be used in the query. For example, if you want to see all recruiters, even if they have no clients, then you should include the recruiter number from the Recruiter table in the design grid. If you want only records with identical values in matching fields, then it does not matter which matching field you select.

Plan Ahead

To Join Tables

If you have determined in the design process that you need to join tables, you will first bring field lists for both tables to the upper Pane of the Query window. Access will draw a line, called a **join line**, between matching fields in the two tables indicating that the tables are related. You then can select fields from either table. Access joins the tables automatically.

The first step is to create a new query and add the Recruiter table to the query. Then, add the Client table to the query. A join line will appear connecting the Recruiter Number fields in the two field lists. This join line indicates how the tables are related; that is, linked through these matching fields. (If you fail to give the matching fields the same name, Access will not insert the line. You can insert it manually, however, by clicking one of the two matching fields and dragging the mouse pointer to the other matching field.)

The following steps create a new query, add the Client table, and then select the appropriate fields.

1

- Click Create on the Ribbon to display the Create tab.

- Click the Query Design button to create a new query.

- Click the Recruiter table in the Show Table dialog box to select the table.

- Click the Add button to add a field list for the Recruiter table to the query (Figure 2–46).

Figure 2–46

2

- Click the Client table in the Show Table dialog box.

- Click the Add button to add a field list for the Client table.

- Close the Show Table dialog box by clicking the Close button.

- Expand the size of the field lists so all the fields in the Recruiter and Client tables appear (Figure 2–47).

Q&A

I didn't get a join line. What should I do?

Ensure that the names of the matching fields are exactly the same, the data types are the same, and the matching field is the primary key in one of the two tables. If all of these are true and you still don't have a join line, you can produce one by pointing to one of the matching fields and dragging to the other matching field.

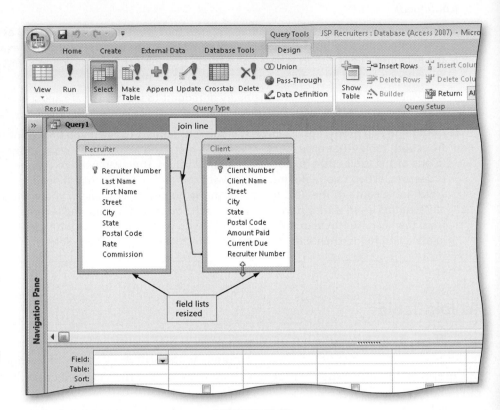

Figure 2–47

3

- In the design grid, include the Recruiter Number, Last Name, and First Name fields from the Recruiter table as well as the Client Number and Client Name fields from the Client table.

- Select Ascending as the sort order for both the Recruiter Number field and the Client Number field (Figure 2–48).

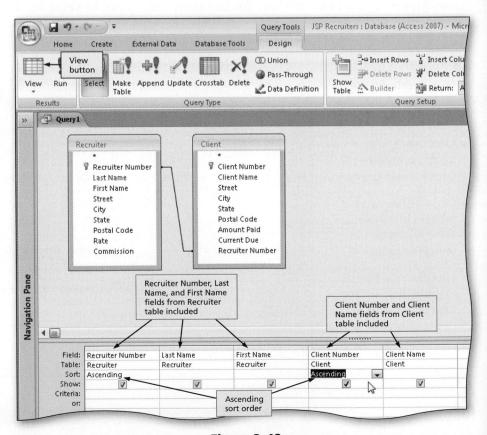

Figure 2–48

4

- View the query results (Figure 2–49).

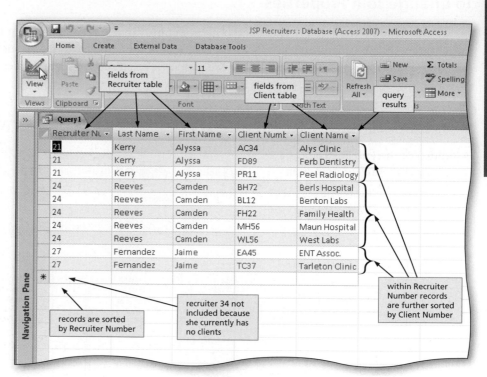

Figure 2–49

To Save the Query

The following steps save the query.

1

- Click the Save button on the Quick Access Toolbar to display the Save As dialog box.

- Type `Recruiter-Client Query` as the query name (Figure 2–50).

2

- Click the OK button to save the query.

Figure 2–50

To Change Join Properties

Normally records that do not match do not appear in the results of a join query. A recruiter such as Jan Lee, for whom no clients currently exist, for example, would not appear. To cause such a record to be displayed, you need to change the **join properties**, which are the properties that indicate which records appear in a join, of the query, as in the following steps.

- Return to Design view.

- Right-click the join line to produce a shortcut menu (Figure 2–51).

Q&A

I don't see Join Properties on my shortcut menu. What should I do?

If Join Properties does not appear on your shortcut menu, you did not point to the appropriate portion of the join line. You will need to point to the correct portion and right-click again.

Figure 2–51

- Click Join Properties on the shortcut menu to display the Join Properties dialog box (Figure 2–52).

Q&A

How do the options in the Join Properties dialog box match the various types of joins described earlier?

Option button 1 gives an inner join, option button 2 gives a left join, and option button 3 gives a right join.

Figure 2–52

3

- Click option button 2 to include all records from the Recruiter table regardless of whether they match any clients.

- Click the OK button.

- View the query results by clicking the View button (Figure 2–53).

- Click the Save button on the Quick Access Toolbar.

Experiment

- Return to Design view, change the Join properties, and select option button 3. View the results to see the effect of this option. When done, return to Design view, change the Join properties, and once again select option button 2.

Figure 2–53

4

- Close the Recruiter-Client Query by clicking the Close 'Recruiter-Client Query' button. Click No if asked to save the changes to the query.

To Create a Report Involving a Join

The following steps create the report shown in Figure 2–54. The records in the report are sorted (ordered) by Client Number within Recruiter Number. To ensure that the records appear in this order, the steps specify that the Recruiter Number and Client Number fields are sort keys.

Figure 2–54

1

- Show the Navigation Pane and be sure the Recruiter-Client Query is selected in the Navigation Pane.

Q&A

I have two copies of Recruiter-Client Query. Does it matter which one I use?

No. There are two copies because the recruiter-Client Query involves two tables. It does not matter which one you select.

- Click Create on the Ribbon to display the Create tab.

- Click the Report Wizard button to display the Report Wizard dialog box (Figure 2–55).

Figure 2–55

2

- Click the Add All Fields button to add all the fields in the Recruiter-Client Query.

- Click the Next button to display the next Report Wizard screen (Figure 2–56).

Figure 2–56

❸

- Because you will not specify any grouping, click the Next button in the Report Wizard dialog box to display the next Report Wizard screen.

- Because you already specified the sort order in the query, click the Next button again to display the next Report Wizard screen.

- Make sure that Tabular is selected as the Layout and Portrait is selected as the Orientation.

- Click the Next button to display the next Report Wizard screen.

- Be sure the Module style is selected.

- Click the Next button to display the next Report Wizard screen.

Figure 2–57

- Erase the current title, and then type Recruiter-Client Report as the new title.

- Click the Finish button to produce the report (Figure 2–57).

❹

- Click the Close button for the Recruiter-Client Report to remove the report from the screen.

To Print a Report

Once you have created a report, you can print it at any time. The layout will reflect the layout you created. The data in the report will always reflect current data. The following step prints the Recruiter-Client Report.

❶ With the Recruiter-Client Report selected in the Navigation Pane, click the Office Button, point to Print on the Office button menu, and then click Quick Print on the Print submenu to print the report.

To Restrict the Records in a Join

Sometimes you will want to join tables, but you will not want to include all possible records. For example, you would like to create a report showing only those clients whose Amount Paid is greater than $20,000, but you do not want the Amount Paid field to appear in the results. In such cases, you will relate the tables and include fields just as you did before. You also will include criteria. To include only those clients whose amount paid is more than $20,000.00, you will include >20000 as a criterion for the Amount Paid field.

The following steps modify the Recruiter-Client query to restrict the records that will be included in the join.

- Open the Recruiter-Client Query in Design view and hide the Navigation Pane.

- Add the Amount Paid field to the query.

- Type >20000 as the criterion for the Amount Paid field and then click the Show check box for the Amount Paid field to remove the check mark (Figure 2–58).

Figure 2–58

- View the query results (Figure 2–59).

- Close the query by clicking the Close 'Recruiter-Client Query' button.

- When asked if you want to save your changes, click the No button.

Figure 2–59

Calculations

If you have determined that a special calculation is required for a query, you then need to determine whether the calculation is an individual record calculation (for example, adding the values in two fields) or a group calculation (for example, finding the total of the values in a particular field on all the records).

JSP Recruiters may want to know the total amount (amount paid plus current due) from each client. This would seem to pose a problem because the Client table does not include a field for total amount. You can calculate it, however, because the total amount is equal to the amount paid plus the current due. A field that can be computed from other fields is called a **calculated field**. A calculated field is an individual record calculation.

JSP also may want to calculate the average amount paid for the clients of each recruiter. That is, they want the average for the clients of recruiter 21, the average for the clients of recruiter 24, and so on. This type of calculation is called a group calculation, because it involves groups of records. In this example, the clients of recruiter 21 would form one group, the clients of recruiter 24 would be a second, and the clients of recruiter 27 form a third group.

The following are guidelines related to calculations in queries.

BTW

Expression Builder
Access includes a tool to help you create complex expressions. If you click Build on the shortcut menu (see Figure 2-60 on the next page), Access displays the Expression Builder dialog box. The dialog box includes an expression box, operator buttons, and expression elements. You use the expression box to build the expression. You can type parts of the expression directly and paste operator buttons and expression elements into the box. You also can use functions in expressions.

Plan Ahead

Determine whether calculations are required.

1. **Determine whether calculations are required.** Examine the query or request to see if there are special calculations to be included. Look for words such as "total," "sum," "compute," or "calculate."

2. **Determine a name for the calculated field.** If calculations are required, decide on the name for the field. Assign a name that helps identify the contents of the field. For example, if you are adding the cost of a number of items, the name "Total Cost" would be appropriate. The name, also called an **alias**, becomes the column name when the query is run.

3. **Determine the format for the calculated field.** Determine how the calculated field should appear. If the calculation involves monetary amounts, you would use the currency format. If the calculated value contains decimals, determine how many decimal places to display.

To Use a Calculated Field in a Query

If you have determined that you need a calculated field in a query, you enter a name (alias) for the calculated field, a colon, and then the expression in one of the columns in the Field row. Any fields included in the expression must be enclosed in square brackets [ ]. For the total amount, for example, you will type Total Amount:[Amount Paid]+[Current Due] as the expression.

You can type the expression directly into the Field row. You will not be able to see the entire entry, however, because the Field row is not large enough. The preferred way is to select the column in the Field row and then use the Zoom command on its shortcut menu. When Access displays the Zoom dialog box, you can enter the expression.

You are not restricted to addition in calculations. You can use subtraction (-), multiplication (*), or division (/). You also can include parentheses in your calculations to indicate which calculations should be done first.

The steps on the next page use a calculated field to display the number, name, amount paid, current due, and the total amount for all clients.

1

- Create a query with a field list for the Client table.

- Add the Client Number, Client Name, Amount Paid, and Current Due fields to the query.

- Right-click the Field row in the first open column in the design grid to display a shortcut menu (Figure 2–60).

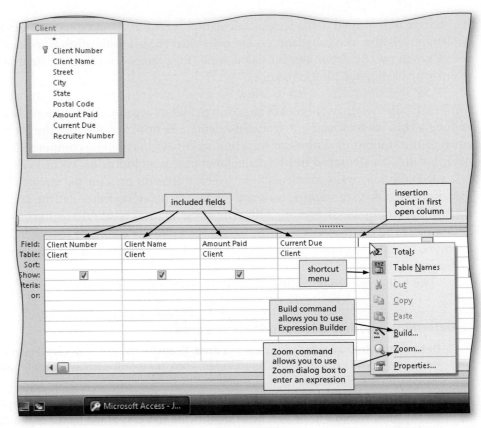

Figure 2–60

2

- Click Zoom on the shortcut menu to display the Zoom dialog box.

- Type `Total Amount:[Amount Paid]+[Current Due]` in the Zoom dialog box (Figure 2–61).

Q&A Do I always need to put square brackets around field names?

If the field name does not contain spaces, square brackets are technically not necessary, although it is still acceptable to use the brackets. It is a good practice, however, to get in the habit of using the brackets.

Figure 2–61

3

- Click the OK button to enter the expression (Figure 2–62).

Figure 2–62

4

- View the query results (Figure 2–63).

Experiment

- Return to Design view and try other expressions. In at least one case, omit the Total Amount and the colon. In at least one case, intentionally misspell a field name. In each case, view the results to see the effect of your changes. When finished, re-enter the original expression.

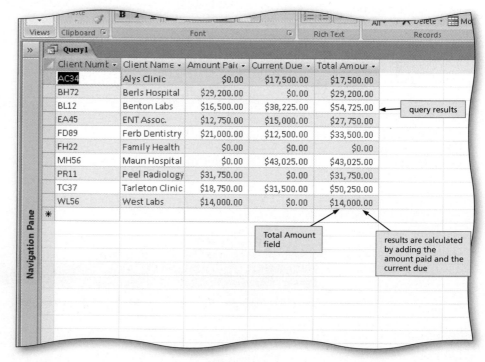

Figure 2–63

Instead of clicking Zoom on the shortcut menu, you can click Build. Access displays the Expression Builder dialog box that provides assistance in creating the expression. If you know the expression you will need, however, it is often easier to enter it using the Zoom command.

To Change a Caption

You can change the way items appear in the results of a query by changing their format. You also can change a query result's heading at the top of a column by changing the caption. Just as when you omitted duplicates, you will make this change by using a property sheet. In the property sheet, you can change the desired property, such as the format, the number of decimal places, or the caption. The following steps change the caption of the Amount Paid field to Paid and the caption of the Current Due field to Due.

- Return to Design view.

- Click Design on the Ribbon to display the Design tab.

- Click the Amount Paid field in the design grid, and then click the Property Sheet button on the Design tab.

- Click the Caption box, and then type `Paid` as the caption (Figure 2–64).

Q&A

My property sheet looks different. What should I do?

If your sheet looks different, you clicked the wrong place and will have to close the property sheet and repeat this step.

Figure 2–64

2

- Close the property sheet by clicking its Close button.

- Click the Current Due field in the design grid, and then click the Property Sheet button on the Design tab.

- Click the Caption box, and then type Due as the caption.

- Close the Property Sheet by clicking its Close button.

- View the query results (Figure 2–65).

3

- Click the Close 'Query1' button to close the query.

- When asked if you want to save your changes, click the No button.

Q&A

What would happen if I clicked the Yes button instead of the No button?

If you had saved the query, the changes you made to the properties would be saved in the database along with the query.

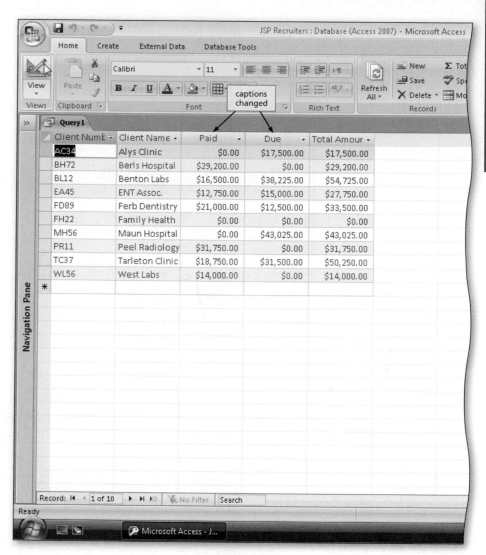

Figure 2–65

Other Ways

1. Right-click field in design grid, click Properties on shortcut menu

Calculating Statistics

For group calculations, Microsoft Access supports several built-in statistics: COUNT (count of the number of records), SUM (total), AVG (average), MAX (largest value), MIN (smallest value), STDEV (standard deviation), VAR (variance), FIRST (first value), and LAST (last value). These statistics are called aggregate functions. An **aggregate function** is a function that performs some mathematical function against a group of records. To use any of these aggregate functions in a query, you include it in the Total row in the design grid. The Total row routinely does not appear in the grid. To include it, click the Totals button on the Design tab.

To Calculate Statistics

The following steps create a new query for the Client table, include the Total row in the design grid, and then calculate the average amount paid for all clients.

- Create a new query with a field list for the Client table.

- If necessary, click Design on the Ribbon to display the Design tab.

- Add the Amount Paid field to the query.

- Click the Totals button on the Design tab to include the Total row in the design grid (Figure 2–66).

Figure 2–66

- Click the Total row in the Amount Paid column to display the Total box arrow.

- Click the Total box arrow to display the Total list (Figure 2–67).

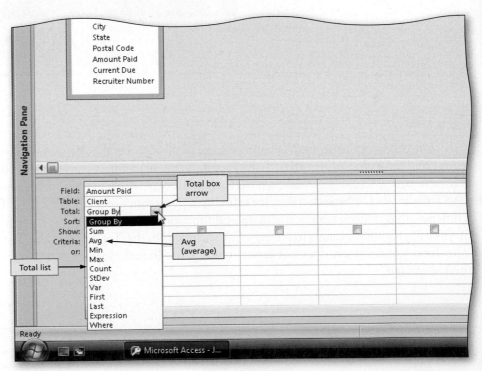

Figure 2–67

3

- Click Avg to indicate that Access is to calculate an average (Figure 2–68).

Figure 2–68

4

- View the query results (Figure 2–69).

Experiment

- Return to Design view and try other aggregate functions. In each case, view the results to see the effect of your selection. When finished, select average once again.

Figure 2–69

To Use Criteria in Calculating Statistics

Sometimes calculating statistics for all the records in the table is appropriate. In other cases, however, you will need to calculate the statistics for only those records that satisfy certain criteria. To enter a criterion in a field, first you select Where as the entry in the Total row for the field, and then enter the criterion in the Criteria row. The following steps use this technique to calculate the average amount paid for clients of recruiter 21.

- Return to Design view.

- Include the Recruiter Number field in the design grid.

- Click the Total box arrow in the Recruiter Number column to produce a Total list (Figure 2–70).

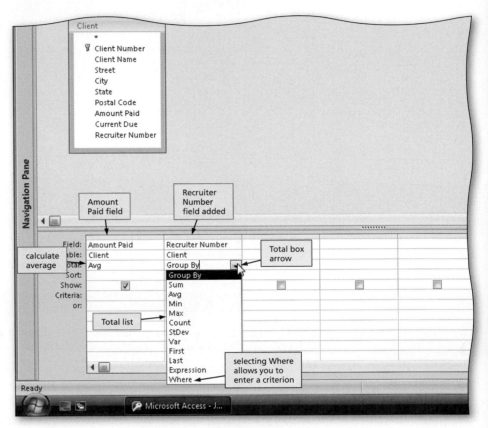

Figure 2–70

- Click Where.

- Type 21 as the criterion for the Recruiter Number field (Figure 2–71).

Figure 2–71

- View the query results (Figure 2–72).

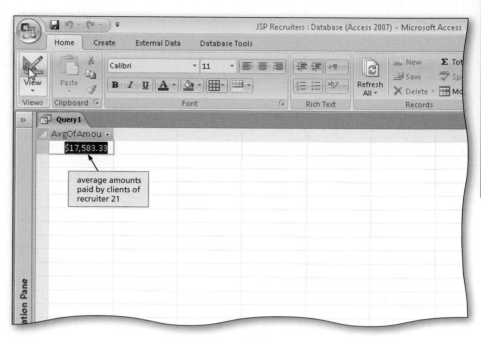

Figure 2–72

To Use Grouping

Another way statistics often are used is in combination with grouping; that is, statistics are calculated for groups of records. You may, for example, need to calculate the average amount paid for the clients of each recruiter. You will want the average for the clients of recruiter 21, the average for clients of recruiter 24, and so on.

Grouping means creating groups of records that share some common characteristic. In grouping by Recruiter Number, for example, the clients of recruiter 21 would form one group, the clients of recruiter 24 would form a second, and the clients of recruiter 27 form a third group. The calculations then are made for each group. To indicate grouping in Access, select Group By as the entry in the Total row for the field to be used for grouping.

The following steps calculate the average amount paid for clients of each recruiter.

- Return to Design view and clear the design grid.

- Include the Recruiter Number field in the query.

- Include the Amount Paid field in the query.

- Select Avg as the calculation in the Total row for the Amount Paid field (Figure 2–73).

Q&A

Why didn't I need to change the entry in the Total Row for the Recruiter Number field?

Group By currently is the entry in the Total row for the Recruiter Number field, which is correct; thus, it was not changed.

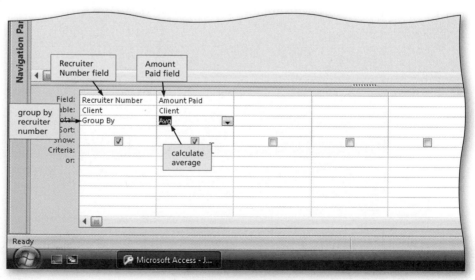

Figure 2–73

2

- View the query results (Figure 2–74).

3

- Close the query.

- Do not save your changes.

Figure 2–74

BTW

Certification
The Microsoft Certified Application Specialist (MCAS) program provides an opportunity for you to obtain a valuable industry credential — proof that you have the Access 2007 skills required by employers. For more information, see Appendix G or visit the Access 2007 Certification Web page (scsite.com/ac2007/cert).

Crosstab Queries

Crosstab queries are useful for summarizing data. A crosstab query calculates a statistic (for example, sum, average, or count) for data that is grouped by two different types of information. One of the types will appear down the side of the resulting datasheet, and the other will appear across the top.

For example, if you have determined that a query must summarize the sum of the amounts paid grouped by both city and recruiter number, you could have cities as the row headings, that is, down the side. You could have recruiter numbers as the column headings, that is, across the top. The entries within the data sheet represent the total of the amounts paid. Figure 2–75 shows a crosstab in which the total of amount paid is grouped by both city and recruiter number with cities down the left-hand side and recruiter numbers across the top. For example, the entry in the row labeled Fort Stewart and in the column labeled 21 represents the total of the amount paid by all clients of recruiter 21 who are located in Fort Stewart.

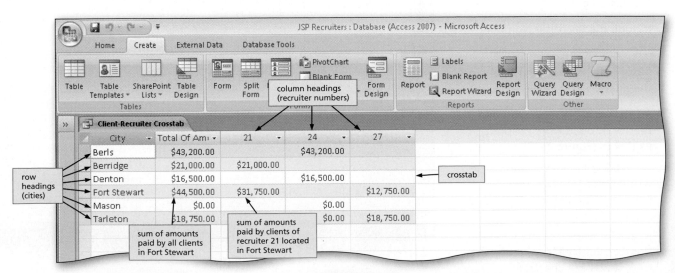

Figure 2–75

To Create a Crosstab Query

The following steps use the Crosstab Query wizard to create a crosstab query.

1

- Click Create on the Ribbon to display the Create tab.

- Click the Query Wizard button to display the New Query dialog box (Figure 2–76).

Figure 2–76

2

- Click Crosstab Query Wizard in the New Query dialog box.

- Click the OK button to display the Crosstab Query Wizard (Figure 2–77).

Figure 2–77

• With the Tables option button selected and the Client table selected, click the Next button to display the next Crosstab Query Wizard screen.

• Click the City field, and then click the Add Field button to select the City field for row headings (Figure 2–78).

Figure 2–78

• Click the Next button to display the next Crosstab Query Wizard screen.

• Click the Recruiter Number field to select the Recruiter Number field for column headings (Figure 2–79).

Figure 2–79

5

- Click the Next button to display the next Crosstab Query Wizard screen.

- Click the Amount Paid field to select the Amount Paid field for calculations.

 Experiment

- Click other fields. For each field, examine the list of calculations that are available. When finished, click the Amount Paid field again.

- Click Sum to select Sum as the calculation to be performed (Figure 2–80).

Q&A My list of functions is different. What did I do wrong?

Either you clicked the wrong field, or the Amount Paid field has the wrong data type. If you mistakenly assigned it the Text data type for example, you would not see Sum in the list of available calculations.

Figure 2–80

6

- Click the Next button to display the next Crosstab Query Wizard screen.

- Type `Client-Recruiter Crosstab` as the name of the query (Figure 2–81).

7

- Click the Finish button to produce the crosstab shown in Figure 2–75 on page AC 122.

- Close the query.

Q&A If I want to view the crosstab at some future date, can I just open the query?

Yes.

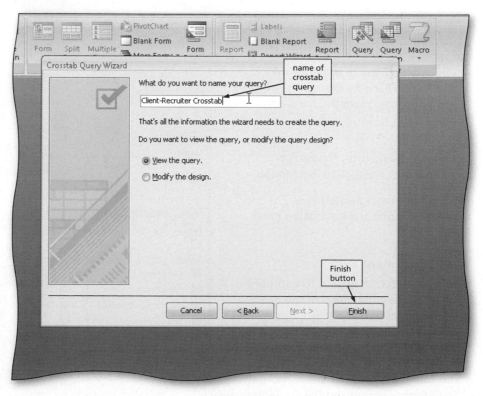

Figure 2–81

To Customize the Navigation Pane

Currently the entries in the Navigation Pane are organized by table. That is, the queries, forms, and reports associated with a particular table appear after the name of the table. In addition, all tables are included. You might want to change the way the information is organized. For example, you might wish to have all the queries appear together, all the forms appear together, and all the reports appear together, regardless of the table on which they are based. The following steps change the organization of the Navigation Pane.

- If necessary, click the Shutter Bar Open/Close Button to show the Navigation Pane.

- Click the Navigation Pane arrow to produce the Navigation Pane menu (Figure 2–82).

Q&A

If the Navigation Pane gets too cluttered, can I hide the objects in a group? For example, if the organization is by table, can I hide the objects (forms, queries, reports) for the table group and only show the table name?

Yes. Click the up arrow on the group bar. The objects under the table group will no longer appear and the up arrow will become a down arrow. To redisplay the objects, click the down arrow.

Figure 2–82

- Click Object Type to organize the Navigation Pane by the type of object rather than by table (Figure 2–83).

- Click the Navigation Pane arrow to produce the Navigation Pane menu.

- Click Tables and Related Views to once again organize the Navigation Pane by table.

 Experiment

- Select different Navigate To Category options to see the effect of the option. With each option you select, select different Filter By Group options to see the effect of the filtering. When you have finished experimenting, select the Tables and Related Views Navigate To Category option and the All Tables Filter By Group option.

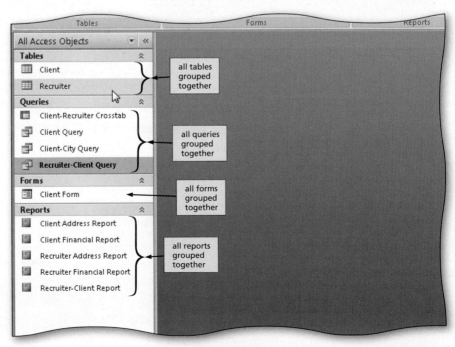

Figure 2–83

To Quit Access

You saved all your changes and are ready to quit Access. The following step quits Access.

1 Click the Close button on the right side of the Access title bar to quit Access.

BTW

Quick Reference
For a table that lists how to complete the tasks covered in this book using the mouse, Ribbon, shortcut menu, and keyboard, see the Quick Reference Summary at the back of this book, or visit the Access 2007 Quick Reference Web page (scsite.com/ac2007/qr).

Chapter Summary

In this chapter you have learned to create queries, enter fields, enter criteria, use text and numeric data in queries, use wildcards, use compound criteria, create parameter queries, sort data in queries, join tables in queries, perform calculations in queries, create crosstab queries, and customize the Navigation Pane. The following list includes all the new Access skills you have learned in this chapter.

1. Use the Simple Query Wizard to Create a Query (AC 78)
2. Use a Criterion in a Query (AC 81)
3. Print the Results of a Query (AC 83)
4. Create a Query in Design View (AC 83)
5. Add Fields to the Design Grid (AC 85)
6. Use Text Data in a Criterion (AC 86)
7. Use a Wildcard (AC 87)
8. Use Criteria for a Field Not Included in the Results (AC 88)
9. Create a Parameter Query (AC 90)
10. Save a Query (AC 91)
11. Use a Saved Query (AC 92)
12. Use a Number in a Criterion (AC 93)
13. Use a Comparison Operator in a Criterion (AC 94)
14. Use a Compound Criterion Involving AND (AC 95)
15. Use a Compound Criterion Involving OR (AC 96)
16. Clear the Design Grid (AC 98)
17. Sort Data in a Query (AC 98)
18. Omit Duplicates (AC 100)
19. Sort on Multiple Keys (AC 101)
20. Create a Top-Values Query (AC 102)
21. Join Tables (AC 105)
22. Save the Query (AC 107)
23. Change Join Properties (AC 108)
24. Create a Report Involving a Join (AC 109)
25. Print a Report (AC 111)
26. Restrict the Records in a Join (AC 112)
27. Use a Calculated Field in a Query (AC 113)
28. Change a Caption (AC 116)
29. Calculate Statistics (AC 118)
30. Use Criteria in Calculating Statistics (AC 120)
31. Use Grouping (AC 121)
32. Create a Crosstab Query (AC 123)
33. Customize the Navigation Pane (AC 126)

If you have a SAM user profile, you may have access to hands-on instruction, practice, and assessment. Log in to your SAM account (http://sam2007.course.com) to launch any assigned training activities or exams that relate to the skills covered in this chapter.

Learn It Online

Test your knowledge of chapter content and key terms.

Instructions: To complete the Learn It Online exercises, start your browser, click the Address bar, and then enter the Web address `scsite.com/ac2007/learn`. When the Access 2007 Learn It Online page is displayed, click the link for the exercise you want to complete and then read the instructions.

Chapter Reinforcement TF, MC, and SA
A series of true/false, multiple choice, and short answer questions that test your knowledge of the chapter content.

Flash Cards
An interactive learning environment where you identify chapter key terms associated with displayed definitions.

Practice Test
A series of multiple choice questions that test your knowledge of chapter content and key terms.

Who Wants To Be a Computer Genius?
An interactive game that challenges your knowledge of chapter content in the style of a television quiz show.

Wheel of Terms
An interactive game that challenges your knowledge of chapter key terms in the style of the television show *Wheel of Fortune*.

Crossword Puzzle Challenge
A crossword puzzle that challenges your knowledge of key terms presented in the chapter.

Apply Your Knowledge

Reinforce the skills and apply the concepts you learned in this chapter.

Using the Query Wizard, Creating a Parameter Query, Joining Tables, and Creating a Report
Instructions: Start Access. Open the The Bike Delivers database that you modified in Apply Your Knowledge in Chapter 1 on page AC 64. (If you did not complete this exercise, see your instructor for a copy of the modified database.)

Perform the following tasks:

1. Use the Simple Query Wizard to create a query for the Customer table. Include the Customer Name, Balance, and Courier Number in the query. Assign the name, Customer Query, to the query.

2. Create a query for the Customer table and add the Customer Number, Customer Name, Courier Number, and Balance fields to the design grid. Sort the records in descending order by Balance. Add a criterion for the Courier Number field that allows the user to enter a different courier each time the query is run. Save the query as Courier Parameter Query.

3. Create a query that joins the Courier and the Customer tables. Add the Courier Number, First Name, and Last Name fields from the Courier table and the Customer Number and Customer Name fields from the Customer table. Sort the records in ascending order by Courier Number and Customer Number. All couriers should appear in the result even if they currently have no customers. Save the query as Courier-Customer Query.

4. Create the report shown in Figure 2–84. The report uses the Courier-Customer Query.

Courier-Customer Report				
Courier Number	Customer Number	First Name	Last Name	Customer Name
102	AS36	Chou	Dang	Asterman Ind.
102	CJ16	Chou	Dang	CJ Gallery
102	ME71	Chou	Dang	Mentor Group
109	AU54	Michelle	Hyde	Author Books
	BL92	Mi	Hyde	Shop

Figure 2–84

5. Submit the revised database in the format specified by your instructor.

Extend Your Knowledge

Extend the skills you learned in this chapter and experiment with new skills. You may need to use Help to complete the assignment.

Creating Crosstab Queries, Creating Queries Using Criteria

Instructions: Start Access. Open the Groom n Fluff database. See the inside back cover of this book for instructions for downloading the Data Files for Students, or see your instructor for information on accessing the files required in this book.

Groom n Fluff is a small pet grooming business. The owner has created an Access database in which to store information about the customers she serves and the pet groomers she employs. You will create the crosstab query shown in Figure 2–85. You also will query the database using specified criteria.

Figure 2–85

Continued >

STUDENT ASSIGNMENTS

Extend Your Knowledge *continued*

Perform the following tasks:

1. Create the crosstab query shown in Figure 2–85 on the previous page. The crosstab groups the average of customers' balances by city and groomer number.

2. Create a query to find all customers who do not live in Grant City. Include the Customer Number, Last Name, and Balance fields in the design grid. Save the query as Not Criteria Query.

3. Create a query to find all customers who do not have a telephone number. Include the Customer Number, Last Name, First Name, Street, and City fields in the query results. Save the query as Missing Values Query.

4. Create a query to find all customers whose balance is between $20.00 and $60.00. Include the Customer Number, Last Name, and Balance fields in the design grid. Save the query as Number Range Query.

5. Create a query to find all customers where the groomer number is 203 or 205 and the balance is greater than $40.00. Include the Customer Number, Last Name, First Name, Balance, and Groomer Number fields in the design grid. Save the query as Compound Criteria Query.

6. Change the database properties, as specified by your instructor. Submit the revised database in the format specified by your instructor.

Make It Right

Analyze a database and correct all errors and/or improve the design.

Correcting Errors in the Query Design

Instructions: Start Access. Open the Keep It Green database. See the inside back cover of this book for instructions for downloading the Data Files for Students, or see your instructor for information on accessing the files required in this book.

Keep It Green is a database maintained by a small landscaping business. The queries shown in Figure 2–86 contain a number of errors that need to be corrected before the queries run properly. The sort query shown in Figure 2–86a displays the query results in the proper order (First Name, Last Name, Street, City) but it is sorted incorrectly. The query results should be sorted by last name within city in ascending order. Also the caption for the Street field should be Address. Save the query with your changes.

When you try to run the join query for the Keep It Green database, the message shown in Figure 2–86b appears. The query joins the Worker table and the Customer table. It also calculates the total amount for each customer. The query should be sorted in alphabetical order by worker last name and customer last name. Correct the error that is causing the message shown in Figure 2–86b and sort the records properly. Save the query with your changes.

Change the database properties, as specified by your instructor. Submit the revised database in the format specified by your instructor.

(a) Incorrect Sort Query

(b) Incorrect Join Query

Figure 2–86

In the Lab

Design, create, modify, and/or use a database following the guidelines, concepts, and skills presented in this chapter. Labs are listed in order of increasing difficulty.

Lab 1: Querying the JMS TechWizards Database

Problem: The management of JMS TechWizards has determined a number of questions it wants the database management system to answer. You must obtain answers to the questions posed by management.

Instructions: Use the database created in the In the Lab 1 of Chapter 1 on page AC 67 for this assignment or see your instructor for information on accessing the files required for this book. Perform the following tasks:

1. Open the JMS TechWizards database and create a new query for the Client table that includes the Client Number, Client Name, and Technician Number fields in the design grid for all clients where the technician number is 23. Save the query as Lab 2-1 Step 1 Query.

2. Create a query that includes the Client Number, Client Name, and Paid fields for all clients located in Liberty Corner with a paid amount greater than $500.00. Save the query as Lab2-1 Step 2 Query.

3. Create a query that includes the Client Number, Client Name, Street, and City fields for all clients whose names begin with Gr. Save the query as Lab 2-1 Step 3 Query.

4. Create a query that lists all cities in descending order. Each city should appear only once. Save the query as Lab 2-1 Step 4 Query.

5. Create a query that allows the user to enter the city to search when the query is run. The query results should display the Client Number, Client Name, and Billed. Test the query by searching for those records where the client is located in Anderson. Save the query as Client-City Query.

Continued >

In the Lab continued

6. Include the Client Number, Client Name, and Billed fields in the design grid. Sort the records in descending order by the Billed field. Display only the top 25 percent of the records in the query result. Save the query as Lab 2-1 Step 6 Query.

7. Join the Technician and the Client table. Include the Technician Number, First Name, and Last Name fields from the Technician table. Include the Client Number, Client Name, and Billed from the Client table. Sort the records in ascending order by technician's last name and client name. All technicians should appear in the result even if they currently have no clients. Save the query as Technician-Client query.

8. Open the Technician-Client query in Design view and remove the Client table. Add the Hourly Rate field to the design grid following the Last Name field. Calculate the number of hours each technician has worked (YTD Earnings/Hourly Rate). Assign the alias Hours Worked to the calculated field. Change the caption for the Hourly Rate field to Rate. Display hours worked as an integer (0 decimal places). Use the Save As command to save the query as Lab 2-1 Step 8 Query.

9. Create a query to display the average billed amount for all clients. Save the query as Lab 2-1 Step 9 Query.

10. Create a query to count the number of clients for technician 23. Save the query as Lab 2-1 Step 10 Query.

11. Create a query to display the average billed amount for each technician. Save the query as Lab 2-1 Step 11 Query.

12. Create the crosstab shown in Figure 2–87. The crosstab groups total of clients' paid amounts by city and technician number. Save the crosstab as City-Technician Crosstab.

13. Submit the revised database in the format specified by your instructor.

City	Total Of Paic	22	23	29
Anderson	$1,005.00	$255.00	$0.00	$750.00
Kingston	$548.50	$548.50	$0.00	
Liberty Corner	$565.00		$565.00	

Figure 2–87

In the Lab

Lab 2: Querying the Hockey Fan Zone Database

Problem: The management of the Hockey Fan Zone store has determined a number of questions it wants the database management system to answer. You must obtain answers to the questions posed by management.

Instructions: Use the database created in the In the Lab 2 of Chapter 1 on page AC 68 for this assignment, or see your instructor for information on accessing the files required for this book. Perform the following tasks:

1. Open the Hockey Fan Zone database and use the query wizard to create a query that includes the Item Number, Description, On Hand, and Cost fields for all records in the Item table. Name the query Lab 2-2 Step 1 Query.

2. Create a query that includes the Item Number, Description, Cost, and Supplier Code fields for all products where the Supplier Code is LG. Save the query as Lab 2-2 Step 2 Query.

3. Create a query that includes the Item Number and Description fields for all products where the description starts with the letter B. Save the query as Lab 2-2 Step 3 Query.

4. Create a query that includes the Item Number and Description field for all products with a cost less than $5.00. Save the query as Lab 2-2 Step 4 Query.

5. Create a query that includes the Item Number and Description field for all products with a selling price greater than $15.00. Save the query as Lab 2-2 Step 5 Query.

6. Create a query that includes all fields for all products with a selling price greater than $10.00 and where the number on hand is fewer than 10. Save the query as Lab 2-2 Step 6 Query.

7. Create a query that includes all fields for all products that have a selling price greater than $15.00 or a supplier code of AC. Save the query as Lab 2-2 Step 7 Query.

8. Join the Supplier table and the Item table. Include the Supplier Code and Supplier Name fields from the Supplier table and the Item Number, Description, On Hand, and Cost fields from the Item table. Sort the records in ascending order by Supplier Code and Item Number. Save the query as Supplier-Item Query. Note that the Report Wizard limits the size of the On Hand column header because it is a number field.

9. Create the report shown in Figure 2–88. The report uses the Supplier-Item query and the Module style.

Supplier-Item Report

Supplier Code	Item Number	Supplier Name	Description	Hand	Cost
AC	5923	Ace Clothes	Jersey	12	$21.45
AC	7810	Ace Clothes	Tee Shirt	32	$9.50
LG	3663	Logo Goods	Ball Cap	30	$11.15
LG	4563	Logo Goods	Earrings	10	$4.50
LG	4593	Logo Goods	Foam Finger	25	$2.95
LG	7930	Logo Goods	Visor	9	$11.95
MN	3683	Mary's Novelties	Bumper Sticker	50	$0.95
MN	6189	Mary's Novelties	Koozies	35	$2.00
MN	6343	Mary's Novelties	Note Cube	7	$5.75

Figure 2–88

10. Create a query that includes the Item Number, Description, On Hand, and Cost fields. Calculate the inventory value (on hand * cost) for all records in the table. Change the caption for the On Hand column to In Stock. Format inventory value as currency with two decimal places. Sort the records in descending order by inventory value. Save the query as Lab 2-2 Step 10 Query.

11. Create a query that calculates and displays the average cost of all items. Save the query as Lab 2-2 Step 11 Query.

12. Create a query that calculates and displays the average cost of items grouped by supplier code. Save the query as Lab 2-2 Step 12 Query.

13. Submit the revised database in the format specified by your instructor.

In the Lab

Lab 3: Querying the Ada Beauty Supply Database

Problem: The management of Ada Beauty Supply has determined a number of questions it wants the database management system to answer. You must obtain answers to the questions posed by management.

Instructions: Use the database created in the In the Lab 3 of Chapter 1 on page AC 69 for this assignment, or see your instructor for information on accessing the files required for this book. For Part 1 and Part 3, save each query using a format similar to the following: Lab 2-3 Part 1a Query, Lab 2-3 Part 3a Query, and so on. Submit the revised database in the format specified by your instructor.

Instructions Part 1: Create a new query for the Customer table and include the Customer Number, Customer Name, Balance, and Amount Paid fields in the design grid. Answer the following questions: (a) Which customers' names begin with C? (b) Which customers are located on Devon? (c) Which customers have a balance of $0.00? (d) Which customers have a balance greater than $200.00 and have an amount paid less than $800.00? (e) Which two customers have the highest balances? (f) For each customer, what is the total of the balance and amount paid amounts?

Instructions Part 2: Join the Sales Rep and the Customer table. Include the Sales Rep Number, First Name, and Last Name from the Sales Rep table and the Customer Number, Customer Name, and Amount Paid from the Customer table in the design grid. Sort the records in ascending order by Sales Rep Number and Customer Number. All sales reps should appear in the result even if they currently have no customers. Save the query as Sales Rep-Customer Query.

Instructions Part 3: Calculate the following statistics: (a) What is the average balance for customers assigned to sales rep 44? (b) What is the total balance for all customers? (c) What is the total amount paid for each sales rep?

Cases and Places

Apply your creative thinking and problem solving skills to design and implement a solution.

• EASIER   •• MORE DIFFICULT

• 1: Querying the Second Hand Goods Database

Use the Second Hand Goods database you created in Cases and Places 1 in Chapter 1 on page AC 71 for this assignment, or see your instructor for information on accessing the files required for this book. Create queries for the following:

a. Find the number and description of all items that contain the word Table.

b. Find the item number, description, and condition of the item that has the earliest posting date.

c. Find the total price of each item available for sale. Show the item description and total price.

d. Find the seller of each item. Show the seller's first name and last name as well as the item description, price, quantity, and date posted. Sort the results by item description within seller last name.

e. Create a parameter query that will allow the user to enter an item description when the query is run. The user should see all fields in the query result.

f. Find all items posted between April 1, 2008 and April 4, 2008. The user should see all fields in the query result.

Submit the revised database in the format specified by your instructor.

• 2: Querying the BeachCondo Rentals Database

Use the BeachCondo Rentals database you created in Cases and Places 2 in Chapter 1 on page AC 71 for this assignment, or see your instructor for information on accessing the files required for this book. Create queries for the following:

a. Find all units that rent for less than $1,000 per week and have at least two bedrooms. The user should see all fields in the query result.

b. Find all units that are on the fourth floor. (Hint: The first digit of the Unit Number field indicates the floor.) Include the Unit Number and the Weekly Rate fields in the query result.

c. Find all units that have more than one bedroom and more than one bathroom and provide linens. Include the Unit Number, Bedrooms, and Weekly Rate fields in the query result.

d. Owner BE20 offers a 15 percent discount on the weekly rate if renters rent for more than one week. What is the discounted weekly rental rate for his units? Your result should include the unit number, bedrooms, bathrooms, sleeps, and discounted weekly rate in your result. Be sure the discounted rate appears as currency.

e. List the owner's first and last name as well as telephone number. Also include the unit number and the weekly rate. All owners should appear in the result even if they currently have no rental units.

f. Find the highest and lowest weekly rate.

Submit the revised database in the format specified by your instructor.

•• 3: Querying the Restaurant Database

Use the restaurant database you created in Cases and Places 3 in Chapter 1 on page AC 71 for this assignment, or see your instructor for information on accessing the files required for this book. Using the Plan Ahead guidelines presented in this chapter, determine at least five questions the conference director might want to ask the database. Using a word processing program, such as Microsoft Word, write the questions in your own words. Then, design the queries for Access. Run and save each query. Submit the Word document and the revised database in the format specified by your instructor.

Continued >

Cases and Places *continued*

•• 4: Designing Queries to Help in Your Job Search

Make It Personal

Use the contacts database you created in Cases and Places 4 in Chapter 1 on page AC 71 for this assignment, or see your instructor for information on accessing the files required for this book. Consider your own personal job situation. What questions would you want to ask this database? Using a word processing program, such as Microsoft Word, write the questions in your own words. Can your database answer the questions that you listed? If it can, design the queries for Access. Run and save each query. In your Word document, identify which questions were posed to Access and which questions could not be answered. For questions that could not be answered, explain why your database cannot answer the question. Submit the Word document and the revised database in the format specified by your instructor.

•• 5: Creating Queries to Analyze Data

Working Together

Obtain a copy of the weather page of your local newspaper. As a team, choose 30 cities of interest. Create a database that contains one table and has five fields (City, State or Province, High Temp, Low Temp, Sky). Use the newspaper's abbreviations for Sky; for example, c for cloudy, r for rain and so on. Create queries that do the following:

a. Display the five cities with the highest high temperatures.

b. Calculate the difference between the high and low temperatures for each city.

c. Display the average high and low temperature for all cities.

d. List the states or provinces in your table. Each state or province should appear only once.

Write a one-page paper that explains what the team learned from querying the database and any conclusions you can draw about the data — for example, describe the Sky conditions for the cities with the least difference in high and low temperature. Submit the assignment in the format specified by your instructor.

1 Creating and Editing a Presentation

Objectives

You will have mastered the material in this chapter when you can:

- Start and quit PowerPoint
- Describe the PowerPoint window
- Select a document theme
- Create a title slide and text slides with single- and multi-level bulleted lists
- Save a presentation
- Copy elements from one slide to another

- View a presentation in Slide Show view
- Open a presentation
- Display and print a presentation in grayscale
- Check spelling
- Use PowerPoint Help

1 | Creating and Editing a Presentation

What Is Microsoft Office PowerPoint 2007?

Microsoft Office PowerPoint 2007 is a complete presentation graphics program that allows you to produce professional-looking presentations (Figure 1–1). A PowerPoint **presentation** also is called a **slide show**.

PowerPoint contains several features to simplify creating a slide show. For example, the results-oriented user interface can boost productivity by making tasks and options readily accessible. Professionally designed standard layouts help you save time by formatting and creating content. You then can modify these layouts to create custom slides to fit your specific needs. To make your presentation more impressive, you can add diagrams, tables, pictures, video, sound, and animation effects. Additional PowerPoint features include the following:

- **Word processing** — Create bulleted lists, combine words and images, find and replace text, and use multiple fonts and type sizes.
- **Outlining** — Develop your presentation using an outline format. You also can import outlines from Microsoft Word or other word processing programs.
- **Charting** — Create and insert charts into your presentations and then add effects and chart elements.
- **Drawing** — Form and modify diagrams using shapes such as arcs, arrows, cubes, rectangles, stars, and triangles. Then apply Quick Styles to customize and add effects. Arrange these objects by sizing, scaling, and rotating.
- **Inserting multimedia** — Insert artwork and multimedia effects into your slide show. The Microsoft Clip Organizer contains hundreds of media files, including pictures, photos, sounds, and movies.
- **Saving to the Web** — Save presentations or parts of a presentation in HTML format so they can be viewed and manipulated using a browser. You can publish your slide show to the Internet or to an intranet.
- **E-mailing** — Send your entire slide show as an attachment to an e-mail message.
- **Collaborating** — Share your presentation with friends and coworkers. Ask them to review the slides and then insert comments that offer suggestions to enhance the presentation.
- **Preparing delivery** — Rehearse integrating PowerPoint slides into your speech by setting timings, using presentation tools, showing only selected slides in a presentation, and packaging the presentation for a CD.

This latest version of PowerPoint has many new features to increase your productivity. Graphics and other shape effects allow you to add glow, shadowing, 3-D effects, and other appealing visuals. Typography effects enhance the design's impact. PowerPoint themes apply a consistent look to each graphic, font, and table color in an entire presentation. Digital signatures enable you to verify that no one has altered your presentation since you created it, and the Document Inspector removes private data, such as comments and hidden text.

PowerPoint gives you the flexibility to make presentations using a projection device attached to a personal computer or using overhead transparencies. In addition, you can take advantage of the World Wide Web and run virtual presentations on the Internet. PowerPoint also can create paper printouts of the individual slides, outlines, and speaker notes.

Project Planning Guidlines

The process of developing a presentation that communicates specific information requires careful analysis and planning. As a starting point, establish why the presentation is needed. Next, analyze the intended audience for the presentation and their unique needs. Then, gather information about the topic and decide what to include in the presentation. Finally, determine the presentation design and style that will be most successful at delivering the message. Details of these guidelines are provided in Appendix A. In addition, each project in this book provides practical applications of these planning considerations.

Project — Presentation with Bulleted Lists

In Project 1, you will follow proper design guidelines and learn to use PowerPoint to create, save, and print the slides shown in Figures 1–1a through 1–1e on this page and the next. The objective is to produce a presentation, called A World Beneath the Waves, to help the Student Government Association (SGA) President, Dave Ehlin, promote the annual spring break diving and snorkeling trip to Cabo San Lucas, Mexico. This slide show presents the highlights of this trip and promotes the included amenities, tour prices, and the inviting Pacific waters. Some of the text will have formatting and color enhancements. In addition, you will print handouts of your slides to distribute to students.

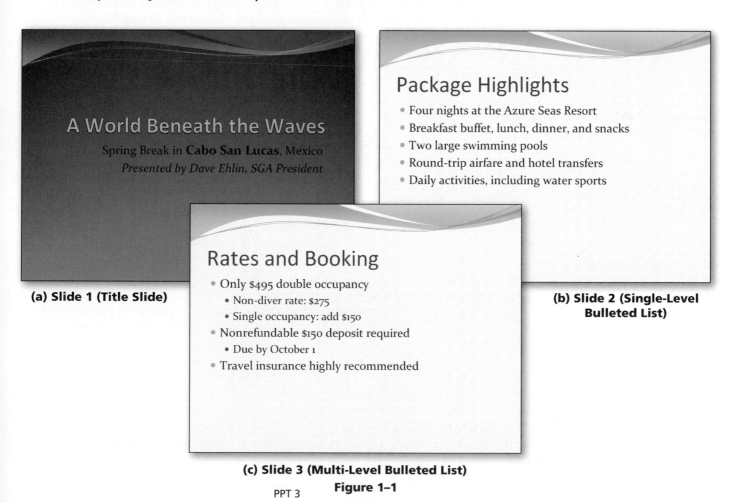

(a) Slide 1 (Title Slide)

(b) Slide 2 (Single-Level Bulleted List)

(c) Slide 3 (Multi-Level Bulleted List)

PPT 3   **Figure 1–1**

(d) Slide 4 (Multi-Level Bulleted List)   **(e) Slide 5 (Closing Slide)**

Figure 1–1 (continued)

PowerPoint allows you to produce slides to use in an academic, business, or other environment. One of the more common uses of these slides is to enhance an oral presentation. A speaker may desire to convey information, such as urging students to participate in a food drive, explaining first aid, or describing the changes in an employee benefit package. The PowerPoint slides should reinforce the speaker's message and help the audience members retain the information presented. An accompanying handout gives audience members reference notes and review material after the presentation's conclusion.

Overview

As you read this chapter, you will learn how to create the presentation shown in Figure 1–1 by performing these general tasks:

- Select an appropriate document theme.
- Enter titles and text on slides.
- Change the size, color, and style of text.
- View the presentation on your computer.
- Save the presentation so you can modify and view it at a later time.
- Print handouts of your slides.

Plan Ahead

> **General Project Guidelines**
> When creating a PowerPoint document, the actions you perform and decisions you make will affect the appearance and characteristics of the finished document. As you create a presentation such as the project shown in Figure 1–1, you should follow these general guidelines:
>
> 1. **Find the appropriate theme.** The overall appearance of a presentation significantly affects its capability to communicate information clearly. The slides' graphical appearance should support the presentation's overall message. Colors, fonts, and layouts affect how audience members perceive and react to the slide content.
>
> 2. **Choose words for each slide.** Use the less is more principle. The less text, the more likely the slides will enhance your speech. Use the fewest words possible to make a point.
>
> *(continued)*

(continued)

3. **Format specific elements of the text.** Examples of how you can modify the appearance, or **format**, of text include changing its shape, size, color, and position on the slide.

4. **Determine where to save the presentation.** You can store a document permanently, or **save** it, on a variety of storage media including a hard disk, USB flash drive, or CD. You also can indicate a specific location on the storage media for saving the document.

When necessary, more specific details concerning the above guidelines are presented at appropriate points in the chapter. The chapter also will identify the actions performed and decisions made regarding these guidelines during the creation of the slides shown in Figure 1–1.

Plan Ahead

Starting PowerPoint

If you are using a computer to step through the project in this chapter and you want your screen to match the figures in this book, you should change your screen's resolution to 1024 × 768. For information about how to change a computer's resolution, read Appendix E.

Note: If you are using Windows XP, see Appendix F for alternate steps.

BTW

Decreasing Resolution
You may need to decrease your computer's resolution if you know you are going to run your presentation on another computer that uses a lower resolution, such as 800 × 600 or 640 × 480. This lower resolution, however, may affect the appearance of your slides.

To Start PowerPoint

The following steps, which assume Windows Vista is running, start PowerPoint based on a typical installation. You may need to ask your instructor how to start PowerPoint for your computer.

1

- Click the Start button on the Windows Vista taskbar to display the Start menu.

- Click All Programs at the bottom of the left pane on the Start menu to display the All Programs list.

- Click Microsoft Office in the All Programs list to display the Microsoft Office (Figure 1–2).

Figure 1–2

2

- Click Microsoft Office PowerPoint 2007 to start PowerPoint and display a new blank document in the PowerPoint window (Figure 1–3).

- If the PowerPoint window is not maximized, click the Maximize button next to the Close button on its title bar to maximize the window.

Q&A

What is a maximized window?

A maximized window fills the entire screen. When you maximize a window, the Maximize button changes to a Restore Down button. When you restore a maximized window, the Restore Down button changes to a Maximize button.

Figure 1–3

Other Ways

1. Double-click PowerPoint icon on desktop, if one is present
2. Click Microsoft Office PowerPoint 2007 on Start menu

The PowerPoint Window

The PowerPoint window consists of a variety of components to make your work more efficient and documents more professional. These include the document window, Ribbon, Mini toolbar and shortcut menus, Quick Access Toolbar, and Office Button. Some of these components are common to other Microsoft Office 2007 programs; others are unique to PowerPoint.

PowerPoint Window

The basic unit of a PowerPoint presentation is a **slide**. A slide may contain text and objects, such as graphics, tables, charts, and drawings. **Layouts** are used to position this content on the slide. When you open a new presentation, the default **Title Slide** layout appears (Figure 1–4). The purpose of this layout is to introduce the presentation to the audience. PowerPoint includes eight other built-in standard layouts.

The default (preset) slide layouts are set up in **landscape orientation**, where the slide width is greater than its height. In landscape orientation, the slide size is preset to 10 inches wide and 7.5 inches high when printed on a standard sheet of paper measuring 11 inches wide and 8.5 inches high.

The PowerPoint window in Figure 1–4 contains placeholders, a mouse pointer, and a status bar. Other elements that may appear in the window are discussed later in this and subsequent chapters.

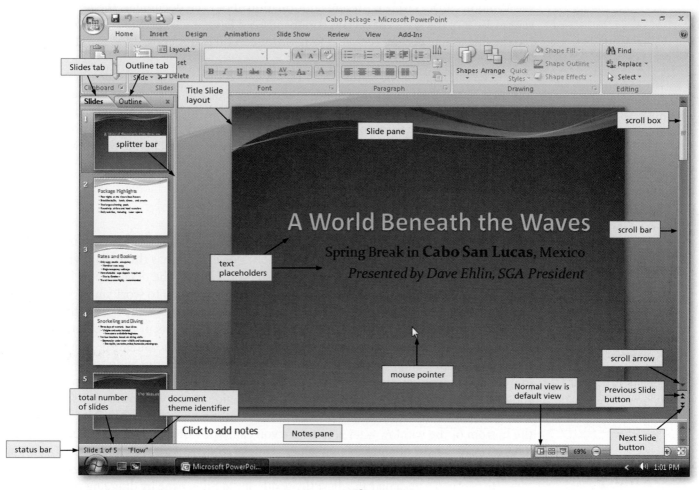

Figure 1–4

PLACEHOLDERS   **Placeholders** are boxes with dotted or hatch-marked borders that are displayed when you create a new slide. All layouts except the Blank slide layout contain placeholders. Depending on the particular slide layout selected, title and subtitle placeholders are displayed for the slide title and subtitle; a content text placeholder is displayed for text, art, or a table, chart, picture, graphic, or movie. The title slide in Figure 1–4 has two text placeholders where you will type the main heading, or title, of a new slide and the subtitle.

MOUSE POINTER   The **mouse pointer** becomes different shapes depending on the task you are performing in PowerPoint and the pointer's location on the screen. The mouse pointer in Figure 1–4 is the shape of a block arrow.

SCROLL BAR   You use the **vertical scroll bar** to display different slides in the document window. When you add a second slide to a presentation, this vertical scroll bar appears on the right side of the Slide pane. On the scroll bar, the position of the **scroll box** reflects the location of the slide in the presentation that is displayed in the document window. A **scroll arrow** is located at each end of a scroll bar. To scroll through, or display different portions of the document in the document window, you can click a scroll arrow or drag the scroll box to move forward or backward through the presentation.

The Previous Slide button and the Next Slide button appear at the bottom of the vertical scroll bar. Click one of these buttons to advance through the slides backwards or forwards.

The **horizontal scroll bar** also may appear. It is located on the bottom of the Slide pane and allows you to display a portion of the slide when the entire slide does not fit on the screen.

STATUS BAR   The **status bar**, located at the bottom of the document window above the Windows Vista taskbar, presents information about the document, the progress of current tasks, and the status of certain commands and keys; it also provides controls for viewing the document. As you type text or perform certain commands, various indicators may appear on the status bar.

The left edge of the status bar in Figure 1–4 shows the current slide number followed by the total number of slides in the document and a document theme identifier. A **document theme** provides consistency in design and color throughout the entire presentation by setting the color scheme, font and font size, and layout of a presentation. Toward the right edge are buttons and controls you can use to change the view of a slide and adjust the size of the displayed document.

PowerPoint Views

The PowerPoint window display varies depending on the view. A **view** is the mode in which the presentation appears on the screen. PowerPoint has three main views: Normal, Slide Sorter, and Slide Show, and also Notes Page. The default view is **Normal view**, which is composed of three working areas that allow you to work on various aspects of a presentation simultaneously. The left side of the screen has a Tabs pane that consists of a **Slides tab** and an **Outline tab** that alternate between views of the presentation in a thumbnail, or miniature, view of the slides and an outline of the slide text. You can type the text of the presentation on the Outline tab and easily rearrange bulleted lists, paragraphs, and individual slides. As you type, you can view this text in the **Slide pane**, which shows a large view of the current slide on the right side of the window. You also can enter text, graphics, animations, and hyperlinks directly in the Slide pane. The **Notes pane** at the bottom of the window is an area where you can type notes and additional information. This text can consist of notes to yourself or remarks to share with your audience. If you want to work with your notes in full page format, you can display them in **Notes Page view**.

In Normal view, you can adjust the width of the Slide pane by dragging the **splitter bar** and the height of the Notes pane by dragging the pane borders. After you have created at least two slides, **scroll bars**, **scroll arrows**, and **scroll boxes** will appear on the right edge of the window.

Ribbon

The **Ribbon**, located near the top of the PowerPoint window, is the control center in PowerPoint (Figure 1–5a). The Ribbon provides easy, central access to the tasks you perform while creating a slide show. The Ribbon consists of tabs, groups, and commands. Each **tab** surrounds a collection of groups, and each group contains related commands.

Figure 1–5(a)

When you start PowerPoint, the Ribbon displays seven top-level tabs: Home, Insert, Design, Animations, Slide Show, Review, and View. The **Home tab**, called the primary tab, contains the more frequently used commands. To display a different tab on the Ribbon, click the top-level tab. That is, to display the Insert tab, click Insert on the Ribbon. To return to the Home tab, click Home on the Ribbon. The tab currently displayed is called the **active tab**.

To display more of the document in the document window, some users prefer to minimize the Ribbon, which hides the groups on the Ribbon and displays only the top-level tabs (Figure 1–5b). To use commands on a minimized Ribbon, click the top-level tab.

Each time you start PowerPoint, the Ribbon appears the same way it did the last time you used PowerPoint. The chapters in this book, however, begin with the Ribbon appearing as it did at the initial installation of the software. If you are stepping through this chapter on a computer and you want your Ribbon to match the figures in this book, read Appendix E.

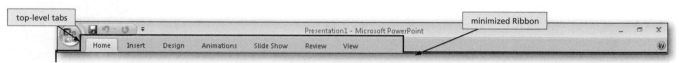

Figure 1–5(b)

In addition to the top-level tabs, PowerPoint displays other tabs, called **contextual tabs**, when you perform certain tasks or work with objects such as pictures or tables. If you insert a picture in a slide, for example, the Picture Tools tab and its related subordinate Format tab appear (Figure 1–6). When you are finished working with the picture, the Picture Tools and Format tabs disappear from the Ribbon. PowerPoint determines when contextual tabs should appear and disappear based on tasks you perform. Some contextual tabs, such as the Chart Tools tab, have more than one related subordinate tab.

Figure 1–6

Commands on the Ribbon include buttons, boxes (text boxes, check boxes, etc.), and galleries (Figure 1–6). A **gallery** is a set of choices, often graphical, arranged in a grid or in a list. You can scroll through choices on an in-Ribbon gallery by clicking the gallery's scroll arrows. Or, you can click a gallery's More button to view more gallery options on the screen at a time. Some buttons and boxes have arrows that, when clicked, also display a gallery; others always cause a gallery to be displayed when clicked. Most galleries support **live preview**, which is a feature that allows you to point to a gallery choice and see its effect in the document - without actually selecting the choice (Figure 1–7).

BTW

Minimizing the Ribbon
If you want to minimize the Ribbon, right-click the Ribbon and then click Minimize the Ribbon on the shortcut menu, double-click the active tab, or press CTRL+F1. To restore a minimized Ribbon, right-click the Ribbon and then click Minimize the Ribbon on the shortcut menu, double-click any top-level tab, or press CTRL+F1. To use commands on a minimized Ribbon, click the top-level tab.

Figure 1–7

Some commands on the Ribbon display an image to help you remember their function. When you point to a command on the Ribbon, all or part of the command glows in shades of yellow and orange, and an Enhanced ScreenTip appears on the screen. An **Enhanced ScreenTip** is an on-screen note that provides the name of the command, available keyboard shortcut(s), a description of the command, and sometimes instructions for how to obtain help about the command (Figure 1–8). Enhanced ScreenTips are more detailed than a typical ScreenTip, which usually only displays the name of the command.

Figure 1–8

The lower-right corner of some groups on the Ribbon has a small arrow, called a **Dialog Box Launcher**, that when clicked displays a dialog box or a task pane with additional options for the group (Figure 1–9). When presented with a dialog box, you make selections and must close the dialog box before returning to the document. A **task pane**, by contrast, is a window that can remain open and visible while you work in the document.

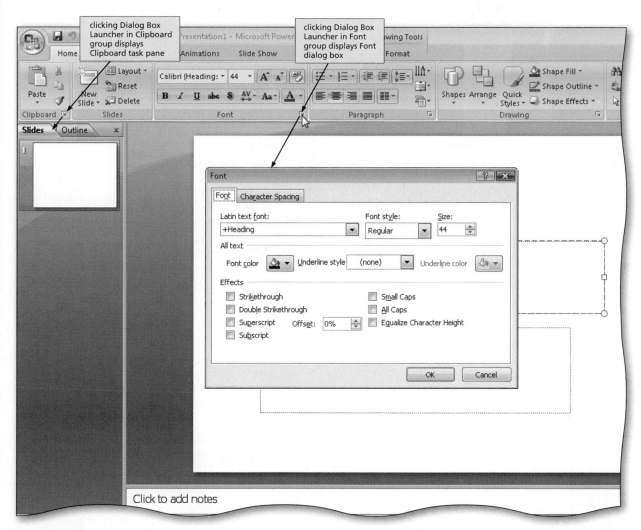

Figure 1–9

Mini Toolbar and Shortcut Menus

The **Mini toolbar**, which appears automatically based on tasks you perform, contains commands related to changing the appearance of text in a slide. All commands on the Mini toolbar also exist on the Ribbon. The purpose of the Mini toolbar is to minimize mouse movement. For example, if you want to use a command that currently is not displayed on the active tab, you can use the command on the Mini toolbar - instead of switching to a different tab to use the command.

When the Mini toolbar appears, it initially is transparent (Figure 1–10a on the next page). If you do not use the transparent Mini toolbar, it disappears from the screen. To use the Mini toolbar, move the mouse pointer into the toolbar, which causes the Mini toolbar to change from a transparent to bright appearance (Figure 1–10b on the next page).

BTW

Turning Off the Mini Toolbar
If you do not want the Mini toolbar to display, click the Office Button, click the PowerPoint Options button on the Office Button menu, and then clear the 'Show Mini Toolbar on selection' check box in the Popular panel.

(a) Transparent Mini Toolbar

(b) Bright Mini Toolbar

Figure 1–10

A **shortcut menu**, which appears when you right-click an object, is a list of frequently used commands that relate to the right-clicked object. When you right-click a scroll bar, for example, a shortcut menu appears with commands related to the scroll bar. If you right-click an item in the document window, PowerPoint displays both the Mini toolbar and a shortcut menu (Figure 1–11).

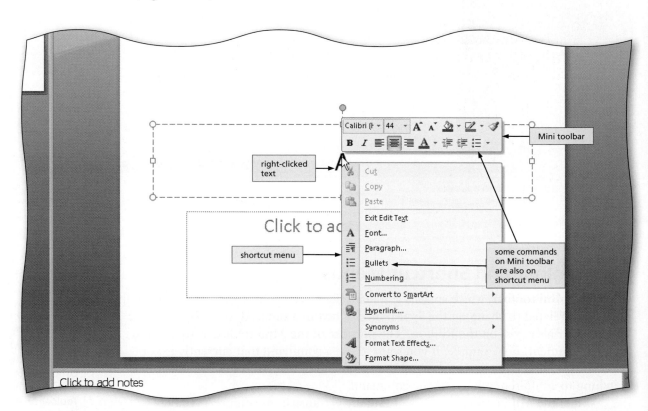

Figure 1–11

Quick Access Toolbar

The **Quick Access Toolbar**, located by default above the Ribbon, provides easy access to frequently used commands (Figure 1–12a). The commands on the Quick Access Toolbar always are available, regardless of the task you are performing. Initially, the Quick Access Toolbar contains the Save, Undo, and Redo commands. If you click the Customize Quick Access Toolbar button, PowerPoint provides a list of commands you quickly can add to and remove from the Quick Access Toolbar (Figure 1–12b).

Figure 1–12(a) Quick Access Toolbar above Ribbon

Figure 1–12(b) Customize Quick Access Toolbar

Quick Access Toolbar Commands
To add a Ribbon command to the Quick Access Toolbar, right-click the command on the Ribbon and then click Add to Quick Access Toolbar on the shortcut menu. To delete a command from the Quick Access Toolbar, right-click the command on the Quick Access Toolbar and then click Remove from Quick Access Toolbar on the shortcut menu. To display the Quick Access Toolbar below the Ribbon, right-click the Quick Access Toolbar and then click Place Quick Access Toolbar below the Ribbon on the shortcut menu.

You also can add other commands to or delete commands from the Quick Access Toolbar so that it contains the commands you use most often. As you add commands to the Quick Access Toolbar, its commands may interfere with the document title on the title bar. For this reason, PowerPoint provides an option of displaying the Quick Access Toolbar below the Ribbon (Figure 1–12c).

Figure 1–12(c) Quick Access Toolbar below Ribbon

Each time you start PowerPoint, the Quick Access Toolbar appears the same way it did the last time you used PowerPoint. The chapters in this book, however, begin with the Quick Access Toolbar appearing as it did at the initial installation of the software. If you are stepping through this chapter on a computer and you want your Quick Access Toolbar to match the figures in this book, you should reset your Quick Access Toolbar. For more information about how to reset the Quick Access Toolbar, read Appendix E.

Office Button

While the Ribbon is a control center for creating documents, the **Office Button** is a central location for managing and sharing documents. When you click the Office Button, located in the upper-left corner of the window, PowerPoint displays the Office Button menu (Figure 1–13). A **menu** contains a list of commands.

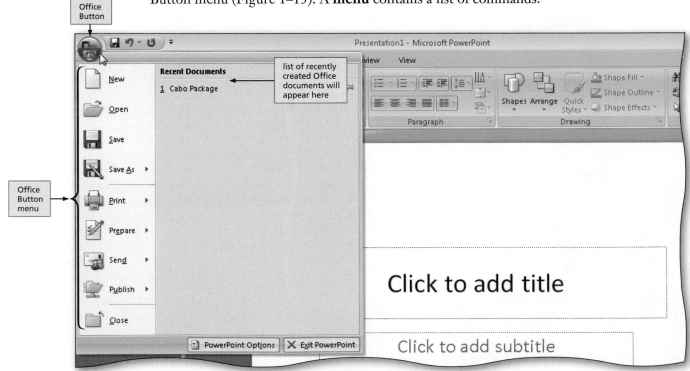

Figure 1–13

When you click the New, Open, Save As, and Print commands on the Office Button menu, PowerPoint displays a dialog box with additional options. The Save As, Print, Prepare, Send, and Publish commands have an arrow to their right. If you point to this arrow, PowerPoint displays a **submenu**, which is a list of additional commands associated with the selected command (Figure 1–14). For the Prepare, Send, and Publish commands that do not display a dialog box when clicked, you can point either to the command or the arrow to display the submenu.

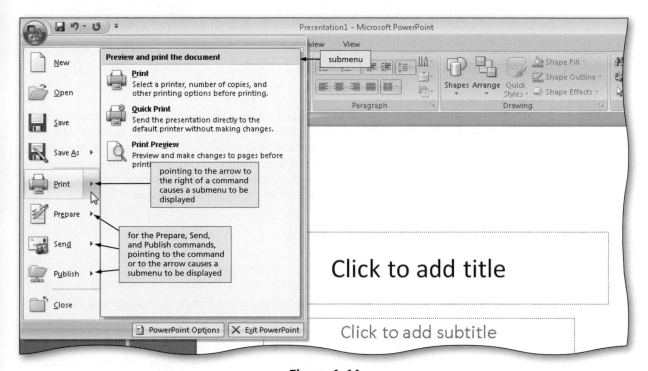

Figure 1–14

Key Tips

If you prefer using the keyboard instead of the mouse, you can press the ALT key on the keyboard to display a **Key Tip badge**, or keyboard code icon, for certain commands (Figure 1–15). To select a command using the keyboard, press its displayed code letter, or **Key Tip**. When you press a Key Tip, additional Key Tips related to the selected command may appear. For example, to select the New command on the Office Button menu, press the ALT key, then press the F key, then press the N key.

Figure 1–15

To remove the Key Tip badges from the screen, press the ALT key or the ESC key until all Key Tip badges disappear, or click the mouse anywhere in the PowerPoint window.

Choosing a Document Theme

You easily can give a presentation a professional and consistent appearance by using a document theme. This collection of formatting choices includes a set of colors (the color theme), a set of heading and content text fonts (the font theme), and a set of lines and fill effects (the effects theme). These themes allow you to choose and change the appearance of all the slides or individual slides in your presentation.

Plan Ahead

> **Find the appropriate theme.**
> In the initial steps of this project, you will select a document theme by locating a particular built-in theme in the Themes group. You could, however, apply a theme at any time while creating the presentation. Some PowerPoint slide show designers create presentations using the default Office Theme. This blank design allows them to concentrate on the words being used to convey the message and does not distract them with colors and various text attributes. Once the text is entered, the designers then select an appropriate document theme.

To Choose a Document Theme

The document theme identifier shows the theme currently used in the slide show. PowerPoint initially uses the **Office Theme** until you select a different theme. The following steps change the theme for this presentation from the Office Theme to the Flow document theme.

- Click Design on the Ribbon to display the Design tab (Figure 1–16).

Figure 1–16

2

- Click the More button in the Themes gallery to expand the gallery, which shows more Built-In theme gallery options (Figure 1–17).

🔍 **Experiment**

- Point to various document themes in the Themes gallery and watch the colors and fonts change on the title slide.

Q&A

Are the themes displayed in a specific order?

Yes. They are arranged in alphabetical order running from left to right. If you point to a theme, a ScreenTip with the design's name appears on the screen.

Q&A

What if I change my mind and do not want to select a new theme?

Click anywhere outside the All Themes gallery to close the gallery.

Figure 1–17

3

- Click the Flow theme to apply this theme to Slide 1 (Figure 1–18).

Q&A

If I decide at some future time that this design does not fit the theme of my presentation, can I apply a different design?

Yes. You can repeat these steps at any time while creating your presentation.

Figure 1–18

Creating a Title Slide

With the exception of a blank slide and a slide with a picture and caption, PowerPoint assumes every new slide has a title. Many of PowerPoint's layouts have both a title text placeholder and at least one content placeholder. To make creating a presentation easier, any text you type after a new slide appears becomes title text in the title text placeholder. The following steps create the title slide for this presentation.

Plan Ahead

> **Choose the words for the slide.**
> No doubt you have heard the phrase, "You get only one chance to make a first impression." The same philosophy holds true for a PowerPoint presentation. The title slide gives your audience an initial sense of what they are about to see and hear. It is, therefore, extremely important to choose the text for this slide carefully. Avoid stating the obvious in the title. Instead, create interest and curiosity using key ideas from the presentation.
> Some PowerPoint users create the title slide as their last step in the design process so that it reflects the tone of the presentation. They begin by planning the final slide in the presentation so that they know where and how they want to end the slide show. All the slides in the presentation should work toward meeting this final slide.

To Enter the Presentation Title

As you begin typing text in the title text placeholder, the title text also is displayed in the Slide 1 thumbnail in the Slides tab. PowerPoint **line wraps** text that exceeds the width of the placeholder. The presentation title for Project 1 is A World Beneath the Waves. This title creates interest by introducing the concept of exploring the life under water. The following step creates the slide show's title.

- Click the label, Click to add title, located inside the title text placeholder to select the placeholder (Figure 1–19).

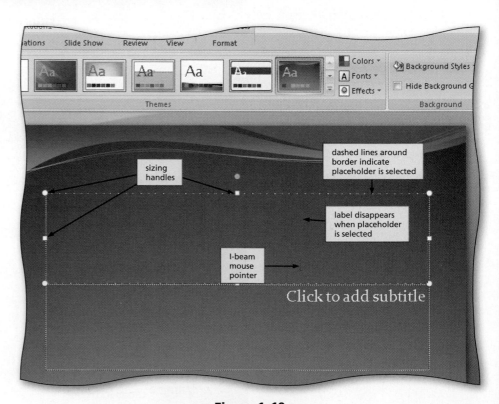

Figure 1–19

2

• Type A World Beneath the Waves in the title text placeholder. Do not press the ENTER key (Figure 1–20).

Q&A

What if a button with two lines and two arrows appears on the left side of the title text placeholder?

The **AutoFit** button displays because PowerPoint attempts to reduce the size of the letters when the title text does not fit on a single line. If you are creating a slide and need to squeeze an extra line in the text placeholder, you can click this button to resize the existing text in the placeholder so the spillover text will fit on the slide.

Figure 1–20

Correcting a Mistake When Typing

If you type the wrong letter, press the BACKSPACE key to erase all the characters back to and including the one that is incorrect. If you mistakenly press the ENTER key after typing the title and the insertion point is on the new line, simply press the BACKSPACE key to return the insertion point to the right of the letter s in the word Waves.

When you install PowerPoint, the default setting allows you to reverse up to the last 20 changes by clicking the Undo button on the Quick Access Toolbar. The ScreenTip that appears when you point to the Undo button changes to indicate the type of change just made. For example, if you type text in the title text placeholder and then point to the Undo button, the ScreenTip that appears is Undo Typing. For clarity, when referencing the Undo button in this project, the name displaying in the ScreenTip is referenced. You can reapply a change that you reversed with the Undo button by clicking the Redo button on the Quick Access Toolbar. Clicking the Redo button reverses the last undo action. The ScreenTip name reflects the type of reversal last performed.

Paragraphs

Subtitle text in the subtitle text placeholder supports the title text. It can appear on one or more lines in the placeholder. To create more than one subtitle line, you press the ENTER key after typing some words. PowerPoint creates a new line, which is the second paragraph in the placeholder. A **paragraph** is a segment of text with the same format that begins when you press the ENTER key and ends when you press the ENTER key again. This new paragraph is the same level as the previous paragraph. A **level** is a position within a structure, such as an outline, that indicates the magnitude of importance. PowerPoint allows for five paragraph levels.

To Enter the Presentation Subtitle Paragraph

The first subtitle paragraph links to the title by giving specific details about the vacation location, and the second paragraph gives information about the person who will be speaking to the audience. The following steps enter the presentation subtitle.

- Click the label, Click to add subtitle, located inside the subtitle text place-holder to select the placeholder (Figure 1–21).

dashed lines around border indicate placeholder is selected

label disappears when placeholder is selected

Figure 1–21

- Type Spring Break in Cabo San Lucas, Mexico and then press the ENTER key.

- Type Presented by Dave Ehlin, SGA President but do not press the ENTER key (Figure 1–22).

Q&A Why do red wavy lines appear below the words, Cabo and Ehlin?

The lines indicate possible spelling errors.

subtitle text entered in placeholder

red wavy lines indicate possible misspelled words

Figure 1–22

Plan Ahead

Identify how to format specific elements of the text.

Most of the time, you use the document theme's text attributes, color scheme, and layout. Occasionally, you may want to change the way a presentation looks, however, and still keep a particular document theme. PowerPoint gives you that flexibility.

Graphic designers use several rules when formatting text.

- Avoid all capital letters, if possible. Audiences have difficulty comprehending sentences typed in all capital letters, especially when the lines exceed seven words. All capital letters leaves no room for emphasis or inflection, so readers get confused about what material deserves particular attention. Some document themes, however, have a default title text style of all capital letters.

- Avoid text with a font size less than 24 point. Audience members generally will sit a maximum of 50 feet from a screen, and at this distance 24-point type is the smallest size text they can read comfortably without straining.

- Make careful color choices. Color evokes emotions, and a careless color choice may elicit the incorrect psychological response. PowerPoint provides a color palette with hundreds of colors. The built-in document themes use complementary colors that work well together. If you stray from these themes and add your own color choices, without a good reason to make the changes, your presentation is apt to become ineffective.

Formatting Characters in a Presentation

Recall that each document theme determines the color scheme, font and font size, and layout of a presentation. You can use a specific document theme and then change the characters' formats any time before, during, or after you type the text.

Fonts and Font Styles

Characters that appear on the screen are a specific shape and size. Examples of how you can modify the appearance, or **format**, of these typed characters on the screen and in print include changing the font, style, size, and color. The **font**, or typeface, defines the appearance and shape of the letters, numbers, punctuation marks, and symbols. **Style** indicates how the characters are formatted. PowerPoint's text font styles include regular, italic, bold, and bold italic. **Size** specifies the height of the characters and is gauged by a measurement system that uses points. A **point** is 1/72 of an inch in height. Thus, a character with a point size of 36 is 36/72 (or 1/2) of an inch in height. **Color** defines the hue of the characters.

This presentation uses the Flow document theme, which uses particular font styles and font sizes. The Flow document theme default title text font is named Calibri. It has a bold style with no special effects, and its size is 56 point. The Flow document theme default subtitle text font is Constantia with a font size of 26 point.

BTW

Formatting Words
To format one word, position the insertion point anywhere in the word. Then make the formatting changes you desire. The entire word does not need to be selected for the change to occur.

To Select a Paragraph

You can use many techniques to format characters. When you want to apply the same formats to multiple words or paragraphs, it is efficient to select the desired text and then make the desired changes to all the characters simultaneously. The first formatting change you will make will apply to the second paragraph of the title slide sub-title. The following step selects this paragraph.

1

- Triple-click the paragraph, Presented by Dave Ehlin, SGA President, in the subtitle text placeholder to select the paragraph (Figure 1–23).

Q&A

Can I select the paragraph using a technique other than triple-clicking?

Yes. You can move your mouse pointer to the left of the first paragraph and then drag it to the end of the line.

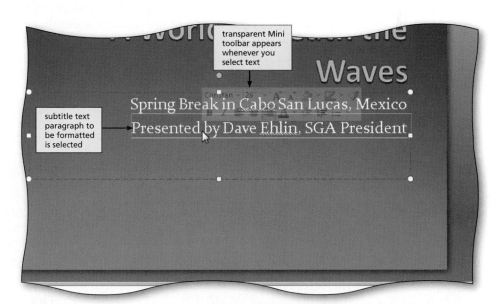

Figure 1–23

To Italicize Text

Different font styles often are used on slides to make them more appealing to the reader and to emphasize particular text. Italic type, used sparingly, draws the readers' eyes to these characters. The following step adds emphasis to the second line of the subtitle text by changing regular text to italic text.

- With the subtitle text still selected, click the Italic button on the Mini tool-bar to italicize that text on the slide and on the slide thumbnail (Figure 1–24).

Q&A

If I change my mind and decide not to italicize the text, how can I remove this style?

Select the italicized text and then click the Italic button. As a result, the Italic button will not be selected, and the text will not have the italic font style.

Figure 1–24

Other Ways
1. Right-click selected text, click Font on shortcut menu, click Italic in Font style list   2. Click Home tab, click Italic in Font group   3. Press CTRL+I

To Select Multiple Paragraphs

Each of the subtitle lines is a separate paragraph. As previously discussed, PowerPoint creates a new paragraph each time you press the ENTER key. To change the character formatting in both paragraphs, it is efficient to select the desired text and then make the desired changes to all the characters simultaneously.

The next formatting change you will make will apply to both title slide subtitle paragraphs. The following step selects the first paragraph so that you can format both paragraphs concurrently.

- With the second subtitle text paragraph selected, press the CTRL key and then triple-click the first subtitle text paragraph, Spring Break in Cabo San Lucas, Mexico, to select both paragraphs (Figure 1–25).

Q&A

Can I use a different technique to select both subtitle text paragraphs?

Yes. Click the placeholder border so that it appears as a solid line. When the placeholder is selected in this manner, formatting changes will apply to all text in the placeholder.

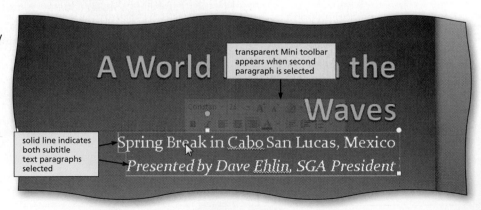

Figure 1–25

**Plan
Ahead**

> **Identify how to format specific elements of the text.**
> When selecting text colors, try to limit using red. At least 15 percent of men have difficulty distinguishing varying shades of green or red. They also often see the color purple as blue and the color brown as green. This problem is more pronounced when the colors appear in small areas, such as slide paragraphs or line chart bars.

To Change the Text Color

PowerPoint allows you to use one or more text colors in a presentation. To add more emphasis to the title slide subtitle text, you decide to change the color. The following steps add emphasis to both subtitle text paragraphs by changing the font color from white to dark blue.

- With both paragraphs selected, click the Font Color arrow on the Mini toolbar to display the palette of Theme Colors and Standard Colors (Figure 1–26).

Q&A

If the Mini toolbar disappears from the screen, how can I display it once again?

Right-click the text, and the Mini toolbar should appear.

Figure 1–26

- Click the Dark Blue button in the Standard Colors row on the Mini toolbar (row 1, column 9) to change the font color to dark blue (Figure 1–27).

Q&A

Why did I select the color, dark blue?

Dark blue is one of the 10 standard colors associated with every document theme, and it works well with the shades of blue already on the slide. An additional consideration is that dark colors print well.

Figure 1–27

- Click outside the selected area to deselect the two paragraphs.

Other Ways

1. Right-click selected text, click Font on shortcut menu, click Font color button, click Dark Blue in Standard Colors row
2. Click Home tab, click Font Color arrow in Font group, click Dark Blue in Standard Colors row

To Select a Group of Words

PowerPoint designers use many techniques to format characters. To apply the same formats to multiple words or paragraphs, they select the desired text and then make the desired changes to all the characters simultaneously.

To add emphasis to the vacation destination, you want to increase the font size and change the font style to bold for the words, Cabo San Lucas. You could perform these actions separately, but it is more efficient to select this group of words and then change the font attributes. The following steps select a group of words.

- Position the mouse pointer immediately to the left of the first character of the text to be selected (in this case, the C in Cabo) (Figure 1–28).

Figure 1–28

- Drag the mouse pointer through the last character of the text to be selected (in this case, the s in Lucas) (Figure 1–29).

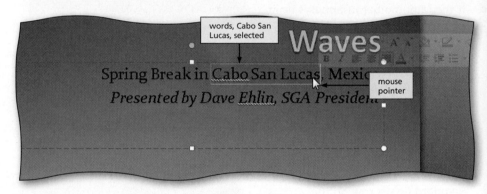

Figure 1–29

To Increase Font Size

To add emphasis, you increase the font size for Cabo San Lucas. The Increase Font Size button on the Mini toolbar increases the font size in preset increments. The following step uses this button to increase the font size.

- Click the Increase Font Size button on the Mini toolbar once to increase the font size of the selected text from 26 to 28 point (Figure 1–30).

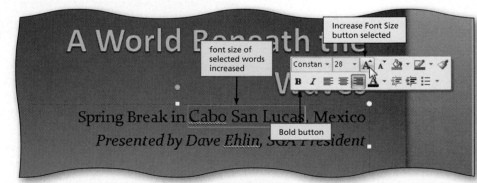

Figure 1–30

Other Ways

1. Click Home tab, click Increase Font Size button in Font group
2. Click Home tab, click Font Size box arrow, click new font size
3. Press CTRL+SHIFT+>

To Bold Text

Bold characters display somewhat thicker and darker than those that display in a regular font style. Clicking the Bold button on the Mini toolbar is an efficient method of bolding text. To add more emphasis to the vacation destination, you want to bold the words, Cabo San Lucas. The following step bolds this text.

 1

- Click the Bold button on the Mini toolbar to bold the three selected words (Figure 1–31).

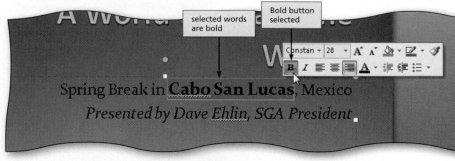

Figure 1–31

Other Ways

1. Click Home tab, click Bold button in Font group
2. Press CTRL+B

Identify how to format specific elements of the text.
Avoid line wraps. Your audience's eyes want to stop at the end of a line. Thus, you must plan your words carefully or adjust the font size so that each point displays on only one line.

Plan Ahead

To Decrease the Title Slide Title Text Font Size

The last word of the title text, Waves, appears on a line by itself. For aesthetic reasons, it is advantageous to have this word appear with the rest of the title on a single line. One way to fit text on one line is to decrease the font size. The process is similar to increasing the font size. Clicking the Decrease Font Size button on the Mini toolbar decreases the size in preset increments. The following steps decrease the font size from 56 to 48 point.

 1

- Select the title slide title text, A World Beneath the Waves (Figure 1–32).

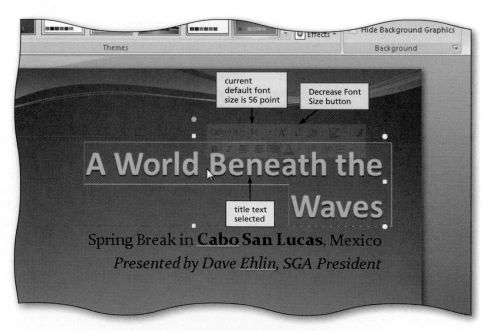

Figure 1–32

2
- Click the Decrease Font Size button on the Mini toolbar twice to decrease the font size from 56 to 48 point (Figure 1–33).

Figure 1–33

Saving the Project

While you are building a presentation, the computer stores it in memory. When you save a presentation, the computer places it on a storage medium such as a USB flash drive, CD, or hard disk. A saved presentation is referred to as a **file**. A **file name** is the name assigned to a file when it is saved.

It is important to save the presentation frequently for the following reasons:

- The presentation in memory will be lost if the computer is turned off or you lose electrical power while PowerPoint is open.

- If you run out of time before completing your project, you may finish your presentation at a future time without starting over.

Plan Ahead

Determine where to save the document.
When saving a document, you must decide which storage medium to use.

- If you always work on the same computer and have no need to transport your projects to a different location, then your computer's hard drive will suffice as a storage location. It is a good idea, however, to save a backup copy of your projects on a separate medium in case the file becomes corrupted or the computer's hard drive fails.

- If you plan to work on your projects in various locations or on multiple computers, then you should save your projects on a portable medium, such as a USB flash drive or CD. The projects in this book use a USB flash drive, which saves files quickly and reliably and can be reused. CDs are easily portable and serve as good backups for the final versions of projects because they generally can save files only one time.

BTW

Saving in a Previous PowerPoint Format
To ensure that your presentation will open in an earlier version of PowerPoint, you must save your file in PowerPoint 97–2003 format. Files saved in this format have the .ppt extension.

To Save a Presentation

You have performed many tasks and do not want to lose the work completed thus far. Thus, you should save the presentation. The following steps save a presentation on a USB flash drive using the file name, Cabo Package.

Note: If you are using Windows XP, see Appendix F for alternate steps.

1

- With a USB flash drive connected to one of the computer's USB ports, click the Save button on the Quick Access Toolbar to display the Save As dialog box. (Figure 1–34).

- If the Navigation pane is not displayed in the Save As dialog box, click the Browse Folders button to expand the dialog box.

- If a Folders list is displayed below the Folders button, click the Folders button to remove the Folders list.

Q&A Do I have to save to a USB flash drive?

No. You can save to any device or folder. A **folder** is a specific location on a storage medium. You can save to the default folder or a different folder. You also can create your own folders, which is explained later in this book.

Figure 1–34

2

- Type Cabo Package in the File name box to change the file name. Do not press the ENTER key after typing the file name (Figure 1–35).

Q&A What characters can I use in a file name?

A file name can have a maximum of 260 characters, including spaces. The only invalid characters are the backslash (\), slash (/), colon (:), asterisk (*), question mark (?), quotation mark ("), less than symbol (<), greater than symbol (>), and vertical bar (|).

Q&A What are file properties and tags?

File properties contain information about a file such as the file name, author name, date the file was modified, and tags. A tag is a file property that contains a word or phrase about a file. You can organize and locate files based on their file properties.

Figure 1–35

- If Computer is not displayed in the Favorite Links section, drag the top or bottom edge of the Save As dialog box until Computer is displayed.

- Click Computer in the Favorite Links section to display a list of available drives (Figure 1–36).

- If necessary, scroll until UDISK 2.0 (E:) appears in the list of available drives.

Q&A Why is my list of drives arranged and named differently?

The size of the Save As dialog box and your computer's configuration determine how the list is displayed and how the drives are named.

Q&A How do I save the file if I am not using a USB flash drive?

Use the same process, but select your desired save location in the Favorite Links section.

Figure 1–36

- Double-click UDISK 2.0 (E:) in the Computer list to select the USB flash drive, Drive E in this case, as the new save location (Figure 1–37).

Q&A What if my USB flash drive has a different name or letter?

It is very likely that your USB flash drive will have a different name and drive letter and be connected to a different port. Verify the device in your Computer list is correct.

Figure 1–37

5

- Click the Save button in the Save As dialog box to save the presentation on the USB flash drive with the file name, Cabo Package (Figure 1–38).

Q&A How do I know that the project is saved?

While PowerPoint is saving your file, it briefly displays a message on the status bar indicating the amount of the file saved. In addition, your USB drive may have a light that flashes during the save process.

Q&A Why is .pptx displayed immediately to the right of the file name?

Depending on your Windows Vista settings, .pptx may be displayed after you save the file. The file type .pptx is a PowerPoint 2007 document. Previous versions of PowerPoint had a file type of .ppt.

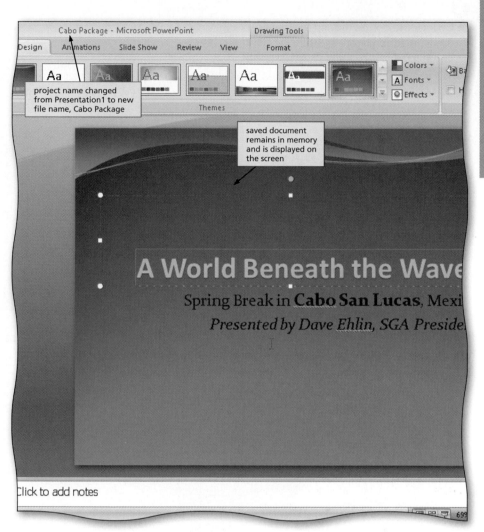

Figure 1–38

Other Ways

1. Click Office Button, click Save, type file name, click Computer, select drive or folder, click Save button

2. Press CTRL+S or press SHIFT+F12, type file name, click Computer, select drive or folder, click Save button

Adding a New Slide to a Presentation

With the title slide for the presentation created, the next step is to add the first text slide immediately after the title slide. Usually, when you create a presentation, you add slides with text, graphics, or charts. Some placeholders allow you to double-click the placeholder and then access other objects, such as media clips, charts, diagrams, and organization charts. You can change the layout for a slide at any time during the creation of a presentation.

To Add a New Text Slide with a Bulleted List

When you add a new slide, PowerPoint uses the Title and Content slide layout. This layout provides a title placeholder and a content area for text, art, charts, and other graphics. A vertical scroll bar appears in the Slide pane when you add the second slide so that you can move from slide to slide easily. A thumbnail of this slide also appears in the Slides tab. The following steps add a new slide with the Title and Content slide layout.

1

- Click Home on the Ribbon to display the Home tab (Figure 1–39).

Figure 1–39

2

- Click the New Slide button in the Slides group to insert a new slide with the Title and Content layout (Figure 1–40).

Q&A Why does the bullet character display a blue dot?

The Flow document theme determines the bullet characters. Each paragraph level has an associated bullet character.

Q&A I clicked the New Slide arrow instead of the New Slide button. What should I do?

Click the Title and Content slide thumbnail in the layout gallery.

Figure 1–40

Other Ways
1. Press CTRL+M

> **Choose the words for the slide.**
> All presentations should follow the 7 × 7 rule which states that each slide should have a maximum of seven lines, and each line should have a maximum of seven words. PowerPoint designers must choose their words carefully and, in turn, help viewers read the slides easily.

Plan Ahead

Creating a Text Slide with a Single-Level Bulleted List

The information in the Slide 2 text placeholder is presented in a bulleted list. All the bullets appear at the same paragraph level, called the first level.

To Enter a Slide Title

PowerPoint assumes every new slide has a title. The title for Slide 2 is Package Highlights. The following step enters this title.

1
- Click the label, Click to add title, to select it and then type `Package Highlights` in the placeholder. Do not press the ENTER key (Figure 1–41).

Q&A What are those six icons grouped in the middle of the slide?

You can click one of the icons to insert a specific type of content: table, chart, SmartArt graphic, picture, clip art, or media clip.

Figure 1–41

To Select a Text Placeholder

Before you can type text into the text placeholder, you first must select it. The following step selects the text placeholder on Slide 2.

1
- Click the label, Click to add text, to select the text placeholder (Figure 1–42).

Q&A Why does my mouse pointer have a different shape?

If you move the mouse pointer away from the bullet, it will change shape.

Figure 1–42

Other Ways
1. Press CTRL+ENTER

To Type a Single-Level Bulleted List

The content placeholder provides an area for the text characters. When you click inside a placeholder, you then can type or paste text. If your text exceeds the size of the placeholder, PowerPoint will attempt to make the text fit by reducing the text size and line spacing. **Line spacing** is the amount of vertical space between the lines of text.

As discussed previously, a bulleted list is a list of paragraphs, each of which is preceded by a bullet. A paragraph is a segment of text ended by pressing the ENTER key. The next step is to type the single-level bulleted list, which consists of five paragraphs (Figure 1–1b on page PPT 3). The following steps create a single-level bulleted list.

- **Type** Four nights at the Azure Seas Resort **and then press the** ENTER **key to begin a new bulleted first-level paragraph (Figure 1–43).**

Q&A

Can I delete bullets on a slide?

Yes. If you do not want bullets to display on a particular paragraph, click the Bullets button in the Paragraph group on the Home tab or right-click the paragraph and then click the Bullets button on the Mini toolbar.

Figure 1–43

- **Type** Breakfast buffet, lunch, dinner, and snacks **and then press the** ENTER **key.**

- **Type** Two large swimming pools **and then press the** ENTER **key.**

- **Type** Round-trip airfare and hotel transfers **and then press the** ENTER **key.**

- **Type** Daily activities, including water sports **but do not press the** ENTER **key (Figure 1–44).**

Q&A

I pressed the ENTER key in error, and now a new bullet appears after the last entry on this slide. How can I remove this extra bullet?

Press the BACKSPACE key.

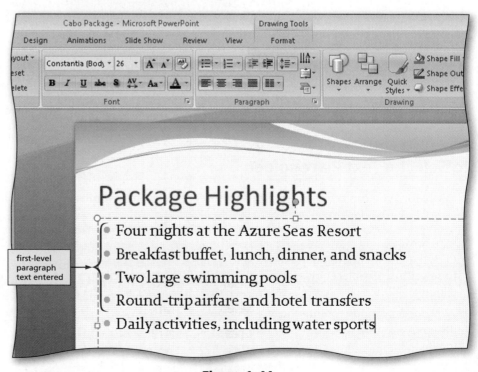

Figure 1–44

Creating a Text Slide with a Multi-Level Bulleted List

Slides 3 and 4 in Figure 1–1 on pages PPT 3–4 contain more than one level of bulleted text. A slide that consists of more than one level of bulleted text is called a **multi-level bulleted list slide**. Beginning with the second level, each paragraph indents to the right of the preceding level and is pushed down to a lower level. For example, if you increase the indent of a first-level paragraph, it becomes a second-level paragraph.

Creating a text slide with a multi-level bulleted list requires several steps. Initially, you enter a slide title in the title text placeholder. Next, you select the content text placeholder. Then, you type the text for the multi-level bulleted list, increasing and decreasing the indents as needed. The next several sections add a slide with a multi-level bulleted list.

To Add a New Slide and Enter a Slide Title

When you add a new slide to a presentation, PowerPoint keeps the same layout used on the previous slide. PowerPoint assumes every new slide has a title. The title for Slide 3 is Rates and Booking. The following steps add a new slide (Slide 3) and enter a title.

- Click the New Slide button in the Slides group on the Home tab to insert a new slide with the Title and Content layout (Figure 1–45).

Figure 1–45

- Click the title text placeholder and then type `Rates and Booking` in this placeholder. Do not press the ENTER key (Figure 1–46).

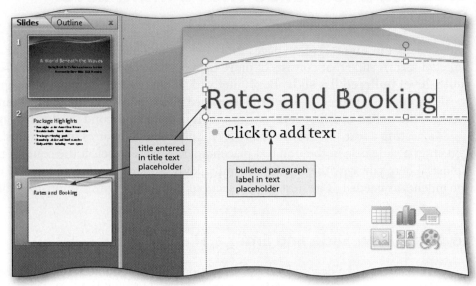

Figure 1–46

Other Ways

1. Press SHIFT+CTRL+M

To Type a Multi-Level Bulleted List

In a multi-level bulleted list, a lower-level paragraph is a subset of a higher-level paragraph. It usually contains information that supports the topic in the paragraph immediately above it.

The next step is to select the content text placeholder and then type the multi-level bulleted list, which consists of six entries (Figure 1–1c on page PPT 3). Creating a lower-level paragraph is called **demoting** text; creating a higher-level paragraph is called **promoting** text. The following steps create a list consisting of three levels.

- Click the bulleted paragraph text placeholder.

- Type `Only $495 double occupancy` and then press the ENTER key (Figure 1–47).

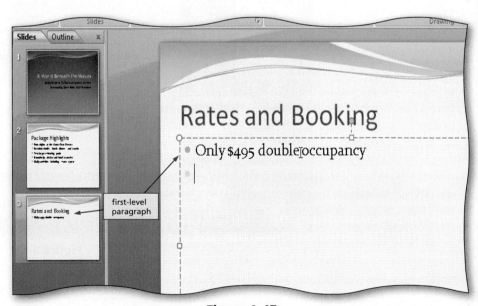

Figure 1–47

2

- Click the Increase List Level button in the Paragraph group to indent the second paragraph below the first and create a second-level paragraph (Figure 1–48).

Q&A

Why does the bullet for this paragraph have a different size and color?

A different bullet is assigned to each paragraph level.

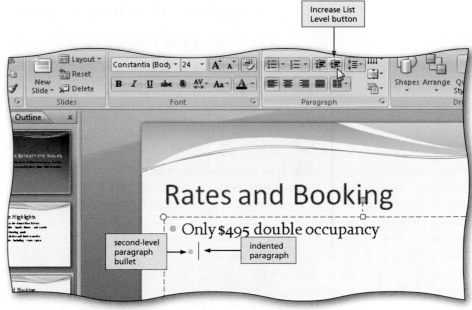

Figure 1–48

3

- Type Non-diver rate: $275 and then press the ENTER key to add a new paragraph at the same level as the previous paragraph.

- Type Single occupancy: add $150 and then press the ENTER key (Figure 1–49).

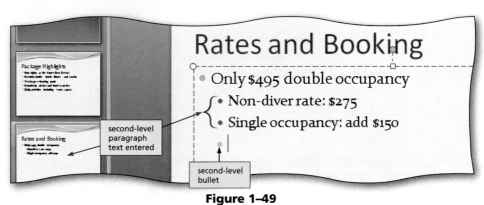

Figure 1–49

4

- Click the Decrease List Level button in the Paragraph group so that the second-level paragraph becomes a first-level paragraph (Figure 1–50).

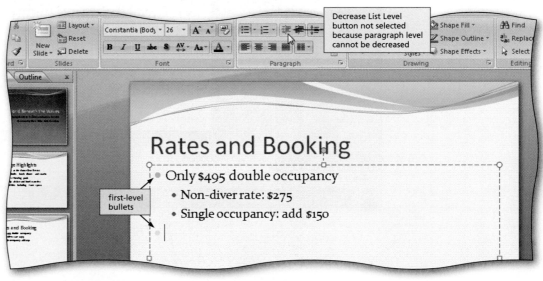

Other Ways

1. Press TAB to promote paragraph; press SHIFT+TAB to demote paragraph

Figure 1–50

To Type the Remaining Text for Slide 3

The following steps complete the text for Slide 3.

1 Type `Nonrefundable $150 deposit required` and then press the ENTER key.

2 Click the Increase List Level button in the Paragraph group to demote the paragraph.

3 Type `Due by October 1` and then press the ENTER key.

4 Click the Decrease List Level button in the Paragraph group to promote the paragraph.

5 Type `Travel insurance highly recommended` but do not press the ENTER key (Figure 1–51).

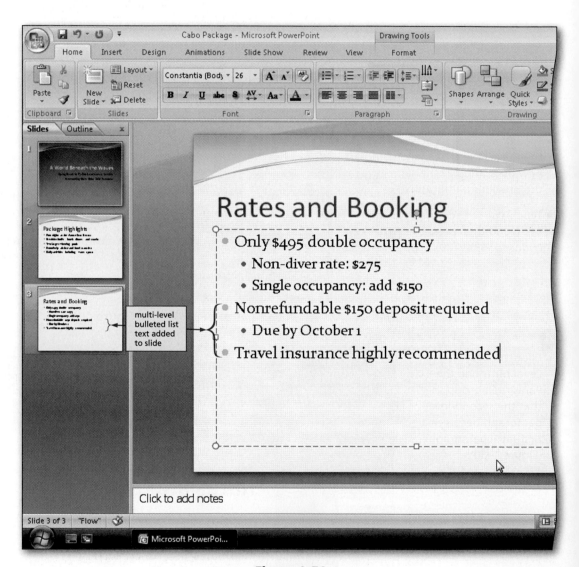

Figure 1–51

To Create Slide 4

Slide 4 is the final multi-level bulleted text slide in this presentation. It has three levels. The following steps create Slide 4.

1 Click the New Slide button in the Slides group.

2 Type `Snorkeling and Diving` in the title text placeholder.

3 Press CTRL+ENTER to move the insertion point to the text placeholder.

4 Type `Three days of two-tank boat dives` and then press the ENTER key.

5 Click the Increase List Level button. Type `Weights and tanks included` and then press the ENTER key (Figure 1–52).

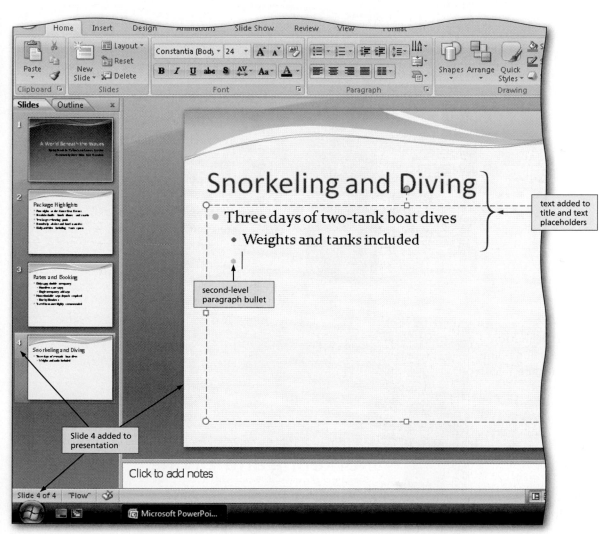

Figure 1–52

To Create a Third-Level Paragraph

Slide 4 contains detailed information about the particular dives. Each additional paragraph becomes more specific and supports the information in the paragraph above it.

The next line in Slide 4 is indented an additional level, to the third level. The following steps demote the text to a third-level paragraph.

1

- Click the Increase List Level button so that the second-level paragraph becomes a third-level paragraph (Figure 1–53).

Figure 1–53

2

- Type Instructors available for beginners and then press the ENTER key to create a second third-level paragraph (Figure 1–54).

Figure 1–54

3

- Click the Decrease List Level button two times so that the insertion point appears at the first level (Figure 1–55).

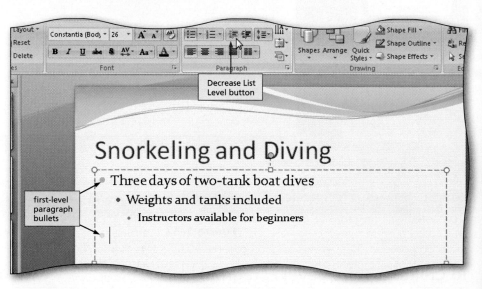

Figure 1–55

To Type the Remaining Text for Slide 4

The next three paragraphs concern what divers and snorkelers will view. The following steps type the remaining text for Slide 4.

1 Type `Various locations based on diving skills` and then press the ENTER key.

2 Press the TAB key to increase the indent to the second level.

3 Type `Spectacular underwater wildlife and landscapes` and then press the ENTER key.

4 Press the TAB key to increase the indent to the third level.

5 Type `See squids, sea turtles, snakes, barracudas, and stingrays` but do not press the ENTER key (Figure 1–56).

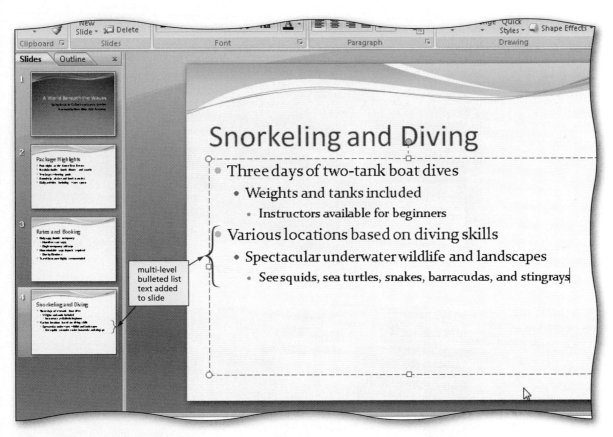

Figure 1–56

Choose the words for the slide.

After the last bulleted list slide in the slide show appears during a slide show, the default PowerPoint setting is to end the presentation with a **black slide**. This black slide appears only when the slide show is running and concludes the slide show, so your audience never sees the PowerPoint window. It is a good idea, however, to end the presentation with a final, closing slide to display at the end of the presentation. This slide ends the presentation gracefully and should be an exact copy, or a very similar copy, of your title slide. The audience will recognize that the presentation is drawing to a close when this slide appears. It can remain on the screen when the audience asks questions, approaches the speaker for further information, or exits the room.

Plan Ahead

Ending a Slide Show with a Closing Slide

All the text slides are created for the Cabo Package slide show. This presentation thus far consists of a title slide, one text slide with a single-level bulleted list, and two text slides with a multi-level bulleted list. A closing slide that resembles the title slide is the final slide to create.

To Duplicate a Slide

When two slides contain similar information and have the same format, duplicating one slide and then making minor modifications to the new slide saves time and increases consistency.

Slide 5 will have the same layout and design as Slide 1. The most expedient method of creating this slide is to copy Slide 1 and then make minor modifications to the new slide. The following steps duplicate the title slide.

1

• Click the Slide 1 thumbnail in the Slides tab to display Slide 1 (Figure 1–57).

Figure 1–57

2

• Click the New Slide arrow in the Slides group on the Home tab to display the Flow layout gallery (Figure 1–58).

Figure 1–58

3
- Click Duplicate Selected Slides in the Flow layout gallery to create a new Slide 2, which is a duplicate of Slide 1 (Figure 1–59).

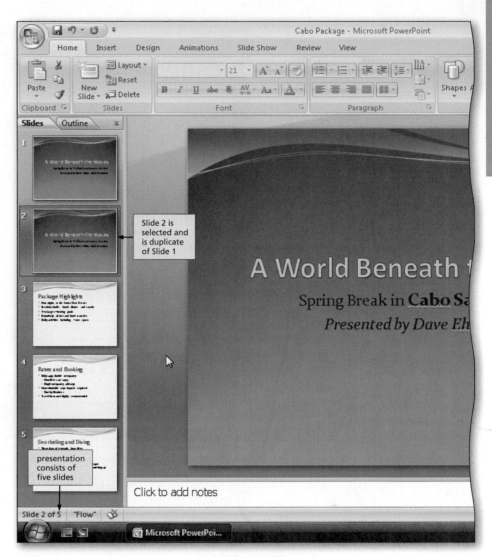

Figure 1–59

To Arrange a Slide

The new Slide 2 was inserted directly below Slide 1 because Slide 1 was the selected slide. This duplicate slide needs to display at the end of the presentation directly after the final title and content slide.

Changing slide order is an easy process and is best performed in the Tabs pane. When you click the slide thumbnail and begin to drag it to a new location, a line indicates the new location of the selected slide. When you release the mouse button, the slide drops into the desired location. Hence, this process of dragging and then dropping the thumbnail in a new location is called **drag and drop**. You can use the drag-and-drop method to move any selected item, including text and graphics. The following step moves the new Slide 2 to the end of the presentation so that it becomes a closing slide.

- With Slide 2 selected, drag the Slide 2 slide thumbnail in the Slides pane below the last slide thumbnail (Figure 1–60).

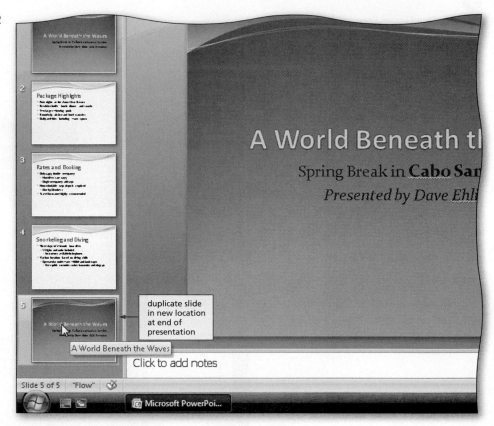

Other Ways

1. Click slide icon on Outline tab, drag icon to new location
2. In Slide Sorter view click slide thumbnail, drag thumbnail to new location

Figure 1–60

To Delete All Text in a Placeholder

To keep the ending slide clean and simple, you want only the slide show title, A World Beneath the Waves, to display on Slide 5. The following steps delete both paragraphs in the subtitle placeholder.

- With Slide 5 selected, click the subtitle text placeholder to select it (Figure 1–61).

Figure 1–61

2

- Click the subtitle text placeholder border to change the border from a dashed line to a solid line (Figure 1–62).

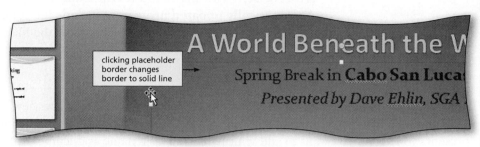

Figure 1–62

3

- Click the Cut button in the Clipboard group on the Home tab to delete all the text in the subtitle text placeholder (Figure 1–63).

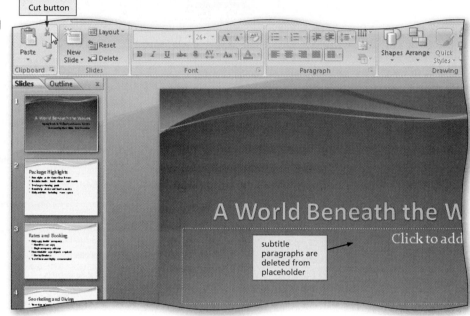

Figure 1–63

Other Ways

1. Right-click selected text, click Cut on shortcut menu
2. Select text, press DELETE key
3. Select text, press CTRL+X

Changing Document Properties and Saving Again

PowerPoint helps you organize and identify your files by using document properties, which are the details about a file. **Document properties**, also known as **metadata**, can include such information as the project author, title, or subject. **Keywords** are words or phrases that further describe the document. For example, a class name or document topic can describe the file's purpose or content.

Document properties are valuable for a variety of reasons:

- Users can save time locating a particular file because they can view a document's properties without opening the document.
- By creating consistent properties for files having similar content, users can better organize their documents.
- Some organizations require PowerPoint users to add document properties so that other employees can view details about these files.

Five different types of document properties exist, but the more common ones used in this book are standard and automatically updated properties. **Standard properties**

BTW

Converters for Earlier PowerPoint Versions
The Microsoft Web site has updates and converters if you are using earlier versions of PowerPoint. The Microsoft Office Compatibility Pack for Word, Excel and PowerPoint 2007 File Format will allow you to open, edit, and save Office 2007 documents that you receive without saving them in the earlier version's file format.

are associated with all Microsoft Office documents and include author, title, and subject. **Automatically updated properties** include file system properties, such as the date you create or change a file, and statistics, such as the file size.

To Change Document Properties

The **Document Information Panel** contains areas where you can view and enter document properties. You can view and change information in this panel at any time while you are creating a document. Before saving the presentation again, you want to add your name and class name as document properties. The following steps use the Document Information Panel to change document properties.

1

- Click the Office Button to display the Office Button menu.

- Point to Prepare on the Office Button menu to display the Prepare submenu (Figure 1–64).

Q&A What other types of actions besides changing properties can you take to set up a document for distribution?

The Prepare submenu provides commands related to sharing a document with others, such as allowing or restricting people to view and modify your document, checking to see if your presentation will run in earlier versions of PowerPoint, and searching for hidden personal information.

Figure 1–64

2

- Click Properties on the Prepare submenu to display the Document Information Panel (Figure 1–65).

Q&A Why are some of the document properties in my Document Information Panel already filled in?

The person who installed Microsoft Office 2007 on your computer or network may have set or customized the properties.

Figure 1–65

3

• Click the Author text box, if necessary, and then type your name as the Author property. If a name already is displayed in the Author text box, delete it before typing your name.

• Click the Subject text box, if necessary delete any existing text, and then type your course number and section as the Subject property (Figure 1–66).

Q&A

What types of document properties does PowerPoint collect automatically?

PowerPoint records such details as how long you worked at creating your project, how many times you revised the document, and what fonts and themes are used.

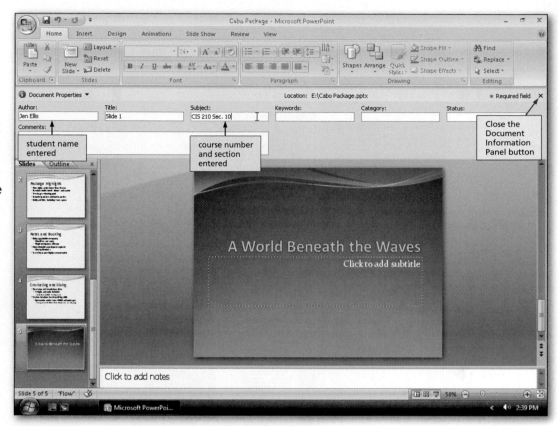

Figure 1–66

4

• Click the Close the Document Information Panel button so that the Document Information Panel no longer is displayed.

To Save an Existing Presentation with the Same File Name

Saving frequently cannot be overemphasized. You have made several modifications to the presentation since you saved it earlier in the chapter. When you first saved the document, you clicked the Save button on the Quick Access Toolbar, the Save As dialog box appeared, and you entered the file name, Cabo Package. If you want to use the same file name to save the changes made to the document, you again click the Save button on the Quick Access Toolbar. The following step saves the presentation again.

1

• Click the Save button on the Quick Access Toolbar to overwrite the previous Cabo Package file on the USB flash drive (Figure 1–67).

Q&A

Why did the Save As dialog box not appear?

PowerPoint overwrites the document using the settings specified the first time you saved the document. To save the file with a different file name or on different media, display the Save As dialog box by clicking the Office Button and then clicking Save As on the Office Button menu. Then, fill in the Save As dialog box as described in Steps 2 through 5 on pages PPT 27 through PPT 29.

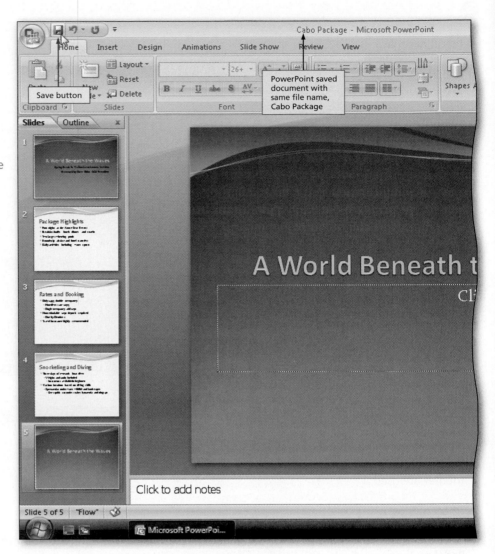

Figure 1–67

Other Ways

1. Press CTRL+S or press SHIFT+F12, press ENTER

Moving to Another Slide in Normal View

When creating or editing a presentation in Normal view, you often want to display a slide other than the current one. You can move to another slide using several methods.

- Drag the scroll box on the vertical scroll bar up or down to move through the slides in the presentation.
- Click the Next Slide or Previous Slide button on the vertical scroll bar. Clicking the Next Slide button advances to the next slide in the presentation. Clicking the Previous Slide button backs up to the slide preceding the current slide.
- On the Slides tab, click a particular slide to display that slide in the Slide pane.

To Use the Scroll Box on the Slide Pane to Move to Another Slide

Before continuing with developing this project, you want to display the title slide by dragging the scroll box on the vertical scroll bar. When you drag the scroll box, the **slide indicator** shows the number and title of the slide you are about to display. Releasing the mouse button shows the slide. The following steps move from Slide 5 to Slide 1 using the scroll box on the Slide pane.

- Position the mouse pointer on the scroll box.

- Press and hold down the mouse button so that Slide: 5 of 5 A World Beneath the Waves appears in the slide indicator (Figure 1–68).

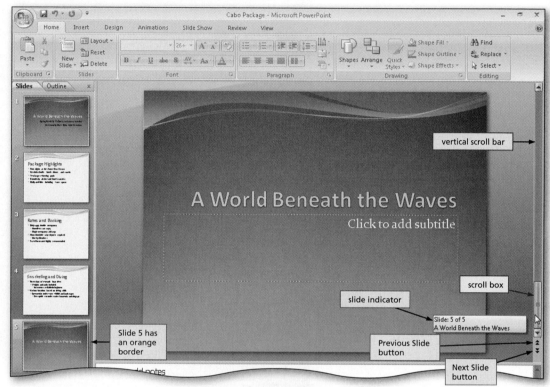

Figure 1–68

- Drag the scroll box up the vertical scroll bar until Slide: 1 of 5 A World Beneath the Waves appears in the slide indicator (Figure 1–69).

Figure 1–69

• Release the mouse button so that Slide 1 appears in the Slide pane and the Slide 1 thumbnail has an orange border in the Slides tab (Figure 1–70).

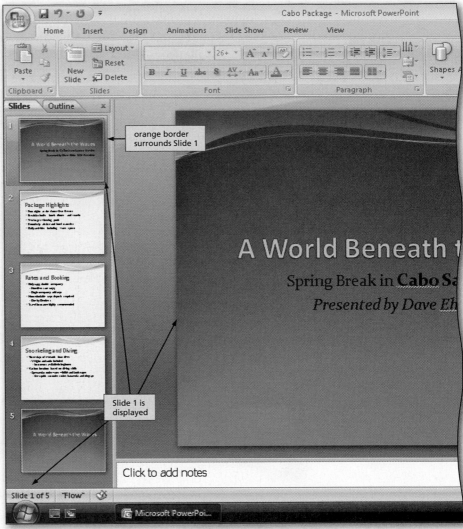

Figure 1–70

Other Ways

1. Click Next Slide button or Previous Slide button to move forward or back one slide
2. Press PAGE DOWN or PAGE UP to move forward or back one slide

Viewing the Presentation in Slide Show View

The Slide Show button, located in the lower-right corner of the PowerPoint window above the status bar, allows you to show a presentation using a computer. The computer acts like a slide projector, displaying each slide on a full screen. The full-screen slide hides the toolbars, menus, and other PowerPoint window elements.

To Start Slide Show View

When making a presentation, you use **Slide Show view**. You can start Slide Show view from Normal view or Slide Sorter view. Slide Show view begins when you click the Slide Show button in the lower-right corner of the PowerPoint window on the status bar. PowerPoint then shows the current slide on the full screen without any of the PowerPoint window objects, such as the menu bar or toolbars. The following steps start Slide Show view.

1

- Point to the Slide Show button in the lower-right corner of the PowerPoint window on the status bar (Figure 1–71).

Figure 1–71

2

- Click the Slide Show button to display the title slide (Figure 1–72).

Q&A

Where is the PowerPoint window?

When you run a slide show, the PowerPoint window is hidden. It will reappear once you end your slide show.

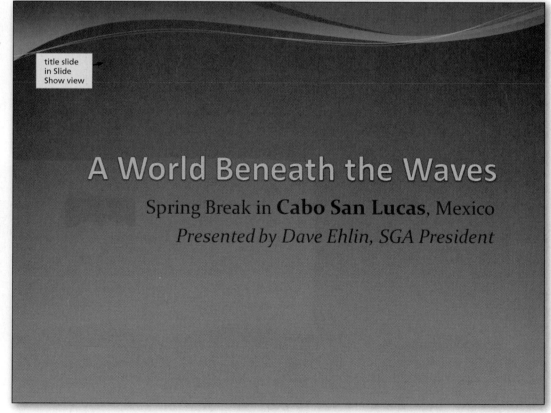

Figure 1–72

Other Ways

1. Click Slide Show tab, click From Beginning button in Start Slide Show group
2. Press F5

To Move Manually through Slides in a Slide Show

After you begin Slide Show view, you can move forward or backward through the slides. PowerPoint allows you to advance through the slides manually or automatically. During a slide show, each slide in the presentation shows on the screen, one slide at a time. Each time you click the mouse button, the next slide appears. The following steps move manually through the slides.

- Click each slide until Slide 5 (A World Beneath the Waves) is displayed (Figure 1–73).

Q&A

I see a small toolbar in the lower-left corner of my slide. What is this toolbar?

The Slide Show toolbar appears when you begin running a slide show and then move the mouse pointer. The buttons on this toolbar allow you to navigate to the next slide, the previous slide, to mark up the current slide, or to change the current display.

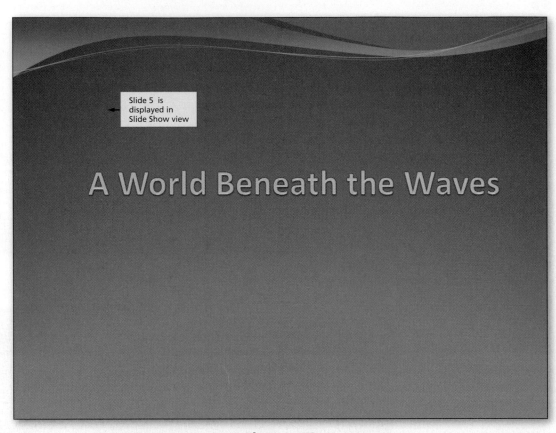

Slide 5 is displayed in Slide Show view

A World Beneath the Waves

Figure 1–73

- Click Slide 5 so that the black slide appears with a message announcing the end of the slide show (Figure 1–74).

Q&A

How can I end the presentation at this point?

Click the black slide to return to Normal view in the PowerPoint window or press the ESC key.

End of slide show, click to exit.

message announces end of slide show

Figure 1–74

Other Ways

1. Press PAGE DOWN to advance one slide at a time, or press PAGE UP to go back one slide at a time

2. Press RIGHT ARROW or DOWN ARROW to advance one slide at a time, or press LEFT ARROW or UP ARROW to go back one slide at a time

3. If Slide Show toolbar is displayed, click Next Slide or Previous Slide button on toolbar

To Display the Pop-Up Menu and Go to a Specific Slide

Slide Show view has a shortcut menu, called a **pop-up menu**, that appears when you right-click a slide in Slide Show view. This menu contains commands to assist you during a slide show.

When the pop-up menu appears, clicking the Next command moves to the next slide. Clicking the Previous command moves to the previous slide. Pointing to the Go to Slide command and then clicking the desired slide allows you to move to any slide in the presentation. The Go to Slide submenu contains a list of the slides in the presentation. You can go to the requested slide by clicking the name of that slide. Additional pop-up menu commands allow you to change the mouse pointer to a ballpoint or felt tip pen or highlighter that draws in various colors, make the screen black or white, create speaker notes, and end the slide show. The following steps go to the title slide (Slide 1) in the Cabo Package presentation.

1

• With the black slide displaying in Slide Show view, right-click the slide to display the pop-up menu.

2

• Point to Go to Slide on the pop-up menu, and then point to 2 Package Highlights in the Go to Slide submenu (Figure 1–75).

Q&A

Why does my pop-up menu appear in a different location on my screen?

The pop-up menu appears near the location of the mouse pointer at the time you right-click.

3

• Click 2 Package Highlights to display Slide 2.

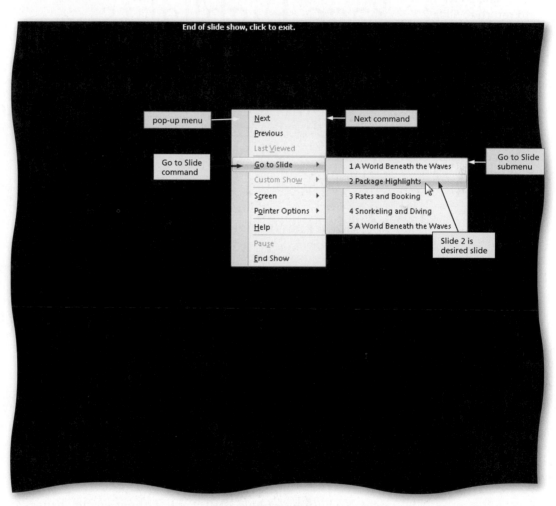

Figure 1–75

To Use the Pop-Up Menu to End a Slide Show

The End Show command on the pop-up menu ends Slide Show view and returns to the same view as when you clicked the Slide Show button. The following steps end Slide Show view and return to Normal view.

- Right-click Slide 2 and then point to End Show on the pop-up menu (Figure 1–76).

- Click End Show to return to Slide 2 in the Slide pane in Normal view.

- If the Microsoft Office PowerPoint dialog box appears, click the Yes button.

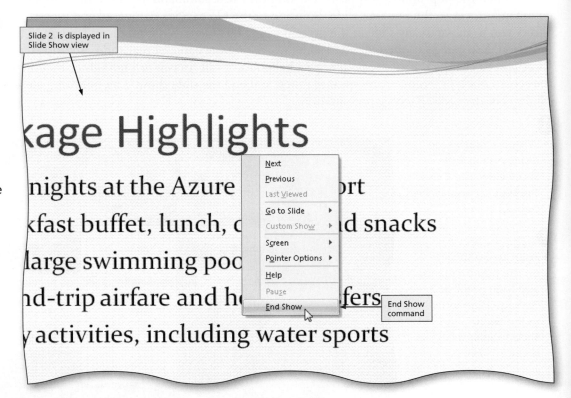

Figure 1–76

Other Ways

1. Press ESC (shows slide last viewed in Slide Show view)

Quitting PowerPoint

When you quit PowerPoint, if you have made changes to a presentation since the last time the file was saved, PowerPoint displays a dialog box asking if you want to save the changes you made to the file before it closes that window. The dialog box contains three buttons with these resulting actions:

- Yes button — Saves the changes and then quits PowerPoint
- No button — Quits PowerPoint without saving changes
- Cancel button — Closes the dialog box and redisplays the presentation without saving the changes

If no changes have been made to an open presentation since the last time the file was saved, PowerPoint will close the window without displaying a dialog box.

To Quit PowerPoint with One Document Open

You saved the presentation prior to running the slide show and did not make any changes to the project. The presentation now is complete, and you are ready to quit PowerPoint. When you have one document open, the following steps quit PowerPoint.

1

Point to the Close button on the right side of the PowerPoint title bar (Figure 1–77).

2

• Click the Close button to quit PowerPoint.

Q&A What if I have more than one PowerPoint document open?

You would click the Close button for each open document. When you click the last open document's Close button, PowerPoint also quits. As an alternative, you could click the Office Button and then click the Exit PowerPoint button on the Office Button menu, which closes all open PowerPoint documents and then quits PowerPoint.

Figure 1–77

Other Ways

1. With one document open, double-click Office Button

2. Click Office Button, click Exit PowerPoint on Office Button menu

3. With one document open, right-click Microsoft

PowerPoint button on Windows Vista taskbar, click Close on shortcut menu

4. With one document open, press ALT+F4

Starting PowerPoint and Opening a Presentation

Once you have created and saved a presentation, you may need to retrieve it from your storage medium. For example, you might want to revise the document or print it. Opening a presentation requires that PowerPoint is running on your computer.

To Start PowerPoint

The following steps, which assume Windows Vista is running, start PowerPoint.

1 Click the Start button on the Windows Vista taskbar to display the Start menu.

2 Click All Programs at the bottom of the left pane on the Start menu to display the All Programs list and then click Microsoft Office in the All Programs list to display the Microsoft Office list.

3 Click Microsoft Office PowerPoint 2007 on the Microsoft Office list to start PowerPoint and display a new blank presentation in the PowerPoint window.

4 If the PowerPoint window is not maximized, click the Maximize button on its title bar to maximize the window.

Note: If you are using Windows XP, see Appendix F for alternate steps.

To Open a Presentation from PowerPoint

Earlier in this chapter you saved your project on a USB flash drive using the file name, Cabo Package. The following steps open the Cabo Package file from the USB flash drive.

1

• With your USB flash drive connected to one of the computer's USB ports, click the Office Button to display the Office Button menu (Figure 1–78).

Q&A What files are shown in the Recent Documents list?

PowerPoint displays the most recently opened document file names in this list. If the name of the file you want to open appears in the Recent Documents list, you could click it to open the file.

Figure 1–78

2

• Click Open on the Office Button menu to display the Open dialog box.

• If the Folders list is displayed below the Folders button, click the Folders button to remove the Folders list.

• If necessary, click Computer in the Favorite Links section and then scroll until UDISK 2.0 (E:) appears in the list of available drives.

• Double-click UDISK 2.0 (E:) to select the USB flash drive, Drive E in this case, as the new open location.

• Click Cabo Package to select the file name (Figure 1–79).

Q&A How do I open the file if I am not using a USB flash drive?

Use the same process, but be certain to select your device in the Computer list.

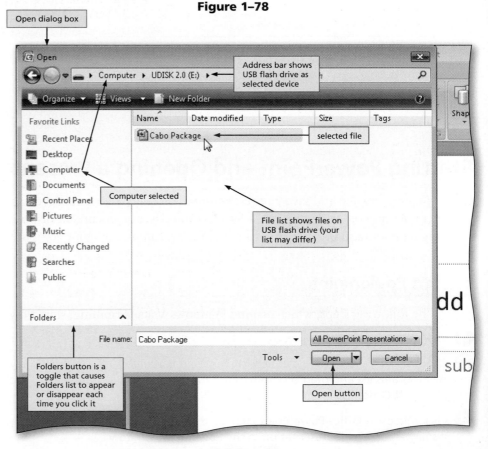

Figure 1–79

3

- Click the Open button to open the selected file and display Slide 1 in the PowerPoint window (Figure 1–80).

Q&A

Why are the PowerPoint icon and name on the Windows Vista taskbar?

When you open a PowerPoint file, a PowerPoint program button is displayed on the taskbar. The button contains an ellipsis because some of its contents do not fit in the allotted button space. If you point to a program button, its entire contents appear in a ScreenTip, which in this case would be the program name followed by the file name.

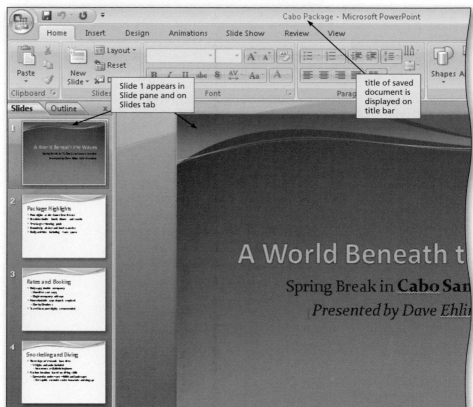

Figure 1–80

Other Ways

1. Click Office Button, double-click file name in Recent Documents list
2. Press CTRL+O, select file name, press ENTER

Checking a Presentation for Spelling Errors

After you create a presentation, you should check it visually for spelling errors and style consistency. In addition, you use PowerPoint's Spelling tool to identify possible misspellings. Do not rely on the spelling checker to catch all your mistakes. While PowerPoint's spelling checker is a valuable tool, it is not infallible. You should proofread your presentation carefully by pointing to each word and saying it aloud as you point to it. Be mindful of commonly misused words such as its and it's, through and though, and to and too.

PowerPoint checks the entire presentation for spelling mistakes using a standard dictionary contained in the Microsoft Office group. This dictionary is shared with the other Microsoft Office applications such as Word and Excel. A **custom dictionary** is available if you want to add special words such as proper names, cities, and acronyms. When checking a presentation for spelling errors, PowerPoint opens the standard dictionary and the custom dictionary file, if one exists. When a word appears in the Spelling dialog box, you can perform one of several actions.

Table 1–1 Spelling Dialog Box Buttons and Actions		
Button Name	**When To Use**	**Action**
Ignore	Word is spelled correctly but not found in dictionaries	Continues checking rest of the presentation but will flag that word again if it appears later in document
Ignore All	Word is spelled correctly but not found in dictionaries	Ignores all occurrences of the word and continues checking rest of presentation
Change	Word is misspelled	Click proper spelling of the word in Suggestions list. PowerPoint corrects word, continues checking rest of presentation, but will flag that word again if it appears later in document.
Change All	Word is misspelled	Click proper spelling of word in Suggestions list. PowerPoint changes all occurrences of misspelled word and continues checking rest of presentation.
Add	Add word to custom dictionary	PowerPoint opens custom dictionary, adds word, and continues checking rest of presentation.
Suggest	Correct spelling is uncertain	Lists alternative spellings. Click the correct word from the Suggestions box or type the proper spelling. Corrects the word and continues checking the rest of the presentation.
AutoCorrect	Add spelling error to AutoCorrect list	PowerPoint adds spelling error and its correction to AutoCorrect list. Any future misspelling of word is corrected automatically as you type.
Close	Stop spelling checker	PowerPoint closes spelling checker and returns to PowerPoint window.

To Check Spelling

The standard dictionary contains commonly used English words. It does not, however, contain many proper names, abbreviations, technical terms, poetic contractions, or antiquated terms. PowerPoint treats words not found in the dictionaries as misspellings. The following steps check the spelling on all slides in the Cabo Package presentation.

- Click Review on the Ribbon to display the Review tab (Figure 1–81).

Figure 1–81

2

- Click the Spelling button in the Proofing group to start the spelling checker and display the Spelling dialog box (Figure 1–82).

Figure 1–82

3

- Click the Ignore button to skip the word, Cabo (Figure 1–83).

Q&A

Cabo is not flagged as a possible misspelled word. Why not?

Your custom dictionary contains the word, so it is recognized as a correct word.

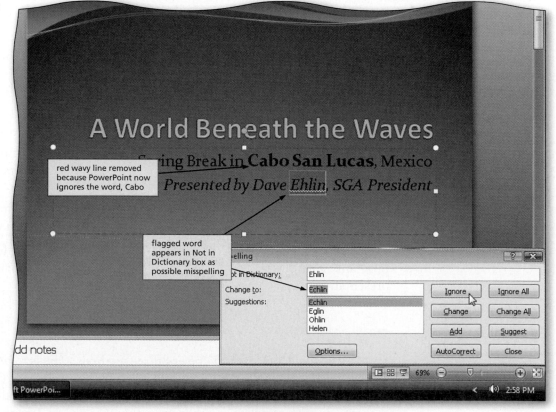

Figure 1–83

4

- Click the Ignore button to skip the word, Ehlin.

- When the Microsoft Office PowerPoint dialog box appears, click the OK button to close the spelling checker and return to the current slide, Slide 1, or to the slide where a possible misspelled word appeared.

- Click the slide to remove the box from the word, Ehlin (Figure 1–84).

Figure 1–84

Correcting Errors

After creating a presentation and running the spelling checker, you may find that you must make changes. Changes may be required because a slide contains an error, the scope of the presentation shifts, or the style is inconsistent. This section explains the types of errors that commonly occur when creating a presentation.

BTW

Certification
The Microsoft Certified Application Specialist (MCAS) program provides an opportunity for you to obtain a valuable industry credential – proof that you have the PowerPoint 2007 skills required by employers. For more information see Appendix G or visit the PowerPoint 2007 Certification Web page (scsite.com/ppt2007/cert).

Types of Corrections Made to Presentations

You generally make three types of corrections to text in a presentation: additions, deletions, and replacements.

- Additions are necessary when you omit text from a slide and need to add it later. You may need to insert text in the form of a sentence, word, or single character. For example, you may want to add the presenter's middle name on the title slide.

- Deletions are required when text on a slide is incorrect or no longer is relevant to the presentation. For example, a slide may look cluttered. Therefore, you may want to remove one of the bulleted paragraphs to add more space.

- Replacements are needed when you want to revise the text in a presentation. For example, you may want to substitute the word, their, for the word, there.

Editing text in PowerPoint basically is the same as editing text in a word processing program. The following sections illustrate the most common changes made to text in a presentation.

Deleting Text

You can delete text using one of three methods. One is to use the BACKSPACE key to remove text just typed. The second is to position the insertion point to the left of the text you wish to delete and then press the DELETE key. The third method is to drag through the text you wish to delete and then press the DELETE key. Use the third method when deleting large sections of text.

Replacing Text in an Existing Slide

When you need to correct a word or phrase, you can replace the text by selecting the text to be replaced and then typing the new text. As soon as you press any key on the keyboard, the selected text is deleted and the new text is displayed.

PowerPoint inserts text to the left of the insertion point. The text to the right of the insertion point moves to the right (and shifts downward if necessary) to accommodate the added text.

Displaying a Presentation in Grayscale

Printing handouts of a presentation allows you to use them to make overhead transparencies. The Color/Grayscale button on the Color/Grayscale group on the View tab shows the presentation in black and white before you print. Pure Black and White alters the slides' appearance so that black lines display on a white background. Shadows and other graphical effects are hidden. Grayscale shows varying degrees of gray.

To Display a Presentation in Grayscale

The Color/Grayscale button on the Color/Grayscale group on the View tab changes from color bars to shades of black, called grayscale, and white. After you view the text objects in the presentation in grayscale, you can make any changes that will enhance printouts produced from a black and white printer or photocopier. The following steps display the presentation in grayscale.

1

• Click View on the Ribbon to display the View tab (Figure 1–85).

Figure 1–85

- Click Grayscale in the Color/Grayscale group to display Slide 1 in grayscale in the Slide pane (Figure 1–86).

Figure 1–86

- Click the Next Slide button four times to view all slides in the presentation in grayscale (Figure 1–87).

Figure 1–87

- Click the Back To Color View button in the Close group to return to the previous tab and display Slide 5 with the default Flow color scheme (Figure 1–88).

Figure 1–88

Printing a Presentation

After you create a presentation, you often want to print it. A printed version of the presentation is called a **hard copy** or **printout**.

Printed copies of your presentation can be useful for the following reasons:

- Many people prefer proofreading a hard copy of the presentation rather than viewing the slides on the screen to check for errors and readability.

- Someone without computer access or who could not attend your live presentation can view the slides' content.

- Copies can be distributed as handouts to people viewing your presentation.

- Hard copies can serve as reference material if your storage medium is lost or becomes corrupted and you need to re-create the presentation.

It is a good practice to save a presentation before printing it, in the event you experience difficulties with the printer.

To Print a Presentation

With the completed presentation saved, you may want to print it. The following steps print all five completed presentation slides in the saved Cabo Package project.

- Click the Office Button to display the Office Button menu.

- Point to Print on the Office Button menu to display the Print submenu (Figure 1–89).

Q&A

Can I print my presentation in black and white to conserve ink or toner?

Yes. Click the Office Button, point to the arrow next to Print on the Office Button menu, and then click Print Preview on the Print submenu. Click the Options button on the Print Preview tab, point to Color/Grayscale on the Options button menu, and then click Pure Black and White on the Color/Grayscale submenu. Click the Print button on the Print submenu.

Figure 1–89

2

- Click Quick Print on the Print submenu to print the slides.

- When the printer stops, retrieve the hard copy of the five Cabo Package slides (Figures 1–90a through 1–90e).

Q&A

How can I print multiple copies of my document other than clicking the Print button twice?

Click the Office Button, point to Print on the Office Button menu, click Print on the Print submenu, increase the number in the Number of copies box, and then click the OK button.

Q&A

Do I have to wait until my presentation is complete to print it?

No, you can follow these steps to print your slides at any time while you are creating your presentation.

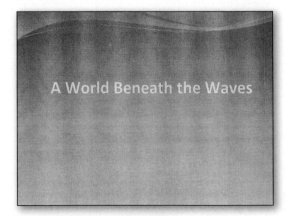

(a) Slide 1

(b) Slide 2

(c) Slide 3

(d) Slide 4

(e) Slide 5

Figure 1–90

Other Ways

1. Press CTRL+P

BTW

Quick Reference
For a table that lists how to complete the tasks covered in this book using the mouse, Ribbon, shortcut menu, and keyboard, see the Quick Reference Summary at the back of this book, or visit the PowerPoint 2007 Quick Reference Web page (scsite.com/ppt2007/qr).

Making a Transparency

With the handouts printed, you now can make overhead transparencies using one of several devices. One device is a printer attached to your computer, such as an inkjet printer or a laser printer. Transparencies produced on a printer may be in black and white or color, depending on the printer. Another device is a photocopier. Because each of these devices requires a special transparency film, check the user's manual for the film requirement of your specific device, or ask your instructor.

PowerPoint Help

At any time while using PowerPoint, you can find answers to questions and display information about various topics through **PowerPoint Help**. Used properly, this form of assistance can increase your productivity and reduce your frustrations by minimizing the time you spend learning how to use PowerPoint.

This section introduces you to PowerPoint Help. Additional information about using PowerPoint Help is available in Appendix C.

BTW

PowerPoint Help
The best way to become familiar with PowerPoint Help is to use it. Appendix C includes detailed information about PowerPoint Help and exercises that will help you gain confidence in using it.

To Search for PowerPoint Help

Using PowerPoint Help, you can search for information based on phrases such as save a presentation or format a chart, or key terms such as copy, save, or format. PowerPoint Help responds with a list of search results displayed as links to a variety of resources. The following steps, which use PowerPoint Help to search for information about using document themes, assume you are connected to the Internet.

1

- Click the Microsoft Office PowerPoint Help button near the upper-right corner of the PowerPoint window to open the PowerPoint Help window.

- Type document theme in the Type words to search for text box at the top of the PowerPoint Help window (Figure 1–91).

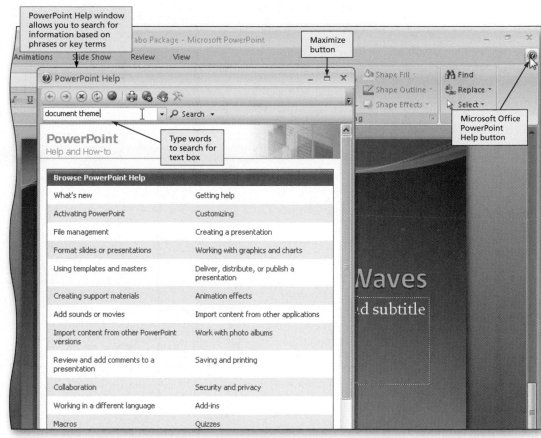

Figure 1–91

2

- Press the ENTER key to display the search results.

- Click the Maximize button on the PowerPoint Help window title bar to maximize the Help window (Figure 1–92).

Q&A

Where is the PowerPoint window with Slide 1?

PowerPoint is open in the background, but the PowerPoint Help window is overlaid on top of the Microsoft PowerPoint window. When the PowerPoint Help window is closed, the slide will reappear.

Figure 1–92

3

- Click the 'Apply or customize a document theme' link to display information regarding applying or customizing themes (Figure 1–93).

Q&A

What is the purpose of the buttons at the top of the Power-Point Help window?

Use the buttons in the upper-left corner of the PowerPoint Help window to navigate through the Help system, change the display, show the PowerPoint Help table of contents, and print the contents of the window.

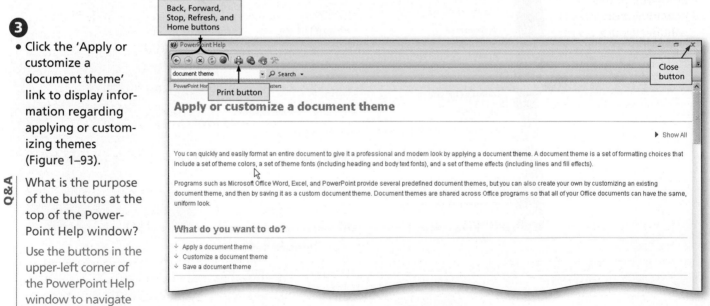

Figure 1–93

4

- Click the Close button on the PowerPoint Help window title bar to close the PowerPoint Help window and display Slide 5.

Other Ways

1. Press F1

To Quit PowerPoint

The following steps quit PowerPoint.

1 Click the Close button on the right side of the title bar to quit PowerPoint; or, if you have multiple PowerPoint documents open, click the Office Button and then click the Exit PowerPoint button on the Office Button menu to close all open documents and quit PowerPoint.

2 If necessary, click the No button in the Microsoft Office PowerPoint dialog box so that any changes you have made are not saved.

Chapter Summary

In this chapter you have learned how to apply a document theme, create a title slide and text slides with bulleted lists, format text, view the presentation in Slide Show view, and print slides as handouts. The items listed below include all the new PowerPoint skills you have learned in this chapter.

1. Start PowerPoint (PPT 5)
2. Choose a Document Theme (PPT 16)
3. Enter the Presentation Title (PPT 18)
4. Enter the Presentation Subtitle Paragraph (PPT 20)
5. Select a Paragraph (PPT 21)
6. Italicize Text (PPT 22)
7. Select Multiple Paragraphs (PPT 22)
8. Change the Text Color (PPT 23)
9. Select a Group of Words (PPT 24)
10. Increase Font Size (PPT 24)
11. Bold Text (PPT 25)
12. Decrease the Title Slide Title Text Font Size (PPT 25)
13. Save a Presentation (PPT 27)
14. Add a New Text Slide with a Bulleted List (PPT 29)
15. Enter a Slide Title (PPT 31)
16. Select a Text Placeholder (PPT 31)
17. Type a Single-Level Bulleted List (PPT 32)
18. Add a New Slide and Enter a Slide Title (PPT 33)
19. Type a Multi-Level Bulleted List (PPT 34)
20. Create a Third-Level Paragraph (PPT 37)
21. Duplicate a Slide (PPT 40)
22. Arrange a Slide (PPT 41)
23. Delete All Text in a Placeholder (PPT 42)
24. Change Document Properties (PPT 44)
25. Save an Existing Presentation with the Same File Name (PPT 45)
26. Use the Scroll Box on the Slide Pane to Move to Another Slide (PPT 47)
27. Start Slide Show View (PPT 49)
28. Move Manually through Slides in a Slide Show (PPT 50)
29. Display the Pop-Up Menu and Go to a Specific Slide (PPT 51)
30. Use the Pop-Up Menu to End a Slide Show (PPT 52)
31. Quit PowerPoint with One Document Open (PPT 53)
32. Open a Presentation from PowerPoint (PPT 54)
33. Check Spelling (PPT 55)
34. Display a Presentation in Grayscale (PPT 59)
35. Print a Presentation (PPT 61)
36. Search for PowerPoint Help (PPT 63)

If you have a SAM user profile, you may have access to hands-on instruction, practice, and assessment. Log in to your SAM account (http://sam2007.course.com) to launch any assigned training activities or exams that relate to the skills covered in this chapter.

Learn It Online

Test your knowledge of chapter content and key terms.

Instructions: To complete the Learn It Online exercises, start your browser, click the Address bar, and then enter the Web address scsite.com/ppt2007/learn. When the Office 2007 Learn It Online page is displayed, click the link for the exercise you want to complete and then read the instructions.

Chapter Reinforcement TF, MC, and SA
A series of true/false, multiple choice, and short answer questions that test your knowledge of the chapter content.

Flash Cards
An interactive learning environment where you identify chapter key terms associated with displayed definitions.

Practice Test
A series of multiple choice questions that test your knowledge of chapter content and key terms.

Who Wants To Be a Computer Genius?
An interactive game that challenges your knowledge of chapter content in the style of a television quiz show.

Wheel of Terms
An interactive game that challenges your knowledge of chapter key terms in the style of the television show *Wheel of Fortune*.

Crossword Puzzle Challenge
A crossword puzzle that challenges your knowledge of key terms presented in the chapter.

Apply Your Knowledge

Reinforce the skills and apply the concepts you learned in this chapter.

Modifying Character Formats and Paragraph Levels
Instructions: Start PowerPoint. Open the presentation, Apply 1-1 Keep Your Cool, from the Data Files for Students. See the inside back cover of this book for instructions on downloading the Data Files for Students, or contact your instructor for more information about accessing the required files.

The two slides in the presentation stress the importance of drinking plenty of water on hot days. The document you open is an unformatted presentation. You are to modify the document theme and text, indent the paragraphs, and format the text so the slides look like Figure 1–94.

Perform the following tasks:
1. Change the document theme to Trek. Note that the Trek theme uses all capital letters for the title text. On the title slide, use your name in place of Student Name and bold and italicize your name. Increase the title text font size to 44 point.

(a) Slide 1 (Title Slide)
Figure 1–94

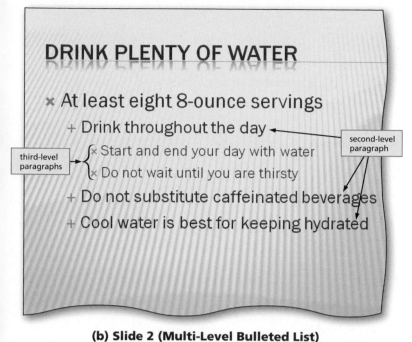

(b) Slide 2 (Multi-Level Bulleted List)
Figure 1–94 (continued)

2. On Slide 2, increase the indent of the second, fifth, and sixth paragraphs (Drink throughout the day; Do not substitute caffeinated beverages; Cool water is best for keeping hydrated) to second-level paragraphs. Then change paragraphs three and four (Start and end your day with water; Do not wait until you are thirsty) to third-level paragraphs.

3. Check the spelling, and then display the revised presentation in grayscale.

4. Change the document properties, as specified by your instructor. Save the presentation using the file name, Apply 1-1 Drink Water. Submit the revised document in the format specified by your instructor.

Extend Your Knowledge

Extend the skills you learned in this chapter and experiment with new skills. You may need to use Help to complete the assignment.

Changing Slide Theme and Text

Instructions: Start PowerPoint. Open the presentation, Extend 1-1 Nutrition, from the Data Files for Students. See the inside back cover of this book for instructions on downloading the Data Files for Students, or contact your instructor for more information about accessing the required files.

You will choose a theme (Figure 1–95), format slides, and create a closing slide.

Figure 1–95

Perform the following tasks:
1. Apply an appropriate document theme.

2. On Slide 1, use your name in place of Student Name. Format the text using techniques you learned in this chapter, such as changing the font size and color and also bolding and italicizing words.

Continued >

STUDENT ASSIGNMENTS

Extend Your Knowledge *continued*

3. On Slide 2, adjust the paragraph levels so that the lines of text are arranged under vegetable and fruit categories. Edit the text so that the slide meets the 7 × 7 rule, which states that each line should have a maximum of seven words, and each slide should have a maximum of seven lines.

4. On Slides 3 and 4, create paragraphs and adjust the paragraph levels.

5. Create an appropriate closing slide using the title slide as a guide.

6. Change the document properties, as specified by your instructor. Save the presentation using the file name, Extend 1-1 Fruit and Vegetables.

7. Add the Print button to the Quick Access Toolbar and then click this button to print the slides.

8. Delete the Print button from the Quick Access Toolbar.

9. Submit the revised document in the format specified by your instructor.

Make It Right

Analyze a presentation and correct all errors and/or improve the design.

Correcting Formatting and List Levels

Instructions: Start PowerPoint. Open the presentation, Make It Right 1-1 Indulge, from the Data Files for Students. See the inside back cover of this book for instructions on downloading the Data Files for Students, or contact your instructor for more information about accessing the required files.

Correct the formatting problems and errors in the presentation while keeping in mind the guidelines presented in this chapter.

Perform the following tasks:

1. Change the document theme from Metro, shown in Figure 1–96, to Opulent.

2. On Slide 1, replace the words, Fall Semester, with your name. Format your name so that it displays prominently on the slide.

3. Move Slide 2 to the end of the presentation so that it becomes the new Slide 4.

4. Use the spell checker to correct the misspellings. Analyze the slides for other word usage errors that the spell checker did not find.

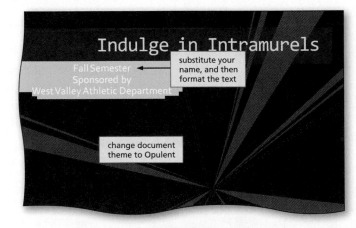

Figure 1–96

5. On Slide 2, increase the Slide 2 title (Athletic Events) font size to 40. Make the indent levels for paragraphs 2, 4, and 6 the same level.

6. On Slide 3, change the title text (Awards Ceremony) font size to 40. Make the indent levels for paragraphs 3 and 5 the same level.

7. Change the document properties, as specified by your instructor. Save the presentation using the file name, Make It Right 1-1 Intramurals.

8. Submit the revised document in the format specified by your instructor.

In the Lab

Design and/or create a presentation using the guidelines, concepts, and skills presented in this chapter. Labs 1, 2, and 3 are listed in order of increasing difficulty.

Lab 1: Creating a Presentation with Bulleted Lists

Problem: Many of the important steps you will take in your life are influenced by your credit report. Buying a car, renting an apartment, and even applying for a job often require a credit check. Your credit score can make or break your ability to obtain the goods you truly want and need. One of your assignments in your economics class is to give a speech about establishing credit. You develop the outline shown in Figure 1–97 and then prepare the PowerPoint presentation shown in Figures 1–98a through 1–98d.

Instructions: Perform the following tasks.

1. Create a new presentation using the Aspect document theme.

2. Using the typed notes illustrated in Figure 1–97, create the title slide shown in Figure 1–98a using your name in place of Marc Kantlon. Italicize your name. Decrease the font size of the title paragraph, Give Yourself Some Credit, to 40. Increase the font size of the first paragraph of the subtitle text, Understanding Your Credit Report, to 28.

3. Using the typed notes in Figure 1–97, create the three text slides with bulleted lists shown in Figures 1–98b through 1–98d.

Give Yourself Some Credit
Understanding Your Credit Report
Marc Kantlon
Economics 101

Credit Report Fundamentals
Generated by three companies
Experian, Equifax, TransUnion
Factors
How much you owe to each company
Payment history for each company
Includes utilities, medical expenses, rent

How FICO Is Calculated
Range - 760 (excellent) to 620 (poor)
35% - Payment history
30% - Amounts owed
15% - Credit history length
10% - New credit
10% - Credit types

Improve Your FICO Score
Pay bills on time
Avoid opening many new accounts
Open only if you intend to use
Keep balances low
Less than 25% of credit limit
Review credit report yearly

Figure 1–97

Continued >

4. On Slide 3, change the font color of the number, 760, to green and the number, 620, to red.

5. Check the spelling and correct any errors.

6. Drag the scroll box to display Slide 1. Click the Slide Show button to start Slide Show view. Then click to display each slide.

7. Change the document properties, as specified by your instructor. Save the presentation using the file name, Lab 1-1 Credit.

8. Submit the document in the format specified by your instructor.

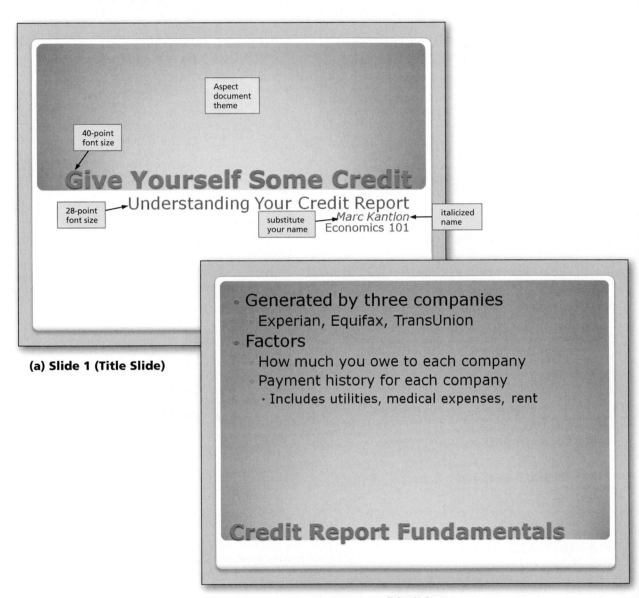

(a) Slide 1 (Title Slide)

(b) Slide 2

Figure 1–98

(c) Slide 3

(d) Slide 4

Figure 1–98 (continued)

In the Lab

Lab 2: Creating a Presentation with Bulleted Lists and a Closing Slide

Problem: Hybrid vehicles have received much attention in recent years. Everyone from environmentalists to movie stars are driving them, and potential buyers wait for months until the vehicles arrive in dealers' showrooms. You work part-time at Midwest State Bank, and the loan department manager, Jen Westbrook, has asked you to develop a PowerPoint presentation to accompany her upcoming speech. She hands you the outline shown in Figure 1–99 and asks you to create the presentation shown in Figures 1–100a through 1–100e.

Is a Hybrid Car Right for You?
Jen Westbrook, Midwest State Bank Loan Department Manager

Are They a Good Value?
    Depends upon your driving habits
    Government offers tax credits
    Excellent resale value
    Efficient gas consumption

What Is Their Gas Mileage?
    Depends upon make and size
            City: Ranges from 18 to 60 mpg
            Highway: Ranges from 21 to 66 mpg
    Actual mileage affected by driving patterns

What Makes Them Work?
    Use two motors
        Gas
            Smaller, more efficient than traditional vehicle
        Electric
            Gives gas engine extra power boost
            May power car entirely

See me for your next car purchase
    Jen Westbrook, Midwest State Bank Loan Department Manager

Figure 1–99

Continued >

In the Lab *continued*

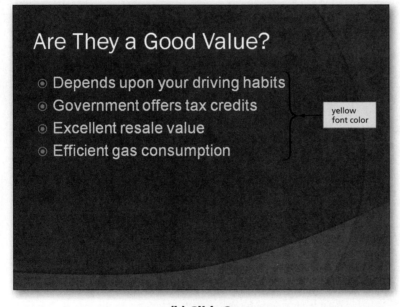

(a) Slide 1 (Title Slide)

(b) Slide 2

Figure 1–100

Instructions: Perform the following tasks.

1. Create a new presentation using the Technic document theme.

2. Using the typed notes illustrated in Figure 1–99, create the title slide shown in Figure 1–100a using your name in place of Jan Westbrook. Bold your name. Italicize the title, Is a Hybrid Car Right for You?, and increase the font size to 54. Change the font color of the title text to green and the subtitle text to yellow.

3. Using the typed notes in Figure 1–99, create the three text slides with bulleted lists shown in Figures 1–100b through 1–100d. Change the color of all the bulleted list paragraph text to yellow.

4. Duplicate the title slide and then move the new closing slide to the end of the presentation. Change the Slide 5 title text, increase the font size to 66, and remove the italics.

5. Check the spelling and correct any errors.

6. Drag the scroll box to display Slide 1. Click the Slide Show button to start Slide Show view. Then click to display each slide.

7. Change the document properties, as specified by your instructor. Save the presentation using the file name, Lab 1-2 Hybrids.

8. Submit the revised document in the format specified by your instructor.

What Is Their Gas Mileage?

- ◉ Depends upon make and size
  - • City: Ranges from 18 to 60 mpg
  - • Highway: Ranges from 21 to 66 mpg
- ◉ Actual mileage affected by driving patterns

yellow font color

(c) Slide 3

What Makes Them Work?

- ◉ Use two motors
  - • Gas
    - ○ Smaller, more efficient than traditional vehicle
  - • Electric
    - ○ Gives gas engine extra power boost
    - ○ May power car entirely

yellow font color

new closing slide

(d) Slide 4

Jen Westbrook, Midwest State Bank Loan Department Manager

text not italicized

SEE ME FOR YOUR NEXT CAR PURCHASE

66-point font size

(e) Slide 5 (Closing Slide)

Figure 1–100 (continued)

In the Lab

Lab 3: Creating and Updating Presentations

Problem: Bobbie Willis, the public relations director for the South Haven Park District, plans activities every season for community residents and promotes the offerings using a PowerPoint presentation. The new seminars for senior citizens this spring are quilting and t'ai chi. Adults can register for gourmet cooking lessons and kickball. Teens can enroll in sailing and fencing lessons.

South Haven Park District
New Spring Seminars
Bobbie Willis, Director

Seniors' Seminars
    Quilting
        Quilts made from donated fabrics
        Sewing machines provided
    T'ai Chi
        Gentle warm-ups
        12 slow, continuous movements
        Easy cool-down exercises

Adults' Seminars
    Almost Gourmet
        Learn techniques from a professional chef
            Everyone prepares and enjoys the dinners
                Come hungry!
    Kickball
        Learn techniques and rules

Teens' Seminars
    Sailing
        Sail a 30-foot sailboat at your first class
    Fencing
        Three levels
            Level 1 – Beginning Foil
            Level 2 – Foil, Epee, and Saber
            Level 3 – Open Strip Fencing

Figure 1–101

Instructions Part 1: Using the outline in Figure 1–101, create the presentation shown in Figure 1–102. Use the Oriel document theme. On the title slide shown in Figure 1–102a, type your name in place of Bobbie Willis, increase the font size of the title paragraph, South Haven Park District, to 60 and change the text font style to italic. Increase the font size of the subtitle paragraph, New Spring Seminars, to 32, and change the font size of the subtitle paragraph with your name to 37 or to a size that displays all the text on one line. Create the three text slides with multi-level bulleted lists shown in Figures 1–102b through 1–102d.

    Correct any spelling mistakes. Change the document properties, as specified by your instructor. Save the presentation using the file name, Lab 1-3 Part One Spring Seminars. Display the presentation in grayscale.

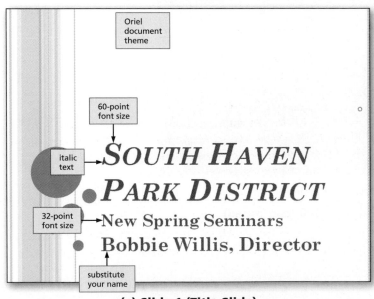

(a) Slide 1 (Title Slide)
Figure 1–102

(b) Slide 2

(c) Slide 3

(d) Slide 4

Figure 1–102 (continued)

Instructions Part 2: The South Haven Park District staff members want to update this presentation to promote the new Fall seminars. Modify the presentation created in Part 1 to create the presentation shown in Figure 1–103. To begin, save the current presentation with the new file name, Lab 1-3 Part Two Fall Seminars. Change the document theme to Civic. On the title slide, remove the italics from the title paragraph, South Haven Park District, decrease the font size to 44, and bold the text. Change the first subtitle paragraph to New Fall Seminars. Then change your title in the second subtitle paragraph to Executive Director and change the font size of the entire paragraph to 28.

On Slide 2, change the first first-level paragraph, Quilting, to Quilting for the Holidays. Change the first second-level paragraph, Quilts made from donated fabrics, to Quilts will be raffled at Annual Bazaar. Change the title of the second seminar to Intermediate T'ai Chi.

On Slide 3, change the first second-level paragraph under Almost Gourmet to Holiday feasts and parties. Then change the second-level paragraph under Kickball to Seminar concludes with single elimination tournament.

On Slide 4, change the first class from Sailing to Climbing and then change the course description second-level paragraph to Covers verbal signals, rope, knots, harnesses, belaying.

Continued >

In the Lab *continued*

Correct any spelling mistakes, and then view the slide show. Change the document properties, as specified by your instructor. Display the presentation in grayscale. Submit both Part One and Part Two documents in the format specified by your instructor.

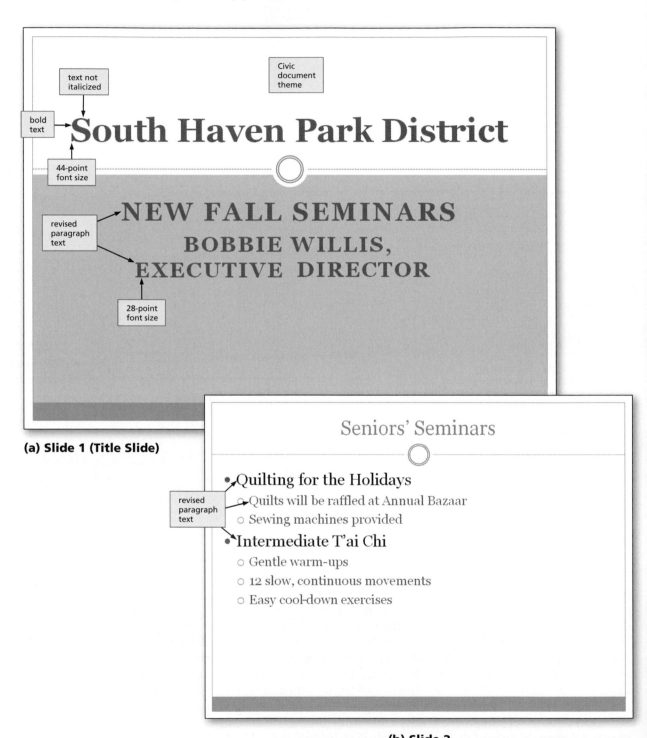

(a) Slide 1 (Title Slide)

(b) Slide 2

Figure 1–103

(c) Slide 3

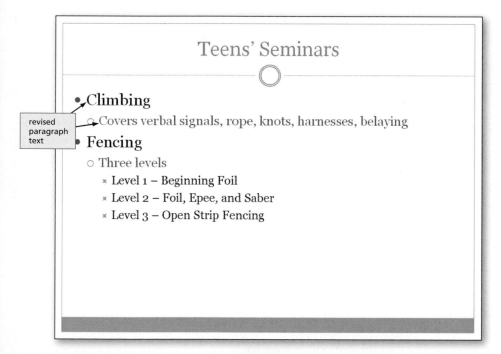

(d) Slide 4

Figure 1–103 (continued)

Cases and Places

Apply your creative thinking and problem solving skills to design and implement a solution.

• Easier   •• More Difficult

Note: Remember to use the 7 × 7 rule as you design the presentations: a maximum of seven words on a line and a maximum of seven lines on one slide.

• 1: Design and Create an Ocean and Seas Presentation

Salt water covers more than two-thirds of the Earth's surface. This water flows freely between the Earth's five oceans and seas, which all are connected. In preparation for your next snorkeling and diving adventure, you have been reading about the oceans and seas. You decide to prepare a PowerPoint presentation to accompany a speech that is required in your Earth Science class. You create the outline shown in Figure 1–104 about these waters. Use this outline along with the concepts and techniques presented in this chapter to develop and format a slide show with a title slide and three text slides with bulleted lists. Be sure to check spelling.

Water, Water, Everywhere
The Earth's Oceans and Seas
Jamel Thomas
Earth Science 203

Major Bodies of Water
    Four oceans: Pacific, Atlantic, Indian, and Arctic
        Pacific is largest and deepest
           64,186,300 square miles
           12,925 feet average depth
  Fifth ocean delimited in 2000
        Southern Ocean north of Antarctica

Coral Reefs
    Form in shallow, warm seas
    Made of coral polyps' skeletons
      Grow on top of old skeletons
    Spend adult lives fixed to same spot
    Coral diseases increasing dramatically past 10 years
      Responding to onset of bacteria, fungi, viruses

Ocean Zones
    Sunlit (down to 650 feet)
        Sea plants and many animals
    Twilight (down to 3,300 feet)
      Many different fish
    Sunless (down to 13,100 feet)
        Animals feed on dead food from above

Figure 1–104

• 2: Design and Create an Industrial Revolution Presentation

The Industrial Revolution changed the way people worked and lived in many parts of the world. With its roots in Britain in the 18th century, the Industrial Revolution introduced new machines, steam power, and trains. As part of your World History homework assignments, you develop the outline shown in Figure 1–105 about the Industrial Revolution and then create an accompanying PowerPoint presentation. Use the concepts and techniques presented in this chapter to develop and format this slide show with a title slide, three text slides with bulleted lists, and a closing slide. Be sure to check spelling.

The Industrial Revolution
1700 - 1850
Sonia Banks
World History 108

British Inventors
   First machines spun and wove cloth quickly
      Wealthy businessmen built factories
        Spinning Jenny machine spun 16 threads simultaneously
   Angered people who made cloth at home
      Luddites protested by smashing machines
        Led by Ned Ludd

Steam Power
   James Watt invented first steam engine in 1782
      Hundreds of his engines used throughout Britain
   George Stephenson designed steam train, The Rocket
      Peak speed: 30 mph
      Used to transport goods in 1829

Coal Mining
   Coal needed to boil water to create steam
   Mining towns boomed
      Deep mines dug
      Men, women, and children worked long hours
        Many people killed and injured

Figure 1–105

Continued >

Cases and Places *continued*

•• 3: Design and Create a Recycling Presentation

Many communities require recycling of household waste. Residents are required to separate paper, plastics, and glass and put each material in special bins or bags. Electronic equipment also can be recycled. Your community has developed a special program for broken or obsolete computers and peripherals, office equipment and products, small home appliances, and entertainment equipment. These items include personal computers, printers, cellular telephones, toasters, televisions, DVD players, and video game consoles. Community officials will be collecting these items during the next two Fridays at your local police station and a nearby shopping center. They will not accept air conditioners, humidifiers, and hazardous wastes. Using the concepts and techniques presented in this chapter, develop a short PowerPoint presentation to show at various businesses and offices in your community. Emphasize that recycling is important because electronic products have very short useful lives. They produce waste and may contain hazardous materials, but many components can be salvaged. Include one slide with acceptable products and another with unacceptable products.

•• 4 Design and Create Your Favorite or Dream Car Presentation

Make It Personal

Ever since Henry Ford rolled the first Model T off his assembly line in 1908, people have been obsessed with cars. From the sporty Corvette to the environmentally friendly Prius, everyone has a favorite car or dream car. Use the concepts and techniques presented in this chapter to create a slide show promoting a particular vehicle. Include a title slide, at least three text slides with bulleted lists, and a closing slide. Format the text using colors, bolding, and italics where needed for emphasis. Be sure to check spelling.

•• 5: Design and Create a Financial Institutions Presentation

Working Together

Financial institutions such as banks, savings and loans, and credit unions offer a variety of products. Have each member of your team visit, telephone, or view Web sites of three local financial institutions. Gather data about:

1) Savings accounts

2) Checking accounts

3) Mortgages

4) Certificates of deposit

After coordinating the data, create a presentation with at least one slide showcasing each financial institution. As a group, critique each slide. Submit your assignment in the format specified by your instructor.

2 | Creating a Presentation with Illustrations and Shapes

Objectives

You will have mastered the material in this chapter when you can:

- Create slides from a blank presentation
- Change views to review a presentation
- Change slide layouts
- Add a background style
- Insert, move, and size clip art
- Insert a photograph from a file
- Delete a placeholder

- Change font color
- Format text using the Format Painter
- Add and size a shape
- Apply Quick Styles to placeholders and shapes
- Select slide transitions
- Preview and print an outline and handout

2 | Creating a Presentation with Illustrations and Shapes

Introduction

In our visual culture, audience members enjoy viewing effective graphics. Whether reading a document or viewing a PowerPoint presentation, people increasingly want to see photographs, artwork, graphics, and a variety of type. Researchers have known for decades that documents with visual elements are more effective than those that consist of only text because the illustrations motivate audiences to study the material. People remember at least one-third more information when the document they are seeing or reading contains visual elements. These graphics help clarify and emphasize details, so they appeal to audience members with differing backgrounds, reading levels, attention spans, and motivations.

BTW

Delivery Skills
While illustrations and shapes help audience members retain important points in a slide show, keep in mind that a speaker's presentation skills are the most effective part of a presentation. The presenter's posture, eye contact, volume, gestures, and rate establish the tone and tempo of the presentation. A good presentation rarely overcomes poor delivery skills.

Project — Presentation with Illustrations and a Shape

The project in this chapter follows graphical guidelines and uses PowerPoint to create the presentation shown in Figure 2–1. This slide show, which discusses identity theft, has a variety of illustrations and visual elements inserted on a gray background. Clip art and photographs add interest. Transitions help one slide flow gracefully into the next during a slide show. Slide titles have a style that blends well with the background and illustrations. The slide handouts include an outline of the slides and print all four slides on one page.

This presentation uses Quick Styles, which are collections of formatting options for objects and documents. The Quick Styles, like the document themes introduced in Chapter 1, are created by Microsoft's visual designers and give your presentation a professional look. When you rest your mouse pointer on a Quick Style thumbnail in the Quick Style gallery, you will see how the various colors, fonts, and effects are combined, and you can select the image that best fits the impression you want to present in your slide show.

Overview

As you read through this chapter, you will learn how to create the presentation shown in Figure 2–1 by performing these general tasks:

- Create a new presentation from a blank presentation.
- Review presentation in a variety of views.
- Insert and format shapes.
- Insert photographs and clips.
- Print an outline and a handout.

Protect Your Good Name

Reduce Your Risk of Identity Theft

(a)

Reduce Access to Personal Data

- Shred credit card offers
- Use a locked mailbox
- Mail envelopes *inside* the post office
- Remove listing from telephone directory

(b)

Internet and Security Safeguards

- Install a firewall
- Install and update virus protection software
- Never respond to phishing e-mail
- Use credit, not debit, cards when shopping

(c)

Beware of 'Shoulder Surfers'

Shield your hand when entering your PIN

Thieves may be watching with binoculars

(d)

Figure 2–1

Plan
Ahead

General Project Guidelines

When creating a PowerPoint presentation, the actions you perform and decisions you make will affect the appearance and characteristics of the finished document. As you create a presentation with illustrations, such as the project shown in Figure 2–1, you should follow these general guidelines:

1. **Focus on slide text content.** Give some careful thought to the words you choose to use. Some graphic designers advise starting with a blank screen so that the document theme does not distract from or influence the words.

2. **Use single quotation marks.** PowerPoint slides generally use a single quotation mark in several instances.

   - The introduction of an unfamiliar term

   - A quotation

   - Nicknames

   - Composition titles

3. **Adhere to copyright regulations.** Copyright laws apply to printed and Web-based materials. You can copy an existing photograph or artwork if it is in the public domain, if your company owns the graphic, or if you have obtained permission to use it. Be certain you have the legal right to use a desired graphic in your presentation.

4. **Use color effectively.** Your audience's eyes are drawn to color on a slide. Used appropriately, color can create interest by emphasizing material and promoting understanding. Be aware of symbolic meanings attached to colors, such as red generally representing danger, electricity, and heat.

5. **Use serif fonts for titles and sans serif fonts for body text.** Typefaces are divided into two categories: serif and sans serif. A serif letter generally has thin and thick areas, with the thin areas at the end of the lines. A sans serif letter generally is the same thickness. The letters in this box are sans serif.

6. **Choose graphics that serve a purpose.** Illustrations and art should help your audience remember and understand information. They should be uncluttered and visually appealing. Determine why you need each graphic and the kind of information it communicates.

7. **Consider graphics for multicultural audiences.** In today's intercultural society, your presentation might be viewed by people whose first language is different from yours. Some graphics have meanings specific to a culture, so be certain to learn about your intended audience and their views.

   When necessary, more specific details concerning the above guidelines are presented at appropriate points in the chapter. The chapter also will identify the actions you perform and decisions made regarding these guidelines during the creation of the presentation shown in Figure 2–1.

Starting PowerPoint

Chapter 1 introduced you to starting PowerPoint, selecting a document theme, creating slides with bulleted lists, and printing a presentation. The following steps summarize starting a new presentation. To start PowerPoint, Windows Vista must be running. If you are using a computer to step through the project in this chapter and you want your screen to match the figures in this book, you should change your computer's resolution to 1024 × 768. For more information about how to change a computer's resolution, see Appendix E.

To Start PowerPoint

Note: If you are using Windows XP, see Appendix F for alternate steps.

1 Click the Start button on the Windows Vista taskbar to display the Start menu.

2 Click All Programs at the bottom of the left pane on the Start menu to display the All Programs list and then click Microsoft Office in the All Programs list.

3 Click Microsoft Office PowerPoint 2007 to start PowerPoint and display a new blank presentation in the PowerPoint window.

4 If the PowerPoint window is not maximized, click the Maximize button next to the Close button on its title bar to maximize the window.

Plan Ahead

Focus on slide text content.
Once you have researched your presentation topic, many methods exist to begin developing slide content.

- Select a document theme and then enter text, illustration, and tables.

- Open an existing presentation and modify the slides and theme.

- Import an outline created in Microsoft Word.

- Start with a blank presentation that uses the default Office Theme. Consider this practice similar to an artist who begins creating a painting with a blank, white canvas.

Experiment using different methods of developing the initial content for slides. Experienced PowerPoint users sometimes find one technique works better than another to stimulate creativity or help them organize their ideas in a particular circumstance.

Creating Slides from a Blank Presentation

In Chapter 1, you selected a document theme and then typed the content for the title and text slides using single- and multi-level bulleted lists. In this chapter, you will type the slide content for the title and text slides, select a background, and then format the text.

To Create a Title Slide

Recall from Chapter 1 that the title slide introduces the presentation to the audience. In addition to introducing the presentation, this project uses the title slide to capture the audience's attention by using title text and a shape, which is a movable, resizable graphical element. You will add this shape after you have typed the text for all four slides. The following step creates the slide show's title.

1 Type `Protect Your Good Name` in the title text placeholder (Figure 2–2 on the next page).

BTW

Introducing the Presentation
Before your audience enters the room, start the presentation and display Slide 1. This slide should be visually appealing and provide general interest in the presentation. An effective title slide gives a good first impression.

Figure 2–2

Use sans serif fonts for content text.
When a new slide is displayed during your presentation, your audience members focus on the title and then read the words in the content placeholder. Generally more words appear in the content placeholder, so designers use sans serif typefaces to decrease reading time.

To Create the First Text Slide with a Single-Level Bulleted List

The first text slide you create in Chapter 2 describes tips for helping prevent thieves from accessing personal information. The four suggestions are displayed as second-level paragraphs. The following steps add a new slide (Slide 2) and then create a text slide with a single-level bulleted list.

1 Click the New Slide button in the Slides group.

2 Type `Reduce Access to Personal Data` in the title text placeholder.

3 Press CTRL+ENTER, type `Shred credit card offers` in the content text placeholder, and then press the ENTER key.

4 Type `Use a locked mailbox` and then press the ENTER key.

5 Type `Mail envelopes inside the post office` and then press the ENTER key.

6 Type `Remove listing from telephone directory` but do not press the ENTER key.

7 Italicize the word, inside, in the third bulleted paragraph (Figure 2–3).

Figure 2–3

To Create the Second Text Slide with a Single-Level Bulleted List

The second text slide contains suggestions to help computer users protect their sensitive electronic files from cyber-intruders. The following steps add a new slide (Slide 3) and then create a text slide with a single-level bulleted list.

1 Click the New Slide button in the Slides group.

2 Type `Internet and Security Safeguards` in the title text placeholder.

3 Press CTRL+ENTER, type `Install a firewall` in the content text placeholder, and then press the ENTER key.

4 Type `Install and update virus protection software` and then press the ENTER key.

5 Type `Never respond to phishing e-mail` and then press the ENTER key.

6 Type `Use credit, not debit, cards when shopping` but do not press the ENTER key (Figure 2–4).

Figure 2–4

Plan Ahead

Use single quotation marks.
Type an apostrophe for the single quotation mark. PowerPoint generally will invert the first single quotation mark, making it an open-quotation mark, after you type a second single quotation mark, which then becomes a close-quotation mark.

To Create the Third Text Slide with a Single-Level Bulleted List

The final text slide in your presentation provides information to protect people using an automatic teller machine (ATM). "Shoulder surfers" position themselves near an ATM and often use binoculars and cameras to capture a user's personal identification number (PIN). The following steps add a new slide (Slide 4) and then create a text slide with two second-level bulleted paragraphs.

1 Click the New Slide button in the Slides group.

2 Type `Beware of 'Shoulder Surfers'` in the title text placeholder.

3 Press CTRL+ENTER, type `Shield your hand when entering your PIN` in the content text placeholder, and then press the ENTER key.

4 Type `Thieves may be watching with binoculars` but do not press the ENTER key (Figure 2–5).

Figure 2–5

To Choose a Background Style

Now that the basic text paragraphs for the title and three text slides have been entered, you need to make design decisions. In creating Project 1, you chose a theme that determined the colors, fonts, and effects. You also can select these elements individually without choosing a theme. In Project 2, you will choose a background that fits the tone of your presentation and then choose fonts and effects. PowerPoint provides 12 white, ivory, blue, and black **background styles**. Background styles have designs that may include color, shading, patterns, and textures. **Fill effects** add pattern and texture to a background, which add depth to a slide. The following steps add a background style to all slides in the presentation.

1

- Click Design on the Ribbon to display the Design tab.

- Click the Background Styles button in the Background group to display the Background Styles gallery (Figure 2–6).

Experiment

- Point to various styles themes in the Background Styles gallery and watch the backgrounds changes on the slide.

Q&A

Are the backgrounds displayed in a specific order?

Yes. They are arranged in order from white to black running from left to right. The first row has solid backgrounds; the middle row has darker fills at the bottom; the bottom row has darker fills on the sides. If you point to a background, a ScreenTip with the background's name appears on the screen.

Figure 2–6

2

- Click Background Style 12 to apply this background to all the slides (Figure 2–7).

Figure 2–7

Q&A

If I decide later that this background style does not fit the theme of my presentation, can I apply a different background?

Yes. You can repeat these steps at any time while creating your presentation.

Q&A

What if I want to apply this background style to only one slide?

When the gallery is displaying, right-click the desired style and then click Apply to Selected Slides.

Note: If you are using Windows XP, see Appendix F for alternate steps.

To Save a Presentation

You have performed many tasks to create the slide show and do not want to risk losing the work completed thus far. Accordingly, you should save the presentation. For a detailed example of the procedure summarized below, refer to pages PPT 27 through PPT 29 in Chapter 1.

1 With a USB flash drive connected to one of the computer's USB ports, click the Save button on the Quick Access Toolbar to display the Save As dialog box.

2 Type `Identity Theft` in the File name text box to change the file name. Do not press the ENTER key after typing the file name. If Computer is not displayed in the Favorite Links section, drag the top or bottom edge of the Save As dialog box until Computer is displayed. Click Computer in the Favorite Links section.

3 Double-click your USB flash drive in the list of available drives.

4 Click the Save button in the Save As dialog box to save the presentation on the USB flash drive with the file name, Identity Theft.

Changing Views to Review a Presentation

In Chapter 1, you displayed slides in Slide Show view to evaluate the presentation. Slide Show view, however, restricts your evaluation to one slide at a time. Recall from Chapter 1 that Slide Sorter view allows you to look at several slides at one time, which is why it is the best view to use to evaluate a presentation for content, organization, and overall appearance. After reviewing the slides, you can change the view to Normal view to continue working on the presentation.

To Change the View to Slide Sorter View

You can review the four slides in this presentation all in one window. The following step changes the view from Normal view to Slide Sorter view.

- Click the Slide Sorter button at the lower right of the PowerPoint window to display the presentation in Slide Sorter view (Figure 2–8).

Q&A

Why is Slide 4 selected?

It is the current slide in the slide pane.

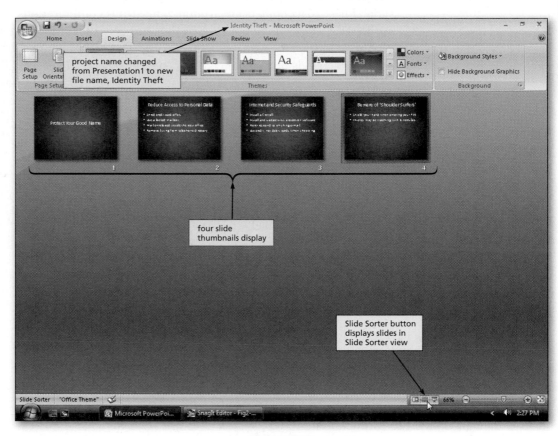

Figure 2–8

To Change the View to Normal View

You can make changes to text in Normal view and on the Outline tab. It is best, however, to change the view to Normal view when altering the slide layouts and formats so you can see the results of your changes. Switching between Slide Sorter view and Normal view helps you review your presentation, assess whether the slides have an attractive design and adequate content, and are organized for the most impact. The following steps change the view from Slide Sorter view to Normal view.

- Click the Normal button at the lower right of the PowerPoint window to display the presentation in Normal view (Figure 2–9).

Figure 2–9

Using the Find Command
Rather than viewing all the slides in your presentation to look for a particular word or phrase you typed, use the Find command to locate this text. Click the Home tab, click the Find button in the Editing group, type the text in the Find what text box, and then click the Find Next button.

Changing Layouts

When you developed this presentation, PowerPoint applied the Title Slide layout for Slide 1 and the Title and Content layout for the other three slides in the presentation. These layouts are the default styles. A **layout** specifies the arrangement of placeholders on a slide. These placeholders are arranged in various configurations and can contain text, such as the slide title or a bulleted list, or they can contain content, such as SmartArt graphics, pictures, charts, tables, shapes, and clip art. The placement of the text, in relationship to content, depends on the slide layout. You can specify a particular slide layout when you add a new slide to a presentation or after you have created the slide.

Using the **Layout gallery**, you can choose a slide layout. The nine layouts in this gallery have a variety of placeholders to define text and content positioning and formatting. Three layouts are for text: Title Slide, Section Header, and Title Only. Five are for text and content: Title and Content, Two Content, Comparison, Content with Caption, and Picture with Caption. The Blank layout has no placeholders. If none of these standard layouts meets your design needs, you can create a **custom layout**. A custom layout specifies the number, size, and location of placeholders, background content, and optional slide and placeholder-level properties.

When you change the layout of a slide, PowerPoint retains the text and objects and repositions them into the appropriate placeholders. Using slide layouts eliminates the need to resize objects and the font size because PowerPoint automatically sizes the objects and text to fit the placeholders.

To Change the Slide Layout to Two Content

Notice the slides have a significant amount of space and look plain. These observations indicate a need to add visual interest to the slides. The next several sections improve the presentation by changing layouts and adding clip art and photos. Before you add these graphical elements, you must change the slide layouts.

Adding clip art and a photograph to Slides 2, 3, and 4 requires two steps. First, change the slide layouts and then insert the clip or photo into the content placeholders. The following steps change the slide layout on Slide 2 from Title and Content to Two Content.

1
- Click the Previous Slide button on the vertical scroll bar twice to display Slide 2.

- Click Home on the Ribbon to display the Home tab.

- Click the Layout button in the Slides group on the Home tab to display the Layout gallery (Figure 2–10).

Figure 2–10

2

- Click Two Content to apply that layout to Slide 2 (Figure 2–11).

Q&A

Why did the bulleted list move to the left placeholder?

PowerPoint assumes you want your bulleted list to display on the left side of your slide. If you want the list to display on the right side, you will need to move the placeholders on the slide.

Figure 2–11

To Change the Slide Layout to Two Content

Slide 3 also will have a bulleted list and a graphic element, so the layout needs to change to accommodate this slide content. The following steps change the Slide 3 layout to Two Content.

1 Click the Next Slide button.

2 Click the Layout button in the Slides group on the Home tab to display the Layout gallery.

3 Click Two Content to apply the layout to Slide 3 (Figure 2–12).

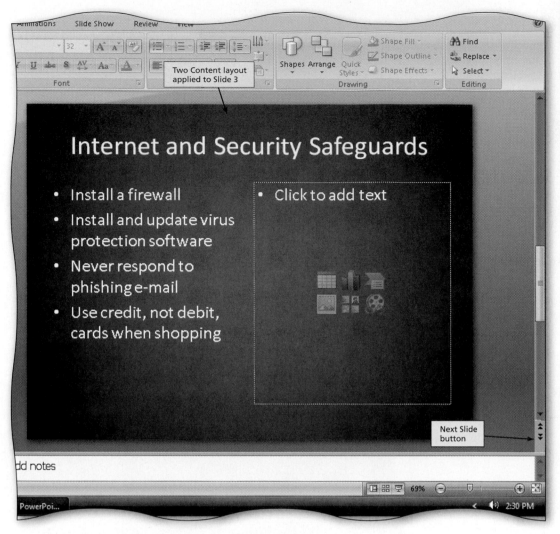

Figure 2-12

To Change the Slide Layout to Picture with Caption

The Slide 4 text discusses exercising caution while using an automatic teller machine (ATM). You have a photograph of a person using an ATM, and you want to display this graphic prominently on the slide. The Picture with Caption layout serves this purpose well, so the layout needs to change to accommodate this slide content. The following steps change the Slide 4 layout to Picture with Caption.

1 Click the Next Slide button.

2 Click the Layout button in the Slides group.

3 Click Picture with Caption to apply the layout to Slide 4 (Figure 2–13).

Q&A Why did the font size of the title and bulleted list text decrease?

PowerPoint reduced the font size to make room for the large upper content placeholder. You can increase the font size of this text if you desire.

Figure 2–13

Inserting Clip Art and Photographs into Slides

A **clip** is a single media file, including art, sound, animation, and movies. Adding a clip can help increase the visual appeal of many slides and can offer a quick way to add professional-looking graphic images and sounds to a presentation without creating these files yourself. This art is contained in the **Microsoft Clip Organizer**, a collection of drawings, photographs, sounds, videos, and other media files shared with Microsoft Office applications. The **Office Collections** contains all these media files included with Microsoft Office.

You also can add your own clips to slides. You can insert these files directly from a storage medium, such as a USB flash drive. In addition, you can add them to the other files in the Clip Organizer so that you can search for and reuse these images, sounds, animations, and movies. When you create these media files, they are stored on your hard disk in **My Collections**. The Clip Organizer will find these files and create a new collection with these files. Two other locations for clips are Shared Collections and Web Collections. Files in the **Shared Collections** typically reside on a shared network file server and are accessed by multiple users. The **Web Collections** clips reside on the Microsoft Clip Art and Media Home page on the Microsoft Office Online Web site. They are available only if you have an active Internet connection.

BTW

Importing Clips
Previous versions of PowerPoint imported clips automatically the first time a user desired to insert clips. PowerPoint 2007 requires the user to import the clips on first use by clicking the Organize clips link in the Clip Art task pane, clicking the File menu in the Favorites – Microsoft Clip Organizer dialog box, pointing to Add Clips to Organizer in the File menu, and then clicking Automatically.

The Clip Art Task Pane

You can add clips to your presentation in two ways. One way is by selecting one of the slide layouts that includes a content placeholder with a Clip Art button. A second method is by clicking the Clip Art button in the Illustrations area on the Insert tab. Clicking the Clip Art button opens the Clip Art task pane. The **Clip Art task pane** allows you to search for clips by using descriptive keywords, file names, media file formats, and clip collections. Specific file formats could be for clip art, photographs, movies, and sounds. Clips are organized in hierarchical **clip collections**, which combine topic-related clips into categories, such as Academic, Business, and Technology.

Clips have one or more keywords associated with various entities, activities, labels, and emotions. In most instances, the keywords give the name of the clip and related categories. For example, an image of a cow in the Animals category has the keywords animals, cattle, cows, dairies, farms, and Holsteins. You can enter these keywords in the Search for text box to find clips when you know one of the words associated with the image. Otherwise, you may find it necessary to scroll through several categories to find an appropriate clip.

To Insert a Clip from the Clip Organizer into a Content Placeholder

Depending on the installation of the Microsoft Clip Organizer on your computer, you may not have the clip art used in this chapter. Contact your instructor if you are missing clips used in the following steps. If you have an open connection to the Internet, clips from the Microsoft Office Online Web site will display automatically as the result of your search results.

With the Two Content layout applied to Slide 2, you insert clip art into the right content placeholder. The following steps insert clip art of a shredder into the content placeholder on Slide 2.

- Click the Previous Slide button twice to display Slide 2.

- Click the Clip Art button in the content placeholder to display the Clip Art task pane.

- Click the Search for text box in the Clip Art task pane, delete any letters that are present, and then type shredder in the Search for text box (Figure 2–14).

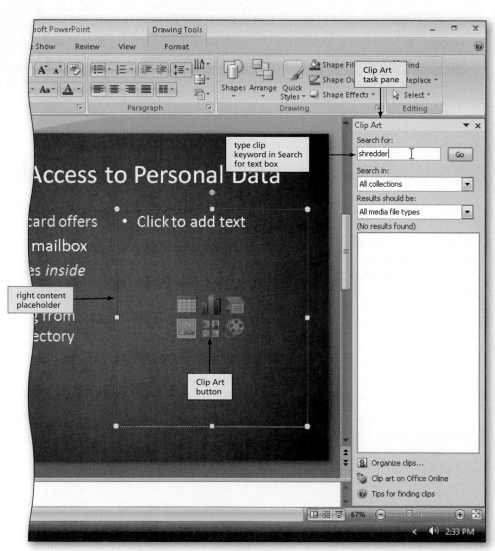

Figure 2–14

2

- Click the Go button so that the Microsoft Clip Organizer will search for and display all pictures having the keyword, shredder.

- If necessary, click the Yes button if a Microsoft Clip Organizer dialog box appears asking if you want to include additional clip art images from Microsoft Office Online.

- If necessary, scroll down the list to display the shredder clip shown in Figure 2–15

- Click the clip to insert it into the right content placeholder (Figure 2–15).

Q&A

What if the shredder image displayed in Figure 2–15 is not shown in my Clip Art task pane?

Select a similar clip. Your clips may be different depending on the clips installed on your computer and if you have an open connection to the Internet.

Q&A

What is the blue globe image that displays in the lower-left corner of the clips in the Clip Art task pane?

The globe indicates that the image was obtained from the Microsoft Office Online Web site.

Figure 2–15

Adhere to copyright regulations.
You have permission to use the clips from the Microsoft Clip Organizer. If you want to use a clip from another source, be certain you have the legal right to insert this file in your presentation. Read the copyright notices that accompany the clip and are posted on the Web site. The owners of these images and files often ask you to give them credit for using their work, which may be satisfied by stating where you obtained the images.

Plan Ahead

Photographs and the Clip Organizer

In addition to clip art, you can insert pictures into a presentation. These may include scanned photographs, line art, and artwork from compact discs. To insert a picture into a presentation, the picture must be saved in a format that PowerPoint can recognize. Table 2–1 identifies some of the formats PowerPoint recognizes.

You can import files saved with the .emf, .gif, .jpg, .png, .bmp, .rle, .dib, and .wmf formats directly into PowerPoint presentations. All other file formats require separate filters that are shipped with the PowerPoint installation software and must be installed. You can download additional filters from the Microsoft Office Online Web site.

Table 2–1 Primary File Formats PowerPoint Recognizes	
Format	**File Extension**
Computer Graphics Metafile	.cgm
CorelDRAW	.cdr, .cdt, .cmx, and .pat
Encapsulated PostScript	.eps
Enhanced Metafile	.emf
FlashPix	.fpx
Graphics Interchange Format	.gif
Hanako	.jsh, .jah, and .jbh
Joint Photographic Experts Group (JPEG)	.jpg
Kodak PhotoCD	.pcd
Macintosh PICT	.pct
PC Paintbrush	.pcx
Portable Network Graphics	.png
Tagged Image File Format	.tif
Windows Bitmap	.bmp, .rle, .dib
Microsoft Windows Metafile	.wmf
WordPerfect Graphics	.wpg

To Insert a Photograph from the Clip Organizer into a Slide

Next you will add a photograph to Slide 3. You will not insert this picture into a content placeholder, so it will display in the center of the slide. Later in this chapter you will resize this picture and then delete the right placeholder because it is not being used. To start the process locating this photograph, you do not need to click the Clip Art button icon in the content placeholder because the Clip Art task pane already is displayed. The following steps add a photograph to Slide 3.

1 Click the Next Slide button to display Slide 3.

2 Click the Search for text box in the Clip Art task pane and then delete the letters in the text box.

3 Type `credit card` and then click the Go button.

4 If necessary, scroll down the list to display the picture of a credit card shown in Figure 2–16 and then click the photograph to insert it into Slide 3 (Figure 2–16).

Q&A Why is my photograph so large on the slide?

The photograph was inserted into the slide and not into a content placeholder. You will resize the picture later in this chapter.

Figure 2–16

To Insert a Photograph from a File into a Slide

The final image to insert in the presentation is a photograph on Slide 4. This slide uses the Picture with Caption layout, so the picture will display in the top placeholder. The following steps add a picture from the Data Files for Students. See the inside back cover of this book for instructions on downloading the Data Files for Students, or contact your instructor for more information on accessing the required files. The following steps insert a photograph of a student using an automatic teller machine (ATM).

Note: If you are using Windows XP, see Appendix F for alternate steps.

- Click the Next Slide button to display Slide 4.

- Click the Close button in the Clip Art task pane so that it no longer is displayed (Figure 2–17).

Figure 2–17

2

- Click the Insert Picture from File icon in the content placeholder to display the Insert Picture dialog box.

- If the Folders list is displayed below the Folders button, click the Folders button to remove the Folders list.

- With your USB flash drive connected to one of the computer's USB ports, if necessary, click Computer in the Favorite Links section and then scroll until UDISK 2.0 (E:) appears in the list of available drives.

- Double-click UDISK 2.0 (E:) to select the USB flash drive, Drive E in this case, as the device that contains the picture.

- Click ATM to select the file name (Figure 2–18).

Q&A
What if the photograph is not on a USB flash drive?

Use the same process, but select the device containing the photograph in the Favorite Links section.

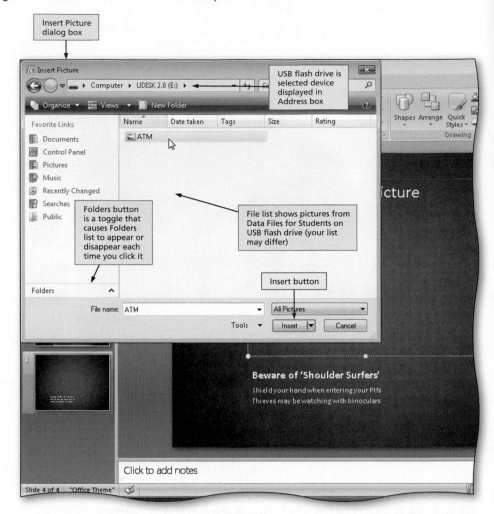

Figure 2–18

3

- Click the Insert button in the dialog box to insert the picture into Slide 4 (Figure 2–19).

Figure 2–19

Resizing Clip Art and Photographs

Sometimes it is necessary to change the size of clip art. **Resizing** includes both enlarging and reducing the size of a clip art graphic. You can resize clip art using a variety of techniques. One method involves changing the size of a clip by specifying exact dimensions in a dialog box. Another method involves dragging one of the graphic's sizing handles to the desired location. A selected graphic appears surrounded by a **selection rectangle**, which has small squares and circles, called **sizing handles** or move handles, at each corner and middle location.

To Resize Clip Art

On Slide 2, much space appears around the clip, so you can increase its size. The photograph on Slide 3 is too large for the slide, so you should reduce its size. To change the size, drag the corner sizing handles to view how the clip will look on the slide. Using these corner handles maintains the graphic's original proportions. Dragging the square sizing handles alters the proportions so that the graphic becomes more or less high or more or less wide. The following steps increase the size of the Slide 2 clip using a corner sizing handle.

1

- Click the Previous Slide button two times to display Slide 2.

- Click the shredder clip to select it and display the selection rectangle.

- Point to the upper-left corner sizing handle on the clip so that the mouse pointer shape changes to a two-headed arrow (Figure 2–20).

Figure 2–20

- Drag the sizing handle diagonally toward the center of the slide until the mouse pointer is positioned approximately as shown in Figure 2–21.

Q&A What if the clip is not the same size shown in Figure 2–21?

Repeat Steps 1 and 2.

Figure 2–21

- Release the mouse button to resize the clip. If necessary, select the clip and then use the ARROW keys to position the clip as shown in Figure 2–21.

- Click outside the clip to deselect it (Figure 2–22).

Q&A What happened to the Picture Tools and Format tabs?

When you click outside the clip, PowerPoint deselects the clip and removes the Picture Tools and Format tabs from the screen.

Q&A What if I want to return the clip to its original size and start again?

With the graphic selected, click the Reset button in the Slides group on the Home tab.

Figure 2–22

To Resize a Photograph

The credit card picture in Slide 3 fills the middle of the slide and covers some text, so you should reduce its size. The following steps resize this photograph using a sizing handle.

1 Click the Next Slide button to display Slide 3.

2 Click the credit card photograph to select it.

3 Drag the upper-left corner sizing handle on the photograph diagonally inward until the photograph is resized approximately as shown in Figure 2–23.

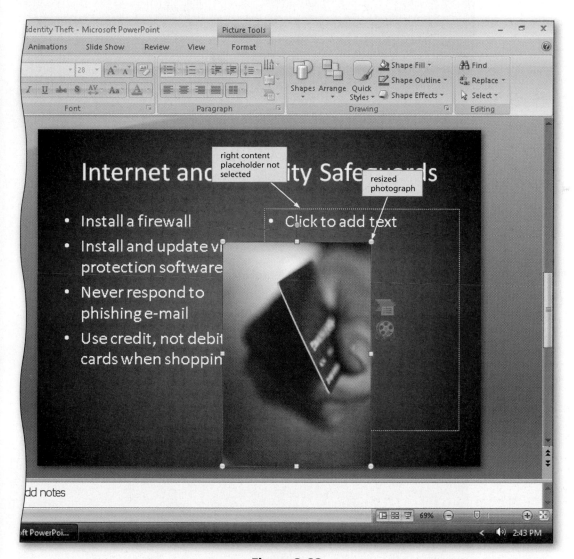

Figure 2–23

To Delete a Placeholder

The credit card photograph was inserted into the slide and not into a content placeholder. The right content placeholder, therefore, is not needed, so you can delete it from the slide. The following steps delete this placeholder.

1

- Click the right content placeholder to select it.

- Click the edge of the placeholder so the border is displayed as a solid line (Figure 2–24).

Figure 2–24

2

- Press the DELETE key to delete the placeholder from Slide 2 (Figure 2–25).

Figure 2–25

To Move Clips

After you insert clip art or a picture on a slide, you may want to reposition it. The credit card photograph on Slide 3 and the shredder clip on Slide 2 could be centered in the spaces between the bulleted text and the right edge of the slide. The following steps move these graphics.

1

- Click the credit card photograph on Slide 3 to select it and then press and hold down the mouse button.

- Drag the photograph diagonally upward toward the word, Safeguards (Figure 2–26).

Figure 2–26

2

- Click the Previous Slide button to display Slide 2.

- Click the shredder clip to select it, press and hold down the mouse button, and then drag the photograph toward the right side of the slide (Figure 2–27).

Figure 2–27

Inserting Special Characters
You can insert characters not found on your keyboard, such as the Euro sign (€), the copyright sign (©), and Greek capital letters (e.g., Δ, Ε, Θ). To insert these characters, click the Insert tab on the Ribbon, and then click the Symbol button in the Text group. When the Symbol dialog box is displayed, you can use the same font you currently are using in your presentation, or you can select another font. The Webdings, Webdings 2, and Webdings 3 fonts have a variety of symbols.

To Save an Existing Presentation with the Same File Name

You have made several changes to your presentation since you last saved it. Thus, you should save it again. The following step saves the presentation again.

 Click the Save button on the Quick Access Toolbar to overwrite the previous Identity Theft file on the USB flash drive.

Formatting Title and Content Text

Choosing well-coordinated colors and styles for text and objects in a presentation is possible by using **Quick Styles**, which are defined combinations of formatting options. The styles in the Quick Styles Gallery have a wide variety of font, background, and border colors. You even can create a custom Quick Style and give it a unique name. Once you select a particular Quick Style and make any other font changes, you then can copy these changes to other text using the **Format Painter**. The Format Painter allows you to copy all formatting changes from one object to another.

To Format Title Text Using Quick Styles

The 42 Quick Styles are displayed in thumbnails in the Quick Style gallery. When you place your mouse pointer over a Quick Style thumbnail, PowerPoint changes the text and shows how the Quick Style affects the formatting. The title text in this presentation will have a light orange background, a dark orange border, and black letters. The following steps apply a Quick Style to the title text.

- Click the Slide 2 title text placeholder to select it.

- Click the Quick Styles button in the Drawing group on the Home tab to display the Quick Styles gallery. Point to the Subtle Effect – Accent 6 Quick Style (row 4, column 7) to display a live preview of the style (Figure 2–28).

 Experiment

- Point to various styles in the Quick Styles gallery and watch the format of the text, backgrounds, and borders change in the placeholder.

Figure 2–28

2

• Click the Subtle
Effect – Accent 6
Quick Style (row 4,
column 7) to apply
this format to the
title text placeholder
(Figure 2–29).

Figure 2–29

To Format Remaining Title Text Using Quick Styles

Once you have applied a Quick Style to one title text placeholder, it is a good idea to use the same style for consistency. The following steps apply the Subtle Effect – Accent 6 Quick Style to the title text placeholder on Slides 3 and 4.

1 Click the Next Slide button to display Slide 3. Click the title text placeholder and then click the Quick Styles button in the Drawing group to display the Quick Styles gallery.

2 Click the Subtle Effect – Accent 6 Quick Style (row 4, column 7) to apply this format to the title text placeholder.

3 Click the Next Slide button to display Slide 4. Click the title text placeholder, click the Quick Styles button, and then click the Subtle Effect – Accent 6 Quick Style (row 4, column 7) to apply this format to the title text placeholder (Figure 2–30).

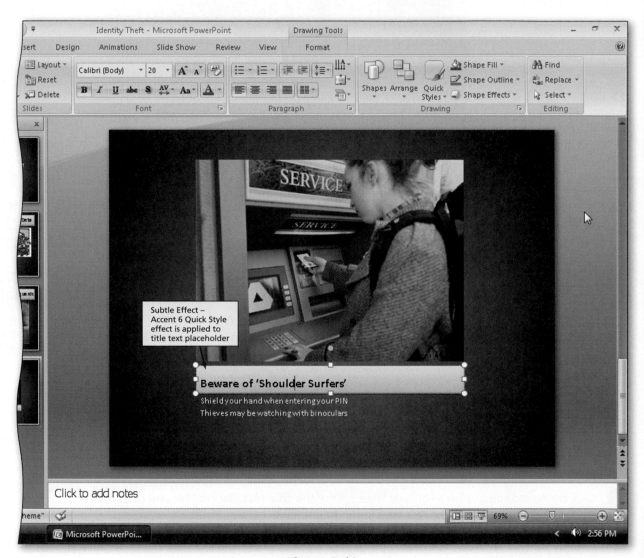

Figure 2–30

Plan
Ahead

Use serif fonts for titles.
The design guidelines for title text differ from the guidelines for content body text. You would like your audience members to remember the main points of your presentation, and you can help their retention by having them read the title text more slowly than they read the words in the content text placeholder. The uneven lines in serif typefaces cause eye movement to slow down. Designers, therefore, often use serif fonts for the slide title text.

To Change the Heading Font

The default Office Theme heading and body text font is Calibri with a font size of 28 point. Calibri is a sans serif font, and designers recommend using a serif font to draw more attention to the slide title text. The following steps change the font from Calibri to Cambria.

1

- Click the Previous Slide button two times to display Slide 2. Triple-click the title text paragraph. With the text selected, click the Font box arrow in the Font group on the Home tab to display the Font gallery (Figure 2–31).

Will the fonts in my Font gallery be the same as those in Figure 2–31?

Your list of available fonts may differ, depending on the type of printer you are using.

2

- Scroll through the Font gallery, if necessary, and then point to Cambria (or a similar font) to display a live preview of the title text in Cambria font.

Experiment

- Point to various fonts in the Font gallery and watch the font of the title text change in the document window.

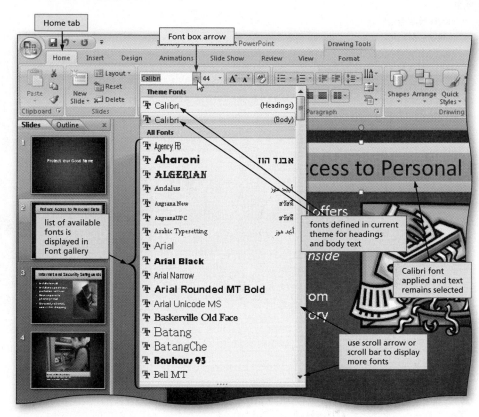

Figure 2–31

3

- Click Cambria (or a similar font) to change the font of the selected text to Cambria (Figure 2–32).

Figure 2–32

Other Ways
1. Click Font box arrow on Mini toolbar, click desired font in Font gallery	in Font list or type a font in Font box, click OK button	list or type a font in Font box, click OK button
2. Right-click selected text, click Font on shortcut menu, click Font tab, select desired font	3. Click Dialog Box Launcher in Font group, click Font tab, select desired font in Font	4. Press CTRL+SHIFT+F, click Font tab, select desired font in the Font list, click OK button

To Shadow Text

A **shadow** helps the letters display prominently by adding a shadow behind the text. The following step adds a shadow to the selected title text, Reduce Access to Personal Data.

- With the text selected, click the Text Shadow button in the Font group on the Home tab to add a shadow to the selected text (Figure 2–33).

Q&A

How would I remove a shadow?

You would click the Shadow button a second time, or you immediately could click the Undo button on the Quick Access Toolbar.

Figure 2–33

To Change Font Color

Color is used to emphasize or draw attention to specific text. The following step changes the title text font color from black to dark red.

- With the text selected, click the Font Color box arrow in the Font group on the Home tab to display the Font Color gallery (Figure 2–34).

Q&A

What is the difference between the colors shown in the Theme Colors area and the Standard Colors?

The ten colors in the top row of the Theme Colors area are two text, two background, and six accent colors in the Office Theme; the five colors in each column under the top row display different transparencies. The ten standard colors are available in every document theme.

Figure 2–34

2
● Point to the Dark Red color in the Standard Colors row to display a live preview of the title text in a Dark Red color (Figure 2–35).

Experiment
● Point to various colors in the Font Color gallery and watch the title text color change in the slide.

3
● Click Dark Red to change the title text font color.

Q&A How would I change a color?
You would click the Font Color box arrow and then select another color in the Font Color gallery.

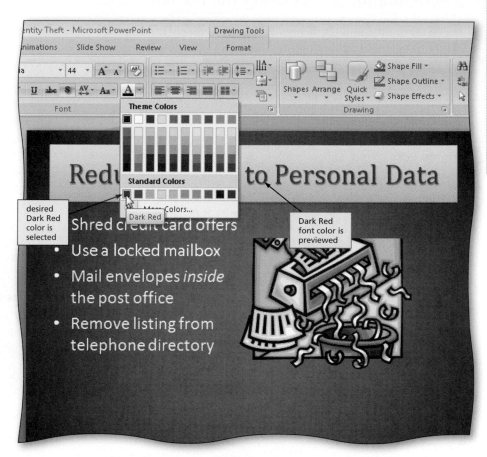

Figure 2–35

Other Ways	
1. Click Font color box arrow on Mini toolbar, click desired color in Font Color gallery 2. Right-click selected text, click Font on shortcut menu, click Font tab, select desired color in Font color list, click OK button	3. Click Dialog Box Launcher in Font group, click Font tab, select desired color in Font color list, click OK button 4. Press CTRL+SHIFT+F, click Font tab, select desired color in Font color list, click OK button

Format Painter

To save time and avoid formatting errors, you can use the Format Painter to apply custom formatting to other places in your presentation quickly and easily. You can use this feature in three ways:

● To copy only character attributes, such as font and font effects, select text that has these qualities.

● To copy both paragraph attributes, such as alignment and indentation and character attributes, select the entire paragraph.

● To apply the same formatting to multiple words, phrases, or paragraphs, double-click the Format Painter button and then select each item you want to format. You then can press the ESC key or click the Format Painter button to turn off this feature.

BTW
Deleting WordArt
If you decide you no longer want the WordArt text to display on your slide, select this text, click the Format tab on the Ribbon, click the Quick Styles button, and then click Clear WordArt.

To Format Slide 3 Text Using the Format Painter

To save time and duplicated effort, you quickly can use the Format Painter to copy formatting attributes from the Slide 2 title text and apply them to Slides 3. The following steps use the Format Painter to copy formatting features.

- With the Slide 2 title text still selected, double-click the Format Painter button in the Clipboard group in the Home tab (Figure 2–36).

- Move the mouse pointer off the Ribbon.

Q&A

Why did my mouse pointer change shape?

The mouse pointer changed shape by adding a paint brush to indicate that the Format Painter function is active.

Figure 2–36

- Click the Next Slide button to display Slide 3. Triple-click the title text placeholder to apply the format to all the title text (Figure 2–37).

Figure 2–37

To Format Remaining Title Text

Once you have applied formatting characteristics to one text placeholder, you should maintain consistency and apply the same formats to the other title text characters. The following steps use the Format Painter to change the font and font color and apply a shadow to the Slide 4 and Slide 1 title text.

1 Click the Next Slide button to display Slide 4. Triple-click the title text placeholder to apply the format to all title text characters.

Q&A What happened to all the letters in my title?

The Format Painter applied a style that does not fit in the current placeholder. You will adjust the font size so that all the words are displayed.

2 Click the Previous Slide button three times to display Slide 1. Triple-click the title text placeholder to apply the format to all title text characters.

3 Press the ESC key to turn off the Format Painter feature (Figure 2–38).

Other Ways

1. Click Format Painter button on Mini toolbar

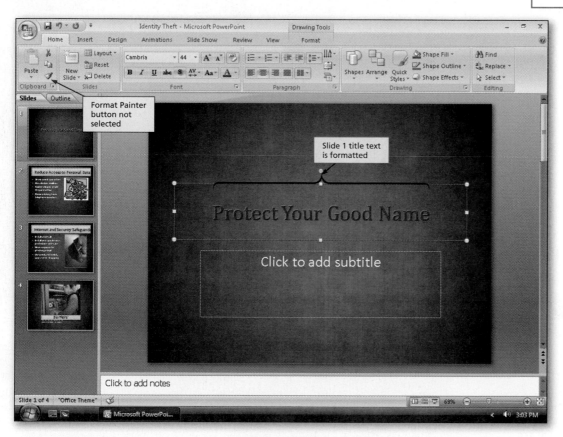

Figure 2–38

To Size Slide 4 Text

The Slide 4 title text placeholder is too small to accommodate the formatting characteristics you applied to the text. The text will fit if you reduce the font size. In addition, the body text should be enlarged for readability. The following steps adjust the size of the Slide 4 title and body text.

1 Click the Next Slide button three times to display Slide 4.

2 Select both body text paragraphs in the content text placeholder and then click the Increase Font Size button on the Mini toolbar four times to increase the font size to 24 point.

3 Triple-click the title text placeholder and then click the Decrease Font Size button on the Mini toolbar three times to reduce the font size to 32 point.

4 Click the slide anywhere outside the placeholders to deselect it (Figure 2–39).

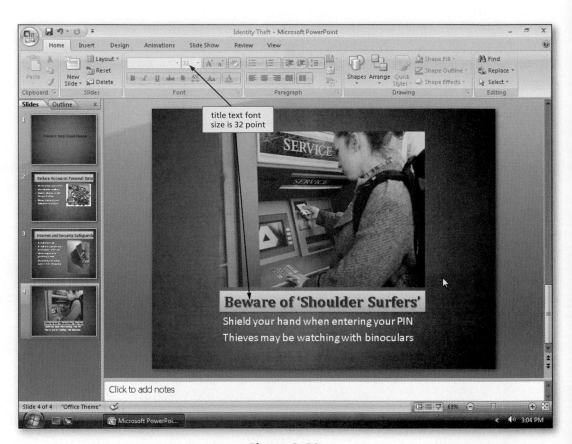

Figure 2–39

Adding and Formatting a Shape

One method of getting the audience's attention at the start of a slide show is to have graphical elements on the title slide. PowerPoint provides a wide variety of shapes that can add visual interest to a slide. Shape elements include lines, basic geometrical shapes, arrows, equation shapes, flowchart symbols, stars, banners, and callouts.

Slide 1 in this presentation is enhanced in a variety of ways. First, the title text font size is increased to aid readability and to catch the audience's attention. Then a shape is inserted below the title text with additional formatted text. Finally, the subtitle text placeholder is deleted because it no longer is needed.

To Increase Title Slide Font Size

The title on a slide should be large enough to stimulate the audience's interest and announce the topic of the presentation. The following steps increase the Slide 1 title text.

1 Click the Previous Slide button three times to display Slide 1.

2 Select the Slide 1 title text, Protect Your Good Name. Click the Increase Font Size button on the Mini toolbar six times until the font size is 80 point (Figure 2–40).

3 Click the slide anywhere outside the title text placeholder to deselect it.

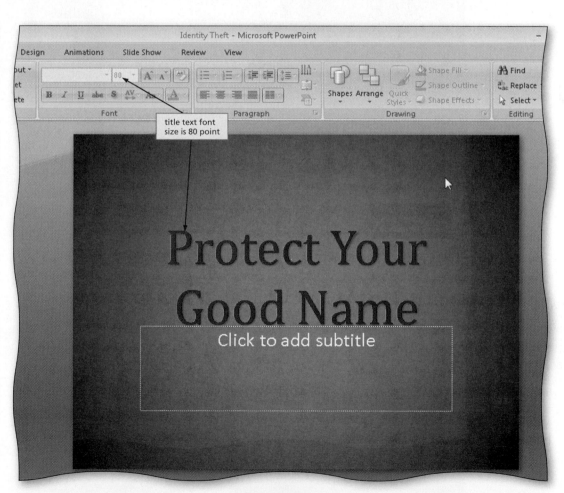

Figure 2–40

To Add a Shape

After adding a shape to a slide, you can change its default characteristics by adding text, bullets, numbers, and Quick Styles. You also can combine multiple shapes to create a more complex graphic. The following steps add a banner shape to Slide 1.

- Click the Shapes button in the Drawing group on the Home tab to display the Shapes gallery. Point to the Wave banner shape in the Stars and Banners area (Figure 2–41).

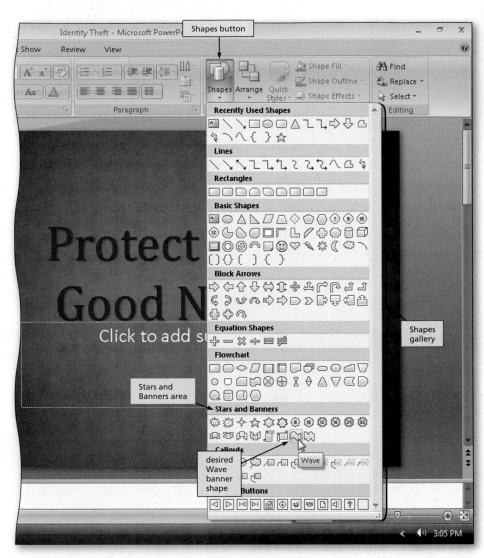

Figure 2–41

- Click the Wave shape (Figure 2–42).

Q&A

Why did my pointer change shape?

The pointer changed to a plus shape to indicate the Wave shape has been added to the Clipboard.

Figure 2–42

3

- Click Slide 1 anywhere below the title text to insert the Wave shape (Figure 2–43).

Figure 2–43

Other Ways

1. Click More button in Insert Shapes group on Format tab in Drawing Tools tab

To Resize a Shape

The next step is to resize the Wave shape. The shape should be enlarged so that it appears prominently on the slide and can hold the subtitle text. The following steps resize the selected Wave shape.

1

- With the Wave shape still selected, point to the lower-right corner sizing handle on the picture so that the mouse pointer shape changes to a two-headed arrow (Figure 2–44).

 Q&A What if my shape is not selected?

To select a shape, click it.

Figure 2–44

2

- Drag the sizing handle diagonally outward and downward until the Wave shape is the approximate size of the one shown in Figure 2–45.

Figure 2–45

3

- Release the mouse button to resize the shape (Figure 2–46).

Q&A What if the shape is the wrong size?

Repeat Steps 1 and 2.

Q&A What if I want to move the shape to a different location on the slide?

With the shape selected, press the ARROW keys or drag the shape to the desired location.

Other Ways

1. Enter shape height and width in Height and Width text boxes in Size group on Format tab in Drawing Tools contextual tabs

2. Click Dialog Box Launcher in Size group on Format tab in Drawing Tools contextual tabs, click Size tab, enter desired height and width values in text boxes, click Close button

Figure 2–46

To Add Text to a Shape

The banner shape is displayed on Slide 1 in the correct location. The next step is to add text stating that the presentation will cover strategies to help prevent identity theft. The following step describes how to add this information to the shape.

1
- With the Wave banner shape selected, type Reduce Your Risk of Identity Theft in the shape (Figure 2–47).

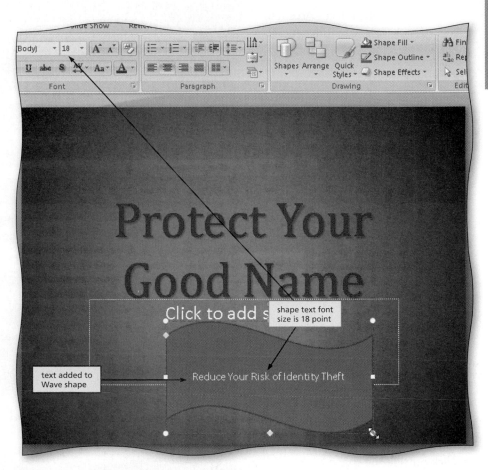

Figure 2–47

To Format Shape Text and Add a Shape Quick Style

Formatting text in a shape follows the same techniques as formatting text in a placeholder. You can change font, font color and size, and alignment, and you also can apply a Shape Quick Style. The following steps describe how to format the shape text by increasing the font size and adding a Shape Quick Style.

1
- Triple-click the Wave shape text to select it and then click the Increase Font Size button on the Mini toolbar five times until the font size is 36 point (Figure 2–48).

Figure 2–48

2

- Click the Shape Quick Styles button in the Drawing group on the Home tab to display the Quick Styles gallery (Figure 2–49).

- Point to the Subtle Effect – Accent 6 Shape Quick Style (row 4, column 7) to display a live preview of the style.

Experiment

- Point to various styles in the Quick Styles gallery and watch the format of the text, backgrounds, and borders change in the Wave shape.

3

- Click the Subtle Effect – Accent 6 Shape Quick Style (row 4, column 7) to apply this format to the shape.

Figure 2–49

4

- Click outside the shape to deselect it (Figure 2–50).

Figure 2–50

To Delete a Placeholder

The subtitle placeholder no longer is necessary on Slide 1 because the shape fills the area below the title text. The following steps delete the Slide 1 subtitle placeholder.

1

• Click the subtitle text placeholder border two times to change the border to a solid line (Figure 2–51).

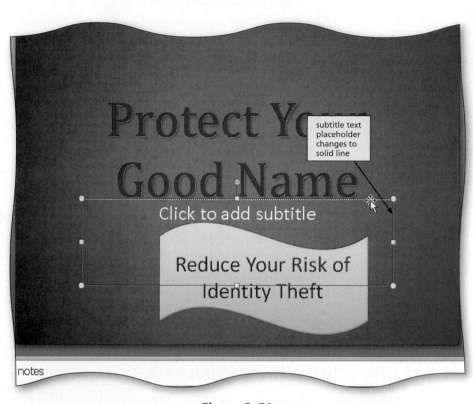

subtitle text placeholder changes to solid line

Figure 2–51

2

• Press the DELETE key to delete the placeholder. If necessary, select the shape and then use the ARROW keys to center the shape under the title text (Figure 2–52).

subtitle text placeholder is deleted

Figure 2–52

Use simple transitions.
Transitions help segue one slide into the next seamlessly. They should not be used decoratively or be something on which an audience member focuses. For consistency, use the same transition throughout the presentation unless you have a special circumstance that warrants a different effect.

Adding a Transition

PowerPoint provides many animation effects to add interest and make a slide show presentation look professional. **Animation** includes special visual and sound effects applied to text or content. A **slide transition** is a special animation effect used to progress from one slide to the next in a slide show. You can control the speed of the transition effect and add a sound.

PowerPoint provides more than 50 different transitions in the Quick Styles group. They are arranged into five categories that describe the types of effects:

- Fades and Dissolves - Blend one slide seamlessly into the next slide
- Wipes - Gently uncover one slide to reveal the next
- Push and Cover - Appear to move one slide off the screen
- Stripes and Bars – Use blinds and checkerboard patterns
- Random – Use vertical and horizontal bars or an arbitrary pattern that changes each time you run the presentation.

To Add a Transition between Slides

In this presentation, you apply the Uncover Right transition in the Wipes category to all slides and change the transition speed to Medium. The following steps apply this transition to the presentation.

1
- Click the Animations tab on the Ribbon and then point to the More button in the Transition to This Slide group (Figure 2–53).

Q&A

Is a transition applied now?

No. The first slide icon in the Transitions group has an orange border, which indicates no transition has been applied.

Figure 2–53

2

- Click the More button to expand the Transitions gallery.

- Point to the Uncover Right transition (row 2, column 2) in the Wipes category in the Transitions gallery to display a live preview of this transition (Figure 2–54).

Experiment

- Point to various styles in the Transitions gallery and watch the transitions on the slide.

Figure 2–54

3

- Click Uncover Right in the Wipes category in the Transitions gallery to apply the Uncover Right transition to the title slide.

Q&A

Why does a star appear next to Slide 1 in the Slides tab?

The star indicates that a transition animation effect is applied to that slide.

- Click the Transition Speed arrow in the Transition to This Slide group on the Animations tab to display three possible speeds: Slow, Medium, and Fast (Figure 2–55).

Figure 2–55

- Click Medium to change the transition speed for Slide 1 to Medium.

- Click the Apply to All button in the Transition to This Slide group on the Animations tab to apply the Uncover Right transition and Medium speed to all four slides in the presentation (Figure 2–56).

Q&A

What if I want to apply a different transition and speed to each slide in the presentation?

Repeat Steps 2 through 5 for each slide individually.

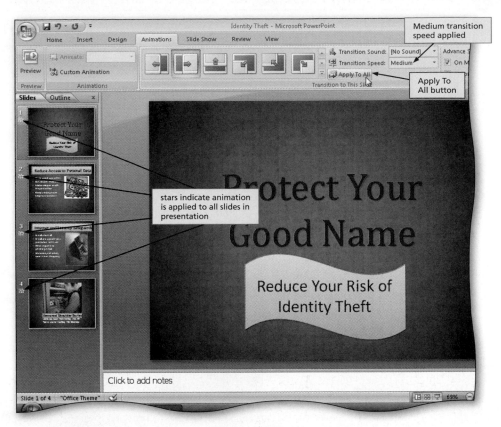

Figure 2–56

To Change Document Properties

Before saving the presentation again, you want to add your name, class name, and some keywords as document properties. The following steps use the Document Information Panel to change document properties.

1 Click the Office Button to display the Office Button menu, point to Prepare on the Office Button menu, and then click Properties on the Prepare submenu to display the Document Information Panel.

2 Click the Author text box, if necessary, and then type your name as the Author property. If a name already is displayed in the Author text box, delete it before typing your name.

3 Click the Subject text box, if necessary delete any existing text, and then type your course and section as the Subject property.

4 Click the Keywords text box, if necessary delete any existing text, and then type identity theft, Internet safeguards, PIN as the Keywords properties.

5 Click the Close the Document Information Panel button so that the Document Information Panel no longer is displayed.

To Save an Existing Presentation with the Same File Name

You have made several changes to the presentation since you last saved it. Thus, you should save it again. The following step saves the document again.

Note: If you are using Windows XP, see Appendix F for alternate steps.

1 Click the Save button on the Quick Access Toolbar to overwrite the previous Identity Theft file on the USB flash drive.

To Run an Animated Slide Show

All changes are complete, and the presentation is saved. You now can view the Identity Theft presentation. The following step starts Slide Show view.

1 Click the Slide Show button to display the title slide (Figure 2–57).

2 Click each slide and view the transition effect and slides.

Figure 2–57

BTW

Quick Reference
For a table that lists how to complete the tasks covered in this book using the mouse, Ribbon, shortcut menu, and keyboard, see the Quick Reference Summary at the back of this book, or visit the PowerPoint 2007 Quick Reference Web page (scsite.com/ppt2007/qr).

Printing a Presentation as an Outline and Handouts

During the development of a lengthy presentation, it often is easier to review an outline in print rather than on the screen. Printing an outline also is useful for audience handouts or when your supervisor or instructor wants to review your subject matter before you develop the presentation fully. In addition, printing two or more slides on one page helps audience members see relationships between slides and also conserves paper. You can preview your print selections to see how your printout will look.

The **Print What list** in the Page Setup group or in the Print dialog box contains options for printing slides, handouts, notes, and an outline. If you want to print handouts, you can specify whether you want one, two, three, four, six, or nine slide images to display on each page. The next two sections preview and then print the presentation outline and the presentation slides as a handout.

To Preview and Print an Outline

Recall that in Chapter 1 each slide printed on a separate page when you clicked Quick Print on the Print submenu. When you want to print other materials, such as an outline, notes, or handouts, you click Print on the Print submenu and select what form of output you desire. The following steps preview and print an outline.

- Click the Office Button to display the Office Button menu.

- Point to Print on the Office Button menu to display the Print submenu (Figure 2–58).

Figure 2–58

2

- Click Print Preview on the Print submenu to display a preview of a slide, handout, or outline of the presentation.

Q&A

Why does the slide preview image vary among slides, handouts, and outlines?

PowerPoint retains the settings last specified for previewing and printing. If, for example, you last specified to print in Grayscale, the current document will print in Grayscale unless you change the setting.

- If an outline is not previewed, click the Print What box arrow in the Page Setup group on the Print Preview tab to display a list of output types in the Print What list (Figure 2–59).

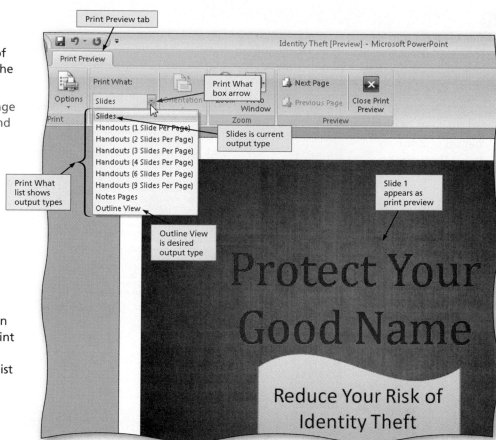

Figure 2–59

3

- Click Outline View in the Print What list if this choice is not already selected.

- Click the Zoom button in the Zoom group on the Print Preview tab to open the Zoom dialog box.

- Click 100% in the Zoom dialog box to change the zoom so that you can read the outline easily on the screen (Figure 2–60).

Q&A

If I change the zoom percentage, will the document print differently?

Changing the zoom has no effect on the printed document.

Figure 2–60

- Click the OK button in the Zoom dialog box to zoom the outline.

- Drag the scroll box on the vertical scroll bar up or down to move through the outline text (Figure 2–61).

Q&A

If I do not want to print my outline now, can I cancel this print request?

Yes. Click the Close Print Preview button in the Print Preview window to return to Normal view.

Figure 2–61

- Click the Print button in the Print group on the Print Preview tab to display the Print dialog box (Figure 2–62).

Q&A

What if my Print dialog box displays a different printer name?

It is likely a different printer name will display. Just ensure that the printer listed is the correct device you want to use to print your outline.

Figure 2–62

6
- Click the OK button to print the outline (Figure 2–63).

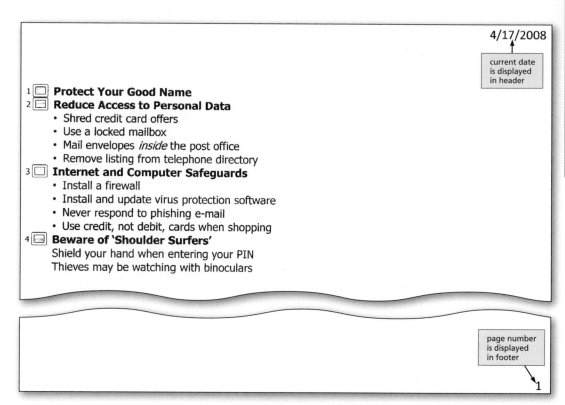

Figure 2–63

Other Ways

1. Drag Zoom slider on status bar
2. Click Zoom button on status bar, select desired zoom percent or type, click OK button

To Preview and Print Handouts

Printing handouts is useful for reviewing a presentation because you can analyze several slides displayed simultaneously on one page. Additionally, many businesses distribute handouts of the slide show before a presentation so the attendees can refer to a copy.

The default slide print order is Horizontal so that Slides 1 and 2, and 3 and 4 are adjacent to each other. You can change this order to Vertical, which shows Slides 1 and 4, and 2 and 3 adjacent to each other, by clicking Options in the Print group on the Print Preview tab and then changing the printing order.

The following steps preview and print presentation handouts.

1 Click the Print What box arrow in the Page Setup group.

2 Click Handouts (4 Slides Per Page) in the Print What list. Drag the scroll box on the vertical scroll bar up or down to move through the page.

3 Click the Print button in the Print group.

4 Click the OK button in the Print dialog box to print the handout (Figure 2–64).

5 Click the Close Print Preview button in the Preview group on the Print Preview tab to return to Normal view.

Figure 2–64

Saving and Quitting PowerPoint

If you made any changes to your presentation since your last save, you should save it again before quitting PowerPoint. The following steps save changes to the presentation and quit PowerPoint.

To Quit PowerPoint

This project is complete. The following steps quit PowerPoint.

1 Click the Office Button and then click the Exit PowerPoint button.

2 If necessary, click the Yes button in the Microsoft Office PowerPoint dialog box so that any changes you have made are saved.

Chapter Summary

In this chapter you have learned how to create slides from a blank presentation, change slide layouts, add a background style, insert clip art and pictures, size graphic elements, apply Quick Styles, select slide transitions, and preview and print an outline and handout. The items listed below include all the new PowerPoint skills you have learned in this chapter.

1. Choose a Background Style (PPT 89)
2. Change the View to Slide Sorter View (PPT 91)
3. Change the View to Normal View (PPT 91)
4. Change the Slide Layout to Two Content (PPT 92)
5. Change the Slide Layout to Picture with Caption (PPT 94)
6. Insert a Clip from the Clip Organizer into a Content Placeholder (PPT 96)
7. Insert a Photograph from the Clip Organizer into a Slide (PPT 98)
8. Insert a Photograph from a File into a Slide (PPT 99)
9. Resize Clip Art (PPT 100)
10. Resize a Photograph (PPT 103)
11. Delete a Placeholder (PPT 104)
12. Move Clips (PPT 105)
13. Format Title Text Using Quick Styles (PPT 106)
14. Format Remaining Title Text Using Quick Styles (PPT 107)
15. Change the Heading Font (PPT 109)
16. Shadow Text (PPT 110)
17. Change Font Color (PPT 110)
18. Format Text Using the Format Painter (PPT 112)
19. Format Remaining Title Text (PPT 113)
20. Add a Shape (PPT 116)
21. Resize a Shape (PPT 117)
22. Add Text to a Shape (PPT 119)
23. Format Shape Text and Add a Shape Quick Style (PPT 119)
24. Add a Transition between Slides (PPT 122)
25. Preview and Print an Outline (PPT 122)
26. Preview and Print Handouts (PPT 129)

 If you have a SAM user profile, you may have access to hands-on instruction, practice, and assessment. Log in to your SAM account (http://sam2007.course.com) to launch any assigned training activities or exams that relate to the skills covered in this chapter.

Learn It Online

Test your knowledge of chapter content and key terms.

Instructions: To complete the Learn It Online exercises, start your browser, click the Address bar, and then enter the Web address `scsite.com/ppt2007/learn`. When the Office 2007 Learn It Online page is displayed, click the link for the exercise you want to complete and then read the instructions.

Chapter Reinforcement TF, MC, and SA
A series of true/false, multiple choice, and short answer questions that test your knowledge of the chapter content.

Flash Cards
An interactive learning environment where you identify chapter key terms associated with displayed definitions.

Practice Test
A series of multiple choice questions that test your knowledge of chapter content and key terms.

Who Wants To Be a Computer Genius?
An interactive game that challenges your knowledge of chapter content in the style of a television quiz show.

Wheel of Terms
An interactive game that challenges your knowledge of chapter key terms in the style of the television show *Wheel of Fortune*.

Crossword Puzzle Challenge
A crossword puzzle that challenges your knowledge of key terms presented in the chapter.

Apply Your Knowledge

Reinforce the skills and apply the concepts you learned in this chapter.

Changing the Background and Adding Photographs and a Quick Style
Instructions: Start PowerPoint. Open the presentation, Apply 2-1 Lifestyle, from the Data Files for Students. See the inside back cover of this book for instructions on downloading the Data Files for Students, or contact your instructor for more information about accessing the required files.

The four slides in the presentation present basic guidelines for maintaining a healthy lifestyle and focus on proper weight, exercise, and food choices. The document you open is an unformatted presentation. You are to add and size photographs, change the background style, change slide layouts, apply a transition, and use the Format Painter so the slides look like Figure 2-65.

Perform the following tasks:
1. Change the background style to Style 11 (row 3, column 3). On the title slide, use your name in place of Student Name and bold and italicize your name and change the font color to orange. Increase the title text font size to 72 point, change the font to Baskerville Old Face, and change the font color to Dark Blue.
2. On Slides 2 and 4, change the layout to Two Content and then insert the photographs shown in Figure 2-65b and 2-65d from the Microsoft Clip Organizer.
3. On Slide 3, change the layout to Picture with Caption and then insert the picture shown in Figure 2-65c from the Microsoft Clip Organizer. Delete the text placeholder. Change the title text font size to 44 point, center this text, and then add the italic font style and shadow effect. Use the Format Painter to format the title text on Slides 2 and 4.
4. Apply the Subtle Effect – Accent 1 Quick Style (row 4, column 2) to the Slides 2, 3, and 4 title text placeholders. Apply the Uncover Left wipe transition (row 2, column 1) to all slides.

5. Check the spelling, and then display the revised presentation in Slide Sorter view.

6. Change the document properties, as specified by your instructor. Save the presentation using the file name, Apply 2–1 Healthy Lifestyle. Submit the revised document in the format specified by your instructor.

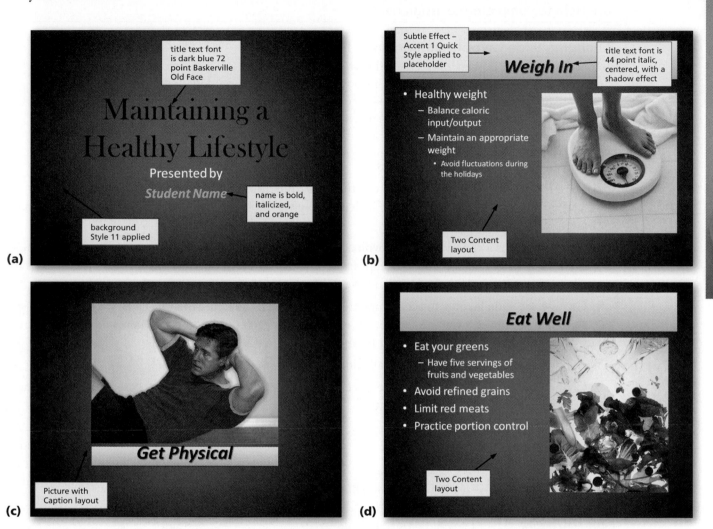

Figure 2–65

Extend Your Knowledge

Extend the skills you learned in this chapter and experiment with new skills. You may need to use Help to complete the assignment.

Changing Slide Layouts and Moving Clips

Instructions: Start PowerPoint. Open the presentation, Extend 2-1 Fats, from the Data Files for Students. See the inside back cover of this book for instructions on downloading the Data Files for Students, or contact your instructor for more information on accessing the required files.

You will choose a background, format slides, and copy clips (Figure 2–66).

Perform the following tasks:

1. Add an appropriate background style.

2. On Slide 1, use your name in place of Student Name. Format the text using techniques you learned and applied in this chapter, such as changing the font size and color and also bolding and italicizing words.

3. Slide 7 contains a variety of clips downloaded from the Microsoft Clip Organizer. Review the slides in the presentation and then move clips from Slide 7 to the appropriate slides. You do not need to use all the clips. Delete Slide 7 when you have finished moving the desired clips to the slides.

4. Change the slide layouts to accommodate the clips. Size the clips when necessary. Edit the text so that each slide meets the 7 × 7 rule, which states that each line should have a maximum of seven words, and each slide should have a maximum of seven lines.

5. Apply an appropriate transition to all slides.

6. Change the document properties, as specified by your instructor. Save the presentation using the file name, Extend 2-1 Enhanced Fats.

7. Submit the revised document in the format specified by your instructor.

variety of clips to consider moving to previous slides in presentation

Figure 2–66

Make It Right

Analyze a presentation and correct all errors and/or improve the design.

Applying Background and Quick Styles

Instructions: Start PowerPoint. Open the presentation, Make It Right 2-1 Safety, from the Data Files for Students. See the back inside cover of this book for instructions on downloading the Data Files for Students, or contact your instructor for more information on accessing the required files.

Correct the formatting problems and errors in the presentation while keeping in mind the guidelines presented in this chapter.

Perform the following tasks:

1. Change the document theme from Verve, shown in Figure 2–67, to Paper. Apply the Style 7 background style (row 2, column 3).

2. On Slide 1, replace the words, Student Name, with your name. Apply a Quick Style to your name and the title text so that they display prominently on the slide.

3. Move Slide 2 to the end of the presentation so that it becomes the new Slide 5.

4. Use the spell checker to correct the misspellings. Analyze the slides for other word usage errors that the spell checker did not find.

5. Adjust the clip art sizes so they do not overlap text and are the appropriate dimensions for the slide content.

6. Select a Quick Style to apply to the Slides 2 through 5 title text. Center the title text and apply a shadow.

7. Apply an appropriate transition to all slides. Change the speed to Slow.

8. Change the document properties, as specified by your instructor. Save the presentation using the file name, Make It Right 2-1 Home Safety.

9. Submit the revised document in the format specified by your instructor.

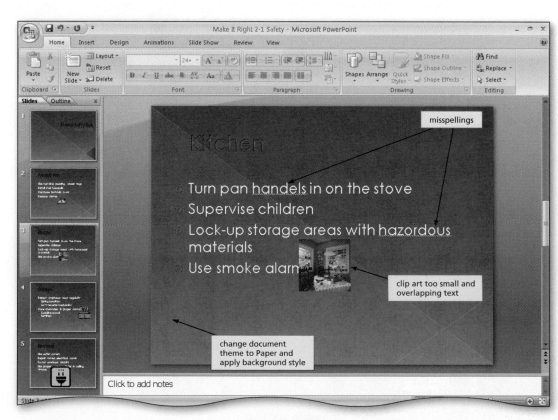

Figure 2–67

In the Lab

Design and/or create a presentation using the guidelines, concepts, and skills presented in this chapter. Labs 1, 2, and 3 are listed in order of increasing difficulty.

Lab 1: Creating a Presentation with a Clip and Shapes

Problem: The ear affects balance while it enables us to hear. This organ can be divided into three parts for analysis: outer, middle, and inner. The outer ear is composed of a flap and the auditory canal. The middle ear has three tiny bones called the auditory ossicles and the eustachian tube, which links the ear to the nose. The inner ear contains the spiral-shaped cochlea and also the semicircular canals and the vestibule, which control balance. You are studying the ear as a unit in your health class, so you decide to develop a PowerPoint slide that names these parts to help you study for a quiz. Create the slide shown in Figure 2–68 from a blank presentation.

Instructions: Perform the following tasks.

1. Apply the Style 6 background style (row 2, column 2) to the slide. Change the layout to Content with Caption. Import the ear diagram clip from the Microsoft Clip Organizer.

2. Type the slide title and caption body text shown in Figure 2–68. Use your name in place of Bill Tracy, and then italicize this text and change the font color to Blue (color 8 in the Standard Colors row). Change the color of the title text to Dark Red (color 1 in the Standard Colors row) and increase the font size to 24.

3. Use the Right Arrow, Left Arrow, Up Arrow, and Down Arrow shapes in the Block Arrow section to point to the parts of the ear shown in Figure 2–68. Add the number to each arrow. Apply the Subtle Effect – Accent 3 Quick Style (row 4, column 4) to each arrow. Change the font size of each arrow text to 24 point and bold these numbers.

4. Check the spelling and correct any errors.

5. Change the document properties, as specified by your instructor. Save the presentation using the file name, Lab 2-1 Ear.

6. Submit the revised document in the format specified by your instructor.

Figure 2–68

In the Lab

Lab 2: Creating a Presentation with Photographs Inserted from a File

Problem: Destructive insects damage specific species of trees throughout the world. You have learned in your Botany 202 class that the Asian Longhorn Beetle, the Emerald Ash Borer, the Gypsy Moth, and the Western Pine Beetle are among trees' biggest pests. One of your assignments in your botany class is to give a speech about common tree pests. You develop the outline shown in Figure 2–69 and then prepare the PowerPoint presentation shown in Figures 2–70a through 2–70f. You have obtained permission from the U.S. Forestry Department to copy photographs from its Web site to your slide show; these photographs are on your Data Files for Students.

Tree Pests
Creatures That Bug Our Trees
Jim DeYoung
Botany 202

Asian Longhorn Beetle
- Native to China
- Transported to United States in infested packing material

Emerald Ash Borer
- Killed 20 million trees in Michigan, Ohio, and Indiana
- Firewood quarantines to prevent new infestations

Gypsy Moth
- Spread to U.S. in 1870
- Oaks and Aspens are most common hosts
- Larva defoliate trees
- Small mammals and birds are predators

Western Pine Beetle
- Infest Ponderosa and Coulter pine trees
  - Mainly Western states
- Tree loss considered normal ecological process

Acknowledgements
- Photos and information courtesy of the USDA Forest Service
  - forestry.about.com

Figure 2–69

Continued >

In the Lab *continued*

Instructions: Perform the following tasks.

1. Create a new presentation using the Foundry document theme. Apply the Style 7 background style (row 2, column 3).

2. Using the typed notes illustrated in Figure 2–69, create the title slide shown in Figure 2–70a using your name in place of Jim DeYoung. Bold your name and apply a shadow.

3. Insert the Isosceles Triangle shape (row 1, column 3 in the Basic Shapes category) in the top center of Slide 1. Size the shape so that the top and bottom align with the edges of the brown area of the slide, as shown in Figure 2–70a.

4. Using the typed notes in Figure 2–69, create the five text slides with bulleted lists shown in Figures 2–70b through 2–70f. Use the Two Content slide layout for Slides 2 through 5 and the Title and Content slide layout for Slide 6.

5. Insert the appropriate pictures from your Data Files for Students on Slides 2 through 5.

6. Apply the Wedge transition (row 1, column 5 in the Wipes category) to all slides. Change the speed to Medium. Check the spelling and correct any errors.

7. Review the slides in Slide Sorter view to check for consistency, and then change the view to Normal.

8. Drag the scroll box to display Slide 1. Click the Slide Show button to start Slide Show view. Then click to display each slide.

9. Change the document properties, as specified by your instructor. Save the presentation using the file name, Lab 2-2 Tree Pests.

10. Submit the document in the format specified by your instructor.

(a)

(b)

Figure 2–70

(c)   (d)

(e)   (f)

Figure 2–70

In the Lab

Lab 3: Creating a Presentation with Clips and Shapes

Problem: Snowboarding's popularity has soared in recent years; even Cameron Diaz and Space Shuttle astronauts have a passion for the sport. But with this increase in snowboarders has come a corresponding increase in injuries. The most common injuries are caused by a failure to follow common sense precautions. In order to maximize the time on the slopes, snowboarders need to prepare for the sport by wearing proper equipment, getting into condition, and snowboarding under control. Bryan Howell owns a local ski and snowboard shop in your town and has asked you to prepare a PowerPoint presentation that he can share with equipment buyers and renters. He hands you the outline shown in Figure 2–71 and asks you to create the presentation shown in Figures 2–72a through 2–72d.

Prepare for Snowboarding Season
    Vertical Slope Shop
    Bryan Howell, Owner

Dress for the Ride
- Loose fitting layers
    – Moisture wicking inner
    – Insulating middle
    – Waterproof outer shell
- Goggles
- Helmet, wrist guards

Get into Condition
- Stretch for 10 minutes
    – Do lateral squats, hops
- Eat complex carbohydrates
- Drink plenty of water
    – Dehydration is common

Snowboard under Control
- Be aware of traffic
    – Where trails merge
- Stick to slopes designed for your ability
- Be aware of changing conditions

Figure 2–71

Instructions: Perform the following tasks.
1. Use the typed notes illustrated in Figure 2–71 to create four slides shown in Figures 2–72a through 2–72d from a blank presentation. Apply the Style 7 background style (row 2, column 3). Use your name in place of Bryan Howell on the title slide shown in Figure 2–72a. Bold your name.
2. Insert the Right Triangle shape (row 1, column 4 in the Basic Shapes category) on Slide 1. With the shape selected, click the Arrange button in the Drawing group on the Home tab, point to Rotate in the Position Objects group, and then click Flip Horizontal to turn the triangle shape. Drag the shape to the lower-right corner of the slide, increase the size to that shown in Figure 2–72a, and apply the Colored Outline - Accent 3 Quick Style (row 1, column 4).

3. Italicize the Slide 1 title text, Prepare for Snowboarding Season, align the text left, and change the font color to Black. Align the subtitle text left and change the font color to Green (color 6 in the Standard Colors row).

4. Add the photographs and clip art shown in Figures 2–72a through 2–72d from the Microsoft Clip Organizer. Adjust the clip sizes when necessary.

5. Change the Slide 2 title text font size to 54 point, change the font to Forte, and then change the color to Green. Use the Format Painter to format the title text on Slides 3 and 4 with the same features as on Slide 2.

6. Apply the Newsflash transition (row 6, column 2 in the Wipes category) to all slides. Change the speed to Medium. Check the spelling and correct any errors.

7. Click the Slide Sorter button, view the slides for consistency, and then click the Normal button.

8. Change the document properties, as specified by your instructor. Save the presentation using the file name, Lab 2-3 Snowboarding.

9. Submit the revised document in the format specified by your instructor.

(a)

(c)

(d)

Figure 2–72

Cases and Places

Apply your creative thinking and problem solving skills to design and implement a solution.

● Easier   ●● More Difficult

Note: Remember to use the 7 × 7 rule as you design the presentations: a maximum of seven words on a line and a maximum of seven lines on one slide.

● 1: Design and Create an Energy Efficiency Presentation

Global demand, industry deregulation, and regional conflicts have increased energy prices. The United States Department of Energy predicts energy use will grow 33 percent by 2030. Despite these staggering numbers, homeowners can undertake relatively simple measures to be energy efficient. Create a presentation using the outline in Figure 2–73. Apply at least three objectives found at the beginning of this chapter to develop the presentation. Add a title slide with a shape and a closing slide that cites your references. Be sure to check spelling.

Home Energy Savings Tips

Save Money While You Help the Environment

Bright Ideas
- Lighting accounts for more than 10 percent of electric bill
- Change to compact florescent lights (CFLs)
  - Use 50-75 percent less energy
  - Last up to ten times longer than conventional bulbs

Keep It Clean
- Wash only *full* loads of clothes and dishes
- Keep dryer vents clean
- Air dry dishes when possible
- Use ENERGY STAR products

Stay Out of Hot Water
- Heating water accounts for 13 percent of energy bill
- Use low-flow fixtures
- Repair leaks
- Lower thermostat
- Insulate heater

References
- www1.eere.energy.gov/consumer/tips/save_energy.html
- www.exeloncorp.com/comedcare/
- www.energystar.gov/]

Figure 2–73

• 2: Design and Create a Hypertension Presentation

According to the National Heart, Lung, and Blood Institute, nearly one-third of American adults are inflicted by the "silent killer," high blood pressure. This disease affects people of all ages and ethnicities. Use the concepts and techniques presented in this chapter to create a presentation following the outline in Figure 2–74, which includes the definition of hypertension and hypertension categories, has tips on controlling high blood pressure, and lists Web sites to view for further information. Insert photographs and clips, and apply a subtle slide transition to all slides. Be sure to check spelling.

Blood Pressure 101
Taking Control of the Silent Killer

Blood Pressure Definition
- Force of blood on vein walls
  o Pressure units: milligrams of mercury (mgHg)
- Defined by two numbers
  o Systolic: Pressure during beats
  o Diastolic: Pressure between beats
- Read as the systolic over diastolic level
  o Example: 125 over 74

Adult Blood Pressure Categories
- Normal
  o Systolic < 120
  o Diastolic < 80
- Prehypertension
  o Systolic 120 – 139
  o Diastolic 80 – 89
- Hypertension
  o Systolic > 140
  o Diastolic > 90

Detection
- No symptoms
- Person must be tested
  o Sphygmomanometer and stethoscope used

Hypertension Prevention Tips
- Eat healthy
  o Fruits, vegetables
  o Low fat diet
- Maintain weight
- Exercise regularly

References
- National Heart, Lung, and Blood Institute
  www.nhlbi.nih.gov
- American Heart Association
  www.americanheart.org/presenter.jhtml

Figure 2–74

Continued >

Cases and Places *continued*

•• 3: Design and Create a Portable Media Player Presentation

Video tape recorders were immensely popular more than three decades ago with several competing standards introduced in the market. Each technology touted different features. Today, the situation is similar with portable media players and cellular telephones that can download music from the Internet or rip files from your computer. Your supervisor at NextPhase Electronics recognizes buyers need assistance learning about these devices. She has asked you to prepare a presentation summarizing one of these players for next month's Saturday Seminar Series at the store. Research a specific portable media player and create a slide for each of the following attributes: featured model, user interface, and finding and loading songs. Select art and photographs from the Microsoft Clip Organizer, and add a title slide and summary slide to complete your presentation. Format the title slide with a shape and the text with colors and bolding where needed for emphasis.

•• 4: Design and Create a Campus Orientation Presentation

Make It Personal

Feedback from new students at your school cites difficulties navigating your campus. Incoming students mention the library, registrar, and health services as locations most often sought. To address these concerns, you volunteered as a member of the New Student Orientation Team to create a presentation and distribute a handout showing frequently accessed areas of the school. Use the concepts and techniques presented in this chapter to develop and format a slide show with a title slide and at least three text slides with bulleted lists. Create a slide for each landmark that briefly describes its location, and use clips and text to annotate it. Obtain a map of your campus and import it as a picture into your presentation. Select slide layouts that permit both the map and a bulleted list to appear on each slide. Use the arrow shapes to indicate the location of the landmark on the map. Add a background style and slide transitions. Be sure to check spelling. Print a handout with two slides on each page to distribute to new students on campus.

•• 5: Design and Create a Wellness Program Presentation

Working Together

Health care costs continue to rise at nearly double the inflation rate. Many health insurance companies are becoming proactive in containing those costs by offering reimbursement for wellness programs. Have each member of your team visit, telephone, or view Web sites of three health insurance companies. Gather information about:

1) Health screenings

2) Fitness center amenities

3) Self-Improvement classes

4) Wellness program benefits

After coordinating the data, create a presentation with a least one slide showcasing each topic. As a group, critique each slide. Submit your assignment in the format specified by your instructor.

Web Feature

Creating Web Pages Using PowerPoint

Objectives

You will have mastered the material in this Web feature when you can:

- Preview and save a presentation as a Web page
- Customize the Quick Access Toolbar
- Display Web pages created in PowerPoint in a browser
- Complete file management tasks within PowerPoint

Web Feature Introduction

The graphic design power of PowerPoint allows you to create vibrant presentations that convey information in a clear, interesting manner. Some of these presentations are created for small, specific audiences, such as student club members planning a fundraising activity. In this case, the presentation may be shown in an office. Other presentations are designed for large, general audiences, such as potential students planning a campus visit. These students can view the presentation on their school's **intranet**, which is an internal network that uses Internet technologies. On a grand scale, you can inform the entire world about the contents of your presentation by posting your slide show to the World Wide Web.

Project — Web Page

Figure 1a shows the presentation describing yoga fundamentals in Slide Sorter view. The Fitness Center director at your school requests that the information in the slide be made available on the school's intranet for employees and student workers to view. In order to accomplish this task, you must save the presentation as a Web page.

You can save a presentation, or a portion of a presentation as a Web page. The saved **Web page** is a snapshot of the presentation. It is similar to a running slide show in that you can view it, but you cannot modify it. In the browser window, the presentation appears as it would in Microsoft PowerPoint, including a Next Slide button you can click to advance the slides. As illustrated in Figure 1, this Web feature shows you how to save a presentation (Figure 1a) as a Web page (Figures 1b through 1e) and view it using your browser.

PowerPoint allows you to **publish presentations**, which is the process of making existing presentations available to others on the World Wide Web or on a company's intranet, when you use the Save As command on the Office Button menu and choose to save a presentation as a Web page. If you have access to a Web server, you can publish Web pages by saving them on a Web server or on an FTP location. To learn more about publishing Web pages on a Web server or on an FTP location using Microsoft Office applications, refer to Appendix D.

This Web feature illustrates how to create and save the Web pages on a USB flash drive, rather than on a Web server. This feature also demonstrates how to preview a presentation as a Web page and create a new folder using the Save As dialog box.

Overview

As you read through this feature, you will learn how to create the yoga Web pages shown in Figures 1b, 1c, 1d, and 1e by performing these general tasks:

- Preview and save PowerPoint presentations as Web pages.
- Add a button to the Quick Access Toolbar.
- Use Windows Explorer to view Web pages.

Using Web Page Preview and Saving a PowerPoint Presentation as a Web Page

At any time during the construction of a presentation, PowerPoint makes it easy to preview how it will display on an intranet or on the World Wide Web by using the Web Page Preview command. When you invoke the Web Page Preview command, it starts your browser and displays the active slide in the presentation as a Web page without saving files. By previewing your slide show, you can decide which features look good and which need modification. The left side of the window includes the navigation frame, which is the outline of the presentation. The outline contains a table of contents consisting of each slide's title text. You can click the Expand/Collapse Outline button below the navigation frame to view the complete slide text. The right side of the window shows the complete slide in the slide frame. The speaker notes, if present, are displayed in the notes frame below the slide frame. Once the preview is acceptable, you then can save the presentation as a Web page. The Web Page Preview command is not available on the Ribbon, but you can add the command to the Quick Access Toolbar.

Figure 1

Plan
Ahead

General Project Guidelines

When creating the yoga Web pages, the actions you perform and decisions you make will affect the appearance and characteristics of the finished presentation. As you create Web pages, such as the project shown in Figure 1, you should follow these general guidelines:

1. **Develop an effective presentation.** Your slide show should provide essential information to a specific audience. Text should be succinct and meaningful. Graphics, such as illustrations, and color should add visual appeal and promote understanding. Ask someone else to view your presentation and give you suggestions for improvements.

2. **Preview and review the Web pages created from your PowerPoint presentation.** Preview the Web page to assess readability and visual interest. Be certain to test your finished Web page document in at least one browser program to check if it looks and works as you intended.

3. **Publish your Web page.** Once you have created a Web page, you can publish it, which makes it available to others on a network, such as the World Wide Web or a company's intranet. Many Internet service providers offer storage space on their Web servers at no cost to their subscribers. The procedures for using Microsoft Office to publish a Web page are discussed in Appendix D.

This Web Feature focuses on the second guideline, identifying the actions you perform and the decisions you make during the creation of the Web pages shown in Figure 1. Chapters 1 and 2 presented details about how to accomplish the goals of the first guideline listed above, and Appendix D presents details about how to achieve the goals of the last guideline.

To Add a Button to the Quick Access Toolbar

Many commands available in PowerPoint are not included on any of the tabs on the Ribbon. You can, however, add such commands to the Quick Access Toolbar. One such command allows you to preview a document in a Web browser. This command, Web Page Preview, needs to be added to the Quick Access Toolbar so that the Web page can be previewed. The following steps add the Web Page Preview command to the Quick Access Toolbar.

- Connect a USB flash drive to one of the computer's USB ports.

- Start PowerPoint and then open the presentation, Yoga, from the Data Files for Students.

- Click the Customize Quick Access Toolbar button to display the Customize Quick Access Toolbar menu (Figure 2).

Figure 2

3

- Click the More Commands command on the Customize Quick Access Toolbar menu.

- When the PowerPoint Options dialog box is displayed, click the 'Choose commands from' box arrow to display the 'Choose commands from' list (Figure 3).

Figure 3

4

- Click Commands Not in the Ribbon in the 'Choose commands from' list to display a list of commands not in the Ribbon (Figure 4).

Figure 4

• Scroll to the bottom of the list, click Web Page Preview, and then click the Add button to add the button to the Quick Access Toolbar (Figure 5).

Figure 5

• Click the OK button to close the PowerPoint Options dialog box and display the Quick Access Toolbar with the Web Page Preview button added to it (Figure 6).

Will the Web Page Preview command be in the Quick Access Toolbar the next time I start PowerPoint?

Yes. When you change the Quick Access Toolbar, the changes remain even after you restart PowerPoint. If you share a computer with somebody else or if the Quick Access Toolbar becomes cluttered, PowerPoint allows you to remove commands from the Quick Access Toolbar. You will remove the Web Page Preview button from the Quick Access Toolbar later in this Web feature.

Figure 6

To Preview the Web Page

The following steps preview the presentation in a browser.

1

• Click the Web Page Preview button on the Quick Access Toolbar to display the Web page in your browser. If the Information Bar dialog box appears, click the Close button. If the security warning appears in the Information bar at the top of the Web page, click it and then click 'Allow Blocked Content' to run the ActiveX controls. If the Information Bar appears asking for an add-on from Microsoft, see your instructor.

Figure 7

• If necessary, click the Maximize button on your browser's title bar (Figure 7).

Q&A What happens when I click the Web Page Preview button?

PowerPoint starts your browser and it displays a preview of how Slide 1 will appear as a Web page (Figure 7). The Web page preview is nearly identical to the display of the slide in PowerPoint.

2

• Click the Full Screen Slide Show button to have Slide 1 fill the entire screen (Figure 8).

Must I always view the full screen of each slide?

Q&A No. Viewing the slides in a full screen helps you review their style and spelling easily and allows you to see how the slides will be displayed when viewed in a browser.

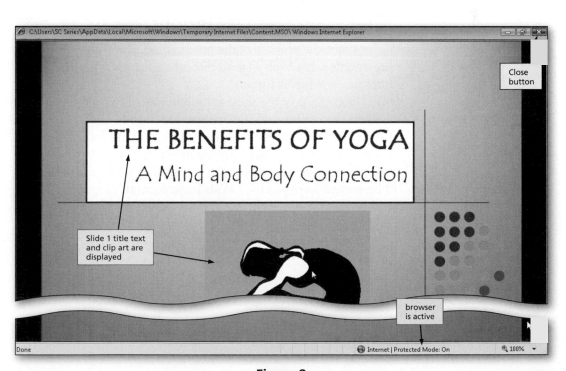

Figure 8

3

- Press the SPACEBAR to display the Slide 2 title text. Continue pressing the SPACEBAR to view each line of Slide 2 body text.

- Continue pressing the SPACEBAR to view each slide in the presentation.

- When the black slide is displayed, press the SPACEBAR again to return to Web Page preview of Slide 1 in the browser window (Figure 9).

- Click the Close button on the right side of the browser title bar to close the browser and make PowerPoint active again.

Figure 9

BTW

Viewing Transitions
If slide transitions do not appear when you are previewing your Web Page, you should check your Web Options settings. To do this, click the Office Button, click the PowerPoint Options button, click Advanced, scroll down and then click the Web Options button in the PowerPoint Options dialog box, if necessary click the General tab in the Web Options dialog box, and then click Show slide animation while browsing if it is not selected already.

Web Page Format Options

Once the preview of the presentation as a Web page is acceptable, you can save the presentation as a Web page so that others can view it using a Web browser, such as Internet Explorer or Mozilla Firefox.

You can save the presentation in one of two Web page formats. Both formats convert the contents of the presentation into HTML (HyperText Markup Language), which is a language browsers can interpret. One format is called **Single File Web Page format**, which saves all of the components of the Web page in a single file with an .mht extension. This format is useful particularly for e-mailing presentations in HTML format. The second format, called **Web Page format,** saves the Web page in a file and some of its components in a folder. This format is useful if you need access to the components, such as illustrations, that comprise the Web page.

To Save a PowerPoint Presentation as a Web Page in a Newly Created Folder

Experienced users organize the files saved on a storage medium, such as a USB flash drive or hard disk, by creating folders. They then save related files in a common folder. PowerPoint allows you to create folders before saving a file using the Save As dialog box. The following steps create a new folder on the USB flash drive and then save the Yoga presentation as a Web page in the new folder.

1

- With the Yoga presentation open, click the Office Button.

- Click Save As on the Office Button menu to display the Save As dialog box (Figure 10).

Figure 10

2

- Type `Yoga Web Page` in the File name text box.

- Click the 'Save as type' box arrow and then scroll down and click Single File Web Page.

- If the name of your USB flash drive does not appear in the Favorite Links section, click Computer in the Favorite Links section and then double-click UDISK 2.0 (E:) (your USB flash drive name and letter may be different).

- Click the New Folder button to create a new folder.

- When PowerPoint displays the new folder named New Folder, type `Web Feature` in the text box (Figure 11).

Figure 11

- Press the ENTER key. If the Microsoft Office PowerPoint dialog box appears, click the Yes button.

Q&A
What does PowerPoint do when I press the ENTER key?

PowerPoint automatically selects the new folder Web Feature in the Address bar. PowerPoint saves all slides in the presentation as Web pages.

4

- Click the Save button to save the presentation in a single file Web page in HTML format in the Web Feature folder on the USB flash drive (Figure 12).

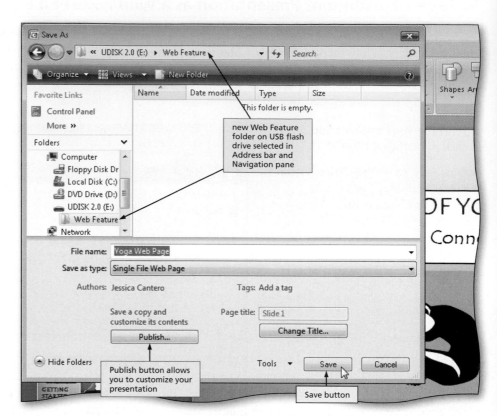

Figure 12

BTW

Certification
The Microsoft Certified Application Specialist (MCAS) program provides an opportunity for you to obtain a valuable industry credential – proof that you have the PowerPoint 2007 skills required by employers. For more information see Appendix G or visit the PowerPoint 2007 Certification Web page (scsite.com/ppt2007/cert).

Publishing Presentations as Web Pages

The Save As dialog box changes when you select Single File Web Page in the 'Save as type' box. When you use the Single File Web Page format, a Save area appears in the dialog box. Within the Save area is a Publish button (Figure 12). Some publishing options allow you to select particular slides for your presentation, display speaker notes, and select which browsers will support your presentation.

In the previous set of steps, the Save button was used to save the PowerPoint presentation as a Web page. The Publish button in the Save As dialog box shown in Figure 12 is an alternative to the Save button. It allows you to customize the Web page further.

If you have access to a Web server that allows you to save files in a Web folder, then you can save the Web page directly on the Web server by clicking the Network folder in the Save in bar of the Save As dialog box (Figure 12). If you have access to a Web server that allows you to save on an FTP site, then you can select the FTP site below FTP locations in the Save in box just as you select any folder on which to save a file. To learn more about publishing Web pages in a Web folder or on an FTP location using Office applications, refer to Appendix D.

After PowerPoint saves the presentation in Step 4, it displays the MHTML file – not the presentation – in the PowerPoint window. PowerPoint can continue to display the presentation in HTML format, because within the MHTML file that it created, it also saved the PowerPoint formats that allow it to display the MHTML file in PowerPoint. This is referred to as **round tripping** the MHTML file back to the application in which it was created.

To Reset the Quick Access Toolbar and Quit PowerPoint

Your work with the PowerPoint presentation is complete. The following steps remove the Web Page Preview button from the Quick Access Toolbar and quit PowerPoint.

1 Click the Customize the Quick Access Toolbar button on the Ribbon.

2 Click the More Commands command.

3 When the PowerPoint Options dialog box is displayed, click the Reset button. If the Reset Customizations dialog box is displayed, click the Yes button.

4 Click the OK button on the PowerPoint Options dialog box to close it.

5 Click the Close button on the Microsoft PowerPoint title bar.

Q&A Do I need to remove the button from the Quick Access Toolbar?

No. For consistency, the Quick Access Toolbar is reset after the added buttons are no longer needed. If you share a computer with others, you should reset the Quick Access Toolbar.

File Management Tools in PowerPoint

In the previous set of steps, PowerPoint automatically navigates to the new folder name in the Save in box when you press the ENTER key after typing the new folder name (Figure 12). It was not necessary to create a new folder earlier in this Web feature. You nevertheless could have saved the Web page on the USB flash drive in the same manner in which you saved files on the USB flash drive in the previous projects. Creating a new folder, however, allows you to organize your work.

Finally, once you create a folder, you can right-click it while the Save As dialog box is active and perform many file management tasks directly in PowerPoint (Figure 13). For example, once the shortcut menu appears, you can rename the selected folder, delete it, copy it, display its properties, and perform other file management functions.

BTW

Quick Reference
For a table that lists how to complete the tasks covered in this book using the mouse, Ribbon, shortcut menu, and keyboard, see the Quick Reference Summary at the back of this book, or visit the PowerPoint 2007 Quick Reference Web page (scsite.com/ppt2007/qr).

Figure 13

To View the Web Page Using a Browser

With the Web page saved in the Web Feature folder on the USB flash drive, you now can view it using a browser. If you want to display or hide the navigation frame, click the Show/Hide Outline button below the outline. Later, if you want to redisplay the navigation frame, click the Show/Hide Outline button again. Similarly, the Show/Hide Notes button below the slide frame allows you to display or conceal the speaker notes, if present, on a particular slide. To review a slide you have seen already, click the Previous Slide button. The following steps view the Yoga Web page using your browser.

- If necessary, connect the USB flash drive to one of the computer's USB ports.

- Click the Start button on the Windows Vista taskbar, click All Programs on the Start menu, and then click Internet Explorer on the All Programs list.

- When the Internet Explorer window appears, type `E:\Web Feature\Yoga Web Page.mht` in the Address bar and then press the ENTER key to display the Web page in your browser (Figure 14). (Your USB flash drive may have a different name and letter).

Figure 14

- If the Internet Explorer dialog box appears, click the OK button, right-click the first Internet Explorer button on the Windows Vista taskbar, and then click Close on the shortcut menu. If a security warning appears in the Information Bar, click it to view the options and then click Allow Blocked Content on the shortcut menu.

- If the Security Warning dialog box is displayed, click the Yes button.

Q&A What are the benefits of using a browser to view a presentation?

You can see from Figures 14 and 15 that a Web page is an ideal way to distribute information to a large group of people. For example, the Web page could be published on a Web server connected to the Internet and made available to anyone with a computer, browser, and the address of the Web page. It also can be e-mailed easily, because the Web page resides in a single file, rather than in a file and folder. Publishing a Web page of a presentation, thus, is an excellent alternative to distributing printed copies of the presentation.

Q&A Can I review a slide I have seen already?

Yes. Click the Previous Slide button.

- Click the Expand/ Collapse Outline button at the bottom of the window to display the text of each slide in outline form in the navigation frame.

- Click the Next Slide button three times to view all four slides in your browser (Figure 15).

Q&A

What if I want to display or hide the navigation and notes frames?

To hide the navigation frame, click the Show/Hide Outline button below the outline. Later, if you want to redisplay the navigation frame, click the Show/Hide Outline button again. Similarly, the Show/Hide Notes button below the slide frame allows you to display or conceal the speaker notes, if present, on a particular slide.

Figure 15

- Click the Close button on the right side of the browser title bar to close the browser.

Feature Summary

This Web feature introduced you to customizing the Quick Access Toolbar, previewing a presentation as a Web page, creating a new folder on a USB flash drive, and viewing a Web page. The items listed below include all the new Office 2007 skills you have learned in this Web feature.

1. Add a Button to the Quick Access Toolbar (PPT 148)
2. Preview the Web Page (PPT 151)
3. Save a PowerPoint Presentation as a Web Page in a Newly Created Folder (PPT 153)
4. Reset the Quick Access Toolbar and Quit Power Point (PPT 155)
5. View the Web Page Using a Browser (PPT 156)

If you have a SAM user profile, you may have access to hands-on instruction, practice, and assessment. Log in to your SAM account (http://sam2007.course.com) to launch any assigned training activities or exams that relate to the skills covered in this feature.

In the Lab

Create a Web page using the guidelines, concepts, and skills presented in this Web feature. Labs are listed in order of increasing difficulty.

Lab 1: Creating a Web Page from the A World Beneath the Waves Presentation

Problem: Dave Ehlin, the Student Government Association (SGA) president, wants to expand the visibility of the A World Beneath the Waves presentation you created in Chapter 1. He believes a Web page would be an excellent vehicle to help promote the spring break trip to Cabo San Lucas, Mexico and has asked you to help transfer the presentation to the Internet.

Instructions:

1. Open the Cabo Package presentation shown in Figure 1–1 on page PPT 5 that you created in Chapter 1. (If you did not create this presentation, see your instructor for a copy.)

2. Add the Web Page Preview command to the Quick Access Toolbar.

3. Review the five slides in the Cabo Package presentation, and then preview the presentation as a Web page. Close the browser.

4. Save the presentation as a single file Web page in a new folder titled Web Feature Exercises using the file name, Lab WF-1 Cabo Package Web Page. Reset the Quick Access Toolbar and then quit PowerPoint.

5. Start your browser. With the Web page located on the USB flash drive, type E:\Web Feature Exercises\Lab WF-1 Cabo Package Web Page.mht in the Address bar (your USB flash drive may have a different name and letter). When the browser displays the Web page, click the Expand/Collapse Outline button at the bottom of the window to display the text of each slide in outline form.

6. Click the Next Slide button at the bottom of the window to view the slides. Close the browser. Submit the assignment as requested by your instructor.

In the Lab

Lab 2: Creating and Printing a Web Page from the Identity Theft Presentation

Problem: The Identity Theft presentation you developed in Chapter 2 could provide useful information for consumers, so you want to save this presentation as a Web page and post it to the Internet.

Instructions:
1. Open the Identity Theft presentation shown in Figure 2–1 on page PPT 83 that you created in Chapter 2. (If you did not create this presentation, see your instructor for a copy.)
2. Add the Web Page Preview command to the Quick Access Toolbar.
3. Review the four slides in the Identity Theft presentation, and then preview the presentation as a Web page. Close the browser.
4. Save the presentation as a Web page (select Web Page in the Save as type box) in the Web Feature Exercises folder using the file name, Lab WF-2 Identity Theft Web Page. Reset the Quick Access Toolbar and then quit PowerPoint. Saving the presentation as a Web page, rather than a single file Web page, will result in an additional folder being added to the Web Feature Exercises folder.
5. Start your browser. With the Web page located on the USB flash drive, type `E:\Web Feature Exercises\Lab WF-2 Identity Theft Web Page.mht` in the Address bar (your USB flash drive may have a different name and letter). When the browser displays the Web page, click the Next Slide button at the bottom of the window to view the slides.
6. Print the Web page by clicking the Print button on the Toolbar.
7. Close the browser. Submit the assignment as requested by your instructor.

Continued >

In the Lab

Lab 3: File Management within PowerPoint

Problem: One of your classmates has asked you to teach him how to perform basic file management tasks from within PowerPoint.

Instructions:

1. Start PowerPoint and then click the Open command on the Office Button menu. When PowerPoint displays the Open dialog box, create a new folder called In the Lab 3 on your USB flash drive.

2. Use the shortcut menu to complete the following tasks: (1) rename the In the Lab 3 folder to In the Lab 3A; (2) show the properties of the In the Lab 3A folder; and (3) delete the In the Lab 3A folder.

Appendix A
Project Planning Guidelines

Using Project Planning Guidelines

The process of communicating specific information to others is a learned, rational skill. Computers and software, especially Microsoft Office 2007, can help you develop ideas and present detailed information to a particular audience.

Using Microsoft Office 2007, you can create projects such as Word documents, Excel spreadsheets, Access databases, and PowerPoint presentations. Computer hardware and productivity software such as Microsoft Office 2007 minimizes much of the laborious work of drafting and revising projects. Some communicators handwrite ideas in notebooks, others compose directly on the computer, and others have developed unique strategies that work for their own particular thinking and writing styles.

No matter what method you use to plan a project, follow specific guidelines to arrive at a final product that presents information correctly and effectively (Figure A–1). Use some aspects of these guidelines every time you undertake a project, and others as needed in specific instances. For example, in determining content for a project, you may decide that a bar chart communicates trends more effectively than a paragraph of text. If so, you would create this graphical element and insert it in an Excel spreadsheet, a Word document, or a PowerPoint slide.

Determine the Project's Purpose

Begin by clearly defining why you are undertaking this assignment. For example, you may want to track monetary donations collected for your club's fundraising drive. Alternatively, you may be urging students to vote for a particular candidate in the next election. Once you clearly understand the purpose of your task, begin to draft ideas of how best to communicate this information.

Analyze Your Audience

Learn about the people who will read, analyze, or view your work. Where are they employed? What are their educational backgrounds? What are their expectations? What questions do they have?

PROJECT PLANNING GUIDELINES

1. DETERMINE THE PROJECT'S PURPOSE
Why are you undertaking the project?

2. ANALYZE YOUR AUDIENCE
Who are the people who will use your work?

3. GATHER POSSIBLE CONTENT
What information exists, and in what forms?

4. DETERMINE WHAT CONTENT TO PRESENT TO YOUR AUDIENCE
What information will best communicate the project's purpose to your audience?

Figure A–1

Design experts suggest drawing a mental picture of these people or finding photographs of people who fit this profile so that you can develop a project with the audience in mind.

By knowing your audience members, you can tailor a project to meet their interests and needs. You will not present them with information they already possess, and you will not omit the information they need to know.

Example: Your assignment is to raise the profile of your college's nursing program in the community. How much do they know about your college and the nursing curriculum? What are the admission requirements? How many of the applicants admitted complete the program? What percent pass the state Boards?

Gather Possible Content

Rarely are you in a position to develop all the material for a project. Typically, you would begin by gathering existing information that may reside in spreadsheets or databases. Web sites, pamphlets, magazine and newspaper articles, and books could provide insights of how others have approached your topic. Personal interviews often provide perspectives not available by any other means. Consider video and audio clips as potential sources for material that might complement or support the factual data you uncover.

Determine What Content to Present to Your Audience

Experienced designers recommend writing three or four major ideas you want an audience member to remember after reading or viewing your project. It also is helpful to envision your project's endpoint, the key fact you wish to emphasize. All project elements should lead to this ending point.

As you make content decisions, you also need to think about other factors. Presentation of the project content is an important consideration. For example, will your brochure be printed on thick, colored paper or transparencies? Will your PowerPoint presentation be viewed in a classroom with excellent lighting and a bright projector, or will it be viewed on a notebook computer monitor? Determine relevant time factors, such as the length of time to develop the project, how long readers will spend reviewing your project, or the amount of time allocated for your speaking engagement. Your project will need to accommodate all of these constraints.

Decide whether a graph, photograph, or artistic element can express or emphasize a particular concept. The right hemisphere of the brain processes images by attaching an emotion to them, so audience members are more apt to recall these graphics long term rather than just reading text.

As you select content, be mindful of the order in which you plan to present information. Readers and audience members generally remember the first and last pieces of information they see and hear, so you should put the most important information at the top or bottom of the page.

Summary

When creating a project, it is beneficial to follow some basic guidelines from the outset. By taking some time at the beginning of the process to determine the project's purpose, analyze the audience, gather possible content, and determine what content to present to the audience, you can produce a project that is informative, relevant, and effective.

Appendix B
Introduction to Microsoft Office 2007

What Is Microsoft Office 2007?

Microsoft Office 2007 is a collection of the more popular Microsoft application software. It is available in Basic, Home and Student, Standard, Small Business, Professional, Ultimate, Professional Plus, and Enterprise editions. Each edition consists of a group of programs, collectively called a suite. Table B-1 lists the suites and their components.
Microsoft Office Professional Edition 2007 includes these six programs: Microsoft Office Word 2007, Microsoft Office Excel 2007, Microsoft Office Access 2007, Microsoft Office PowerPoint 2007, Microsoft Office Publisher 2007, and Microsoft Office Outlook 2007. The programs in the Office suite allow you to work efficiently, communicate effectively, and improve the appearance of the projects you create.

Table B-1

	Microsoft Office Basic 2007	Microsoft Office Home & Student 2007	Microsoft Office Standard 2007	Microsoft Office Small Business 2007	Microsoft Office Professional 2007	Microsoft Office Ultimate 2007	Microsoft Office Professional Plus 2007	Microsoft Office Enterprise 2007
Microsoft Office Word 2007	✓	✓	✓	✓	✓	✓	✓	✓
Microsoft Office Excel 2007	✓	✓	✓	✓	✓	✓	✓	✓
Microsoft Office Access 2007					✓	✓	✓	✓
Microsoft Office PowerPoint 2007		✓	✓	✓	✓	✓	✓	✓
Microsoft Office Publisher 2007				✓	✓	✓	✓	✓
Microsoft Office Outlook 2007	✓		✓				✓	✓
Microsoft Office OneNote 2007		✓				✓		
Microsoft Office Outlook 2007 with Business Contact Manager				✓	✓	✓		
Microsoft Office InfoPath 2007						✓	✓	✓
Integrated Enterprise Content Management						✓	✓	✓
Electronic Forms						✓	✓	✓
Advanced Information Rights Management and Policy Capabilities						✓	✓	✓
Microsoft Office Communicator 2007							✓	✓
Microsoft Office Groove 2007						✓		✓

Microsoft has bundled additional programs in some versions of Office 2007, in addition to the main group of Office programs. Table B–1 on the previous page lists the components of the various Office suites.

In addition to the Office 2007 programs noted previously, Office 2007 suites can contain other programs. Microsoft Office OneNote 2007 is a digital notebook program that allows you to gather and share various types of media, such as text, graphics, video, audio, and digital handwriting. Microsoft Office InfoPath 2007 is a program that allows you to create and use electronic forms to gather information. Microsoft Office Groove 2007 provides collaborative workspaces in real time. Additional services that are oriented toward the enterprise solution also are available.

Office 2007 and the Internet, World Wide Web, and Intranets

Office 2007 allows you to take advantage of the Internet, the World Wide Web, and intranets. The Microsoft Windows operating system includes a **browser**, which is a program that allows you to locate and view a Web page. The Windows browser is called Internet Explorer.

One method of viewing a Web page is to use the browser to enter the Web address for the Web page. Another method of viewing a Web page is clicking a hyperlink. A **hyperlink** is colored or underlined text or a graphic that, when clicked, connects to another Web page. Hyperlinks placed in Office 2007 documents allow for direct access to a Web site of interest.

An **intranet** is a private network, such as a network used within a company or organization for internal communication. Like the Internet, hyperlinks are used within an intranet to access documents, pages, and other destinations on the intranet. Unlike the Internet, the materials on the network are available only for those who are part of the private network.

Online Collaboration Using Office

Organizations that, in the past, were able to make important information available only to a select few, now can make their information accessible to a wider range of individuals who use programs such as Office 2007 and Internet Explorer. Office 2007 allows colleagues to use the Internet or an intranet as a central location to view documents, manage files, and work together.

Each of the Office 2007 programs makes publishing documents on a Web server as simple as saving a file on a hard disk. Once placed on the Web server, users can view and edit the documents and conduct Web discussions and live online meetings.

Using Microsoft Office 2007

The various Microsoft Office 2007 programs each specialize in a particular task. This section describes the general functions of the more widely used Office 2007 programs, along with how they are used to access the Internet or an intranet.

Microsoft Office Word 2007

Microsoft Office Word 2007 is a full-featured word processing program that allows you to create many types of personal and business documents, including flyers, letters, resumes, business documents, and academic reports.

Word's AutoCorrect, spelling, and grammar features help you proofread documents for errors in spelling and grammar by identifying the errors and offering suggestions for corrections as you type. The live word count feature provides you with a constantly updating word count as you enter and edit text. To assist with creating specific documents, such as a business letter or resume, Word provides templates, which provide a formatted document before you type the text of the document. Quick Styles provide a live preview of styles from the Style gallery, allowing you to preview styles in the document before actually applying them.

Word automates many often-used tasks and provides you with powerful desktop publishing tools to use as you create professional looking brochures, advertisements, and newsletters. SmartArt allows you to insert interpretive graphics based on document content.

Word makes it easier for you to share documents for collaboration. The Send feature opens an e-mail window with the active document attached. The Compare Documents feature allows you easily to identify changes when comparing different document versions.

Word 2007 and the Internet   Word makes it possible to design and publish Web pages on the Internet or an intranet, insert a hyperlink to a Web page in a word processing document, as well as access and search the content of other Web pages.

Microsoft Office Excel 2007

Microsoft Office Excel 2007 is a spreadsheet program that allows you to organize data, complete calculations, graph data, develop professional looking reports, publish organized data to the Web, and access real-time data from Web sites.

In addition to its mathematical functionality, Excel 2007 provides tools for visually comparing data. For instance, when comparing a group of values in cells, you can set cell backgrounds with bars proportional to the value of the data in the cell. You can also set cell backgrounds with full-color backgrounds, or use a color scale to facilitate interpretation of data values.

Excel 2007 provides strong formatting support for tables with the new Style Preview gallery.

Excel 2007 and the Internet   Using Excel 2007, you can create hyperlinks within a worksheet to access other Office documents on the network or on the Internet. Worksheets saved as static, or unchanging Web pages can be viewed using a browser. The person viewing static Web pages cannot change them.

In addition, you can create and run queries that retrieve information from a Web page and insert the information directly into a worksheet.

Microsoft Office Access 2007

Microsoft Office Access 2007 is a comprehensive database management system (DBMS). A **database** is a collection of data organized in a manner that allows access, retrieval, and use of that data. Access 2007 allows you to create a database; add, change, and delete data in the database; sort data in the database; retrieve data from the database; and create forms and reports using the data in the database.

Access 2007 and the Internet   Access 2007 lets you generate reports, which are summaries that show only certain data from the database, based on user requirements.

Microsoft Office PowerPoint 2007

Microsoft Office PowerPoint 2007 is a complete presentation graphics program that allows you to produce professional looking presentations. With PowerPoint 2007, you can create informal presentations using overhead transparencies, electronic presentations using a projection device attached to a personal computer, formal presentations using 35mm slides or a CD, or you can run virtual presentations on the Internet.

PowerPoint 2007 and the Internet   PowerPoint 2007 allows you to publish presentations on the Internet or other networks.

Microsoft Office Publisher 2007

Microsoft Office Publisher 2007 is a desktop publishing program (DTP) that allows you to design and produce professional quality documents (newsletters, flyers, brochures, business cards, Web sites, and so on) that combine text, graphics, and photographs. Desktop publishing software provides a variety of tools, including design templates, graphic manipulation tools, color schemes or libraries, and various page wizards and templates. For large jobs, businesses use desktop publishing software to design publications that are **camera ready**, which means the files are suitable for production by outside commercial printers. Publisher 2007 also allows you to locate commercial printers, service bureaus, and copy shops willing to accept customer files created in Publisher.

Publisher 2007 allows you to design a unique image, or logo, using one of more than 45 master design sets. This, in turn, permits you to use the same design for all your printed documents (letters, business cards, brochures, and advertisements) and Web pages. Publisher includes 70 coordinated color schemes; 30 font schemes; more than 10,000 high-quality clip art images; 1,500 photographs; 1,000 Web-art graphics; 340 animated graphics; and hundreds of unique Design Gallery elements (quotations, sidebars, and so on). If you wish, you also can download additional images from the Microsoft Office Online Web page on the Microsoft Web site.

Publisher 2007 and the Internet   Publisher 2007 allows you easily to create a multipage Web site with custom color schemes, photographic images, animated images, and sounds.

Microsoft Office Outlook 2007

Microsoft Office Outlook 2007 is a powerful communications and scheduling program that helps you communicate with others, keep track of your contacts, and organize your schedule. Outlook 2007 allows you to view a To-Do bar containing tasks and appointments from your Outlook calendar. Outlook 2007 allows you to send and receive electronic mail (e-mail) and permits you to engage in real-time communication with family, friends, or coworkers using instant messaging. Outlook 2007 also provides you with the means to organize your contacts, and you can track e-mail messages, meetings, and notes with a particular contact. Outlook's Calendar, Contacts, Tasks, and Notes components aid in this organization. Contact information is available from the Outlook Calendar, Mail, Contacts, and Task components by accessing the Find a Contact feature. **Personal information management (PIM)** programs such as Outlook provide a way for individuals and workgroups to organize, find, view, and share information easily.

Microsoft Office 2007 Help

At any time while you are using one of the Office programs, you can interact with **Microsoft Office 2007 Help** for that program and display information about any topic associated with the program. Several categories of help are available. In all programs, you can access Help by pressing the F1 key on the keyboard. In Publisher 2007 and Outlook 2007, the Help window can be opened by clicking the Help menu and then selecting Microsoft Office Publisher or Outlook Help command, or by entering search text in the 'Type a question for help' text box in the upper-right corner of the program window. In the other Office programs, clicking the Microsoft Office Help button near the upper-right corner of the program window opens the program Help window.

The Help window in all programs provides several methods for accessing help about a particular topic, and has tools for navigating around Help. Appendix C contains detailed instructions for using Help.

Collaboration and SharePoint

While not part of the Microsoft Office 2007 suites, SharePoint is a Microsoft tool that allows Office 2007 users to share data using collaborative tools that are integrated into the main Office programs. SharePoint consists of Windows SharePoint Services, Office SharePoint Server 2007, and, optionally, Office SharePoint Designer 2007.

Windows SharePoint Services provides the platform for collaboration programs and services. Office SharePoint Server 2007 is built on top of Windows SharePoint Services. The result of these two products is the ability to create SharePoint sites. A SharePoint site is a Web site that provides users with a virtual place for collaborating and communicating with their colleagues while working together on projects, documents, ideas, and information. Each member of a group with access to the SharePoint site has the ability to contribute to the material stored there. The basic building blocks of SharePoint sites are lists and libraries. Lists contain collections of information, such as calendar items, discussion points, contacts, and links. Lists can be edited to add or delete information. Libraries are similar to lists, but include both files and information about files. Types of libraries include document, picture, and forms libraries.

The most basic type of SharePoint site is called a Workspace, which is used primarily for collaboration. Different types of Workspaces can be created using SharePoint to suit different needs. SharePoint provides templates, or outlines of these Workspaces, that can be filled in to create the Workspace. Each of the different types of Workspace templates contain a different collection of lists and libraries, reflecting the purpose of the Workspace. You can create a Document Workspace to facilitate collaboration on documents. A Document Workspace contains a document library for documents and supporting files, a Links list that allows you to maintain relevant resource links for the document, a Tasks list for listing and assigning To-Do items to team members, and other links as needed. Meeting Workspaces allow users to plan and organize a meeting, with components such as Attendees, Agenda, and a Document Library. Social Meeting Workspaces provide a place to plan social events, with lists and libraries such as Attendees, Directions, Image/Logo, Things To Bring, Discussions, and Picture Library. A Decision Meeting Workspace is a Meeting Workspace with a focus on review and decision-making, with lists and libraries such as Objectives, Attendees, Agenda, Document Library, Tasks, and Decisions.

Users also can create a SharePoint site called a WebParts page, which is built from modules called WebParts. WebParts are modular units of information that contain a title bar and content that reflects the type of WebPart. For instance, an image WebPart would contain a title bar and an image. WebParts allow you quickly to create and modify a SharePoint site, and allow for the creation of a unique site that can allow users to access and make changes to information stored on the site.

Large SharePoint sites that include multiple pages can be created using templates as well. Groups needing more refined and targeted sharing options than those available with SharePoint Server 2007 and Windows SharePoint Services can add SharePoint Designer 2007 to create a site that meets their specific needs.

Depending on which components have been selected for inclusion on the site, users can view a team calendar, view links, read announcements, and view and edit group documents and projects. SharePoint sites can be set up so that documents are checked in and out, much like a library, to prevent multiple users from making changes simultaneously. Once a SharePoint site is set up, Office programs are used to perform maintenance of the site. For example, changes in the team calendar are updated using Outlook 2007, and changes that users make in Outlook 2007 are reflected on the SharePoint site. Office 2007 programs include a Publish feature that allows users easily to save file updates to a SharePoint site. Team members can be notified about changes made to material on the site either by e-mail or by a news feed, meaning that users do not have to go to the site to check to see if anything has been updated since they last viewed or worked on it. The search feature in SharePoint allows users quickly to find information on a large site.

Appendix C
Microsoft
Office 2007 Help

Using Microsoft Office Help

This appendix shows how to use Microsoft Office Help. At any time while you are using one of the Microsoft Office 2007 programs, you can use Office Help to display information about all topics associated with the program. To illustrate the use of Office Help, this appendix uses Microsoft Office Word 2007. Help in other Office 2007 programs responds in a similar fashion.

In Office 2007, Help is presented in a window that has Web browser-style navigation buttons. Each Office 2007 program has its own Help home page, which is the starting Help page that is displayed in the Help window. If your computer is connected to the Internet, the contents of the Help page reflect both the local help files installed on the computer and material from Microsoft's Web site. As shown in Figure C–1, two methods for accessing Word's Help are available:

1. Microsoft Office Word Help button near the upper-right corner of the Word window
2. Function key F1 on the keyboard

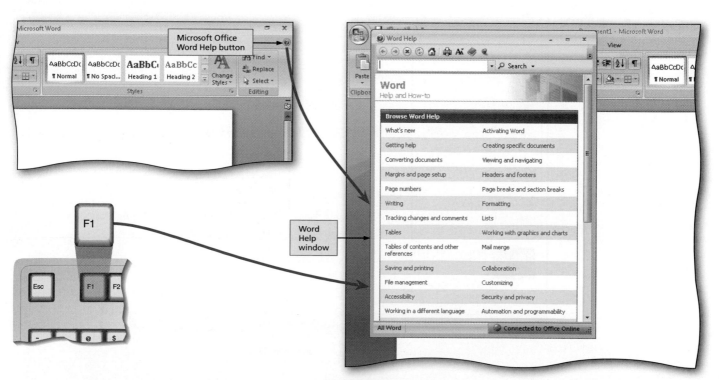

Figure C–1

To Open the Word Help Window

The following steps open the Word Help window and maximize the window.

1

- Start Microsoft Word, if necessary. Click the Microsoft Office Word Help button near the upper-right corner of the Word window to open the Word Help window (Figure C–2).

Figure C–2

2

- Click the Maximize button on the Help title bar to maximize the Help window (Figure C–3).

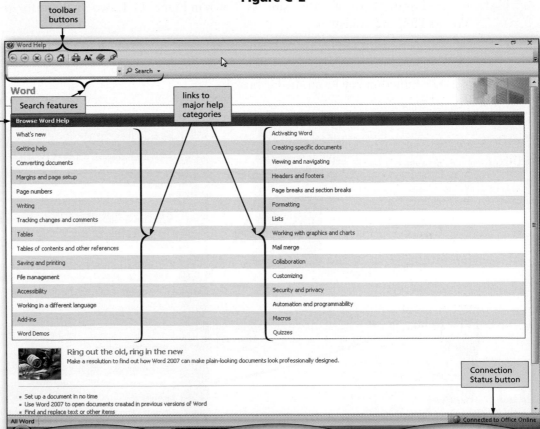

Figure C–3

The Word Help Window

The Word Help window provides several methods for accessing help about a particular topic, and also has tools for navigating around Help. Methods for accessing Help include searching the help content installed with Word, or searching the online Office content maintained by Microsoft.

Figure C–3 shows the main Word Help window. To navigate Help, the Word Help window includes search features that allow you to search on a word or phrase about which you want help; the Connection Status button, which allows you to control where Word Help searches for content; toolbar buttons; and links to major Help categories.

Search Features

You can perform Help searches on words or phrases to find information about any Word feature using the 'Type words to search for' text box and the Search button (Figure C–4a). Click the 'Type words to search for' text box and then click the Search button or press the ENTER key to initiate a search of Word Help.

Figure C–4

Word Help offers the user the option of searching the online Help Web pages maintained by Microsoft or the offline Help files placed on your computer when you install Word. You can specify whether Word Help should search online or offline from two places: the Connection Status button on the status bar of the Word Help window, or the Search button arrow on the toolbar. The Connection Status button indicates whether Help currently is set up to work with online or offline information sources. Clicking the Connection Status button provides a menu with commands for selecting online or offline searches (Figure C–4b). The Connection Status menu allows the user to select whether Help searches will return content only from the computer (offline), or content from the computer and from Office Online (online).

Clicking the Search button arrow also provides a menu with commands for an online or offline search (Figure C–4a). These commands determine the source of information that Help searches for during the current Help session only. For example, assume that your preferred search is an offline search because you often do not have Internet access. You would set Connection Status to 'Show content only from this computer'. When you have Internet access, you can select an online search from the Search menu to search Office Online for information for your current search session only. Your search will use the Office Online resources until you quit Help. The next time you start Help, the Connection Status once again will be offline. In addition to setting the source of information that Help searches for during the current Help session, you can use the Search menu to further target the current search to one of four subcategories of online Help: Word Help, Word Templates, Word Training, and Developer Reference. The local search further can target one subcategory, Developer Reference.

In addition to searching for a word or string of text, you can use the links provided on the Browse Word Help area (Figure C–3 on page APP 10) to search for help on a topic. These links direct you to major help categories. From each major category, subcategories are available to further refine your search.

Finally, you can use the Table of Contents for Word Help to search for a topic the same way you would in a hard copy book. The Table of Contents is accessed via a toolbar button.

Toolbar Buttons

You can use toolbar buttons to navigate through the results of your search. The toolbar buttons are located on the toolbar near the top of the Help Window (Figure C–5). The toolbar buttons contain navigation buttons as well as buttons that perform other useful and common tasks in Word Help, such as printing.

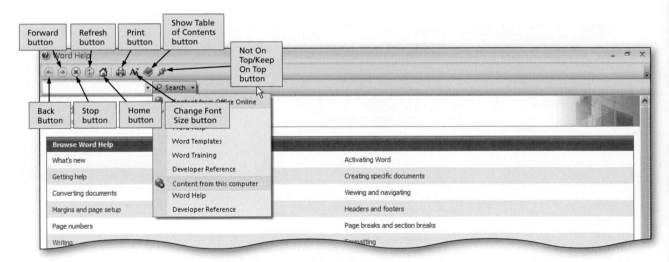

Figure C–5

The Word Help navigation buttons are the Back, Forward, Stop, Refresh, and Home buttons. These five buttons behave like the navigation buttons in a Web browser window. You can use the Back button to go back one window, the Forward button to go forward one window, the Stop button to stop loading the current page, and the Home button to redisplay the Help home page in the Help window. Use the Refresh button to reload the information requested into the Help window from its original source. When getting Help information online, this button provides the most current information from the Microsoft Help Web site.

The buttons located to the right of the navigation buttons — Print, Change Font Size, Show Table of Contents, and Not on Top — provide you with access to useful and common commands. The Print button prints the contents of the open Help window. The Change Font Size button customizes the Help window by increasing or decreasing the size of its text. The Show Table of Contents button opens a pane on the left side of the Help window that shows the Table of Contents for Word Help. You can use the Table of Contents for Word Help to navigate through the contents of Word Help much as you would use the Table of Contents in a book to search for a topic. The Not On Top button is an example of a toggle button, which is a button that can be switched back and forth between two states. It determines how the Word Help window behaves relative to other windows. When clicked, the Not On Top button changes to Keep On Top. In this state, it does not allow other windows from Word or other programs to cover the Word Help window when those windows are the active windows. When in the Not On Top state, the button allows other windows to be opened or moved on top of the Word Help window.

You can customize the size and placement of the Help window. Resize the window using the Maximize and Restore buttons, or by dragging the window to a desired size. Relocate the Help window by dragging the title bar to a new location on the screen.

Searching Word Help

Once the Word Help window is open, several methods exist for navigating Word Help. You can search for help by using any of the three following methods from the Help window:

1. Enter search text in the 'Type words to search for' text box
2. Click the links in the Help window
3. Use the Table of Contents

To Obtain Help Using the Type words to search for Text Box

Assume for the following example that you want to know more about watermarks. The following steps use the 'Type words to search for' text box to obtain useful information about watermarks by entering the word, watermark, as search text. The steps also navigate in the Word Help window.

1

- Type watermark in the 'Type words to search for' text box at the top of the Word Help window.

- Click the Search button arrow to display the Search menu (Figure C-6).

- If it is not selected already, click All Word on the Search menu to select the command. If All Word is already selected, click the Search button arrow again to close the Search menu.

Q&A

Why select All Word on the Search menu?

Selecting All Word on the Search menu ensures that Word Help will search all possible sources for information on your search term. It will produce the most complete search results.

Figure C–6

- Click the Search button to display the search results (Figure C–7).

Q&A

Why do my results differ?

If you do not have an Internet connection, your results will reflect only the content of the Help files on your computer. When searching for help online, results also can change as material is added, deleted, and updated on the online Help Web pages maintained by Microsoft.

Q&A

Why were my search results not very helpful?

When initiating a search, keep in mind to check the spelling of the search text; and to keep your search very specific, with fewer than seven words, to return the most accurate results.

Figure C–7

- Click the 'Brand a document with a watermark or background' link to open the Help document associated with the link in the Help window (Figure C–8).

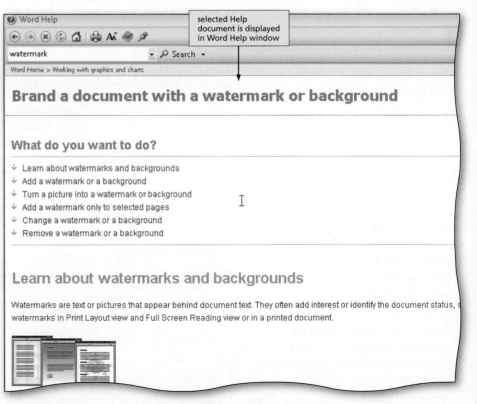

Figure C–8

4

- Click the Home button on the task-bar to clear the search results and redisplay the Word Help home page (Figure C–9).

Figure C–9

To Obtain Help Using the Help Links

If your topic of interest is listed in the Browse Word Help area, you can click the link to begin browsing Word Help categories instead of entering search text. You browse Word Help just like you would browse a Web site. If you know in which category to find your Help information, you may wish to use these links. The following steps find the watermark Help information using the category links from the Word Help home page.

1

- Click the 'Working with graphics and charts' link to open the 'Working with graphics and charts' page.

- Click the 'Brand a document with a watermark or background' link to open the Help document associated with the link (Figure C–10).

Q&A What does the Show All link do?

In many Help documents, additional information about terms and features is available by clicking a link in the document to display additional information in the Help document. Clicking the Show All link opens all the links in the Help document that expand to additional text.

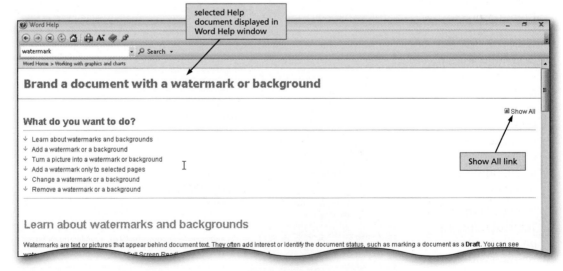

Figure C–10

To Obtain Help Using the Help Table of Contents

A third way to find Help in Word is through the Help Table of Contents. You can browse through the Table of Contents to display information about a particular topic or to familiarize yourself with Word. The following steps access the watermark Help information by browsing through the Table of Contents.

1

- Click the Home button on the toolbar.

- Click the Show Table of Contents button on the toolbar to open the Table of Contents pane on the left side of the Help window. If necessary, click the Maximize button on the Help title bar to maximize the window (Figure C–11).

Figure C–11

2

- Click the 'Working with graphics and charts' link in the Table of Contents pane to view a list of Help subtopics.

- Click the 'Brand a document with a watermark or background' link in the Table of Contents pane to view the selected Help document in the right pane (Figure C–12).

Q&A How do I remove the Table of Contents pane when I am finished with it?

The Show Table of Contents button acts as a toggle switch. When the Table of Contents pane is visible, the button changes to Hide Table of Contents. Clicking it hides the Table of Contents pane and changes the button to Show Table of Contents.

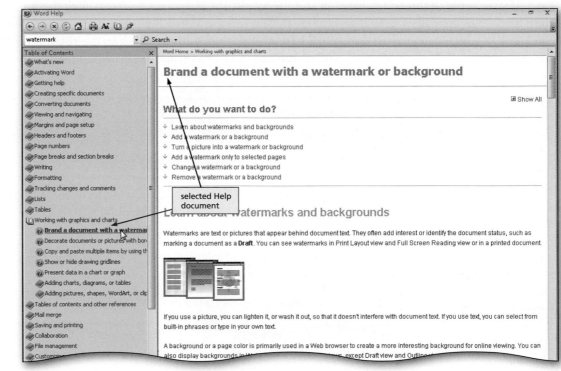

Figure C–12

Obtaining Help while Working in Word

Often you may need help while working on a document without already having the Help window open. For example, you may be unsure about how a particular command works, or you may be presented with a dialog box that you are not sure how to use. Rather than opening the Help window and initiating a search, Word Help provides you with the ability to search directly for help.

Figure C–13 shows one option for obtaining help while working in Word. If you want to learn more about a command, point to the command button and wait for the Enhanced ScreenTip to appear. If the Help icon appears in the Enhanced ScreenTip, press the F1 key while pointing to the command to open the Help window associated with that command.

Figure C–13

Figure C–14 shows a dialog box with a Get help button in it. Pressing the F1 key while the dialog box is displayed opens a Help window. The Help window contains help about that dialog box, if available. If no help file is available for that particular dialog box, then the main Help window opens.

Figure C–14

Use Help

1 Obtaining Help Using Search Text

Instructions: Perform the following tasks using Word Help.

1. Use the 'Type words to search for' text box to obtain help about landscape printing. Use the Connection Status menu to search online help if you have an Internet connection.

2. Click Select page orientation in the list of links in the search results. Double-click the Microsoft Office Word Help window title bar to maximize it. Read and print the information. At the top of the printout, write down the number of links Word Help found.

3. Use the Search menu to search for help offline. Repeat the search from Step 1. At the top of the printout, write down the number of links that Word Help found searching offline. Submit the printouts as specified by your instructor.

4. Use the 'Type words to search for' text box to search for information online about adjusting line spacing. Click the 'Adjust the spacing between a list bullet or number and the text' link in the search results. If necessary, maximize the Microsoft Office 2007 Word Help window. Read and print the contents of the window. Close the Microsoft Office Word Help window. Submit the printouts as specified by your instructor.

5. For each of the following words and phrases, click one link in the search results, click the Show All link, and then print the page: page zoom; date; print preview; Ribbon; word count; and citation. Submit the printouts as specified by your instructor.

2 Expanding on Word Help Basics

Instructions: Use Word Help to better understand its features and answer the questions listed below. Answer the questions on your own paper, or submit the printed Help information as specified by your instructor.

1. Use Help to find out how to customize the Help window. Change the font size to the smallest option and then print the contents of the Microsoft Office Word Help window. Change the font size back to its original setting. Close the window.

2. Press the F1 key. Search for information about tables, restricting the search results to Word Templates. Print the first page of the Search results.

3. Search for information about tables, restricting the search results to Word Help files. Print the first page of the Search results.

4. Use Word Help to find out what happened to the Office Assistant, a feature in the previous version of Word. Print out the Help document that contains the answer.

Appendix D
Publishing Office 2007 Web Pages to a Web Server

With the Office 2007 programs, you use the Save As command on the Office Button menu to save a Web page to a Web server using one of two techniques: Web folders or File Transfer Protocol. A **Web folder** is an Office shortcut to a Web server. **File Transfer Protocol (FTP)** is an Internet standard that allows computers to exchange files with other computers on the Internet.

You should contact your network system administrator or technical support staff at your Internet access provider to determine if their Web server supports Web folders, FTP, or both, and to obtain necessary permissions to access the Web server. If you decide to publish Web pages using a Web folder, you must have the Office Server Extensions (OSE) installed on your computer.

Using Web Folders to Publish Office 2007 Web Pages

When publishing to a Web folder, someone first must create the Web folder before you can save to it. If you are granted permission to create a Web folder, you must obtain the Web address of the Web server, a user name, and possibly a password that allows you to access the Web server. You also must decide on a name for the Web folder. Table D–1 explains how to create a Web folder.

Office 2007 adds the name of the Web folder to the list of current Web folders. You can save to this folder, open files in the folder, rename the folder, or perform any operations you would to a folder on your hard disk. You can use your Office 2007 program or Windows Explorer to access this folder. Table D–2 explains how to save to a Web folder.

Table D–1 Creating a Web Folder
1. Click the Office Button and then click Save As or Open.
2. When the Save As dialog box (or Open dialog box) appears, click the Tools button arrow, and then click Map Network Drive... When the Map Network Drive dialog box is displayed, click the 'Connect to a Web site that you can use to store your documents and pictures' link.
3. When the Add Network Location Wizard dialog box appears, click the Next button. If necessary, click Choose a custom network location. Click the Next button. Click the View examples link, type the Internet or network address, and then click the Next button. Click 'Log on anonymously' to deselect the check box, type your user name in the User name text box, and then click the Next button. Enter the name you want to call this network place and then click the Next button. Click to deselect the 'Open this network location when I click Finish' check box, and then click the Finish button.

Table D–2 Saving to a Web Folder
1. Click the Office Button, click Save As.
2. When the Save As dialog box is displayed, type the Web page file name in the File name text box. Do not press the ENTER key.
3. Click the Save as type box arrow and then click Web Page to select the Web Page format.
4. Click Computer in the Navigation pane.
5. Double-click the Web folder name in the Network Location list.
6. If the Enter Network Password dialog box appears, type the user name and password in the respective text boxes and then click the OK button.
7. Click the Save button in the Save As dialog box.

Using FTP to Publish Office 2007 Web Pages

When publishing a Web page using FTP, you first must add the FTP location to your computer before you can save to it. An FTP location, also called an **FTP site**, is a collection of files that reside on an FTP server. In this case, the FTP server is the Web server.

To add an FTP location, you must obtain the name of the FTP site, which usually is the address (URL) of the FTP server, and a user name and a password that allows you to access the FTP server. You save and open the Web pages on the FTP server using the name of the FTP site. Table D–3 explains how to add an FTP site.

Office 2007 adds the name of the FTP site to the FTP locations list in the Save As and Open dialog boxes. You can open and save files using this list. Table D–4 explains how to save to an FTP location.

Table D–3 Adding an FTP Location
1. Click the Office Button and then click Save As or Open.
2. When the Save As dialog box (or Open dialog box) appears, click the Tools button arrow, and then click Map Network Drive... When the Map Network Drive dialog box is displayed, click the 'Connect to a Web site that you can use to store your documents and pictures' link.
3. When the Add Network Location Wizard dialog box appears, click the Next button. If necessary, click Choose a custom network location. Click the Next button. Click the View examples link, type the Internet or network address, and then click the Next button. If you have a user name for the site, click to deselect 'Log on anonymously' and type your user name in the User name text box, and then click Next. If the site allows anonymous logon, click Next. Type a name for the location, click Next, click to deselect the 'Open this network location when I click Finish' check box, and click Finish. Click the OK button.
4. Close the Save As or the Open dialog box.

Table D–4 Saving to an FTP Location
1. Click the Office Button and then click Save As.
2. When the Save As dialog box is displayed, type the Web page file name in the File name text box. Do not press the ENTER key.
3. Click the Save as type box arrow and then click Web Page to select the Web Page format.
4. Click Computer in the Navigation pane.
5. Double-click the name of the FTP site in the Network Location list.
6. When the FTP Log On dialog box appears, enter your user name and password and then click the OK button.
7. Click the Save button in the Save As dialog box.

Appendix E
Customizing Microsoft Office 2007

This appendix explains how to change the screen resolution in Windows Vista to the resolution used in this book. It also describes how to customize the Word window by changing the Ribbon, Quick Access Toolbar, and the color scheme.

Changing Screen Resolution

Screen resolution indicates the number of pixels (dots) that the computer uses to display the letters, numbers, graphics, and background you see on the screen. When you increase the screen resolution, Windows displays more information on the screen, but the information decreases in size. The reverse also is true: as you decrease the screen resolution, Windows displays less information on the screen, but the information increases in size.

The screen resolution usually is stated as the product of two numbers, such as 1024×768 (pronounced "ten twenty-four by seven sixty-eight"). A 1024×768 screen resolution results in a display of 1,024 distinct pixels on each of 768 lines, or about 786,432 pixels. The figures in this book were created using a screen resolution of 1024×768.

The screen resolutions most commonly used today are 800×600 and 1024×768, although some Office specialists set their computers at a much higher screen resolution, such as 2048×1536.

To Change the Screen Resolution

The following steps change the screen resolution from 1280×1024 to 1024×768. Your computer already may be set to 1024×768 or some other resolution.

- If necessary, minimize all programs so that the Windows Vista desktop appears.

- Right-click the Windows Vista desktop to display the Windows Vista desktop shortcut menu (Figure E–1).

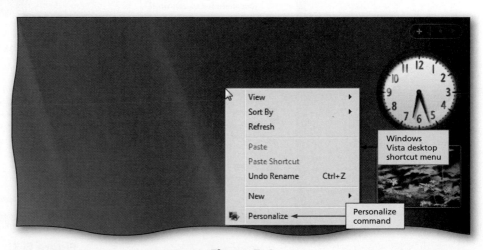

Figure E–1

2

- Click Personalize on the shortcut menu to open the Personalization window.

- Click Display Settings in the Personalization window to display the Display Settings dialog box (Figure E–2).

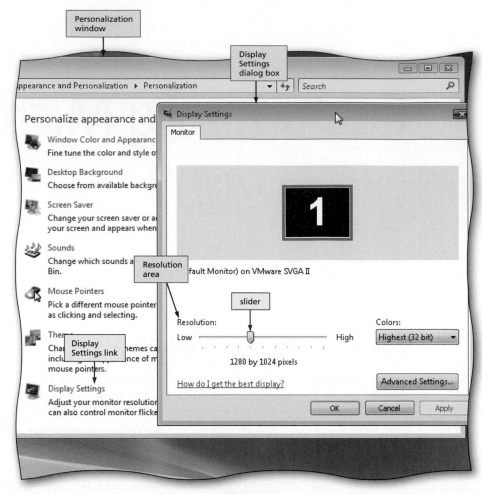

Figure E–2

3

- Drag the slider in the Resolution area so that the screen resolution changes to 1024 × 768 (Figure E–3).

Figure E–3

4

- Click the OK button to change the screen resolution from 1280 × 1024 to 1024 × 768 (Figure E–4).

Figure E–4

5

- Click the Yes button in the Display Settings dialog box to accept the new screen resolution (Figure E–5).

Q&A

What if I do not want to change the screen resolution after seeing it applied after I click the OK button?

You either can click the No button in the inner Display Settings dialog box, or wait for the timer to run out, at which point Windows Vista will revert to the original screen resolution.

- Click the Close button to close the Personalization Window.

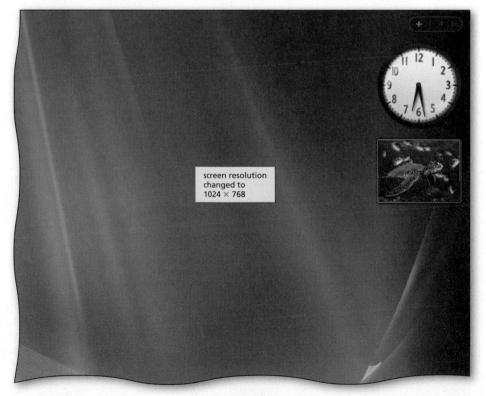

Figure E–5

Screen Resolution and the Appearance of the Ribbon in Office 2007 Programs

Changing the screen resolution affects how the Ribbon appears in Office 2007 programs. Figure E–6 shows the Word Ribbon at the screen resolutions of 800 × 600, 1024 × 768, and 1280 × 1024. All of the same commands are available regardless of screen resolution. Word, however, makes changes to the groups and the buttons within the groups to accommodate the various screen resolutions. The result is that certain commands may need to be accessed differently depending on the resolution chosen. A command that is visible on the Ribbon and available by clicking a button at one resolution may not be visible and may need to be accessed using its group button at a different resolution.

Figure E–6

Comparing the three Ribbons, notice changes in content and layout of the groups and galleries. In some cases, the content of a group is the same in each resolution, but the layout of the group differs. For example, the same buttons appear in the Font and Paragraph groups in the three resolutions, but the layouts differ. The buttons are displayed in three rows at the 800×600 resolution, and in two rows in the 1024×768 and 1280×1024 resolutions. In other cases, the content and layout are the same across the resolution, but the level of detail differs with the resolution. In the Clipboard group, when the resolution increases to 1280×1024, the names of all the buttons in the group appear in addition to the buttons themselves. At the lower resolution, only the buttons appear.

Changing resolutions also can result in fewer commands being visible in a group. Comparing the Editing groups, notice that the group at the 800×600 resolution consists of an Editing button, while at the higher resolutions, the group has three buttons visible. The commands that are available on the Ribbon at the higher resolutions must be accessed using the Editing button at the 800×600 resolution.

Changing resolutions results in different amounts of detail being available at one time in the galleries on the Ribbon. The Styles gallery in the three resolutions presented show different numbers of styles. At 800×600, you can scroll through the gallery three styles at a time, at 1024×768, you can scroll through the gallery four styles at a time, and at 1280×1024, you can scroll through the gallery six styles at a time.

Customizing the Word Window

When working in Word, you may want to make your working area as large as possible. One option is to minimize the Ribbon. You also can modify the characteristics of the Quick Access Toolbar, customizing the toolbar's commands and location to better suit your needs.

To Minimize the Ribbon in Word

The following steps minimize the Ribbon.

- Start Word.

- Maximize the Word window, if necessary.

- Click the Customize Quick Access Toolbar button on the Quick Access Toolbar to display the Customize Quick Access Toolbar menu (Figure E–7).

Figure E–7

- Click Minimize the Ribbon on the Quick Access Toolbar to reduce the Ribbon display to just the tabs (Figure E–8).

Figure E–8

Other Ways

1. Double-click the active Ribbon tab
2. Press CTRL+F1

Customizing and Resetting the Quick Access Toolbar

The Quick Access Toolbar, located to the right of the Microsoft Office Button by default, provides easy access to some of the more frequently used commands in Word (Figure E–7). By default, the Quick Access Toolbar contains buttons for the Save, Undo, and Redo commands. Customize the Quick Access Toolbar by changing its location in the window and by adding additional buttons to reflect which commands you would like to be able to access easily.

To Change the Location of the Quick Access Toolbar

The following steps move the Quick Access Toolbar to below the Ribbon.

- Double-click the Home tab to redisplay the Ribbon.

- Click the Customize Quick Access Toolbar button on the Quick Access Toolbar menu to display the Customize Quick Access Toolbar menu (Figure E–9).

Figure E–9

- Click Show Below the Ribbon on the Quick Access Toolbar menu to move the Quick Access Toolbar below the Ribbon (Figure E–10).

Figure E–10

To Add Commands to the Quick Access Toolbar Using the Customize Quick Access Toolbar Menu

Some of the more commonly added commands are available for selection from the Customize Quick Access Toolbar menu. The following steps add the Quick Print button to the Quick Access Toolbar.

- Click the Customize Quick Access Toolbar button to display the Customize Quick Access Toolbar menu (Figure E–11).

Figure E–11

- Click Quick Print on the Quick Access Toolbar menu to add the Quick Print button to the Quick Access Toolbar (Figure E–12).

Figure E–12

To Add Commands to the Quick Access Toolbar Using the Shortcut Menu

Commands also can be added to the Quick Access Toolbar from the Ribbon. Adding an existing Ribbon command that you use often to the Quick Access Toolbar makes the command immediately available, regardless of which tab is active.

- Click the Review tab on the Ribbon to make it the active tab.

- Right-click the Spelling & Grammar button on the Review tab to display a shortcut menu (Figure E–13).

Figure E–13

2

- Click Add to Quick Access Toolbar on the shortcut menu to add the Spelling & Grammar button to the Quick Access Toolbar (Figure E–14).

Figure E–14

To Add Commands to the Quick Access Toolbar Using Word Options

Some commands do not appear on the Ribbon. They can be added to the Quick Access Toolbar using the Word Options dialog box.

1

- Click the Office Button to display the Office Button menu (Figure E–15).

Figure E–15

2

- Click the Word Options button on the Office Button menu to display the Word Options dialog box (Figure E–16).

Figure E–16

3

- Click Customize in the left pane.

- Click 'Choose commands from' box arrow to display the 'Choose commands from' list.

- Click Commands Not in the Ribbon in the 'Choose commands from' list.

- Scroll to display the Web Page Preview command.

- Click Web Page Preview to select it (Figure E–17).

Figure E–17

Appendix E

4

- Click the Add button to add the Web Page Preview button to the list of buttons on the Quick Access Toolbar (Figure E–18).

Figure E–18

5

- Click the OK button to add the Web Page Preview button to the Quick Access Toolbar (Figure E–19).

Figure E–19

Other Ways

1. Click Customize Quick Access Toolbar button, click More Commands, select commands to add, click Add button, click OK button

To Remove a Command from the Quick Access Toolbar

- Right-click the Web Page Preview button on the Quick Access Toolbar to display a shortcut menu (Figure E–20).

Figure E–20

- Click Remove from Quick Access Toolbar on the shortcut menu to remove the button from the Quick Access Toolbar (Figure E–21).

Figure E–21

Other Ways

1. Click Customize Quick Access Toolbar button, click More Commands, click the command you wish to remove in the Customize Quick Access Toolbar list, click Remove button, click OK button

2. If the command appears on the Customize Quick Access Toolbar menu, click the Customize Quick Access Toolbar button, click the command you wish to remove

To Reset the Quick Access Toolbar

1

- Click the Customize Quick Access Toolbar button on the Quick Access Toolbar.

- Click More Commands on the Quick Access Toolbar menu to display the Word Options Dialog box.

- Click the Show Quick Access Toolbar below the Ribbon check box to deselect it (Figure E–22).

Figure E–22

- Click the Reset button, click the Yes button in the dialog box that appears, and then click the OK button in the Word Options dialog box, to reset the Quick Access Toolbar to its original position to the right of the Office Button, with the original three buttons (Figure E–23).

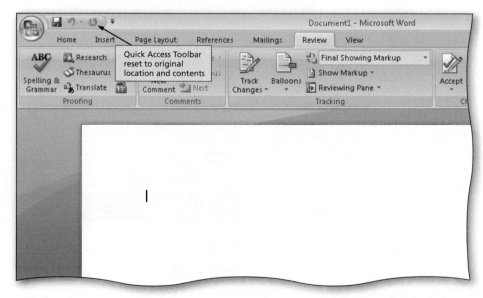

Figure E–23

Changing the Word Color Scheme

The Microsoft Word window can be customized by selecting a color scheme other than the default blue one. Three color schemes are available in Word.

To Change the Word Color Scheme

The following steps change the color scheme.

1

- Click the Office Button to display the Office Button menu.

- Click the Word Options button on the Office Button menu to display the Word Options dialog box.

- If necessary, click Popular in the left pane. Click the Color scheme box arrow to display a list of color schemes (Figure E–24).

Figure E–24

2

- Click Silver in the list.

- Click the OK button to change the color scheme to silver (Figure E–25).

How do I switch back to the default color scheme?

Follow the steps for changing the Word color scheme, and select Blue from the list of color schemes.

Figure E–25

Appendix F

Steps for the Windows XP User

For the XP User of this Book

For most tasks, no differences exist between using Office 2007 under the Windows Vista operating system and using an Office 2007 program under the Windows XP operating system. With some tasks, however, you will see some differences, or need to complete the tasks using different steps. This appendix shows how to Start an Application, Save a Document, Open a Document, Insert a Picture, and Insert Text from a File while using Microsoft Office under Windows XP. To illustrate these tasks, this appendix uses Microsoft Word. The tasks can be accomplished in other Office programs in a similar fashion.

To Start Word

The following steps, which assume Windows is running, start Word based on a typical installation. You may need to ask your instructor how to start Word for your computer.

1

• Click the Start button on the Windows taskbar to display the Start menu.

• Point to All Programs on the Start menu to display the All Programs submenu.

• Point to Microsoft Office on the All Programs submenu to display the Microsoft Office submenu (Figure F–1).

Figure F–1

- Click Microsoft Office Word 2007 to start Word and display a new blank document in the Word window (Figure F–2).

- If the Word window is not maximized, click the Maximize button next to the Close button on its title bar to maximize the window.

- If the Print Layout button is not selected, click it so that your screen layout matches Figure F–2.

Figure F–2

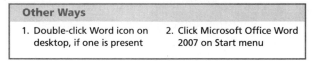

Other Ways
1. Double-click Word icon on desktop, if one is present	2. Click Microsoft Office Word 2007 on Start menu

To Save a Document

After editing, you should save the document. The following steps save a document on a USB flash drive using the file name, Horseback Riding Lessons Flyer.

- With a USB flash drive connected to one of the computer's USB ports, click the Save button on the Quick Access Toolbar to display the Save As dialog box (Figure F–3).

Q&A

Do I have to save to a USB flash drive?

No. You can save to any device or folder. A **folder** is a specific location on a storage medium. You can save to the default folder or a different folder. You also can create your own folders, which is explained later in this book.

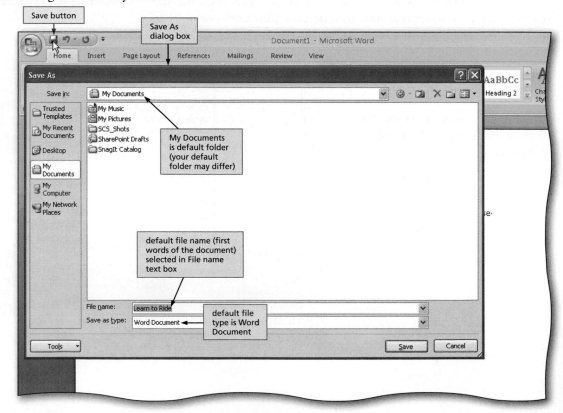

Figure F–3

2

- Type the name of your file (Horseback Riding Lessons Flyer in this example) in the File name text box to change the file name. Do not press the ENTER key after typing the file name (Figure F–4).

Q&A What characters can I use in a file name?

A file name can have a maximum of 255 characters, including spaces. The only invalid characters are the backslash (\), slash (/), colon (:), asterisk (*), question mark (?), quotation mark ("), less than symbol (<), greater than symbol (>), and vertical bar (|).

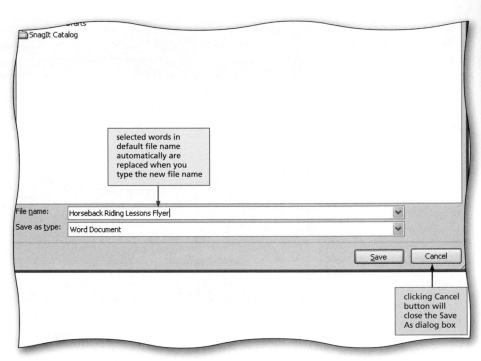

Figure F–4

3

- Click the Save in box arrow to display a list of available drives and folders (Figure F–5).

Q&A Why is my list of files, folders, and drives arranged and named differently from those shown in the figure?

Your computer's configuration determines how the list of files and folders is displayed and how drives are named. You can change the save location by clicking shortcuts on the **My Places bar**.

Q&A How do I save the file if I am not using a USB flash drive?

Use the same process, but be certain to select your device in the Save in list.

Figure F–5

4

- Click UDISK 2.0 (E:) in the Save in list to select the USB flash drive, Drive E in this case, as the new save location (Figure F–6).

- Click the Save button to save the document.

Q&A What if my USB flash drive has a different name or letter?

It is very likely that your USB flash drive will have a different name and drive letter and be connected to a different port. Verify the device in your Save in list is correct.

Figure F–6

Other Ways

1. Click Office Button, click Save, type file name, select drive or folder, click Save button

2. Press CTRL+S or press SHIFT+F12, type file name, select drive or folder, click Save button

To Open a Document

The following steps open the Horseback Riding Lessons Flyer file from the USB flash drive.

1

- With your USB flash drive connected to one of the computer's USB ports, click the Office Button to display the Office Button menu.

- Click Open on the Office Button menu to display the Open dialog box.

- If necessary, click the Look in box arrow and then click UDISK 2.0 (E:) to select the USB flash drive, Drive E in this case, in the Look in list as the new open location.

- Click Horseback Riding Lessons Flyer to select the file name (Figure F–7).

Figure F–7

- Click the Open button to open the document.

Q&A How do I open the file if I am not using a USB flash drive?

Use the same process, but be certain to select your device in the Look in list.

Other Ways

1. Click Office Button, double-click file name in Recent Documents list

2. Press CTRL+O, select file name, press ENTER

To Insert a Picture

The following steps insert a centered picture, which, in this example, is located on a USB flash drive.

1 Position the insertion point where you want the picture to be located. Click Insert on the Ribbon to display the Insert tab. Click the Insert Picture from File button on the Insert tab to display the Insert Picture dialog box.

2 With your USB flash drive connected to one of the computer's USB ports, if necessary, click the Look in box arrow and then click UDISK 2.0 (E:) to select the USB flash drive, Drive E in this case, in the Look in list as the device that contains the picture. Select the file name of the picture file.

3 Click the Insert button in the dialog box to insert the picture at the location of the insertion point in the document.

To Insert Text from a File

The following steps insert text from a file located on the USB flash drive.

1 Click where you want to insert the text. Click Insert on the Ribbon to display the Insert tab. Click the Object button arrow in the Text group to display the Object menu. Click Text from File to display the Insert File dialog box.

2 With your USB flash drive connected to one of the computer's USB ports, if necessary, click the Look in box arrow and then click UDISK 2.0 (E:) to select the USB flash drive, Drive E in this case, in the Look in list as the device that contains the file. Click to select the file name.

3 Click the Insert button in the dialog box to insert the file at the location of the insertion point in the document.

To Create a New Database

The following steps create a database on a USB flash drive.

1 With a USB flash drive connected to one of the computer's USB ports, click Blank Database in the Getting Started with Microsoft Office Access screen to create a new blank database.

2 Type the name of your database in the File Name text box and then click the 'Browse for a location to put your database' button to display the File New Database dialog box.

3 Click the Save in box arrow to display a list of available drives and folders and then click UDISK 2.0 (E:) (your letter may be different) in the Save in list to select the USB flash drive as the new save location.

4 Click the OK button to select the USB flash drive as the location for the database and to return to the Getting Started with Microsoft Office Access screen.

5 Click the Create button to create the database on the USB flash drive with the file name you selected.

To Open a Database

The following steps use the More button to open a database from the USB flash drive.

1 With your USB flash drive connected to one of the computer's USB ports, click the More button to display the Open dialog box.

2 If necessary, click the Look in box arrow and then click UDISK 2.0 (E:) to select the USB flash drive in the Look in list as the new open location. (Your drive letter might be different.)

3 Select the file name. Click the Open button to open the database.

4 If a Security Warning appears, click the Options button to display the Microsoft Office Security Options dialog box. With the option button to enable this content selected, click the OK button to enable the content.

Appendix G
Microsoft Business Certification Program

What Is the Microsoft Business Certification Program?

The Microsoft Business Certification Program enables candidates to show that they have something exceptional to offer – proved expertise in Microsoft Office 2007 programs. The two certification tracks allow candidates to choose how they want to exhibit their skills, either through validating skills within a specific Microsoft product or taking their knowledge to the next level and combining Microsoft programs to show that they can apply multiple skill sets to complete more complex office tasks. Recognized by businesses and schools around the world, more than 3 million certifications have been obtained in more than 100 different countries. The Microsoft Business Certification Program is the only Microsoft-approved certification program of its kind.

What Is the Microsoft Certified Application Specialist Certification?

The Microsoft Certified Application Specialist certification exams focus on validating specific skill sets within each of the Microsoft Office system programs. Candidates can choose which exam(s) they want to take according to which skills they want to validate. The available Application Specialist exams include:

- Using Microsoft® Windows Vista™
- Using Microsoft® Office Word 2007
- Using Microsoft® Office Excel® 2007
- Using Microsoft® Office PowerPoint® 2007
- Using Microsoft® Office Access 2007
- Using Microsoft® Office Outlook® 2007

> For more information and details on how Shelly Cashman Series textbooks map to Microsoft Certified Application Specialist certification, visit scsite.com/off2007/cert.

What Is the Microsoft Certified Application Professional Certification?

The Microsoft Certified Application Professional certification exams focus on a candidate's ability to use the 2007 Microsoft® Office system to accomplish industry-agnostic functions, for example Budget Analysis and Forecasting, or Content Management and Collaboration. The available Application Professional exams currently include:

- Organizational Support
- Creating and Managing Presentations
- Content Management and Collaboration
- Budget Analysis and Forecasting

Index

Quick Reference Summary

In the Microsoft Office 2007 programs, you can accomplish a task in a number of ways. The following four tables (one each for Microsoft Office Word 2007, Microsoft Office Excel 2007, Microsoft Office Access 2007 and Microsoft Office PowerPoint 2007) provide a quick reference to each task presented in this textbook. The first column identifies the task. The second column indicates the page number on which the task is discussed in the book. The subsequent four columns list the different ways the task in column one can be carried out.

Table 1 Microsoft Office Word 2007 Quick Reference Summary

Task	Page Number	Mouse	Ribbon	Shortcut Menu	Keyboard Shortcut
1.5 Line Spacing	WD 86		Line spacing button on Home tab	Paragraph | Indents and Spacing tab	CTRL+5
AutoCorrect Entry, Create	WD 93	Office Button | Word Options button | Proofing | AutoCorrect Options button			
AutoCorrect Options Menu, Display	WD 92	Point to text automatically corrected, point to small blue box, click AutoCorrect Options button			
Bibliographical List, Create	WD 113		Bibliography button on References tab | Insert Bibliography		
Bibliographical List, Modify Source and Update List	WD 117		Manage Sources button on References tab | select source | Edit button		
Bibliography Style, Change	WD 95		Bibliography Style box arrow on References tab		
Bold	WD 34	Bold button on Mini toolbar	Bold button on Home tab	Font | Font tab | Bold in Font style list	CTRL+B
Bullets, Apply	WD 32	Bullets button on Mini toolbar	Bullets button on Home tab	Bullets	ASTERISK KEY | SPACEBAR
Capital Letters	WD 86		Change Case button on Home tab | UPPERCASE	Font	CTRL+SHIFT+A

Table 1   Microsoft Office Word 2007 Quick Reference Summary *(continued)*

Task	Page Number	Mouse	Ribbon	Shortcut Menu	Keyboard Shortcut
Case of Letters, Change	WD 86		Change Case button on Home tab	Font | Font tab	SHIFT+F3
Center	WD 26	Center button on Mini toolbar	Center button on Home tab	Paragraph | Indents and Spacing tab	CTRL+E
Citation Placeholder, Insert	WD 101		Insert Citation button on References tab | Add New Placeholder		
Citation, Insert and Create Source	WD 96		Insert Citation button on References tab | Add New Source		
Citation, Edit	WD 98	Click citation, Citation Options box arrow | Edit Citation			
Close Document	WD 60	Office Button | Close			
Count Words	WD 107	Word Count indicator on status bar	Word Count button on Review tab		CTRL+SHIFT+G
Cut	WD 121		Cut button on Home tab	Cut	CTRL+X
Delete Text	WD 59				DELETE
Dictionary, Custom, View or Modify Entries	WD 127	Office Button | Word Options button | Proofing | Custom Dictionaries button			
Dictionary, Set Custom	WD 127	Office Button | Word Options button | Proofing | Custom Dictionaries button | select desired dictionary name | Change Default button			
Document Properties, Set or View	WD 51	Office Button | Prepare | Properties			
Double-Space Text	WD 87		Line spacing button on Home tab	Paragraph | Indents and Spacing	CTRL+2
Double-Underline	WD 35		Font Dialog Box Launcher on Home tab	Font | Font tab	CTRL+SHIFT+D
Find Text	WD 124	Select Browse Object button on vertical scroll bar | Find icon	Select Find button on Home tab		CTRL+F
Find and Replace Text	WD 123	Select Browse Object button on vertical scroll bar | Find icon | Replace tab	Select Replace button on Home tab		CTRL+H
First-Line Indent Paragraphs	WD 88	Drag First Line Indent marker on ruler	Paragraph Dialog Box Launcher on Home tab | Indents and Spacing tab	Paragraph | Indents and Spacing tab	TAB
Font Size, Change	WD 28	Font Size box arrow on Mini toolbar	Font Size box arrow on Home tab	Font | Font tab	CTRL+SHIFT+P
Font Size, Decrease 1 Point	WD 86			Font | Font tab	CTRL+ [

Table 1 Microsoft Office Word 2007 Quick Reference Summary *(continued)*

Task	Page Number	Mouse	Ribbon	Shortcut Menu	Keyboard Shortcut
Font Size, Increase 1 Point	WD 86			Font	Font tab	CTRL+]
Font, Change	WD 29	Font box arrow on Mini toolbar	Font box arrow on Home tab	Font	Font tab	CTRL+SHIFT+F
Footnote Reference Mark, Insert	WD 100		Insert Footnote button on References tab		CTRL+ALT+F
Footnote, Delete	WD 106	Delete note reference mark in document window	Cut button Home tab		BACKSPACE | BACKSPACE
Footnote, Edit	WD 106	Double-click note reference mark in document window	Show Notes button on References tab		
Footnote, Move	WD 106	Drag note reference mark in document window	Cut button on Home tab | Paste button on Home tab		
Footnote Style, Modify	WD 102		Click footnote text | Styles Dialog Box Launcher | Manage Styles button | Modify button	Style | Footnote Text | Modify button	
Formatting Marks	WD 14		Show/Hide ¶ button on Home tab		CTRL+SHIFT+*
Graphic, Resize	WD 46	Drag sizing handle	Format tab in Picture Tools tab or Size Dialog Box Launcher on Format tab	Size | Size tab	
Hanging Indent, Create	WD 116	Drag Hanging Indent marker on ruler	Paragraph Dialog Box Launcher on Home tab | Indents and Spacing tab	Paragraph | Indents and Spacing tab	CTRL+T
Hanging Indent, Remove	WD 86		Paragraph Dialog Box Launcher on Home tab | Indents and Spacing tab	Paragraph | Indents and Spacing tab	CTRL+SHIFT+T
Header & Footer, Close	WD 83	Double-click dimmed document text	Close Header and Footer button on Design tab		
Header, Display	WD 80	Double-click dimmed header	Header button on Insert tab | Edit Header		
Help	WD 60		Office Word Help button		F1
Insertion Point, Move to Beginning of Document	WD 24	Scroll to top of document, click			CTRL+HOME
Insertion Point, Move to End of Document	WD 25	Scroll to bottom of document, click			CTRL+END
Italicize	WD 36	Italic button on Mini toolbar	Italic button on Home tab	Font	Font tab	CTRL+I
Justify Paragraph	WD 86		Justify button on Home tab	Paragraph | Indents and Spacing tab	CTRL+J

Table 1 Microsoft Office Word 2007 Quick Reference Summary *(continued)*

Task	Page Number	Mouse	Ribbon	Shortcut Menu	Keyboard Shortcut
Left-Align	WD 86		Align Text Left button on Home tab	Paragraph | Indents and Spacing tab	CTRL+L
Move Selected Text	WD 121	Drag and drop selected text	Cut button on Home tab | Paste button on Home tab	Cut | Paste	CTRL+X; CTRL+V
Open Document	WD 56	Office Button | Open			CTRL+O
Page Border, Add	WD 48		Page Borders button on Page Layout tab		
Page Break, Manual	WD 112		Page Break button on Insert tab		CTRL+ENTER
Page Number, Insert	WD 82		Insert Page Number button on Design tab		
Paragraph, Add Space Above	WD 79		Line spacing button on Home tab | Add Space Before (After) Paragraph	Paragraph | Indents and Spacing tab	CTRL+0 (zero)
Paragraphs, Change Spacing Above and Below	WD 50		Spacing Before box arrow on Page Layout tab	Paragraph | Indents and Spacing tab	
Picture Border, Change	WD 45		Picture Border button on Format tab		
Picture Style, Apply	WD 44		Picture Tools and Format tabs | More button in Picture Styles gallery		
Picture, Insert	WD 41		Picture button on Insert tab		
Print Document	WD 54	Office Button | Print | Print			CTRL+P
Print Document Properties	WD 130	Office Button | Print | Print | Print what box arrow			
Quick Style, Create	WD 90		More button in Styles gallery | Save Selection as a New Quick Style	Styles | Save Selection as a New Quick Style	
Quit Word	WD 55	Close button on right side of Word title bar			ALT+F4
Remove character formatting (plain text)	WD 87		Font Dialog Box Launcher on Home tab | Font tab	Font | Font tab	CTRL+SPACEBAR
Remove paragraph formatting	WD 87		Font Dialog Box Launcher on Home tab	Font | Font tab	CTRL+Q
Research Task Pane, Use	WD 128	Hold down ALT key, click word to look up			
Right-Align Paragraph	WD 81		Align Text Right button on Home tab	Paragraph | Indents and Spacing tab	CTRL+R
Rulers, Display	WD 87	View Ruler button on vertical scroll bar	View Ruler on View tab		
Save Document, Same Name	WD 53	Save button on Quick Access Toolbar			CTRL+S
Save New Document	WD 19	Save button on Quick Access Toolbar			CTRL+S

Table 1 Microsoft Office Word 2007 Quick Reference Summary *(continued)*

Task	Page Number	Mouse	Ribbon	Shortcut Menu	Keyboard Shortcut
Select Block of Text	WD 33	Click at beginning of text, hold down SHIFT key and click at end of text to select; or drag through text			CTRL+SHIFT+RIGHT ARROW and/or DOWN ARROW
Select Browse Object Menu, Use	WD 118	Select Browse Object button on vertical scroll bar			ALT+CTRL+HOME
Select Character(s)	WD 120	Drag through character(s)			CTRL+SHIFT+RIGHT ARROW
Select Entire Document	WD 120	Point to left of text and triple-click			CTRL+A
Select Graphic	WD 46	Click graphic			
Select Line	WD 27	Point to left of line and click			SHIFT+DOWN ARROW
Select Lines	WD 30	Point to left of first line and drag up or down			CTRL+SHIFT+DOWN ARROW
Select Paragraph	WD 90	Triple-click paragraph			SHIFT+DOWN ARROW
Select Paragraphs	WD 30	Point to left of first paragraph, double-click, and drag up or down			
Select Sentence	WD 120	Press and hold down CTRL key and click sentence			CTRL+SHIFT+RIGHT ARROW
Select Word	WD 59	Double-click word			CTRL+SHIFT+RIGHT ARROW
Select Words	WD 33	Drag through words			CTRL+SHIFT+RIGHT ARROW
Single-Space Lines	WD 86		Line spacing button on the Home tab	Paragraph | Indents and Spacing tab	CTRL+1
Small uppercase letters	WD 86		Font Dialog Box Launcher on Home tab | Font tab	Font | Font tab	CTRL+SHIFT+K
Sort Paragraphs	WD 200		Sort button on Home tab		
Source, Edit	WD 104	Click citation, Citation Options box arrow | Edit Source			
Spelling and Grammar	WD 125	Spelling and Grammar Check icon on status bar | Spelling	Spelling & Grammar button on Review tab	Right-click flagged text | Spelling	F7
Spelling and Grammar Check as You Type	WD 16	Spelling and Grammar Check icon on status bar		Correct word on shortcut menu	
Style Set, Change	WD 37		Change Styles button on Home tab | Style Set on Change Styles menu		
Styles Task Pane, Open	WD 25		Styles Dialog Box Launcher		ALT+CTRL+SHIFT+S
Styles, Apply	WD 24		Styles gallery		
Styles, Modify	WD 90		Styles Dialog Box Launcher		

Table 1 Microsoft Office Word 2007 Quick Reference Summary *(continued)*

Task	Page Number	Mouse	Ribbon	Shortcut Menu	Keyboard Shortcut
Subscript	WD 86		Font Dialog Box Launcher on Home tab	Font	Font tab	CTRL+EQUAL SIGN
Superscript	WD 86		Font Dialog Box Launcher on Home tab	Font	Font tab	CTRL+SHIFT+PLUS SIGN
Synonym, Find	WD 124		Thesaurus on Review tab	Synonyms	desired word	SHIFT+F7
Theme Colors, Change	WD 39		Change Styles button on Home tab	Colors on Change Styles menu		
Theme Fonts, Change	WD 40		Change Styles button on Home tab	Fonts on Change Styles menu		
Underline	WD 35		Underline button on Home tab	Font	Font tab	CTRL+U
Underline words, not spaces	WD 86				CTRL+SHIFT+W
Zoom	WD 46	Zoom Out and Zoom In buttons on status bar	Zoom button on View tab		

Table 2 Microsoft Office Excel 2007 Quick Reference Summary

Task	Page Number	Mouse	Ribbon	Shortcut Menu	Keyboard Shortcut
AutoCalculate	EX 62	Select range	right-click AutoCalculate area	click calculation			
Bold	EX 38	Bold button on Mini toolbar	Bold button on Home tab or Font Dialog Box Launcher on Home tab	Font tab	Format Cells	Font tab	Bold in Font style list	CTRL+B
Borders	EX 111	Borders button on Mini toolbar	Borders button on Home tab or Alignment Dialog Box Launcher on Home tab	Border tab	Format Cells	Border tab	CTRL+1	B
Cell Style, change	EX 35		Cell Styles button on Home tab		
Center	EX 113	Right-click cell	Center button on Mini toolbar	Center button on Home tab or Alignment Dialog Box Launcher on Home tab	Format Cells	Alignment tab	CTRL+1	A
Center Across Columns	EX 40	Right-click selection	Merge & Center button on Mini toolbar	Merge & Center button on Home tab or Alignment Dialog Box Launcher on Home tab	Format Cells	Alignment tab	CTRL+1	A
Chart, Add	EX 50		Dialog Box Launcher in Charts group on Insert tab		F11
Clear Cell	EX 66	Drag fill handle back	Clear button on Home tab	Clear Contents	DELETE

Table 2 Microsoft Office Excel 2007 Quick Reference Summary *(continued)*

Task	Page Number	Mouse	Ribbon	Shortcut Menu	Keyboard Shortcut
Clear Worksheet	EX 66		Select All button on worksheet | Clear button on Home tab		
Close Workbook	EX 59		Close button on Ribbon or Office Button | Close		CTRL+W
Color Background	EX 110		Fill Color button on Home tab or Font Dialog Box Launcher on Home tab | Fill tab	Format Cells | Fill tab	CTRL+1 | F
Column Width	EX 46, 122	Drag column heading boundary	Home tab | Format button | Column Width	Column Width	ALT+O | C | W
Comma Style Format	EX 44		Comma Style button on Home tab or Number Dialog Box Launcher on Home tab | Accounting	Format Cells | Number tab | Accounting	CTRL+1 | N
Conditional Formatting	EX 119		Conditional Formatting button on Home tab		ALT+O | D
Copy to adjacent cells	EX 27	Select source area | drag fill handle through destination cells	Select source area | click Copy button on Home tab | select destination area | click Paste button on Home tab	Right-click source area | click Copy | right-click destination area | click Paste	
Currency Style Format	EX 116		Currency Style button on Home tab or Format Cells | Number | Currency	Format Cells | Number | Currency	CTRL+1 | N
Cut	EX 64		Cut button on Home tab	Cut	CTRL+X
Date, Format	EX 113		Font Dialog Box Launcher on Home tab | Number tab | Date	Format Cells | Number tab | Date	
Decimal Place, Decrease	EX 115		Decrease Decimal button on Home tab or Number Dialog Box Launcher on Home tab | Number tab | Currency	Format Cells | Number tab | Currency	CTRL+1 | N
Decimal Place, Increase	EX 118		Increase Decimal button on Home tab or Number Dialog Box Launcher on Home tab | Number tab | Currency	Format Cells | Number tab | Currency	CTRL+1 | N
Document Properties, Set or View	EX 55	Office Button | Prepare | Properties			ALT+F | E | P
E-Mail from Excel	EX 142	Office Button | Send | E-Mail			ALT+F | D | E
Embedded Chart, Delete	EX 67				Select chart, press DELETE
Fit to Print	EX 156		Page Setup Dialog Box Launcher on Page Layout tab		ALT+P | SP

Table 2 Microsoft Office Excel 2007 Quick Reference Summary *(continued)*

Task	Page Number	Mouse	Ribbon	Shortcut Menu	Keyboard Shortcut
Font Color	EX 39	Font Color box arrow on Mini toolbar	Font Color button arrow on Home tab or Font Dialog Box Launcher on Home tab	Format Cells | Font tab	CTRL+1 | F
Font Size, Change	EX 38	Font Size box arrow on Mini toolbar	Font Size box arrow on Home tab or Font Dialog Box Launcher on Home tab	Format Cells | Font tab	CTRL+1 | F
Font Size, Increase	EX 39	Increase Font Size button on Mini toolbar	Increase Font Size button on Home tab		
Font Type	EX 36	Font box arrow on Mini toolbar	Font box arrow on Home tab or Font Dialog Box Launcher in Font group on Home tab	Format Cells | Font tab	CTRL+1 | F
Formula Assistance	EX 101	Insert Function button in formula bar	Insert Function button on Formulas tab		CTRL+A after you type function name
Formulas Version	EX 136				CTRL+ACCENT MARK
Full Screen	EX 9		Full Screen button on View tab		ALT+V | U
Function	EX 101	Insert Function button in formula bar	Insert Function button on Formulas tab		SHIFT+F3
Go To	EX 48	Click cell	Find & Select button on Home tab		F5
Help	EX 67 and Appendix C		Microsoft Office Excel Help button on Ribbon		F1
Hide Column	EX 122	Drag column heading boundary	Format button on Home tab | Hide & Unhide or Hide & Unhide button on View tab	Hide	CTRL+0 (zero) to hide CTRL+SHIFT+) to display
Hide Row	EX 126	Drag row heading boundary		Hide	CTRL+9 to hide CTRL+SHIFT+(to display
In-Cell Editing	EX 63	Double-click cell			F2
Margins, Change	EX 130		Margins button on Page Layout tab		
Merge Cells	EX 41		Merge & Center button on Home tab or Alignment Dialog Box Launcher on Home tab	Format Cells | Alignment tab	ALT+O | E | A
New Workbook	EX 67	Office Button | New			CTRL+N
Open Workbook	EX 61	Office Button | Open			CTRL+O
Percent Style Format	EX 118		Percent Style button on Home tab or Number Dialog Box Launcher on Home tab | Percentage	Format Cells | Number tab | Percentage	CTRL+1 | N or CTRL+SHIFT+%
Preview Worksheet	EX 132	Office Button | Print | Print Preview			ALT+F | W | V
Print Worksheet	EX 132	Office Button | Print			CTRL+P

Table 2 Microsoft Office Excel 2007 Quick Reference Summary *(continued)*

Task	Page Number	Mouse	Ribbon	Shortcut Menu	Keyboard Shortcut
Quit Excel	EX 59	Close button on title bar Office Button | Exit Excel			ALT+F4
Range Finder	EX 106	Double-click cell			
Redo	EX 65	Redo button on Quick Access Toolbar			ALT+3 or CTRL+Y
Row Height	EX 125	Drag row heading boundary	Format button on Home tab | Row Height	Row Height	ALT+O | R | E
Save Workbook, New Name	EX 57		Office Button | Save As		ALT+F | A
Save Workbook, Same Name	EX 57	Save button on Quick Access Toolbar	Office Button | Save		CTRL+S
Select All of Worksheet	EX 67	Select All button on worksheet			CTRL+A
Select Cell	EX 15	Click cell or click Name box, type cell reference, press ENTER			Use arrow keys
Shortcut Menu	EX 12	Right-click object			SHIFT+F10
Spell Check	EX 127		Spelling button on Review tab		F7
Split Cell	EX 41		Merge & Center button on Home tab or Alignment Dialog Box Launcher on Home tab | click Merge cells to deselect	Format Cells | Alignment tab | click Merge cells to deselect	ALT+O | E | A
Stock Quotes	EX 138		Existing Connections button on Data tab		ALT+D | D | D
Sum	EX 25	Function Wizard button in formula bar | SUM	Sum button on Home tab	Insert Function button on Formulas tab	ALT+=
Undo	EX 65	Undo button on Quick Access Toolbar			ALT+2, CTRL+Z
Unhide Column	EX 122	Drag hidden column heading boundary to right	Unhide button on View tab	Unhide	ALT+O | C | U
Unhide Row	EX 127	Drag hidden row heading boundary down	Unhide button on View tab	Unhide	ALT+O | R | U
Worksheet Name, Change	EX 141	Double-click sheet tab, type new name		Rename	
Workbook Theme, Change	EX 109		Themes button on Page Layout tab		

Table 3 Microsoft Office Access 2007 Quick Reference Summary

Task	Page Number	Mouse	Ribbon	Shortcut Menu	Keyboard Shortcut
Add New Field	AC 24	Right-click Add New Field in Datasheet	Insert Rows button on Design Tab	Design View | INSERT	
Add Record	AC 30, 38	New (blank) record button	New button on Home tab	Open | Click in field	CTRL+PLUS SIGN (+)
Calculate Statistics	AC 118		Totals button on Design tab		
Change Database Properties	AC 60	Office button | Manage | Database Properties			
Change Primary Key	AC 28	Delete field | Primary Key button	Design View button on Design tab | select field | Primary Key button		
Clear Query	AC 98				Select all entries | DELETE
Close Object	AC 35	Close button for object		Right-click item | Close	
Create Calculated Field	AC 113			Zoom	SHIFT+F2
Create Crosstab Query	AC 123		Query Wizard button on Create tab | Crosstab Query Wizard		
Create Database	AC 14	Blank Database button or Office Button | Save			CTRL+S or SHIFT+F12 or ALT+I
Create Query	AC 78		Query Design button on Create tab		
Create Report	AC 51		Report Wizard button on Create tab		
Create Table	AC 23	Office Button | Save button	Table button on Create tab		CTRL+S or SHIFT+F12
Customize Navigation Pane	AC 126	Navigation Pane arrow | Object Type			
Define Fields in a Table	AC 24		Right-click Add New Field on Datasheet tab | Rename Column	Right-click Add New Field | Rename Column	
Exclude Field from Query Results	AC 112	Show check box			
Field Size	AC 46		Design View button on Design tab | select field | Field Size box		
Format a Calculated Field	AC 116		Property Sheet button on Design tab		
Group in Query	AC 121	Total row or include multiple fields in query			
Include All Fields in Query	AC 85	Double-click asterisk in field list	Query Design button on Create tab | Add All Fields button		
Include Field in Query	AC 85		Query Design button on Create tab | select field | Add Field button		

Table 3 Microsoft Office Access 2007 Quick Reference Summary *(continued)*

Task	Page Number	Mouse	Ribbon	Shortcut Menu	Keyboard Shortcut
Join Tables	AC 105		Query Design button on Create tab | bring field lists for tables into upper pane		
Move to First Record	AC 39	First Record button			
Move to Last Record	AC 39	Last Record button			
Move to Next Record	AC 39	Next Record button			
Move to Previous Record	AC 39	Previous Record button			
New Item	various	Office button | Open			
Omit Duplicates	AC 100	Open Property Sheet, set Unique Values to Yes	Property Sheet button on Design tab | Unique Values	Properties | Unique Values	
Open Database	AC 37	More button | Open button or Office button | double-click file name			CTRL+O
Open Table	AC 26	Open button		Open	
Preview Table	AC 41	Office button | Print | Print Preview			ALT+F, W, V
Print Object	AC 41, 56	Office button | Print | Quick Print or Print			CTRL+P
Quit Access	AC 36	Close button			
Save Form	AC 58	Office button | Save			CTRL+S
Save Query	AC 91	Save button or Office button | Save			CTRL+S
Save Table	AC 27	Save button	Office button | Save	Save	CTRL+S
Search for Access Help	AC 62	Microsoft Office Access Help button			F1
Select Fields for Report	AC 51		Report Wizard button on Create tab | Add Field button		
Simple Query Wizard	AC 78		Query Wizard button on Create tab		
Sort Data in Query	AC 98		Select field in Design grid | Ascending		
Sort on Multiple Keys	AC 101	Assign two sort keys			
Split Form	AC 57		Split Form button on Create tab		
Start Access	AC 12	Start button | All Programs | Microsoft Office | Microsoft Office Access 2007			
Switch Between Form and Datasheet Views	AC 57	Form View or Datasheet View button			
Use AND Criterion	AC 95				Place criteria on same line

Table 3 Microsoft Office Access 2007 Quick Reference Summary *(continued)*

Task	Page Number	Mouse	Ribbon	Shortcut Menu	Keyboard Shortcut
Use Criterion	AC 81	Right-click query | Design View | Criteria row			
Use OR Criterion	AC 96				Place criteria on separate lines

Table 4 Microsoft Office PowerPoint 2007 Quick Reference Summary

Task	Page Number	Mouse	Ribbon	Shortcut Menu	Keyboard Shortcut
Add Shapes	PPT 119		Shapes button on Home tab | select shape		
Add Transition	PPT 122		Transition effect on Animations tab or More button in Transition to This Slide group on Animations tab | select transition		ALT+A | T
Change Size, Clip Art, Photo, or Shape	PPT 101, 103, 117	Drag sizing handles	Dialog Box Launcher in Size group of Format tab | Size tab | enter height and width values or Size group of Format tab | enter height and width values		
Clip Art, Insert	PPT 96	Clip Art icon in slide	Clip Art button on Insert tab		
Demote a Paragraph	PPT 34	Increase List Level button on Mini toolbar	Increase List Level button on Home tab		TAB or ALT+SHIFT+ RIGHT ARROW
Display a Presentation in Grayscale	PPT 59		Grayscale button on View tab		ALT+V | C | U
Document Properties	PPT 44	Office Button | Prepare | Properties			
Document Theme, Choose	PPT 16		More button on Design tab | theme		
End Slide Show	PPT 54			End Show	ESC or HYPHEN
Font, Change	PPT 109	Font button or Font box arrow on Mini toolbar	Font button on Home tab or Font arrow on Home tab | select font or Font Dialog Box Launcher on Home tab | Latin text font arrow on Font tab	Font | Latin text font arrow on Font tab	CTRL+SHIFT+F | Font tab | Latin text font arrow
Font Color	PPT 23, 110	Font Color button or Font Color arrow on Mini toolbar	Font Color button on Home tab or Font Color arrow on Home tab | select color or Font Dialog Box Launcher on Home tab | Font color button on Font tab | select color	Font | Font color button on Font tab | select color	CTRL+SHIFT+F | Font tab | Font color button | select color

Table 4 Microsoft Office PowerPoint 2007 Quick Reference Summary *(continued)*

Task	Page Number	Mouse	Ribbon	Shortcut Menu	Keyboard Shortcut
Font Size, Decrease	PPT 25	Decrease Font Size button or Font Size arrow on Mini toolbar	Decrease Font Size button on Home tab or Font Size arrow on Home tab | size	Font Size arrow | Size	CTRL+SHIFT+LEFT CARET (<)
Font Size, Increase	PPT 24	Increase Font Size button or Font Size arrow on Mini toolbar	Increase Font Size button on Home tab or Font Size arrow on Home tab | size	Font size arrow | Size	CTRL+SHIFT+RIGHT CARET (>)
Help	PPT 63 and Appendix A		Office PowerPoint Help button		F1
Insert Photograph	PPT 98, 99	Insert Picture from File icon on slide	Picture button on Insert tab		
Move Clip Art or Photo	PPT 105	Drag			
Next Slide	PPT 47	Next Slide button on vertical scroll bar			PAGE DOWN
Normal View	PPT 91	Normal View button at lower-right PowerPoint window	Normal button on View tab		ALT+V | N
Open Presentation	PPT 54	Office Button | Open | select file			CTRL+O
Preview Presentation as Web Page	PPT 151	[Assumes Web Page Preview button has been added to Quick Access toolbar] Web Page Preview button			
Previous Slide	PPT 50, 51	Previous Slide button on vertical scroll bar			PAGE UP
Print a Presentation	PPT 61	Office Button | Print			CTRL+P
Print an Outline	PPT 122	Office Button | point to Print | Print Preview | Print What arrow | Outline View			
Promote a Paragraph	PPT 34	Decrease List Level button on Mini toolbar	Decrease List Level button on Home tab		SHIFT+TAB Or ALT+SHIFT+ LEFT ARROW
Quick Access Toolbar, Add Buttons	PPT 148	Customize Quick Access Toolbar button | select from command options			
Quick Access Toolbar, Reset	PPT 154	Customize Quick Access Toolbar button | More Commands | Reset button			
Quit PowerPoint	PPT 53	Double-click Office Button or Close button on title bar or Office Button | Exit PowerPoint		Right-click Microsoft PowerPoint button on taskbar | Close	ALT+F4 Or CTRL+Q
Save a Presentation	PPT 27	Save button on Quick Access toolbar or Office Button | Save			CTRL+S Or SHIFT+F12

Table 4 Microsoft Office PowerPoint 2007 Quick Reference Summary *(continued)*

Task	Page Number	Mouse	Ribbon	Shortcut Menu	Keyboard Shortcut
Save as Web Page	PPT 152	Office Button | Save As | add File name | change Save as type to Single File Web Page | Save button			ALT+F | G or F12
Slide, Add	PPT 29		New Slide button on Home tab or New Slide arrow on Home tab | choose slide type		CTRL+M
Slide, Arrange	PPT 41	Drag slide in Slides tab to new position or in Slide Sorter View drag slide to new position			
Slide, Background	PPT 89		Background Styles button on Design tab | select style	Format Background	
Slide, Duplicate	PPT 40		New Slide arrow on Home tab | Duplicate Selected Slides		
Slide Layout	PPT 92, 94		Layout button on Home tab		
Slide Show View	PPT 49	Slide Show button at lower-right PowerPoint window	Slide Show button on View tab or From Beginning button on Slide Show tab		F5 or ALT+V | W
Slide Sorter View	PPT 91	Slide Sorter View button at lower-right in PowerPoint window	Slide Sorter button on View tab		ALT+V | D
Spelling Check	PPT 55		Spelling button on Review tab		F7
Text, Add Shadow	PPT 110		Text Shadow button on Home tab		
Text, Bold	PPT 25	Bold button on Mini toolbar	Bold button on Home tab		CTRL+B
Text, Change Color	PPT 23	Font Color button or Font Color arrow on Mini toolbar	Font color arrow on Home tab | choose color	Font | Font color button | choose color	
Text, Delete	PPT 42		Cut button on Home tab	Cut	DELETE or CTRL+X or BACKSPACE
Text, Formatting with Quick Styles	PPT 119		Quick Styles button on Home tab | select style		
Text, Italicize	PPT 22	Italic button on Mini toolbar	Italic button on Home tab	Font | Font style arrow | Italics	CTRL+I
Text, Select	PPT 21	Drag to select | double-click to select word | triple-click to select paragraph			SHIFT+DOWN ARROW or SHIFT+RIGHT ARROW

Table 4 Microsoft Office PowerPoint 2007 Quick Reference Summary *(continued)*

Task	Page Number	Mouse	Ribbon	Shortcut Menu	Keyboard Shortcut
Use Format Painter	PPT 112	Format Painter button on Mini toolbar	Double-click Format Painter button on Home tab | select text with a format you want to copy | select other text to apply previously selected format | press ESC to turn off Format Painter		
Zoom for Printing	PPT 128	Drag Zoom slider on status bar or Office Button | point to Print | Print Preview |	Zoom button on View tab | select zoom		
Zoom for Viewing Slides	PPT 127	Drag Zoom slider on status bar	Zoom button on View tab | select zoom		